Understanding Control Flow

Peter A. Buhr

Understanding Control Flow

Concurrent Programming Using μC++

 Springer

Peter A. Buhr
Cheriton School of Computer Science
University of Waterloo
Waterloo, Ontario, Canada

ISBN 978-3-319-25701-3   ISBN 978-3-319-25703-7   (eBook)
DOI 10.1007/978-3-319-25703-7

Library of Congress Control Number: 2016937408

Printed on acid-free paper

This Springer imprint is published by SpringerNature
The registered company is Springer International Publishing AG Switzerland

To Lauri for making life possible.

To Jon for Yosemite.

To Roy and Carl for turning defeat into victory.

To all the people in the acknowledgements for their generous time and patience.

Preface

Learning to program involves progressing through a series of basic concepts; each is fundamentally new and cannot be trivially constructed from previous ones. Programming concepts can be divided into two broad categories: *data* and *control* flow. While many books concentrate on data flow, i.e., data structures and objects, this book concentrates on control flow. The basic control-flow concepts are selection and looping, subroutine and object member call/return, recursion, routine pointer, exception, coroutine, and concurrency; each of these concepts is fundamental because it cannot be trivially constructed from the others. The difficulty in understanding and using these concepts grows exponentially from loops to concurrency, and a programmer must understand all of these concepts to be able to solve the complete gamut of modern programming problems.

Control-flow issues are extremely relevant in modern computer languages and programming styles. In addition to the basic control-flow mechanisms, virtually all new computer languages provide some form of exceptional control-flow to support robust programming. As well, concurrency capabilities are appearing with increasing frequency in both new and old programming languages. The complexity issues and reliability requirements of current and future software demand a broader knowledge of control flow; this book provides that knowledge.

The book starts with looping, and works through each of the different kinds of control-flow concepts, examining why each is fundamental and where it is useful. Time is spent on each concept according to its level of difficulty, with coroutines and concurrency receiving the most time as they should be new to the reader and because of their additional complexity. The goal is to do for control flow what is done for data structures in a data-structure book, i.e., provide a foundation in fundamental control-flow, show which problems require certain kinds of control flow, and which language constructs provide the different forms of control flow. In essence, a good data-structure book should provide its reader with the skills to select the proper data structure from a palette of structures to efficiently solve a problem; this book attempts to provide the same skill for control flow.

The book is intended for students learning advanced control-flow and concurrent programming *at the undergraduate level*. Often the only advanced control-flow students see is concurrency, and this material is usually presented as a secondary issue in an upper-year operating-systems and/or database course. Often the amount of undergraduate time spent on concurrency is only 2 to 3 weeks of classes. Only if a student progresses to graduate school is there an opportunity to obtain additional material on concurrency. However, the need for advanced control-flow and especially concurrency is growing at a tremendous rate. New programming methodologies are requiring new forms of control flow, and new programming languages are supporting these methodologies with new control structures, such as concurrency constructs. Also, all computers now contain multi-threading and multi-cores, while multiple processors and distributed systems are ubiquitous, which all require advanced programming methodologies to take full advantage of the available parallelism. Therefore, all of these advance forms of control flow are becoming basic programming skills needed by all programmers, not just graduate students working in the operating system or database disciplines.

Prerequisites

The material in the book is presented *bottom up*: basic concepts are presented first, with more advanced concepts built slowly and methodically on previous ones. Because many of the concepts are difficult and new to most readers, extra time is spent and additional examples are presented to ensure each concept is understood before progressing to the next. The reader is expected to have the following knowledge:

- intermediate programming experience in some object-oriented language;
- an introduction to the programming language C++.

Furthermore, the kinds of languages discussed in this book are imperative programming languages, such as, Pascal, C, Ada, Modula-3, Java, C#, etc. The reader is expected to have a good understanding of these kinds of languages.

Why C++

This book uses C++ as the base programming-language. The reason is that C++ is becoming one of the dominant programming languages because it:

- is based on C, which has a large programmer and legacy code base,
- is as efficient as C in most situations,
- contains low-level features, e.g., direct memory access, needed for: systems programming, memory management, embedded/real-time,

- has high-level features, e.g., exception handling, objects, polymorphism, and an extensive standard library, which programmers now demand,
- allows direct interaction with UNIX/Windows.

Concurrency in C++

Prior to C++11, C++ did not provide all the advanced control-flow mechanisms needed for modern programming; most importantly, it lacked concurrency features. Early in the development of C++, Bjarne Stroustrup (primary creator of C++), said the following on this point:

> My conclusion at the time when I designed C++ was that no single model of concurrency would serve more than a small fraction of the user community well. I could build a single model of concurrency into C++ by providing language features that directly supported its fundamental concepts and ease its use through notational conveniences. However, if I did that I would favor a small fraction of my users over the majority. This I declined to do, and by refraining from doing so I left every form of concurrency equally badly supported by the basic C++ mechanisms. [8]

True to Stroustrup's opinion, C++11 has adopted a simple, low-level, approach to concurrency. Prior to C++11, many different concurrency approaches for C++ were implemented with only varying degrees of adoption, unlike the C programming language, which has two dominant but incompatible low-level concurrency libraries: pthreads and Win32. Interestingly, concurrency *cannot* be safely added to a language via library code [1, 2, 4, 6], so what is not there, often cannot be added later.

High-Level Concurrency

C++'s simple concurrency limits its future in the parallel domain. Therefore, it is imperative C++ be augmented with high-level concurrency facilities to extend its concurrent-programming base. The ideal scenario is for a single consistent high-level powerful concurrency mechanism; but what should it look like? In theory, any high-level concurrency paradigm/model can be adapted into C++. However, C++ does not support all concurrency approaches equally well, e.g., models such as tuple space, message passing, and channels have no preexisting connection in the language. C++ is fundamentally based on a class model using routine call, and its other features leverage this model. Any concurrency approach matching this C++ model is better served because its concepts interact consistently with the language. In other words, programmers using C++ benefit best from a design that applies the "Principle of Least Astonishment" whenever possible. Therefore, let C++'s design principles dictate which concurrency approaches fit best. For an object-oriented language, thread/stack is best associated with class, and mutual-exclusion/

synchronization with member routines. This simple observation fits many object-oriented languages, and leverages both the existing object-oriented mechanisms and programmer knowledge about them. The resulting concurrency mechanism becomes an extension of the language model, and programmers work from a single model rather than an add-on feature requiring a different way of thinking to use.

μC++

The purpose of this book is to cover advanced control-flow beyond those in C++11. While much of the material in this book is language independent, at some point it is necessary to express the material in a concrete form. Having a concrete mechanisms for use in both examples and assignments provides a powerful bridge between what is learned and how that knowledge is subsequently used in practice. To provide a concrete form, this book uses a dialect of C++, called μC++ , as a vehicle to explain ideas and present real examples.[1] (Download or Github μC++ and install it using command sudo sh u++-6.1.0.sh.) μC++ was developed in response to the need for expressive high-level language facilities to teach advanced control-flow and concurrency [5]. Basically, μC++ extends the C++ programming language [9] in the same way that C++ extends the C programming language. The extensions introduce new objects that augment the existing control flow facilities and provide for light-weight concurrency on uniprocessor and parallel execution on multiprocessor computers. Nevertheless, μC++ has its own design bias, short comings, and idiosyncrasies, which make it less than perfect in all situations. These problems are not specific to μC++, but occur in programming-language design, which involves many compromises to accommodate the practical aspects of the hardware and software environment in which languages execute.

This book does not cover all of the details of μC++, such as how to compile a μC++ program or how to use some of the more complex μC++ options. These details are covered in the μC++ Annotated Reference Manual [3]. When there is a discrepancy between this book and the reference manual, the manual always takes precedence, as it reflects the most recent version of the software. Unfortunately, the current dynamic nature of software development virtually precludes any computer-science textbook from being perfectly up to date with the software it discusses.

---

[1] A similar approach was taken to teach concurrency using a dialect of Pascal, called Pascal-FC (Functionally Concurrent) [7].

Programming Questions

Many of the programming questions at the end of the chapters are quite detailed. (Some might argue they are not detailed enough.) The reason for the detail is that there are just too many ways to write a program. Therefore, some reasonable level of guidance is necessary to know what is required for a solution and for subsequent marking of the assignment.

Acknowledgments

Greg Andrews (SR), Igor Benko and Wim Hesselink (software solutions), Roy Krischer and Richard Bilson (exceptions), Ashif Harji (exceptions, automatic-signal monitors), Ric Holt (deadlock), Doug Lea and David Dice (Java/concurrency), Prabhakar Ragde (complexity) and Robert Holte, Paul Kates, Caroline Kierstead, John Plaice (general discussion and proofreading).

References

1. Boehm, H.J.: Threads cannot be implemented as a library. SIGPLAN Notices **40**(6), 261–268 (2005)
2. Buhr, P.A.: Are safe concurrency libraries possible? Commun. ACM **38**(2), 117–120 (1995)
3. Buhr, P.A.: μC++ annotated reference manual, version 6.1.0. Tech. rep., School of Computer Science, University of Waterloo, Waterloo, Ontario, Canada, N2L 3G1 (2015). http://plg.uwaterloo.ca/~usystem/pub/uSystem/u++-6.1.0.sh
4. Buhr, P.A., Ditchfield, G.: Adding concurrency to a programming language. In: USENIX C++ Technical Conference Proceedings, pp. 207–224. USENIX Association, Portland, Oregon, U.S.A. (1992)
5. Buhr, P.A., Ditchfield, G., Stroobosscher, R.A., Younger, B.M., Zarnke, C.R.: μC++: Concurrency in the object-oriented language C++. Software—Practice and Experience **22**(2), 137–172 (1992)
6. Buhr, P.A., Ditchfield, G., Zarnke, C.R.: Adding concurrency to a statically type-safe object-oriented programming language. SIGPLAN Notices **24**(4), 18–21 (1989). Proceedings of the ACM SIGPLAN Workshop on Object-Based Concurrent Programming, Sept. 26–27, 1988, San Diego, California, U.S.A.
7. Burns, A., Davies, G.: Concurrent Programming. Addison-Wesley (1993)
8. Stroustrup, B.: A perspective on concurrency in C++. In: G.V. Wilson, P. Lu (eds.) Parallel Programming in C++, Scientific and Engineering Computation Series, pp. xxvi–xxvii. MIT Press (1996)
9. Stroustrup, B.: The C++ Programming Language, third edn. Addison-Wesley (1997)

Contents

Chapter 1
Introduction

The purpose of this book is to study and analyse control flow. While the book's main emphasis is on concurrent programming, which is the most complex form of control flow, it is important to lay a strong foundation in all the different forms of control flow that can be used in programming. Separating simpler control-flow issues from concurrency issues allows a step-wise presentation of the aspects of concurrency, rather than presenting all the issues at once and trying to deal with their overwhelming complexity. Therefore, the next three chapters do not deal with concurrency, but with advanced control-flow techniques used in writing both sequential and concurrent programs, and subsequently used throughout this book.

1.1   Control Flow

The following is a list of different kinds of control flow available in modern programming languages by increasing order of complexity:

1. basic control structures,
2. routine/member call/return,
3. recursion,
4. routine pointer,
5. exception,
6. coroutine,
7. concurrency.

Some of the elements in the list are programming language constructs that provide forms of control flow, while other elements are techniques that achieve advanced forms of control flow using the language constructs. The reader should be familiar with the first three items in the list. Each element is discussed briefly now and in detail in subsequent chapters.

© Springer International Publishing Switzerland 2016
P.A. Buhr, *Understanding Control Flow*, DOI 10.1007/978-3-319-25703-7_1

1.2   Basic Control Structures

Selection and looping constructs, such as IF and WHILE statements, are the basic control-flow mechanisms used in a program and taught at the beginning of any programming course. These constructs allow virtually any control-flow patterns *within* a routine. Without these control structures, a computer is nothing more than a calculator, unable to make decisions or repeatedly perform operations on its own. The most general of the basic control structures is the GOTO statement, which allows arbitrary transfers of control. However, arbitrary transfers of control can result in control flow that is difficult to understand. Therefore, certain limits are often placed on the kinds of control flow allowed, possibly by the programming language or the programmers using the language.

1.3   Routine/Member Call/Return

Subroutines, subprograms, functions or procedures are used to parameterize a section of code so that it can be reused without having to copy the code with different variables substituted for the parameters. Routines provide reuse of knowledge and time by allowing other programs to call the routine, dynamically substituting values from different argument variables into parameter variables in the routine computation and subsequently returning one or more results. It is common for one routine to call another, making routines one of the basic building blocks for program construction. Modularization of programs into reusable routines is the foundation of modern software engineering. To support this capability, a programming language allows virtually any contiguous, complete block of code to be factored into a subroutine and called from anywhere in the program; conversely, any routine call is replaceable by its corresponding routine body with appropriate substitutions of arguments for parameters. The ability to support modularization is an important design factor when developing control structures to facilitate software-engineering techniques.

Routine activation (call/invocation) introduces a complex form of control flow. When control reaches a routine call, the current execution context is temporarily suspended and its local state is saved, and the routine starts execution at its beginning along with a new set of its local variables. When the routine returns, its local variables are destroyed and control is implicitly returned to the point of the routine call, reactivating any saved state. As routines call one another, a chain of suspended routines is formed. A call adds to one end of the chain; a return removes from the same end of the chain. Therefore, the chain behaves like a stack, and it is normally implemented that way, with the local storage of each routine allocated consecutively from one end of storage for each call and removed from that same end when the routine returns. In most programming languages, it is impossible to build this call/return mechanism using the basic control-flow constructs; hence, routine call/return is a fundamental mechanism to affect control flow.

```
double std( const double v[ ], int size ) {        double std( const double v[ ], int size ) {
    // compute average                                 double avg() {  // nested routine
    double sum = 0.0;                                      double sum = 0.0;
    for ( int i = 0; i < size; i += 1 ) {                  for ( int i = 0; i < size; i += 1 ) {
        sum += v[i];                                           sum += v[i];
    }                                                      }
    double av = sum / size;                                return sum / size; // average
    // compute standard deviation                      }
    sum = 0.0;                                          double av = avg(), sum = 0.0;
    for ( int i = 0; i < size; i += 1 ) {              for ( int i = 0; i < size; i += 1 ) {
        double diff = v[i] - av;                           double diff = v[i] - av;
        sum += diff * diff;                                sum += diff * diff;
    }                                                  }
    return sqrt( sum / size );                         return sqrt( sum / size ); // std deviation
}                                                  }

              (a) Inline                                    (b) Nested routine
```

Fig. 1.1 Compute standard deviation

Many programming languages also support nested routines (C++ /Java support nested routines indirectly). For example, Fig. 1.1 shows a routine to compute the standard deviation of an array of values. Modularization allows factoring the calculation into a local routine avg, in which variables v and size are global to routine avg but local to routine std. Routine nesting follows the rule that a variable or routine name should exist in the smallest scope of usage to prevent inappropriate or accident usage, or pollute other namespaces. Similar to routine nesting is the notion of a structure (or class) nesting for organizing heterogeneous data types. Like a routine, a structure provides a scope that can be nested to arbitrary depth with other structures, e.g., in Java:

```
class Outer {
    enum RGB { R, G, B };
    int i, j = 0;
    class Inner {            // nest structure
        int i;               // name reuse
        RGB c = RGB.R;       // access local type
        int w = j;           // access local variable
    }
}
```

Nested routines have the same scope relationship as nested structures, where a routine call to std instantiates the outer block, like a declaration of Outer creates the outer structure. In both cases, the inner routine and structure depend on the outer, so it is impossible to call the inner routine without first calling the outer routine, nor is it possible to create the inner structure without first instantiating an outer.

An object is a combination of these two notions: nesting a routine in a structure. Both a routine and a structure define a static declaration scope that can be used in exactly the same way by a routine nested in either context. Therefore, allowing the definition of routines in a structure follows naturally from the static declaration scope present by a structure and the structure instance acts like a routine activation. However, from a control-flow perspective, there is no difference in calling a routine or a member routine of an object. While the environment in which the member routine executes is different from the environment of a routine because the member routine can access an object's context as well as the static context where the object is defined, the control flow is still a basic routine call/return.

1.4 Recursion

While it is common for one routine to call another, it is uncommon for a routine to call itself, either directly or indirectly, but if it does, the calls form a cycle, called recursion. The cycles formed by recursion are analogous to looping with control structures *with the addition that a new instance of the routine is created for each call*.

Recursion is often confusing, and there is a good reason for this: there are very few physical situations where recursion occurs, and therefore, there are no common analogies that a person can use to understand recursion. The most common examples of physical recursion are standing between two parallel mirrors or pointing a T.V. camera at the T.V. screen it is broadcasting to. In theory, there is an infinite number of copies of the original entity; in practice, the number of repeated instances drops off very quickly. Alternatively, it is straightforward to imagine looping as simply doing an operation over and over. For example, in carrying bricks from a truck to a house, a person might make repeated trips carrying one or more bricks at a time. With recursion, a simple analogy cannot be constructed. Essentially a person carries one or more bricks, clones oneself back at the truck, and the clone carries the next load of bricks; after making N trips, there are N copies of the person at the house, and then, $N-1$ of them disappear. While both approaches are equally valid ways of moving the bricks, the latter approach is not the one that would immediately suggest itself to most people.

(Interestingly, recursive data structures, such as a linked list or a tree data structure, have a similar problem. These structures are rarely specified, manipulated or implemented using direct recursive techniques; exceptions are languages where all data and/or objects are implicitly referenced via pointers. In all cases, the data recursion is indirect through an explicit or implicit pointer in the data structure. While it might be argued that this is an implementation issue, the fact that it exists in virtually all programming languages indicates that direct recursive data-structures are more of a concept than a reality.)

While recursion is not always intuitive, the class of problems that require building up state information during the execution of an algorithm may be trivially implemented by a recursive solution. These algorithms use the local state of a routine to implicitly build a stack data-structure that remembers both data and execution state. For example, recursive solutions to many tree-walking algorithms are usually the simplest because the implicit stack created by the routine calls is required by these algorithms and is implicitly managed by the normal routine-call mechanism. By informally decomposing these algorithms into control flow

and implicit data-structure, it is often possible to easily understand their recursive
solutions.

Like all programming techniques, recursion can be abused, e.g., by constructing
a complex recursive solution using the implicit stack, when a different, explicit
data-structure would produce a straightforward solution. An example problem is
the obvious recursive solution for calculating the Fibonacci sequence 0, 1, 1, 2, 3,
5, 8, 13, 21, ...

```
int Fib( int n ) {                      int Fib( int n ) {
    if ( n == 0 )                           int fn = 0, fn1 = 0, fn2 = 1;
        return 0;                           for ( int i = 0; i < n; i += 1 ) {
    else if ( n == 1 )                          fn = fn1 + fn2;
        return 1;                               fn2 = fn1; fn1 = fn;
    else                                    }
        return Fib( n - 1 ) + Fib( n - 2 );     return fn;
}                                       }
```

            (a) Recursion   (b) Looping

The recursive solution (left example) builds multiple stacks to calculate each partial
Fibonacci number in the sequence up to the initial argument value (exponential
complexity in space and time, specifically $\Theta(\phi^n)$), while the looping solution (right
example) uses only 3 variables and n iterations. While excellent recursive solutions
exist for this problem, a novice programmer can unknowingly generate a space
and time inefficient recursive solution because of the implicit aspects of recursion.
Hence, it is essential for a programmer to understand both a control-flow technique
and its underlying details to construct an efficient program.

1.5 Routine Pointer

The argument/parameter mechanism generalizes routines with respect to manipulating data, but the routine code executed for all data is fixed. To further generalize
a routine, it is possible to pass routine arguments, which are called within a routine,
e.g.:

```
double h( double v, double offset ) { return sin( v ) + offset; }
double k( double v, double offset ) { return cos( v ) + offset / 2.0; }
double f( double offset, double N, double g( double v, double offset ) ) {
    double sum = 0.0;
    for ( double x = 0; x <= N; x += 0.1 ) {
        sum = sqrt( 1.0 - pow( g( x, offset ), 2.0 ) );
    }
    return sum;
}
f( 0.1, 0.9, h );        // execute different code within f
f( 0.1, 0.9, k );
```

The previously modularized routine g is now a parameter f, allowing different
routines to be passed into f, which calls the corresponding argument routine within
the loop. Note, it is necessary to pass the offset value as an argument to the parameter

routine g because it is no longer nested, and hence, offset is not a global variable. In many cases, object routine-members are implicitly implemented using routine pointers.

1.6   Exception

Basic control structures allow virtually any control-flow pattern *within* a routine. However, control flow *among* routines is rigidly controlled by the call/return mechanism. If routine X calls routine Z, the normal way for X to affect the control flow of Z is indirectly by passing data arguments to Z. To directly affect control flow, X can pass a routine as an argument to Z, which Z then calls. In the reverse direction, the only way for Z to affect the control flow of X is through its return value and output parameters. One common mechanism is for Z to return a flag, called a **return code**, which X uses to influence its control flow. Note, in both cases, programming conventions are used to implement more sophisticated control flow patterns using only the basic control structures and call/return.

If modularization introduces intermediate routines between X and Z, e.g., if X calls Y and Y calls Z, it becomes much more difficult to use these conventions to allow X and Z to influence each other's control flow. In this general case, all routine calls between X and Z must be modified to pass the necessary extra arguments from X to Z, and the necessary extra return values from Z to X. Transferring this additional information among the intermediate levels can be tedious and error prone, resulting in significant complication (e.g., complex routine coupling).

Exceptions extend call/return semantics to reference code and transfer to this code in the "reverse" direction to a normal routine-call, i.e., Z can return directly to X terminating any intermediate calls, like Y. Instead of passing routines through multiple levels, routines are implicitly passed so the signatures of any intermediate routine are unaffected. As well, control flow is extended to allow a direct transfer from a called routine through multiple intermediate routines back to a specific calling routine. These additional forms of control flow support a variety of programming techniques that cannot be simulated well with basic control-flow mechanisms.

One common programming application where exception is used is dealing with error situations detected in a lower-level routine invocation, allowing the dynamic selection of a corrective routine and possibly a transfer of control to some stable recovery point in the call chain if correction of the original problem is impossible. However, not all exceptions result from errors; some exceptions only indicate infrequently occurring events, which are handled outside of the normal algorithmic control sequence.

1.7 Coroutine

Like exceptions, coroutines provide a new mechanism for transferring control among routines. What differentiates a coroutine from a routine is that a coroutine can suspend its execution and return to the caller *without* terminating. The caller can then resume the coroutine at a later time and it restarts from the point where it suspended, continuing with the local state that existed at the point of suspension.

While this form of control flow may seem peculiar, it handles the class of problems where a routine needs to retain data and execution location between calls, which is useful for coding finite and push-down automata (and more). As well, this flow of control is also the precursor to true tasks but without concurrency problems; hence, a coroutine allows incremental development of these properties [1].

1.8 Concurrency

In all the previous discussions of control flow, there has been the implicit assumption of a single point of execution that moves through the program, controlled by the values in variables and the control structures. As a consequence, a program is only ever executing at one particular location. Concurrency is the introduction of multiple points of execution into a program. As a consequence, a program now has multiple locations where execution is occurring. Reasoning, understanding and coordinating these multiple execution points as they interact and manipulate shared data is what concurrent programming is about.

1.9 Summary

The minimal set of control flow concepts needed in modern programming languages are: basic control flow, (member) routine call/return, recursion, routine pointer, exception, coroutine and concurrency. While not all languages support this set of concepts directly, it is essential to be able to recognize these basic forms, and then adapt, as best as possible, to the specific implementation language/system.

Reference

1. Yeager, D.P.: Teaching concurrency in the programming languages course. SIGCSE BULLETIN **23**(1), 155–161 (1991). The Papers of the Twenty-Second SIGCSE Technical Symposium on Computer Science Education, March. 7–8, 1991, San Antonio, Texas, U.S.A.

Chapter 2
Advanced Control Flow*

This chapter reviews basic control flow and then presents advanced control flow, which is not easily simulated using the basic control structures.

2.1 Basic Control Flow

Basic control-structures allow for virtually any control-flow pattern *within* a routine. The basic control-structures are:

- conditional: if-then-else, case
- looping: while, repeat (do-while), for
- routine: call/return (recursion, routine pointers)

which are used to specify most of the control flow in a program. In fact, only the while-loop is necessary to construct any control flow as it can be used to mimic the others. This assertion is demonstrated by showing the transformations from the if-then-else and repeat-loop constructs to the while-loop:

IF	IF using WHILE	REPEAT	REPEAT using WHILE

if (a > b) {	flag = true;
	while (a > b & flag) {
	  flag = false;
	  b = 2;
	}
		do {
		  x += 1;
			flag = true;
			while (flag | x < 10) {
			  x += 1;
			  flag = false;

} else {	while (flag) {
	  flag = false;
	  b = 7;
		} while (x < 10);	}

}	}		

---

* This chapter is a major revision of "A Case for Teaching Multi-exit Loops to Beginning Programmers" in [6].

© Springer International Publishing Switzerland 2016
P.A. Buhr, *Understanding Control Flow*, DOI 10.1007/978-3-319-25703-7_2

In the if-then-else simulation (left), the flag variable ensures the loop body executes at most once and the second while-loop does not execute if the first one does; in the repeat simulation, the flag variable ensures the loop body executes at least once. The reader can generalize to the case statement, which is a series of disjuncted if-statements, and the for-loop, which is a while-loop with a counter.

Another example of restricted control-flow is any program can be written using a single while-loop, any number of if-statements, and extra variables, where the if-statements re-determine what was happening on the previous loop iteration. However, even though the while-loop can mimic the other control structures or only one while-loop is necessary, it is clear that programming in this manner is awkward. Therefore, there is a significant difference between being able to do a job and doing the job well; unfortunately, it is hard to quantify the latter, and so it is often ignored. A good analogy is that a hammer can be used to insert screws and a screwdriver can pound nails so they are weakly interchangeable, but both tools have their own special tasks at which they excel. This notion of weak equivalence is common in computer science, and should be watched for because it does not take into account many other tangible and intangible factors. Weak equivalences appear repeatedly in this book.

The remainder of this chapter discusses several advanced forms of control flow: multi-exit loop and multi-level exit. Each form allows altering control flow in a way not trivially possible with the basic control-structures. Again, there is a weak equivalence between the new forms of control and the while-loop, but each new form provides substantial advantages in readability, expressibility, maintainability and efficiency, which justifies having specific language constructs to support them.

2.2 GOTO Statement

Conspicuous by its absence from the list of basic control-structures is the GOTO statement. The reason is most programming styles do not advocate the use of the goto, and some modern programming-languages no longer provide a GOTO statement (e.g., Java [10]). However, the much maligned goto is an essential part of control flow and exists implicitly in virtually all control structures. For example, the following shows the implicit GOTO statements in both the if-then-else and while-loop.

Implicit Transfer	Explicit Transfer

if (C) { // false => transfer to else
    ... // then-clause
    // transfer after else
} **else** {
    ... // else-clause
}
	if (! C) goto L1;
	    ... // then-clause
	    goto L2;
	L1:
	    ... // else-clause
	L2:

while (C) { // false => transfer after while
    ... // loop-body
} // transfer to start of while
	L3: **if** (! C) goto L4;
	    ... // loop-body
	    goto L3;
	L4:

For the if-then-else (top), there are two gotos: the first transfers over the then-clause if the condition is false (notice the reversal of the condition with the **not** operator), and the second transfers over the else-clause after executing the then-clause if the condition is true. For the while-loop (bottom), there are also two gotos: the first transfers over the loop-body if the condition is false (notice the reversal of the condition with the **not** operator), and the second transfers from the bottom of the loop-body to before the loop condition. The key point is that programming cannot exist without the goto (unconditional branch) to transfer control. Therefore, it is necessary to understand the goto even when it is used implicitly within high-level control-structures. By understanding the goto, it is possible to know when it is necessary to use it explicitly, and hence, when it is being used correctly.

Given that the goto is essential, why is it a problem? During the initial development of programming, it was discovered that arbitrary transfer of control results in programs that are difficult to understand and maintain:

> For a number of years I have been familiar with the observation that the quality of program-mers is a decreasing function of the density of **go to** statements in the programs they produce [7, p. 147].

During the decade of the 1970s, much work was done to understand the effect of different restrictions on transfer of control with regard to expressibility versus understandability and maintainability. This research has the generic name **structured programming**. The conclusion was that a small set of control structures used with a particular programming style makes programs easier to write and understand, as well as maintain. In essence, a set of reasonable conventions was adopted by programmers, similar to adopting a set of traffic rules for car drivers. Not all structured programming conventions are identical, just as traffic conventions vary from country to country. Nevertheless, the conventions have a large intersection, and therefore, it is only necessary to learn/adjust for any minor differences.

The basis for structured programming is the work of Böhm and Jacopini [5], which shows any arbitrary control-flow written with gotos can be transformed into an equivalent restricted control-flow uses only IF and WHILE control structures. The transformation requires the following modifications to the original goto program:

- copy code fragments of the original program, and
- introduce flag variables used only to affect control flow, and thus, not containing data from the original program.

Interestingly, even when there are no gotos, constructing control flow with just IF and WHILE frequently requires code duplication and the use of flag variables to overcome the limitations of WHILE. For example, when using a WHILE loop, it is often necessary to copy code before the loop and at the end of the loop (see page 15), and to effect early termination of nested WHILE loops, it is often necessary to use flag variables (see page 21). However, copying code has the problem of maintaining consistent copies, i.e., every programmer has experienced the situation of changing the code in one copy but forgetting to make the corresponding change in the other copies. Although this problem is mitigated by putting the duplicated code in a routine, routines introduce additional declarations, calls and execution cost, especially if many parameters are required. Similarly, introducing flag variables requires extra declarations and executable statements to set, test and reset the flags. *In fact, a flag variable used strictly for control flow purposes is the variable equivalent of a* GOTO *statement.* This equivalence exists because modification of a flag variable can be buried in a loop body or even appear in remote parts of the program, and thus, has the same potential to produce unintuitive control flow. This additional complexity is often a consequence of restricting control flow, e.g., only using IF and WHILE.

Peterson, Kasami and Tokura [23] demonstrate some code copying and all flag variables required by the Böhm and Jacopini transformation can be eliminated by using a new control-structure. This control structure involves an EXIT statement and requires labelling some loops (labelled **break** in Java). The EXIT statement transfers control *after* the appropriately labelled control-structure, exiting any intervening (nested) control-structures, e.g.:

```
A: LOOP                    // outer loop A
   ...
   B: LOOP                 // inner loop B
      ...
      WHEN C2 EXIT B       // exit inner loop B
      ...
      WHEN C1 EXIT A       // exit outer loop A
      ...
   END LOOP
   ...
END LOOP
```

EXIT A transfers to the statement after (the END LOOP of) the outer loop labelled A and EXIT B transfers to the statement after the inner loop labelled B. Fundamentally, EXIT is a GOTO but restricted in the following ways:

- EXIT cannot be used to create a loop, i.e., cause a backward branch in the program, which means only looping constructs can be used to create a loop. This restriction is important so all situations resulting in repeated execution of statements are solely delineated by the looping constructs.
- Since EXIT always transfers out of containing control-structures, it cannot be used to branch into a control structure. This restriction is important for languages allowing declarations within the bodies of control structures. Branching into the middle of a control structure may not create the necessary local variables or initialize them.

Therefore, exits are a valuable programming tool to simplify or remove techniques required when control flow is restricted.

Three different forms of exits are identified:

1. one in which control leaves only the current loop control-structure at possibly several different locations, called a **multi-exit** or **mid-test** loop;
2. one in which control leaves multiple levels but to a statically determinable level, called **static multi-level exit**;

3. one in which control leaves multiple levels but to a level that is determined dynamically, called **dynamic multi-level exit**.

In the case of multi-exit loop, the level of exit is determined implicitly, and hence, it is unnecessary to name program levels nor to use that name to exit the loop. However, terminating multiple control-structures either statically or dynamically requires additional naming. Because the multi-exit loop occurs more frequently than the other kinds of exits, and absence of names reduces program complexity, some languages have a specific construct for direct exit from a loop (e.g., unlabelled **break** in C/C++/Java). However, static multi-level exit subsumes multi-exit loop, so having separate constructs for multi-exit and static multi-level exit is a programmer convenience.

2.3 Multi-Exit (Mid-Test) Loop

The anatomy of a loop construct involves two parts: an infinite loop and a mechanism to stop the loop. This anatomy can be seen by decomposing the two most common looping constructs into these two constituent parts. The while-loop (left) is composed of an infinite loop with one exit located at the top (right, Ada [30]):

```
while ( i < 10 ) {      loop                -- infinite loop
                           exit when i >= 10;   -- loop exit
     ...                    ...          ↑ reverse condition
}                       end loop
```

The repeat-loop (left) is composed of an infinite loop with one exit located at the bottom (right):

```
do                      loop                -- infinite loop
     ...                    ...
                           exit when i >= 10;   -- loop exit
while ( i < 10 );       end loop     ↑ reverse condition
```

Both right examples have one important difference, the condition of the **if** statement is reversed relative to the **while** or **do-while**. In this case, the condition specifies why the loop exits instead of why the loop should continue execution.

Unlike the fixed **while** and **do-while** looping constructs, the **loop** construct allows the exit to be located in positions other than the top or bottom of the infinite loop. A multi-exit (mid-test) loop can have one or more exit locations anywhere in the body of the loop. Therefore, the anatomy of a multi-exit loop is:

```
loop
    exit when C1; -- top
       ...
    exit when C2; -- middle
       ...
    exit when C3; -- bottom
end loop
```

The one advantage of loop exit is the ability to change the kind of loop solely by moving the exit line; i.e., no other text in the program needs to be modified.

Given the basic anatomy of a multi-exit loop, what is the best way to implement it in C/C++? An infinite loop can be created in the following ways:

```
while ( true ) {          for ( ;; ) {              do {
   ...                       ...                       ...
}                         }                         } while ( true );
```

In this book, the **for** version (middle) is used because it is more general; i.e., it is easily modified to have a loop index:

```
for ( int i = 0; i < 10; i += 1 ) { // loop index
```

without having to change existing text in the program. If a **while/do-while** construct is used to generate an infinite loop, it must be changed to a **for** construct if a loop index is introduced.[1] This style is used wherever possible in this book, i.e., programs are written and language constructs are used so new text can be inserted or existing text removed without having to change any other text in the program. This approach ensures any errors introduced by a change are only associated with new code, never existing code. (Occasionally it is necessary to violate this style so examples fit.)

The loop exit is done with two statements: **if** and **break**. The **if** statement checks if the loop should stop, and the **break** statement terminates the loop body and continues execution after the end of the loop body. As above, implementing a **while** or **do-while** loop is trivial by placing the exit at the top or bottom of the loop body:

```
for ( ;; ) {  // WHILE        for ( ;; ) {  // REPEAT
   If ( I >= 10 ) break;          ...
   ...                            if ( i >= 10 ) break;
}                             }
```

and the kind of loop can be changed by simply moving the exit location in the loop body. In contrast, changing a while loop to a repeat loop requires modifying several lines, which increases the possibility of introducing errors. A disadvantage is confusion using an **if** statement that does not continue execution in the loop body; i.e., the usual flow of control associated with an **if** statement is not followed in this case because of the exit. Having special syntax, like **exit when** C, removes this confusion. Having to reverse the exit condition from a while loop can be an advantage: most programmers think, talk and document the situations that cause a loop to stop versus continue looping, which often leads to errors specifying the loop conditional expression. For example, when merging two files using high-values, the loop performing the merge exits when both keys become high-value:

```
loop
   exit when f1.key = high and f2.key = high;
```

Using a **while** or **do-while**, the expression must be inverted. Without an understanding of de Morgan's law, many programmers fail to make this transformation correctly, negating the relational operators but not the logical, producing:

---

[1] Alternatively, the loop index could be added to the **while** construct by adding multiple statements. However, this defeats the purpose of having a **for** construct and increases the chance of additional errors when adding or removing the loop index because three separate locations must be examined instead of one.

```
while ( f1.key ~= high & f2.key ~= high ) do
              ↑ should be |
```

Thus, the specification of loop termination in the form of when it should stop rather than when it should continue produces programs that are often easier to write and understand.

The more interesting use of the loop exit is exiting from locations other than the top or bottom of the loop, e.g.:

```
for ( ;; ) {
    ...
    if ( ... ) break;  // middle exit
    ...
}
```

For many programmers, this control flow seems peculiar, but in fact, exits of this form are necessary to eliminate copied code needed with while and repeat loops. The best example of duplicated code is reading until end of file, as in the code fragment:

```
cin >> d; // priming        for ( ;; ) {
while ( ! cin.fail() ) {          cin >> d;
    ...                           if ( cin.fail() ) break;
    cin >> d;                     ...
}                           }
```

The left example shows traditional **loop priming**, which duplicates the reading of data before and at the end of the loop body. The reason for the initial read is to check for the existence of any input data, which sets the end-of-file indicator. However, all duplicate code is a significant software-maintenance problem. The right example uses loop exit to eliminates the duplicate code, and hence, has removed the software-maintenance problem solely by altering the control flow. A similar C++ idiom for this example is:

```
while ( cin >> d ) {  // cin returns status of read
    ...
}
```

but results in side-effects in the expression (changing variable d) and precludes analysis of the input stream (cin) without code duplication, e.g., print the status of stream cin after every read for debugging purposes, as in:

```
while ( cin >> d ) {              for ( ;; ) {
    cout << cin.good() << endl;       cin >> d;
                                      cout << cin.good() << endl;
                                      if ( cin.fail() ) break;
    ...                               ...
}                                 }
cout << cin.good() << endl;
```

In the C++ idiom (left), printing the status of the read, i.e., did it fail or succeed, must be duplicated after the loop to print the status for end-of-file. In the multi-exit case (right), the status is printed simply by inserting one line of code after the read.

Many programmers have a tendency to write an unnecessary **else** with loop exits:

BAD	GOOD	BAD	GOOD

for (;;) {
　S1
　if (C1) {
　　S2
　} else {
　　break;
　}
　S3
}
	for (;;) {
	　S1
	　if (! C1) break;
	　S2
	
	　S3
	}
		for (;;) {
		　S1
		　if (C1) {
		　　break;
		　} else {
		　　S2
		　}
		　S3
		}
			for (;;) {
			　S1
			　if (C1) break;
			
			　S2
			
			　S3
			}

In both examples, the code S2 is logically part of the loop body not part of an **if** statement. Making S2 part of the loop exit is misleading and makes it more difficult to locate the exit points. Hence, it is good programming style to not have an **else** clause associated with a loop exit.

It is also possible to have multiple exit-points from the middle of a loop (left):

```
                        bool flag1 = false, flag2 = false;
for ( ;; ) {            while ( ! flag1 & ! flag2 ) {
  S1                      S1
  if ( C1 ) break;        if ( C1 ) flag1 = true;
                          } else {
  S2                        S2
  if ( C2 ) break;          if ( C2 ) flag2 = true;
                            } else {
  S3                          S3
                            }
                          }
}                       }
```

This loop has two reasons for terminating, such as no more items to search or found the item during the search. Contrast the difference in complexity between these two code fragments that are functionally identical. The while loop (right) requires two flag variables, an awkward conjunction in the loop condition for termination, and testing and setting the flags in the loop body. The reduction in complexity for the multi-exit loop comes solely by altering the control flow.

Finally, an exit can also include code that is specific to that exit (left):

```
                            bool flag1 = false, flag2 = false;
for ( ;; ) {                while ( ! flag1 & ! flag2 ) {
  S1                          S1
  if ( C1 ) { E1; break; }    if ( C1 ) flag1 = true;
                              } else {
  S2                            S2
  if ( C2 ) { E2; break; }      if ( C2 ) flag2 = true;
                                } else {
  S3                              S3
                                }
                              }
}                           }
                            if ( flag1 ) E1; // which exit ?
                            else E2;
```

The statements E1 and E2 in the then-clause of the exiting **if** statement are executed *before* exit from the loop (meaning they are in the scope of loop declarations, like a loop index). For a single exit, any specific exit code can be placed after the loop. For multiple exits with specific exit code for each exit, placing the exit codes after the loop requires additional **if** statements to determine which code should be executed based on the reason for the loop exit (right). In some situations, it is impossible to retest an exit condition after the loop because the exit condition is transitory, e.g., reading a sensor that resets after each read, so flag variables must be used.

2.3.1 Loop-Exit Criticisms

While the multi-exit loop is an extremely powerful control-flow capability, it has its detractors. Critics of the multi-exit loop often claim exits are difficult to find in the loop body. However, this criticism is simply dealt with by outdenting the exit (**eye-candy**), as in all the examples given thus far, which is the same indentation rule used for the **else** of the if-then-else:

```
if ( ... ) {                    if ( ... ) {
    XXX XXX                         XXX XXX
    } else { // not outdented       } else { // outdented, good eye-candy
    XXX XXX                         XXX XXX
}                               }
```

In the left example, it is difficult to locate the else-clause because the **else** keyword is indented at the same level as the statements in the then/else clauses; in the right example, the else-clause is outdented from these statements to make it trivial to locate. In addition (or possibly as an alternative to outdenting), comments can be used to clearly identify loop exits. As well, folding specific exit-code into a loop body can make it difficult to read when the exit-specific code is large. This criticism is justified, and so programmers must decide when such an approach is best.

Critics of multi-exit loop also claim the control-flow is "unstructured", i.e., it does not follow the doctrine originally presented for structured programming, which only uses **if** and **while**. (See [16] for a comprehensive discussion of both sides of the issue.) However, this is a very restricted and conservative view of structured programming and does not reflect current knowledge and understanding in either programming-language design or software engineering. That is, it makes no sense to summarily reject the multi-exit loop when its complexity is virtually equivalent to a while loop and yet it simplifies important coding situations. The key point is to understand the potential techniques available to solve a problem and select the most appropriate technique for each individual case.

2.3.2 Linear Search Example

A good example that illustrates the complexity of control flow is a linear search of an array to determine if a key is present as an element of the array. In addition, if the search finds the key, the position in the array where the key is found must be available for subsequent operations. The two common errors in this search are:

- using an invalid subscript into the array. This problem often happens when the array is full and the key is not present; it is easy to subscript one past the end of the array.
- off-by-one error for the index of the array element when there is a match with the search key. This problem often happens if the loop index is advanced too early or too late with respect to stopping the search after finding the key.

Several solutions to this problem are examined.

The first solution uses only **if-else, while** and basic relational/logical operators:

```
i = -1; found = 0;
while ( i < size - 1 & ! found ) {
    i += 1;
    found = key == list[i];
}
if ( found ) { ...      // found
} else { ...            // not found
}
```

Why must the program be written in this way? First, if the condition of the while-loop is written like this:

```
while ( i < size & key != list[i] )
```

a subscript error occurs when I has the value size because the bitwise logical operator & evaluates both of its operands (and C arrays are subscripted from zero). There is no way around this problem using only **if-else, while** constructs and basic relational/ logical operators. Second, variable i must be incremented *before* key is compared in the loop body to ensure it has the correct value should the comparison be true and the loop stop. This results in the unusual initializing of i to -1, and the loop test succeeding in the range -1 to $size - 2$. Finally, the variable found is used solely for control flow purposes, and therefore, is a flag variable.

Many C programmers believe there is a simple second solution using only the **if-else** and **while** constructs (**for** is used to simplify it even further):

```
for ( i = 0; i < size && key != list[i]; i += 1 ) {}
                     ↑ only executed if i < size
if ( found ) { ...      // found
} else { ...            // not found
}
```

However, there are actually three control structures used here: **if-else, for,** and **&&.** Unlike the bitwise operator &, the operation **&&** is not a traditional operator because it may not evaluate both of its operands; if the left-hand operand evaluates to false, the right-hand operand is not evaluated. By not evaluating list[i] when i has the value size, the invalid subscript problem is removed. Such partial evaluation of an expression is called **short-circuit** or **lazy** evaluation. A short-circuit evaluation is a control-flow construct and not an operator because it cannot be written in the form of a routine as a routine call eagerly evaluates its arguments before being invoked in most programming languages.[2] All operators in C++ can be written in the form of a routine. Therefore, the built-in logical constructs && and || are not operators but rather control structures in the middle of an expression.

Finally, to understand both solutions requires a basic understanding of boolean algebra, i.e., the truth tables for boolean operators ∧ (and) and ∨ (or), and for &&, it is necessary to understand the relationship $false \land ? = false$, and for ||, the relationship $true \lor ? = true$. In some cases, students may not have taken boolean algebra before attempting to write a linear search in a programming course, making the explanation of the linear search doubly difficult.

The third solution uses a multi-exit loop:

```
for ( i = 0; ; i += 1 ) {
    if ( i == size ) break;
    if ( key == list[i] ) break;
}
if ( i == size ) { ...        // not found
} else { ...                  // found
}
```

If the first loop-exit occurs, it is obvious there is no subscript error because the loop is terminated when i has the value size. If the second loop-exit occurs, i must reference the position of the element equal to the key. As well, no direct knowledge of boolean algebra is required (even though the logic of the boolean ∧ occurs implicitly); hence, this form of linear search can be learned very early.

Finally, all the linear-search solutions have an additional test after the search to re-determine the result of the search; i.e., when the search ends, it is known if the key is or is not found in the array, but this knowledge is thrown away. Hence, after the search completes, it is necessary to check again what happened in the search. This superfluous check at the end of the search can be eliminated by folding this code into the search using exit code, e.g.:

```
for ( i = 0; ; i += 1 ) {
    if ( i == size ) { ... /* not found */ break; }
    if ( key == list[i] ) { ... /* found */ break; }
}
```

Again, a programmer has to judge whether folding exit code into the loop body is appropriate for each specific situation with respect to functionality and readability.

The key observation is that a multi-exit loop is a viable alternative to other control-flow techniques, e.g., **while**, flag variables and short-circuit logical operators, and is often simpler to understand, eliminates duplicated code and is equally efficient with respect to runtime performance. As well, multi-exit allows new code

---

[2] Some programming languages, such as Algol 60 [4] and Haskell [13], support deferred/lazy argument evaluation. If C++ had this mechanism, the built-in operators && and || could be written as routines. However, deferred/lazy argument evaluation produces a substantially different kind of routine call, and has implementation and efficiency implications. Interestingly, C++ allows the operators && and || to be overloaded with user-defined versions, but these overloaded versions *do not* display the short-circuit property. Instead, they behave like normal routines with eager evaluation of their arguments. This semantic behaviour can easily result in problems if a user is relying on the short-circuit property. For this reason, operators && and || should never be overloaded in C++. Fundamentally, C++ should not allow redefinition of operators && and || because they do not follow the same semantic behaviour as the built-in versions.

to be inserted between the exits and on exit termination. Accomplishing similar additions, when other constructs are used, requires program restructuring, which introduces the potential for errors.

2.4 Static Multi-Level Exit

A static multi-level exit is one in which control leaves multiple levels of *nested* control-structures to an exit point within the same routine; hence, the exit point is known at compile time, i.e., can be determined before starting program execution. It is the fact that the criteria for completing/terminating a computation is embedded within the nested control-structures that introduces the complexity. Programming languages provide different mechanisms for multi-level exit, some similar to that proposed by Peterson et al. (see Sect. 2.2, p. 10). For example, both μC++ and Java provide a labelled **break** and **continue** statement.

```
L1: {                          // compound, good eye-candy for labels
    ...
    L2: switch ( ... ) {       // switch
      case ...:
        L3: for ( ... ) {      // loop
          ... continue L3; ... // next iteration
          ... break L3; ...    // exit loop
          ... break L2; ...    // exit switch
          ... break L1; ...    // exit compound statement
        } // for
        break;                 // exit switch
        ... // more case clauses
    } // switch
    ...
} // compound
```

Note, a label has routine scope in C/C++/Java, meaning it must be unique within a routine (member), and it must be attached to a statement. For **break**, the target label may be associated with a **for**, **while**, **do**, **switch** or compound ({}) statement; for **continue**, the target label may be associated with a **for**, **while** or **do** statement. While labelled **break/continue** eliminate the explicit use of the **goto** statement to exit multiple levels of control structure, the underlying mechanism to perform the transfer is still a **goto**.

Notice, the simple case of multi-level exit (exiting 1 level) is just a multi-exit loop and could have been done using a **break** without a label. The advantage of using an unlabelled **break** is not having to generate unique labels in a routine for each control structure with an exit. The disadvantage of using an unlabelled **break** is the potential for errors when nested control-structures are added:

```
for ( ;; ) {          for ( ;; ) {                        B: for ( ;; ) {
                        for ( ;; ) { // add new loop          for ( ;; ) {
    ...                   ...                                   ...
  if ( C1 ) break;      if ( C1 ) break; // exit wrong level  if ( C1 ) break B;
    ...                   ...                                   ...
                        } // incorrect exit point             }
}                       } // correct exit point             } // correct exit point
```

```
B1: for ( i = 0; i < 10; i += 1 ) {

    B2: for ( j=0; j<10; j += 1 ) {
        ...
        if ( ... ) break B2;  // outdent

        ... // rest of loop
    if ( ... ) break B1;  // outdent

        ... // rest of loop


    } // for

    ... // rest of loop

} // for
```

```
bool flag1 = false;
for ( i = 0; i < 10 && ! flag1; i += 1 ) {
    bool flag2 = false;
    for ( j=0; j<10 && ! flag1 && ! flag2; j += 1 ) {
        ...
        if ( ... ) flag2 = true;
        else {
            ... // rest of loop
            if ( ... ) flag1 = true;
            else {
                ... // rest of loop .
            } // if
        } // if
    } // for
    if ( ! flag1 ) {
        ... // rest of loop
    } // if
} // for
```

Fig. 2.1 Contrast multi-loop exit with basic control structures

Here, the unlabelled break must be transformed into a labelled break to maintain correct control flow.

As stated previously (page 12), without multi-level exit, flag variables are required to achieve equivalent control flow. Fig. 2.1 shows that if two nested loops must exit to different levels depending on certain conditions, there is a significant difference between the multi-loop exit and using only **if-else** and **while**. Each loop requires a flag variable for termination. If an additional nested loop is added between the existing two loops, an additional flag variable must be introduced and set, tested, and reset in the new and containing loops. Similarly, removing a nested loop requires removing all occurrences of its associated flag variable. Hence, changes of this sort are tedious and error-prone. In contrast, the multi-level exit version has no flag variables, which reduces both complexity and execution cost; as well, nested loops can be added or removed without changing existing code. Notice the exaggerated outdenting scheme for termination of the outer loop, which shows exactly the level the exit transfers to. Remember, a program is a utilitarian entity; indentation should reflect this and not be just an esthetic consideration.

The mechanism providing this flexibility is the labelled exit, but unlike μC++/Java, C++ does not have a labelled **break** (or **continue**). Hence, the previous multi-level exit example must be written as follows in C++:

```
for ( i = 0; i < 10; i += 1 ) {
    for ( j = 0; j < 10; j += 1 ) {
        ...
        if ( ... ) goto L2;
        ...
    if ( ... ) goto L1;
        ...
    } // for
    L2: ;                    // exit point, bad eye-candy
    ...
} // for
L1: ;                        // exit point
```

duplication	no duplication	
| ```
if ( C1 ) {
    S1;
    if ( C2 ) {
        S2;
        if ( C3 ) {
            S3;
        } else
            S4;
    else
        S4;
else
    S4;
``` | ```
C: {
    if ( C1 ) {
        S1;
        if ( C2 ) {
            S2;
            if ( C3 ) {
                S3;
                break C;
            }
        }
    }
    S4; // only once
}
``` | ```
if ( C1 ) {
    S1;
    if ( C2 ) {
        S2;
        if ( C3 ) {
            S3;
            goto C:
        }
    }
}
S4; // only once
C: ;
``` |

Fig. 2.2 Nested if-statements

There are several points to note. First, because the **break** statement exits only one level, a **goto** statement *must* be used to exit multiple levels. The **goto** transfers control to the corresponding label, terminating any control structures between the **goto** and the label. Second, labels L1 and L2 are necessary to denote the transfer points of the exit but their location is at the *end* of the terminated control-structure rather than the beginning. In the example, a label is associated with a null statement by putting a semicolon after the label, making the label independent of any statement that might be moved or removed.

The advantage of the labelled **break/continue** is allowing static multi-level exits without having to use the **goto** statement and ties control flow to the target control-structure rather than an arbitrary point in a program. Furthermore, the location of the label at the *beginning* of the target control-structure informs the reader (eye candy) of complex control-flow occurring in the body of the control structure. With **goto**, the label at the end of the control structure fails to convey this important clue early enough to the reader. Finally, using an explicit target for the transfer instead of an implicit target allows new nested loop or **switch** constructs to be added or removed without affecting other constructs.

Fig. 2.2 shows this discussion applies equally well to a series of nested if-statement with common **else** clauses, e.g., print an error message if any one of the conditions fails. The goal is to remove the duplicate code S4. Using a routine is one approach, but requires factoring the duplicate code into a routine with necessary parameters. Instead, the problem is solved in situ by changing the control flow. The labelled **break** or **goto** jumps over the common code if control reaches the inner most **if** statement. Otherwise, if one of the **if** statements is false, the common code is executed.

An alternative mechanism for performing some forms of exit is to use **return** statements in a routine body, as in:

```
int rtn( ... ) {
    ... return expr$_1$; ...
    ... return expr$_2$; ...
}
```
```

Non-nested Returns	Nested Returns
``int rtn(int x, int y) {
if (x < 3) return 3;
if (x == 3) return y;
x += 1;
if (x > y) {
x = y + y;
} else {
x += 3;
}
return x;
}```	```int rtn(int x, int y) {
if (x > 3) {
x += 1;
if (x > y) {
x = y;
} else {
return x + 3;
}
return x + y;
} else if (x < 3) {
return 3;
} else {
return y;
}
}```

Fig. 2.3 Nested return-statements

These **return** statements may appear in nested control-structures, and hence, cause termination of both the control structures and the routine. But since **return** terminates a routine, using it for all exit situations in a routine is impossible. As with exits, return points should be highlighted by outdenting or comments to make them easy to locate. Fig. 2.3 shows it is sometimes possible to factor multiple returns towards the beginning of a routine to eliminate nesting. This approach can enhance readability and understandability by reducing the number of return points and nested control-structures with return points.

In summary, while multi-exit loops appear often, static multi-level exits appear infrequently. Do not expect to find many static multi-level exits even in large programs. Nevertheless, they are extremely concise and execution-time efficient when needed; use them, but do not abuse them.

2.5 Routine

Routines, subroutines, subprograms, functions or procedures are used to parameterize a section of code so it can be reused without having to copy the code with different variables substituted for the parameters. Routines provide reuse of knowledge and time by allowing other programs to call the routine, dynamically binding actual argument variables to formal parameter variables for the computation of the routine. It is common for one routine to call another, making routines one of the basic building blocks for program construction. Modularization of programs into reusable routines is the foundation of modern software engineering. To support this capability, a programming language allows virtually any contiguous, complete block of code to be factored into a subroutine and called from anywhere in the program; conversely, any routine call is replaceable by its corresponding routine

body with appropriate substitutions of arguments for parameters. The ability to
support modularization is an important design factor when developing control
structures to facilitate software-engineering techniques.

Routine activation (call/invocation) introduces a complex form of control flow.
When control reaches a routine call, the current execution context is temporarily
suspended and its local state is saved, and the routine starts execution at its beginning
along with a new set of its local variables, called a **routine activation** or **stack
frame**.

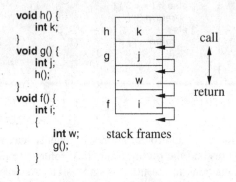

```
void h() {
    int k;
}
void g() {
    int j;
    h();
}
void f() {
    int i;
    {
        int w;
        g();
    }
}
```

Note, a language construct defining a declaration scope, i.e., one that can have local
declarations, also generates a stack frame that is treated as a call. When a routine
returns, it implicitly returns to the point of the routine call, reactivating any saved
state. From the control perspective, the programmer does not have to know where a
routine is or how to get back to the call; it just happens. In fact, there is no magic, the
compiler/linker stores the location of the routine at each call site. When a routine
call occurs, this location is used to transfer to the routine and the location of the
call is saved so the routine can transfer back. As routines call one another, a chain of
suspended routines is formed. A call adds a routine activation, containing a routine's
local-state, to one end of the chain; a return removes an activation from the same end
of the chain, destroying the routine's local-state. Therefore, the chain behaves like a
stack, and it is normally implemented that way. In most programming languages,
it is impossible to build this call/return mechanism using the basic control-flow
constructs; hence, routine call/return is a fundamental mechanism to affect control
flow.

In general, routine-call complexity depends on the references within the routine.
If a routine is self-contained, i.e., it only references parameters and local variables:

```
int rtn( int p ) {          // self-contained: local variable references
    int i = 0;
    {   int j = 1;
        {   int k = 2;
            cout << p << i << j << k << endl;
        }
    }
}
```

then the routine does not depend on its lexical context (surrounding code) to execute.
In this case, local variable references are statically determined and bound at compile
time, even though there may be multiple instances of rtn on the stack (recursion).

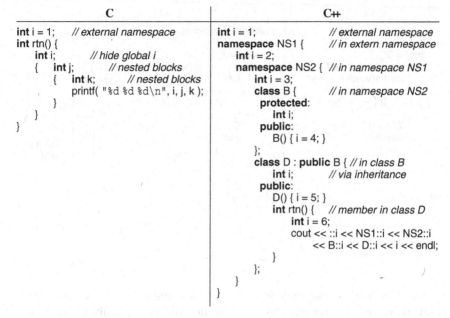

C	C++
| ```
int i = 1;      // external namespace
int rtn() {
    int i;      // hide global i
    {   int j;      // nested blocks
        {   int k;      // nested blocks
            printf( "%d %d %d\n", i, j, k );
        }
    }
}
``` | ```
int i = 1;              // external namespace
namespace NS1 {         // in extern namespace
    int i = 2;
    namespace NS2 {  // in namespace NS1
        int i = 3;
        class B {       // in namespace NS2
            protected:
            int i;
            public:
            B() { i = 4; }
        };
        class D : public B {  // in class B
            int i;              // via inheritance
            public:
            D() { i = 5; }
            int rtn() {      // member in class D
                int i = 6;
                cout << ::i << NS1::i << NS2::i
                     << B::i << D::i << i << endl;
            }
        };
    }
}
``` |

Fig. 2.4 Lexical scopes

These fixed references are possible because a routine activation has a pointer to its stack frame (like an object **this** pointer) and all local variables are at fixed offsets from this pointer (base-displacement addressing).

However, the lexical scoping of a programming language allows a routine to reference variables and routines not defined within it (see Fig. 2.4). The lexical scope of a routine in C (left) is only one level, the external namespace, due to the lack of nested routines (see also Fig. 1.1, p. 3). This additional scope level still has fixed references to it because there is only one instance of the external namespace so the compiler can generate a fixed address for any reference; such a pointer is called a lexical link or access link [3, § 7.3.7]. The lexical scope of a member routine in C++ (right) is significantly more complex: a routine can have inheritance nesting in one or more classes,[3] which can be nested in one or more namespaces. Nevertheless, references within a member routine are still fixed even though there can be multiple routine activations and object instances. Again, each routine activation has a pointer to its stack frame, and a pointer to its containing object instance, i.e. **this**, and there is only one instance of each namespace so the compiler can statically generate references to each variable using offsets within frames/objects or fixed lexical links to namespaces.

This issue is generalized further for languages with more complex lexical scoping, such as nested routines, classes and resumption exceptions (see page 87). Nested routines are examined for both GNU C and C++11 in Fig. 2.5. The nested

---

[3] While classes can be lexically nested, there is no lexical scoping.

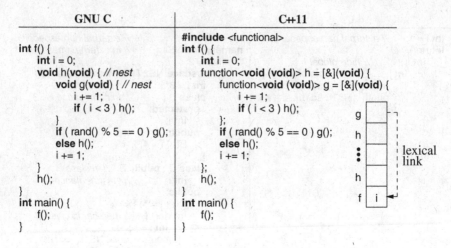

GNU C	C++11

```
int f() {
    int i = 0;
    void h(void) { // nest
        void g(void) { // nest
            i += 1;
            if ( i < 3 ) h();
        }
        if ( rand() % 5 == 0 ) g();
        else h();
        i += 1;
    }
    h();
}
int main() {
    f();
}
```

```
#include <functional>
int f() {
    int i = 0;
    function<void (void)> h = [&](void) {
        function<void (void)> g = [&](void) {
            i += 1;
            if ( i < 3 ) h();
        };
        if ( rand() % 5 == 0 ) g();
        else h();
        i += 1;
    };
    h();
}
int main() {
    f();
}
```

Fig. 2.5 Nested routines

routine g increments the variable f::i, which is accessible in its lexical scope. However, unlike the previous cases, the location of i is not easily found or at a static location because there is an unknown distance on the stack from g to f because the number of recursive calls to h between them is determined dynamically. Hence, when g is called it must be implicitly passed a lexical link, which is a pointer to f's stack frame to access i. Furthermore, unlike the single external area, there may be multiple calls to f on the stack (assume f is recursive), where each one of these calls generates a g with a lexical link to its specific instance of f. Thus, it is impossible to have a static pointer to f, as for the external area, because there can be multiple fs. Lexical links are a standard technique in the implementation of nested routines to give a routine access to variables from the lexical context of its definition [8, Section 9.5].

2.6 Recursion

A **recursive algorithm** is a problem-solving approach that subdivides a problem into two major components:

1. A recursive case, where an instance of the problem is solved by reapplying the algorithm on a refined set of data,
2. and a base case, where an instance of the problem is solved directly.

There is a strong analogy between a recursive algorithm and the mathematical principle of induction. The class of problems suitable for divide-and-conquer solutions lends itself to recursive algorithms because the data is subdivided into smaller and smaller pieces, until there is only one value or a small number of values that can be manipulated directly. When a recursive algorithm is implemented as a program, a technique called **recursion** is used where a routine calls itself directly or indirectly, forming a call cycle. A direct example of recursion is routine X calling itself any number of times; an indirect example is routine X calling Y, routine Y calling Z, and routine Z calling back to X, and this cycle occurs any number of times. Hence, programs without call cycles are non-recursive and programs with call cycles are recursive.

Many programmers find designing, understanding and coding recursion to be difficult (see also page 4), even though the call mechanism does not differentiate between calls forming and not forming cycles.

You cannot be *taught* to think recursively, but you can *learn* to think recursively [31, p. 92].

The difficulty occurs because recursive programs form a more complex dynamic program-structure than non-recursive programs. For non-recursive programs, the set of calls form an acyclic graph; for recursive programs, the set of calls form a cyclic graph. Hence, it is the dynamic structure (cycles versus no cycles) that denotes recursion not the call mechanism, which is identical for all calls. And it is the cycles in the call graph that make it more difficult to understand recursive programs, simply because acyclic graphs are simpler than cyclic ones.

The simplest form of recursion is similar to looping:

Looping	Recursion	
`int i = 0;`	`loop( 0 );`	*// initialization / start recursion*
`for ( ;; ) {`	`void loop( int i ) {`	
`int j = i + 3;`	`int j = i + 3;`	*// local variable*
`...`		*// loop body / repeated statements*
`if ( i == N ) break;`	`if ( i == N ) return`	*// loop test / base case*
`...`		*// loop body / repeated statements*
`i += 1;`	`loop( i + 1 );`	*// increment loop-index / argument*
`}`	`}`	*// no operations after return*

Initializing the loop index corresponds to the initial call to begin the recursion. The test to stop looping corresponds to the base case of the recursion to stop further calls. Incrementing the loop index at the end of the loop corresponds to the recursive call at the end of the routine passing an incremented argument. Of course the loop index and recursive parameter can be an arbitrary entity, such as a pointer traversing a linked list.

This simple form of recursion is called **tail recursion**, where a recursive routine ends solely with a single call to itself, i.e., no other operations can occur after the call except returning a result. What is special about this case? From outside the routine, there is nothing special, i.e., a caller is pending (stopped) waiting for state to be returned so it can process it. However, from inside the routine, the caller sees it call itself at the end. Hence, the next stack frame in the recursion is identical in structure to the current frame, where the arguments are bound to the parameters at each call. As well, no computation after the return means returns can cascade, i.e., the return value is returned, then returned, then returned, etc. without needing to restart callers as there is no future computation, until the initial caller is restarted. Therefore, an optimization of reusing the current stack frame is possible where the argument expression i + 1 is bound to the next i of the call and other local variables

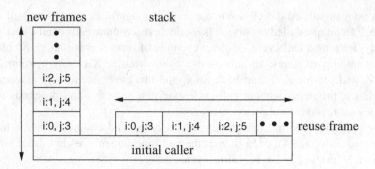

Fig. 2.6 Tail recursion/continuation passing

are reinitialized at the start of the routine, but the location and size of these variables
are the same as the previous frame. Hence, the parameters can be mutated for the
next call after evaluating the argument expression(s), and any local state is mutated
during initialization of the next call.

Fig. 2.6 shows how this optimization can continue independent of recursion: if
control does not need to return to a routine for further computation, the next call can
continue on the top of the stack. This style of programming is called **continuation
passing**. Continuation passing can be explicit by always passing any state previously
needed to the next call, making prior stack frames unnecessary. Taken ad nauseam, a
program can execute with a single stack frame, at the high cost of pushing sufficient
state forward on each call to perform the next portion of the computation. In general,
programmers balance the mix of state saving and state forwarding to efficiently
perform computations.

However, recursion is more powerful than looping because of its ability to
remember both data and execution state. In the previous looping example, there is a
single loop-index variable i and all loop transfers are to static locations (start or end
of loop). In the previous recursion example, each routine call creates a new instance
of the routine's local variables, which includes parameters, and stores the return
location for each call even though the return point is the same for all calls (except
the first call); hence, there are $N+1$ instances of parameter variable i, local variable j
and a corresponding number of return locations. (Why $N+1$ rather than N?) Hence,
the left example uses $O(1)$ storage while the right example uses $O(N)$ storage, and
there is an $O(N)$ cost for creating and removing these variables. Therefore, using
tail recursion to implement a simple loop may not produce the same efficiency.
However, tail recursion is easily transformed into a loop, removing any recursion
overhead. Most compilers implicitly convert a tail-recursive routine into its looping
counterpart; some languages guarantee this conversion so programmers know tail
recursive solutions are efficient, e.g., Scheme [1, § 3.5].

In detail, recursion exploits the ability to remember both data and execution
state (return points) created via routine calls; both capabilities are accomplished
implicitly through the routine-call stack. Data is explicitly remembered via parameters and local variables created on each call to a routine. Execution state is

implicitly remembered via the call/return mechanism, which saves the caller's location on the stack so a called routine knows where to return. Visualizing the implicit state information pushed and popped on the call-stack during recursion may help understand recursion is just normal call/return with cycles in the call graph manipulating an implicit stack data-structure.

Non-tail recursive situations can take advantage of the additional power of recursion. A simple example is reading an arbitrary number of values and printing them in reverse order:

Looping/Array	Looping/Stack	Recursion

```
void printRev() {             void printRev() {             void printRev() {
   int n, v[100]; // dimension    stack<int> s; int v;           int v;
   for ( n=0; n<100; n+=1 ) {     for ( ;; ) {                   // front side
      cin >> v[n];                   cin >> v;                   cin >> v;
      if ( cin.fail() ) break;       if ( cin.fail() ) break;    if ( cin.fail() ) return;
                                     s.push( v );                printRev();
   }                             }
   for ( n-=1; n>=0; n-=1 ) {     for ( ; ! s.empty(); s.pop() ) {   // back side
      cout << v[n] << endl;          cout << s.top() << endl;    cout << v << endl;
   }                             }
}                             }                             }
```

What is interesting about this problem is that *all* values must be read and stored before any printing can occur because the last value appears first.

The looping solution using an array (left) creates a fixed-size array to store the values during reading. Normally, this array is over-dimensioned to handle the worst case number of input values (wasting storage), and the program fails if the worst case is exceeded. As well, the loop index must be managed carefully as it is easy to generate an off-by-one error with the zero-origin arrays in C++.

Alternatively, a variable-sized data-structure can be used to store the values to eliminate the fixed-sized array problems. The looping solution using a stack (centre) creates the simplest data-structure needed to solve this problem, allowing the values to be accessed in Last-In First-Out (LIFO) order.[4] As well, this solution has no explicit loop index, so off-by-one errors are eliminated.

The recursive solution (right) uses the implicit routine-call stack to replace the explicit stack for storing the input values, and replaces the two **for** loops (input/output) by an input and output phase retaining execution-state. In general, recursive control-flow is divided into a front side (before) and a back side (after) for each recursive call. The front side is like a loop going in the forward direction over parameter data, and the back side is like a loop going in the reverse direction over the parameter data with possibly a return value. In this program, the action on the front side of the recursion is to allocate a new local variable v on the stack to remember data and to read a value into this variable. The action on the back side of the recursion is to print the value read and deallocate the local variable, which occurs

---

[4] While a variable-sized array, e.g., C++ Standard Library vector, is also possible, it is more complex and expensive than is needed for this problem.

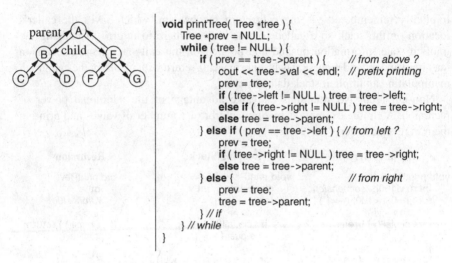

```
void printTree( Tree *tree ) {
    Tree *prev = NULL;
    while ( tree != NULL ) {
        if ( prev == tree->parent ) {      // from above ?
            cout << tree->val << endl;   // prefix printing
            prev = tree;
            if ( tree->left != NULL ) tree = tree->left;
            else if ( tree->right != NULL ) tree = tree->right;
            else tree = tree->parent;
        } else if ( prev == tree->left ) { // from left ?
            prev = tree;
            if ( tree->right != NULL ) tree = tree->right;
            else tree = tree->parent;
        } else {                           // from right
            prev = tree;
            tree = tree->parent;
        } // if
    } // while
}
```

Fig. 2.7 Bidirectional tree traversal

in reverse order to the front-side action. The print on the back side of the recursion makes this program non-tail recursive. Note, an arbitrary amount of work can occur between the front and back side of a particular recursion step during intervening recursive (and non-recursive) calls.

If the problem is changed to require more general access to the data, such as printing the values in the forward order for an even number of values and reverse order for an odd number of values, there is no direct recursive solution. The reason is that for an even number of values, the values must be printed on the front side of the recursion, but all the values must be read *before* it is known if there are an even number of them, and by then, all the front-side actions have occurred. Hence, an explicit data-structure is required, like a deque, which allows efficient forward and backward access to the values. If a problem requires even more general access to the data, e.g., efficient random access, an array data-structure is needed.

The next example shows a more complex use of the ability of recursion to implicitly remember data and execution location. In theory, tree traversal, i.e., visiting all nodes of a tree data structure, requires both parent and child links, where a parent link moves up the branch of a tree and a child link moves down the branch of a tree. Fig. 2.7 shows a tree traversal for a tree with bidirectional links. The traversal keeps track of the previous node visited and uses that information along with the current and parent nodes to determine whether to traverse up or down the tree. The amount of storage needed for the traversal is the tree parameter and the prev pointer, as each tree node already contains the parent/child pointers.

If a tree node has no parent pointer, it is impossible to walk up the tree, and hence, to traverse the tree. Traversing a unidirectional tree (child only links) requires a stack to temporarily hold a pointer to the node above the current node (parent link), and this stack has a maximum depth of the tree height. This temporary stack

Looping/Stack	Recursion

```
struct State {
    Tree *t;                    // parameter
    int es;                     // execution state
    State( Tree *t, int es ) : t( t ), es( es ) {}
};
void printTree( Tree *tree ) {
    stack<State> cs;
    int es;

    for ( ;; ) {
        if ( tree == NULL ) {       // general case ?
        if ( cs.empty() ) break;    // final return ?
            tree = cs.top().t;      // parent
            es = cs.top().es;       // prior exec state
            cs.pop();               // pop stack frame
        } else {                    // normal return
            es = 0;                 // call
        } // if
        switch( es ) {              // execution state ?
          case 0:                   // call
            cout << tree->val << endl; // prefix
            cs.push( State( tree, 1 ) );
            tree = tree->left;
            break;
          case 1:                   // return from left
            cs.push( State( tree, 2 ) );
            tree = tree->right;
            break;
          case 2:                   // return from right
            tree = NULL;            // cause return
        } // switch
    } // for
}
```

```
// prefix traversal
void printTree( Tree *tree ) {
    if ( tree != NULL ) {
        cout << tree->val << endl;
        printTree( tree->left );
        printTree( tree->right );
    } // if
}
```

Fig. 2.8 Unidirectional tree traversal

can be an explicit data-structure or implicit using the call-stack. Fig. 2.8 shows a
tree traversal for a tree with unidirectional links. The looping solution (left) uses
an explicit stack to store the parent node and three possible execution states. (Note,
the structure of the looping solution accurately mimics the flow of the control in
the recursive solution.) The recursive solution (right) uses the routine-call stack to
implicitly store the parameter variable tree (data state) and whether the left or right
branch was last visited (execution state). In detail, the recursive solution generates
the following information on the call stack during a tree traversal (l ⟹ go left, r ⟹
go right, _ ⟹ print):

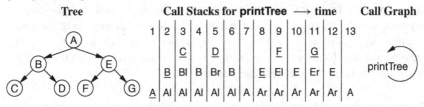

Hence, when control is at level N of the tree, level $N - 1$ of the call stack has the
equivalent of a back (parent) pointer in parameter variable tree to allow walking up

```
int partition( int array[ ], int left, int right, int pivotIndex ) {
    int pivotValue = array[pivotIndex];
    swap( array[pivotIndex], array[right] );              // move pivot to end
    int storeIndex = left;
    for ( int i = left; i < right; i += 1 ) {
        if ( array[i] < pivotValue ) {
            swap( array[storeIndex], array[i] );
            storeIndex += 1;
        }
    }
    swap( array[right], array[storeIndex] );              // move pivot back
    return storeIndex;
}
void quicksort( int array[ ], int left, int right ) {
    if ( right <= left ) return;                          // base case, one value
    int pivotIndex = partition( array, left, right, ( right + left ) / 2 );
    quicksort( array, left, pivotIndex - 1 );             // sort left half
    quicksort( array, pivotIndex + 1, right );            // sort right half
}
```

Fig. 2.9 Recursive quick sort

a tree (when a call returns) without explicit back-pointers in the tree. As well, each call stores its return location on the call stack (l for the call with the left subtree and r for the call with the right subtree). Hence, when control returns from level N of the tree, the return location at $N - 1$ of the call stack implicitly indicates which branch of the tree has been traversed. Most importantly, the explicit stack and complex control-flow in the looping solution becomes implicit in the recursive solution using the call stack and front/back side of the recursion. Hiding these details in the recursive solution clearly illustrates the power of the routine-call to retain both data and execution state. This complexity is further hidden in the simple call graph for the recursive tree-traversal, which is only a single cycle, making the recursive solution seem magical.

Another non-tail-recursive example is quick sort [12] (see Fig. 2.9), which employs double recursion like a tree traversal. The recursive algorithm chooses a pivot point in an array of unsorted values. Then all values less than the pivot are partitioned to the left of it and all greater values to the right of it, which means the pivot is now in its sorted location. After partitioning, quick sort is called recursively to sort the set of values on both sides of the pivot. The base case for the recursion is when there is only a single value to be sorted, which is a sorted set.

Note, in both tree traversal and quick sort, the structure of the data (tree, array) remains fixed throughout the recursion; only data within the data structure and auxiliary variables associated with the recursion change. However, recursive solutions to some problems may even restructure the data, such as balancing a binary tree, which reshapes the tree. Changing the data structure during traversal can increase the complexity of the recursive algorithm because elements may move and reappear at new locations. Correspondingly, the program recursion may need to increase in complexity to deal with these cases.

Table 2.1 Péter/Robinson values, $\infty \approx$ extremely large value

m\n	0	1	2	3	4	...n
0	1	2	3	4	5	$n+1$
1	2	3	4	5	6	$n+2$
2	3	5	7	9	11	$2n+3$
3	5	13	29	61	125	$2^{n+3}-3$
4	13	65533	$2^{65536}-3$	$2^{2^{65536}}-3$	∞	$\underbrace{2^{2^{\cdot^{\cdot^{2}}}}}_{n+3\ twos}-3$
5	65533	$\underbrace{2^{2^{\cdot^{\cdot^{2}}}}}_{65536\ twos}-3$	∞	∞	∞	∞
$\vdots$ m	∞	∞	∞	∞	∞	∞

Interestingly, it is possible for even simple recursion to cause extreme blowup (see also page 5). For example, Ackermann's function [2]:

$$A(a,b,n) = \begin{cases} a+b & \text{if } n=0 \\ n-1 & \text{if } b=0 \text{ and } n=1,2 \\ a & \text{if } b=0 \text{ and } n>2 \\ A(a,A(a,b-1,n),n-1) & \text{if } n>0 \text{ and } b>0 \end{cases}$$

and its simplified two-parameter variant created by Rózsa Péter [22] and Raphael M. Robinson [25] (which is often incorrectly called Ackermann's function):

$$A(m,n) = \begin{cases} n+1 & \text{if } m=0 \\ A(m-1,1) & \text{if } n=0 \\ A(m-1,A(m,n-1)) & \text{if } m>0 \text{ and } n>0 \end{cases}$$

only use addition and subtraction, but very quickly generate extremely deep recursion and correspondingly very large values due to an exponential effect (see Table 2.1).

This example illustrates that recursion can very succinctly generate extremely complex forms of control flow; therefore, recursion needs to be used carefully, with a full understanding of its storage and execution implications.

2.7 Functional Programming

Functional programming is a style of programming that avoids keeping explicit state by returning values from routines and using immutable variables, i.e., **const** variables that are write-once read-only. One consequence of this programming style is the need to use recursion to perform repeated operations versus looping, which has a mutable loop counter. Specialized programming languages exist that

Mutable Summation	Immutable Summation	
C++ & Looping	C++ & Recursion	Haskell & Recursion
```template<typename T>``` `T sum( list<T> *lst ) {` `T acc = 0;` `for ( list<T> *p = lst;` `p != 0; p = p->next )` `acc += p->val;` `return acc;` `}`	```template<typename T>``` `T sum( list<T> *lst ) {` `if ( lst == 0 ) return 0;` `else return lst->val +` `sum( lst->next );` `}`	`sum lst =` `if null lst then 0` `else (head lst) +` `sum (tail lst)`

Fig. 2.10 Sum list elements

facilitate the functional-programming style, e.g., Lisp [28], Scheme [24], ML [20], Haskell, by supporting a programming style that precludes mutable variables. The main advantage of functional programming is a simplified yet powerful model of computation, which allows easy verification, optimization and parallelization of programs. This discussion focuses solely on the use of recursion to replace mutable variables.

Fig. 2.10 shows a looping and a recursive solution for summing the integer elements of a list in C++ and a recursive solution in Haskell[5]. The C++ solution uses the following list data-structure, similar to that used in most functional systems:

```
template<typename T>
  struct list {
    T val;       // data
    list *next;  // next list element
    list( T val, list *next ) : val( val ), next( next ) {}
};
```

For simplicity, the fields in the structure are accessed directly rather than through accessor routines. Both summing examples are generic and work with any list containing a type with a zero (0) value and plus (+) operator. The recursion eliminates the two mutable variables, acc and p, in the looping solution. Mutable variable acc is replaced by $N + 1$ return values and p is replaced by $N + 1$ parameter values resulting from the $N + 1$ recursive calls to process a list of elements. Because the recursion is not tail recursive, there is no trivial optimization of the recursive programs into the more efficient looping version with mutable state. The program can be converted into tail recursion by changing the interface and restructuring the code:

```
template<typename T>
  T sum( list<T> *lst, T val ) {                        // two parameters versus one
    if ( lst == 0 ) return val;
    else return sum( lst->next, val + lst->val ); // compute sum on front side
}
```

The tail-recursive solution computes the sum on the front side of the recursion, while the non-tail-recursive solution computes on the back side. While the original

---

[5]Haskell commonly uses pattern-matching versus **if** statements, but there is no semantic difference between these mechanisms.

non-tail-recursive solution has an intuitive structure, the tail-recursive form requires a complex solution for a simple problem. It is possible to regain the original interface by using a helper routine to perform the sum, but that further increases the complexity of the solution. In fact, many compilers can implicitly optimize the non-tail-recursive solution into its more complex form, which retains the simple solution while achieving looping efficiency.

Fig. 2.11 shows two mutable-list and two immutable-list versions for reversing a list in C++. The first mutable-list version uses looping and assumes the list is a deque (doubly linked). The loop traverses the list bidirectionally to its midpoint using two indices, swapping the values from the front and back halves of the list nodes during the traversal. The only difficult part is determining the list midpoint for a list with an even number of values. The second mutable-list solution uses recursion to walk through the list and assumes the list is only singly linked with a list header containing a pointer to the start and end of the list. During the front side of the recursion, the head of the list is removed and remembered. During the back side of the recursion, the node removed on the front side is added to the end of the list. In both cases, the original list is modified to generate the reversed list; in the first approach, the node values are changed, while in the second case, the link fields are changed.

The immutable-list solutions both duplicate the list in reversed order, which is the functional approach. The first immutable-list version uses looping (non-functional) and assumes the list is only singly linked with a list header only containing a pointer to the start of the list. As each node is traversed in the original list, a copy of the node is made and added to the head of the reversed list. The second immutable-list version uses recursion to replace the loop (functional). However, this solution requires access to both the original and the reverse list so it requires two parameters, which changes the routine's signature. The solution hides the second parameter by using a helper routine. During the front side of the recursion, the head of the list is copied and added to the head of the reversed list. During the back side of the recursion, the reversed list is returned. In both cases, the original list is unmodified and new reverse list is generated.

Quicksort is another example where it is possible to have a mutable version that sorts the array of values in place by interchanging values in the array (see Fig. 2.9, p. 32), or immutable version that copies the value into a sorted array, which is subsequently returned. For example, in Haskell, an immutable quicksort can be written as:

```
quicksort [] = []
quicksort( p:xs ) = quicksort [x|x <- xs,x < p] ++ [p] ++ quicksort [x|x <- xs,x >= p]
```

Here two patterns are used to deal with the case where the list is empty [], which returns an empty set [], or non-empty, which returns a new sorted list. In the second case, the argument is divided into its head, p, and the rest of the list, xs, using s:xs, and p becomes the pivot. The new sorted list is constructed by concatenating three lists: the quicksort of a new list with values less than the pivot, [x|x <- xs,x < s], a new list containing the pivot [s], and the quicksort of a new list with values greater than or

Iteration

Mutable List	Immutable List
| ```cpp
template<typename T>
 deque<T> &reverse( deque<T> &l ) {
   T *fwd, *bwd, *prev;
   for ( fwd = l.head(), bwd = l.tail();
         fwd != bwd && prev != fwd;
         fwd = l.succ( fwd ),
         bwd = l.pred( bwd ) ) {
     swap( fwd->value, bwd->value );
     prev = bwd; // used for even test
   }
   return l;
}
``` | ```cpp
template<typename T>
 queue<T> *reverse( const queue<T> &l ) {
   queue<T> *r = new queue<T>;
   for ( T *fwd = l.head();
         fwd != NULL;
         fwd = l.succ( fwd ) ) {
     r->addHead( new T( fwd->value ) );
   }
   return r;
}
``` |

Recursion

Mutable List	Immutable List
| ```cpp
template<typename T>
 queue<T> &reverse( queue<T> &l ) {
   if ( l.empty() ) return l;
   else {
     T *front = l.dropHead();
     queue<T> &t = reverse( l );
     t.addTail( front );
     return t;
   }
}
``` | ```cpp
template<typename T>
 queue<T> *helper( queue<T> *r, T *node ) {
   if ( node == NULL ) return r;
   else {
     r->addHead( new T( node->value ) );
     return helper( r, node->next );
   }
}
template<typename T>
 queue<T> *reverse( const queue<T> &l ) {
   queue<T> *r = new queue<T>;
   return helper( r, l.head() );
}
``` |

Fig. 2.11 Reverse list elements

equal to the pivot, [x|x <- xs,x >= s]. Note, at each level of the recursion, new lists are created that are subsequently sorted rather than modifying the original list of values. The key observation is that functional programming relies on immutable values to achieve its goals of verification, optimization and parallelizing of programs. Recursion is used instead of mutable loop-indices for iteration and creating/copying new data structures is used instead of reusing existing ones.

Finally, as mentioned in Sect. 2.6, p. 26, many programmers find recursion difficult, and hence, struggle to understand and create recursive algorithms and programs. For these programmers, a functional programming-language presents a daunting environment because of the heavy use of recursion. Nevertheless, functional programming techniques are ideal for solving certain kinds of problems. When these techniques are used properly and in the right circumstances, it is possible to create succinct and elegant solutions to complex problems.

2.8   Routine Pointers

The flexibility and expressiveness of a routine comes from abstraction through the argument/parameter mechanism, which generalizes a routine across any argument variables of matching type. However, the code within the routine is the same for all data in these variables. To generalize a routine further, it is necessary to pass code as an argument, which is executed within the routine body. Most programming languages allow a routine to be passed as a parameter to another routine for further generalization and reuse. Java only has routines contained in class definitions so routine pointers must be accomplished indirectly via classes.

C/C++	Java
`typedef int (*RP)( int );`	`interface RP { int p( int i ); }`
`int f( int v, RP p ) {`	`class F {`
`    return p( v*2 ) + 2; }`	`    static int f( int v, RP p ) { return p.p( v * 2 ) + 2; } }`
`int g( int i ) { return i-1; }`	`class G implements RP { public int p( int i ) { return i-1; } }`
`int h( int i ) { return i / 2; }`	`class H implements RP { public int p( int i ) { return i / 2; } }`
`cout << f( 4, g ) << endl;`	`System.out.println( F.f( 4, new G() ) );`
`cout << f( 4, h ) << endl;`	`System.out.println( F.f( 4, new H() ) );`

As for data parameters, routine parameters are specified with a type (return type, and number and types of parameters), and any routine matching that type can be passed as an argument. Routine f is generalized to accept any routine argument of the form: returns an **int** and takes an **int** parameter. Within the body of f, the parameter p is called with an appropriate **int** argument, and the result of calling p is further modified before it is returned. The types of both routines g and h match the second parameter type of f, and hence, can be passed as arguments to f, resulting in f performing different computations rather than a fixed computation.

Fig. 2.12 shows a routine that plots arbitrary functions rather than having a specific function embedded within the routine. Specifically, the plot routine takes start and end points along the X-axis, minimum and maximum points along the Y-axis for scaling, and a function to plot. The X range is divided into 50 intervals, with a star plotted at a scaled distance above/below the X-axis for the Y value returned from the function. Note, the plot has the X-axis rotated along the normal Y-axis so the plot can be arbitrarily long; therefore, the Y-axis is rotated along the normal X-axis, and hence is restricted by the width of the screen or paper.

A routine parameter is passed as a constant reference; in general, it makes no sense to change or copy routine code, like copying a data value. (There are esoteric situations where code is changed or copied during execution, called self-modifying code, but it is rare.) C/C++ requires the programmer to explicitly specify the reference via a pointer, while other languages implicitly create a reference.

A common source of confusion and errors in C/C++ is specifying the type of a routine. A routine type has the routine name and its parameters embedded within the return type, mimicking the way the return value is used at the routine's call site. For example, a routine that takes an integer parameter and returns a routine that takes an integer parameter and returns an integer is declared/used as follows:

```
#include <iostream>
#include <iomanip>
#include <cmath>
using namespace std;

void plot( double start, double end, double min, double max, double(*f)( double ) ) {
    double points = 50;                           // number of points along X-axis
    double inc = (end - start) / points, range = 1.0 / (max - min),
        offset = -min, height = points;
    cout << fixed << " (" << setw(5) << "X" << " , " << setw(5) << "Y" << ") " << endl;
    for ( double x = start; x <= end; x += inc ) {
        double y = f( x );                         // Y range
        int graph = height * (offset + y) * range;  // Y range scaled into integer domain
        cout << " (" << setw(5) << setprecision(2) << x
            << " , " << setw(5) << setprecision(1) << y << ") "
            << setw(graph) << "*" << endl;
    }
    cout << endl << endl;                          // space between graphs
}
double poly( double x ) { return 7 * pow( x, 2 ) + 2 * x + 1; }

int main() {
    plot( 0, 4 * M_PI, -1, 1, sin );               // plot library and user functions
    plot( 0, 4 * M_PI, -1, 1, cos );
    plot( -1.4, 1.4, -6, 6, tan );
    plot( -1.5, 1.25, 0, 10, poly );
}
```

Fig. 2.12 Graph functions

```
int ( *f( int p ) )( int ) { ... return g; } // return routine
int i = f( 3 )( 4 ); // call returned routine
```

Essentially, the return type is wrapped around the routine name in successive layers
(like an onion). While attempting to make the two contexts consistent was a laudable
goal, it did work out in practice. The problem is further exacerbated because routine
pointers are defined as a pointer but treated as a reference, and hence, automatically
dereferenced, allowing the direct call f(3) versus the indirect call (*f)(3).

Two important uses of routine parameters are fixup (see also Sect. 3.1, p. 62) and
call-back routines. A **fixup routine** is passed to another routine and is called if an
unusual situation is encountered during a computation. For example, when inverting
a matrix, the matrix may not be invertible if its determinant is 0, i.e., the matrix is
singular. Instead of halting the program if a matrix is found to be singular, the invert
routine calls a user supplied fixup routine to see if it is possible to recover and
continue the computation with some form of correction (e.g., modify the matrix):

```
int singularDefault( int matrix[ ][10], int rows, int cols ) { abort(); }
int invert( int matrix[ ][10], int rows, int cols,
        int (*singular)( int matrix[ ][10], int rows, int cols ) = singularDefault ) {
    ... if ( determinant( matrix, rows, cols ) == 0 ) {
        correction = singular( matrix, rows, cols ); // possible correction
    } ...
}
int fixup( int matrix[ ][10], int rows, int cols ) { return 0; }
invert( matrix, 10, 10, fixup ); // fixup rather than abort
```

The fixup routine generalizes the invert routine because the corrective action is specified for each call, and that action can be tailored to a particular usage. By giving the fixup parameter a default value, most calls to invert need not provide a fixup argument.

A **call-back routine** is used in event programming. When an event occurs, one or more call-back routines are called (triggered) and each one performs an action specific for that event. For example, a graphical user interface has an assortment of interactive "widgets", such as buttons, sliders and scrollbars. When a user manipulates the widget, events are generated representing the new state of the widget, e.g., a button changes from up to down, and the widget remembers the new state. A program registers interest in state transitions for different widgets by supplying a call-back routine, and each widget calls its registered call-back routine(s) when the widget changes state. Normally, a widget passes the new state of the widget to each call-back routine so it can perform an appropriate action, e.g.:

```
int callback( /* information about event */ ) {
    // examine event information and perform appropriate action
    // return status of callback action
}
...
registerCB( closeButton, callback );
```

Event programming with call-backs is straightforward until the call-back routine has multiple states that change depending on the number of times it is called or previous argument values. In this case, it is necessary to retain data and execution state information between invocations of the call-back routine, which can result in an awkward coding style (see also functor page 40 and coroutine Sect. 4, p. 125).

Another area where routine pointers are used implicitly is implementing virtual-routine members. Consider an object containing data and routine members, e.g.:

```
class Base {
    int x, y;              // data members
    virtual void m1(...);  // routine members
    virtual void m2(...);
};
```

The following are three implementation approaches for objects of type Base.

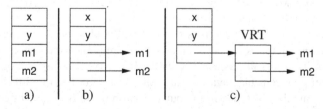

Implementation a) (left) has each object containing data fields x and y, and copies of routines m1 and m2. However, for N objects of type Base, there are N copies of routines m1 and m2, which are constant, i.e., the code for m1 and m2 does not change during execution and each routine can be tens, hundreds or thousands of bytes long. To remove the routine duplication, implementation b) (middle) factors out the constant values from each object and replaces them with a routine pointer to a constant routine value. While this approach results in significant savings in storage, each object still duplicates M routine pointers, where M is the number of routine members in the object (two for Base). Implementation c) (right) removes this final duplication by factoring out the common routine pointers into a virtual-routine table (VRT), and each object of type Base points to this common table. Therefore, routine pointers are used implicitly in the implementation of objects containing virtual routine members. Complex variants of the VRT are used to handle multiple and virtual inheritance [29, § 3.5.1].

As mentioned, it is possible to return a routine pointer as well as pass it as an argument, e.g.:

```
double g( double i ) { return i - 1.0; }
double h( double i ) { return i / 2.0; }
double ( *f( int i ) )( double ) {      // returns a pointer to a routine taking
    return i == 0 ? g : h;              //    a double and returning a double
}
```

However, returning a nested routine is complex because of lexical references:

GNU C	C++11
```int (*f(int i))(int) { int w = 2; int g(int j) { return i + w + j; } return g;}```	```function<int (int)> f(int i) { int w = 2; function<int (int)> g = [&](int j) { return i + w + j; }; return g;}```

Nested routine g accesses the parameter i and local variable w. However, when g is returned, routine f terminates and i and w are removed from the stack. As a result, when g is finally called, it references invalid storage.

To make this capability work, in general, requires a mechanism called a **closure**, which does not exist in C and only recently added to C++11, but does exist in other programming languages (first-class routines). The closure is an instance of the environment needed by g to make it work after it is returned from f. In essence, the closure retains information about a particular instance of f's environment existing when g is returned. In this case, the closure is an instance of parameter i and local variable w, and g would need a pointer to this closure as well as any lexical links that existed when the closure was created.

Fig. 2.13 shows a closure can be simulated with a class and made to look like a routine with a functor. A **functor** is a class redefining the function-call operator, which allows its object instances to be called like a routine. In the example, the closure object preserves the environment within f, so after f has terminated, g can be called any number of times in the outer environment. The same effect can be achieved in C++11 by explicitly asking the compiler to make a copy closure for the nested routine g:

```
function<int ( int )> g = [ = ](int j) {      // capture non-local symbols by value
    return i + w + j;
};
cout << f( 3 )( 4 ) << endl;                  // temporary Closure
function<int ( int )> c = f( 3 );             // retain Closure
cout << c( 4 ) + c( 7 ) << endl;             // call g twice
```

```
class Closure {
    int i, w;
public:
    Closure( int i, int w ) : i( i ), w( w ) {}
    int operator()( int j ) { return i + w + j; } // functor
};
Closure f( int i ) {
    int w = 2;
    return Closure( i, w );                    // capture
}
cout << f( 3 )( 4 ) << endl;                   // temporary Closure
Closure c = f( 3 );                            // retain Closure
cout << c( 4 ) + c( 7 ) << endl;               // call g twice
```

Fig. 2.13 Functor

However, a functor is not interchangeable with a routine pointer even if both have the same signature. Functors and routine pointers are only interchangeable through template parameters, where different code is generated for each.

2.9 Iterator

Iterative control flow repeatedly performs an action over a set of data. In some situations, the notion of iteration is abstracted, i.e., it is performed indirectly rather than directly using looping or recursion. One important example is when the elements of a data structure are not directly accessible. For example, a data structure may be implemented such that its elements are structured via a linked-list or a tree. Abstraction requires the data structure interface to be independent of the implementation. Hence, a user cannot construct a loop that accesses any of the link fields in the data structure because the implementation is allowed to change, which precludes any form of direct traversal. Therefore, an indirect abstract mechanism is needed to traverse the structure without requiring direct access to the internal representation. Such indirect traversal is provided by an iterator (or generator or cursor) object. A key requirement of indirect traversal is the ability to retain both data and execution state information between calls, e.g., to remember the current location in the traversal between one call to advance the traversal to the next. In some languages, special constructs exist that building special generator objects for iterating [11, 17, 21, 26, 27]. In C++, iterators are created through companion types of a basic data-structure. For example, the C++ Standard Library (stdlib) provides iterator types for many of its data structures. The kinds of traversal provided by an iterator are often those most efficiently possible for the associated data structure. For example, the iterator for a singly linked list may only provide unidirectional traversal (i.e., from head to tail), whereas the iterator for doubly linked list may provide bidirectional traversal (i.e., from head to tail or tail to head). While it is possible to provide reverse traversal of a singly linked list or random access to a

```
int main() {
    list<int> il;                                    // doubly-linked list
    for ( int i = 0; i < 10; i += 1 ) { il.push_back( i ); } // create list elements
    list<int>::iterator fr;                          // forward iterator
    list<int>::reverse_iterator rv;                  // reverse iterator
    for ( fr = il.begin(), rv = il.rbegin(); fr != il.end(); ++fr, ++rv ) { // bidirectionally print
        cout << *fr << " " << *rv << endl;
    }
    for ( fr = il.begin(); fr != il.end(); ++fr ) { il.erase( fr ); } // remove list elements
}
```

Fig. 2.14 List/iterator

doubly linked list, the cost for these operations can be very expensive; therefore, it is better to change to a more efficient data structure to obtain the necessary iterator access.

Fig. 2.14 demonstrates creating and using a C++ standard-library list and its iterator. This list is doubly-linked, i.e., each node has forward and backward pointers, which allow it to be traversed bidirectionally (forward or backwards). Two kinds of bidirectional iterator, iterator and reverse_iterator, are used to simultaneously traverse the list. An iterator is assigned a starting point, often the beginning/end of the list: begin/rbegin. The prefix operators ++/-- provide the bidirectional movement of an iterator's internal cursor to the next/previous node or to a fictitious node past the end/beginning of the list: end/rend. The forward iterator, iterator, advances from the starting point towards the end of the list, while the reverse iterator, reverse_iterator, advances from the starting point towards the beginning of the list. Because the iterator is an object, there can be multiple iterators instantiated, where each iterator is iterating independently over the same or a completely different list.

To accomplish iteration, the iterator objects fr and rv are closures retaining state information about the traversal in member variables between calls to the traversal operators, ++/--, such as the list being traversed and the current location of the traversal in the list. In effect, the iterator manages a cursor in the closure that moves in a particular direction during the list traversal. Because an iterator can retain arbitrary information between calls, it is possible for some iterators to continue traversing even as elements are being removed (see the last loop in Fig. 2.14). However, the control flow in operators ++/-- cannot be a loop traversing the data structure because it must return after each iteration terminating the loop; hence, the code must be structured sequentially and is controlled by internal execution-state information retain between calls to the iterator movement-operations. This control flow is necessary because a routine member cannot retain state between calls (see also Sect. 4.5, p. 136).

There are two basic kinds of iterators: one that brings the data to the action is called an **external iterator**, and one that brings the action to the data is called an **internal iterator** [9, p. 260]. The previous iterators, iterator/reverse_iterator, are external iterators, i.e., the data is extracted (directly or indirectly) from the data structure and then some action is performed using the data or changing the data. An internal iterator is often called a **mapping iterator** or **applicative iterator** because it maps or applies an action onto each node of the data structure during traversal. For example, the specific recursive printTree routine in Fig. 2.8, p. 31 can be generalized into an internal iterator for performing any action across a complete traversal of the tree data-structure by using a routine pointer, e.g.:

```
template<typename T, typename Action> void map( Tree<T> *tree, Action act ) {
    if ( tree == NULL ) return      // base case ?
        act( tree->data );          // prefix, perform action on data in node
        map( tree->left, act );
        map( tree->right, act );
}
void print( Data &d ) { cout << d << endl; } // action
Tree tree;
map( tree, print );                  // bring action to data: print tree
```

By passing a different routine/functor to the iterator, it is possible to perform a user specified action at each node during the traversal.

Given the two forms of iterator, what are their advantages and disadvantages? In general, an external iterator is simpler than an internal iterator with respect to the following situations:

- not traversing the entire data structure;
- accessing state at the point of traversal;
- traversing multiple data structures and performing some action on the values from each, e.g., comparing two data structures for equality.

For example, Fig. 2.15a shows an external iterator where the loop traverses at most the first 10 nodes of the list, and performs different actions depending on state information local to the traversal context, i.e., variables m and i. Fig. 2.15b shows it is possible to generalize an internal iterator to handle this scenario using a closure to access the state local at the traversal context and to manage its loop counter.

Therefore, there is only a weak equivalence between the two kinds of iterators. External iterators are more general than internal iterators, but simple internal iterators hide more of the traversal details, and hence, are often easier to use.

2.10 Dynamic Multi-Level Exit

Basic and advanced control-structures allow for virtually any control-flow patterns *within* a routine, called a **local transfer**. Modularization states any contiguous, complete block of code can be factored into a routine and called from anywhere in the program (modulo lexical scoping rules). However, modularization fails when factoring exits, in particular, multi-level exits.

```
int i, m = 5;                                  class Closure {
list<int> l;                                       int i, &m;
list<int>::iterator fr;  // forward iterator   public:
for ( i = 0, fr = l.begin(); i < 10 && fr != l.end();    Closure( int &m ) : m( m ), i( 0 ) {}
        i += 1, ++fr ) {                           bool operator()( int &fr ) {
    if ( *fr != m )    // non-matching elements       if ( i == 10 ) return false;
    else *fr += i;     // matching elements           if ( fr != m ) cout << fr << endl;
}                                                      else fr += i;
                                                       i += 1;
                                                       return true;
                                                   }
                                               } c( m );
if ( i < 10 )      // all front elements processed    if ( map( l, c ) ) ...
else               // only front 10 list elements     else ...

        (a) External                                      (b) Internal
```

Fig. 2.15 Kinds of iterator

```
B1: for ( i = 0; i < 10; i += 1 ) {        void rtn( ... ) {
    ...
    ┌─────────────────────────────────┐        ┌─────────────────────────────────┐
    │ B2: for ( j = 0; j < 10; j += 1 ) {│        │ B2: for ( j = 0; j < 10; j += 1 ) {│
    │     ...                          │        │     ...                          │
    │     if ( ... ) break B1;         │        │     if ( ... ) break B1;         │
    │     ...                          │        │     ...                          │
    │ }                                │        │ }                                │
    └─────────────────────────────────┘        └─────────────────────────────────┘
    ...                                    }
}                                          B1: for ( i = 0; i < 10; i += 1 ) {
                                               ...
                                               rtn( ... )
                                               ...
                                           }
```

The inner loop is factored into routine rtn, but fails to compile because the label B1 is in another routine, and labels only have routine scope. (There is a good reason for this restriction.) Hence, control flow *among* routines is rigidly controlled by the call/return mechanism, e.g., given A calls B calls C, it is impossible to transfer directly from C back to A, terminating B in the transfer. Dynamic multi-level exit extends call/return semantics to transfer in the *reverse* direction to normal routine calls, called **non-local transfer**, and allow modularization of static multi-level exit (see Sect. 3.7.2, p. 77).

The control-flow pattern being introduced by non-local transfer is calling a routine and having multiple forms of return. That is, when a routine call returns normally, i.e., control transfers to the statement after the call, it indicates normal completion of the routine's algorithm; whereas, one or more exceptional returns, i.e., control transfers to statements not after the call, indicate some form of ancillary completion (but not necessarily an error). For example, Fig. 2.16 shows a Fortran program with alternate returns from a subroutine. Subroutine AltRet has a normal return and two alternate returns, named 1 and 2. While normal return always transfers to the statement after the call, the caller can specify where the alternative returns transfer on each call, in this case lines labelled 10 and 20. Hence, there are three forms of return from AltRet, normal completion and two exceptional completions, and the actions for each form are controlled at the call. This pattern is

```
C   Two alternate return parameters, denoted by * and named 1 and 2
      subroutine AltRet( c, *, * )
         integer c;
         if ( c == 0 ) return   ! normal return
         if ( c == 1 ) return 1 ! alternate return
         if ( c == 2 ) return 2 ! alternate return
      end
C   Statements labelled 10 and 20 are alternate return points
         call AltRet( 0, *10, *20 )
         print *, "normal return 1"
         call AltRet( 1, *10, *20 )
         print *, "normal return 2"
         return
10       print *, "alternate return 1"
         call AltRet( 2, *10, *20 )
         print *, "normal return 3"
         return
20       print *, "alternate return 2"
         stop
      end
```

Fig. 2.16 Fortran alternate return from subroutine

just a generalization of what occurs with multi-exit loop and multi-level exit, where control structures may end with or without an exceptional transfer of control from within them. The pattern also addresses the fact that algorithms can have multiple outcomes, and separating the outcomes from one another makes it easy to read and maintain a program. However, this pattern does not handle the case of multiple levels of nested modularization, where a new modularized routine wants to have an alternate return not to its direct caller but rather an indirect caller several stack frame below it. For example, if AltRet is further modularized, the new routine has to have an alternate return to AltRet and then another alternate return to its caller. Rather than this two-step operation, it is simpler for the new modularized routine to bypass the intermediate step and transfer directly to the caller of AltRet. To accomplish a multiple-step return requires a more complex non-local transfer, which transfers in the same reverse direction as **return** but can return multiple times to an alternate return-point.

The underlying mechanism for non-local transfer is presented in C pseudo-code in Fig. 2.17 using a label variable L, which contains both a pointer to a routine activation on the stack and a transfer point within the routine. In the example, the first nonlocal transfer from f transfers to the static label L1 in the activation record for h, terminating f's activation. The second nonlocal transfer from f transfers to the static label L2 in the activation record for h, terminating the activation records for f and g. Note, the value of the label variable is not statically/lexically determined like a normal label within a routine. Hence, nonlocal transfer, **goto** L in f, involves a two-step operation: direct control flow to the specified routine activation on the stack; and then go to the transfer point (label) within the routine. A consequence of the transfer is that blocks activated between the **goto** and the label value are terminated because of stack unwinding. PL/I [14] is one of a small number of languages (Beta [19],

C pseudo-code	Control Flow
| ```
label L;
void f( int i ) {
    // non-local return
    if ( i == ... ) goto L;
}
void g( int i ) {
    if ( i > 1 ) { g( i - 1 ); return; }
    f( i );
}
void h( int i ) {
    if ( i > 1 ) { h( i - 1 ); return; }
    L = L1; // dynamic transfer-point
    f( 1 ); goto S1;
L1: // handle L1 non-local return
S1: // continue normal execution
    L = L2; // dynamic transfer-point
    g( 1 ); goto S2;
L2: // handle L2 non-local return
S2: // continue normal execution
}
``` | 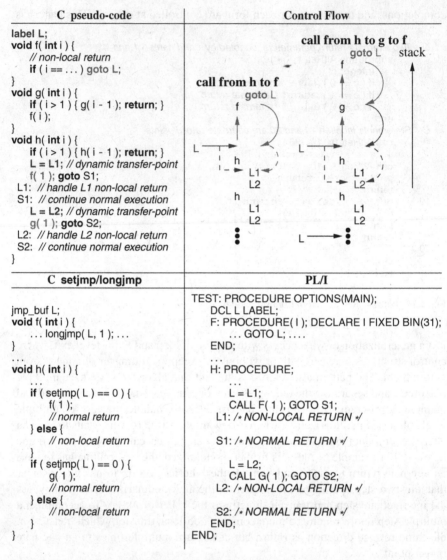 |

C setjmp/longjmp	PL/I
| ```
jmp_buf L;
void f( int i ) {
    ... longjmp( L, 1 ); ...
}
...
void h( int i ) {
    ...
    if ( setjmp( L ) == 0 ) {
        f( 1 );
        // normal return
    } else {
        // non-local return
    }
    if ( setjmp( L ) == 0 ) {
        g( 1 );
        // normal return
    } else {
        // non-local return
    }
}
``` | ```
TEST: PROCEDURE OPTIONS(MAIN);
    DCL L LABEL;
    F: PROCEDURE( I ); DECLARE I FIXED BIN(31);
        ... GOTO L; ....
    END;
    ...
    H: PROCEDURE;
        ...
        L = L1;
        CALL F( 1 ); GOTO S1;
    L1: /* NON-LOCAL RETURN */

    S1: /* NORMAL RETURN */

        L = L2;
        CALL G( 1 ); GOTO S2;
    L2: /* NON-LOCAL RETURN */

    S2: /* NORMAL RETURN */
    END;
END;
``` |

Fig. 2.17 Dynamically-scoped transfer-points (nonlocal transfer)

C [15]) supporting nonlocal transfer among dynamic blocks through the use of label variables. PL/I and Beta provide nonlocal transfer via a language control-flow mechanism, while C uses a library approach.

For example, in Fig. 2.17, the C program (left bottom) uses the library routine setjmp to store the current execution context in variable L, which is within the scope of the call to setjmp, setjmp returns a zero value, and a call is made to routine f. Routine f may execute a transfer using the library routine longjmp to the execution-context variable, transferring out of f, through any number of additional scope levels, back within the saved scope of setjmp, which now returns a nonzero value to
```

indicate alternate return. However, having setjmp return once for the explicit setup call and implicitly again after the longjmp makes this library approach for nonlocal transfer obscure and confusing. The code associated with alternate execution resets execution-context variable L and calls g, which may return normally or to the new alternate code. The PL/I program (right bottom) uses a label variable and works identically to the C pseudo-code (left top). The key is that the transfer point for the longjmp or GOTO is unknown statically; it is determined by the dynamic value of the execution context or label variable.

Unfortunately, nonlocal transfer is too general, allowing branching to almost anywhere, resulting in the structured programming problem. This lack of discipline can make programs less maintainable and error-prone [18, p. 102]. Therefore, a restricted form of nonlocal transfer (**goto**) is necessary, similar to the restrictive form of the local **goto** using labelled break (see Sect. 2.4, p. 20). The next chapter presents different mechanisms to control nonlocal transfer to make it fit into the structured-programming methodology.

2.11 Summary

There is a weak equivalence between the basic and advanced control-structures because simulating advanced control-structures with basic ones is both awkward and inefficient in most cases. Multi-exit loop eliminates duplicated code, which is a maintenance problem. Static multi-level exit allows the elimination of flag variables, which are the variable equivalent of the **goto** statement. As well, static multi-level exit can simulate multi-exit, i.e., multi-exit is a subset (one level exit) of static multi-level exit (multiple levels); nevertheless, some languages provide separate constructs for multi-exit and static multi-level exit. The GOTO statement can be used to simulate both multi-exit and static multi-level exit if these specific control structures do not exist in a programming language. While the GOTO statement can be easily misused, resulting in control flow that is extremely difficult to follow, it can be used for legitimate purposes. Any legitimate purpose *must* satisfy the two restrictions of not creating a loop and not branching into a control structure (see page 11). Therefore, the GOTO should not be maligned or removed from programming languages unless other strongly equivalent constructs are provided. Even more advanced forms of exit are possible when the transfer point is determined dynamically due to routine call. There is a weak equivalence between control structures and routines because control structures can only simulate routine calls via copying code and textually substituting arguments for parameters. Therefore, routines are a fundamental component in control flow. Recursion is a simple extension of basic routine call, i.e., a routine can call itself directly or indirectly, and it is possible because of the basic stack implementation of routine activations. Functional programming uses recursion as the looping mechanism to eliminate mutable data. Routine pointers generalize a routine beyond data parameters allowing the code executed by a routine call to change dynamically. Routine pointers are the basis for many other programming mechanisms, like virtual routines in object-oriented programming. Returning routine pointers presents problems for nested routines that reference local state, requiring a closure mechanism to capture this local state. Iterators combine a number of control-flow techniques (most importantly a closure) to traverse an abstract and encapsulated data-structure. Iterators may be external or internal, defining who controls the iteration: the client using the iterator or the iterator itself, leading to a weak equivalence between them. Selecting the best control flow for implementing an algorithm is crucial for readability, efficiency and maintainability; but the selection process can only be done if a programmer is aware of the possibilities and understands how each works.

2.12   Questions

1. State the three basic forms of control structures.
2. The following C/C++ code fragment is valid:

   ```
   // assume i, a, b, c, and d are of type int
   switch ( i ) {          // unusual switch statement
     case 0:
       if ( a > b ) {
         case 1:
         for ( c = 0; c < 10; c += 1 ) {
           case 2:
             d += 1;
         } // for
       } // if
   } // switch
   ```

   a. Outline very briefly the control flow in this code fragment when i takes on values 0, 1, 2, 4. (Do not explain what the code fragment is trying to accomplish, only what the control flow is doing.)
   b. Explain what control-flow problem this form of control introduces, and why this problem results in both comprehension and technical difficulties.
   c. Find the popular name of a similar *unusually* usage of the **switch** statement.

3. Any program using basic control-flow constructs can be transformed into an equivalent program using only the **while** construct. Rewrite each of the following C++ control structures using **ONLY** expressions (including operators & and |) and **while** statements so that it preserves the exact same execution sequence. The statements **if/else, switch, for, do, break, continue, goto, throw** or **return**, and the operators &&, || or ? are not allowed. New variables may be created to accomplish the transformation.

a. **if/else** conditional

```
if ( C ) {
    S1
} else {
    S2
}
```

b. **switch** conditional

```
switch ( i ) {
    case 1:
    S1
    case 2:
    S2
    break;
    default:
    S3
}
```

c. **do/while** loop

```
do {
    S1
} while ( C );
```

d. **for** loop

```
for ( int i = 0; i < 10; i += 1 ) {
    S1
}
```

4. Any program using basic control-flow constructs can be transformed into an equivalent program using only the **while** construct. Rewrite the C++ program in Fig. 2.18 using **ONLY** expressions (including operators & and |) and **while** statements so that it preserves the exact same execution sequence. The statements **if/else, switch, for, do, break, continue, goto, throw** or **return**, and the operators **&&, ||** or **?** are not allowed. New variables may be created to accomplish the transformation. Output from the transformed program must be identical to the original program.

5. Rewrite the following C++ program in Fig. 2.19, p. 51 using **ONLY** expressions (including operators & and |), **one while**, and any number of **if/else** statements so that it preserves the exact same execution sequence. The statements **switch, for, do, break, continue, goto, throw** or **return**, and the operators **&&, ||** or **?** are not allowed. New variables may be created to accomplish the transformation. Output from the transformed program must be identical to the original program.

6. Explain the notion of *weak equivalence*.

7. Rewrite an **if/else** and **while** loop using **goto** statements.

8. Convert the C++ program in Fig. 2.20, p. 51 from using **goto** to using only basic control-structures:

9. Define the term *structured programming*.

10. Böhm and Jacopini demonstrated any arbitrary control-flow written with gotos can be transformed into an equivalent restricted control-flow uses only **if** and **while** control structures. What two program modifications are required for the transformation?

11. What is a *flag variable* and why are flag variables a problem?

12. The following code fragment contains duplicate code; show how it can be eliminated.

```
int x
cin >> x;              // duplicate
while ( ! cin.fail() ) {
    S1;
    cin >> x;          // duplicate
}
```

13. Why is a flag variable the variable equivalent of a **goto** statement?

```
#include <iostream>
#include <cstdlib>              // atoi
using namespace std;

int main( int argc, char *argv[ ] ) {
    int v1, v2 = 2;
    switch ( argc ) {
      case 3:
        v2 = atoi( argv[2] );
        if ( v2 < 2 || 100 < v2 ) goto usage;
      case 2:
        v1 = atoi( argv[1] );
        if ( v1 < 1 || 100 < v1 ) goto usage;
        break;
      usage:
      default:
        cerr << "Usage: " << argv[0] << " v1 (1-100) [ v2 (2-100) ] " << endl;
        exit( EXIT_FAILURE );
    }
    int i = v1, j = v2, k = 7;
    cout << boolalpha;
    if ( i > 27 ) {
        j = 10;
        cout << j << " " << k << endl;
    } else {
        k = 27;
        cout << j << " " << k << endl;
    }
    for ( ;; ) {
        cin >> i;
        cout << cin.good() << endl;
        if ( cin.fail() ) break;
        cout << i << endl;
    }
}
```

Fig. 2.18 Only while

14. Give two restrictions on static multi-level exit that makes it an acceptable programming language construct, i.e., it cannot be misused like a **goto**.

15. What control-flow pattern is necessary to eliminate all flag variables, and what safe construct provides this pattern?

16. A loop exit in C++ is created with the **if** and **break** statements; however, there are *good* and *bad* ways to code the loop exit in a loop. Rewite the loop bodies in each of the following code fragments to use the *good* pattern for loop exit and explain why the change is better:

a.
```
for ( int i = 0;; i += 1 ) {
    if ( key == list[i] ) {
        break;
    } else {
        cout << list[i] << endl;
    }
}
```

b.
```
for ( int i = 0;; i += 1 ) {
    if ( key != list[i] ) {
        cout << list[i] << endl;
    } else {
        break;
    }
}
```

```cpp
#include <iostream>
using namespace std;

int main() {
    char ch;
    int g, b;
    cin >> noskipws;                          // turn off white space skipping
    for ( ;; ) {                              // loop until eof
        for ( g = 0; g < 5; g += 1 ) {        // groups of 5 blocks
            for ( b = 0; b < 4; b += 1 ) {    // blocks of 4 characters
                for ( ;; ) {
                    cin >> ch;                // read one character
        if ( cin.fail() ) goto fini;          // eof ?
                    if ( ch != '\n' ) break;  // ignore newline
                } // for
                if ( ch == '\t' ) ch = ' ';   // convert tab to blank
                cout << ch;                   // print character
            } // for
            cout << "  ";                     // block separator
        } // for
        cout << endl;                         // group separator
    } // for
  fini: ;
    if ( g != 0 || b != 0 ) cout << endl;
} // main
```

Fig. 2.19 One while and if/else

```cpp
int c[2] = { 1, 1 }, turn = 1;

void dekker( int me, int other ) {
    int i = 0;
  A1:
    c[me] = 0;
  L1:
    if ( c[other] == 0 ) {
        if ( turn == me ) goto L1;
        c[me] = 1;
      B1:
        if ( turn == other ) goto B1;
        goto A1;
    }
    CS();
    turn = other;
    c[me] = 1;
    i += 1;
    if ( i <= 1000000 ) goto A1;
}
```

Fig. 2.20 Goto program

17. Rewrite the following code using only **if/else** and **while** to eliminate the exits from the middle of the loop.

```
for ( ;; ) {
    S1
    if ( i >= 10 ) { E1; break; }
    S2
    if ( j >= 10 ) { E2; break; }
    S3
}
```

18. Describe an indentation technique (eye-candy) so exits in a loop body are easy to read.

19. Write a linear search that looks up a key in an array of elements, and if the key does not appear in the array, it is added to the end of the array; otherwise, if the key does exist the number of times it has been looked up is recorded by incrementing a counter associated with the element in the array. Use the following data structures:

```
struct elem {
    int data;      // data value examined in the search
    int occ;       // number of times data is looked up
};
```

Use a multi-exit loop with exit code in the solution and terminate the program if adding an element results in exceeding the array size.

20. a. Explain how the short-circuit *AND* (&&) and *OR* (||) work.

    b. Use de Morgan's law to convert this **while** loop into an equivalent **for** (;;) loop with an exit using a **break**.

    ```
    while ( Values[i] != HighValue && Values[i] <= Max ) { ... }
    ```

    c. What is the inconsistency between the built-in operators && and ||, and user defined versions of these operators?

21. What is *static* about **break** and labelled **break**?

22. Rewrite the following program removing the labelled breaks.

```
B1: for ( i = 0; i < 10; i += 1 ) {
    B2: for ( j=0; j<10; j += 1 ) {
        ...
        if ( ... ) break B2;  // outdent
            ... // rest of loop
    if ( ... ) break B1;  // outdent
        ... // rest of loop
    } // for
    ... // rest of loop
} // for
```

23. a. Transform routine do_work in Fig. 2.21 so it preserves the same control flow but removes the **for** and **goto** statements, and replaces them with **ONLY** expressions (including & and |), **if/else** and **while** statements. The statements **switch, for, do, break, continue, goto, throw** or **return**, and the operators &&, || or ? are not allowed. In addition, setting a loop index to its maximum value, to force the loop to stop is not allowed. Finally, copying significant amounts of code or creating subroutines is not allowed, i.e., no transformation where the code grows exponentially with the number of nested loops. New

```
#include <cstdlib>              // atoi
#include <iostream>
using namespace std;

// volatile prevents dead-code removal
void do_work( int C1, int C2, int C3, int L1, int L2, volatile int L3 ) {
    for ( int i = 0; i < L1; i += 1 ) {
        cout << "S1 i:" << i << endl;
        for ( int j = 0; j < L2; j += 1 ) {
            cout << "S2 i:" << i << " j:" << j << endl;
            for ( int k = 0; k < L3; k += 1 ) {
                cout << "S3 i:" << i << " j:" << j << " k:" << k << " : ";
          if ( C1 ) goto EXIT1;
                cout << "S4 i:" << i << " j:" << j << " k:" << k << " : ";
            if ( C2 ) goto EXIT2;
                cout << "S5 i:" << i << " j:" << j << " k:" << k << " : ";
              if ( C3 ) goto EXIT3;
                cout << "S6 i:" << i << " j:" << j << " k:" << k << " : ";
            } // for
          EXIT3:;
            cout << "S7 i:" << i << " j:" << j << endl;
        } // for
      EXIT2:;
        cout << "S8 i:" << i << endl;
    } // for
  EXIT1:;
} // do_work

int main( int argc, char *argv[] ) {
    int times = 1, L1 = 10, L2 = 10, L3 = 10;
    switch ( argc ) {
      case 5:
        L3 = atoi( argv[4] );
        L2 = atoi( argv[3] );
        L1 = atoi( argv[2] );
        times = atoi( argv[1] );
        break;
      default:
        cerr << "Usage: " << argv[0] << " times L1 L2 L3" << endl;
        exit( EXIT_FAILURE );
    } // switch

    for ( int i = 0; i < times; i += 1 ) {
        for ( int C1 = 0; C1 < 2; C1 += 1 ) {
            for ( int C2 = 0; C2 < 2; C2 += 1 ) {
                for ( int C3 = 0; C3 < 2; C3 += 1 ) {
                    do_work( C1, C2, C3, L1, L2, L3 );
                    cout << endl;
                } // for
            } // for
        } // for
    } // for
} // main
```

Fig. 2.21 Static multi-level exit

variables may be created to accomplish the transformation. Output from the transformed program must be identical to the original program.

b.   i. Compare the original and transformed program with respect to performance by doing the following:

- Remove (comment out) *all* the print (cout) statements in the original and transformed version.
- Time the execution using the time command:

```
% time ./a.out
3.21u 0.02s 0:03.32 100.0%
```

(Output from time differs depending on the shell, but all provide user, system and real time.) Compare the *user* time (3.21u) only, which is the CPU time consumed solely by the execution of user code (versus system and real time).

- Use the program command-line argument (if necessary) to adjust the number of times the experiment is performed to get execution times approximately in the range 0.1 to 100 s. (Timing results below 0.1 s are inaccurate.) Use the same command-line value for all experiments.
- Run both the experiments again after recompiling the programs with compiler optimization turned on (i.e., compiler flag -O2). Include all 4 timing results to validate the experiments.

ii. State the observed performance difference between the original and transformed program, without and with optimization.

iii. Speculate as to the reason for the performance difference between the coding styles.

iv. Does compiler optimization affect either coding style? (Yes/No answer).

24. Why is it good practice to label all exits?

25. The following form of control flow appears occasionally:

```
if C1 then
    S1
    if C2 then
        S2
        if C3 then
            S3
        else
            S4
        endif
    else
        S4
    endif
else
    S4
endif
```

Notice, if any of the conditions are false, the same code is executed (often printing an error message or back-tracking), resulting in code duplication. One way to deal with the code duplication is to put code S4 into a routine and call it. Alternatively, imagine fixing this duplication with a labelled **if** for use in the

else clause, where the **else** terminates all **if** statements up to the corresponding labelled one, as in:

```
L1: if C1 then
        S1
        if C2 then
            S2
            if C3 then
                S3
        else L1 // terminates 3 if statements
        S4
    endif
```

In this example, all 3 **if** statements transfer to the same **else** clause if the conditional is false. Unfortunately, the syntactic form of the **if** statement in C/C++ makes it impossible to implement this extension. Explain the problem.

26. Explain the control flow of *call/return*.
27. What is *modularization*, and why is it the basic building block of software engineering.
28. Why may a block require a stack frame?
29. Why do stack frames form a stack?
30. Explain the term *lexical scope*, and give two explanations of different lexical scoping.
31. Why do nested routines need a *lexical link*?
32. Explain the control flow that occurs with *recursion*
33. Convert the following looping form of factorial into a recursive form.

```
unsigned long long int factorial( int n ) {
    for ( unsigned long long int fact = 1; n > 1; n -= 1 ) {
        fact *= n;
    }
    return fact;
}
```

34. What is *tail recursion*?
35. What is meant by the *front* and *back* side in recursion?
36. What class of problems are handled best by recursive solutions?
37. Convert the following recursive form of the Euclidean algorithm computing greatest common-divisor into a looping form.

```
int gcd( int x, int y ) {
    if ( y == 0 ) {
        return x;
    } else {
        return gcd( y, x % y );
    }
}
```

38. What two properties define *functional programming*
39. Convert the following generic, mutable summation routine into one that is an immutable summation routine.

```
template<typename T>
T sum( list<T> *lst ) {
    T acc = 0;
    for ( list<T> *p = lst;
          p != 0; p = p->next )
        acc += p->val;
    return acc;
```

40. Routine pointers introduce what new form of generalization in a routine.
41. What is the problem with routine pointer syntax in C/C++?
42. Explain the term *fixup* and *call back* routine.
43. What is the relationship between routine pointers and virtual routines?
44. How are virtual routines implemented in object-oriented languages to conserve space?
45. Why is returned a nested routine complex?
46. What is a *functor* and explain its purpose?
47. What is an iterator and why must it save state between invocations?
48. Explain *mapping* and *application* iterator.
49. What is a *non-local transfer*?
50. a. Transform the program in Fig. 2.22 replacing **throw/catch** with longjmp/setjmp. Except for a jmp_buf variable to replace the exception variable created by the **throw**, no new variables may be created to accomplish the transformation. Output from the transformed program must be identical to the original program, **except for one aspect, which you will discover in the transformed program**.

    b. i. Compare the original and transformed program with respect to performance by doing the following:
        * Compile the original **throw/catch** and setjmp/longjmp programs without print statements.
        * Time each execution using the time command:

            ```
            % time ./a.out
            3.21u 0.02s 0:03.32 100.0%
            ```

            (Output from time differs depending on the shell, but all provide user, system and real time.) Compare the *user* time (3.21u) only, which is the CPU time consumed solely by the execution of user code (versus system and real time).
        * Use the program command-line arguments to adjust the amount of program execution to get execution times in the range 10 to 100 s. (Timing results below 1 s are inaccurate.) Use the same command-line values for all experiments, if possible; otherwise, increase/decrease the arguments as necessary and scale the difference in the answer.
        * Run both the experiments again after recompiling the programs with compiler optimization turned on (i.e., compiler flag -O2). Include all 4 timing results to validate the experiments.

```cpp
#include <iostream>
using namespace std;
#include <cstdlib>                              // exit, atoi

struct T {
    ~T() { cout << "~T" << endl; }
};
struct E {};
int hc, gc, fc, kc;

void f( volatile int i ) {                      // volatile, prevent dead-code optimizations
    T t;
    cout << "f enter" << endl;
    if ( i == 3 ) throw E();
    if ( i != 0 ) f( i - 1 );
    cout << "f exit" << endl;
    kc += 1;                                    // prevent tail recursion optimization
}
void g( volatile int i ) {
    cout << "g enter" << endl;
    if ( i % 2 == 0 ) f( fc );
    if ( i != 0 ) g( i - 1 );
    cout << "g exit" << endl;
    kc += 1;
}
void h( volatile int i ) {
    cout << "h enter" << endl;
    if ( i % 3 == 0 ) {
        try {
            f( fc );
        } catch( E ) {
            cout << "handler 1" << endl;
            try {
                g( gc );
            } catch( E ) {
                cout << "handler 2" << endl;
            }
        }
    }
    if ( i != 0 ) h( i - 1 );
    cout << "h exit" << endl;
    kc += 1;
}
int main( int argc, char *argv[] ) {
    switch ( argc ) {
      case 4: fc = atoi( argv[3] );             // f recursion depth
      case 3: gc = atoi( argv[2] );             // g recursion depth
      case 2: hc = atoi( argv[1] ); break;      // h recursion depth
      default: cerr << "Usage: " << argv[0] << " hc gc fc" << endl;
               exit( EXIT_FAILURE );
    }
    if ( hc < 0 || gc < 0 || fc < 0 ) {
        cerr << "Input less than 0" << endl;
        exit( EXIT_FAILURE );
    }
    h( hc );
}
```

Fig. 2.22 Throw/catch

      ii. State the observed performance difference between the original and
        transformed program, without and with optimization.
     iii. Speculate as to the reason for the performance difference.

51. Why does modularization (refactoring) cause problems with multi-level exit?
52. Explain why a label variable for non-local transfer must be a tuple of two values.
53. Why does longjmp not work properly in C++?

References

1. Abelson, H., Adams IV, N.I., Bartley, D.H., Brooks, G., Dybvig, R.K., Friedman, D.P., Halstead, R., Hanson, C., Haynes, C.T., Kohlbecker, E., Oxley, D., Pitman, K.M., Rozas, G.J., Jr., G.L.S., Sussman, G.J., Wand, M., *Ed. by* Richard Kelsey, Clinger, W., Rees, J.: Revised⁵ report on the algorithmic language Scheme. SIGPLAN Not. 33(9), 26–76 (1998)
2. Ackermann, W.: Zum hilbertschen aufbau der reellen zahlen. Math. Ann. 99(1), 118–133 (1928)
3. Aho, A.V., Lam, M.S., Sethi, R., Ullman, J.D.: Compilers: Principles, Techniques, and Tools, 2nd edn. Addison-Wesley Longman Publishing, Boston, MA, USA (2006)
4. Backus, J.W., Bauer, F.L., Green, J., Katz, C., McCarthy, J., Naur, P., Perlis, A.J., Rutishauser, H., Samuelson, K., Vauquois, B., Wegstein, J., van Wijngaarden, A., Woodger, M.: Revised report on the algorithmic language algol 60. Commun. ACM 6(1), 1–17 (1963)
5. Böhm, C., Jacopini, G.: Flow diagrams, turing machines and languages with only two formation rules. Commun. ACM 9(5), 366–371 (1966)
6. Buhr, P.A.: A case for teaching multi-exit loops to beginning programmers. SIGPLAN Not. 20(11), 14–22 (1985)
7. Dijkstra, E.W.: Go to statement considered harmful. Commun. ACM 11(3), 147–148 (1968). Reprinted in [32] pp. 29–36.
8. Fischer, C.N., LeBlanc, Jr., R.J.: Crafting a Compiler. Benjamin Cummings (1991)
9. Gamma, E., Helm, R., Johnson, R., Vlissides, J.: Design Patterns: Elements of Reusable Object-Oriented Software. Professional Computing Series. Addison-Wesley, Boston (1995)
10. Gosling, J., Joy, B., Steele, G., Bracha, G.: The Java Language Specification, 2nd edn. Addison-Wesley, Boston (2000)
11. Griswold, R.E., Griswold, M.T.: The Icon Programming Language. Prentice-Hall, Englewood Cliffs (1983)
12. Hoare, C.A.R.: Algorithms 63/64: Partition/quicksort. Commun. ACM 4(7), 321 (1961)
13. Hudak, P., Fasel, J.H.: A gentle introduction to haskell. SIGPLAN Not. 27(5), T1–53 (1992)
14. International Business Machines: OS and DOS PL/I Reference Manual, 1st edn. (1981). Manual GC26-3977-0
15. Kernighan, B.W., Ritchie, D.M.: The C Programming Language, 2nd edn. Prentice Hall Software Series. Prentice-Hall, Englewood Cliffs (1988)
16. Knuth, D.E.: Structured programming with go to statements. ACM Comput. Surv. 6(4), 261–301 (1974). DOI http://doi.acm.org/10.1145/356635.356640
17. Liskov, B., Atkinson, R., Bloom, T., Moss, E., Schaffert, J.C., Scheifler, R., Snyder, A.: CLU Reference Manual. Lecture Notes in Computer Science, vol. 114. Springer, New York (1981)
18. MacLaren, M.D.: Exception handling in PL/I. SIGPLAN Not. 12(3), 101–104 (1977). Proceedings of an ACM Conference on Language Design for Reliable Software, March 28–30, 1977, Raleigh, North Carolina, U.S.A.
19. Madsen, O.L., Møller-Pedersen, B., Nygaard, K.: Object-oriented Programming in the BETA Programming Language. Addison-Wesley, Boston (1993)
20. Milner, R.: A theory of type polymorphism in programming. J. Comput. Syst. Sci. 17, 348–375 (1978)

21. Murer, S., Omohundro, S., Stoutamire, D., Szyperski, C.: Iteration abstraction in sather. ACM Trans. Progr. Lang. Syst. **18**(1), 1–15 (1996)
22. Péter, R.: Konstruktion nichtrekursiver funktionen. Math. Ann. **1**(111), 42–60 (1935)
23. Peterson, W.W., Kasami, T., Tokura, N.: On the capabilities of while, repeat, and exit statements. Commun. ACM **16**(8), 503–512 (1973)
24. Rees, J., Clinger, W.: Revised[3] report on the algorithmic language Scheme. SIGPLAN Not. **21**(12), 37–79 (1986)
25. Robinson, R.M.: Recursion and double recursion. Bull. Am. Math. Soc. **54**, 987–993 (1948)
26. van Rossum, G.: Python Reference Manual, Release 2.5. Python Software Foundation (2006). Fred L. Drake, Jr., editor
27. Schemenauer, N., Peters, T., Hetland, M.L.: Simple generators. Tech. rep. (2001). http://www.python.org/peps/pep-0255.html
28. Steele, G.: COMMON LISP: The Language. Digital Press, New York (1984)
29. Stroustrup, B.: The Design and Evolution of C++. Addison-Wesley, Boston (1994)
30. United States Department of Defense: The Programming Language Ada: Reference Manual, ANSI/MIL-STD-1815A-1983 edn. (1983). Springer, New York
31. Weissman, C.: Lisp 1.5 Primer. Dickenson Publishing, Belmont (1967)
32. Yourdon, E.N. (ed.): Classics in Software Engineering. Yourdon Press, New York (1979)

Chapter 3
Exceptions*

Multi-exit loop and multi-level exit demonstrate the power of advanced control flow to reduce program complexity (flag variables) and eliminate duplicate code. However, these control structures preclude modularity (code factoring), which is essential for software engineering. For example, the left code has three nested loops and an exit from the inner most loop.

Multi-level Exit   **Refactored Loops**

```
A: for ( ... ) {
     int i;




B: for ( ... ) {
     int j;




C: for ( ... ) {
     int k;
     ... if ( i < j && k > i ) break A;
```

```
void X() {
    A: for ( ... ) {
      int i;
      Y( i );

void Y( int i ) {
    B: for ( ... ) {
      int j;
      Z( i, j );

void Z( int i, int j ) {
    C: for ( ... ) {
      int k;
      ... if ( i < j && k > i ) break A;
```

Assume the loops are refactored from bottom-up, making each loop into a routine: the inner most loop C is placed into routine Z with two parameters to access variables i and j from the containing scope, the middle loop B is placed into routine Y with one parameter to access variable i from the containing scope, and the outer most loop A is placed into routine X. Of course, the refactored code on the right fails because the

---

* This chapter is a revision of "Exception Handling" in [4] ©2002 Elsevier Science. Portions reprinted by permission.

© Springer International Publishing Switzerland 2016

P.A. Buhr, *Understanding Control Flow*, DOI 10.1007/978-3-319-25703-7_3

break statement refers to label A in a different routine scope, which is disallowed. It is disallowed because a label is a constant within a routine not a variable. To make it work requires a label variable composed of two parts: a routine activation on the stack and a transfer point (label) within a routine (see Sect. 2.10, p. 43). If a program is written as a single large routine, taking full advantage of basic and advanced control flow, it is optimal with respect to execution performance. However, while some code duplication can be eliminated through advanced control-structures, there is significant code duplication as there is no mechanism to reuse code in the form of modularized routines. Hence, there is a dilemma: use advanced control for program simplification and elimination of duplicate code but preclude certain forms of modularity, or have complex programs with some duplication but allow arbitrary modularity. Clearly, to support modularity for advanced control, the routine-call mechanism must be enhanced to support different kinds of returning, just as multi-level exit supports different kinds of termination of multiple control structures. This chapter discusses how the routine call is extended, and how the resulting mechanism provides for modularity.

3.1   Traditional Approaches

Before examining advance routine-call, it is worth examining its alternative, i.e., how to reestablish the equivalent control flow after modularization when the original code contains a multi-level exit.

return code: This technique has a routine return a special value on completion indicating normal or exceptional execution. A common use of a return code is to indicate an error situation. For example, the C output routine, printf, normally returns an integer indicating the number of characters transmitted, or returns a negative value if an output or encoding error occurs. Fig. 3.1 shows the simulation for the initial example using return codes and flag variables, multiple **return** and **break** and nonlocal transfer. Again, the use of flag variables results in significant code complexity, while the multiple **return** and **break** is simpler. Note, routines Y and Z now return a value, i.e., the return code, which must be tested after each call. If a refactored routine already returns a value, it may be necessary to return the return code via an output parameter that modifies a corresponding argument at the call:

```
int Z( int i, int j, int &retcode ) {
    ...
    ... if ( i < j && k > i ) { retcode = -1; return; }
    ...
    retcode = 0;
}
```

Alternative approaches include returning a structure containing the result and return code, or possibly changing the return type to have multiple values [6]:

```
val, rc = Z( 3, 4 );        // return result and return code
```

Flag Variables & Return Codes	Flag Variables & return/break	Non-local Transfer
| ```c
void X() {
    bool flag = false;
    for ( ! flag && ... ) {
        int i;
        if (Y(i) == -1) flag = true;
        else { ... }
    }
}
int Y( int i ) {
    bool flag = false;
    for ( ! flag && ... ) {
        int j;
        if (Z(i,j) == -1) flag = true;
        else { ... }
    }
    if ( ! flag ) { ... }
    return flag ? -1 : 0;
}
int Z( int i, int j ) {
    bool flag = false;
    for ( ! flag && ... ) {
        int k;
        ...
        if (i<j && k>i) flag = true;
        else { ... }
    }
    if ( ! flag ) { ... }
    return flag ? -1 : 0;
}
``` | ```c
void X() {
    for ( ... ) {
        int i;
        if ( Y( i ) == -1 ) break;
        ...
    }
}
int Y( int i ) {
    for ( ... ) {
        int j;
        if (Z(i, j) == -1) return -1
        ...
    }
    ...
    return 0;
}
int Z( int i, int j ) {
    for ( ... ) {
        int k;
        ...
        if ( i < j && k > i ) return -1;
        ...
    }
    ...
    return 0;
}
``` | ```c
label L;
void X() {
    L = A;
    for ( ... ) {
        int i;
        Y( i );
        ...
    } A: ;
}
void Y( int i ) {
    for ( ... ) {
        int j;
        Z( i, j );
        ...
    }
    ...
}
void Z( int i, int j ) {
    for ( ... ) {
        int k;
        ...
        if (i<j && k>i) goto L;
        ...
    }
}
``` |

Fig. 3.1 Simulate multi-level exit after refactoring

However, all of these approaches change the signature of the routine, which may require updating all calls or at least recompiling the calls.

status flag: This technique has a routine set a shared (global) variable with a special value indicating normal or exceptional execution during the routine. The value remains in the shared variable as long as it is not overwritten by another routine. For example, many UNIX library routines indicate a specific error by storing a predefined integer value (e.g., 5 means I/O error) into the global variable errno. Fig. 3.2 shows the simulation for the initial example using a status flag and flag variables or multiple **return** and **break**. Again, the use of flag variables results in significant code complexity, while the multiple **return** and **break** is simpler. Note, routines Y and Z do not return a value, but the status flag must be tested after each call. What is not mentioned is when to reset the status flag. For this example, the flag can be reset at the end of X, but that assumes no other usage of the status flag by other routines that may need the value to propagate further along the call chain. In general, there is no way to know if the status flag can safely be reset without total knowledge of all routines that are called.
```

Global Status Flag	Return & Break
| ```
bool status = false;
void X() {
    for ( ! status && ... ) {
        int i;
        Y( i );
        if ( ! status )
            { ... }
    }
}
void Y( int i ) {
    for ( ! status && ... ) {
        int j;
        Z( i, j );
        if ( ! status )
            { ... }
    }
    if ( ! status ) { ... }
}
void Z( int i, int j ) {
    for ( ! status && ... ) {
        int k;
        ...
        if ( i < j && k > i ) status = true;
        else { ... }
    }
    if ( ! status ) { ... }
}
``` | ```
bool status = false;
void X() {
    for ( ... ) {
        int i;
        Y( i );
        if ( status ) break;
        ...
    }
}
void Y( int i ) {
    for ( ... ) {
        int j;
        Z( i, j );
        if ( status ) return
        ...
    }
    ...
}
void Z( int i, int j ) {
    for ( ... ) {
        int k;
        ...
        if ( i < j && k > i ) { status = true; return; }
        ...
    }
    ...
}
``` |

Fig. 3.2 Simulate multi-level exit with global status flag

fixup routine: This technique takes the *opposite* approach from the previous two. Instead of terminating a routine, an attempt is made to correct the exceptional issue locally at the point where it occurs. The corrective action is provided through a routine pointer (see Sect. 2.8, p. 37) to a correction routine; the routine pointer is either a default argument, an argument passed by the caller, or accessed via a global variable. The computation detecting the exceptional issue calls the appropriate fixup routine passing any necessary information so it can compute a corrective result. The fixup routine returns a corrective result so the computation can continue or uses a return code or status flag to indicate a correction could not be generated. Fig. 3.3 shows the simulation for corrective actions using a local and global fixup definition. The local-fixup approach requires passing the fixup routine through all levels to the point of the exceptional case. A local fixup-routine can be used as an alternative, instead of the one passed into a routine. This technique allows the corrective action to be determined dynamically, e.g.:

```
rtn( a, b, c > 3 ? fixup1 : fixup2 );  // fixup routine determined dynamically
```

The trivial case for this technique is to only pass a fixup value rather than a routine. However, it is rare for the fixup result to be pre-computable, and hence, independent of the specific exceptional issue. The global-fixup approach usually

Local Fixup (nested routine)	Global Fixup
| | ```
int (*fixup)( ... );        // global fixup pointer
int fixup1( ... ) { ... }   // global fixup routines
int fixup2( ... ) { ... }
``` |

```
void X() {                         void X() {
    for ( ... ) {                      for ( ... ) {
        int i;                             int i;
        int fixup1( ... ) { ... } // nested    int (*temp)( ... ) = fixup; // save fixup
                                               fixup = fixup1;  // set fixup pointer
        Y( i, fixup1 );                    Y( i );
        ...                                fixup = temp; ... // reset fixup
    }                                  }
}                                  }
void Y( int i, int (*fixup)( ... ) ) {   void Y( int i ) {
    for ( ... ) {                      for ( ... ) {
        int j;                             int j;
        int fixup2( ... ) { ... } // nested    int (*temp)( ... ) = fixup; // save fixup
                                               fixup = fixup2;  // set fixup pointer
        Z( i, j, fixup2 );                 Z( i, j );
        ...                                fixup = temp; ... // reset fixup
    }                                  }
}                                  }
void Z( int i, int j, int (*fixup)( ... ) ) {   void Z( int i, int j ) {
    for ( ... ) {                      for ( ... ) {
        int k;                             int k;
        ...                                ...
        if ( i < j && k > i )              if ( i < j && k > i )
            correction = fixup( ... );         correction = fixup( ... );
        ...                                ...
    }                                  }
}                                  }
```

Fig. 3.3 Simulate corrective action

has one or more global fixup-variables that are set and reset to different fix routines. It is good practice to save and restore the previous value of a global fixup-variable so that other routines using the variable work correctly.

The UNIX library routines often use a combination of return code and status flag by returning a negative or zero value to indicate an exceptional condition occurred and using the status variable, errno, to indicate the specific kind of error.

```
if ( printf(...) < 0 ) {        // check return code for error
    perror( "printf:" );        // errno describes specific error
    abort();                    // terminate program
}
```

C++ provides a global fixup routine through the following global routine-pointer:

```
typedef void (*new_handler)();
```

Any fixup routine assigned to this global pointer is called by operator **new** when a request for storage cannot be satisfied. When called, the fixup routine must make more storage available and then return, or perform more complex exception handling. Since this particular fixup routine does not take any parameters, changes must occur using global variables or a functor rather than a routine (see
```

Sect. 3.15.2, p. 111). A similar kind of global fixup is provided by UNIX systems for signal handling, where a signal handler deals with ancillary situations that occur infrequently, e.g.:

```
void sigIOHandler( int sig, siginfo_t *sfp, struct ucontext *cxt ) { ... }
signal( SIGIO, sigIOHandler );
```

The call to signal registers the signal-handler (fixup) routine sigIOHandler to be called after completion of an I/O operation, called a SIGIO event. When the handler is called, it is passed information appropriate to the particular signal and the execution context at the time of the signal. The signal handler must then perform an appropriate action to deal with the completed I/O operation before execution continues.

Unfortunately, these traditional techniques have significant drawbacks:

- Checking a return code or status flag is optional, so it can be delayed or even omitted, which can cause a cascade of errors later in the program's execution. Hence, traditional techniques are passive rather than active.
- The return code technique often encodes exceptional values among normal returned values, which artificially enlarges the range of valid values independent of the computation. Hence, changing a value representing an exceptional value into a normal return value or vice versa can result in interactions between the normal and exception-handling code, even though the two cases should be independent.
- Testing and handling the return code or status flag is often performed locally, i.e., immediately after a routine call, to prevent loss of information and to ensure a problem is dealt with immediately. However, handling a problem immediately is not always the best solution. First, local handling can make a program difficult to read as each routine call results in multiple statements, obscuring the fundamental algorithm. Second, local handling can be inappropriate, especially for library routines, because a local action, e.g., terminating the program, may be inappropriate for the program calling the routine. Hence, local handling is not always desirable since lower-level code does not necessarily know the exact context and/or reasons for its invocation.
- Third, local fixup routines increases the number of parameters, and hence the cost of each call, and may be passed through multiple levels enlarging parameter lists even when the fixup routine is not used. Local with fixup routines can work well, but at the cost of increasing the number of parameters, and hence the cost of each call. But for nonlocal handling, fixup routines have a problem similar to return codes. For intermediate-level routines in a call chain, local fixup routines must be passed through these levels enlarging parameter lists even when the fixup routine may not be applicable. This effect results in unnecessary coupling of routine prototypes between low, intermediate and high level routines, e.g., changing the type of a fixup routine causes the prototypes of multiple routines to change. Finally, changes may be impossible for legacy routine in a call chain requiring the pass-through of fixup routines from a high to low level.

- The alternative to local handling is nonlocal handling, meaning the problem is handled further down the call stack, rather than at the original call site. However, to allow nonlocal handling by a calling routine, the return or status values from *all* local calls within a routine must be folded into the single return and/or status values for a routine, requiring no overlap among values, and possibly significantly enlarging the set of returned values. As a result, it is difficult to generate unique return/status values, and the routine that finally handles the exception must be able to decode the value to determine the situation that generated it, which can result in tight coupling between high and low level routines.
- A status flag can be overwritten before the previous condition is checked or handled. This problem is exacerbated in a concurrent environment because of sharing issues.
- Global fixup routines, often implemented using a global routine-pointer, have identical problems with status flags. In particular, because the pointer values can change in many places to perform different fixup actions, programmers must follow a strict convention of saving and restoring the previous routine value to ensure no local computation changes the environment for a previous one. Relying on programmers to follow conventions is always extremely error prone. Also, shared global variables do not work in concurrent contexts.

Traditional solutions for indicating multiple return-options from a routine are ad-hoc, add significant complexity to a program and require diligence by a programmer to be aware of and properly deal with them. Since many of the alternate return-options indicate error situation, it is common for programs to fail rather than recover or terminate gracefully because the error goes undetected by the caller. For example, virtually all calls to printf in C programs never subsequently check the return code. Given that multiple return-options is a necessary form of control flow, often hidden in the form of return codes and status flags, it needs to be supported properly by the programming language so it is easier for programmers to handle these cases.

3.2 Exception Handling

Many programming languages provide enhanced routine-call mechanisms, often referred to as **exception handling**, but this name is misleading because there is little agreement on what an exception is. Attempts have been made to define exceptions in terms of errors but an error itself is also ill-defined. Instead of struggling to define which phenomenon are or are not exceptional (abnormal), this discussion treats exception handling as a control-flow mechanism, where an exception is a component of an **exception handling mechanism** (EHM) that specifies program behaviour after an exceptional issue has been detected.

The control flow generated by an EHM encompasses both multi-exit loop, static multi-level exit and dynamic multi-level exit, which covers multiple return-options from a routine. The goal is to make certain programming tasks easier, in particular, writing robust programs. Robustness results because exceptions are active rather than passive phenomenon, forcing programs to react immediately when an exceptional issue occurs. This dynamic redirection of control flow indirectly forces programmers to think about the consequences of an exceptional issue when designing and writing programs. The cost of using exceptions should be no different than the cost of rigorously using traditional approaches. The problem is that traditional approaches are not used rigorously so exceptions appear costly as they force rigor (i.e., exceptions cannot be ignored unless explicitly done so). The extra rigor provides an enormous benefit in program reliability; nevertheless, an EHM is not a panacea and only as good as the programmer using it. Unfortunately, even with the availability of modern EHMs, many systems and programmers still handle an exceptional issues using return codes and status flags (although this is slowly changing).

An **exceptional event** is an event that is (usually) known to exist but which is *ancillary* to an algorithm. Because it is ancillary, an exceptional event may be forgotten or ignored without causing a direct failure, e.g., an arithmetic overflow can occur during a computation without generating a program error, but result in erroneous results. In other situations, the exceptional event always occurs but with a low frequency, e.g., encountering end-of-file when reading data. Essentially, a programmer must decide on the level of frequency that moves an event from the algorithmic norm to an exceptional case. Once this decision is made, the mechanism to deal with the exceptional event is best moved out of the normal algorithmic code and handled separately. The mechanism to accomplish this separation is the EHM.

EHMs exist in most modern programming languages, e.g., ML, CLU, Mesa [23], Ada, Modula-3 [2], Java, C# [10] and C++. Fundamentally, all EHMs require the following three language constructs:

1. A label, bound statically or dynamically to a particular statement, that can be used to uniquely identify a transfer point. Often label or type names are used. C++ allows *any* type name to be used as a label; other programming languages restrict which names can be used.
2. A statement to transfer control from a statically or dynamically nested control-structure to an exception label in a different statically or dynamically nested control-structure. C++ provides the **throw** statement.
3. An implicit or explicit clause or statement that is the target of the transfer raised from within a statically or dynamically created block. C++ provides the **try** statement with **catch** clauses as the targets.

The key property in most EHMs is that the point where control flow transfers may only be *known* at execution time (i.e., determined dynamically), and hence, an exception is often a dynamic multi-level exit.

Fig. 3.4 shows an example of refactoring a code block containing labels and how the EHM for C++ generates a dynamic multi-level exit using an exception. The **throw** statement in routine f may raise an exception of type E1 or E2 depending on the value of a random number. When an exception is raised, control exits routine f because

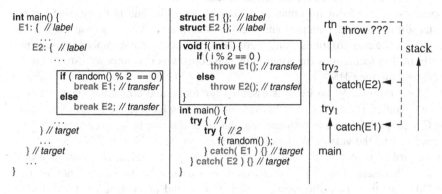

Fig. 3.4 Simple exception

there is no target labelled statement for E1 or E2 in the scope of f. Control transfers down the call stack, to either the block created for the **try** statement associated with the labelled statement (**catch** clause) for either E1 or E2. If the exception is not handled by the first **try** block, the exception continues down the stack to the next **try** block. Only when the exception labelled target or the bottom of the stack is reached does the search stop. Notice it is impossible to determine statically where the statement **throw** transfers control; control may transfer to the first or second **catch** clause depending on the value generated by the random-number generator. It is this fact that differentiates dynamic and static multi-level exit.

3.3 EHM Objectives

The failure of return codes and status flags as an informal (ad hoc) EHM argues strongly for a formal EHM supported by the programming language, which must:

1. be able to change control flow without requiring additional testing and transfers, after an exceptional issue is determined,
2. provide a mechanism to prevent a failed/incomplete operation from continuing, and
3. strive to be orthogonal to other language features, i.e., the EHM features should be able to be used in any reasonable context without unnecessary restrictions.

The first objective targets readability and programmability by eliminating multiple checking of return codes and flags, and removing the need to pass fixup routines or have complex control-logic within normal code to deal with exceptional cases. The second objective provides a transfer from the exceptional event that disallows returning if an operation is non-resumable, directing control flow away from an operation where local information is possibly corrupt. The last objective targets extensibility to add, change, and remove exceptions with minimal effects on existing code and programs using them. Nevertheless, specific implementation and optimization techniques for some language constructs can impose restrictions on constructs in the EHM.

More importantly, an EHM is essential for sound and efficient code generation by a compiler. If a compiler is unaware of exception handling, e.g., setjmp/longjmp in C, it may perform code optimizations that *invalidate* the program, needing cryptic concepts like the **volatile** declaration qualifier (see Sect. 12.6, p. 631). Because of these problems, nonlocal transfer is unacceptable as an EHM. However, nonlocal transfer is essential in an EHM, otherwise it is impossible to achieve the first two EHM objectives, i.e., alleviating explicit testing and preventing return to a non-resumable operation.

3.4   Execution Environment

The structure of the execution environment has a significant effect on an EHM, i.e., an object-oriented concurrent environment requires a more complex EHM than a non-object-oriented sequential environment. For example, objects declared in a block may have destructors, and these destructors must be executed no matter how the block ends, either by normal or exceptional block termination.

```
class T {
    int *i;
    T() { i = new int[10]; ... }
    ~T() { delete [] i; ... } // must free storage
};
{
    T t;
    ... if ( ... ) throw E();
    ...
} // destructor must be executed
```

As well, a control structure may have a finally clause that must always be executed no matter how it ends, either by normal or exceptional block termination.

```
try {
    infile = new Scanner( new File( "abc" ) ); // open input file
    ... if ( ... ) throw new E();
    ...
} finally { // always executed
    infile.close();           // must close file
}
```

Hence, the EHM becomes more complicated since terminating a block containing local objects with destructors (and recursively if these objects contain local objects) or control structures with finally clauses must be executed. Another example is that sequential execution has only one stack; therefore, it is simple to define consistent and well-formed semantics for exceptional control flow. However, a complex execution-environment involves advanced objects (e.g., continuation, coroutine, task), each with its own separate execution stack (see Sect. 4.7.2, p. 146). Given multiple stacks, the EHM semantics for this environment must be more sophisticated, resulting in more complexity. For example, when an exception is raised, the current stack is traversed down to its base searching for an appropriate handler. If no handler is found, it is possible to continue propagating the exception from the current stack to another object's stack. The choice for selecting the point of continuation depends on the particular EHM strategy. Hence, the complexity and design of the execution environment significantly affects the complexity and design of its EHM.

3.5 Terminology

A programming entity with a stack is called an **execution**, because it has the potential to perform all basic and advanced control-flow independently of other executions. A name representing an exceptional event is an **exception type**. An **exception** is an instance of an exception type, and is generated by executing a language or system operation indicating an ancillary (exceptional) situation for a particular execution entity. **Raise (throw)** is the special operation that creates an exception, denoting the ancillary condition the programmer cannot or does not want to handle via conventional control flow. Some exceptions cannot be raised by the programmer, e.g., only the runtime system may raise predefined exceptions such as hardware exceptions. Normally, an exception may be raised at any point during a program's execution. The execution entity raising the exception is the **source execution**. The execution entity that changes control flow due to a raised exception is the **faulting execution**.

Propagation directs control flow from the source execution to a handler that matches the exception in the faulting execution. A **propagation mechanism** is the set of rules used to locate and match an exception with a handler. A **local exception** is when an exception is raised and handled by the same execution entity, i.e, the source and faulting executions are the same. A **nonlocal exception** is when the source and faulting executions are different. A **synchronous exception** is a local or nonlocal exception where the source and faulting executions are performed by the same thread of control (i.e., sequentially). An **asynchronous exception** is a nonlocal exception where the source and faulting executions are performed by different threads of control (i.e., concurrently), and it is the most advanced form of nonlocal exception. Unlike a local raise, which flows directly into propagation, an asynchronous raise separates the execution paths of raise and propagation on the source and faulting executions, respectively. That is, a nonlocal/asynchronous exception may be delayed, until the faulting execution begins propagation at some appropriate time.

A handler has two components:

1. A value for comparison with the raised exception to determine if the handler is qualified to deal with it.
2. An inline (nested) block of code responsible for dealing with a matching exception.

A handler catches an exception when propagation transfers there; a handler may match with one or more exceptions. It is possible that another exception is raised (new propagation) or the current exception is reraised (continue propagation) while executing the handler. Reraise terminates the current handling of a caught exception and continues its propagation from the handler's context. Reraise is useful if a handler detects it is incapable of (completely) handling an exception and needs to propagate the same exception to a handler further down the stack. Reraise is often provided by a raise statement without an exception type, e.g.:

```
catch ( E e ) {
    ... throw; ...     // no exception type
}
```

Here, the implicit exception for the reraise is the exception from the original raise. A handler has handled an exception only if the handler completes rather than raising another exception. Unlike returning from a routine, there may be multiple return mechanisms for a handler (see Sect. 3.9, p. 101). Depending on the return mechanism, control may return after the raise or the handler; in the latter case, the blocks on the stack from the start of propagation to the handler are removed from the stack, called stack unwinding. A guarded block is a language unit with associated handlers, e.g., try-block in C++/Java; an unguarded block is a language unit without handlers.

In summary, an EHM = *exception type* + *raise* (exception) + *propagation* + *handler*, where *exception type* represents a kind of exceptional event, *raise* instantiates an exception of the exception type in the source execution and finds the faulting execution, *propagation* finds an appropriate handler for the exception in the faulting execution, and that *handler* handles the exceptional event or raises the same or another exception.

3.6 Control-Flow Taxonomy

Before examining exception handing in detail, it is interesting to look at the underlying mechanisms affecting call-return. Specifically, it is possible to categorize call-return via two general properties:

static/dynamic call: The routine at the call is looked up statically (compile-time) or dynamically (runtime) [8]. For example, assume C supports nested routines:

```
void f() {
    void h() {}          // f::h
    void g() {           // f::g
        h();             // call h ?
    }
    void k( void (*p)() ) {  // routine parameter
        void h() {}      // k::h
        p();             // call supplied routine
    }
    k( g );              // pass g and called in k
}
```

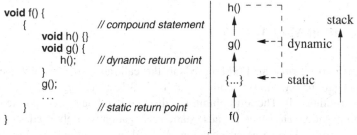

Now, the difference between static and dynamic call occurs after g is indirectly called from k through parameter p. When g is invoked, it calls routine h, but which h? For static call, during compilation of g the name h is looked up in the lexical context, which is the h defined in f because the h in k is inaccessible by the lexical scope rules (gcc provides nested routines with static call). For dynamic call, during execution of g, the name h is looked up in the dynamic context, which is the h defined in k because the call occurs inside of k through parameter p. Essentially, dynamic call searches for a routine definition with the same name as the call name closest on the stack. While dynamic call may seem unusual, it provides a form of polymorphism, allowing a routine call to vary dynamically depending on the caller, e.g., to generalize pre-compiled library routines.[1] Finally, variables can be statically or dynamically looked up with exactly the same issues as for routines.

Interestingly, this polymorphism is subtly different from the polymorphism provided by virtual members of an object accessed by an object reference. When a virtual member is called through an object reference, it is not known statically which member is called, as it depends on the particular object referenced. However, (usually) no search is required to look up the member in the object; the member's location is known at compile time (e.g., virtual-routine vector). Hence, this case is only a partial dynamic call.[2]

static/dynamic return: After a routine completes, it returns to its static (definition) or dynamic (call) context. For example, assume C supports nested routines:

```
void f() {
    {                    // compound statement
        void h() {}
        void g() {
            h();         // dynamic return point
        }
        g();
        ...
    }                    // static return point
}
```

---

[1]The original Lisp programming language uses dynamic call, but newer versions of Lisp, e.g., Scheme, provide both static and dynamic call.

[2]Some object-oriented programming languages, e.g., Smalltalk [12] and Self [1], actually do a full dynamic call involving a search for the member's location in the object.

Table 3.1 Static/dynamic call/return constructs

	Call/Raise	
Return/Handled	Static	Dynamic
Static	1. Sequel	3. Termination
Dynamic	2. Routine	4. Routine pointer, virtual routine, resumption

the difference between static and dynamic return occurs after h is called from g. Assume h has static return, during compilation of h the lexical context for h is remembered as the return point, which means when h returns from the call in g, control transfers to the statement after the end of the block defining h, i.e., after the compound statement. Notice, no matter where h is called (directly or indirectly), the block containing its lexical context must exist because h can only be referenced from within the block in which it is defined. Also, during the transfer to the end of the compound statement, the stack is unwound, removing the routine activations for h and then g. Hence, static return is extremely powerful because it allows terminating multiple routine activations without programmatically returning from each routine. Assume h has dynamic return, during execution of h the dynamic routine making the call is remembered as the return point, which means when h returns from the call in g, control transfers to the statement after the call. In this case, only the top routine activation on the stack is removed, and control continues after the call in the activation that is now at the top of the stack, which is the behaviour for normal routine-call in most languages.

These two control-flow properties can be combined in four ways, resulting in the following language constructs. Case 2 is already familiar as it is a normal routine, with static name lookup at the call and a dynamic return. The other three cases contain all the extant forms of exception handling, and each is discussed in detail. An EHM may provide all or only a subset of these three possible cases.

3.7 Exception Models

It is common to classify an EHM based on the call/raise property that occurs during propagation, i.e., the two columns in Table 3.1, excluding case 2 because it is normal routine call. The left column is called static propagation and the right dynamic propagation. However, because static propagation is rarely used, dynamic propagation is often known as propagation. As well, it is common to classify an EHM based on the return/handled property that occurs after propagation, i.e., the two rows in Table 3.1, excluding case 2 because it is normal routine call. The top row is called terminate semantics as control cannot return to the point of the call/raise because the routine activations on the stack are removed during propagation. Termination models are implemented using nonlocal transfer. However, because static termination is rarely used, dynamic termination is often known as termination.

```
A: for ( ;; ) {                    for ( ;; ) {           // loop A
                                       sequel S1( ... ) { ... }
    B: for ( ;; ) {                    void M1( ... ) {
                                           ...
                                           if ( ... ) S1( ... );
                                           ...
        C: for ( ;; ) {            }
                                   for ( ;; ) {           // loop B
            ...                        sequel S2( ... ) { ... }
            if ( ... ) { break A; }    C: for ( ;; ) {
            ...                            M1( ... );      // modularize
        if ( ... )  { break B; }          if ( ... ) S2( ... );  // modularize
            ...                            ...
        if ( ... ) { break C; }           if ( ... ) break C;
            ...                            ...
        }                              }
    }                              } // S2 static return
}                              } // S1 static return
```

Fig. 3.5 Static-exit modularization

The bottom row is called resume semantics as control returns to the point of
the call/raise because the routine activations on the stack are not removed during
propagation. Cases 1, 3 and 4 of Table 3.1 are discussed in detail.

3.7.1   Static Propagation/Termination

Static call and return (case 1 in Table 3.1) is based on Tennent's sequel construct [28,
p. 108]. A sequel is a routine, including parameters but no return value, where the
routine name is looked up lexically at the call site but control returns to the end of
the block in which the sequel is declared (static return) rather than after the sequel
call.[3] In this case, return is along the lexical structure of the program versus the
routine activations on the call stack. Note, a sequel requires routine nesting within
the program's lexical structure (which C++ does not have).

The original purpose of the sequel was not exception handling; it was modularization of static exits (see Sect. 2.10, p. 43). In the left example of Fig. 3.5, it
is impossible to modularize any code containing a labelled **break** statement. The
reason is the transfer points only have meaning in the routine where a **break** is
located. For example, if **break** A is modularized into another routine, it is no longer
a static exit because the routine can be called from other locations where a different
label A is defined or there is no label A. In the right example of Fig. 3.5, the sequels

---

[3] An alternate design for the sequel is to have two forms of return: normal and exceptional. A
normal **return** is dynamic, like a routine; an exceptional return, using a raise, is static.

Monolithic Compilation	Separate Compilation

`{ // new block`
`  sequel StacKOvfl(...) {...} // handler`
`  class stack {`
`    void push( int i ) {`
`      ... if (...) StacKOvfl(...); ...`
`    }`
`    ...`
`  };`
`  stack s;      // create stack`
`  for ( ... ) {`
`    ... s.push( 3 ); ... // overflow ?`
`  }`
`} // StacKOvfl transfers here`
	`class stack {   // library code`
	`  int (*StacKOvfl)(int);`
	`  stack( sequel of(...) ) : StacKOvfl(of) {...}`
	`  void push( int i ) {`
	`    ... if ( ... ) StacKOvfl(...); ...`
	`  }`
	`};`
	
	`{              // user code`
	`  sequel myStacKOvfl(...) {...} // handler`
	`  stack s( myStacKOvfl );`
	`  ... s.push( 3 ); ... // possible overflow ?`
	`} // myStacKOvfl transfers here`

Fig. 3.6 Sequel compilation structure

S1 and S2 are used to allow modularization of two code fragments containing static
exits. After sequel S2 is called, any return transfers to the end of the loop labelled B,
terminating two nested loops, because the body of loop B contains the definition of
S2. After sequel S1 is called from within M1, any return transfers to the end of the
loop labelled A, terminating the call to M1 and the three nested loops because the
body of loop A contains the definition of S1. Clearly, a programmer must statically
nest a sequel in the block it is to terminate.

With respect to exception handling, static return provides a crucial feature that is
unavailable with dynamic return: the ability to terminate multiple routine activations
with a single return. The left example in Fig. 3.6 shows an example of how a
sequel can be used to provide exception handling [16, 17]. The sequel overflow is
defined along with the class stack. Inside stack::push, the sequel overflow is called
if the current push operation cannot be performed because of insufficient storage
for the stack (imagine an array implementation of the stack with a finite number of
elements). After stack s is created, the **for** loop begins to push elements onto the
stack, which could result in a stack overflow. If push calls overflow, control returns
to the end of the compound statement because it contains the definition of sequel
overflow. Hence, the advantage of the sequel is the handler is statically known (like
static multi-level exit), and in some cases, can be as efficient as a direct transfer
(**goto**). If a handler behaves like a sequel, the handling action for each raise can be
determined at compile time (statically).

The problem with static return for exception handling is that it only works for
monolithic code, i.e., code not subdivided for separate compilation. For example,
library and user code have disjoint static contexts, e.g., if stack is separately
compiled in a library, the sequel call in push no longer knows the static blocks
containing calls to push. To overcome this problem, a sequel can be made a
parameter of stack (right example in Fig. 3.6), and the stack creator provides a fixup
routine as an argument. Now when StacKOvfl is called inside stack::push, control
transfers to the lexical location of the sequel passed as an argument, in this case
to the end of the block containing myStacKOvfl. However, when a sequel is passed
as an argument, the handler is no longer known statically at the raise because the

parameter changes with each argument value. Furthermore, adding the sequel to a routine's prototype has the same problems as fixup routines (see Sect. 3.1, p. 62) and can inhibit reuse (see Sect. 3.8.5, p. 94).

3.7.2 Dynamic Propagation/Termination

Dynamic call and static return (case 3 in Table 3.1, p. 74) differs from a sequel in that the handler name at the raise is looked up during execution unlike a static call (see Fig. 3.4, p. 69). The advantage of dynamic call is that it offers an additional form of polymorphism to generalize exception handling (see Sect. 3.6, p. 72) by searching for handlers installed in guarded blocks on the stack. As well, dynamic call works for separate compilation because the lexical context is not required.

The following are disadvantages for dynamic propagation but in some cases are considered advantages:

Visibility   An exception can propagate through a scope where it is invisible and then back into a scope where it is visible. For example, if routine A calls B and B calls C, C can raise an exception that is unknown to B but caught by A. It has been suggested this behaviour is undesirable because a routine, i.e., B, is indirectly propagating an exception it does not know [25]. Some language designers believe an exception should never be propagated into a scope where it is unknown, or if allowed, the exception should lose its identity and be converted into a general failure exception. However, there are significant reuse restrictions resulting from preventing such propagation (see Sect. 3.8.5, p. 94), or if the exception is converted to a general exception, the loss of specific information may preclude proper handling of the exception at a lower-level of abstraction. As well, in software engineering, it is considered tight coupling [26] for higher-level code to catch a specific rather than general exception (see Sect. 3.8.2, p. 90).

Dynamic-Handler Selection   The handler chosen to match a raised exception is determined dynamically. Hence, a programmer seldom knows statically which handler may be selected, making the program difficult to trace and the EHM harder to use [16, 20, 25, 30]. However, when raising an exception it is rare to know which specific action has to be taken because a routine can be called from many different locations; otherwise, it is unnecessary to define the handler in a separate place, i.e., bound to a guarded block lower on the call stack. Therefore, the uncertainty of a handling action when an exception is raised is not introduced by an EHM but by the problem and its solution. For example, a library normally defines exception types and raises them without providing handlers; the library client provides the specific handlers for the exception in the application. Similarly, the return code technique does not allow the library writer to know the action taken by a client. When an EHM facility is used correctly, the control flow of propagation, the handler selection, and its execution should be understandable.

Ada	C++	nonlocal transfer
procedure main **is**		
E : exception;	**struct** E {};	**label** L;
procedure f **is begin**	**void** f() {	**void** f() {
raise E;	throw E();	goto L;
end f;	}	}
begin	**int** main() {	**int** main() {
	try {	L = L1; // set transfer-point
f;	f();	f(); **goto** S1;
exception when E =>	} **catch**(E) {	L1: ;
-- handler	// handler	// handler
	}	S1: ;
end main;	}	}

Fig. 3.7 Terminate

The terminate approach *restricts* nonlocal transfer similar to the way labelled break restricts local transfer: no backward branching and no branching into a block (see Sect. 2.2, p. 10). After dynamic propagation to locate a handler, if the handler completes, control flow continues as if the incomplete operation in the guarded block terminated without encountering the exception, i.e., static return like a sequel. Hence, the handler acts as an alternative operation for its guarded block. This model is the most popular form of restricted nonlocal transfer, appearing in Ada, C++ , ML [22], Modula-3 and Java [14]. Terminate is often likened to a *reverse* routine call, particularly when argument/parameters are available (see Sect. 3.8.4, p. 93). Essentially, the raise acts like a call and the handler acts like a routine, but control flows down the stack rather than up. Some EHMs divide propagation into one level and multiple levels [19, p. 547] [30, p. 218], i.e., control transfers from the raise to the immediate caller (one level) or from the raise to any nested caller (multiple levels). However, this distinction is artificial and largely stems from a desire to support exception lists (see Sect. 3.8.5, p. 94).

For example, in Fig. 3.7, the Ada program (left) defines an exception type E and a procedure f in the scope of procedure main and then calls f. Procedure f executes a raise of the exception, transferring out of f, through any number of blocks on the stack, to the handler at the end of main. The C++ program (middle) also defines an exception type E. Routine f executes a raise (**throw**) of the exception, transferring out of f, through any number of blocks on the stack, to the handler at the end of the **try** statement in main. The nonlocal transfer (right) shows the low-level approach of the **goto**. Notice that termination achieves the first two EHM objectives in Sect. 3.3, p. 69, without the drawbacks of nonlocal transfer.

Interestingly, because C++ allows any type to be used as an exception type, it seems to provide additional generality, i.e., there is no special exception type in the language. However, in practice, this generality is almost never used. First, using a built-in type like **int** as an exception type is dangerous because the type has no inherent meaning for any exceptional event. That is, one library routine can raise **int** to mean one thing and another routine can raise **int** to mean another; a handler catching **int** may misunderstand the meaning of the exception. To prevent this ambi-

	Retry	Simulation
1	**char** readfiles(**char** *files[ ], **int** N) {	**char** readfiles(**char** *files[ ], **int** N) {
2	**int** i = 0, sum, value;	**int** i = 0, sum, value;
3	ifstream infile;	ifstream infile;
4	infile.open(files[i]);	infile.open(files[i]);
5	sum = 0;	sum = 0;
6		**while** (**true**) {
7	**try** {	**try** {
8	infile >> value;	infile >> value;
9	sum += value; ...	sum += value; ...
10	} retry(Eof) {	} **catch**(Eof) {
11	i += 1;	i += 1;
12	infile.close();	infile.close();
13	**if** (i == N) **goto** Finished;	**if** (i == N) **break**;
14	infile.open(files[i]);	infile.open(files[i]);
15	}	}
16	Finished: ;	}
17	}	}

Fig. 3.8 Retry

guity, programmers create specific types describing the exception, e.g., overflow, underflow, etc. Second, these specific exception types can very rarely be used in normal computations, so the sole purpose of these types is for raising unambiguous exceptions. In essence, C++ programmers ignore the generality available in the language and follow a convention of creating explicit exceptions types. Therefore, having a specific exception type in a programming language is not a restriction and provides additional documentation, discriminating between conventional and exception types, while providing the compiler with exact knowledge about types rather than having to infer it from the program, i.e., is **int** a number or an exception.

A modification to the terminate model is the retry model, which restarts the failed operation, creating an implicit loop in the control flow. There must be a clear beginning for the operation to be restarted. The beginning of the guarded block is usually the restart point and there is hardly any other sensible choice. The left example of Fig. 3.8 shows a **retry** handler by extending the C++ exception mechanism; the example reads numbers from multiple files and sums the values. For this example, pretend that C++ raises an exception-type Eof for end-of-file, and the **retry** handler completes by jumping to the start of the **try** block. The handler is supposed to remove the exceptional event in the **retry** handler so the operation can continue. In the example, it opens the next file so reading can continue until all files are read. Mesa, Exceptional C [11], and Eiffel [21] provide retry semantics through a **retry** statement only available in the handler clause.

As mentioned, establishing the operation restart point is essential; reversing lines 5 and 7 in the figure generates a subtle error with respect to the exceptional but not normal execution, i.e., the sum counter is incorrectly reset on retry. This error can be difficult to discover because control flow involving propagation occurs infrequently. In addition, when multiple handlers exist in the handler clause, these handlers must use the same restart point, making retrying more difficult to use.

C++	μC++
| ```
ifstream infile;
ofstream outfile;
outfile.exceptions( ios_base::failbit );
infile.exceptions( ios_base::failbit );
switch ( argc ) {
  case 3:
    try {
      outfile.open( argv[2] );
    } catch( ios_base::failure ) {...}
    // fall through to handle input file
  case 2:
    try {
      infile.open( argv[1] );
    } catch( ios_base::failure ) {...}
    break;
  default:
    ...
} // switch
string line;
try {
  for ( ;; ) {  // loop until end-of-file
    getline( infile, line );
    outfile << line << endl;
  }
} catch ( ios_base::failure ) {}
``` | ```
ifstream infile;
ofstream outfile;


switch ( argc ) {
  case 3:
    try {
      outfile.open( argv[2] );
    } catch( uFile::Failure ) {...}
    // fall through to handle input file
  case 2:
    try {
      infile.open( argv[1] );
    } catch( uFile::Failure ) {...}
    break;
  default:
    ...
} // switch
string line;

for ( ;; ) {
  getline( infile, line );
  if ( infile.fail() ) break;
  outfile << line << endl;
}
``` |

Fig. 3.9 I/O exceptions

   While the retry model provides additional functionality, it can be easily simulated
with a loop and the termination model (see right example of Fig. 3.8) [11, p. 834].
The transformation is straightforward by nesting the guarded block in a loop with
a loop-exit in the handler. In general, rewriting is superior to using retry so that all
looping is the result of looping constructs, not hidden in the EHM. Because of the
above problems and that it can be simulated easily with termination and looping,
retry seldom appears in an EHM.

   As mentioned, exceptions are useful for many kinds of ancillary event, e.g., many
aspects of I/O can raise exceptions versus returning return-codes. Fig. 3.9 shows
how I/O in C++ can be toggled to use exceptions and μC++ always uses exceptions
for I/O errors. In C++, ios::exception is a mask indicating which stream state-flags
(e.g., failbit, badbit, etc.) throw an exception. Setting the failbit for exceptions raises
the ios_base::failure exception for failure to open a file, read a data value, or end-of-
file, i.e., all cases where the failbit is normally set. μC++ provides its own exceptions
for network and file I/O errors (see [3, § 5.10]), but no exception for end-of-file.

   It is a common misconception that only one exception may propagate at a time;
in fact, an arbitrary number of propagating exceptions can be generated. Just like
multiple routines can be called, multiple exceptions can be propagating. Remember,
propagation of an exception does not complete until the exception is handled, i.e.,
the handler must complete rather than raise another exception. An exception must
remain pending during execution of a handler because the handler may reraise the

caught exception, and hence, continue its propagation. However, a handler can create guarded blocks or call routines that create guarded blocks, and then an exception can be raised that is caught by one of handlers associated with these guarded block, which can create more guarded blocks and raise more exceptions. For example, in:

```
struct E {};                          h  ↗
int cnt = 3;                          f
void f( int i ) {                     f
    if ( i == 0 ) throw E();          h  ↗  throw E₂
    try {                             f
        f( i - 1 );                   f
    } catch( E ) { // handler h       h  ↗  throw E₁
        cnt -= 1;                     f
        if ( cnt > 0 ) f( 2 );        f
    }
}
int main() { f( 2 ); }
```

there is a recursive call to f in the handler, which creates another guarded block. After the recursion descends three levels, an exception E is raised, which unwinds the third call and is caught by the **try** for the second call. The handler executes at the top of the stack, replacing the unwound stack frame for the third call. Since cnt is greater than 0, a new recursion is started with f, and the process repeats two more times, until cnt is 0. When cnt is 0, there are three handlers on the stack, each having caught an exception E, and none of the handlers has handled their caught exception. Hence, there are three propagations in progress at this time. As the handlers and calls to f complete, stack unwinds and the propagations complete.

Another common misconception is that a C++ destructor cannot raise an exception. For example, in:

```
struct E {};
struct C {
    ~C() { throw E(); }                              y's destructor
};                                                   | throw E
try {                  // outer try        inner try          x's destructor
    C x;               // raise on deallocation   | y          | throw E
    try {              // inner try        outer try          outer try
        C y;           // raise on deallocation   | x          | x
    } catch( E ) {...} // inner handler
} catch( E ) {...}     // outer handler
```

the outer **try** block creates an instance x and the inner **try** creates an instance y. When the inner **try** block ends, y's destructor is called, which raises an exception E, unwinds the destructor and **try** stack-frames, and is handled by the inner **catch**. When the inner handler completes, control continues and the outer **try** block ends, so x's destructor called, which raises an exception E, unwinds the destructor and **try** stack-frames, and is handled at outer **catch**. Therefore, the destructors behave the same as any other routine with respect to exception handling. However, a destructor *cannot* raise an exception during propagation. For example, in:

```
try {
    C x;              // raise on deallocation
    throw E();
} catch( E ) {...}
```

the **try** block creates an instance x and raises an exception E. Propagation unwinds the **try** stack-frame, which invokes x's destructor. The destructor raises another exception E without a handler to deal with first exception, which causes the program to terminate because the first exception cannot be dropped and another started; each exception has to be handled. This case is no different than raising an exception which has no handler; propagation reaches the base of the stack without finding a handler and the program terminates. Conceptually, the first exception can be postponed, but the second exception may remove its handlers during its stack unwinding making this approach infeasible.

Finally, Modula-3 transforms routine call (case 2 in Table 3.1, p. 74) into dynamic-propagation/termination (case 3) by implicitly rewriting a return into a raise of exception return-exception:

RETURN(v)   ⇒   **RAISE** return-exception(v)

and by rewriting a routine call as:

```
VAR v : routine-type;
TRY
    rtn(...);
EXCEPT
    return-exception( v ) => (* routine result is assigned to v *)
END
```

The reason given for this transformation is to unify interactions between **RETURN** and **RAISE** in the EHM. While this transformation is a laudable goal, there is little practical benefit. Specifically, the transformation turns a simple static call into a complex dynamic call, and a simple dynamic return into a static return from the handler after the routine call in the guarded block.

3.7.3   Dynamic Propagation/Resumption

Dynamic call and return (case 4 in Table 3.1, p. 74) differs from termination by returning to the point of the exception raise. Fig. 3.10 shows the resuming model (and the equivalent version using fixup routines), where control flow transfers from the raise point to a handler to correct an incomplete operation, and then *back* to the raise point to continue execution. Resumption is often likened to a *normal* routine call, particularly when argument/parameters are available, as both return to the dynamic location of the call [9, 11]. However, a routine call is statically bound, whereas a resumption raise is dynamically bound.

Resumption is used in cases where fixup and continuation are possible. For example, in large scientific applications, which run for hours or days, there are "error" situations where it is unacceptable to terminate the program, such as

Resumption	Fixup

struct E {};   // label
void f(...) **resume**(E) {
  ... resume E(); // raise
  // control returns here
}
int main() {
  try {
    f(...);
  } **catch**(E) {...} // handler 1
  try {
    f(...);
  } **catch**(E) {...} // handler 2
}
	void f(void (*fixup)()) {
	  fixup()
	  // control returns here
	}
	void fixup1() { ... } // handler 1
	void fixup2() { ... } // handler 2
	int main() {
	  f(fixup1);
	  f(fixup2);
	}

Fig. 3.10 Resumption

computational problems like zero divide, overflow/underflow, etc. and logical situations like a singular matrix. Instead, these problems are dealt with locally by calling a fixup routine, which often logs the problem and then performs a fixup action allowing execution to continue. While a fixup may result in a compromised result, an approximation may suffice and many hours of computer time are salvaged.

Possibly the first programming language to introduce resumption was PL/I.[4] For example, in Fig. 3.11, the PL/I-like program declares the built-in on-condition ZERODIVIDE in the scope of procedure TEST at line 1. This example applies equally well to user defined on-conditions. An on-condition is like a routine name that is dynamically scoped, i.e., a call to ZERODIVIDE (by the hardware on division by zero) selects the closest instance on the call stack rather than selecting an instance at compile time based on lexical scope. In detail, each on-condition has a stack, on which handler bodies are pushed, and a call to an on-condition executes the top handler (unless the condition is disabled). However, when an ON CONDITION statement is executed, it *replaces* the top element of the stack with a new handler routine (rather than push a new one), which is destructive. Handler routines are only pushed when control flow enters a procedure or block within the lexical scope of on-condition variables by duplicating the top element of each stack. When flow of control leaves a procedure or block, the stacks are implicitly popped so any on-units set up inside a block disappear. This style of setting up handlers is unusual among EHMs.

Stepping through the code in Fig. 3.11:

1. The definition of the built-in on-condition ZERODIVIDE in the body of procedure TEST creates a stack with a system default handler. This definition is superfluous because it already exists in the language preamble.

---

[4] A common misconception about the ON CONDITION is that its semantics are termination rather than resumption. PL/I only provides termination via nonlocal **goto**, which requires programmers to construct a termination model by convention.

```
         TEST: PROCEDURE OPTIONS(MAIN);
    1        DCL ZERODIVIDE CONDITION; /* default handler D */
             F: PROCEDURE;
                A = B / 0; /* call H1 */
    4           ON CONDITION(ZERODIVIDE) RETURN 2; /* H2 */
                A = B / 0; /* call H2 */
    5        END;

    2        ON CONDITION(ZERODIVIDE) RETURN 1; /* H1 */
             A = B / 0; /* call H1 */
    3        CALL F();
             END;
```

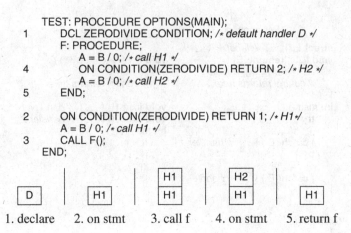

1. declare   2. on stmt   3. call f   4. on stmt   5. return f

Fig. 3.11 PL/I-like resumption

2. The ON CONDITION statement for ZERODIVIDE replaces the default handler at
   the top of ZERODIVIDE's stack with a user handler-routine. The PL/I mechanism
   for returning a result from the handler routine is simplified for this example.
   Within TEST there is an implicit call to condition ZERODIVIDE via the hardware
   when the expression B / 0 is executed, which invokes the top handler, the handler
   executes, and the value 1 is returned for this erroneous expression. Therefore, A
   is assigned the value 1.
3. The call to procedure F duplicates the element of the ZERODIVIDE stack. At the
   start of F, there is an implicit call to condition ZERODIVIDE via the hardware
   when the expression B / 0 is executed, which performs the same handler action
   as before.
4. The ON CONDITION statement for ZERODIVIDE in f then replaces the handler at
   the top of ZERODIVIDE's stack, and this handler is signalled as before.
5. When F returns, the top (local) handler is popped from ZERODIVIDE's stack.

This facility provides polymorphism by allowing a fixed name, ZERODIVIDE, to
have different handlers associated with it based on the dynamic versus the static
structure of the program.

Liskov and Snyder [19, p. 549], and Mitchell and Stroustrup [27, p. 392] argue
against the resumption model but their reasons are largely anecdotal. Goodenough's
resumption model is extensive and complex, and Mesa's resumption is based on
this model [30, pp. 235-240]. However, a resumption model can be as simple as
dynamic routine call, which is easy to implement in languages with nested routines.
For languages without nested routines, like C++, it is still possible to construct
a simple resumption model [3, 5, 11]. There are only two technical issues that
present difficulties with resumption: recursive resuming during propagation and
accessing the resumption handler's lexical scope when an exception is caught. Both
of these technical issues have reasonable solutions. Hence, while resumption has
been rejected by some language designers, it is a viable and useful mechanism in an
EHM.

Recursive Resuming   With termination, the handlers in previous scopes disappear as the stack is unwound; with resumption, the stack is not unwound leaving in place handlers in previous scopes. The presence of resumption handlers in previous scopes can cause a situation called recursive resuming, if the handler or routines called by the handler raise the same exception it just caught, e.g.:

```
try {
    ... resume R(); ...
} catch( R ) {... resume R(); ...} // handler
```

The try block resumes R, which is caught by handler, and the blocks on the call stack are:

```
... → try{} catch( R ) → raise1
... → try{} catch( R ) → handler → raise2
... → try{} catch( R ) → handler → handler → raise3 ...
```

The handler resumes R again, searching from the top of the stack, which finds the catch just below it for R, and invokes the handler again, which continues until the runtime stack overflows. However, programmer intuition says this code is not recursive: lexically, the second resume should not find its containing handler. While recursive resuming is similar to infinite recursion, it is more difficult to discover, both at compile time and at runtime, because of the dynamic choice of a handler. An asynchronous exception compounds the difficulty as it can cause recursive resuming where it is impossible otherwise because the exception can be delivered at any time. Note, even if a resumption handler resumes the exception it handles, which guarantees activating the same resumption handler again, (infinite) recursive resuming may not happen because the handler can take a different execution path as a result of a modified execution state. MacLaren briefly discusses the recursive resuming problem in the context of PL/I [20, p. 101], and the problem exists in Exceptional C [11] and μSystem [5]. Nor is it impossible to prevent recursive resuming via appropriate semantics during propagation. The mechanisms in Mesa [23, p. 143] and VMS [15, pp. 90-92] represent the two main approaches for solving this problem.

Mesa propagation prevents recursive resuming by not reusing an active, unhandled handler, i.e., once a handler for a block is entered it is marked as unhandled and not used again. Marking prevents the above recursion because the handler can only be used once:

```
... → try{} catch( R ) → raise1
... → try{} catch( R ) → handler → raise2
```

Therefore, propagation of the second raise skips handler as it is marked, and a handler further down the stack is found. However, the Mesa approach can be confusing because handlers further down the stack from a marked handler remain eligible.

```
try {                   // outer
    try {               // inner
        ... resume R1(); ...
    } catch( R2 ) {... resume R2(); ...}       // handler2
} catch( R1 ) {... resume R2(); ...}           // handler1
```

... → **try**{} catch(R1) → **try**{} catch(R2) → raise R1
... → **try**{} catch(R1) → **try**{} catch(R2) → handler1 → raise R2
... → **try**{} catch(R1) → **try**{} catch(R2) → handler1 → handler2 → raise R2

After the raise of R1 in the inner **try** block and catch in the outer **try** block, handler1 is marked ineligible but the handler for R2 remains eligible. Therefore, the raise of R2 in handler1 is caught by the inner try block, which is very confusing based on the lexical structure of the **try** blocks.

The VMS exception model solves the recursive resuming problem, but without the Mesa problem, by marking all handlers examined during propagation not just the one catching the exception. For the simple recursive resuming example, Mesa and VMS perform the same marking, as there is only one handler examined and it is marked. In the confusing Mesa case, VMS marking produces the following:

... → **try**{} catch(R1) → **try**{} catch(R2) → raise R1
... → **try**{} catch(R1) → **try**{} catch(R2) → handler1 → raise R2

After the raise of R1 in the inner **try** block and catch in the outer **try** block, both handler1 and handler2 are examined, and hence, marked ineligible. Therefore, propagation of the second raise skips both marked handlers, and a handler further down the stack is found.

Neither approach precludes infinite recursions with respect to propagation, e.g.:

```
void f() {
    try {
        ... resume R; ...
    } catch( R ) f();      // handler
}
```

each call to f creates a new **try** block to handle the next recursion, resulting in an infinite number of handlers:

f → **try**{} catch(R) → handler() → f → **try**{} catch(R) → handler() ...

As a result, there is always an eligible handler to catch the next exception in the recursion, which is a programming error with respect to recursion not propagation.

All handlers are considered unmarked when propagating nonlocal exceptions as the exception is unrelated to any existing propagation. Hence, propagation searches every handler on the runtime stack. Finally, marking does not affect termination propagation because marked resumption handlers are removed during stack unwinding.

Lexical Context   When a handler executes, its static context must be established to access variables and routines lexically accessible in the handler. For example, in:

```
struct E {};
void f( int i ) {
    int x = i;
    if ( i == 1 ) resume E();        // base case
    else if ( i == 3 )               // setup handler
        try {
            f( i - 1 );              // recursion
        } catch( E ) { x = 0; }      // handler
    else f( i - 1 );                 // recursion
}
```

```
handler ┐
f_x 1
f_x 2        lexical link
try catch
f_x 3   ◄─── x 0
f_x 4
f_x 5
```

the call f(5), generates five recursive calls, and a guarded block is setup on the third call. Each call creates a local variable x on the stack. On the last call, a resumption exception is raised. The propagation matches the catch clause for the guarded block but does not unwind the stack because of resumption. The handler executes at the top of stack and sets x to 0; but which x as there are five x's on the stack? The correct x is the third one where the guarded block was created because of lexical scoping rules. Therefore, a lexical link (see page 25) must exist from the handler to its lexical scope in the third stack frame to locate x for the assignment. Fundamentally, a resumption handler behaves like a nested routine, except it is invoked as the result of a raise rather than a call. Lexical links are usually unnecessary in the case of termination as the intermediate stack frames are discarded before execution of the handler. In this case, the handler executes in the same lexical context in which it is defined. Hence, implementing resumption can have an inherent additional cost (lexical links); furthermore, languages without nested routines (e.g., C/C++) would need to add lexical links to support resumption, which can increase the cost of all routine calls.

In fact, the lexical context for resumption handlers has been cited as a source of confusion and complexity [11, p. 833] [27, pp. 391-392]. Confusion results from unexpected values being accessed due to differences between static and dynamic contexts, and complexity from the need for lexical links. Interestingly, both these issues are also related to nested routines. For example, the following is the previous example converted from a resumption exception to a fixup routine (see page 63):

```
void fx1() {}                      // default fixup
void f( int i, void (*fixup)() ) { // fixup versus resumption
    int x = i;
    if ( i == 1 ) fixup();         // base case, correction
    else if ( i == 3 ) {
        void fx2() { x = 0; }      // nested routine
        f( i - 1, fx2 );           // recursion, change fixup
    } else f( i - 1, fixup );      // recursion, pass along fixup
}
```

These two programs generate identical dynamic situations. The nested routine fx2 acts like the resumption handler, references the local variable x, and it is invoked at the top of the stack, like the handler, to perform a corrective action. Hence, complexity for supporting resumption is not an issue for languages with

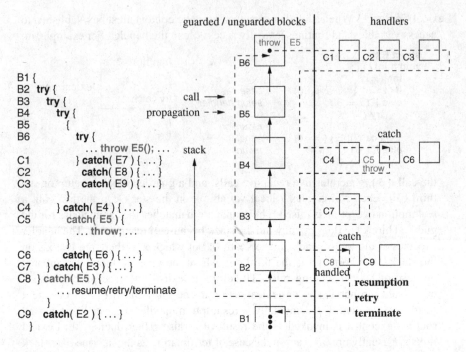

Fig. 3.12 Dynamic propagation

nested routines as lexical links are already required. For languages without nested routines, it is still possible to provide lexical links for resumption handlers, but at a potentially significant cost. If lexical links are not provided, resumption handlers are still possible but must be specified separately from the guarded block, affecting readability and ease of use (see Sect. 3.15.2, p. 111).

In summary, Fig. 3.12 illustrates all aspects of an EHM with the different forms of dynamic propagation. There are six blocks on the stack B1–B6. Blocks B1, B3 and B5 are unguarded and blocks B2, B4 and B6 are guarded blocks. An exception E5 is created and raised in block B6 at the top of the stack. Propagation checks the exception with the handlers for block B6 and no match is found. Propagation continues through block B5, which is unguarded, and onto block B4, where a match is found for catch C5. The handler for C5 decides to reraise the caught exception, and propagation continues through the unguarded block B3 to block B2, where a match is found for catch C8. The handler for C8 handles the exception, and the three different forms of dynamic propagation (resumption, retry, termination) can occur. For resumption, control returns to the point after the raise; for retry, control restarts the guarded block B2 after dealing with the failure; for termination, control continues in block B1 after **try** block B2, which has the C8-handler that statically returned.

3.8 EHM Features

The previous discussion covers the fundamental features of an EHM. Additional features are presented that make an EHM easier to use (see also [5, 9, 13, 18]). Some of these features can have a significant impact on the design of the EHM.

3.8.1 Handler Association

Goodenough's seminal paper on exception handling suggests a handler, enclosed in brackets [...], can be associated with programming units as small as a subexpression and as large as a routine [13, pp. 686–7], e.g.:

```
D = (A + B)[OVERFLOW: /* handle overflow */] + C; /* subexpression */

DO WHILE ( ... );                                /* statement */
    ... /* read and process */
END; [ENDFILE: /* handle end-of-file */]

P : PROCEDURE(...);                              /* routine */
BEGIN;
    ...
END; [ERROR: /* handle error */]
```

For handlers associated with expressions or functions, a mechanism must exist to return a result so execution can continue, which requires additional constructs [13, p. 690]:

```
D = (A + B)[OVERFLOW: EXIT(0);] + C;
```

returns 0 if expression $A + B$ overflow so the remainder of the calculation can continue. Between expression and routine handler association is a language's notion of a block, i.e., the facility that combines multiple statements into a single unit, such as {...} or begin...end. While the granularity of a block is coarser than an expression, the need for fine-grained handling is usually rare. As well, having multiple handlers, which may contain arbitrarily complex code, in the middle of an expression can be difficult to read.

```
G = ((A + B) - C) * ((D / E) + F) ...;    G = ((A + B)[OVERFLOW: ... EXIT(0); ]
                                               - C)[UNDERFLOW: ... EXIT(1); ] * (
                                              (D / E)[ZERODIVIDE: ... EXIT(3); ]
                                               + F) ...;
```

In this situation, it is not much different to subdivide the expression into multiple blocks with appropriate handlers:

```
try { t1 = a + b; } catch( Overflow ) { ... t1 = 0; }
try { t1 = t1 - c; } catch( Underflow ) { ... t1 = 1; }
try { t2 = d / e; } catch( Zerodivide ) { ... t2 = 2; }
g = t1 * ( t2 + f );
```

Having to create temporary variables is the downside of block granularity but it does provide a mechanism to return a value from the handler. Because the block has medium granularity, can simulate other forms, and is used in many modern programming languages (C++ , Java, C#), handlers are only associated with blocks.

Multiple handler clauses can be bound to one block, e.g.:

```
try {
    // guarded block
} catch( E1 ) {       // multiple handlers for guarded block
    // handler1
} catch( E2 ) {
    // handler2
}
```

The propagation mechanism determines the order handler clauses bound to a guarded block are searched.

The scope of the handler clauses for a guarded block varies among languages. For example, in Ada, the handler clause is nested inside a guarded block, and hence, can access variables declared in it, while a C++ handler executes in a scope outside its guarded block making variables in the guarded block inaccessible, e.g.:

Ada	C++
x : integer; -- *outer*	**int** x; // *outer*
begin	**try** {
x : integer; -- *inner*	**int** x; // *inner*
exception when Others =>	} **catch**(...) {
x := 0; -- *inner x*	x = 0; // *outer x*
end;	}

Notice, variable x in the handler clause is different between the two languages. By moving the handler and possibly adding another nested block, the same semantics can be accomplished in either language, as long as a handler can be associated with any nested block.

3.8.2 Derived Exception-Type

An exception type can be derived from another exception type, just like deriving a subclass from a class, providing a kind of polymorphism among exception types. The exception-type hierarchy that is created is also useful to organize exception types, similar to a class hierarchy in object-oriented languages, e.g.:

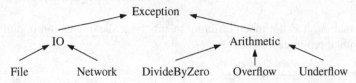

A programmer can then choose to handle an exception at different degrees of specificity along the hierarchy; derived exception-types support a more flexible programming style, and hence, significantly enhance an EHM. For example, higher-level code should catch general exceptions to reduce coupling to the specific implementation at the lower levels; unnecessary coupling may force changes in higher-level code when low-level code changes. A consequence of derived exception-types is that multiple exceptions may match, e.g.:

```
catch( Arithmetic )
```

matches all three derived exception-types: DivideByZero, Overflow, and Underflow. To handle this case, most propagation mechanisms perform a simple linear search of the handler clause for a guarded block and select the first matching handler, so the order of catch clauses in the handler clause becomes important, e.g.:

```
try {
     ...
} catch( Overflow ) {      // must appear first
     // handle overflow
} catch( Arithmetic )
     // handle other arithmetic issues
}
```

An important design question is whether to allow derivation from multiple exception types, called **multiple derivation**, which is similar to multiple inheritance of classes. While Cargill [7] and others argue against multiple inheritance among classes in object-oriented programming, multiple inheritance among derived exception-types is different. For example, consider the following multiple inheritance among derived exception-types [18, p. 19]:

```
exception NetworkErr, FileErr;
exception NetworkFileErr : NetworkErr, FileErr; // multiple derivation
```

which derives NetworkFileErr from NetworkErr and FileErr. While this looks reasonable, there are subtle problems:

```
try {
     ... throw NetworkFileErr ...
} catch( NetworkErr ) ...     // close network connection
    catch( FileErr ) ...      // close file
```

If NetworkFileErr is raised, neither of the handlers may be appropriate to handle the raised exception, but more importantly, which handler in the handler clause should be chosen because of the inheritance relationship? Executing both handlers may look legitimate, but indeed it is not. If a handler clause has a handler only for FileErr, does it mean that it cannot handle NetworkFileErr completely and should raise NetworkErr afterwards? The example shows that handling an exception having multiple parents may be inappropriate. If an exception cannot be caught by one of its parents, the derivation becomes moot. Therefore, multiple derivation is a questionable feature for derived exception-types as it introduces significant complications into the semantics with little benefit.

Finally, with derived exception-types, it is best to catch an exception by reference. For example, in:

```
struct B {...};
struct D : public B {...}; // add fields
try {                                        try {
    throw D(); // _Throw in uC++                 throw D(); // _Throw in uC++
} catch( B e ) { // truncation               } catch( B &e ) { // no truncation
    // cannot down-cast                          ... dynamic_cast<D>(e) ...
}                                            }
```

exception-type D is derived from B with additional data fields. In the left example, a derived object of type D is raised, but the exception is caught at the matching handler by value in a base object of type B. As a result, the exception object is truncated from type D to type B, possibly losing data and precluding calls to members specific to D, i.e., the truncation prevents down-cast from the base to the derived type. For resumption, catching by value precludes returning values back to the raise point. In the right example, the exception is caught by reference, and therefore, the original raised object is not truncated. As a result, the exception object can be down-cast to any derived type to assess all fields and member-routines, and changes to the derived exception-object take effect back at the raise point for resumption.

3.8.3 Catch-Any

Catch-any is a mechanism to match any exception propagating through a guarded block, e.g.:

```
try {
    ...
} catch( E ) {              // handle specific exceptions
    ...
} catch(...) {              // catch any remaining exceptions
    // general cleanup
}
```

For termination, this capability is often used as a general cleanup when a non-specific exception occurs during a guarded-block's execution. For resumption, this capability allows a guarded block to gather or generate information about control flow passing through a guarded block, but only in one direction, i.e., during the raise versus the resumption. With exception-type inheritance, catch-any can be provided by the root exception-type, e.g., **catch**(Exception) in Java. When there is no predefined exception-type hierarchy, special syntax is necessary, e.g., **catch**(...) in C++.

Java block finalization:

```
try {
    ...
} catch( E ) { ... }
... // other catch clauses
} finally { ... } // always executed
```

is executed on *both* normal and exceptional termination, providing additional catch-any capabilities plus dealing with the non-exceptional case. Interestingly,

Finalization	Routine Simulation	Destructor Simulation

int main() {
  int f = open(. . .);
  try {
    // file operations
  } finally {
    close(f);
  }
}
	void cleanup(int &f) {
	  close(f);
	}
	int main() {
	  int f = open(. . .);
	  try {
	    // file operations
	    cleanup(f);
	  } catch(. . .) {
	    cleanup(f);
	  }
	}
		struct cleanup {
		  int &f;
		  cleanup(int &f) : f(f) {}
		  ~cleanup() { close(f); }
		};
		int main() {
		  int f = open(. . .);
		  {
		    cleanup v(f);
		    // file operations
		  }
		}

Fig. 3.13   Finalization

finalization is difficult to mimic with other language features that handle finalization, like destructors in C++. The left example, in Fig. 3.13 shows how a finally clause can be used to ensure an open file is closed regardless of how the block manipulating the file ends. The simulations in the centre and right examples both have a problem preventing duplication of the cleanup code, which forces the use of a routine or object destructor for the cleanup. Unfortunately, this approach makes accessing local variables in the block containing the **try** statement difficult from the cleanup routine or destructor. For systems with nested routines and classes, the references can be direct; otherwise, variables must be explicitly passed to the cleanup routine/class.

3.8.4   Exception Parameters

Of almost equal importance to the control flow provided by exceptions is the ability to pass information from the raise to the handler (which is also true for a routine). Without this capability, it is difficult to communicate the reason for raising an exception and/or where the exception was raised. Without this information, a handler may not be able to determine the extent of the problem and if recovery is possible.

Exception parameters enable a source execution to transfer information in and out of the faulting execution's handler, just like routine parameters and results. An exception parameter can be read-only, write-only and read-write. While information can be passed via shared objects, exception parameters eliminate side effects and locking in a concurrent environment. Ada has no parameters, C (via setjmp/longjmp) has a single integer parameter, Modula-3 and C++ have a single object-parameter containing arbitrary values, ML and Mesa have multiple parameters.

Parameter specification for an exception-type depends on the form of its definition. In Mesa and Modula-3, a technique similar to routine parameters is used:

```
exception E( int );        // exception definition with parameter
throw E( 7 ) ...           // integer argument supplied at raise
catch( E( int p ) ) ...    // integer parameter p received in handler
```

In C++, an object type is the exception-type and an object instance is created to contain any parameters, as in:

```
struct E {
    int i;                 // parameter
    E(int p) { i = p; }
};
void rtn(...) { ... throw E( 7 ); ... } // object argument supplied at raise
int main() {
    try {
        ... rtn(...); ...
    } catch( E p ) {       // object parameter p received in handler
        // use p.i
    }
}
```

In all cases, it is possible to have parameters that are routines (or member routines), and these routines can perform special operations. For example, by convention or with special syntax, an argument or member routine can be used as a **default handler**, which is called if the faulting execution does not find a handler during propagation, as in:

```
void f(...) {...}
exception E( ... ) default( f );       // special syntax, default routine f
struct E { ... void default() {...}; };  // special name, default member
```

Other specialized operations are conceivable.

3.8.5   Exception List

An **exception list**,[5] in Goodenough, CLU, Modula-3, Java and C++, is part of a routine's prototype and specifies which exception types may propagate from the routine to its caller. For example, in the routine prototype:

```
int rtn() throw(E1,E2);
```

the exception list, **throw(E1,E2)**, indicates that only exception types E1 and E2 are raised to any caller of rtn. The purpose of the exception list is to make it possible to ameliorate the visibility problem associated with dynamic propagation (see Sect. 3.7.2, p. 77). First, the union of all exception lists of called routines defines all possible kinds of exceptions that can propagate into the caller's scope. Second, the exception list for the caller's scope restricts which exception types from its called routines can pass to the next level and which ones must be handled within the routine. Therefore, when an exception is raised, it is known statically that all

---

[5]Called an **exception specification** in C++.

blocks traversed during propagation are aware of this particular exception's type, and that the exception is ultimately handled at some point during propagation. From an implementation standpoint, the compiler checks the static call-graph of a program to ensure every raised exception ultimately propagates into a guarded block with an appropriate handler, except possibly for the main routine, which may be able to propagate exceptions to the language's runtime system. Therefore, exception lists can be used to establish invariants about control flow, such as unnecessary **try** blocks. For example, in:

```
int f() throw();        // throws no exceptions
int rtn() {
    try {               // unnecessary try block
        f();
    } catch( E ) {...}
}
```

f's definition states it throws no exceptions. Therefore, it is possible to formally reason that the **try** block in routine rtn is superfluous and elide it.

A consequence of exception lists is that nonlocal handling requires intermediate routines in a call graph to list all exception types that may propagate through it from lower-level to higher-level routines, in which the exception type is ultimately handled. In some cases, the exception types associated with nonlocal handling have little or no meaning at the intermediate levels. So while these exception types are syntactically visible to intermediate routines, they are semantically invisible. The result is unwanted coupling between low and intermediate-level routines, i.e., a change to a lower-level routine raising an exception may cause a cascade of changes in exception lists for intermediate-level routines, where these changes may be largely irrelevant. Another consequence of exception lists is that handlers must ultimately exist for all possible exception types. This may result in the main routine of a program having a guarded block with a large or a catch-any handler clause to deal with exception types not handled lower in the call graph, with corresponding coupling problems. Some languages allow certain (hardware) exceptions, not listed in the program, to be propagated to the language's runtime system. The assumption is that the runtime system may have a default handler for these exceptions, which performs some appropriate action.

Unfortunately, the formality of statically checked exception-lists can become annoying to programmers, resulting in their circumventing much its benefits. For example, it is common in Java programs to see the following idioms that negate the benefits of statically checked exception-lists. One idiom is to have a try block with an empty handler for an exception type, as in:

```
try { wait(); } catch( InterruptedException ex ) { /* empty handler */ }
```

The handler is empty because the exception occurs rarely and/or the programmer has no obvious action to perform should the exception occur; however, without the handler the program does not compile. An alternative idiom to deal with this situation is over-relaxing the routine's exception-list by specifying the root of the exception-type hierarchy, i.e., throws Exception, which allows any exception to propagate from a routine. Here, the programmer is pushing the issue onto the next level simply to make progress. However, this approach can be disruptive to other developers calling this routine as now they are required to deal with more exceptions seemingly unrelated to their code. The conclusion is that the rigid specification and handling adherence required by statically-checked exception-lists may be too high a requirement for many programming situations, and hence, programmers find ways to relax these requirements to simplify program construction, which negates the purpose of exception lists.

An alternative approach to static checking of exception lists is dynamic checking, or a combination of static and dynamic checking. During propagation, at each routine activation, a comparison is made of the raised exception with the routine's exception-list. If the raised exception does not appear in the exception list, it is a runtime violation and some appropriate semantics action must occur. For example, the program can be terminated, the specific exception can be changed to a general failure exception which conceptually appears in all exception lists, or a special user supplied routine is called to take some action. Terminating the program can be inappropriate in many programming situations. Converting the specific raised exception to the failure exception precludes any chance of handling the specific exception-type and only complicates any recovery, especially when a raised exception has parameters that are lost in the conversion. Calling a special routine is only useful if the routine can act like a fixup routine indicating the propagation can (or cannot) continue. From a software engineering perspective, the dynamic approach is less attractive because there is now the potential for a runtime error versus a compile-time error.

C++ supports dynamic checking of exception lists, with one statically checked case: static checking occurs when overriding virtual routines:

```
struct B {
    virtual void f() throw(E);
};
struct D : B {
    void f(); // static error
};
```

The definition of D::f is checked statically and fails because it allows all exception types, whereas B::f allows only exception type E. Otherwise, all verification of checked exception types occurs dynamically during propagation, so at each routine activation during propagation, a comparison is made of the raised exception type with the routine's exception-list. If the comparison fails to find the raised exception type in the exception list, the special routine unexpected is called, which must not return but can raise another exception. C++ explicitly chose to perform dynamic checking over static checking to allow programmers to control the execution behaviour when an exception list is violated through the unexpected routine. Otherwise, C++ could have adopted a static checking approach.

Interestingly, static checking cannot cover all possible situations where exceptions can be raised. Many hardware-specific failures resulting in exceptions can occur at any time, making it impossible to know statically which exception types can occur within a routine. In addition, a nonlocal exception may be propagated at essentially any time, making it impossible to know statically which exception types can occur within a routine. An exception type that is allowed to propagate even when it is not in an exception list is called unchecked. An unchecked exception-type is allowed to propagate into and out of a scope where it is invisible, which is the visibility problem for dynamic propagation. Java supports unchecked exception-types by having all exception types organized into a hierarchy divided into checked and unchecked; an exception type can be derived from either branch of the hierarchy using exception-type derivation. Only checked exception-types can appear in exception lists, and hence, are statically checked. C++ does not have unchecked exception-types but rather unchecked routines, i.e., a routine without an exception list means this routine has all exception types in its exception list, and hence, any exception can pass through this routine.

While exception lists are a useful software engineering mechanism to further specify a routine's behaviour, exception lists can constrain polymorphism [27, p. 394], having a significant feature interaction between the EHM and a language's type system. For example, consider the simplified C++ template routine sort:

```
template<typename T> void sort( T items[] ) {
    // using bool operator<( const T &a, const T &b );
}
```

using the operator routine < in its definition. There are two possibilities with respect to raising exceptions:

1. sort may directly or indirectly raise exceptions
2. operator routine < used by sort may raise exceptions

If sort raises exceptions, it must have an exception list, e.g.:

```
template<typename T> void sort( T items[] ) throw(E1) {
    // using bool operator<( const T &a, const T &b );
}
```

If routine < raises exceptions, static checking requires all of its exception types must be caught in sort or appear in sort's exception list. For languages requiring explicit specification of all required routines as part of a template definition (e.g., Ada, Haskell), it is possible to build on this facility to extend static exception-checking. For example, extending the syntax for the the template routine sort to:

```
template<typename T> void sort( T items[] ) throw(E1)
    // require routine with exception list
    with bool operator<( const T &a, const T &b ) throw(E2);
```

implies all < routines used by sort can throw exception type E2, which sort must handle or include in its exception list. However, any type T with an operator routine < with a larger exception list than sort expects cannot be sorted, constraining reuse. A slightly more general approach is to relax the constraints on the required routines but compensate by specifying which exceptions are caught within sort, as in:

```
template<typename T> void sort( T items[] ) throw(E1), catch(E2)
    with bool operator<( const T &a, const T &b ) throw(E2), catch(E3);
```

This prototype states sort allows E1 to escape from it but catches exception-type E2 within its body, including those that might be generated by any required routine it might call. A similar specification is made by operator routine < with respect to exception-types E2 and E3. This additional information still allows static checking of exceptions but reduces the constraints on the prototypes for the required routines. For example, any set of required routines that raises at most exception types E1 and E2 is applicable because these exception types are either caught in sort or appear in sort's exception list. Similarly, operator routine < can call any routine that raises at most exception types E2 and E3. However, reuse is still constrained because the set of exception types that can be raised by the required routines is restricted to those specified in the exception and catch lists.

A general solution is suggested but only for languages that have complete access to all source code (or its equivalent); hence, this solution is not applicable for systems where only partial information about a definition is available at a declaration. The approach is to extend the syntax for instantiation of a template routine by adding an exception list:

```
sort( v ) throw(E4); // instantiate with exception list
```

implying sort's exception list is extended with exception type E4 in this context, which allows a routine < raising E4 to be used. In C++, this extension could work because a template is expanded as if "inlined", so conceptually a new sort routine is generated for each instantiation; hence, there are actually multiple versions of sort, each with a different prototype. This additional information at the call makes it possible for the compiler to statically determine which exception types propagate *through* sort and *into* the local context of its calls. However, this solution imposes a significant burden on the definition of sort, as it can no longer make certain assumptions about which exceptions may or may not occur in particular contexts. Hence, sort must be designed to be more robust with respect to failure points in its execution to allow this approach.

Static checking of exception lists also constrain reuse for arguments of routine pointers (functional style) and/or polymorphic methods or routines (object-oriented style), e.g.:

```
                                          class B {
                                             virtual int g() throw() {}
int f( int (*p)(...) throw() ) {             int f() { ... g(); ... }
    ... *p(...); ...                      };
}                                         class D : public B {
int g() throw(E) { throw E(); }              int g() throw(E) { throw E(); }
int h(...) {                                 int h() {
    try {                                        try {
        ... f( g ); ...                              ... f(); ...
    } catch( E ) ...                             } catch( E ) ...
}                                            }
                                          };
```

The left example illustrates arguments of routine pointers, where routine h calls f passing argument g, and f calls g with the potential to raise exception type E. Routine h is clearly capable of handling the exception because it has an appropriate **try** block and is aware the version of g it passes to f may raise the exception. However, this reasonable case is precluded because the prototype of the argument routine g is less restrictive than the parameter variable p of f. Similarly, the right example illustrates object-oriented dynamic dispatch, where the derived class replaces member g, which is called from member B::f. Member routine D::h calls B::f, which calls D::g with the potential to raise exception type E. Member D::h is clearly capable of handling the exception because it has an appropriate **try** block and it created the version of g raising the exception. However, this reasonable case is precluded because the prototype of D::g is less restrictive than B::g. If f in the left example or B in the right example are pre-compiled in a library, there is no option to expand the prototypes to allow this reuse scenario. Nor is it reasonable to expand the prototype for every routine. In fact, doing so makes the program less robust because the prototype now covers too broad a range of exception types.

In general, programmers do not want to inhibit reuse, nor do they want to write seemingly unnecessary specifications, but they also want good software-engineering practice, such as static exception-list checking. Unfortunately, these are conflicting goals. In many cases, because the number of exceptions are large and their occurrence is rare, programmers under-constraint a routine by allowing any exception to propagate out of it, which is the default behaviour in C++. While this approach simplifies programming, it defeats the software-engineering goal of providing static exception-checking. At some point, unspecified exceptions must be dealt with. Either the main routine of a program must catch all exceptions and do something appropriate or possibly the language preamble (implicit lexical scope in which a program is compiled) implicitly does this. In either case, if too many exceptions are deferred to this point, the purpose of static exception-list checking is largely circumvented.

Finally, Sect. 3.7.1, p. 75 mentions sequels can be passed as arguments to pre-compiled routines to perform exception handling. Similarly, some schemes for simulating resumption involve passing fixup routines, which are called to correct a problem. However, the list of sequel or fixup routine parameters is similar to an exception list because it makes a routine's prototype more restrictive, which constrains reuse.

3.8.6 Bound Exceptions and Conditional Handling

In Ada, an exception type declared in a generic package creates a new instance for each package instantiation, e.g.:

```
generic package Stack is
    overflow : exception; ...
end Stack;
package S1 is new Stack;  - - new overflow
package S2 is new Stack;  - - new overflow
begin
    ... S1.push(...); ... S2.push(...); ...
exception
    when S1.overflow => ...   - - catch overflow for S1
    when S2.overflow => ...   - - catch overflow for S2
```

Hence, it is possible to distinguish which stack raised the overflow without passing data to the handler. In object-oriented languages, the class is used as a unit of modularity for controlling scope and visibility. Similarly, it makes sense to associate exception types with the class that raises them, as in:

```
class file {
    struct FileErr { ... };            // nested exception type
```

However, is the exception type associated with the class or objects instantiated from it? As above, the answer affects the capabilities for catching the exception, as in:

```
file f;
try {
    ... f.read(...); ...               // may raise FileErr
} catch( f.FileErr ) ...               // option 1
    catch( file::FileErr ) ...         // option 2
```

In option 1, each file object has its own FileErr exception type. Hence, this **catch** clause *only* deals with FileErr events raised by object f, i.e., the handler is for an exception bound to a particular object, called a **bound exception**. This specificity prevents the handler from catching the same exception bound to a different object. In option 2, only one FileErr exception type exists for *all* objects created by type file. Hence, this **catch** clause deals with FileErr events regardless of which file object raises it. Both facilities are useful but the difference between them is substantial and leads to an important robustness issue. Finally, an exception type *among* classes is simply handled by declaring the exception type outside of the classes and referencing it within the classes.

Bound exceptions cannot be trivially mimicked by other mechanisms. Deriving a new exception type for each file object (e.g., f_FileErr from FileErr) results in an explosion in the total number of exception types, and cannot handle dynamically allocated objects, which have no static name. Passing the associated object as an argument to the handler and checking if the argument is the bound object, as in:

```
struct FileErr { file *fp; };
catch( FileErr e ) {                   // fp is passed from the raise
    if ( e.fp == &f ) ...              // deal only with f
    else throw                         // reraise exception
```

requires programmers to follow a coding convention of reraising the exception if the bound object is inappropriate [5]. Such a coding convention is unreliable, significantly reducing robustness. In addition, mimicking becomes infeasible for derived exception-types, as in:

```
struct B { obj o; );                   // base exception-type
struct D : public B {...};             // derived exception-type
obj o1, o2;
try {
```

```
    ... throw D(...);                  |  // bound form
} catch( D e ) {                       |  } catch( o1.D ) {
    if ( e.o == &o1 ) ...   // deal only with o1
    else throw              // reraise exception
} catch( B e ) {                       |  } catch( o2.B ) {
    if ( e.o == &o2 ) ...   // deal only with o2
    else throw              // reraise exception
```

When exception type D is raised, the problem occurs when the first handler catches the derived exception-type and reraises if the object is inappropriate. The reraise immediately terminates the current guarded block, which precludes the handler for the base exception-type in that guarded block from being considered. Therefore, the "catch first, then reraise" approach is an incomplete substitute for bound exceptions.

Finally, it is possible to generalize the concept of the bound exception with conditional handling [24], as in:

```
catch( E e ) when( e.o == 5 && x < y ) . . . // exception data and local variables
```

where the when clause specifies a general conditional expression that must also be true before the handler is chosen, and the object(s) in the conditional does not have to be the object containing the exception-type definition, as for bound exceptions. Conditional handling can mimic bound exceptions simply by checking if the object parameter is equal to the desired object.

```
catch( f.FileErr )          catch( FileErr e ) when( e.fp == &f )
```

For bound exceptions, the raising object is implicitly passed to the handler; for conditional handling, any necessary data must be explicitly passed as an argument or embedding in the exception at the raise. Furthermore, there is only a coincidental connection between the exception and conditional object(s) versus the statically nested exception-type in the bound object.

3.9 Choosing an Exception Model

A programmer needs to choose the exception model (see Sect. 3.7, p. 74), termination or resumption, for dealing with an exceptional event. In general, the decision depends on whether the exception is fixable (return to raise point) or unfixable (recover at higher level), implying resumption or termination models, respectively. There are a number of different ways to specify the exception model:

1. At the definition of the exception type, as in:

```
terminate E1;          // specific definition
resume E2;
try {
    ... throw E1;      // generic raise
    ... throw E2;
} catch( E1 ) ...      // generic handler
  catch( E2 ) ...
```

   Associating the propagation model at exception-type definition means the raise and handler can be generic. In this approach, there is a **partitioning** of exception types, as in Goodenough [13] with ESCAPE and NOTIFY, μSystem [5] with exceptions and interventions, and Exceptional C [11] with exceptions and signals. The advantage of partitioning is the exception definition reflects the nature of the exceptional event, e.g., UNIX signals SIGBUS or SIGTERM always lead to termination of an operation, and hence, can be declared as termination-only. Indeed, partitioning removes the mistake of using the wrong kind of raise and/or handler.

2. At the raise of the exception, as in:

```
exception E;            // generic definition
try {
   ... terminate E;     // specific raise
   ... resume E;
} catch( E ) ...        // generic handler
```

Associating the exception model at the raise means the exception type and handler can be generic. In this approach, an exception type can be used for either kind of propagation, i.e., exception type E implies termination or resumption depending on the raise. The generic handler catching the exception must behave according to the exception model associated with the raise of the exception. As a result, it is almost mandatory to have a runtime facility in the handler to determine the kind of raise, as different actions are usually taken for each.

Without partitioning, every exception type becomes **dual** as it can be raised with either form of exception model, which has the following advantages. First, without dual exception-types, two different exception types may have to be declared, one being terminate-only and the other resume-only. These two exception types are apparently unrelated without a naming convention; using a single dual exception-type establishes the relationship. Second, using a dual exception-type instead of resume-only for some exceptional events allows a resume exception-type to be terminated when no resumption handler is found. This effect can be achieved through a default resumption handler that raises a termination exception.

3. At the handler, as in:

```
exception E;            // generic definition
try {
   ... raise E;         // generic raise
} terminate( E ) ...    // specific handler
try {
   ... raise E;         // generic raise
} resume( E ) ...       // specific handler
```

Associating the exception model at the handler means the exception type and raise can be generic. In this approach, an exception type can be used for either kind of propagation, i.e., exception type E can imply termination or resumption depending on the handler. Note that stack unwinding must be delayed until the handler is found because that is the point when the kind of propagation is determined. However, it is ambiguous to have the two handlers appear in the same handler clause for the same exception.

```
exception E;            // generic definition
try {
   ... raise E;         // generic raise
} terminate( E ) ...    // ambiguous choice
  resume( E ) ...
```

In fact, the choice of handling model can be further delayed using an unwind statement available only in the handler to trigger stack unwinding, as in:

```
exception E;          // generic definition
try {
   ... raise E;       // generic raise
} catch( E ) {        // generic handler
   if (...) unwind;   // => termination
   ...                // => resumption
}
```

In this form, a handler implies resumption unless an unwind is executed resulting in termination. The unwind capability in VMS [15, Chapter 4] and any language with nonlocal transfer can support this approach. Both forms have implications with respect to the implementation because stack unwinding must be delayed, which can have an effect on other aspects of the EHM.

Unfortunately, this approach violates the EHM objective of preventing an incomplete operation from continuing, i.e., it is impossible at the raise point to ensure control flow does not return.

It is possible to combine these approaches to further define the exception model.

Approaches 1 & 2	Approaches 2 & 3

terminate E1; // specific definition
resume E2;
try {
   ... terminate E1; // specific raise
   ... resume E2;
} catch(E1) ... // generic handler
  catch(E2) ... // generic handler
	exception E1, E2; // generic definition
	try {
	   ... terminate E1; // specific raise
	   ... resume E2;
	} terminate(E1) ... // specific handler
	  resume(E2) ...

In the left example, the exception model is specified by both the exception type and at raise, which must agree. The generic handler catching the exception must behave according to this specified exception model. As mentioned, it is almost mandatory to have a runtime facility in the handler to determine the exception model to ensure the correct action is taken. In general, it is better software engineering to partition the handler code for each kind of exception model rather than combine it in a single handler. In the right example, the exception model for the generic exception-type is made specific at the raise and the handler, which must agree. In this form, the handler code is partitioned for each kind of exception model. (The EHM in μC++, see Sect. 3.12, p. 107, uses this approach.) It is also possible to combine all three approaches, as in:

```
terminate E1;         // specific definition
resume E2;
try {
   ... terminate E1;  // specific raise
   ... resume E2;
} terminate( E1 ) ... // specific handler
  resume( E2 ) ...
```

While pedantic, the redundancy of this approach helps in reading the code because the definition specifies the kind of the exception model (especially when the exception type is part of an interface). As well, it is unnecessary to have a mechanism in the handler to determine the kind of raised exception. The EHM in μSystem [5] uses all three locations to specify the exception model.

Finally, in an EHM where terminating and resuming coexist, it is possible to partially override their semantics by raising an exception within a handler, as in:

```
try {                              try {
   ... resume E1;                     ... terminate E1;
} catch( E1 ) terminate E2;        } catch( E1 ) resume E2;
```

In the left example, the terminate overrides the resuming and forces stack unwinding, starting with the stack frame of the handler (frame on the top of the stack), followed by the stack frame of the block that originally resumed the exception. In the right example, the resume cannot override the terminate because the stack frames are already unwound, so the new resume starts with the handler stack frame.

3.10   Derived Exception Implications

With derived exception-types and partitioned exceptions, there is the issue of deriving one kind of exception type from another, e.g., terminate from resume, called **heterogeneous derivation**. If the derivation is restricted to exception types of the same kind it is called **homogeneous derivation**. Homogeneous derivation is straightforward and easy to understand. Heterogeneous derivation is complex but more flexible because it allows deriving from any kind of exception type, so all exception types can appear in one hierarchy.

The heterogeneous derivation and partitioning generate the following derivations:

parent	terminate	resume	dual	dual	terminate	resume
	↓	↓	↓	↓	↓	↓
derived	resume	terminate	resume	terminate	dual	dual
option	1		2		3	

In option 1, the kind of exception type is different when the derived exception-type is raised and the parent is caught. For example, when a resume-only exception type is caught by a terminate-only handler, it could unwind the stack, but that invalidates resumption at the raise point. When a terminate-only exception type is caught by a resume-only handler, it could resume the exception, but that invalidates the termination at the raise point. In option 2, problems occur when the handler for the dual exception-type attempts to perform an unwind or resume on an exception of the wrong kind, resulting in the option 1 problems. In option 3, there is neither an obvious problem nor an advantage if the dual exception-type is caught by the more specific parent. In most cases, it seems that heterogeneous derivation does not simplify programming and may confuse programmers; hence, it is a questionable feature.

3.11 Propagation Mechanism

The propagation mechanism in an EHM is complex because, while searching for a matching handler, multiple handlers may exist on the stack, and among these handlers, multiple may match the raised exception. When there are multiple matching handlers, some criteria must exist to select among them. This criteria should be simple and efficient to implement, and easy for a programmer to comprehend. Three criteria are examined: partial or full pass, exception kind (termination/resumption) matching, specificity versus generality.

partial/full pass: For partial pass, the search starts at the top of the stack and checks each guarded block until a match occurs; the handler associated with the match is executed. This approach gives precedence to handlers higher on the call stack, so an exception is handled by a handler closest to the block where propagation of the exception starts. Usually, operations higher on the stack are more specific while those lower on the call stack are more general. Handling an exception is often easier and more precise in a specific context than in a general context. This propagation approach also minimizes the amount of stack searching and unwinding when raising an exception, so it is efficient to implement. For full pass, the search proceeds from the top to bottom of the stack, making a list of all matching handlers; the set of matching handlers is than analyzed further to decide which is the most appropriate. This approach gives precedence to the most appropriate handler currently installed regardless of its location on the stack with respect to the block where propagation of the exception starts. The most appropriate handler is supposed to provide the best possible correction. However, it becomes increasingly difficult for a programmer to understand which correction will occur, significantly increasing program complexity. Because of its simplicity and ease of understanding, most programming languages adopt the partial-pass approach.

The same argument that applies among handlers on the stack applies among handlers associated with a guarded block, because a guarded block can have multiple matching handlers. The propagation mechanism can perform a partial pass through these handlers and select the first matching one, or examine all the handlers for the guarded block and select the best possible one.

Given partial pass, a programmer must lexically order handlers in a guarded block to achieve the correct effect, and install general handlers at the bottom of the stack and specific handlers at the top. Given full pass, a programmer must have the most appropriate handler on the stack. While the latter approach seems simpler, it significantly reduces the ability to control the scope of handling, e.g., during a call to a library routine, handlers are installed to deal with exceptional events, but these handlers are ignored because of "more appropriate" handlers further down the stack.

exception kind: Termination and resumption are very different ways to deal with exceptional events (see Sect. 3.9, p. 101); therefore, it is important to incorporate this information in selecting a handler. When the propagation mechanism can determine the exception kind either from the exception type or the kind of raise, this information is then available as a matching criteria during the search. As well, non-generic handlers are necessary at a guarded block to apply the exception-kind information in the matching. For generic handlers, the exception kind must be determined *after* the match within the handler by querying the exception or establishing the exception kind dynamically via a mechanism like unwind.

specificity/generality: Exception mechanisms like inheritance and bound exceptions can result in multiple eligible handlers.

1. The exception type is derived from another exception type (see Sect. 3.8.2, p. 90):

```
terminate B;
terminate D : B;
try {
    ... terminate D;
} terminate( D ) ... // more specific
  terminate( B ) ...
```

2. The exception is bound to an object rather than to a class (see Sect. 3.8.6, p. 99):

```
try {
    ... f.read(); ...
} terminate( f.FileErr ) ... // more specific
  terminate( file.FileErr ) ...
```

3. The exception is bound to the same object and derived from another exception type:

```
class foo {
    terminate B;
    terminate D : B;
    void m() { ... terminate D; }
    ...
foo f;
try {
    ... f.m();
} terminate( f.D ) ... // more specific
  terminate( f.B ) ...
```

In this case, it may be infeasible to tell which handler in a handler clause is more specific:

```
try {
    ...
} terminate( D ) ... // equally specific
  terminate( f.B ) ...
```

Here, there is a choice between a derived exception-type and a bound, base exception-type.

In general, partial is better than full pass when looking for a matching handler as it produces tighter coupling between the raise and the handler, and provides more precise control over handling. For matching, the exception type should be used first, when supported by the exception model, because it finds a handler specifically tailored to resolve the exception event. It is still possible for a default resumption handler to override resuming (see Sect. 3.9, p. 101) and raise a termination exception. Specificity is next to select the most precise handler to deal with an event. If an exception model does have cases where handlers in the same handler clause are equally specific, the most common resolution technique is the position of a handler in a handler clause, e.g., select the first equally matching handler.

3.12 μC++ EHM

The following features characterize the μC++ EHM, and differentiate it from the C++ EHM:

- μC++ exceptions are generated from a specific kind of type, which can be thrown and/or resumed. All exception types are also grouped into a hierarchy by publicly inheriting among the exception types. μC++ extends the C++ set of predefined exception-types[6] covering μC++ exceptional runtime and I/O events.
- μC++ restricts raising of exceptions to the specific exception-types; C++ allows any instantiable type to be raised.
- μC++ supports two forms of raising, throwing (terminating) and resuming; C++ only supports throwing. All μC++ exception-types can be either thrown or resumed. μC++ adopts the VMS marking scheme to eliminate recursive resuming (see page 86). Essentially, μC++ follows a common rule for throwing and resuming: between a raise and its handler, each handler is eligible only once.
- μC++ supports two kinds of handlers, termination and resumption, which match with the kind of raise; C++ only supports termination handlers. Unfortunately, resumption handlers have some restrictions because of the lack of nested routines in C++.
- μC++ supports raising of nonlocal and asynchronous exceptions so that exceptions can be used to affect control flow *among* coroutines and tasks. The μC++ kernel implicitly polls for both kinds of exceptions at the soonest possible opportunity. It is also possible to (hierarchically) block these kinds of exceptions when delivery would be inappropriate or erroneous.

3.13   Exception Type

While C++ allows any type to be used as an exception type, μC++ restricts exception types to those defined by **_Event**, which has all the properties of a **class**:

---

[6]std::bad_alloc, std::bad_cast, std::bad_typeid, std::bad_exception, std::basic_ios::failure, etc.

```
_Event exception-type name {
   ...
};
```

As well, every exception type must have a public default and copy constructor.

3.13.1   Creation and Destruction

An exception is the same as a class object with respect to creation and destruction:

```
_Event E { ... };
E e;                        // local exception
_Resume e;                  // resumption raise
E *ep = new E;              // dynamic exception
_Resume *ep;                // resumption raise
delete ep;
_Throw E();                 // termination raise of temporary local exception
```


3.13.2   Inherited Members

Each exception type, if not derived from another exception type, is implicitly derived from the event type uBaseEvent, e.g.:

```
_Event exception-type name : public uBaseEvent ...
```

where the interface for the base-class uBaseEvent is:

```
class uBaseEvent {
  protected:
    uBaseEvent( const char *const msg = " " );
    void setMsg( const char *const msg );
  public:
    enum RaiseKind { ThrowRaise, ResumeRaise };

    const char *const message() const;
    const uBaseCoroutine &source() const;
    const char *const sourceName() const;
    RaiseKind getRaiseKind();
    void reraise() const;
    virtual uBaseEvent *duplicate() const;
    virtual void defaultTerminate();
    virtual void defaultResume();
};
```

The constructor routine uBaseEvent has the following form:

uBaseEvent(const char *const msg = " ") − creates an exception with specified
   message, which is printed in an error message if the exception is not handled.
   The message is copied when an exception is created so it is safe to use within
   an exception even if the context of the raise is deleted.

The member setMsg is an alternate way to associate a message with an exception.

The member message returns the string message associated with an exception. The member source returns the coroutine/task that raised the exception; if the exception has been raised locally, the value NULL is returned. In some cases, the coroutine or task may be deleted when the exception is caught so this reference may be undefined. The member sourceName returns the name of the coroutine/task that raised the exception; if the exception has been raised locally, the value "*unknown*" is returned. This name is copied from the raising coroutine/task when an exception is created so it is safe to use even if the coroutine/task is deleted. The member getRaiseKind returns whether the exception is thrown (ThrowRaise) or resumed (ResumeRaise) at the raise. The member reraise either rethrows or reresumes the exception depending on how the exception was originally raised. The member duplicate returns a copy of the raised exception, which can be used to raise the same exception in a different context after it has been caught; the copy is allocated on the heap, so it is the responsibility of the caller to delete the exception.

The member defaultTerminate is implicitly called if an exception is thrown but not handled; the default action is to call uAbort to terminate the program with the supplied message. The member defaultResume is implicitly called if an exception is resumed but not handled; the default action is to throw the exception, which begins the search for a termination handler from the point of the initial resume. In both cases, a user-defined default action may be implemented by overriding the appropriate virtual member.

3.14 Raising

There are two raising mechanisms: throwing and resuming; furthermore, raising can be done locally, nonlocally or concurrently (see Sect. 4.10, p. 162). The kind of raising for an exception is specified by the raise statements:

```
_Throw [ exception-type ] ;
_Resume [ exception-type ] [ _At uBaseCoroutine-id ] ;
```

If _Throw has no *exception-type*, it is a rethrow, meaning the currently thrown exception continues propagation. If there is no current thrown exception but there is a currently resumed exception, that exception is thrown. Otherwise, the rethrow results in a runtime error. If _Resume has no *exception-type*, it is a reresume, meaning the currently resumed exception continues propagation. If there is no current resumed exception but there is a currently thrown exception, that exception is resumed. Otherwise, the reresume results in a runtime error. The optional _At clause allows the specified exception or the currently propagating exception (reresume) to be raised at another coroutine or task. Nonlocal and concurrent raise is restricted to resumption because the raising execution-state is often unaware of the current state for the handling execution-state. Resumption allows the handler the greatest flexibility in this situation because it can process the exception as a resumption or rethrow the exception for termination (which is the default behaviour, see Sect. 3.13.2).

Exceptions in μC++ are propagated differently from C++. In C++, the **throw** statement creates a copy of the static type of the exception, and propagates the copy. In μC++, the **_Throw** and **_Resume** statements create a copy of dynamic type of the exception, and propagates the copy. For example:

C++	μC++
class B {};	**_Event** B {};
class D : **public** B {};	**_Event** D : **public** B {};
void f(B &t) {	**void** f(B &t) {
throw t;	**_Throw** t;
}	}
D m;	D m;
f(m);	f(m);

in the C++ program, routine f is passed an object of derived type D but throws a copy of an object of base type B, because the static type of the operand for throw, t, is of type B. However, in the μC++ program, routine f is passed an object of derived type D and throws a copy of the original object of type D. This change makes a significant difference in the organization of handlers for dealing with exceptions by allowing handlers to catch the specific rather than the general exception-type.

Note, when subclassing is used, it is better to catch an exception by reference:

catch(E e) {...} // catch by value   **catch**(E &e) {...} // catch by reference

Otherwise, the exception is truncated from its dynamic type to the static type specified at the handler, and cannot be down-cast to the dynamic type. Notice, catching truncation is different from raising truncation, which does not occur in μC++.

3.15 Handler

A handler catches an exception and attempts to deal with the exceptional event. Each handler is in the handler clause of a guarded block. μC++ supports two kinds of handlers, termination and resumption, which match with the kind of raise. An unhandled exception is dealt with by an exception default-member (see Sect. 3.13.2, p. 108).

3.15.1 Termination

A termination handler is a corrective action *after* throwing an exception during execution of a guarded block. In μC++, a termination handler is specified identically to that in C++: **catch** clause of a **try** statement. (The details of termination handlers can be found in a C++ textbook.) Fig. 3.14 shows how C++ and μC++ throw an exception to a termination handler. The differences are using **_Throw** instead of **throw**, throwing the dynamic type instead of the static type, and requiring a special exception type for all exceptions.

C++	μC++
| ```
class E {
    public:
        int i;
        E( int i ) : i( i ) {}
};

void f() {
    throw E( 3 );
}
int main() {
    try {
        f();
    } catch( E e ) {
        cout << e.i << endl;
        throw;
    } // try
}
``` | ```
_Event E {
    public:
        int i;
        E( int i ) : i( i ) {}
};

void f() {
    _Throw E( 3 );
}
void uMain::main() {
    try {
        f();
    } catch( E e ) {
        cout << e.i << endl;
        _Throw;
    } // try
}
``` |

Fig. 3.14   C++ versus μC++ terminating propagation

3.15.2   Resumption

A **resumption handler** is an intervention action *after* resuming an exception during
execution of a guarded block. Unlike normal routine calls, the call to a resumption
handler is dynamically bound rather than statically bound, so different corrections
can occur for the same static context. To provide resumption, μC++ extends the **try**
block to include resumption handlers, where the resumption handler is denoted by
a **_CatchResume** clause at the end of a **try** block:

```
try { ...
} _CatchResume( E1 & ) { ... }   // must appear before catch clauses
  // more _CatchResume clauses
  _CatchResume( ... ) { ... }    // must be last _CatchResume clause
  catch( E2 & ) { ... }          // must appear after _CatchResume clauses
  // more catch clauses
  catch( ... ) { ... }           // must be last catch clause
```

Any number of resumption handlers can be associated with a **try** block, but must
precede any **catch** handlers in a **try** statement. Like **catch**(...), **_CatchResume**(...)
must appear at the end of the list of the resumption handlers. A resumption
handler is, in effect, a nested routine called from the raise site when an exception
is propagated with resumption; when the resumption handler completes, control
returns back to the point of the raise.

A resumption handler can access any types and variables visible in its local
scope, but it cannot perform a **break, continue** or **return** from within the handler.
A resumption handler is a corrective action so a computation can continue. If
a correction is impossible, the resumption handler should throw an appropriate
exception not step into an enclosing block to cause the stack to unwind. There may
be recovery actions closer to the raise point that can better deal with the problem.

```
_Event E {
public:
    int &r;                         // reference to something
    E( int &r ) : r( r ) {}
};
void f() {
    int x;
    ... _Resume E( x ); ... // set exception reference to point to x
}
void g() {
    try {
        f();
    } _CatchResume( E &e ) {
        ... e.r = 3; ...            // change x at raise via reference r
    }
}
```

Fig. 3.15 Handler updating raise context

Fig. 3.15 shows how values at the raise site can be modified directly in the handler if variables are visible in both contexts, or indirectly through reference or pointer variables in the caught exception. The change occurs by passing a pointer/reference to a variable in the raise content to the handler, through which the variable further down the stack is modified.

Finally, μC++ marks resumption handlers during propagation to prevent recursive resuming (see page 86); termination handlers are not marked.

```
try {
    ... _Resume R; ...
} _CatchResume( R ) _Throw R(); // handler1
    catch( R ) ...                // handler2
```

```
... → try{} _CatchResume(R), catch(R) → _Resume R
... → try{} _CatchResume(R), catch(R) → handler1 → _Throw R
... → try{} _CatchResume(R), catch(R) → handler2
```

After the resuming raise of R and catch by handler1, handler1 is marked ineligible because it is a resumption handler, but termination handler2 remains eligible for the **try** block. Therefore, the throwing raise of R in handler2 unwinds handler1 from the the stack to the try block where the exception is caught by handler2.

3.15.3 Termination/Resumption

The form of the raise dictates the set of handlers examined during propagation:

- terminating propagation (**_Throw**) only examines termination handlers (**catch**),
- resuming propagation (**_Resume**) only examines resumption handlers (**_CatchResume**). However, the standard default resumption handler converts resuming into terminating propagation (see Sect. 3.13.2, p. 108).

Often the set of exception types for termination and resumption handlers are disjoint because each exception type has a specific action. However, it is possible for the set of exception types in each handler set to overlap. For example, the exception type R appears in both the termination and resumption handler-sets:

```
_Event E {};
void rtn() {
    try {
        _Resume E();
    }   _CatchResume( E & ) { _Throw E(); }   // H1
        catch( E & ) { ... }                   // H2
    }
}
```

The body of the **try** block resumes exception-type E, which is caught by resumption-handler _**CatchResume**(E) and handler H1 is invoked. The blocks on the call stack are now (stack grows from left to right):

rtn → **try** _**CatchResume**(E),**catch**(E) → H1

Handler H1 throws E and the stack is unwound until the exception is caught by termination-handler **catch**(E) and handler H2 is invoked.

rtn → H2

The termination handler is available because resuming did not unwind the stack.

Finally, there is an interesting interaction between resuming, defaultResume (see Sect. 3.13.2, p. 108), and throwing.

```
_Event R {};
void rtn() {
    try {
        _Resume R();          // resume not throw
    } catch( R & ) { ... }    // H1, no _CatchResume!!!
    }
}
```

which results in the following call stack:

rtn → **try**{} **catch**(R) → defaultResume

When R is resumed, there is no eligible handler (or there is a handler but it is marked ineligible). However, when the base of the stack is reached, defaultResume is called, and its default action is to throw R. Terminating propagation then unwinds the stack until there is a match with the **catch** clause in the **try** block.

3.16 Bound Exceptions

In μC++, every exception derived from the basic exception type can potentially be bound. Binding occurs implicitly when using μC++'s raising statements, i.e., _**Resume** and _**Throw**. In the case of a local raise, the binding is to the object in whose member routine the raise occurs. Fig. 3.16 shows how an exception raised in a call to Datafile.read() is bound to Datafile; an exception raised in a call to Logfile.read() is bound to Logfile. If the raise occurs inside a static member routine or in a free routine, there is no binding. In the case of a nonlocal raise, the binding is to the

```
file Datafile, Logfile;
try {
    ... Datafile.read(); ...
    ... Logfile.read(); ...
} catch ( Datafile.IOError ) {
    // handle Datafile IOError
} catch ( Logfile.IOError ) {
    // handle Logfile IOError
} catch ( IOError ) {
    // handler IOError from other objects
}
```

Fig. 3.16 Bound exceptions

coroutine/task executing the raise. The first two **catch** clauses qualify the exception type with an object to specialize the matching. That is, only if the exception is generated by the specified object does the match occur. The "catch-any" handler, ..., does not have a bound form. It is now possible to differentiate between the specified files and still use the unqualified form to handle the same exception type generated by any other objects.

3.16.1 Matching

A bound handler matches when the binding at the handler clause is identical to the binding associated with the currently propagated exception *and* the exception type in the handler clause is identical to or a base-type of the currently propagated exception type.

Bound handler clauses can be mixed with normal (unbound) handlers; the standard rules of lexical precedence determine which handler matches if multiple are eligible. Any expression that evaluates to an *lvalue* is a valid binding for a handler, but in practice, it only makes sense to specify an object that has a member function capable of raising an exception. Such a binding expression may or may not be evaluated during matching, and in the case of multiple bound-handler clauses, in undefined order. Hence, care must be taken when specifying binding expressions containing side-effects.

3.16.2 Termination

Bound termination handlers appear in the C++ **catch** clause:

catch(*raising-object . exception-declaration*) { ... }

In the previous example, **catch**(Logfile.IOError) is a catch clause specifying a bound handler with binding Logfile and exception-type IOError.

Table 3.2 Inheritance among exception types

Base		Public only/NO multiple inheritance
Derived	Struct/class	Event
Struct/Class	√	X
Event	√	√

3.16.3 Resumption

Bound resumption handlers appear in the μC++ **_CatchResume** clause (see Sect. 3.15.2, p. 111):

    _CatchResume(raising-object . exception-declaration) { ... }

3.17 Inheritance

Table 3.2 shows the forms of inheritance allowed among C++ types and μC++ exception-types. First, the case of *single* public inheritance among homogeneous kinds of exception type, i.e., base and derived type are the both **_Event**, is supported in μC++ (major diagonal), e.g.:

    _Event Ebase {};
    _Event Ederived : public Ebase {}; // homogeneous public inheritance

In this case, all implicit functionality matches between base and derived types, and hence, there are no problems. Public derivation of exception types is for building the exception-type hierarchy, and restricting public inheritance to only exception types enhances the distinction between the class and exception hierarchies. Single private/protected inheritance among homogeneous kinds of exception types is not supported:

    _Event Ederived : private Ebase {};   // homogeneous private inheritance, not allowed
    _Event Ederived : protected Ebase {}; // homogeneous protected inheritance, not allowed

because each exception type must appear in the exception-type hierarchy, and hence must be a subtype of another exception type. Neither **private** nor **protected** inheritance establishes a subtyping relationship. Second, the case of *single* private/protected/public inheritance among heterogeneous kinds of type, i.e., base and derived type of different kind, is supported in μC++ only if the base kind is an ordinary class, e.g.:

    class Cbase {};   // only struct/class allowed

    _Event Ederived : public Cbase {}; // heterogeneous public inheritance

An example for using such inheritance is different exception types using a common logging class. The ordinary class implements the logging functionality and can be reused among the different exception types.

Heterogeneous inheritance from exception types by other kinds of class, exception type, coroutine, mutex or task, is not allowed, e.g.:

```
_Event Ebase {};

struct StructDerived      : public Ebase {};   // not allowed
class ClassDerived        : public Ebase {};   // not allowed
_Coroutine CorDerived     : public Ebase {};   // not allowed
_Monitor MonitorDerived   : public Ebase {};   // not allowed
_Task TaskDerived         : public Ebase {};   // not allowed
```

A structure/class cannot inherit from an exception type because operations defined for exception types may cause problems when accessed through a class object. This restriction does not mean exception types and non-exception-types cannot share code. Rather, shared code must be factored out as an ordinary class and then inherited by exception types and non-exception-types, e.g.:

```
class CommonBase {...};

class ClassDerived        : public CommonBase {};
_Event Ederived           : public CommonBase {};
```

Multiple inheritance is allowed for private/protected/public inheritance of exception types from **struct/class** for the same reason as single inheritance.

3.18   Summary

Static and dynamic name binding, and static and dynamic transfer points can be combined to form the following different language constructs:

	call/raise	
return/handled	static	dynamic
static	1. sequel	3. termination
dynamic	2. routine	4. resumption

These four constructs succinctly cover all the kinds of control flow associated with routines and exceptions. Raising, propagating and handling an exception are the three core control-flow mechanisms of an EHM. There are two useful handling models: termination and resumption. For safety, an EHM should provide matching exception models: terminating and resuming. Handlers should be partitioned with respect to the handling models to provide better abstraction. Marking handlers solves the recursive resuming problem and provides consistent propagation semantics with termination, making it the best choice for an EHM with resumption. Homogeneous derivation of exception types, catch-any and reraise, exception parameters, and bound/conditional handling all improve programmability and extensibility.

There is a weak equivalence between multi-exit/static multi-level and exceptions. Suffice it to say exceptions can only be simulated with great difficulty using simpler control structures. The simulation usually involves routines returning return-codes and complex return-code checking after routine calls, which makes the program extremely difficult to understand and maintain. But most importantly, return code checking is optional, and hence, leaves open the possibility for programmer error. On the other hand, it is fairly easy to simulate both multi-exit and static multi-level exit with dynamic multi-level exit. However, dynamic multi-level exit is usually more costly than multi-exit and static multi-level exit. This cost appears in several different forms, such as increased compilation cost, larger executable programs, and/or increased execution time. Several implementation schemes exist for zero-cost entry of a guarded block (**try** construct in C++), but this should not be confused with the total cost of implementing exceptions. Thus, there is strong justification for having both a static and dynamic multi-level exit construct in a programming language.

3.19 Questions

1. Why do routines need different kinds of returning?
2. Name and explain three traditional solutions for implementing alternate kinds of returning.
3. Convert the C++ program in Fig. 3.17 from using local fix-up routines to one using only a single global fixup pointer, e.g.:

   ```
   int (*fixup)( int );
   ```

   That is, remove the fixup parameter from routines rtn1 and rtn2 so they have the following signatures:

   ```
   int rtn1( int p );
   int rtn2( int p );
   ```

   and use the global fixup pointer to call the appropriate fixup routine. The transformed program must exhibit the same execution behaviour as the original. You are allowed to make local copies of the global fixup pointer.
4. What is an *exception handling mechanism*.
5. Explain how the features in a programming language affect the exception handling mechanism.
6. Explain the difference between the source and faulting execution.
7. Explain the difference among *local* and *nonlocal* exception.
8. Explain the difference among *synchronous* and *asynchronous* exception.
9. Explain the difference between *raise* and *reraise* of an exception.
10. Explain static/dynamic call and static/dynamic return.
11. Explain the difference between termination and resumption exception handling.
12. Convert the C++ program in Fig. 3.18, p. 119 from dynamic multi-level exits to one using only:

    - basic control structures (**if/else, while/do/for, switch**), flag variables,
    - multi-exit and static multi-level exit (basic control structures plus **break/continue/goto**) with no flag variables.

```
#include <iostream>
using namespace std;

int myfixup1( int i ) { return i + 2; }
int myfixup2( int i ) { return i + 1; }
int myfixup3( int i ) { return i + 3; }

int rtn2( int p, int (*fixup)( int ) );                    // forward declaration

int rtn1( int p, int (*fixup)( int ) ) {
    if ( p <= 0 ) return 0;                                // base case
        if ( p % 2 != 0 ) {                                // even ?
            p = rtn2( p - 1, myfixup2 );
        } else {
            p = rtn1( p - 2, myfixup3 );
        }
        if ( p % 3 != 0 ) p = fixup( p );
        cout << p << " ";
        return p + 1;
}
int rtn2( int p, int (*fixup)( int ) ) {
    if ( p <= 0 ) return 0;                                // base case
        if ( p % 3 != 0 ) {                                // even ?
            p = rtn2( p - 2, myfixup1 );
        } else {
            p = rtn1( p - 1, myfixup2 );
        }
        if ( p % 2 != 0 ) p = fixup( p );
        cout << p << " ";
        return p + 2;
}
int main() {
        cout << rtn2( 30, myfixup1 ) << endl;
}
```

Fig. 3.17 Local fixup

The return type of routine rtn may be changed.

13. After a sequel is executed, from where does the control flow continue?
14. Explain how passing fix-up routines can be used to simulate resumption, as in:

```
int fixup( float x, float y );
void rtn( int p, float m, int (*fixup)( float, float ) );
rtn( i, r, fixup ); // pass fix-up routine as argument
```

15. Local fixup routines (ones passed as parameters) increase the number of routine parameters and may need to be passed through multiple levels of routine calls to the point of usage. Explain how these two problems are eliminated with resumption exceptions.
16. Explain how *recursive resuming* can arise.
17. How can *recursive resumption* be prevented?
18. Why do resumption handlers need lexical links?
19. In exception handling, a *resumption handler* is an inline (nested) routine responsible for handling a raised exception. Therefore, understanding issues

```
#include <iostream>
#include <cstdlib>      // access: rand, srand
#include <unistd.h>     // access: getpid
using namespace std;

void rtn( int i ) {
    if ( rand() % 5 == 0 ) throw i;
}
int main( int argc, char *argv[ ] ) {
    int seed = getpid();
    if ( argc == 2 ) seed = atoi( argv[1] );
    srand( seed );
    try {
        for ( int i = 0; i < 10; i += 1 ) {
            rtn( i );
        }
    } catch( int ex ) {
        cout << "single loop:" << ex << endl;
    }
    try {
        for ( int i = 0; i < 10; i += 1 ) {
            for ( int j = 0; j < 10; j += 1 ) {
                rtn( j );
            }
        }
    } catch( int ex ) {
        cout << "double loop:" << ex << endl;
    }
}
```

Fig. 3.18 Exception handling

associated with nested routines is important. In particular, nested routines allow references to global variables in outer scopes, e.g.:

```
void h( int p ) {
    int hv = 10;            // hv is a global variable for g
    void g( int p ) {       // nest routine
        hv = 5              // global reference from g to hv
```

However, recursion results in multiple instances of the global variable on the stack. When eventually a nested routine is called and makes its global reference, which of the multiple global instances is the reference accessing?

The C program in Fig. 3.19 prints a stack trace of its recursive calls.

```
frame#   call     &hv             &gv             fram:hv fram:gv
===============================================================
2        h(2,0)   0x7fff4d0f7368
3        h(1,0)   0x7fff4d0f7318
4        h(0,0)   0x7fff4d0f72c8
5        g(1,0)   0x7fff4d0f72c8   0x7fff4d0f7278   __
6        g(0,0)   0x7fff4d0f72c8   0x7fff4d0f7228   __
7        h(1,1)   0x7fff4d0f71d8
8        h(0,1)   0x7fff4d0f7188
9        g(1,1)   0x7fff4d0f7188   0x7fff4d0f7138   __
10       g(0,1)   0x7fff4d0f7188   0x7fff4d0f70e8   __
```

```
// MUST USE FILE-NAME SUFFIX ".c" AND COMPILE WITH gcc
#include <stdio.h>

int main() {
    unsigned int frameno = 1;                           // main is the first frame

    void h( int p, int call ) {                          // nest routine
        int hv = 10;

        void g( int p, int call ) {                      // nest routine
            int gv = 100;

            void f( int p ) {                            // nest routine
                frameno += 1;
                printf( "%d\tf(%d)\t%p\t%p\t__\t__\n", frameno, p, &hv, &gv );
                if ( p != 0 ) f( p - 1 );
            } // f

            frameno += 1;
            printf( "%d\tg(%d,%d)\t%p\t%p\t__\n", frameno, p, call, &hv, &gv );
            if ( p != 0 ) g( p - 1, call );              // non-base case, recurse
            if ( p == 0 && call == 0 ) h( 1, 1 );        // base of recursion, call h
            if ( p == 0 && call == 1 ) f( 1 );           // base of recursion, call f
        } // g

        frameno += 1;
        printf( "%d\th(%d,%d)\t%p\t\t\t\n", frameno, p, call, &hv );
        if ( p != 0 ) h( p - 1, call );                  // non-base case, recurse
        if ( p == 0 && call == 0 ) g( 1, 0 );            // base of recursion, call g
        if ( p == 0 && call == 1 ) g( 1, 1 );            // base of recursion, call g
    } // h

    printf( "frame#\tcall\t&hv\t\t&gv\t\tfram:hv\tfram:gv\n"
            "===============================================\n" );
    h( 2, 0 );
} // main
```

Fig. 3.19 Nested routines

```
11      f(1)      0x7fff4d0f7188    0x7fff4d0f70e8    __    __
12      f(0)      0x7fff4d0f7188    0x7fff4d0f70e8    __    __
```

The number on the left denotes the level of the stack call-frame (there are 12 calls including the call to main), then the routine name (h, g or f) with its parameter value for the call, and finally the address of the variables hv and gv visible in that frame.

a.   i.   Compile and run the C program in Fig. 3.19.

ii. Copy the output into a file.

iii. In the last two columns, replace the underscores with the frame number where the referenced hv and gv variable is declared (allocated). For example, the top stack-frame for f(0) (frame number 12) has a reference to gv; which frame on the stack (denoted by its frame number) allocated this particular gv variable? Hint, it must be one of the frames for routine g because gv is declared at the start of g.

```
_Event E{};
_Coroutine X {
    void main() {
        _Enable {
            try {
                suspend();
            } xxx( E ) {
                // do nothing
            }
        }
    } // main
  public:
    X() { resume(); }
    void next() { resume(); }
};
_Coroutine Y {
    void main() {
        X x;
        yyy E() _At x;
        x.next();
    } // main
  public:
    Y() { resume(); }
};
void uMain::main() {
    Y y;
}
```

Fig. 3.20 Resumption control flow

b. Define the term *lexical* (*access/static*) link and explain how it is used to access global variables from a nested-routine's stack-frame.

20. For *nonlocal resumption*, where does control return after the handler completes?
21. How are handlers associated with guarded blocks in C++?
22. Give two reasons why *derived exception-types* are an important feature to have in an exception-handling mechanism.
23. Is it easy to simulate Java's finally clause in C++?
24. Explain why *exception parameters* are a useful feature of an exception handling mechanism.
25. What is a checked and unchecked exception in Java?
26. Give an advantage and disadvantage of using exception lists when defining routines.
27. How do exception lists constrain polymorphism?
28. Explain the purpose of the μC++ **_Enable** and **_Disable** statements.
29. Given the code in Fig. 3.20:

    a. Explain from where control continues if the exception is a termination exception and a matching handler is found.
    b. Explain from where control continues if the exception is a resumption exception and a matching handler is found.

```
#include <iostream>
using namespace std;

_Event H {                              // uC++ exception type
  public:
    int &i;                             // pointer to fixup variable at raise
    H( int &i ) : i( i ) {}
};
void f( int &i ) {
  cout << "f " << i << endl;
  if ( rand() % 5 == 0 ) _Resume H( i );  // require correction ?
  try {
    i -= 1;
    if ( 0 < i ) f( i );                // recursion
  } _CatchResume( H &h ) {
    cout << "f handler " << h.i << endl;
    h.i -= 1;
    f( h.i );
  }
}
void uMain::main() {
  int times = 25, seed = getpid();
  switch ( argc ) {
    case 3: seed = atoi( argv[2] );     // allow repeatable experiment
    case 2: times = atoi( argv[1] );    // control recursion depth
    case 1: break;                      // defaults
    default:
      cerr << "Usage: " << argv[0] << " times seed" << endl;
      exit( EXIT_FAILURE );
  }
  srand( seed );                        // fixed or random seed
  try {
    f( times );
  } _CatchResume( H &h ) {
    cout << "root " << h.i << endl;
  }
}
```

Fig. 3.21 Resumption with no fixup simulation

    c. If a matching handler is not found for a resumption exception, what would have happened?

    d. What is the purpose of the **_Enable** block in X?

    e. Why is there a call to x.next() after the exception is raised?

30. In languages without resumption exceptions, resumption can be simulated by explicitly passing handler routines as arguments (often called fixup routines), which are called where the resumption exception is raised. Given the μC++ program in Fig. 3.21:

    a. Explain why this program *cannot* be simulated *solely* by passing fixup routines (routine pointers to handlers) among the routines. That is, no global variables or add additional parameters other than the fixup routine are allowed.

    b. Construct a simulation of the program in C++ by passing handler functors rather than handler routines among the routines. Do not use **void** * to represent a routine pointer because C++ does not guarantee a **void** * can hold a routine pointer. For example, on some systems, routine pointers are actually a structure with 2 or more fields. As well, do not use a counter to keep track of the stack depth.

References

1. Agesen, O., Bak, L., Chambers, C., Chang, B.W., Hølzle, U., Maloney, J.H., Smith, R.B., Ungar, D., Wolczko, M.: The SELF 3.0 Programmer's Reference Manual. Sun Microsystems, Inc., and Stanford University (1993)
2. Birrell, A., Brown, M.R., Cardelli, L., Donahue, J., Glassman, L., Gutag, J., Harning, J., Kalsow, B., Levin, R., Nelson, G.: Systems Programming with Modula-3. Prentice Hall Series in Innovative Technology. Prentice-Hall, Englewood Cliffs (1991)
3. Buhr, P.A.: μC++ annotated reference manual, version 6.1.0. Tech. rep., School of Computer Science, University of Waterloo, Waterloo, Ontario, Canada, N2L 3G1 (2015). http://plg.uwaterloo.ca/~usystem/pub/uSystem/u++-6.1.0.sh
4. Buhr, P.A., Harji, A., Mok, W.Y.R.: Exception handling. In: Zelkowitz, M.V. (ed.) Advances in COMPUTERS, vol. 56, pp. 245–303. Academic Press, London (2002)
5. Buhr, P.A., Macdonald, H.I., Zarnke, C.R.: Synchronous and asynchronous handling of abnormal events in the μSystem. Softw. Pract. Exp. **22**(9), 735–776 (1992)
6. Buhr, P.A., Till, D., Zarnke, C.R.: Assignment as the sole means of updating objects. Softw. Pract. Exp. **24**(9), 835–870 (1994)
7. Cargill, T.A.: Does C++ really need multiple inheritance? In: USENIX C++ Conference Proceedings, pp. 315–323. USENIX Association, San Francisco, California, U.S.A. (1990)
8. Costanza, P.: Dynamic scoped functions as the essence of AOP. SIGPLAN Not. **38**(8), 29–35 (2003)
9. Drew, S.J., Gough, K.J.: Exception handling: Expecting the unexpected. Comput. Lang. **20**(2) (1994)
10. ECMA International Standardizing Information and Communication Systems: C# Language Specification, Standard ECMA-334, 4th edn. (2006)
11. Gehani, N.H.: Exceptional C or C with exceptions. Softw. Pract. Exp. **22**(10), 827–848 (1992)
12. Goldberg, A., Robson, D.: Smalltalk-80: The Language and Its Implementation. Addison-Wesley, Reading (1983)
13. Goodenough, J.B.: Exception handling: Issues and a proposed notation. Commun. ACM **18**(12), 683–696 (1975)
14. Gosling, J., Joy, B., Steele, G., Bracha, G.: The Java Language Specification, 2nd edn. Addison-Wesley, Reading (2000)
15. Kenah, L.J., Goldenberg, R.E., Bate, S.F.: VAX/VMS Internals and Data Structures Version 4.4. Digital Press, Bedford (1988)
16. Knudsen, J.L.: Exception handling – a static approach. Softw. Pract. Exp. **14**(5), 429–449 (1984)
17. Knudsen, J.L.: Better exception handling in block structured systems. IEEE Softw. **4**(3), 40–49 (1987)
18. Koenig, A., Stroustrup, B.: Exception handling for C++. J. Object-Oriented Program. **3**(2), 16–33 (1990)
19. Liskov, B.H., Snyder, A.: Exception handling in CLU. IEEE Trans. Softw. Eng. **SE-5**(6), 546–558 (1979)
20. MacLaren, M.D.: Exception handling in PL/I. SIGPLAN Not. **12**(3), 101–104 (1977). Proceedings of an ACM Conference on Language Design for Reliable Software, March 28–30, 1977, Raleigh, North Carolina, U.S.A.

21. Meyer, B.: Eiffel: The Language.   Prentice Hall Object-Oriented Series. Prentice-Hall, Englewood Cliffs (1992)
22. Milner, R., Tofte, M.: Commentary on Standard ML. MIT Press, Cambridge (1991)
23. Mitchell, J.G., Maybury, W., Sweet, R.: Mesa language manual. Tech. Rep. CSL–79–3, Xerox Palo Alto Research Center (1979)
24. Mok, W.Y.R.: Concurrent abnormal event handling mechanisms. Master's thesis, University of Waterloo, Waterloo, Ontario, Canada, N2L 3G1 (1997). http://plg.uwaterloo.ca/pub/theses/-MokThesis.ps.gz
25. Motet, G., Mapinard, A., Geoffroy, J.C.: Design of Dependable Ada Software. Prentice Hall, Englewood Cliffs (1996)
26. Stevens, W.P., , Myers, G.J., Constantine, L.L.: Structured design. IBM Syst. J. **13**(2), 115–139 (1974)
27. Stroustrup, B.: The Design and Evolution of C++. Addison-Wesley, Reading (1994)
28. Tennent, R.D.: Language design methods based on semantic principles. Acta Inf. **8**(2), 97–112 (1977). Reprinted in [29]
29. Wasserman, A.I. (ed.): Tutorial: Programming Language Design. Computer Society Press, Los Alamitos (1980)
30. Yemini, S., Berry, D.M.: A modular verifiable exception-handling mechanism. ACM Trans. Progr. Lang. Syst. **7**(2), 214–243 (1985)

Chapter 4
Coroutine

As mentioned in Sect. 1.1, p. 1, a routine call cannot be constructed out of basic control flow constructs. Therefore, a routine call is a fundamental control flow mechanism. What characterizes a routine is that it always starts execution from the beginning (top), executes until it returns normally or abnormally (exception), and its local variables only persist for a single invocation. A routine temporarily suspends its execution when it calls another routine, which saves the local state of the caller and reactivates it when the called routine returns. But a routine cannot temporarily suspend execution and return to *its* caller. Interestingly, there exist problems where a routine needs to retain state, both data and execution location, *between* routine calls. Basically, a routine implementing these kinds of problems needs to remember something about what it was doing the last time it was called. These kinds of problems cannot be adequately implemented using normal routines. Two simple examples are presented to illustrate the kinds of situations where a routine needs to retain both data and execution state between calls.

4.1 Fibonacci Series

A series generator, like the Fibonacci series, must remember prior calculations to generate the next value in the series. To demonstrate this situation, the Fibonacci series is used and is defined as follows:

$$f(n) = \begin{cases} 0 & n = 0 \\ 1 & n = 1 \\ f(n-1) + f(n-2) & \text{otherwise} \end{cases}$$

producing the sequence of numbers: 0,1,1,2,3,5,8,13,21,34, etc. Ignoring the problem of stopping, Fig. 4.1 shows a direct solution for producing the Fibonacci series.

© Springer International Publishing Switzerland 2016
P.A. Buhr, *Understanding Control Flow*, DOI 10.1007/978-3-319-25703-7_4

int main() {

```
int fn, fn1, fn2;
fn = 0;  fn1 = fn;                    // 1st case
cout << fn << endl;
fn = 1;  fn2 = fn1;  fn1 = fn;        // 2nd case
cout << fn << endl;
for ( ;; ) {                          // infinite loop
    fn = fn1 + fn2;  fn2 = fn1;  fn1 = fn; // general case
    cout << fn << endl;
}
```

}

Fig. 4.1 Fibonacci direct

The difficulty comes in modularizing this code into a fibonacci routine, so each time the routine is called, it produces the next Fibonacci number in the series. This abstraction provides a Fibonacci generator, which can be placed in a library with other series generators for use by math or statistics programmers. Notice the modularization moves the location of output. In the original version the output is external, i.e., written to a file; in the modularized version the output is internal, i.e., returned from each call to the generator routine. The problem occurs when the fibonacci routine returns after each call–it forgets where it is in the series. Several possible solutions are presented to illustrate the problems in implementing the Fibonacci generator.

4.1.1   Routine Solution

The first solution in Fig. 4.2 uses global state to remember information between routine calls. The main routine calls fibonacci to get the next number in the Fibonacci series, which is then printed. Since the routine fibonacci cannot remember information between calls, information must be remembered in global variables, which are accessed in the fibonacci routine. The global variables can be divided into two kinds: those holding data used in calculations and those used to control execution during each call (flag variables as discussed in Sect. 2.2, p. 10). In this case, the variables fn, fn1 and fn2 hold data while the variable, state, holds control-flow information. The purpose of the data variables is the same as in the initial, simple solution; it is the control flow variable, state, that is new and requires explanation. The definition of fibonacci has three states: two special cases to start the third general case. Each of these three states is denoted by the three values taken on by variable state. When fibonacci is called, it checks the value of state to determine what code should be executed. After a block of code is executed, state is changed to indicate the next block of code executed on a subsequent call to fibonacci. Thus, state is initialized to the starting state, and after two calls, state no longer changes because the general case can be executed from that point onwards.

```
int fn, fn1, fn2, state = 1;        // global variables

int fibonacci() {
    switch (state) {
    case 1:
        fn = 0;  fn1 = fn;
        state = 2;
        break;
    case 2:
        fn = 1;  fn2 = fn1;  fn1 = fn;
        state = 3;
        break;
    case 3:
        fn = fn1 + fn2;  fn2 = fn1;  fn1 = fn;
        break;
    }
    return fn;
}
int main() {
    for ( int i = 1; i <= 10; i += 1 ) {
        cout << fibonacci() << endl;
    }
}
```

Fig. 4.2 Fibonacci routine, shared variables and explicit state

While this program works, it has problems. First, the use of global variables
violates the encapsulation of the generator because the variables can be accessed
or changed by users. (C aficionados would move the global variables into fibonacci
with storage class **static** but that does not solve the remaining problems.) Second,
because there is only one set of global (or **static**) variables for fibonacci, there
can only be one sequence of Fibonacci numbers generated in a program. It is
possible to imagine situations where multiple sequences of Fibonacci numbers have
to be simultaneously generated in a single program. Third, explicitly managing
the execution control information is tedious and error-prone. For a simple program
like fibonacci, the number of states is small and manageable; however, for complex
programs with many states, flattening the program structure into sequential blocks
of code controlled by execution-state variables can completely hide the fundamental
algorithm. Structuring a program into this flattened form corresponds to having only
one controlling loop (possibly for the entire program), and each time through the
loop, flag variables and **if** statements specify different blocks of code to execute.
In fact, any program can be flattened and any flattened program can be written
with multiple loops; hence, there is a weak equivalence between both forms.
Nevertheless, writing a flattened program is not recommended (unless forced to)
because, in general, it obscures the algorithm, making the program difficult to
understand and maintain.

```
class Fibonacci {
    int fn, fn1, fn2, state;        // class variables
public:
    Fibonacci() : state(1) {}
    int next() {
        switch (state) {
          case 1:
            fn = 0;  fn1 = fn;
            state = 2;
            break;
          case 2:
            fn = 1;  fn2 = fn1;  fn1 = fn;
            state = 3;
            break;
          case 3:
            fn = fn1 + fn2;  fn2 = fn1;  fn1 = fn;
            break;
        }
        return fn;
    }
};
int main() {
    Fibonacci f1, f2;
    for ( int i = 1; i <= 10; i += 1 ) {
        cout << f1.next() << " " << f2.next() << endl;
    }
}
```

Fig. 4.3 Fibonacci class, explicit execution state

4.1.2   Class Solution

The problems of global variables and allowing multiple Fibonacci generators can
be handled by creating fibonacci objects from a class definition, as in Fig. 4.3.
(Alternatively, a structure containing the class state can be explicitly passed to the
fibonacci routine.) The global variables from the routine fibonacci are made class
variables in the fibonacci class. It is now possible to generate multiple Fibonacci
generators by instantiating multiple instances of the class, each with its own set of
variables to generate a sequence of Fibonacci numbers. The member next is invoked
to obtain each number in the sequence, and it uses the class variables of the object to
retain state between invocations. Note, a member routine cannot retain state between
calls any more than a routine can, so some form of global variable is necessary. The
main program can now create two Fibonacci generators and print out two sequences
of Fibonacci numbers. Notice the class solution still requires explicit management
of the execution-state information so no improvement has occurred there.

4.1.3 Coroutine Solution

To remove the execution control information requires a coroutine. The first description of a coroutine was:

> ... an autonomous program which communicates with adjacent modules as if they were input or output subroutines. Thus, coroutines are subroutines all at the same level, each acting as if it were the master program when in fact there is no master program [1, p. 396].

and the coroutine concept was developed in parallel by Melvin E. Conway and Joel Erdwinn. A Fibonacci coroutine-solution cannot be presented in C++, as it does not support coroutines; hence, it is necessary to switch to μC++. Only a short explanation of the μC++ coroutine is presented at this time, so as not to interrupt the Fibonacci example. A detailed description of a μC++ coroutine is presented later in Sect. 4.7, p. 145.

A μC++ coroutine type has all the properties of a **class**. The general form of the coroutine type is the following:

```
_Coroutine coroutine-name {
    ...              // implementation variables and members
    void main();     // coroutine main (distinguished member)
public:
    ...              // interface members
};
```

A coroutine is an object created from a coroutine type in which execution of its distinguish member routine can be suspended and resumed; this distinguished member is named main and is called the **coroutine main**. Execution of a coroutine main may be suspended as control leaves it, only to carry on from that point when control returns at some later time. Hence, a coroutine main is not restarted at the beginning on each activation and its local variables are preserved while it is suspended. It is distinguished because it has special properties that none of the other member routines have and only the member routine called main in a μC++ coroutine has special properties. (In a normal C++ program, the routine main is a distinguished routine because the program begins execution there.)

A coroutine main has its own **execution state**, which is the state information needed to retain information while the coroutine main is suspended. An execution state is either **active** or **inactive**, depending on whether or not it is currently being executed. In practice, an execution state consists of the data items created by a coroutine, including its local data and routine activations, and a current execution location, which is initialized to a starting point (member main). The routine activations are often maintained in a contiguous stack, which constitutes the bulk of an execution state and is dynamic in size. This stack is the area where the local variables and execution location are preserved when an execution state is inactive. When flow of control transfers from one execution state to another, it is called a **context switch**, which involves saving the state of the active coroutine, making it inactive, and restoring the inactive state of the next coroutine, making it active. In general, the overhead for a context switch is 2–3 times more expensive than the overhead for a routine call (i.e., excluding execution of the code within the routine).

Normally, a coroutine is only activated indirectly through its interface members, which directly interact with the coroutine's main; hence, the visibility of main is usually **private** or **protected**. The decision to make the coroutine main **private** or **protected** depends solely on whether derived classes can reuse the coroutine main or must supply their own. This structure allows a coroutine type to have multiple public member routines to service different kinds of requests that are statically type-checked. A coroutine main cannot have parameters or return a result, but the same effect can be accomplished indirectly by passing values through the coroutine's variables, called **communication variables**, which are accessible from both the coroutine's member and main routines. Like a routine or class, a coroutine can access all the external variables of a C++ program and variables allocated in the heap. Also, any **static** member variables declared within a coroutine are shared among all instances of that coroutine type.

Fig. 4.4 shows the Fibonacci coroutine and a driver routine. The general structure is similar to the class solution but with the following differences. The type for Fibonacci is now **_Coroutine** instead of **class**. The code from the previous Fibonacci::next member is now in private member Fibonacci::main, which is the "distinguish member routine" (coroutine main) referred to in the coroutine definition. The program main routine, i.e., where the program begins, is the same as before, except it is now a member of a special anonymous coroutine with type uMain (explained in more detail in Chap. 5, p. 191).

The next member makes a call to a special coroutine member, resume, which performs a context switch to start execution at the beginning of member main the first time it is executed, and thereafter, activate (context switch to) the coroutine main at its point of last suspension.

context switch

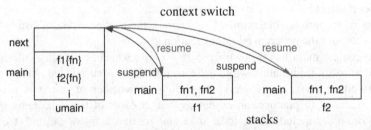

stacks

In detail, the first call to next resumes execution of the coroutine main, causing Fibonacci::main to start on its own stack and allocate local variables fn1 and fn2, and then the communication variable fn and the local variable fn1 are initialized. Now the other special coroutine member, suspend, is executed, which causes control to context switch from the coroutine main, without deallocating the local variables fn1 and fn2, to the top of the stack of the last resuming coroutine, which reactivates after the call to resume in Fibonacci::next. Whereupon, member next also returns, passing back the value in the communication variable fn, which is the first Fibonacci number. The second call to member next resumes the coroutine main, which returns from the first call to suspend, and it then performs the next calculation, suspends back to the

```
#include <iostream>
using namespace std;
_Coroutine Fibonacci {  // : public uBaseCoroutine
    int fn;                // used for communication
    void main() {          // distinguished member

        int fn1, fn2;       // retained between resumes
        fn = 0; fn1 = fn;
        suspend();          // return to last resume
        fn = 1; fn2 = fn1; fn1 = fn;
        suspend();          // return to last resume
        for ( ;; ) {
            fn = fn1 + fn2; fn2 = fn1; fn1 = fn;
            suspend(); // return to last resume
        }

    }
  public:
    int next() {
        resume();           // transfer to last suspend
        return fn;
    }
};
void uMain::main() {   // argc, argv class variables
    Fibonacci f1, f2;
    for ( int i = 1; i <= 10; i += 1 ) {
        cout << f1.next() << " " << f2.next() << endl;
    }
    uRetCode = 3;       // optional, return code
}
```

Fig. 4.4 Fibonacci coroutine, no explicit execution state

last resume, and returns the next Fibonacci number. The third call of next resumes the coroutine main, which returns from the second suspend, enters the general loop, performs the next general calculation, and suspends back to the last resume with the next Fibonacci number. All subsequent calls to next cause resumption at the third suspend, which then performs the next general calculation, and suspends back to the last resume to return a Fibonacci number. Notice, the Fibonacci algorithm has no explicit control variables to remember where to execute, which is the point behind using a coroutine. Just as a routine knows where to return to when it is called, a coroutine knows where to reactivate when it is suspended. This capability means the information explicitly managed by execution-state variables is implicitly managed by the resume/suspend mechanism of a coroutine, allowing direct modularizing of the initial external-output solution in Sect. 4.1, p. 125 into an internal-output solution in the coroutine main.

There are several additional points to note about programming with coroutines. First, to communicate information between a member routine and the coroutine main requires class variables, like the variable fn. Data is copied from the member routine into the communication variable so that it can be accessed by the coroutine main, and vice versa for returning values. This additional step in communication is the price to be paid for statically type-checked communication. Second, all the variables used to store data between activations of the coroutine main should be declared in the coroutine main, e.g., variables fn1 and fn2. While these variables *could* be defined as class variables, this violates encapsulation of the coroutine main, making the variables appear as if they can be read or written by other members of the coroutine. (In other words, never make a variable more visible than is needed.) Finally, it is normal programming style to delete a coroutine that is suspended. For example, when uMain::main terminates, the two local coroutines, f1 and f2, are automatically deleted even though both are suspended in their coroutine main. Deleting a suspended coroutine is no different than deleting a normal class object filled with values.

A coroutine's destructor is invoked when the block containing the coroutine declaration terminates or by an explicit **delete** statement for a dynamically allocated coroutine. If the coroutine is not terminated when it is deallocated, termination is forced *before* executing the destructor, which unwinds the coroutine's stack executing any destructors for objects on the stack. A consequence of this semantics is that the destructor may not resume a coroutine, so it is asymmetric with the coroutine's constructor (see Sect. 4.2).

4.2   Formatting

A formatting routine for generating specific output may need to remember the prior printing location and values to decide how the next value is formatted and printed. To demonstrate this situation, a formatting program is used that reads characters (ignoring newline characters), formats them into blocks of 4 characters, and groups the blocks of characters into groups of 5. For example, given the input:

```
abcdefghijklmnopqrstuvwxyzabcdefghijklmnopqrstuvwxyz
```

the program generates the following output:

```
abcd  efgh  ijkl  mnop  qrst
uvwx  yzab  cdef  ghij  klmn
opqr  stuv  wxyz
```

A direct and routine solution for producing the formatted output appears in Fig. 4.5.

As for the Fibonacci program, the difficulty comes in modularizing this code into a routine so that each time the routine is called with a character, it produces the correct formatted output. Both data and execution state need to be retained between successive calls, i.e., the values of variables b and g, and the locations within nested **for** loops. Routine fmtLines shows an example of flattening the structure of an algorithm (the loop is in the program's main routine reading characters). There are really three nested loops that have been flattened into assignments and **if** statements.

Fig. 4.6, p. 134a shows the class version that accepts single characters and formats them. While it solves the encapsulation and multiple instances issues, it still manages the execution state explicitly. Fig. 4.6, p. 134b shows the equivalent coroutine solution. The prt member calls resume, which performs a context switch to start execution at the beginning of member main the first time it is executed,

```
int main() {                                          int g, b;              // global variables
    int g, b;                                         void fmtLines( char ch ) {
    char ch;                                              if ( ch != -1 ) { // not EOF ?
    cin >> noskipws;    // do not skip white space            if ( ch == ' \n' ) return;
                                                              cout << ch;       // character
    for ( ;; ) {             // for as many characters       b += 1;
        for ( g = 0; g < 5; g +=1 ) { // groups              if ( b == 4 ) {    // block ?
            for ( b = 0; b < 4; b += 1 ) { // blocks             cout << " "; // separator
                for ( ;; ) { // for newline characters           b = 0;
                    cin >> ch; // read one character            g += 1;
            if ( cin.fail() ) goto fini; // eof ? multi-level exit  }
                    if ( ch != ' \n' ) break; // ignore      if ( g == 5 ) {    // group ?
                }                                                cout << endl; // separator
                cout << ch; // character                        g = 0;
            }                                                } else {
            cout << " ";       // block separator                if ( g != 0 || b != 0 )
        }                                                            cout << endl;
        cout << endl;          // group separator            }
    }                                                 }
                                                      int main() {
fini: ;                                                   char ch;
    if ( g != 0 || b != 0 ) cout << endl; // special      cin >> noskipws;
}                                                         for ( ;; ) {
                                                              cin >> ch;
                                                              if ( cin.fail() ) break;
                                                              fmtLines( ch );
                                                          }
                                                          fmtLines( -1 );
                                                      }
```

(a) Direct   (b) Routine

Fig. 4.5 Output formatters

and thereafter, activate (context switch to) the coroutine main at its point of last
suspension.

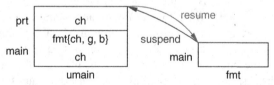

Like the Fibonacci coroutine, the code in member prt is moved into the coroutine
main. However, the structure of the algorithm is now coded as two nested loops,
plus an outer infinite loop to handle any number of characters. Notice the structure
of this program is almost the same as the initial solution in Fig. 4.6. Think about
how the formatter programs would be altered to print a row of asterisks after every
10 lines of output. The program in Fig. 4.6a must continue to flatten the control flow,
while the program in Fig. 4.6b can use the direct equivalent to a modified version of
Fig. 4.5a.

```
class FmtLines {
   int g, b;
public:
   void prt( char ch ) {
      if ( ch == '\n' ) return;
      cout << ch;    // character
      b += 1;
      if ( b == 4 ) { // block ?
         cout << "  "; // block separator
         b = 0;
         g += 1;
      }
      if ( g == 5 ) { // group ?
         cout << endl; // group separator
         g = 0;
      }
   }
```

```
   FmtLines() : g( 0 ), b( 0 ) {}
   ~FmtLines() {
      if ( g != 0 || b != 0 ) cout << endl;
   }
};
```

                     (a) Class

```
_Coroutine Format {
   char ch;
   int g, b;
   void main() {
```
```
      for ( ;; ) {     // for as many characters
         for ( g = 0; g < 5; g += 1 ) { // groups
            for ( b = 0; b < 4; b += 1 ) { // blocks
               for ( ;; ) { // for newline characters
                  suspend();
                  if ( ch != '\n' ) break; // ignore
               }
               cout << ch; // print character
            }
            cout << "  "; // block separator
         }
         cout << endl;      // group separator
      }
```
```
   }
public:
   FmtLines(){ resume(); } // eliminate priming read
   ~FmtLines() {
      if ( g != 0 || b != 0 ) cout << endl;
   }
   void prt( char ch ) {
      FmtLines::ch = ch;
      resume();
   }
};
```

                     (b) Coroutine

Fig. 4.6 Output formatters

A new technique is used in the coroutine formatter to obtain the same structure
as the version in Fig. 4.6b. Note the resume in the constructor of FmtLines. This
resume allows the coroutine main to start *before* any members are called. For the
formatter, all the loops are started before the coroutine main suspends back to finish
construction. At this point, no character has been passed to the coroutine to be
formatted. When the next resume occurs from member prt, the first character is
available *after* the suspend, just like reading from a file generates the first character
after the first input operation. This subtle change eliminates the equivalent priming
read. Without this technique, the coroutine main does not start until the first resume
in prt, so the coroutine has to initialize itself *and* process a character. If this priming-
read effect is retained (by removing the resume from the constructor), the innermost
looping code of the formatter's coroutine main must be changed to:

```
for ( ;; ) {
   if ( ch != '\n' ) break;
      suspend();
}
cout << ch;
suspend();
```

Here the suspends appear *after* processing of a character rather than *before*. If the program in Fig. 4.5, p. 133a is written using a priming read, then this form of the coroutine would be its equivalent. Both forms are valid and depend on the specific problem and programmer.

4.3   Coroutine Construction

Notice for both the Fibonacci and the formatter programs, the coroutine directly expresses the structure of the original algorithm, rather than restructuring the algorithm to fit the available control structures. In fact, one of the simplest ways to write a coroutine is to first write (and test) a stand-alone program that follows the basic structure of reading data, processing the data, and writing the result. This program can be converted into a coroutine by putting the code for processing the data into the coroutine main, replacing the reads and/or writes with calls to suspend, and providing communication variables and interface members to transfer data in/out of the coroutine. The decision about which of the reads or writes to convert depends on whether the program is consuming or producing. For example, the Fibonacci program consumes nothing and produces (generates) Fibonacci numbers, so the writes are converted to suspends; the formatter program directly consumes characters and only indirectly produces output (as a side-effect), so the reads are converted to suspends.

4.4   Correct Coroutine Usage

In general, new users of coroutines have difficulty using the ability of the coroutine to remember execution state. As a result, unnecessary computation is performed to determine execution location or unnecessary flag variables appear containing explicit information about execution state. An example of unnecessary computation occurs in this coroutine, which is passed each digit of a 10-digit number and sums up the even and odd digits separately:

Explicit Execution State	Implicit Execution State
```for (int i = 0; i < 10; i += 1) { if (i % 2 == 0) even += digit; else odd += digit; suspend(); }```	```for (int i = 0; i < 5; i += 1) { even += digit; suspend(); odd += digit; suspend(); }```

The left code fragment uses explicit execution-state by testing the loop counter for even or odd values to determine which block of code to execute in the loop body. The right code fragment reduces the loop iterations to 5, and suspends twice for

```
void main() {
    int fn1, fn2, state = 1;
    for ( ;; ) {
        switch (state) {
        case 1:
            fn = 0;  fn1 = fn;
            state = 2;
            break;
        case 2:
            fn = 1;  fn2 = fn1;  fn1 = fn;
            state = 3;
            break;
        case 3:
            fn = fn1 + fn2;  fn2 = fn1;  fn1 = fn;
            break;
        }
        suspend();
    }
}
```

Fig. 4.7 Unnecessary flag variable

each iteration, once for an even and once for an odd digit. While the difference between these examples may appear trivial, the right example illustrates thinking in the implicit execution-state style versus explicit, and hence, takes full advantage of the coroutine.

Fig. 4.7 shows an example of an unnecessary flag variable, which is based on the Fibonacci generator presented in Sect. 4.1.2, p. 128. This coroutine main uses explicit flag variables to control execution state and a single suspend at the end of an enclosing loop. None of the coroutine's capabilities for remembering execution state are used, and the structure of the program is lost by the loop flattening. While the presence of resume/suspend uses the coroutine main, it is necessary to do more than just *activate* the coroutine main to demonstrate an understanding of retaining data and execution state within a coroutine.

4.5 Iterator

Another example where a routine needs to retain both data and execution state between calls is an iterator. Section 2.9, p. 41 introduced two forms of iterator: internal and external. Creating an internal iterator, bring the action to the data, is usually straightforward because it is similar in structure to a stand-alone program, i.e., obtaining input directly from the data structure within the iterator and applying the action directly to the input, e.g.:

```
template<typename T, typename Action> void map( Tree<T> *tree, Action act ) {
    if ( tree != NULL ) {           // general case ?
        act( tree->data );          // prefix, perform action on data in node
        map( tree->left, act );
        map( tree->right, act );
    } // if
}
void print( Data &d ) { cout << d.f << endl; } // action
Tree<Data> tree;
map( tree, print );                 // print tree
```

However, creating an external iterator, bring the data to the action, is more complex because the data is not processed directly; instead, it is returned for processing at the point of iteration, like the Fibonacci generator (see Sect. 4.1, p. 125). Specifically, note the recursion in map to implicitly retain both data and execution state during traversal. To transform map to an external iterator requires a coroutine to allow recursion to traverse the tree, and yet, return control back for each node of the traversal.

Fig. 4.8 shows a simple iterator type for a prefixed tree traversal. Note, a tree does not have the notion of a first (begin) and last (end) element because each kind of traversal, prefixed, infixed, or postfixed, has different start and end elements. To detect the end of traversal, the iterator has an end member. Like the previous iterator, the tree iterator manages a *cursor*, next, that moves up and down the branches of the tree between successive calls to operator ++. Notice the iterator constructor performs an initial resume so the cursor is at the left most node in the tree to start the traversal, which allows a dereference of the iterator variable before a call to operator ++. Operator ++ resumes the coroutine main to get the next node in the tree. Member nextNode performs the recursive traversal of the tree, suspending back to operator ++ for each node in the traversal. Therefore, the resume in operator ++ normally activates the coroutine main in one of the recursive invocations of nextNode, where it suspended. When member nextNode finishes the traversal, it returns to the call in iterator::main, which completes the traversal by setting next to NULL.

Without the combination of recursion and coroutining, the implementation of an external tree-iterator is very awkward, requiring the explicit creation and manipulation of a stack and retaining complex data and execution-state. Hence, the external tree-iterator convincingly illustrates the need for coroutines to build advanced external iterators.

4.6 Parsing

The general concept of parsing, which is important in many problem areas, is another example of needing to retain data and execution state between calls. For example, a tokenizer routine reads characters and combines them into tokens, e.g., identifiers, numbers, punctuation, etc., and returns each token. The tokenizer may need to retain state between calls to handle multi-part tokens and tokens that are

```
template<typename T> class Tree {
    T data;
    Tree *left, *right;
  public:
    _Coroutine iterator {
        Tree *next;                              // cursor to element returned by ++
        void nextNode( Tree *node ) {            // prefix tree traversal
            if ( node != NULL ) {                // base case, traversal complete ?
                next = node;                     // remember next location
                suspend();                       // activate resumer
                nextNode( node->left );          // search left branch
                nextNode( node->right );         // search right branch
            }
        }
        void main () {
            nextNode( next );                    // start recursion
            next = NULL;                         // indicate traversal is complete
        }
      public:
        iterator( Tree<T> *tree ) {
            next = tree;                         // set cursor to root of tree
            resume();                            // prepare for first deference
        }
        void operator++() { resume(); }          // activate coroutine
        T operator*() { return next->data; }     // return copy of data
        bool end() { return next == NULL; } // traversal finished ?
    }; // iterator
    ...
}; // Tree
void uMain::main() {
    Tree<char> *root;
    // create tree
    Tree<char>::iterator it( root );
    for ( ; ! it.end(); ++it ) {                 // external tree traversal
        cout << *it << endl;
    }
}
```

Fig. 4.8 Tree iterator

sensitive to context. Another example is a parser routine that is passed a sequence of individual characters to determine if a string of characters matches some pattern. The parser routine may also need to retain state between calls to handle complex inter-relationships among the characters of the pattern. Both of these kinds of problems are amenable to solutions using a coroutine because of its ability to retain both data and execution state between calls. Interestingly, there is a significant body of work covering different kinds of parsing; this section discusses how traditional parsing approaches relate to the coroutine.

The simplest traditional mechanism for parsing is the finite automaton:

> The finite automaton (FA) is a mathematical model of a system, with discrete inputs and outputs. The system can be in any of a finite number of internal configurations or "states." The state of the system summarizes the information concerning past inputs that is needed to determine the behavior of the system on subsequent inputs [2, p. 13].

Essentially, an FA is a simple computer consisting of:

- a finite set of states,
- a set of transitions among states, labelled with characters from a fixed alphabet,
- start and end states.

An FA can be represented as a directed graph, called a **transition diagram**, using the following symbols:

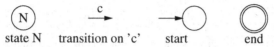

state N   transition on 'c'   start   end

The meaning of each graph element is illustrated using an example: the transition diagram representing the FA for a North-American phone-number is (where 'd' is any decimal digit):

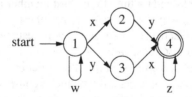

which matches the finite set of phone numbers, such as:

```
(555)123-4567
123-4567
```

The start state does not involve a character; rather it is a pseudo-transition to begin the FA. State 1 is entered from the start state, and if the first character is a ' (', the FA transitions to state 2 or if the first character is a digit, 0–9, the FA transitions to state 7 (skipping the area code). The remaining transitions are all based on the following characters. The end state indicates a complete phone number.

In general, a state may have multiple transitions emanating from it and may cycle back to any state, including itself. For example:

start ⟶ (1) ... (with states 2, 3, 4 and transitions x, y, w, z)

matches an infinite set of strings, such as:

```
wxyz
wwyxz
wxyzzzzz
wwwwxyzzz
```

Multiple emanating transitions provide different choices for the next character, while cycles allow repetition of character sequences. There can be multiple end states.

An FA with the property that for any given state and character there is exactly one unique transition is called a **deterministic FA** (DFA). Any DFA can be represented by a **transition table**. For example, the FA for the previous North-American phone-number is a DFA with the following transition table (empty boxes represent error states):

Character	State													
	1	2	3	4	5	6	7	8	9	10	11	12	13	14
(	2													
d(igit)	7	3	4	5		7	8	9		11	12	13	14	
)					6									
-									10					

If the FA transitions to an error state, it cannot accept the character, indicating the string is unmatchable by the FA. As well, a transition involving a character not in the transition table is equivalent to entering an error state. It is possible to build a universal scanner for any transition table to determine if a string is recognized by a DFA:

```
state = 1;
for ( ;; ) {
    cin >> ch;                          // read characters one at a time
    if ( cin.fail() ) break;            // complete scan ? (no more characters)
    state = transTable[ch][state];      // use transition table to determine next action
    if ( state == ERROR ) break;        // invalid state ?
}
cout << (state is an end-state ? "" : "no ") << "match" << endl;
```

Tools exists to automatically create a transition table for an FA, e.g., UNIX lex.

If such a tool is unavailable or inappropriate, it is possible to directly convert an FA into a program. Fig. 4.9 shows two direct conversions of the FA for a phone number. Fig. 4.9a is a stand-alone program reading characters one at a time (external input) and checking if the string of characters is a phone number. Fig. 4.9b modularizes the stand-alone program into a coroutine, where the characters of the phone number are passed one at a time to the next member (internal input), which returns the current status of the scan. Notice how the coroutine main retains its execution location and reactivates there when it is resumed, e.g., when parsing groups of digits, the coroutine suspends in the middle of a **for** loop, which counts the number of digits, and reactivates within the particular loop when resumed. In both cases, the handling of characters after a phone number is accepted is problem specific. The program/coroutine can continue accepting characters and ignore them; alternatively, the program/coroutine can just end. As well, certain practical parsing situation need to know the "end-of-string", which can be denoted with a special character like newline. This case can be represented in an FA by adding the "end-of-string" character and associated states.

The transition graphs of an FA can be described in a more compact form, called a regular expression, which has 3 basic operations (where x and y can be a character or regular expression):

- concatenation: x y meaning x *and* y,
- union: x | y meaning x *or* y,
- (Kleene) closure: x* meaning 0 or more concatenations of x.

(a) Stand-alone:

```
enum Status { GOOD, BAD };

char ch;
Status status = BAD;

fini: {
    cin >> ch;
    if ( ch == '(' ) {
        for ( i = 0; i < 3; i += 1 ) {
            cin >> ch;
            if ( ! isdigit(ch) ) { break fini; }
        } // for
        cin >> ch;
        if ( ch != ')' ) { break fini; }
        cin >> ch;
    } // if
    for ( i = 0; i < 3; i += 1 ) {
        if ( ! isdigit(ch) ) { break fini; }
        cin >> ch;
    } // for
    if ( ch != '-' ) { status = BAD; break fini; }
    for ( i = 0; i < 4; i += 1 ) {
        cin >> ch;
        if ( ! isdigit(ch) ) { break fini; }
    } // for
    status = GOOD;
    // more characters ?
} // block
cout << endl << "status:" << status << endl;
```

(b) Coroutine:

```
_Coroutine PhoneNo {
  public:
    enum Status { GOOD, BAD };
  private:
    char ch;   // character passed by cocaller
    Status status; // current status of match
    void main() {
        int i;
        status = BAD;
        if ( ch == '(' ) {  // area code ?
            for ( i = 0; i < 3; i += 1 ) {  // 3 digits
                suspend();          // get digit
                if ( ! isdigit(ch) ) { return; }
            } // for
            suspend();              // get ')'
            if ( ch != ')' ) {return;} // ')' ?
            suspend();              // get digit
        } // if
        for ( i = 0; i < 3; i += 1 ) {  // 3 digits
            if ( ! isdigit(ch) ) { return; }
            suspend();              // get digit or '-'
        } // for
        if ( ch != '-' ) { return; } // '-' ?
        for ( i = 0; i < 4; i += 1 ) {  // 4 digits
            suspend();              // get digit
            if ( ! isdigit(ch) ) { return; }
        } // for
        status = GOOD;
        // more characters ?
    }
  public:
    Status next( char c ) {
        ch = c;
        resume();
        return status;
    }
};
```

(a) Stand-alone   (b) Coroutine

Fig. 4.9 Direct FA conversion: phone number

Parenthesis may be used for grouping. For example, the expression, $('x' \mid ('y' \ 'z'))^*$, specifies the infinite set of strings containing zero or more $'x'$ characters or $'yz'$ strings, such as:

```
x
yzyz
xxxyz
yzyzxxxyzxxx
```

Additional operations are sometimes added:

- positive closure: x^+ meaning 1 or more concatenations of x,
- enumeration: x^n meaning n concatenations of x.

These additional operators can be derived from the basic operations, although awkwardly, because regular expressions cannot directly count or remember an arbitrary amount of characters (no auxiliary variables).

The regular expression for the North-American phone-number is:

$d = \text{'0' | '1' | '2' | '3' | '4' | '5' | '6' | '7' | '8' | '9'}$

$phoneno = (\ '\ ('\ d^3\ ')'\ d^3\ '-'\ d^4\ )\ |\ (\ d^3\ '-'\ d^4\ )$

Notice the regular-expression syntax is a simpler representation than the corresponding FA. The following are general guidelines for converting a regular expression to a direct program (see Fig. 4.9 for examples):

- Concatenation is performed by a sequence of checks.
- Alternation is performed by a disjunction of checks using an **if** statement.
- Closure and enumeration are performed by looping.

In fact, the coroutine is more powerful than an FA, and can use mechanisms like counting and auxiliary variables to simplify recognition of strings for a DFA. Hence, it is often unnecessary and inefficient to transform every aspect of an FA directly into a coroutine, i.e., state-for-state translation can result in the poor stylistic approaches discussed in Sect. 4.4, p. 135. Often the transformation from a regular expression for an FA to a coroutine is direct and efficient. Using counting and auxiliary variables in the coroutine can further simplify aspects of the conversion.

An FA that can make nondeterministic choices for accepting input characters is called a **nondeterministic finite automaton** (NFA). For example, consider an NFA described by the regular expression ('x' | 'y')* 'x' 'x', which is a string of zero or more x or y characters ending with two consecutive x characters, e.g.:

```
xx
yxx
xxx
xyxxyyxx
```

The transition diagram and table for an NFA accepting these strings are:

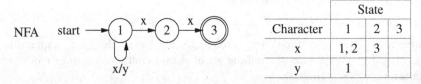

Character	State 1	State 2	State 3
x	1, 2	3	
y	1		

Notice in state 1, the character x can return back to state 1 or transition to state 2. Hence, there is no unique transition at this point in the NFA, which can be seen in the transition table by the two possible states for character x for state 1. Therefore, the simple approach of generating a transition table and using a universal scanner does not work. Interestingly, all NFAs can be converted by appropriate transformations into a DFA (see [2, Section 2.3]), and the transition table for that DFA can be used for scanning. Unlike a DFA, an NFA cannot be converted state-for-state into a coroutine because of the nondeterminism; converting the NFA to a DFA and then to a coroutine is still unlikely to be a good approach. Rather the coroutine should take advantage of counting and auxiliary variables. For example, the coroutine main to recognize the above NFA is:

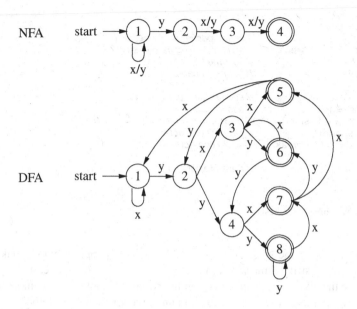

Fig. 4.10 NFA versus DFA

```
char prev = 'y';
for ( ;; ) {
    status = ch == 'x' && prev == 'x' ? GOOD : BAD;
    prev = ch;          // remember last character
    suspend();          // assume characters are x/y
}
```

Here, the coroutine uses auxiliary variables to retain the last two characters scanned to determine if both are x. Note, even though an NFA may not represent the best implementation for parsing, it is often a convenient mechanism to express and reason about certain parsing problems.

For the previous example, the complexity of the NFA and its equivalent DFA is the same, allowing the use of the DFA's transition table for scanning:

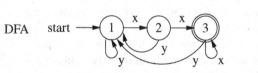

	State		
Character	1	2	3
x	2	3	3
y	1	1	1

However, for some NFA, the equivalent DFA can grow exponentially, making it impractical to use its transition table. Consider the NFA described by the regular expression $('x' | 'y')^* 'y' ('x' | 'y')^{n-1}$, where the nth symbol from the end of the input must be a y. For $n = 3$, the NFA and its equivalent DFA are in Fig. 4.10.

It is easy to see this NFA grows linearly in n. However, its DFA grows exponentially in n because it is necessary to remember the last n characters to determine whether the nth character is a y. As an automaton has no memory, it is necessary to encode each combination of the n trailing characters as a state, resulting

```
status = BAD;
int cnt = 0;
for ( ;; ) {                          // scan opening parenthesis
  if ( ch == ')' ) break;             // start of closing parenthesis ?
  cnt += 1;                           // assume ' ('
  suspend();                          // get next character
}
for ( ;; ) {                          // scan closing parenthesis
  cnt -= 1;                           // assume ' )'
  if ( cnt == 0 ) { status = GOOD; break; }; // balanced ?
  suspend();                          // get next character
  if ( ch != ')' ) { break; };        // invalid character
}
suspend();                            // return result
// more characters ?
```

Fig. 4.11 Matching parenthesis

in 2^n states. Hence, the DFA's transition table grows exponentially in n making its use for scanning strings impractical for larger values of n. As above, the coroutine can replace the NFA's nondeterminism with auxiliary variables to remember the last n characters. For example, the coroutine main to recognize the above NFA is:

```
list<char> prev;                      // or an array of size n
for ( ;; ) {
  prev.push_back( ch );               // remember character
  if ( prev.size() > n ) { prev.pop_front( ); } // only retain last n characters
  status = prev.size() == n && prev.front() == 'y' ? GOOD : BAD;
  suspend();                          // assume characters are x/y
}
```

Here, the number of auxiliary variables is linear in n. For practical parsing problems, the number of auxiliary variables to replace an NFA's nondeterminism is at most linear in the number of states of the NFA.

There are also problems, such as matching balanced parentheses, that cannot be handled by a FA. While it is possible to write a regular representation for a fixed n, $'('^n')'^n$, or set of n:

$$'('^1')'^1 \mid '('^2')'^2 \mid '('^3')'^3 \mid '('^4')'^4 \mid \ldots$$

the general form $'('^+')'^+$ does not ensure the number of opening and closing parentheses are equal. An FA can be made more powerful by allowing an auxiliary stack to remember characters, called a **push-down automaton**. To match balanced parentheses, an open parenthesis is pushed onto the stack and popped off for each closing parenthesis. Once more, a coroutine can directly mimic a push-down automaton by creating an auxiliary stack. Fig. 4.11 shows how to match parentheses with a single auxiliary variable that counts, which a push-down automaton cannot do. The coroutine stops as soon as balanced parentheses are matched.

In summary, parsing is a complex class of problems for which automata are powerful tools; however, the finite and push-down automata are only simple computers, resulting in restricted programming models. Even with a more powerful computer, the ideas, concepts, and understanding provided by automata and regular expressions are applicable in many parsing contexts and present a succinct way to represent these situations with many provable properties. However, when implementing parsing problems, a programming language usually provides a less restricted programming model than those dictated by the different kinds of FA. A parsing program is allowed to have a finite number/kind of auxiliary variables and perform arbitrary arithmetic operations, which is almost equivalent to the most general model of computing, called a Turing machine. Hence, the actual implementation of parsing problems is not constrained by the limitations of the FA; a programmer is free to step outside of the FA programming model, producing simpler and more efficient solutions that only use the FA as a guide. Within a coroutine, a programmer can use auxiliary variables and arbitrary arithmetic, which is why the coroutine can have simpler solutions than an FA for complex parsing problems. But it is the ability of the coroutine to directly represent the execution "state" of an automaton that makes it the ideal tool for directly representing FA, and hence, programming the entire class of parsing problems.

4.7 Coroutine Details

The following μC++ coroutine details are presented to understand subsequent examples or to help in solving questions at the end of the chapter.

4.7.1 Coroutine Creation and Destruction

A coroutine is the same as a class object with respect to creation and destruction, e.g.:

```
_Coroutine C {
    void main() ...        // coroutine main
    public:
    void r( ... ) ...
};
C *cp;                     // pointer to a coroutine
{ // start a new block
    C c, ca[3];            // local creation
    cp = new C;            // dynamic creation
    ...
    c.r( ... );            // call a member routine that activates the coroutine
    ca[1].r( ... );
    cp->r( ... );
    ...
} // c, ca[0], ca[1] and ca[2] are deallocated
...
delete cp; // cp' s instance is deallocated
```

When a coroutine is created, the appropriate coroutine constructor and, if there is inheritance, any base-class constructors are executed in the normal order. The stack component of the coroutine's execution-state is created and the starting point (activation point) is initialized to the coroutine's main routine visible by the inheritance scope rules from the coroutine type; however, the main routine does not start execution until the coroutine is activated by one of its member routines. The location of a coroutine's variables–in the coroutine's data area or in member routine main–depends on whether the variables must be accessed by member routines other than main. Once main is activated, it executes until it activates another coroutine or terminates. The coroutine's point of last activation may be outside of the main routine because main may have called another routine; the routine called could be local to the coroutine or in another coroutine. This issue is discussed further in several example programs.

The coroutine property of a coroutine type, i.e., its execution state, is independent of its object properties. If a coroutine is never resumed, its execution state is never used (and hence, may not be implicitly allocated); in this case, the coroutine behaves solely as an object. A coroutine terminates when its main routine terminates, and its execution state is no longer available (and hence, may be implicitly deleted). After termination, the coroutine behaves as an object, *and cannot be resumed again*. It is possible to determine if a coroutine is terminated by calling getState(), which returns one of Halt, Active, Inactive, where Halt implies terminated. Because a coroutine begins and ends as an object, calls to member routines that manipulate coroutine variables are possible at these times.

When a coroutine terminates, it activates the coroutine that caused main to *start* execution. This choice ensures that the starting sequence is a tree, i.e., there are no cycles. Control flow can move in a cycle among a group of coroutines but termination always proceeds back along the branches of the starting tree. This choice for termination does impose certain requirements on the starting order of coroutines, but it is essential to ensure that cycles can be broken at termination. This issue is discussed further in several example programs. Finally, attempting to activate a terminated coroutine is an error.

4.7.2   Inherited Members

Each coroutine type, if not derived from some other coroutine type, is implicitly derived from the coroutine type uBaseCoroutine, e.g.:

```
_Coroutine coroutine-name : public uBaseCoroutine {   // implicit inheritance
    ...
};
```

where the interface for the base-class uBaseCoroutine is:

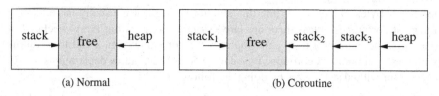

(a) Normal

(b) Coroutine

Fig. 4.12 Storage allocation

```
_Coroutine uBaseCoroutine {
protected:
    void resume();
    void suspend();
public:
    uBaseCoroutine();
    uBaseCoroutine( unsigned int stacksize );
    void verify();
    const char *setName( const char *name );
    const char *getName() const;
    enum State { Halt, Active, Inactive };
    State getState() const;
    uBaseCoroutine &starter() const;
    uBaseCoroutine &resumer() const;
};
```

The protected member routines resume and suspend are discussed in Sect. 4.7.3, p. 149.

The overloaded constructor routine uBaseCoroutine has the following forms:

uBaseCoroutine() –creates a coroutine with the default stack size.

uBaseCoroutine(**unsigned int** stacksize) –creates a coroutine with the specified stack size (in bytes).

Unlike a normal program with a single execution-state, a coroutine program has multiple execution-states, and hence, multiple stacks for each coroutine's routine activations. Managing a single stack can be done simply and implicitly for normal programs, as in Fig. 4.12a. The storage is divided into three areas: the stack for routine activations, the heap for dynamically allocated variables (i.e., variables created with **new**), and the free currently unused storage. Normally, the stack and heap storage grow towards one another until they meet; at which time the program normally terminates with an error. However, managing multiple stacks is significantly more complex and may require some explicit involvement from the programmer, as in Fig. 4.12b. There is no simple technique to allow each stack to grow dynamically into the free area, as for a normal program. Any technique allowing each coroutine stack to grow dynamically requires compiler and runtime support, which is beyond what μC++ provides. Instead, in μC++, each coroutine stack is a fixed size and cannot grow, which requires the programmer to ensure the stack for each coroutine is large enough when the coroutine is created. If no stack size is specified, the default value is architecture dependent, but is usually at least 32K bytes of storage. While this amount is small, it is usually large enough for most coroutines unless there are large variables (e.g., a big array) declared in the coroutine main or a deep call graph for the coroutine (e.g., a call to a routine with deep recursion). A coroutine type can be designed to allow declarations of it to specify individual stack sizes by doing the following:

```
_Coroutine C {
  public:
    C() : uBaseCoroutine( 8192 ) {};  // default 8K stack
    C( unsigned int size ) : uBaseCoroutine( size ) {};  // user specified stack size
    ...
};
C x, y( 16384 );     // x has an 8K stack, y has a 16K stack
```

μC++ attempts to check if a coroutine overflows its stack during execution, but there are a few situations it cannot detect. One of these situations is when the top of one stack overflows onto the bottom of the next coroutine's stack, arbitrarily modifying this stack. In this case, an error may not occur until the modified coroutine moves back down its stack to the point of corruption. At this point, an unusual error may occur completely unrelated to the coroutine that overflowed its stack and caused the problem. Such an error is extremely difficult to track down. One way to detect possible stack overflows is through the member verify, which checks whether the current coroutine has overflowed its stack; if it has, the program terminates. To completely ensure the stack size is never exceeded, a call to verify must be included after each set of declarations, as in the following:

```
void main() {
  ...           // declarations
  verify();     // check for stack overflow
  ...           // code
}
```

Thus, after a coroutine has allocated its local variables, a check is made that its stack has not overflowed. Clearly, this technique is not ideal and requires additional work for the programmer, but it does handle complex cases where the stack depth is difficult to determine and can be used to help debug possible stack overflow situations.

The member routine setName associates a name with a coroutine and returns the previous name. *The name is not copied so its storage must persist for the duration of the coroutine.* The member routine getName returns the string name associated with a coroutine. If a coroutine has not been assigned a name, getName returns the type name of the coroutine. μC++ uses the name when printing any error message, which is helpful in debugging.

The member routine getState returns the current state of a coroutine's execution, which is one of the enumerated values Halt, Active or Inactive. (When accessed from outside of a coroutine type, these enumerated values must be qualified with uBaseCoroutine::.)

The member routine starter returns the coroutine's starter, i.e., the coroutine that performed the first resume of this coroutine (see Sect. 4.7.1, p. 145). The member routine resumer returns the coroutine's last resumer, i.e., the coroutine that performed the last resume of this coroutine (see Sect. 4.7.3).

The routine:

```
uBaseCoroutine &uThisCoroutine();
```

is used to determine the identity of the coroutine executing this routine. Because it returns a reference to the base coroutine type, uBaseCoroutine, this reference can only be used to access the public routines of type uBaseCoroutine. For example, a routine can check whether the allocation of its local variables has overflowed the stack of a coroutine that called it by performing the following:

```
int rtn( ... ) {
    ...                     // declarations
    uThisCoroutine().verify();    // check for stack overflow
    ...                     // code
}
```

As well, printing a coroutine's address for debugging purposes must be done like this:

```
cout << "coroutine:" << &uThisCoroutine() << endl;  // notice the ampersand (&)
```

4.7.3 Coroutine Control and Communication

Control flow among coroutines is specified by the protected members resume and suspend. These members are protected to prevent one coroutine from directly resuming or suspending another coroutine, as in c.resume(). Rather, a coroutine should package these operations as in the following:

- A call to resume may appear in any member of the coroutine, but normally it is used only in the public members.
- A call to suspend may appear in any member of the coroutine, but normally it is used only in the coroutine main or non-public members called directly or indirectly from the coroutine main.

The action performed by members resume and suspend is composed of two parts. The first part inactivates the coroutine calling the member and the second part activates another coroutine.

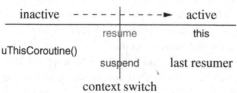

control flow semantics

Both resume and suspend inactivate the current coroutine (denoted by uThisCoroutine). The second part activates a difference coroutine depending on the specific member. Member resume activates the current coroutine object, i.e., the coroutine specified by the implicit **this** variable. Member suspend activates the coroutine that previously executed a call to resume for the coroutine executing the suspend, *ignoring any resumes of a coroutine to itself.* In effect, these special members cause control flow to transfer among execution states, which involves context switches.

It is important to understand that calling a coroutine's member by another coroutine does not cause a switch to the other coroutine. A switch only occurs when a resume is executed in the other coroutine's member. Therefore, printing &uThisCoroutine() in the other coroutine's member always prints the *calling* coroutine's address; printing **this** in the other coroutine's member always prints the *called* coroutine's address (which is the coroutine that resume switches to). Hence, there is a difference between who is executing and where execution is occurring.

4.8   Semi- and Full Coroutine

Coroutines can be structured in two different ways:

1. The semi-coroutine [3, p. 4,37] structure acts asymmetrically, like non-recursive subroutines performing call and return. The first coroutine activates the second coroutine by calling one of the members in the second coroutine that performs a resume; the second coroutine implicitly activates the first coroutine by performing a suspend. Just as a return for a routine implicitly knows its last caller, a suspend for a coroutine implicitly knows the last coroutine that resumed it.

2. The full coroutine structure acts symmetrically, like recursive subroutines performing calls that involve a cycle. The first coroutine activates the second coroutine by calling one of the members of the second coroutine that performs a resume; the second coroutine activates the first coroutine by directly or indirectly calling one of the members of the first coroutine, which then performs a resume. The difference between recursion and full-coroutining is that each invocation of a routine creates a new instance of the routine, while full-coroutining only cycles among preexisting coroutines.

Hence, a full coroutine is part of a resume cycle, while a semi-coroutine never participates in a resume cycle. A full coroutine is allowed to perform semi-coroutine operations because it subsumes the notion of the semi-coroutine; i.e., a full coroutine can use suspend to activate the member routine that activated it or resume to itself, but it must always form a resume cycle with other coroutines.

Fig. 4.13 compares the general control flow available from routines, semi-coroutines and full coroutines. In the figure, vertices represent instances of routines or coroutines, and arcs represent call/return or suspend/resume or resume/resume control flow. On the left, multiple routine calls form a non-branching tree of suspended routines where call goes up the branch allocating a new vertex and return goes down the branch deallocating the current vertex. Even when routines use recursion, there is still only a non-branching tree because each new instance is created at the top of the tree. In the middle, semi-coroutines allow the tree to branch because each coroutine has its own execution state, which allows it to persist

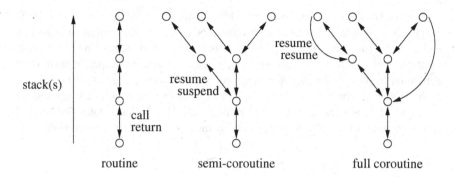

Fig. 4.13 Activation structure

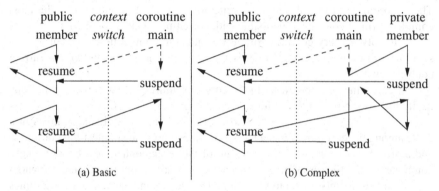

Fig. 4.14 Semi-coroutine control flow

between calls and form another call/return branch. Resuming forks up a branch and suspending joins back to a branch point. On the right, full coroutines allow cycles to form, creating a network graph with arbitrary topology. Each kind of coroutine control-flow is discussed in detail.

4.8.1 Semi-Coroutine

The most common form of coroutine structure is the semi-coroutine; all the examples presented thus far are semi-coroutines. Semi-coroutines are somewhat like routines in that the resumes and suspends move to and from a coroutine like a call and return move to and from a routine. This basic flow of control is illustrated in Fig. 4.14a. At each resume, the complete state of the resumer is retained on the stack of the cocaller, including the call to the coroutine's member that executes the resume. At each suspend, the complete state of the suspender is retained on the stack of the coroutine.

A more complex example appears in Fig. 4.14b, which shows that the coroutine main can be suspended outside of its code body. That is, the coroutine main can call a private member, for example, which then suspends the coroutine (see routine nextNode in Fig. 4.8, p. 138). In this case, when the coroutine suspends, there is an activation for the private member on the coroutine's stack along with the coroutine main. When the coroutine is resumed, it reactivates execution at its last suspension point, which continues in the private member with all of its local state. The number of suspended routine calls is limited only by the stack size of the coroutine main.

4.8.2   Full Coroutine

The less common form of coroutine structure is the full coroutine; it is the most complex form of control flow possible with coroutines. This form of control flow is useful in solving very complex forms of sequential control-flow; as well, understanding full-coroutine control-flow is the first step in understanding concurrent control-flow.

Full coroutines are somewhat like recursive routines in that the coroutine calls itself directly or indirectly to form a cycle. *However, unlike recursion, a new instance of the coroutine is not created for each call*; control simply flows in a cycle among the coroutines, like a loop. Fig. 4.15 shows the simplest full coroutine, and a driver routine, as well as a diagram of the basic control flow between these components. Starting in member uMain::main, the full coroutine fc is created and a call is made to member mem to activate it. The mem member immediately resumes the coroutine main, which makes the anonymous coroutine for uMain::main inactive and starts the coroutine associated with the object of the member call, fc. Control transfers to the beginning of fc's main member because it is the first resume (dashed line in the diagram), and the anonymous coroutine for uMain::main is remembered as the starting coroutine for subsequent termination (discussed shortly).

The full coroutine's main member makes a call to its own member mem. This call implicitly suspends member fc::main (part of a normal routine call) and starts a new instance of mem on fc's execution-state. The resume in mem makes fc inactive and activates the coroutine associated with the object of the member call, fc, but does not create a new instance of it. Hence, fc does a context switch to itself and execution continues after the resume; effectively, the resume does nothing but costs something, i.e., the time to do the context switch. The call to mem returns back to fc::main. Follow this flow of control in the diagram of Fig. 4.15. The key point is that resume reactivates the current coroutine, i.e., **this**, wherever it is suspended. Since, the coroutine main can call other routines before it suspends, it may reactivate completely outside of its own code, as is also possible with semi-coroutines. Given this description of resume, explain what occurs for the call to resume in fc::main?

Finally, there is a call to suspend and a return from the coroutine's main. The suspend starts by inactivating the coroutine that invokes it, and then activates the coroutine that most recently executed a call to resume for this coroutine.

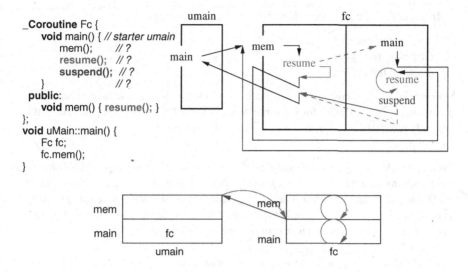

```
_Coroutine Fc {
    void main() { // starter umain
        mem();      // ?
        resume();   // ?
        suspend();  // ?
    }             // ?
public:
    void mem() { resume(); }
};
void uMain::main() {
    Fc fc;
    fc.mem();
}
```

Fig. 4.15 Basic full coroutine control flow

Since the coroutine that last executed a call to resume is fc, the suspend would result in fc context switching to itself (like a resume). While this semantics is consistent with the definition of suspend, it means the original resumer coroutine, uMain::main, is now lost because it is overwritten by the resume of the coroutine to itself. Now the ability to activate a coroutine's last resumer is useful, and this capability is lost only when a coroutine resumes itself, which is neither necessary nor useful, so μC++ makes an exception when performing a resume: a resume of a coroutine to itself does not overwrite the last resumer of the coroutine. Given this exception, the suspend makes active the anonymous coroutine for uMain::main, which continues after the resume in mem, returns from the call fc.mem(), and uMain::main ends, with an unterminated coroutine fc. If the call to suspend is removed and a return occurs from the coroutine's main, fc::main returns. Up to this point, the coroutine main has not terminated; the coroutine is just deleted (from stack/heap) while suspended, which is perfectly fine. However, when a coroutine's main terminates, a special termination rule applies, which activates the coroutine that *first* resumed (cocalled/activated) a coroutine. For semi-coroutines, the starter is often the last (only) resumer, so it appears like the coroutine main implicitly suspends on termination. For full-coroutines, the starter is often *not* the last resumer, so it does *not* appear like the coroutine main implicitly suspends on termination. For fc, the starter coroutine is the anonymous coroutine for uMain::main, so fc terminates and cannot be resumed again; then, the anonymous coroutine for uMain::main is made active, it continues the resume in mem, returns from the call fc.mem(), and uMain::main ends, with a terminated coroutine fc. When uMain::main ends, the special termination rule resumes its starter and the program subsequently terminates.

In general, there are three phases to any full coroutine program:

1. starting the cycle
2. executing the cycle
3. stopping the cycle

Starting the cycle is complicated as each coroutine needs to know at least one other coroutine to form a cycle, for example, fc knows y, y knows fc. The problem is the mutually recursive references, i.e., the declarations need to be:

```
Fc x(y), y(x);
```

but the first declaration fails because of the *definition before use rule* of C++, that is, y is passed as an argument to fc *before* it is defined. Clearly, switching the order of declaration of fc and y does not help. There are several ways to solve this problem. The mechanism presented here is to declare the first instance without a partner and pass it a partner after the other coroutines are created, as in:

```
Fc x, y(x);       // only y gets a partner now
x.partner(y);     // x gets its partner after y is declared
```

The cycle is now closed by the call to x.partner, which initializes x's partner. Once the cycle is created, coroutines x and y can resume around the cycle by calling each other's member routines that do resumes. Stopping can be as complex as starting, because it is necessary to activate uMain for the program to finish (unless exit is used). The semantic rule of resuming a coroutine's starter always provides a path back to uMain, and it is unnecessary to terminate all coroutines as they can be deleted while suspended.

4.8.3   Ping/Pong

Fig. 4.16 shows two coroutines that form a cycle, and a driver routine, as well as a diagram of the basic control flow among these components. This example illustrates how to build full coroutines and understand the control flow with two identical coroutines.

The cycle creation is started in uMain::main using the partner method, where ping is created without a partner, and pong is create with partner ping. Then, umain calls the partner member of ping, passing pong. ping sets its partner to pong, closing the cycle. Notice the class variable part is a pointer rather than a reference. A pointer is required because a reference can only be initialized when an object is created through constructor initialization. Since the constructor cannot be used to initialize all the partner values because of the mutually recursive reference, a pointer type must be used.

Now the cycle is created, umain resumes ping, which is the first resume, so umain becomes ping's starter and umain becomes inactive and control begins in ping's coroutine main. Execution around the cycle begins by ping calling cycle in pong, which resumes pong. Since this resume is the first for pong, ping becomes pong's

```
_Coroutine PingPong {
    const char *name;
    const unsigned int N;
    PingPong *part;
    void main() { // ping' s starter umain, pong' s starter ping
        for ( unsigned int i = 0; i < N; i += 1 ) {
            cout << name << endl;
            part->cycle();
        }
    }
  public:
    PingPong( const char *name, unsigned int N, PingPong &part =
        *(PingPong *)0 ) : name( name ), N( N ), part( &part ) {}
    void cycle() { resume(); }
    void partner( PingPong &part ) { PingPong::part = &part; resume(); }
};
void uMain::main() {
    enum { N = 20 };
    PingPong ping( "ping", N ), pong( "pong", N, ping );
    ping.partner( pong );
}
```

Fig. 4.16 Complex full coroutine

starter for subsequent termination and control begins in pong's coroutine main.
Follow the flow of control between the two coroutines at the bottom of Fig. 4.16,
where the dashed lines are the first resume (cocall).

ping's coroutine main creates local variable i that is retained between subsequent
activations of the coroutine, and executes 20 calls to cycle in the partner coroutine.
Resume$_2$ in pong's cycle member resumes its coroutine main, which makes ping
inactive and makes pong active, but does not create a new instance of it. Hence, ping
only does a context switch to pong. Control transfers to the beginning of pong's

coroutine main because it is the first resume (dashed line in the diagram), and coroutine ping is remembered as the starting coroutine for subsequent termination.

pong's coroutine main creates local variable i that is retained between subsequent activations of the coroutine, and executes 20 calls to cycle in the partner coroutine. Resume$_1$ in ping's cycle member resumes its coroutine main, which makes pong inactive and makes ping active, but does not create a new instance of it. Hence, pong only does a context switch to ping, and first the cycle is now executed.

Control transfers to the location of ping's last inactivation after resume$_2$ in member pong's cycle, which returns to ping's coroutine main for the next call to pong's cycle. Resume$_2$ in pong's cycle member makes ping inactive and activates the coroutine associated with the object of the member call, which context switches to pong. Control transfers to the location of pong's last inactivation after resume$_1$ in member ping's cycle, which returns to pong's coroutine main for the next call to ping's cycle. Trace along the flow lines of Fig. 4.16 until you have found the cycle and understand why resume$_1$ and resume$_2$ transfer control to where they do. It might help to write down for each resume which coroutine is inactivating so it is easy to see why it reactivates where it does.

Stopping the cycle occurs when ping finishes first because it started first. When ping's main finishes, the special termination rule applies so ping resumes its starter umain in ping's partner member (dashed line in the diagram); umain then terminates with a terminated coroutine ping and unterminated coroutine pong. As stated previously, there is nothing wrong with deallocating a suspended coroutine; it is no different than deallocating an object. Assume ping's declaration is changed to ping("ping", N + 1). Now pong ends first, the special termination rule applies so pong resumes its starter ping in pong's cycle member (dashed line in the diagram). ping ends second, the special termination rule applies so ping resumes its starter umain in ping's partner member. umain terminates with terminated coroutines ping and pong.

It is important to understand this program to understand further examples. Therefore, before reading on, make sure you understand the control flow in this program.

4.9   Producer-Consumer Problem

The producer-consumer problem is a standard problem, that is, it is a problem that represents a class of problems. All problems in that class can be solved using some variation on the basic solution to the standard problem. This book discusses several standard problems and presents one or more basic solutions. One of the main skills the reader must develop is the ability to identify standard problems within a problem and adapt standard solutions to solve these problems. This approach is significantly faster than solving problems directly from first principles.

The producer-consumer problem is very simple: a producer generates objects and a consumer receives these objects. It does not matter what the objects are or what the consumer does with them, as long as the producer and consumer agree on the kind of object. When the producer is only calling the consumer there are no cycles in the control flow. If the producer calls the consumer *and* the consumer calls the producer, there is a cycle in the control flow. Both semi- and full coroutine producer and consumer solutions are discussed, which illustrate these two cases.

4.9.1 Semi-coroutine Solution

Fig. 4.17 shows a semi-coroutine producer and consumer, and a driver routine, as well as a diagram of the basic control flow among these components. Starting in member uMain::main, the consumer cons is created followed by the producer prod. Since the solution is semi-coroutining, only the consumer needs to be passed to the producer so the producer can reference the consumer, making starting straightforward. Next, a call is made to the start member of the producer to start the producer coroutine. The number of values generated by the producer is passed as the argument (5 in the program).

The start member in Prod communicates the number of elements to be produced to the coroutine main by copying the parameter to a class variable, which is accessible to the member main. Next, a resume is executed, which makes the anonymous coroutine for uMain::main inactive and starts the coroutine associated with the object of the member call, prod. Control transfers to the beginning of prod's main member because it is the first resume (dashed line in the diagram), and the anonymous coroutine for uMain::main is remembered as the starting coroutine for subsequent termination.

The producer's main member creates local variables that are retained between subsequent activations of the coroutine. Then it executes N iterations of generating two random integer values between 0–99, printing the two values, calling the consumer to deliver the two values, and printing the status returned from the consumer. Normally, the values generated are more complex and the status from the consumer is examined to determine if there is a problem with the delivered values; however, neither of these points is important to understand the control flow between producer and consumer in this example.

The call from the producer to the consumer's delivery member transfers data from producer to consumer. When delivery is called, it is the producer coroutine, prod, executing the member. The values delivered by the producer are copied into communication variables in the consumer and a resume is executed. The resume makes prod inactive and activates the coroutine associated with the object of the member call, cons. Control transfers to the beginning of cons's main member because it is the first resume (dashed line in the diagram), and coroutine prod is remembered as the starting coroutine for subsequent termination.

The consumer's main member creates local variables that are retained between subsequent activations of the coroutine. Then it iterates until the done flag is set, printing the two values delivered, incrementing the status for returning, printing the

```
_Coroutine Cons {                              _Coroutine Prod {
   int p1, p2, status;   // communication         Cons &cons;      // communication
   bool done;                                     int N;

   void main() { // starter prod                  void main() { // starter umain
      // 1st resume starts here                       // 1st resume starts here
      int money = 1;                                  int i, p1, p2, status;
      for ( ;; ) {                                    for ( i = 1; i <= N; i += 1 ) {
       if ( done ) break;                              p1 = rand() % 100;
         cout << "cons receives: " <<                  p2 = rand() % 100;
            p1 << ", " << p2;                           cout << "prod delivers: " <<
         cout << " and pays $" <<                          p1 << ", " << p2 << endl;
            money << endl;                              status = cons.delivery( p1, p2 );
         status += 1;                                   cout << "prod status: " <<
         suspend(); // activate delivery/stop              status << endl;
         money += 1;                                  }
      }                                               cout << "prod stops" << endl;
      cout << "cons stops" << endl;                   cons.stop();
   }                                              }
public:                                         public:
   Cons() : status(0), done(false) {}              Prod( Cons &c ) : cons(c) {}
   int delivery( int p1, int p2 ) {                void start( int N ) {
      Cons::p1 = p1;                                  Prod::N = N;
      Cons::p2 = p2;                                  resume();           // activate main
      resume();            // activate main        }
      return status;                             };
   }
   void stop() {                                 void uMain::main() {
      done = true;                                  Cons cons;      // create consumer
      resume();            // activate main        Prod prod( cons ); // create producer
   }                                               prod.start( 5 );   // start producer
};                                              }
```

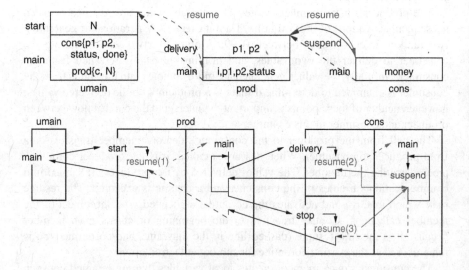

Fig. 4.17 Semi-coroutine: producer-consumer

amount it pays for the values, suspending and incrementing the amount of money for the next payment. The suspend makes cons inactive and activates the coroutine that last resumed it, namely prod. Control transfers to the point where prod was last made inactive and it continues, which is in member delivery after the resume.

The delivery member returns the status value to the call in prod's main member, where the status is printed. The loop then repeats calling delivery, where each call resumes the consumer coroutine. When the consumer is made active it continues after the point where it was last made inactive, which is the suspend in cons's main member.

After iterating N times, the producer calls the stop member in cons. When stop is called, it is the producer coroutine, prod, executing the member. The done flag is set to stop the consumer's execution and a resume is executed. The resume makes prod inactive and activates the coroutine associated with the object of the member call, cons. Control transfers after the last inactive point in cons, which is the suspend in cons's main member. The consumer prints a termination message and its main member terminates. When main terminates, the special termination rule applies, which activates the coroutine that *first* resumed (activated) this coroutine. For cons, the starting coroutine was prod, so cons terminates and cannot be resumed again, and prod reactivates after the resume in consumer member stop (dashed line in the diagram).

The stop member returns and prod's main member terminates. When main terminates, the special termination rule applies, which activates the coroutine that *first* resumed this coroutine. For prod, the starting coroutine was the anonymous coroutine for uMain::main, so prod terminates and cannot be resumed again, and the anonymous coroutine for uMain::main reactivates after the resume in start. The start member returns and uMain::main terminates, activating the coroutine that *first* started it. Hence, this example illustrates terminating all coroutines rather than having uMain::main end with suspended coroutines.

Trace through the program and diagram to see the control flow. The dashed lines at the end of each main show the implicit resume when a coroutine terminates, which go in the reverse direction to the dashed lines that started each coroutine main on the first resume. These lines go back to the coroutine that started the coroutine originally; remember, it is not the order of declaration, but who starts whom. Is the Prod::start member necessary or could the number of loop iterations be passed to Prod::Prod along with the consumer? Depending on your answer to the previous question, does Prod need to be a coroutine or could it be a class?

4.9.2   Full Coroutine Solution

Fig. 4.18 shows a full coroutine producer and consumer coroutine, and a driver routine, along with the stack structure and basic control flow between the producer and consumer. (Actually, the code for member Cons::main must be placed after the definition of Prod because of mutual references.) Starting in member uMain::main,

```
_Coroutine Cons {                                    _Coroutine Prod {
    Prod &prod;          // communication                Cons *cons;          // communication
    int p1, p2, status;                                  int N, money, receipt;
    bool done;                                           void main() { // starter umain
    void main() { // starter prod                            // 1st resume starts here
        // 1st resume starts here                            int i, p1, p2, status;
        int money = 1, receipt;                              for ( i = 0; i < N; i += 1 ) {
        for ( ;; ) {                                             p1 = rand() % 100;
            if ( done ) break;                                   p2 = rand() % 100;
            cout << "cons receives: " <<                         cout << "prod delivers: " <<
                p1 << ", " << p2;                                    p1 << ", " << p2 << endl;
            cout << " and pays $" <<                             status = cons->delivery(p1, p2);
                money << endl;                                   cout << "prod payment of $" <<
            status += 1;                                             money << endl;
            receipt = prod.payment(money);                      cout << "prod status: " <<
            cout << "cons receipt #" <<                              status << endl;
                receipt << endl;                                 receipt += 1;
            money += 1;                                      }
        }                                                    cons->stop();
        cout << "cons stops" << endl;                        cout << "prod stops" << endl;
    }                                                    }
public:                                               public:
    Cons( Prod &p ) : prod(p), status(0),                Prod() : receipt(0) {}
                     done(false) {}                      int payment( int money ) {
    int delivery( int p1, int p2 ) {                         Prod::money = money;
        Cons::p1 = p1;  // activate cons in                  resume();       // activate Cons::delivery
        Cons::p2 = p2;  // Cons::main 1st time               return receipt;
        resume();       // and afterwards cons          }
        return status;  // in Prod::payment            void start( int N, Cons &c ) {
    }                                                        Prod::N = N;  cons = &c;
    void stop() {                                            resume();       // activate umain
        done = true;                                     }
        resume();       // Prod::payment            };
    }                                                void uMain::main() {
};                                                       Prod prod;  Cons cons( prod );
                                                         prod.start( 5, cons );
                                                     }
```

Fig. 4.18 Full coroutine: producer-consumer

the consumer cons is created followed by the producer prod. Since the solution is full coroutining, the consumer needs to be passed to the producer so the producer can reference the consumer, and vice versa. This mutual reference is accomplished using the approach mentioned in Sect. 4.8.2, p. 152, that is, pass the final partner after the other coroutines are created. In this example, the partner member is combined with the start member. A call is then made to the start member of the producer to start the producer coroutine, passing both the number of values generated by the producer and the partner for prod.

The start member in Prod communicates both the number of elements to be produced and the consumer to the coroutine main by copying the parameters to class variables, which are accessible to the member main. Next, a resume is executed, which makes the anonymous coroutine for uMain::main inactive and starts the coroutine associated with the object of the member call, prod. Control transfers to the beginning of prod's main member because it is the first resume (dashed line in the diagram), and the anonymous coroutine for uMain::main is remembered as the starting coroutine for subsequent termination.

The producer's main member creates local variables that are retained between subsequent activations of the coroutine. Like the semi-coroutine version, the main member executes N iterations of generating two random integer values between 0–99, printing the two values, calling the consumer to deliver the two values, and printing the status returned from the consumer.

The call from the producer to the consumer's delivery member transfers data from producer to consumer. When delivery is called, it is the producer coroutine, prod, executing the member. The values delivered by the producer are copied into communication variables in the consumer and a resume is executed. The resume makes prod inactive and activates the coroutine associated with the object of the member call, cons. Control transfers to the beginning of cons's main member because it is the first resume (dashed line in the diagram), and coroutine prod is remembered as the starting coroutine for subsequent termination.

The consumer's main member creates local variables that are retained between subsequent activations of the coroutine. The main member iterates until the done flag is set, printing the two values delivered, incrementing the status for returning, printing the amount it pays for the values, calling back to the producer's payment member, printing the receipt from the producer, and incrementing the amount of money for the next payment.

It is the call from the consumer to the producer's payment member that makes this a full coroutine solution because it forms a cycle between producer and consumer. When payment is called, it is the consumer coroutine, cons, executing the member. The value delivered by the consumer is copied into a communication variable, the value is printed, and a resume is executed. The resume makes cons inactive and activates the coroutine associated with the object of the member call, prod. Control transfers to the point where prod was last made inactive and it continues, which is in member delivery after the resume.

The delivery member returns the status value at the call in prod's main member, where the status is printed. The loop then repeats calling delivery, where each call

resumes the consumer coroutine. When the consumer is made active it continues
after the point where it was last made inactive, which is the resume in payment. The
consumer increments the receipt and returns the receipt value to the call in cons's
main member. The loop then repeats calling payment, where each call resumes the
producer coroutine.

After iterating N times, the producer calls the stop member in cons. When stop
is called, it is the producer coroutine, prod, executing the member. The done flag is
set to stop the consumer's execution and a resume is executed. The resume makes
prod inactive and activates the coroutine associated with the object of the member
call, cons. Control transfers after the last inactive point in cons, which is the resume
in payment, which returns with the last receipt. The consumer prints the last receipt,
terminates its loops because done is true, prints a termination message and its main
member terminates. When main terminates, the special termination rule applies,
which activates the coroutine that *first* resumed (activated) this coroutine. For cons,
the starting coroutine was prod, so cons terminates and cannot be resumed again,
and prod reactivates after the resume in stop (dashed line in the diagram).

The stop member returns and prod's main member terminates. When main
terminates, the special termination rule applies, which activates the coroutine that
first resumed this coroutine. For prod, the starting coroutine was the anonymous
coroutine for uMain::main, so prod terminates and cannot be resumed again, and the
anonymous coroutine for uMain::main reactivates after the resume in start. The start
member returns and uMain::main terminates, activating the coroutine that *first* started
it. Hence, this example illustrates terminating all coroutines rather than having
uMain::main end with suspended coroutines.

Trace through the starting of the two coroutines until both coroutine main
routines are running. At this point, the full coroutine cycle begins. Trace through the
full coroutine cycle to see how it passes both control and data between the producer
and consumer. Note, the resume in member payment activates the execution state
of Prod::main and it continues in member Cons::delivery. Similarly, the resume in
member delivery activates the execution state of Cons::main and it continues in
member Prod::payment. Finally, trace through the stopping sequence to see how the
full coroutine cycle is broken allowing the coroutines to terminate programmatically
instead of deleting suspended coroutines in uMain::main.

The decision to use full coroutining relates to the need for mutually recursive
references among the objects, i.e., there is a call cycle, where these calls need to
resume their associated coroutine; otherwise semi-coroutining can be used.

4.10   Nonlocal Propagation

A local exception within a coroutine behaves like an exception within a routine
or class, with one nonlocal difference. An exception raised and not handled
inside a coroutine terminates it and implicitly raises a nonlocal exception of type

uBaseCoroutine::UnHandledException at the coroutine's last resumer rather than performing the default action of aborting the program. For example, in:

```
_Event E {};
_Coroutine C {
    void main() { _Throw E(); }
  public:
    void mem() { resume(); }
};
void uMain::main() {
    C c;
    try {
        c.mem();
    } _CatchResume( uBaseCoroutine::UnhandledException ) {...}
}
```

the call to c.mem resumes coroutine c, and then inside c.main an exception is raised that is not handled locally by c. When the exception of type E reaches the top of c's stack without finding an appropriate handler, coroutine c is terminated and the nonlocal exception of type uBaseCoroutine::UnHandledException is implicitly raised at uMain, since it is c's last resumer. This semantics reflects the fact that the last resumer is most capable of understanding and reacting to a failure of the operation it just invoked. Furthermore, the last resumer can always be activated because it became inactive when it did the last resume. Finally, when the last resumer is activated, the implicitly raised nonlocal exception is immediately delivered because the context switch back to it *implicitly enables* uBaseCoroutine::UnHandledException, which triggers the propagation of the exception.

A nonlocal exception can be used to affect control flow with respect to *sequential* execution *among* coroutines. That is, a source execution raises an exception at a faulting execution; propagation occurs in the faulting execution. The faulting execution polls at certain points to check for pending nonlocal-exceptions; when nonlocal exceptions are present, the oldest matching exception is propagated, i.e., First-In First-Out (FIFO) service, as if it had been raised locally at the point of the poll. Nonlocal exceptions among coroutines are possible because each coroutine has its own execution-state (stack). For example, in Fig. 4.19 coroutine C is started in its constructor so it can enable nonlocal exceptions and suspend after initialization. uMain then raises a nonlocal exception Since coroutine control-flow is sequential, the exception type E is not propagated immediately. In fact, the exception can only be propagated the next time coroutine c becomes active. Hence, uMain must make a call to c.mem so mem resumes c, and the pending exception propagates from the suspend and is caught by the handler for E. If multiple nonlocal-exceptions are raised at a coroutine, the exceptions are delivered serially but only when the coroutine becomes active. Note, *nonlocal exceptions are initially turned off for a coroutine*, so handlers can be set up *before* any nonlocal exception can be propagated. Propagation of nonlocal exceptions is turned on via the **_Enable** statement (see Sect. 5.11.1, p. 217). To ensure nonlocal exceptions are enabled, the constructor for C resumes C::main to execute the **_Enable** statement *before* any calls to the coroutine can occur. Since, C::main has started and is suspended in the **for**

```
_Event E {};
_Coroutine C {
    void main() {
        try {
            _Enable {   // allow nonlocal exceptions
                ... suspend(); ...
            }              // disable all nonlocal exceptions
        } catch( E ) { ... }
    }
    public:
        C() { resume(); }    // prime loop
        void mem() { resume(); }
};
void uMain::main() {
    C c;
    _Resume E() _At c;  // exception pending
    c.mem();            // trigger exception
}
```

Fig. 4.19 Nonlocal propagation

loop, the nonlocal exception thrown by uMain propagates out of the call to suspend to the catch clause for the exception of type E.

4.11 Summary

There exist a class of problems that experience major control-flow problems when the location of either the input or output is changed by modularizing the code into a routine or class, e.g., series generators, print-formatters, tokenizers, parsers, and iterators. When written as a stand-alone program, these problems can be constructed with the basic control-flow constructs; however, when modularized, the solutions require the ability to remember information between module invocations. Depending on the implementation mechanism used, both data and execution-state can be retained across calls. While it is straightforward to understand how to retain and use saved data (information) between calls, it is more difficult to appreciate the notion of retaining execution state between calls. And yet, it is the ability to preserve the execution state and its associated context between calls that is the more powerful concept, and which significantly simplifies the implementation of this class of problems. The coroutine is one of a small number of programming-language constructs that supports saving both data and execution-state across calls to its members and the coroutine main, and hence, it provides an ideal modularization mechanism for this class of problems.

Coroutines do not appear often in a program, but when needed, they are invaluable. A coroutine cannot be simulated with simpler constructs without violating encapsulation or coding explicit execution states, both of which are unacceptable tradeoffs of the weak equivalence between coroutines and routines or classes. Coroutines are divided into two kinds: semi and full. A semi-coroutine is the most common kind of coroutine. It suspends and resumes to and from the coroutine main like a call and return moves to and from a routine. A full coroutine appears infrequently and in esoteric situations, like a device driver in an operating system. It forms call cycles like a recursive routine, and therefore, is more complex to create and understand. Finally, routines and coroutines may interact freely, i.e., routines may call coroutines, which may call routines, and calls may be recursive within routines or coroutines; all combinations of interactions are possible.

4.12   Questions

1. Explain the fundamental change in call/return control-flow provided by coroutines. Give a simple example.
2. What class of problems is best implemented using coroutines?
3. Explain the difference between a *semi-coroutine* and a *full-coroutine*.
4. Explain when a context switch occurs in coroutining and what happens during a context switch with respect to the coroutine's state.
5. Both suspend() and resume() members are composed of two parts with respect to the actions taken in inactivating and reactivating coroutines. Explain exactly which coroutine is inactivated and which is reactivated for each member.
6. Why is main in a coroutine normally a private/protected member?
7. What is special about the first resume() of a coroutine?
8. Give an advantage for restricting the placement of resume() to within a coroutine's member routines.
9. Explain why a programmer might want to put a resume in a coroutine's constructor.
10. Why does a coroutine need its own stack?
11. When is a coroutine's stack created?
12. Explain the difference between stackless and stackfull coroutines.
13. What is the special termination rule for coroutines in μC++?
14. Explain the 3 basic phases in all full coroutine programs (also necessary in a semi-coroutine program, too).
15. Both the suspend and resume members are composed of two parts with respect to the actions taken in inactivating and reactivating coroutines. Explain exactly which coroutine is inactivated and which is activated for each special coroutine member.
16. How can a coroutine be simulated in a language that does not provide them?
17. Write a *semi-coroutine* with the following public interface (you may only add a public destructor and private members):

```
_Coroutine grammar {
    char ch;                    // character passed by cocaller
    int status;                 // current status of match: 0, 1, 2
  public:
    int next( char c ) {
        ch = c;
        resume();
        return status;
    }
};
```

which verifies a string of characters matches the language $x_1(x_2x_3)^+x_1$, that is, a character x_1, followed by one or more pairs of characters x_2x_3, followed by the character x_1, where $x_1 \neq x_2$, e.g.:

valid strings	invalid strings
xyzx	x
ababaa	ababa
a b ba	a bba
xyyyyx	xyx
#@%@%@%#	##@#@#

After creation, the coroutine is resumed with a series of characters from a string (one character at a time). The coroutine returns a value for each character:

- 0 means continue sending characters, may yet be a valid string of the language,
- 1 means the characters form a valid string of the language and no more characters can be sent,
- 2 means the last character resulted in a string not of the language.

After the coroutine returns a value of 1 or 2, it must terminate; sending more characters to the coroutine after this point is undefined.

Write a program grammar that checks if a string is in the above language. The shell interface to the grammar program is as follows:

grammar [filename]

(Square brackets indicate optional command line parameters, and do not appear on the actual command line.) If no input file name is specified, input comes from standard input. Output is sent to standard output. *For any specified command-line file, check it exists and can be opened. You may assume I/O reading and writing do not result in I/O errors.*

The program should:

- read a line from the file,
- create a grammar coroutine,
- pass characters from the input line to the coroutine one at time while the coroutine returns 0,
- print an appropriate message when the coroutine returns 1 or 2,
- terminate the coroutine,

- print out result information, and
- repeat these steps for each line in the file.

If there are any additional characters (including whitespace) on a line after the coroutine returns 1 or 2, print an appropriate warning message about the additional characters. For every non-empty input line, print the line and the string yes if the line is in the language and the string no otherwise; print an appropriate warning for an empty input line (i.e., a line containing only '\n'). The following is some example output:

```
"xyzx" : "xyzx" yes
"ababaa" : "ababaa" yes
"a b ba" : "a b ba" yes
"xyyyyx" : "xyyyyx" yes
"#@%@%@%#" : "#@%@%@%#" yes
"xyyyyxabc" : "xyyyyx" yes -- extraneous characters "abc"
"x" : "x" no
"xab" : "xab" no
"" : Warning! Blank line.
"abab" : "abab" no
"a bba" : "a b bb" no -- extraneous characters "a"
"xyx" : "xyx" no
"##@#@#" : "##" no -- extraneous characters "@#@#"
```

18. Write a *semi-coroutine* with the following public interface (you may only add a public destructor and private members):

```
_Coroutine FloatConstant {
    public:
        enum Status { CONT, MATCH, ERROR };    // possible status
    private:
        Status status;                         // current status of match
        char ch;                               // character passed by cocaller
        void main();                           // coroutine main
    public:
        Status next( char c ) {
            ch = c;                            // communication in
            resume();                          // activate
            return status;                     // communication out
        }
};
```

which verifies a string of characters corresponds to a C++ floating-point constant described by the following grammar:

floating-constant : $sign_{opt}$ *fractional-constant exponent-part$_{opt}$ floating-suffix$_{opt}$* |
   $sign_{opt}$ *digit-sequence exponent-part floating-suffix$_{opt}$*
fractional-constant :   *digit-sequence$_{opt}$* "." *digit-sequence* | *digit-sequence* "."
exponent-part :   { "e" | "E" } $sign_{opt}$ *digit-sequence*
sign :   "+" | "-"
digit-sequence :   *digit* | *digit-sequence digit*
floating-suffix :   "f" | "l" | "F" | "L"
digit :   "0" | "1" | "2" | "3" | "4" | "5" | "6" | "7" | "8" | "9"

where X_{opt} means $X \mid \epsilon$ and ϵ means empty. In addition, there is a maximum of 16 digits for the mantissa (non-exponent digits) and 3 digits for the characteristic (exponent digits). For example, the following are valid C/C++ floating-point constants:

```
123.456
-.099
+555.
2.7E+1
-3.555E-12
```

After creation, the coroutine is resumed with a series of characters from a string (one character at a time). The coroutine returns a status for each character:

- CONT means continue sending characters, may yet be a valid string of the language,
- MATCH means the characters currently form a valid substring of a floating-point constant (e.g., 1., .1) but more characters can be sent (e.g., e12),
- ERROR means the last character resulted in a string that is not a floating-point constant.

If there are no more characters to pass to the coroutine while the coroutine is returning CONT, the text is not a floating-point constant. If there are no more characters to pass to the coroutine while the coroutine is returning MATCH, the text is a floating-point constant. If there are characters to pass to the coroutine while the coroutine is returning CONT or MATCH, the text may be a floating-point constant. If there are characters to pass to the coroutine while the coroutine is returning MATCH but the string is complete (e.g., 1.0F), the next character passed to the coroutine returns a value of ERROR. If the coroutine returns ERROR, the text is not a floating-point constant. After the coroutine returns a value of ERROR, it must terminate; sending more characters to the coroutine after this point is undefined.

Write a program floatconstant that checks if a string is a floating-point constant. The shell interface to the floatconstant program is as follows:

floatconstant [infile]

(Square brackets indicate optional command line parameters, and do not appear on the actual command line.) If no input file name is specified, input comes from standard input. Output is sent to standard output. For any specified command-line file, check it exists and can be opened. You may assume I/O reading and writing do not result in I/O errors.

The program should:

- read a line from the file,
- create a FloatConstant coroutine,
- pass characters from the input line to the coroutine one at time while the coroutine returns CONT or MATCH,
- stop passing characters when there are no more or the coroutine returns ERROR,
- terminate the coroutine,
- print out result information, and
- repeat these steps for each line in the file.

For every non-empty input line, print the line, how much of the line is parsed, and the string yes if the string is a valid floating-point constant and the string no otherwise. If there are extra characters on a line after parsing, print these characters with an appropriate warning. Print an appropriate warning for an empty input line, i.e., a line containing only '\n'. The following is some example output:

```
"+1234567890123456." : "+1234567890123456." yes
"+12.E-2" : "+12.E-2" yes
"-12.5" : "-12.5" yes
"12." : "12." yes
"-.5" : "-.5" yes
".1E+123" : ".1E+123" yes
"-12.5F" : "-12.5F" yes
"" : Warning! Blank line.
"a" : "a" no
"+." : "+." no
" 12.0" : " " no, extra characters "12.0"
"12.0  " : "12.0 " no, extra characters "  "
"1.2.0a" : "1.2." no, extra characters "0a"
"0123456789.0123456E-0124" : "0123456789.0123456" no, extra characters "E-0124"
```

Assume a *valid* floating-point constant starts at the beginning of the input line, i.e., there is no leading whitespace. See the C library routine isdigit(c), which returns true if character c is a digit.

19. Write a *semi-coroutine* to verify a string of bytes is a valid Unicode Transformation Format 8-bit character (UTF-8). UTF-8 allows any universal character to be represented while maintaining full backwards-compatibility with ASCII encoding, which is achieved by using a variable-length encoding. The following table provides a summary of the Unicode value ranges in hexadecimal, and how they are represented in binary for UTF-8.

Unicode ranges	UTF-8 binary encoding
000000-00007F	0xxxxxxx
000080-0007FF	110xxxxx 10xxxxxx
000800-00FFFF	1110xxxx 10xxxxxx 10xxxxxx
010000-10FFFF	11110xxx 10xxxxxx 10xxxxxx 10xxxxxx

(UTF-8 is restricted to U+10FFFF so it matches the constraints of the UTF-16 character encoding.) For example, the symbol £ is represented by Unicode value 0xA3 (binary 1010 0011). Since £ falls within the range of 0x80 to 0x7FF, it is encoded by the UTF-8 bit string 110xxxxx 10xxxxxx. To fit the character into the eleven bits of the UTF-8 encoding, it is padded on the left with zeroes to 00010100011. The UTF-8 encoding becomes 11000010 10100011, where the x's are replaced with the 11-bit binary encoding giving the UTF-8 character encoding 0xC2A3 for symbol £. Note, UTF-8 is a minimal encoding; e.g., it is incorrect to represent the value 0 by any encoding other than the first one. Use unformatted I/O to read the Unicode bytes and the public interface given in Fig. 4.20 (you may only add a public constructor/destructor and private members)

```
_Coroutine Utf8 {
  public:
    _Event Match {
    public:
      unsigned int unicode;
      Match( unsigned int unicode ) : unicode( unicode ) {}
    };
    _Event Error {};
  private:
    union UTF8 {
      unsigned char ch;              // character passed by cocaller
      struct {                        // types for 1st UTF-8 byte
        unsigned char dt : 7;        // data
        unsigned char ck : 1;        // check
      } t1;
      struct {
        unsigned char dt : 5;        // data
        unsigned char ck : 3;        // check
      } t2;
      struct {
        // YOU FIGURE IT OUT
      } t3;
      struct {
        // YOU FIGURE IT OUT
      } t4;
      struct {                        // type for extra UTF-8 bytes
        // YOU FIGURE IT OUT
      } dt;
    } utf8;
    // YOU MAY ADD PRIVATE MEMBERS
  public:
    // YOU MAY ADD CONSTRUCTOR/DESTRUCTOR IF NEEDED
    void next( unsigned char c ) {
      utf8.ch = c;                    // insert character into union for analysis
      resume();
    }
};
```

Fig. 4.20 UTF-8 interface

After creation, the coroutine is resumed with a series of bytes from a string (one byte at a time). The coroutine suspends after each byte or throws one of these two exceptions:

- Match means the bytes form a valid encoding and no more bytes can be sent,
- Error means the bytes form an invalid encoding and no more bytes can be sent.

Throw Error for an incorrectly encoded-byte or a correct encoding that falls outside the accepted range. For example, the bytes 0xe09390 (11100000 1001 0011 1001 000) form a 3-byte UTF-8 character (known from the first byte). However, the character is invalid because its value 0x4d0 (xx010011 xx010000) < 0x800, the lower bound for a 3-byte UTF-8 character. This error can be detected at the second byte, but all three bytes must be read to allow finding the start of the next UTF-8 character for a sequence of UTF-8 characters or extra characters in this question.

After the coroutine throws an exception, it must terminate; sending more bytes to the coroutine after this point is undefined.

Write a program utf8 that checks if a string follows the UTF-8 encoding. The shell interface to the utf8 program is as follows:

    utf8 [filename]

(Square brackets indicate optional command line parameters, and do not appear on the actual command line.) If no input file name is specified, input comes from standard input. Output is sent to standard output. Issue appropriate runtime error messages for incorrect usage or if a file cannot be opened.

The input file contains an unknown number of UTF-8 characters separated by newline characters. Hence, the value 0xa cannot be a UTF-8 character as it denotes newline (' \n'). For every non-empty input line, print the bytes of the UTF-8 character in hexadecimal as each is checked. If a valid UTF-8 character is found, print "valid" followed by the Unicode value of the UTF-8 character in hexadecimal; if an invalid UTF-8 character is found, print "invalid". If there are any additional bytes on a line after determining if a byte sequence is valid/invalid, the coroutine throws Match or Error, print an appropriate warning message and the additional bytes in hexadecimal. Print a warning for an empty input line (i.e., a line containing only ' \n'). **Hint:** to print a character in hexadecimal use the following cast:

    char ch = 0xff;
    std::cout << std::hex << (unsigned int)(unsigned char)ch << std::endl;

The following is example output:

    0x23 : valid 0x23
    0x23 : valid 0x23. Extra characters 0x23
    0xd790 : valid 0x5d0
    0xd7 : invalid
    0xc2a3 : valid 0xa3
    : Warning! Blank line.
    0xb0 : invalid
    0xe0e3 : invalid
    0xe98080 : valid 0x9000
    0xe98080 : valid 0x9000. Extra characters 0xfff8
    0xe09390 : invalid
    0xff : invalid. Extra characters 0x9a84
    0xf09089 : invalid
    0xf0908980 : valid 0x10240
    0x1 : valid 0x1

WARNING: On little-endian architectures (e.g., like AMD/Intel x86), the compiler reverses the bit order; hence, the bit-fields in variable utf8 above must be reversed. While it is unfortunate C/C++ bit-fields lack portability across hardware architectures, they are the highest-level mechanism to manipulate bit-specific information. Your assignment will only be tested on a little endian computer.

20. Write a *semi-coroutine* to sort a set of values into ascending order using a binary-tree insertion method. This method constructs a binary tree of the data values, which can subsequently be traversed to retrieve the values in sorted order. Construct a binary tree without balancing it, so that the values 25, 6, 9, 5, 99, 100, 101, 7 produce the tree:

```
     25
  6     99
 5  9      100
 7          101
```

By traversing the tree in infix order—go left if possible, return value, go right if possible—the values are returned in sorted order. Instead of constructing the binary tree with each vertex having two pointers and a value, build the tree using a coroutine for each vertex. Hence, each coroutine in the tree contains two other coroutines and a value. (A coroutine must be self-contained, i.e., it cannot access any global variables in the program.)

The coroutine has the following interface (you may only add a public destructor and private members):

```
template<typename T> _Coroutine Binsertsort {
    const T Sentinel;          // value denoting end of set
    T value;                   // communication: value being passed down/up tree
    void main();               // YOU WRITE THIS ROUTINE
  public:
    Binsertsort( T Sentinel ) : Sentinel( Sentinel ) {}
    void sort( T value ) {     // value to be sorted
        Binsertsort::value = value;
        resume();
    }
    T retrieve() {             // retrieve sorted value
        resume();
        return value;
    }
};
```

Assume type T has operators == and <= (or <), and public default and copy constructor. Each value for sorting is passed to the coroutine via member sort. When passed the first value, v, the coroutine stores it in variable pivot. Each subsequent value is compared to pivot. If v <= pivot, a Binsertsort coroutine called less is resumed with v; if v > pivot, a Binsertsort coroutine called greater resumed with v. Each of the two coroutines, less and greater, creates two more coroutines in turn. The result is a binary tree of identical coroutines. The coroutines less and greater must not be created by calls to **new**, i.e., no dynamic allocation is necessary in this coroutine.

The end of the set of values is signaled by passing the value Sentinel; Sentinel is initialized when the sort coroutine is created via its constructor. (The Sentinel is not considered to be part of the set of values.) When a coroutine receives a value of Sentinel, it indicates end-of-unsorted-values, and the coroutine resumes its left branch (if it exists) with a value of Sentinel, prepares to receive the sorted values from the left branch and pass them back up the tree until it receives a value of Sentinel from that branch. The coroutine then passes up its pivot value.

Next, the coroutine resumes its right branch (if it exists) with a value of Sentinel, prepares to receive the sorted values from the right branch and pass them back up the tree until it receives a value of Sentinel from that branch. Finally, the coroutine passes up a value of Sentinel to indicate end-of-sorted-values and the coroutine terminates. (Note, the coroutine does not print out the sorted values it simply passes them to its resumer.)

Remember to handle the special cases where a set of values is 0 or 1, e.g., Sentinel being passed as the first or second value to the coroutine. These cases must be handled by the coroutine versus special cases in the uMain::main program. Show Binsertsort can sort any type (like a structure with multiple values forming the key) providing operator == and <= (or similar operations depending on your implementation).

The executable program is named binsertsort and has the following shell interface:

binsertsort unsorted-file [sorted-file]

(Square brackets indicate optional command line parameters, and do not appear on the actual command line.) The type of the input values and the sentinel value are provided as preprocessor variables.

- If the unsorted input file is not specified, print an appropriate usage message and terminate. The input file contains lists of unsorted values. Each list starts with the number of values in that list. For example, the input file:

```
8 25 6 8 5 99 100 101 7
3 1 3 5
0
10 9 8 7 6 5 4 3 2 1 0
```

contains 4 lists with 8, 3, 0 and 10 values in each list. (The line breaks are for readability only; values can be separated by any white-space character and appear across any number of lines.)

Assume the first number in the input file is always present and correctly specifies the number of following values. Assume all following values are correctly formed so no error checking is required on the input data, and none of the following values are the Sentinel value.
- If no output file name is specified, use standard output. Print the original input list followed by the sorted list, as in:

```
25 6 8 5 99 100 101 7
5 6 7 8 25 99 100 101

1 3 5
1 3 5
```

blank line from list of length 0 (not actually printed)
blank line from list of length 0 (not actually printed)

```
9 8 7 6 5 4 3 2 1 0
0 1 2 3 4 5 6 7 8 9
```

for the previous input file. End each set of output with a blank line.

• Print an appropriate error message and terminate the program if unable to open
  the given files.
21. Write a semi-coroutine that extracts messages (i.e., byte sequences of a speci-
    fied format) from a byte stream. The coroutine is resumed for every byte read
    from the stream. When a complete message has been identified, the coroutine
    makes the message available to the cocaller and terminates.

    A message starts with an STX character (octal value 002), followed by up to
    64 bytes of data, an ETX character (octal value 003), and a 2-byte check sum
    (CHS). For example (all values are in octal):

    002, |145,142,147, ... ,135,|003, |164,031
    STX | data |ETX |CHS

Characters such as ETX may appear in the message but they will be preceded
by an ESC character (octal value 033). When an ESC character is found in the
message, it is ignored and the next character is read as is. Messages may be
separated by arbitrary bytes; in this assignment, you should assume that the
bytes between messages are different from STX.

    Embed the coroutine in a test program that reads a byte stream from standard
input, and writes only the data portions of the identified messages on separate
lines to standard output. The test program should check that each message was
transmitted correctly by performing the following calculation on the data bytes
of the message and comparing the result with the CHS value.

$$\sum_{i=1}^{n} byte_i \quad \text{where } n \text{ is the number of bytes in the message.}$$

Do NOT include control characters STX, ETX, ESC or the CHS bytes in this
summation. The only exception to this rule is if one of the control characters
is escaped in the data portion of the message. If the message was transmitted
incorrectly, print an appropriate error message along with the message.

    Do not attempt to print files that contain control characters (e.g., STX, ETX,
ESC) directly on the line printer. Use the following command sequence to print
files containing control characters:

    od -av *your-test-file* | lpr *regular printer options BUT NO file name*

22. Write a program that filters a stream of text. The filter semantics are specified
    by command-line options. The program creates a *semi-coroutine* filter for each
    command-line option joined together in a pipeline with a reader filter at the
    input end of the pipeline, followed by the command-line filters in the middle of
    the pipeline (maybe zero), and a writer filter at the output end of the pipeline.
    Control passes from the reader, through the filters, and to the writer, ultimately
    returning back to the reader. One character moves along the pipeline at any
    time. For example, a character starts from the reader filter, may be deleted or
    transformed by the command-line filters, and any character reaching the writer
    filter is printed.

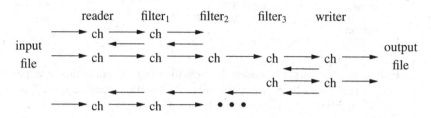

(In the following, you may not add, change or remove prototypes or given members; you may add a destructor and/or private and protected members.)

Each filter must inherit from the abstract class Filter:

```
_Coroutine Filter {
protected:
    static const unsigned char End_Filter = '\377';
    unsigned char ch;
public:
    void put( unsigned char c ) {
        ch = c;
        resume();
    }
};
```

which ensures each filter has a put routine that can be called to transfer a character along the pipeline.

The reader reads characters from the specified input file and passes these characters to the first coroutine in the filter:

```
_Coroutine Reader : public Filter {
    // YOU MAY ADD PRIVATE MEMBERS
public:
    Reader( Filter *f, istream *i );
};
```

The reader constructor is passed the next filter object, which the reader passes one character at a time from the input stream, and an input stream object from which the reader reads characters. No coroutine calls the put routine of the reader; all other coroutines have their put routine called.

The writer is passed characters from the last coroutine in the filter pipeline and writes these characters to the specified output file:

```
_Coroutine Writer : public Filter {
    // YOU MAY ADD PRIVATE MEMBERS
public:
    Writer( ostream *o );
};
```

The writer constructor is passed an output stream object to which this filter writes characters that have been filtered along the pipeline. No filter is passed to the writer because it is at the end of the pipeline.

All other filters have the following interface:

```
_Coroutine filter-name : public Filter {
    // YOU MAY ADD PRIVATE MEMBERS
    public:
        filter-name( Filter *f, ... );
};
```

Each filter constructor is passed the next filter object, which this filter passes one character at a time after performing its filtering action, and "..." is any additional information needed to perform the filtering action.

The pipeline is built by uMain from writer to reader, in reverse order to the data flow. Each newly created coroutine is passed to the constructor of its predecessor coroutine in the pipeline. The reader's constructor resumes itself to begin the flow of data, and it calls the put routine of the next filter to begin moving characters through the pipeline to the writer. Normal characters, as well as control characters (e.g., '\n', '\t'), are passed through the pipeline. When the reader reaches end-of-file, it passes the sentinel character '\377' through the pipeline and then terminates. Similarly, each coroutine along the filter must pass the sentinel character through the pipeline and then terminate. The writer does not print the sentinel character. uMain ends when the reader declaration completes, implying all the input characters have been read and all the filter coroutines are terminated. The reader coroutine can read characters one at a time or in groups; the writer coroutine can write characters one at a time or in groups.

Filter options are passed to the program via command line arguments. For each filter option, create the appropriate coroutine and connect it into the pipeline. If no filter options are specified, then the output should simply be an echo of the input from the reader to the writer. *Assume all filter options are correctly specified, i.e., no error checking is required on the filter options.*

The filter options that must be supported are:

-h   The *hex dump* option replaces each character in the stream with its corresponding ASCII 2-hexadecimal digit value. For example, the character 'a' is transformed into the two characters '6' and '1', as 61 is the ASCII hexadecimal value for character 'a'. The hexadecimal filter also formats its output by transforming two characters into 4 hexadecimal digits, adding one space, transforming two characters into 4 hexadecimal digits, adding three spaces, repeating this sequence four times, and adding a newline. For example, this input sequence:

The quick brown fox jumps over the lazy dog.

generates the following:

```
5468 6520    7175 6963    6b20 6272    6f77 6e20
666f 7820    6a75 6d70    7320 6f76    6572 2074
6865 206c    617a 7920    646f 672e    0a
```

Note, it is possible to convert a character to its hexadecimal value using a simple, short expression.

-s   The *capitalize* option capitalizes the first letter of every sentence. A
sentence starts with the letter following whitespace (space, tab, newline)
(isspace) characters after a period, question mark, or exclamation point.
If the starting letter is lowercase (islower), the filter transforms the letter
to uppercase. The first letter character in the pipeline is a special case and
should be capitalized even though there is no preceding whitespace.

-w   The *whitespace* option removes all spaces and tabs (isblank) from the
start and end of lines, and collapses multiple spaces and tabs within a line
into a single space. Lines are delimited by the newline character ($'\n'$).

-T *base-width*   The *triangle* option arranges the characters in the input
stream into a *triangle* shape. (Assume a space separates -T and *base-
width*.) The triangle is isosceles with a base width of *base-width* characters. The base width must be odd; increment an even value so it is odd.
For example, this input sequence:

  The_quick_brown_fox_jumps_over_the_lazy_dog.

and a base width of 9, generates the following:

```
T
he_
quick
_brown_
fox_jumps

_
ove
r_the
_lazy_d
og.
```

Progressively fewer spaces are added before characters to form a triangle
until a row of 9 characters (base-width) is reached and then a newline is
added. There are no spaces added at the end of each line. A tab or newline
input character is changed to a single space. The triangles are repeated
until the input ends, forming a connected chain.

The order in which filter options appear on the command line is significant,
i.e., the left-to-right order of the filter options on the command line is the first-to-
last order of the filter coroutines. As well, a filter option may appear more than
once in a command. Each filter should be constructed without regard to what
any other filters do, i.e., there is no communication among filters using global
variables; all information is passed using member put. **Hint:** scan the command
line left-to-right to locate and remember the position of each option, and then
scan the option-position information right-to-left (reverse order) to create the
filters with their specified arguments.

The executable program is to be named filter and has the following shell
interface:

filter [*-filter-options ...*] [infile [outfile]]

(Square brackets indicate optional command line parameters, and do not appear
on the actual command line.) If filter options appear, assume they appear *before*
the file names. Terminate the program for unknown or insufficient command
arguments, or if an input or output file cannot be opened. Assume any given
argument values are correctly formed, i.e., no error checking is required for
numeric values. If no input file name is specified, input from standard input and
output to standard output. If no output file name is specified, output to standard
output.

23. Write a generic *binary search-tree* and *semi-coroutine* iterators to traverse this
tree using an external iterator. The binary search-tree has two parts: the generic
tree container and the nodes held within the container.

   Each node within the tree container must inherit from the following abstract
type:

```
class Treeable {
    friend class TFriend;
    Treeable *parent, *left, *right;
  public:
    Treeable() { parent = left = right = NULL; }
};
```

so it has a parent pointer, and left and right child pointers. The concrete type (T)
(derived type) must provide operators:

```
T *T::operator=( T & );
bool operator==( T, T );
bool operator<( T, T );
bool operator>( T, T );
ostream &operator<<( ostream &, T & );
```

which are assignment, equality, greater and less than, and output. These
operations are used in copying nodes, inserting and removing nodes from the
binary search-tree, and printing the contents of a node. A node can appear in
only one tree at a time.

   The tree is generic in the nodes it contains:

```
template<typename T> class Tree : protected TFriend {
  public:
    Tree();                         // create empty tree
    virtual ~Tree();                // delete tree nodes
    virtual T *top() const;         // return root node of the tree
    virtual void insert( T * );     // insert a node into the tree (do not copy node)
    virtual void remove( T * );     // remove a node from the tree
};
```

The constructor creates an empty tree after allocation, and the destructor deletes
any tree nodes so the tree is empty for deallocation. In addition, member top
returns the root of the tree, member insert adds a node to the tree (does not
copy the node), and member remove removes a node from the tree. Nodes with
duplicate values may appear in the tree but a node can appear in only one tree.
(Please acknowledge any sources if you copy a binary search-tree algorithm.)

For encapsulation reasons, it is important that users cannot directly access the
pointers in Treeable. Normally these fields would be made **private** and the Tree
type would be a **friend** of Treeable. However, when Tree is a generic type, there
is no single type that can be specified as the friend in Treeable because there are
an infinite number of Tree types. One trick around this problem is to create an
intermediate type, which is the friend, and the intermediate type supplies access
to the private information via inheritance: The intermediate type TFriend:

```
class TFriend {
  protected:
    Treeable *&parent( Treeable *tp ) const {
      return tp->parent;
    }
    Treeable *&left( Treeable *tp ) const {
      return tp->left;
    }
    Treeable *&right( Treeable *tp ) const {
      return tp->right;
    }
};
```

has been used above as the friend of Treeable and its descendants have access
to the private information through TFriend's member routines. In this case, the
access is total, i.e., both read and write, but the technique can be applied in other
cases giving only read or write access as appropriate.

To further ensure abstraction and encapsulation, an iterator is used to traverse
the tree so it is unnecessary to know the internal structure of the tree. This
abstract tree-iterator is used to create specific iterators for accessing the nodes
of a tree:

```
template<typename T> _Coroutine treeIter : protected TFriend {
  public:
    treeIter();
    treeIter( const Tree<T> & );
    virtual void over( const Tree<T> & );
    virtual bool operator>>( T *& );
};
```

The first constructor creates an iterator that works with any tree of type Tree<T>.
The second constructor creates an iterator that is bound to a specific tree of type
Tree<T>. Member over is used to set the tree that is traversed by the iterator (used
with the first constructor). Member >> returns the next node in the traversal
through its parameter and returns **true** if there are more nodes in the tree or
false otherwise (i.e., there are no more nodes in the tree).

Create the following specific iterators for the tree:

a. A preorder tree-iterator coroutine, which returns the tree nodes one at a time
   using a preorder traversal of the tree:

```
template<typename T> _Coroutine preorderTreeIter : public treeIter<T> {
  public:
    preorderTreeIter();
    preorderTreeIter( const Tree<T> & );
};
```

b. An inorder tree-iterator coroutine, which returns the tree nodes one at a time
using an inorder traversal of the tree:

```
template<typename T> _Coroutine inorderTreeIter : public treeIter<T> {
  public:
    inorderTreeIter();
    inorderTreeIter( const Tree<T> & );
};
```

c. A postorder tree-iterator coroutine, which returns the tree nodes one at a time
using a postorder traversal of the tree:

```
template<typename T> _Coroutine postorderTreeIter : public treeIter<T> {
  public:
    postorderTreeIter();
    postorderTreeIter( const Tree<T> & );
};
```

In addition, create the following non-member routines:

a. A non-member routine to recursively delete *all* the nodes of the tree:

```
template<typename T> static void deleteTree( Tree<T> & );
```

b. A non-member routine to recursively print *all* the nodes of the tree:

```
template<typename T> static void printTree( const Tree<T> & );
```

Use inorder traversal for printing the tree.

c. A non-member routine to recursively duplicate (copy) *all* the nodes of the
tree:

```
template<typename T> static void copyTree(Tree<T> &to, const Tree<T> &from);
```

The first parameter is where the copy is made and the second parameter is
where the copy comes from. Delete any existing nodes in the first parameter
before copying the values from the second.

d. A non-member routine to determine whether the fringe (leaf nodes) of two
trees are the same independent of the tree structure.

```
template<typename T> bool sameFringe( const Tree<T> &, const Tree<T> & );
```

e. Design another non-member routine using the tree iterators to perform some
useful action on a tree or trees.

Create appropriate tests illustrating the use of the tree iterators and non-
member routines, such as creating one or more trees and manipulating them.

HINT: several casts are necessary from type Treeable to T when using members left and right in TFriend. Why can these be static casts but are guaranteed
safe? (Include the answer to this question in the program documentation.)

24. Write a *full coroutine* that plays the following card game. Each player takes
a number of cards from a deck of cards and passes the remaining deck to the
player on the left if the number of remaining cards is odd, or to the right if the
number of remaining cards is even. A player must take at least one card and no
more than a certain maximum. The player who takes the last cards wins. If the

```
Players: 5   Cards: 188              Players: 6   Cards: 136
P0     P1     P2     P3     P4       P0     P1     P2     P3     P4     P5
       8:180> 2:178> 2:176> 3:173<                        4:132> 5:127<
4:153< 6:157< 8:163< 2:171< 7:146>                 7:118> 2:125<
3:143< 2:121< 8:123< 8:131< 4:139<                 8:110> 6:104> 7:97<
8:113<               1:110> 2:111<          3:86>  2:89<  6:91<
1:103<                      6:104>          5:72>  6:77<  3:83<
1:99<                       3:100>   3:62>  4:65<  3:69<
6:92>  5:87<                1:98>           4:58>  1:57<
4:83<                       3:80>           3:54>  1:53<
4:76>  7:69<                        2:45<   6:47<                3:40>  2:43>
4:65<  1:50>  4:51<  8:55<  2:63<   6:32>   4:28>  3:25<                2:38>
       3:42>  5:45<                 5:16>   4:21<
       5:32>  5:37<                         4:12>  2:10>  3:7<
              2:30>  2:28>  5:23<           7:0#
              1:14>  8:15<
       5:0#   4:5<   5:9<
```

Fig. 4.21 Card game: example output

number of cards is less than or equal to the maximum, a play always takes all the cards to win.

The interface for a Player is (you may only add a public destructor and private members):

```
_Coroutine Player {
    // YOU MAY ADD PRIVATE MEMBERS
public:
    Player( Printer &printer, unsigned int id );
    void start( Player &lp, Player &rp );
    void play( unsigned int deck );
};
```

The constructor is passed a reference to a printer object and an identification number assigned by the main program. (Use values in the range 0 to $N-1$ for identification values.) To form the circle of players, the start routine is called for each player from uMain::main to pass a reference to the player on the left and right; the start routine also resumes the player coroutine to set uMain as its starter (needed during termination). The play routine receives the deck of cards passed among the players.

All output from the program is generated by calls to a printer, excluding error messages. The interface for the printer is (you may add only a public destructor and private members):

```
class Printer {
    // YOU MAY ADD PRIVATE MEMBERS
public:
    Printer( const unsigned int NoOfPlayers, const unsigned int NoOfCards );
    void prt( const unsigned int id, const unsigned int took );
};
```

The printer attempts to reduce output by condensing the play along a line. Figure 4.21 shows two example outputs from different runs of the program.

Each column is assigned to a player, and a column entry indicates a player's current play "taken:remaining:direction", indicating:

a) the number of cards taken by a player,
b) the number of cards remaining in the deck,
c) the direction the remaining deck is passed, where "<" means to the left, ">" means to the right, and "#" means the game is over.

Player information is buffered in the printer until a play would overwrite a buffer value. At that point, the buffer is flushed (written out) displaying a line of player information. The buffer is cleared by a flush so previously stored values do not appear when the next player flushes the buffer and an empty column is printed. All column spacing can be accomplished using the standard 8-space tabbing; **do not build and store strings of text for output**.

The main program plays G games sequentially, i.e., one game after the other, where G is a command line parameter. For each game, N players are created, where N is a random integer in the range from 2 to 10 inclusive, and one player is passed a deck containing M cards, where M is a random integer in the range from 10 to 200 inclusive. The player passed the deck of cards begins the game, and each player follows the simple strategy of taking C cards, where C is a random integer in the range from 1 to 8 inclusive, until there are less than or equal to 8 cards. **Do not spend time developing complex strategies to win.** At the end of each game, it is unnecessary for a player's coroutine main to terminate but ensure each player is deleted before starting the next game.

The executable program is named cardgame and has the following shell interface:

```
cardgame [ G [ S ] ]
```

G is the number of card games to be played (≥ 0). If no value for G is specified, assume 5. S is the starting seed for the random number generator to allow reproducible results (> 0). If no value for S is specified, initialize the random number generator with an arbitrary seed value (e.g., getpid() or time). Check all command arguments for correct form (integers) and range; print an appropriate usage message and terminate the program if a value is missing or invalid.

25. Write a *full coroutine* that simulates the game of Hot Potato. The game consists of an umpire and a number of players. The umpire starts a *set* by tossing the *hot* potato to a player. What makes the potato *hot* is the timer inside it. The potato is then tossed among the players until the timer goes off. A player never tosses the potato to themselves. The player holding the potato when the timer goes off is eliminated. The potato is then given back to the umpire, who resets the timer in the potato, and begins the game again with the remaining players, unless only one player remains, which the umpire declares the winner.

   · The potato is the item tossed around by the players and it also contains the timer that goes off after a random period of time. The interface for the Potato is (you may only add a public destructor and private members):

```
class Potato {
  public:
    Potato( unsigned int maxTicks = 10 );
    void reset( unsigned int maxTicks = 10 );
    bool countdown();
};
```

The constructor is optionally passed the maximum number of ticks until the timer goes off. The potato chooses a random value between 1 and this maximum for the number of ticks. Member reset is called by the umpire to re-initialize the timer to reuse the potato. Member countdown is called by the players, and returns **true** if the timer has gone off and **false** otherwise. Rather than use absolute time to implement the potato's timer, make each call to countdown be one tick of the clock.

The interface for a Player is (you may only add a public destructor and private members):

```
_Coroutine Player {
    void main();
  public:
    typedef ... PlayerList; // container type of your choice
    Player( Umpire &umpire, unsigned int Id, PlayerList &players );
    unsigned int getId();
    void toss( Potato &potato );
};
```

The type PlayerList is a C++ standard-library container of your choice, containing all the players still in the game. The constructor is passed the umpire, an identification number assigned by the main program, and the container of players still in the game. The member getId returns a player's identification number. If a player is not eliminated while holding the *hot* potato, then the player chooses another player, excluding itself, at random from the list of players and tosses it the potato using its toss member. Use the following approach for the random selection:

```
do {
    next = rand() % numPlayersLeft;
} while ( next == me );
```

The interface for the Umpire is (you may only add a public destructor and private members):

```
_Coroutine Umpire {
    void main();
  public:
    Umpire( Player::PlayerList &players );
    void set( unsigned int player );
};
```

The umpire creates the potato. Its constructor is passed the container with the players still in the game. When a player determines it is eliminated, i.e., the timer went off while holding the potato, it calls set, passing its player identifier so the umpire knows the set is finished. The umpire removes the eliminated player from the list of players, but does not delete the player because it might be used to play some other game. Hence, player coroutines are created and deleted in the main program. The umpire then resets the potato and tosses it to a randomly selected player to start the next set; this toss counts with respect to the timer in the potato.

The executable program is named hotpotato and has the following shell interface:

hotpotato players [seed]

players is the number of players in the game and must be between 2 and 20, inclusive. seed is a value for initializing the random number generator using routine srand. When given a specific seed value, the program must generate the same results for each invocation. If the seed is unspecified, use a random value like the process identifier (getpid) or current time (time), so each run of the program generates different output. When present, assume each argument is an integer value, but it may not be in range; print an appropriate usage message and terminate the program if a value is missing or outside its range. The driver creates the umpire, the players players, with player identifiers from 0 to players–1, and the container holding all the players. It then starts the umpire by calling set with one of the player identifiers, which implies that player has terminated, but since it is still on the list, the game starts with all players.

Make sure that a coroutine's public methods are used for passing information to the coroutine, but not for doing the coroutine's work.

The output should show a dynamic display of the game, i.e., the set number, each player taking their turn (Id identifies a player), and who gets eliminated for each set and the winning player. Output must be both concise and informative, e.g.:

```
5 players in the match
  POTATO will go off after 9 tosses
Set 1:   U -> 4 -> 0 -> 3 -> 2 -> 0 -> 1 -> 4 -> 0 -> 2 is eliminated
  POTATO will go off after 8 tosses
Set 2:   U -> 4 -> 3 -> 0 -> 3 -> 0 -> 3 -> 0 -> 3 is eliminated
  POTATO will go off after 10 tosses
Set 3:   U -> 1 -> 4 -> 0 -> 4 -> 1 -> 4 -> 1 -> 0 -> 4 -> 0 is eliminated
  POTATO will go off after 10 tosses
Set 4:   U -> 1 -> 4 -> 1 -> 4 -> 1 -> 4 -> 1 -> 4 -> 1 -> 4 is eliminated
1 wins the Match!
```

26. A *token-ring algorithm* is used in a distributed system to control access to a shared transmission channel. Multiple nodes, called *stations*, communicate with each other using a shared channel, which forms a ring among stations. Stations can only communicate unidirectionally with each other using the ring, i.e, a station can only directly transmit data to its immediate successor in the ring. A *token* is passed between stations around the ring and a station can only send data when it holds the token. There is only one token in the system, which is passed around the ring until a station has data to send. Write a simulation where each station is represented by a full coroutine. Assume all of the coroutines are identical, distinguishable only by their identification number (id), so there is only one type of full coroutine. Finally, coroutines are structured around the ring in increasing order by their id numbers.

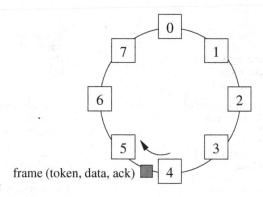

frame (token, data, ack)

Fig. 4.22 Token ring with 8 stations

A token ring with 8 stations is illustrated in Fig. 4.22. The ring represents
the shared transmission channel. The unit of transmission is called a *frame*.
The frame is currently being transmitted from Station 4 to Station 5, clockwise
around the ring. There are three types of frames: *token*, *data*, and *ack* (for
acknowledgment). A token frame represents the right to send, subject to the
priority mechanism explained below. When a station receives the token frame,
it can conceptually hold the token and then send a data frame. The data frame
carries the source and destination id numbers of the sender and receiver stations.
This data frame is then transmitted around the ring until the destination station
is reached. The destination station conceptually removes the data frame and
immediately generates an acknowledgment (ack) frame that is sent around the
ring back to the sender by swapping the source and destination fields in the data
frame. After receiving an ack frame, the source station must forward the token
to its neighbour and wait for the token to return (after at least one transmission
round), before transmitting another data frame or making another reservation
(see below).

The token-ring algorithm has a priority mechanism to control traffic around
the ring. All frames carry a priority field, which is used to reserve the channel
for pending send-requests with a certain priority. Each send request arrives with
a specified priority. When a station has a pending send-request, it compares the
request priority with the current priority in the incoming frame and uses the
following rules:

a. If the frame is a data or ack frame and the frame priority is less than the
   request priority, the station saves the frame priority value (including 0) and
   replaces it with its request priority when forwarding the frame.
b. If the frame is a token frame and the frame priority is less or equal than the
   request priority, the station can send its data frame. If there is a saved priority

```
_Coroutine Station {
    struct Frame {
        enum { Token, Data, Ack } type;          // type of frame
        unsigned int src;                        // source id
        unsigned int dst;                        // destination id
        unsigned int prio;                       // priority
    } frame;

    static unsigned int requests;                // total send requests (if needed)
    void data( Frame frame );                    // pass frame
    void main();                                 // coroutine main
  public:
    Station( unsigned int id );
    void setup( Station *nexthop );              // supply next hop
    void sendreq( unsigned int round, unsigned int dst,
                  unsigned int prio );           // store send request
    void start();                                // inject token and start
}; // Station
```

Fig. 4.23 Station interface

value, the data frame priority is set to the saved priority value (see previous rule) and the saved priority value is deleted. Otherwise the data frame priority is set to the token priority. Note that this rule can never increase the frame priority.

c. Otherwise, the station must not change the frame priority.

The rules for a pending request are summarized in the following table:

Frame priority	Frame type		
	Token	Data or Passing Ack	Ack To Self
Higher than request	Wait	Wait	Wait
Equal to request	Send	Wait	Wait
Lower than request	Send	Reserve	Wait

In this simulation, time is measured in transmission rounds, starting from 0. Each station increments its local round counter whenever a frame (or the combination of data + ack frame) makes a full transmission round and arrives back at the station. In combination with the priority mechanism, this means frames are not always sent during the requested round.

The executable program is named tokenring and has the following shell interface:

```
tokenring S [ F ]
```

S is the number of stations (coroutines) in the ring and must be a positive integer. Station Ids are numbered 0..S-1. The program must support 2-100 stations. F is an optional file name for reading send requests. If the file name is not present, input must be read from standard input.

Write a *full coroutine* with the interface given in Fig. 4.23 (you may add only a public destructor and private members). To form the ring of stations, uMain::main calls the setup member for each station to pass a pointer to the coroutine's next hop. After uMain::main initializes the ring, it reads all send requests from the given input source and calls sendreq to store send requests at the respective source station. Each station must store all its send requests at the beginning and work through them during the simulation. After processing the input file, uMain::main calls the start member of Station 0 to start the simulation. The start member creates a token frame with priority 0 and activates (resumes) the coroutine. Each station then performs the protocol processing by calling the data member of its successor with a frame, and the data member must resume the coroutine for processing the frame (i.e., protocol processing must be done on each coroutine's stack).

A station generates data frames for transmission from external *send requests* that it receives at creation from umain via calls to Station::sendreq. A send request becomes *pending* in the specified round until it can be transmitted around the ring. At each station, send requests are processed in the order of their specified rounds. If multiple send requests are given for the same round, they are processed in the order of input. The input is provided in the following format:

    <round> <src> <dst> <prio>

with

    <round> transmission round
    <src>   source id
    <dst>   destination id
    <prio> priority

For example, given input:

    1 1 3 0
    1 2 1 0
    1 3 1 4
    10 4 2 7

For round 1, station 1 has a send request to station 3 with priority 0. For round 1, station 2 has a send request to station 1 with priority 0. For round 1, station 3 has a send request to station 1 with priority 4. Because the request at station 3 has a higher priority than the request at station 2, it is served first. For round 10, station 4 has a send request to station 2 with priority 7. A valid send request must have:

- 0 <= round : round number must be positive
- src != dst : sending to self is unnecessary
- src < stations : send must be from existing station
- dst < stations : send must be to existing station

Output is written to standard output and shows a dynamic log of transmitted messages for each round:

    <round> p<prio> : <type> [<src> <dst>] ...

with

```
<round>  transmission round
<prio>   priority
<type>   "tok" for token, "d" for data, or "a" ack
<src>    source id for data and ack types
<dst>    destination id for data and ack types
```

The output for the above input with 4 stations is:

```
$ tokenring 4 input
ignoring bad send request: 10 4 2 7
round  s:0      s:1       s:2       s:3
0      p0:tok   p0:tok    p0:tok    p0:tok
1      p0:tok   p0:d1,3   p0:d1,3   p4:a3,1
2      p4:a3,1  p4:tok    p4:tok    p0:d3,1
3      p0:d3,1  p0:a1,3   p0:a1,3   p0:tok
4      p0:tok   p0:tok    p0:d2,1   p0:d2,1
5      p0:d2,1  p0:a1,2   p0:tok
```

where each column is separated by a tab (`'\t'`). Notice, the last line of the input is invalid because station number is not in the range 0..3 for 4 stations.

Devise a mechanism to properly hand back control to uMain::main after the last acknowledgment has been received by the last sender. uMain::main must delete all dynamically allocated memory.

27. Write a *full coroutine* called merge that works with another instance of itself to merge together two sorted arrays of integer values in ascending order, producing a third sorted array. Duplicate values may appear in the merged arrays.

The merge coroutine has the following public interface (you may add only a public destructor and private members):

```
_Coroutine merge {
  public:
    merge();
    void start( merge *partner, int sortValues[ ], int mergedValues[ ] );
    void mergeTo( int limit, int nextPos );
};
```

The start member is used to initialize the coroutine and has the following parameters: a pointer to its partner coroutine, one of the sorted arrays to be merged, and the third array into which the merged values are placed. Assume that mergedValues is large enough to hold the values from the two sorted arrays. A sentinel value of 99999999 can be inserted as an end-of-array value in sortValues. It will not appear as a regular value in sortValues, and it must not be copied to mergedValues.

The main program reads the necessary data, creates two instances of merge and then calls the start member for each. The start member saves its parameter values but does not resume the coroutine. The main program then compares the first values in each of the sorted arrays, and then calls the mergeTo member of the instance of merge that is passed the array containing the smaller value, passing it the larger of the first array values and 0, respectively. The mergeTo member resumes the coroutine. The merge that is resumed now copies from its sorted array into the merged array all values that are less than or equal to the limit. When this is complete, the current merge calls the mergeTo member of the other instance, passing the value that caused the current instance to stop merging, i.e., the first value in its array that is greater than limit and the first empty location in mergedValues. The second merge then does exactly what the first merge did, i.e., copy values from its sorted array into mergedValues until a value is greater than limit. The two merges pass control back and forth until both have copied all their sorted values into the merged array. Remember, when a merge has completed copying all its values, it must allow the other merge to complete its copying. Depending on which merge finishes first, one of the merges may not have finished its main member when control returns to uMain::main; this is fine as that merge is deleted when uMain::main terminates. The main program then prints the result of the merge from the mergedValues array.

HINT: The merge algorithm is extremely simple; if you write a substantial number of lines of code to do the merge operation itself, something is wrong.

The executable program is named merge and has the following shell interface:

merge *sorted-infile1 sorted-infile2 [merged-outfile]*

(Square brackets indicate optional command line parameters, and do not appear on the actual command line.)

- If the two sorted input files are not specified, print an appropriate usage message and terminate. An input file contains a list of sorted values. Each list starts with the number of values in that list. For example, the input file:

    8 -5 6 7 8 25 99 100 101

    contains a list with 8 values in it. (The placement of numbers above is for readability only; values can be separated by any white-space character and appear across any number of lines.) Both lists of sorted values from each file are to be read into arrays. You must handle an arbitrary number of values in a list. (HINT: GNU C++ allows arrays to be dynamically dimensioned.)

    Assume the first number in the input file is always present and correctly specifies the number of following values; assume all following values are correctly formed and sorted so no error checking is required on the input data.

    The UNIX jot and sort commands may be useful in preparing test data.
- If no merge output file name is specified, use standard output. The format of the output is the same as the input file so that the output of one merge can be used as the input to another.

For any specified command-line file, check it exists and can be opened. You may assume I/O reading and writing do not result in I/O errors.

NOTE: there is an existing UNIX command called merge so during testing ensure you invoke your program and not the UNIX one.

References

1. Conway, M.E.: Design of a separable transition-diagram compiler. Commun. ACM **6**(7), 396–408 (1963)
2. Hopcroft, J.E., Ullman, J.D.: Introduction to Automata Theory, Languages and Computation. Addison-Wesley, Reading (1979)
3. Marlin, C.D.: Coroutines: A Programming Methodology, a Language Design and an Implementation, *Lecture Notes in Computer Science, Ed. by G. Goos and J. Hartmanis*, vol. 95. Springer, New York (1980)

Chapter 5
Concurrency

While coroutines are important in their own right, they also introduce one of the basic forms of control flow found in concurrent programming, which is suspending execution and subsequently resuming it while retaining state information during the suspension. What differentiates concurrency from coroutining is multiple execution points in a program that behave independently of one another.

In the past, coroutines have been *associated* with concurrency [4, § 3]:

> In essence, coroutines are concurrent processes in which process switching has been completely specified, rather than left to the discretion of the implementation [2, p. 8].

However, coroutines execute with a single point of execution, and hence, coroutining is *not* concurrency. While coroutining and concurrency share the ability to retain execution state between calls, coroutining never experiences the same problems nor is there the same power as concurrency. In essence, once task switching is completely specified rather than left to the discretion of the implementation, there is no longer independent execution, and hence, neither concurrency nor processes.

This chapter begins with general information on concurrency and several definitions needed in further explanations, starting with these:

- A **thread** is an independent sequential execution path through a program. Conceptually, a thread has at one end the point of execution that is moving through the program, and the path taken by that point of execution forms a trail through the program. This analogy can be likened to a *thread of consciousness*, which is the train of thoughts that lead to an idea or answer. Often a thread is illustrated by a needle with a thread trailing behind it showing where the point of the needle has been in the program. The most important property of a thread, and the aspect producing concurrency, *is scheduling execution separately and independently among threads.*
- A **process** is a program component that combines a thread and an execution state into a single programming language or operating system construct.
- A **task** is similar to a process except it is reduced along some dimension (like the difference between a boat and a ship: one is physically smaller than the other).

© Springer International Publishing Switzerland 2016
P.A. Buhr, *Understanding Control Flow*, DOI 10.1007/978-3-319-25703-7_5

It is often the case that a process is an operating system construct having its own
memory, while a task is a programming language construct that shares a common
memory with other tasks. A task is sometimes called a light-weight process or
LWP, which emphasizes the reduced stature.

- Parallel execution is when two or more operations occur simultaneously, which
  can *only* occur when multiple processors (CPUs) are present. It is the threads of
  control associated with processes and tasks, executing on multiple processors,
  that results in parallel execution. Hence, without multiple processors there can
  be no parallel execution.
- Concurrent execution is any situation in which execution of multiple processes
  or tasks *appears* to be performed in parallel. Again, it is the threads of control
  associated with processes and tasks that results in concurrent execution.

μC++ provides tasks, while an operating system, such as UNIX, provides processes.
Since μC++ is used in this book, the term task is used unless there is an important
reason to distinguish between a process and a task. Nevertheless, all of the
discussion concerning a task applies equally to a process (although the reverse is
not necessarily true).

5.1 Why Write Concurrent Programs

In general, concurrent programs are more complex to write and debug than an
equivalent sequential program. The main reason to write a concurrent program is to
decrease the execution time of a program through parallelism. However, this is only
possible when there are multiple processors. Interestingly, it may be the case that
making a program concurrent *increases the cost of execution*, just like modularizing
a program into multiple routines might increase execution cost because of additional
routine call overhead. Therefore, for certain problems, a sequential program is
appropriate; for other problems, dividing it into multiple executing tasks may be
the natural way of creating a solution. What is crucial is that an algorithm expressed
concurrently can immediately take advantage of any available hardware parallelism.
On the other hand, a sequential program can never take advantage of available
parallelism. Thus, in certain situations, it is reasonable to spend the time and effort
to construct parallel algorithms and write concurrent programs to implement them
in anticipation of available hardware parallelism, otherwise much of the advantage
of new multiprocessor computers is unrealized.

5.2 Why Concurrency Is Complex?

Concurrency is inherently complex; no amount of "magic" can hide the complexity.
If you read or hear that concurrent programming can be made as simple as sequential
programming, *don't believe it*! Information and complexity theory show that it is
impossible for this to be true. Here are some reasons why:

Understanding   While people can do several things concurrently and in parallel, the number is small because of the difficulty in managing and coordinating them. This fact is especially true when things interact with one another. Hence, reasoning about multiple streams of execution and their interactions is much more complex than sequential reasoning.

Specifying   How can/should a problem be broken up so that parts of it can be solved at the same time as other parts? How and when do these parts interact or are they independent? If interaction is necessary, what information must be communicated during an interaction? Do certain interactions interfere with one another?

Debugging   Concurrent operations proceed at varying speeds and in non-deterministic order, hence execution is not entirely anticipatable nor repeatable.

An example to illustrate some of these problems is moving furniture out of an apartment. In general, moving requires multiple people (parallelism) and lots of coordination and communication. If the moving truck is rented by the hour and pizza has to be purchased for all the helpers, there is incentive to maximize the parallelism with as few helpers as possible.

Understanding

- How many helpers?

  The number of helpers depends on how many friends you have or how much money you have or both, for example, 1,2,3, ... N helpers, where N is the number of items of furniture. With N helpers, each person picks up one item and moves it, which is highly parallel. Is there any point in having more than N helpers? Yes, because some items are large and need multiple people to carry them; in fact, this is usually the reason why a single person cannot move on their own.

- How many trucks?

  Like helpers, it is conceivable to have a truck for each item, assuming each helper can also drive, but such a scheme is impractical. Another consideration is that a single large truck might be better than many small trucks, but more expensive to hire. Alternatively, a single small truck might require a large number of trips, slowing down the entire moving process. A medium truck or a couple of small trucks might be the most efficient and cost-effective form of transportation.

Specifying

- Who does what and when?

  Given a set of M helpers, who does what and when? All workers may not be equal, so there may be restrictions on certain workers with respect to certain jobs. For example, the person that drives the truck must know how to drive and have a driver's license. Heavy items should usually be moved by the strongest people to avoid damage to the item, the house/apartment, and the people carrying the item. As well, the order in which items are moved can make a difference depending on the size and shape of the truck, and who is available to carry them.

- Where are the bottlenecks?

A bottleneck is interference resulting from interaction among tasks or the resources the tasks are using; it often imposes a maximum on the amount of possible concurrency. The term bottleneck refers to pouring liquid out of a bottle: a liquid cannot be poured faster than the size of the bottle's neck, regardless of how large the bottle or what is in the bottle. Some examples of bottlenecks are the door out of a room, items in front of other items, and large items. Imagine if there are N helpers, and each picks up an item and they all rush to the door at the same time. Clearly, the more helpers, the more coordination is required among them. While it is true that some helpers can work in small groups and others can work alone, there must be some overall coordination or major problems arise at the bottlenecks.

- What communication is necessary among the helpers?

During the course of the move, communication is used as the mechanism to provide coordination. Orders are given to specify which items to take next, that some items are fragile and need special care, and that big items need several helpers working together. The amount of communication should be as brief and concise as possible; if helpers are communicating, they are probably not working.

Debugging

- How to detect and deal with problems?

Many problems can occur during a move. What differentiates a move from a program is that problems must be dealt with during the move. In the case of a program, problems are dealt with in the next run of the program; only rarely is a program debugged during its execution and allowed to continue. Still, in the case of moving, understanding problems in the current move can help prevent the same problems occurring in the next move. (Experience is recognizing when you have made the same mistake, twice.)

However, many problems are move specific and timing specific. Even given the same move done multiple times, different problems can occur. For example, two people might arrive simultaneously at a doorway in one move but not in another, or the sofa is not in front of the stove in one move but it is in another, or some communication is lost in one move but not in another. In other words, no two moves are identical (even from the same location), and similarly no two runs of a concurrent program are identical. Therefore, even after carefully planning what appears to be a problem free move, a problem might appear because of a minute difference in timing at some point in the move that is apparently unrelated to the problem situation. Therefore, guaranteeing a problem free move requires understanding of the dynamics of the move over time not just a static description of the move algorithm. The same is true for concurrent programs.

It is these kinds of problems that make specifying concurrent algorithms, and subsequently testing and debugging them difficult and frustrating. One peculiar situation is called a "Heisenbug" [5], named after the German physicist Werner Karl Heisenberg. For example, when a print statement is added to a failing concurrent program to determine what is wrong, the program works; when the print statement is removed, the program continues to fail. In this situation, the act of observing the concurrent system changes the timing of the program in a subtle way so the error case does not occur. In certain difficult cases, the only way to find such an error is to perform thought experiments to try to imagine the case that is failing.

As this example illustrates, managing and coordinating concurrency and parallelism is difficult but essential in certain situations. In effect, a good manager is someone who can deal with high levels of concurrency and parallelism among employees; a good concurrent programmer must also be a good manager.

5.3 Concurrent Hardware

Hardware structure dictates several aspects of concurrency. While esoteric hardware designs exist, only three basic designs are examined.

1. Concurrent execution of tasks is possible on a computer that has only one CPU, called a **uniprocessor**.

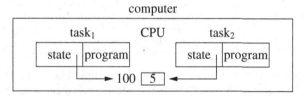

There can be no parallelism in this structure because there is only one CPU. But parallelism can be simulated by rapidly switching the CPU back and forth among tasks at non-deterministic program locations providing concurrency. Switching involves a context switch from task to task, which saves the state of the currently executing task and restores the state of the next task so it can execute. Different names for this technique are **multitasking** for multiple tasks, **multiprocessing** for multiple processes, or **pseudo-parallelism** for either scheme. Unlike coroutining, there is no control over where or when a process or task is suspended and another resumed. In fact, it is this phenomenon that introduces all the difficulties in concurrent programs; programs must be written to work regardless of non-deterministic ordering of program execution. Switching can happen explicitly but conditionally when calling a library routine; i.e., the library routine may or may not perform a context switch depending on state that is hidden from the caller. Hence, the caller cannot predict if a context switch will occur. Switching can also happen implicitly because of an external interrupt that is independent of program execution, such as a timer interrupt; i.e., after a period of time, called a time-slice, a task can be interrupted between any two instructions and control switches to another task. Hence, the execution of a task is not continuous; rather it is composed of a series of discrete time-slices, which occur at non-deterministic time intervals. If interrupts affect scheduling of tasks (i.e., change the order of execution), the scheduling is called preemptive, otherwise the scheduling is non-preemptive. In either case, a programmer may not be able to predict execution order, unlike coroutines, although the granularity of the context-switch points is at the instruction level for preemptive scheduling and at the routine level for non-preemptive scheduling, making it more difficult to reason about execution behaviour in the former.

Because memory is shared, tasks can pass data and addresses to one another during communication. What is crucial is that an address can be dereferenced by another CPU and get the same data. For example, if one task executing on a particular CPU passes the memory address 100 to another task executing on another CPU, both tasks can dereference the address 100 and get the same memory location in the shared memory, and hence, access the same value 5.

2. True parallelism is only possible when a computer has multiple CPUs, called a multiprocessor. In this structure, the CPUs share the same memory, called a shared-memory multiprocessor:

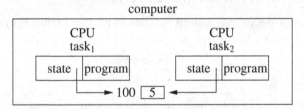

Most computers use this structure for input/output (I/O). For example, a disk controller often has its own CPU and can directly read and write memory, called direct memory access (DMA). Because there are multiple CPUs, there can be parallelism between program execution and I/O operations. Therefore, virtually all computers are in fact multiprocessors with other CPUs hidden in I/O devices. However, because these additional CPUs are not available for running user programs, these computers are uniprocessor from the user's perspective but multiprocessor from the hardware and operating system perspective.

3. Finally, different computers have separate CPUs and separate memories:

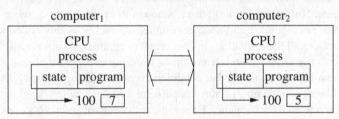

Processes or tasks that run on different computers run in parallel with each other. If there is a connection between the computers, communication among them is possible; a system of interconnected computers has non-shared memory, called a distributed system. While non-shared memory systems have the same concurrency issues as shared, they have the additional problem of being unable to dereference addresses passed from another computer. For example, if one task executing on one computer passes the memory address 100 to another task executing on another computer, the data at location 100 is probably different on both computers. Therefore, either all data must be passed by value among computers or addresses must be specially marked, so when dereferenced, data is fetched from the computer that the address originated from. Thus, linked data structures, like a list or tree, are very difficult to manipulate on a distributed system.

Finally, it is possible to combine the different hardware structures, such as a distributed system composed of uniprocessor and multiprocessor computers.

It is sufficient to examine the first case, which is the simplest, as it generates virtually all of the concurrency issues and problems that arise with the latter two cases. Furthermore, μC++ provides support for only the first two cases.

5.4 Execution States

As mentioned, a thread does not execute from start to end in an uninterrupted sequence; a thread may be interrupted multiple times during its execution, possibly to share the CPU with other threads, but there may be other reasons, too. Even a sequential program very seldomly executes from start to end without interruption because most operating systems are multiprocessing. Hence, the operating system interrupts each sequential program at various points during it execution and switches to another, which in turn may be another sequential program or a concurrent program containing multiple threads, each of which may be interrupted during their execution. Because of these interruptions, a thread goes through multiple state transitions during its execution, and it is important to discuss the states and transitions briefly as they are relevant in further discussion.

At any moment in its lifetime, a thread is in one of 5 states

```
                (scheduler)
    new ──────▶ ready ◀────▶ running ──────▶ halted
                   ▲            │
                   └─ blocked ──┘
                      (waiting) ◀─┘
```

new   When a thread is created it enters the system in the new state. In this state, the system initializes all aspects of the thread, such as allocating storage, loading executable code, etc., before execution begins.

ready   After a thread has been initialized, it is now ready for execution when a
   CPU becomes available. While waiting for an available CPU, the thread is in the
   ready state. A ready thread is not executing, it only has the *potential* to execute.
running   When a CPU begins executing a ready thread, the thread's state changes
   to the running state and its execution state to active (see Sect. 4.1.3, p. 129). As
   long as a thread is executing, its state is running. There can only be as many
   running threads as there are CPUs.
blocked   If a thread has to wait for another thread or a user to type in input data,
   it may block itself so that other threads may execute. In these situations, a thread
   voluntarily gives up the CPU because it cannot make further progress at this time
   and its state changes to the blocked state. When a thread is blocked, it is not
   eligible for execution until it is explicitly marked as ready, which only happens
   when the event that the thread is waiting for has occurred.
halted   When a thread finishes execution, either successfully or unsuccessfully, it
   is moved to the halted state. At this time, the system cleans up all outstanding
   aspects of the thread, such as freeing storage, closing files, printing output, etc.
   Only then can the thread be deallocated.

As mentioned, transitions of state are initiated in response to events (interrupts),
such as:

timer alarm   When a timer expires it indicates that it may be time to switch to
   another thread. Notice that the timer is running in parallel with the execution of
   the current thread. In this case, a thread moves directly from the running to the
   ready state. The thread is not blocked because it can still continue to execute if it
   had a CPU; it has simply been moved back to the ready state to wait its turn for
   access to a CPU.
I/O completion   For example, a user finishes typing and presses the "Return" or
   "Enter" key to complete a read from a terminal. If a thread has blocked itself
   waiting for an I/O completion, the subsequent completion changes the thread's
   state to ready. Notice that after the event's completion the thread is only ready to
   execute; it must always wait its turn for access to a CPU.
exception   If a program exceeds some limit (CPU time, etc.) or generates an error,
   it is moved from the running to the halted state and the system cleans up after it
   (e.g., close files, free storage, etc.).

A thread may experience thousands of these transitions during its execution
depending on what it is doing and how long it executes. Understanding a thread's
states and the transitions among states is important in understanding concurrent
execution. For example, non-deterministic "ready ↔ running" transitions can cause
basic sequential operations to be unsafe:

```
int i = 0;
task0          task1
i += 1         i += 1
```

If the increment is implemented with single inc i instruction, transitions can only
occur before or after instruction, not during execution of the instruction; in this

```
        task₀                    task₁
1st iteration
ld   r1,i    (r1 <- 0)
add r1,#1   (r1 <- 1)
                        1st iteration
                        ld   r1,i    (r1 <- 0)
                        add r1,#1   (r1 <- 1)
                        st   r1,i    (i  <- 1)
                        2nd iteration
                        ld   r1,i    (r1 <- 1)
                        add r1,#1   (r1 <- 2)
                        st   r1,i    (i  <- 2)
                        3rd iteration
                        ld   r1,i    (r1 <- 2)
                        add r1,#1   (r1 <- 3)
                        st   r1,i    (i  <- 3)
1st iteration
st   r1,i    (i  <- 1)
```

Fig. 5.1 Failure sequence

case, each increment is unaffected by another. However, if the increment is wrapped by a load-store sequence:

```
ld   r1,i     // load into register 1 the value of i
add r1,#1    // add 1 to register 1
st   r1,i     // store register 1 into i
```

transitions can occur during the sequence. Regardless of how the increment is implemented, if both tasks increment 10 times, the expected result is 20. However, this expectation is only true for the single instruction and false for the load-store sequence. There are many failure cases for load-store sequence where i does not reach 20. To demonstrate a failure, it is important to remember a context switch saves and restores registers for each task (and coroutine).

Fig. 5.1 shows the sequence of execution on a uniprocessor that fails to reach a total of 20; assume i has the value 0 at the start of the sequence: Task₀ starts an increment by copying the value 0 from i into register r1, and adding one to the copy, giving 1. Before the copy can be stored back into variable i, task₀ is interrupted by a time-slice, its registers and other state is stored, and task₁ is scheduled for execution. Task₁ then copies the value 0 from i and performs three consecutive increments of variable i, so the value of i is 3. Task₁ is now interrupted by a time-slice, its registers and other state is stored, and task₀ is scheduled for execution. Task₀ restarts execution at exactly the place it left off with the state saved before its time-slice. As a result, the value 1 in register r1 is stored over the value 3 in variable i. Therefore, the first 3 iterations of task₁ are lost. While the operating system makes transitions among processes largely invisible for sequential programs, this is not the case for concurrent programs. Hence, sequential operations, however small (increment), are unsafe in a concurrent program. Therefore, a programmer has to be aware of a thread's states and transitions.

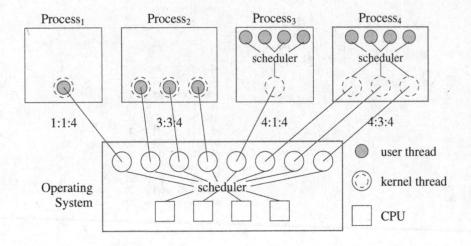

Fig. 5.2 Threading model

5.5   Threading Model

For multiprocessor systems, Fig. 5.2 shows a possible threading model defining the relationship between threads and CPUs. In general, the operating system (OS), bottom level, manages CPUs, providing logical access via kernel threads (virtual processors) *scheduled* across the CPUs. When a sequential program is run, the OS creates a process ($Process_1$) with a single kernel thread. The OS normally allows multiple programs to be started, each with its own process (i.e., memory and kernel thread), providing multiprocessing. These kernel threads are time-sliced across one or more CPUs available from the hardware.

A process itself may have multiple kernel threads ($Process_2$) to provide concurrency within it, as well as among processes. When multiple CPUs are available, the kernel threads within a process can provide parallelism. Because the kernel threads are within a processes, the tasks executing with these threads can share data via pointers.

It is possible to recursively apply this execution structure within a process ($Process_3$). A program may have user threads that are scheduled on its process's kernel threads using an internal scheduling mechanism. For example, the time-slice for a kernel thread can be subdivided into smaller units, and each unit executes one or more user tasks within the process, just like the OS does for kernel threads. User threads are a low-cost structuring mechanism, like routines, objects, coroutines (versus high-cost kernel thread). If there are multiple kernel threads in a process, these kernel threads can provide parallelism but at the user thread level ($Process_4$).

Relationships in the threading model are denoted by user:kernel:CPU, where:

- 1:1:C (kernel threading) – 1 user thread maps to 1 kernel thread.
- M:M:C (generalize kernel threading) – M × 1:1 kernel threads. (Java/Pthreads)

- N:1:C (user threading) – N user threads map to 1 kernel thread. (no parallelism)
- N:M:C (user threading) – N user threads map to M kernel threads. (μC++)

Often the CPU number (C) is omitted.

It is possible to recursively apply the execution structure to an arbitrary number of levels. For example, nano threads can be added on top of user threads, and virtual machines can be added below OS. In general, 4 levels is about the maximum number of useful levels on a computer.

5.6 Concurrent Systems

There are three major approaches for specifying concurrency in a program:

1. those attempting to *discover* concurrency in an otherwise sequential program, e.g., by parallelizing loops and access to data structures [3].
2. those that provide concurrency through *implicit* constructs, which a programmer uses to build a concurrent program
3. those that provide concurrency through *explicit* constructs, which a programmer uses to build a concurrent program

The first approach is extremely appealing because a programmer continues to write sequential programs and they are automatically made concurrent. Furthermore, existing sequential programs, regardless of their age, can be automatically converted as well (often referred to as parallelizing "dusty decks[1]"). Unfortunately, there is a fundamental limit to how much parallelism can be found and current techniques only work on certain kinds of programs. In the second approach, concurrency is accessed indirectly via specialized mechanisms. Essentially, a programmer gives hints about potential concurrency in a program via mechanisms like pragmas or parallel **for**. The concurrency system uses these hints to subdivide sequential components in a program (like a loop body) into tasks. When the program executes, the system decides on the form of concurrency and the number of threads, so all concurrency is implicitly managed. In the third approach, concurrency is directly accessed and explicitly managed by the program through concurrency constructions in the programming language. The program decides on the form of concurrency, the number of tasks, and when tasks are created and destroyed. Approaches 1 and 2 are always built from approach 3. In general, concurrency needs to be explicit to solve all the different kinds of concurrency problems. While both implicit and explicit approaches are complementary, and hence, can appear together in a single programming language, the limitations of the implicit approach require some form of explicit approach always be available to achieve maximum concurrency.

---

[1]The "deck" part refers to the time when programs were punched onto cards making the stack of cards for a program a "deck" of cards. The "dusty" part simply means the card deck is old enough to have gathered dust.

Currently, μC++ only provides an explicit approach, but nothing in its design precludes adding an implicit approach as well.

Within the explicit approaches, some languages provide a single technique or paradigm (see Chap. 13, p. 637) that must be used to solve all concurrent problems. While a particular paradigm may be very good for solving certain kinds of problems, it may be awkward or preclude other kinds of solutions. Therefore, a good concurrent system must support a variety of different concurrency paradigms, while at the same time not requiring the programmer to work at too low a level. As stated before, there is no simple solution to concurrency that requires little or no work on the part of the programmer; as the amount of concurrency increases, so does the complexity to express and manage it. *There is no free lunch!*

5.7 Speedup

As mentioned, the main purpose of concurrency is to decrease the execution time of a program through parallelism. The following are some high-level ways to quantify the expected decrease in execution time and to help understand where decreases come from in a program.

Program speedup is defined by $S_C = T_1/T_C$, where C is the number of CPUs and T_1 is the sequential execution. For example, if 1 CPU takes 10 s, $T_1 = 10$, then 4 CPUs take 2.5 s, $T_4 = 2.5 \Rightarrow S_4 = 10/2.5 = 4$ times speedup. Fig. 5.3 shows different kinds of speedup. Super-linear speedup implies doubling the number of processors more than doubles the program speed, which is impossible in practice. Linear speedup is the ideal form of speedup, and implies doubling the number of processors doubles the program speed. Due to administrative cost and hardware interactions, linear speedup is seldom achieved. Sub-linear speedup implies doubling the number of processors less than doubles the program speed. This speedup is a very common outcome of a concurrent program because concurrent overhead plus computation costs are always greater than the cost of sequential execution, which flattens the line. Non-linear speedup often implies a sub-linear speedup that reaches a peak and then asymptotically approaches a limit as more processors are added. This speedup is also a very common outcome of a concurrent program when some part of the computation or hardware saturates, resulting in the peak and the very slow speedup after this point.

There are three basic aspects affecting speedup (assume sufficient parallelism for all concurrency):

1. amount of concurrency
2. critical path among concurrency
3. scheduler efficiency

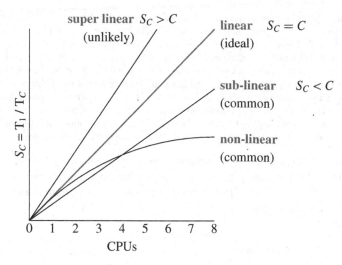

Fig. 5.3 Speedup

Concurrency

Every concurrent algorithm/program is composed of sequential and concurrent sections, e.g., sequentially read matrix, concurrently subtotal rows, sequentially total subtotals. Amdahl's law (Gene Amdahl) is used to find the maximum expected improvement to an overall system when parts of the system improve, which allows it to predict theoretical maximum speedup as multiple processors are added to concurrent sections. If the time for the concurrent section of a program is P, then the rest of the execution time is sequential $1 - P$. Using Amdahl's law, the maximum speedup using C CPUs is:

$$S_C = \frac{1}{(1-P)+P/C} \quad where\ T_1 = 1, T_C = sequential + concurrent$$

That is, the time for the sequential section plus the time for the concurrent section divided by the amount of available parallelism (i.e., number of CPUs). As C goes to infinity, P/C goes to 0, so the maximum speedup is $1/(1 - P)$, i.e., time for the sequential section. Interestingly, speedup falls rapidly as the sequential section $(1 - P)$ increases, even for large C. For example, given a sequential section taking 0.1 units (10 %), $S_C = 1/(1 - .9)$ so maximum speedup is 10 times, regardless of C, even though 90 % of the program is concurrent. Still, an order of magnitude increase in performance is excellent.

Interestingly, Amdahl only gave a literal description of the law attributed to him. The actual mathematical formula was created by someone else.

> The first characteristic of interest is the fraction of the computational load which is associated with data management housekeeping. This fraction has been very nearly constant for about ten years, and accounts for 40 % of the executed instructions in production runs.

In an entirely dedicated special purpose environment this might be reduced by a factor of two, but it is highly improbably that it could be reduced by a factor of three. The nature of this overhead appears to be sequential so that it is unlikely to be amenable to parallel processing techniques. Overhead alone would then place an upper limit on throughput of five to seven times the sequential processing rate, even if the housekeeping were done in a separate processor. The non-housekeeping part of the problem could exploit at most a processor of performance three to four times the performance of the housekeeping processor. A fairly obvious conclusion which can be drawn at this point is that the effort expended on achieving high parallel processing rates is wasted unless it is accompanied by achievements in sequential processing rates of very nearly the same magnitude [1, p. 483].

Therefore, concurrent programming consists of minimizing the sequential component $(1 - P)$. For example, assume an algorithm/program has 4 sequential stages: $t1 = 10$, $t2 = 25$, $t3 = 15$, $t4 = 50$ (time units), and a programmer manages to concurrently speedup sections $t2$ by 5 times and $t4$ by 10 times.

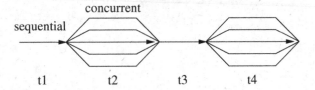

Therefore, $T_C = 10 + 25 / 5 + 15 + 50 / 10 = 35$ (time units), so speedup = $100 / 35 = 2.86$ times. Hence, the large reductions for $t2$ and $t4$ have only minor effect on total speedup. Finally, the formula does not consider any increasing costs for the concurrency, i.e., administrative costs, so the result are optimistic.

Critical Path

While sequential sections bound speedup, concurrent sections are also bound by the **critical path** of computation, which is the longest sequential path among the concurrent paths.

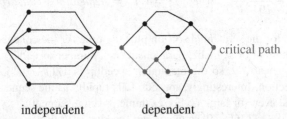

If all the threads in a concurrent section are created together and do not interact there is **independent execution**, and the critical paths for all threads are essentially equal. Hence, the time to execute any thread is approximately the time to execute all threads for that section. However, if the threads in a concurrent section are created at different times and interact there is **dependent execution**, and the critical paths among the threads are different lengths. Hence, the time to execute the thread with the longest critical path is approximately the time to execute that section. Essentially, the longest path bounds speedup.

Scheduler

At each level in the threading model (see Sect. 5.5, p. 200) is a scheduler controlling when a thread at that level is executed by a thread at the level below it. Since this scheduler is often built into each level of the threading model, there is usually little or no control over it. This scheduler can significantly affect efficiency through ordering of execution, e.g.:

- greedy scheduling : run a thread as long as possible before context switching (not very concurrent).
- LIFO scheduling : give priority to newly waiting tasks (starvation).

So a programmer may organize the structure of a concurrent program so it executes in a particular ordering to achieve good performance. But the scheduler may change the execution ordering for different reasons, resulting in poor ordering for certain programs. As a result, expected speed in the program is unrealized.

Therefore, it is difficult to achieve significant speedup for many algorithms/programs. In general, benefit comes when many programs achieve some speedup so there is an overall improvement on a multiprocessor computer.

5.8   Basic Concurrent Programming

It is now time to introduce concurrent programming, one of the most difficult forms of control flow to understand and master. Concurrent programming requires the ability to specify the following 3 mechanisms in a programming language.

1. thread creation and termination;
2. thread synchronization;
3. thread communication.

Each of these mechanisms is discussed in detail.

5.8.1   Thread Creation/Termination

The first and most important aspect of concurrent programming is how to start a new thread of control. The two ingredients needed are a new thread and a location for the new thread to start execution. In theory, there is no reason to restrict the starting point of a thread, for example, a thread could start in the middle of an expression.

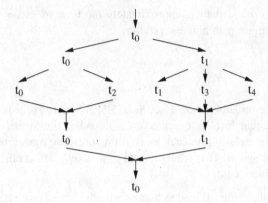

Fig. 5.4 Thread graph

In practice, there are practical considerations for the implementation that preclude such generality. (Think of restricting the starting point of a thread like restricting the target of a GOTO statement.)

5.8.2   Thread Graph

It is possible to visualize the creation/termination of threads graphically by a **thread graph**. The purpose of the graph is to show the lifetime of a thread. New thread creation is represented by forks in the graph, and termination is represented by joins in the graph (see Fig. 5.4). Starting at the top (root) of the graph with an initial thread task t_0, it creates a new task t_1 with its own thread. The creation is denoted by the fork in the graph with t_0 continuing execution along the left branch and t_1 starting along the right branch. Task t_0 then creates a new task, t_2, and both tasks proceed. Similarly, task t_1 creates two new tasks, t_3 and t_4, and all three tasks proceed. At some point in time, independent of the length of the arcs in the graph, tasks t_0 and t_2 join (synchronize), task t_2 terminates, and task t_0 proceeds. Similarly, tasks t_1, t_3 and t_4 join, tasks t_3 and t_4 terminate, and task t_1 proceeds. Finally, tasks t_0 and t_1 join, task t_1 terminates, and task t_0 proceeds.

Thread graphs are useful for understanding the basic structure of a concurrent system. Knowing the creation and termination relationships among tasks defines this basic structure. As mentioned, the arcs in the graph do not represent absolute time, only relative time with respect to creation and termination. Additional graphs are presented that display other kinds of important information in a concurrent system. While these kinds of graphs are not used extensively, either in this book or in practical concurrent programming, they are useful at this early stage of understanding.

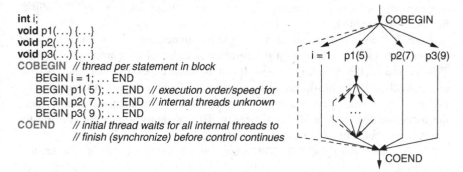

```
int i;
void p1(...) {...}
void p2(...) {...}
void p3(...) {...}
COBEGIN  // thread per statement in block
    BEGIN i = 1; ... END
    BEGIN p1( 5 ); ... END  // execution order/speed for
    BEGIN p2( 7 ); ... END  // internal threads unknown
    BEGIN p3( 9 ); ... END
COEND       // initial thread waits for all internal threads to
            // finish (synchronize) before control continues
```

Fig. 5.5 COBEGIN/COEND and thread graph

5.8.3   COBEGIN/COEND

One mechanism for creating/terminating threads is the COBEGIN ... COEND statement,[2] where "CO" stands for concurrent. COBEGIN creates a block out of a statement list, just like BEGIN ("{" in C++); the difference is that each statement is executed concurrently. That is, a new thread is created for each statement, which starts execution at the beginning of the statement and terminates at the end of the statement. Furthermore, the thread that starts the COBEGIN blocks at the COEND until all the threads created in the block have terminated. Fig. 5.5 shows an example COBEGIN/COEND and its corresponding thread graph. The fact that the initial thread is implicitly blocked during the COBEGIN is illustrated in the graph by a dashed line. What can be inferred from the thread graph about routine p1? Note, COBEGIN can only create a tree of processes (more formally a lattice, i.e., a tree with top and bottom root).

The most important point is that, once the threads are started, their execution with respect to one another is no longer under strict programmer control. After the COBEGIN, the threads associated with statements may continue in any order and at any speed, and threads may continue simultaneously, if the program is running on a multiprocessor. If only one thread is running, the others are in the ready state waiting their turn to become running. (Devise a situation where all threads are in the ready state.) In fact, the initial thread may get all the way to the end of COEND with none of the internal threads having started execution. Many other possible execution sequences may occur, where each thread takes several turns being blocked, ready and running, so that the execution of the internal threads are interleaved many times. This apparent lack of control during execution is often disconcerting to many programmers and is one of the most difficult aspects of concurrent programming to

---

[2] Another common name for this statement is PARBEGIN ... PAREND where "PAR" stands for parallel. However, this name is misleading because there is no parallelism when the program is run on a uniprocessor computer, only concurrency.

come to grips with. In fact, much of the subsequent discussion involves controlling the order of execution.

Note, it is usually the case that a single assignment or even small groups of assignments do not benefit from concurrency because of concurrency overhead. That is, the cost of creating a new thread is more expensive than the cost of executing the code by the thread. For concurrency to achieve a performance benefit, the amount of work performed by a thread must be significantly greater than the administrative cost of the concurrency. This phenomenon is not specific to concurrency, but is true for managing any work.

Finally, one drawback of COBEGIN is creating a dynamic number of new threads of control. For example, if the number of threads to be created is read in, it is necessary to use a recursive routine to construct a dynamic number of nested scopes, as in:

```
void loop( int N ) {
    if ( N != 0 ) {
        COBEGIN
            BEGIN p1( ... ); END
            BEGIN loop( N - 1 ); END // recursive call
        COEND // wait for return of recursive call
    }
}
cin >> N;
loop( N );
```

Here, the thread graph is an unbalanced binary tree with one branch running p1 and other branch running the call to routine loop.

5.8.4   START/WAIT

An alternative approach for creating/terminating threads is the START and WAIT statements.[3] START is like COBEGIN, but only creates a single thread and the thread always starts by executing a routine call:

auto handle = START(*routine-name, comma-separated-argument-list*);

The call must specify any arguments needed by the routine. Note, a routine is often chosen as the thread starting point because it is a well-defined building block in program composition and is an equally well-defined unit of execution. Since any segment of code can be modularized into a routine, there is no fundamental restriction on the code a thread may execute; however, a new name often has to be created and code has to be restructured into a routine. As well, START returns a **handle** (opaque value representing an object) to identify the new thread. A WAIT

---

[3] Another common name for these statements are "fork" and "join" because the calling thread splits into two threads after executing it and subsequently reconnects on termination. However, these names have existing meaning and connotations in UNIX for starting a process.

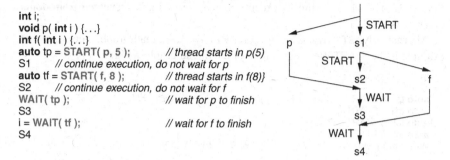

```
int i;
void p( int i ) {...}
int f( int i ) {...}
auto tp = START( p, 5 );        // thread starts in p(5)
S1      // continue execution, do not wait for p
auto tf = START( f, 8 );        // thread starts in f(8)}
S2      // continue execution, do not wait for f
WAIT( tp );                     // wait for p to finish
S3
i = WAIT( tf );                 // wait for f to finish
S4
```

Fig. 5.6 START/WAIT and thread graph

statement is like COEND, but waiting for only one thread, associated with a handle, to finish:

optional-return-value = WAIT(*handle*);

The optional return-value is for retrieving the result from a started function.

Fig. 5.6 shows an example START/WAIT and its corresponding thread graph. The key difference from COBEGIN/COEND is the initial thread does not block at the START and wait for its termination. How many threads are created after the second START? There are three: the initial thread that starts the program, and the two new ones running in p and f, respectively. Is it possible to start multiple threads running in the same routine, such as f? This problem is similar to that identified for coroutines: creation of multiple instances of the same coroutine (see Sect. 4.1.2, p. 128). If so, how is it possible to wait for the different threads and retrieve their specific result?

Notice the routine calls generated by START is now broken into two parts. The first part starts the call, specifying any necessary arguments, the second part appears in the WAIT, waiting for completion of the call, and where appropriate, retrieving a result. This division indicates the temporal nature of the call and that it is possible to perform other work between the two parts. In a sequential program, these two aspects are combined because the caller waits for the result. Finally, when control reaches a WAIT statement it may not have to wait if the specified routine has already finished.

Unlike COBEGIN/COEND, which can only generate a tree thread-graph, START/ WAIT can generate an arbitrary thread graph. The thread graph in Fig. 5.6 is not a tree, and hence, the same control flow cannot be generated using COBEGIN/ COEND, achieving the same level of concurrency. The following is a best-effort approximation of the thread graph:

```
COBEGIN
    p( 5 );
    BEGIN S1; COBEGIN f( 8 ); S2; COEND END // wait for f!
COEND
S3; S4;
```

Draw the thread graph for this code to visualize that the graphs are not equivalent. Furthermore, try altering the code to see if you can achieve equivalent thread graphs. Finally, additional threads must be created because the thread executing the

COBEGIN is blocked during its execution, and therefore, is prevented from doing other work.

Alternatively, START/WAIT can construct any tree thread-graph. The following example is the START/WAIT equivalent of the thread graph in Fig. 5.5, p. 207.

```
int i;
...
auto tp0 = START( [&]() { i = 1; ... } );          // COBEGIN
auto tp1 = START( p1, 5 );
auto tp2 = START( p2, 7 );
auto tp3 = START( p3, 9 );
WAIT( tp0 ); WAIT( tp1 ); WAIT( tp2 ); WAIT( tp3 );   // COEND
```

5.8.5 Termination Synchronization

It is rare in concurrent programming to start a task and then ignore it. An example might be a task that prints out some values; however, such a thread has a side effect independent of the program's execution. Normally, a task is working on behalf of another task, and it returns results to be used in further computations. The creator of a new thread needs to know, at the very minimum, when the computation is done, and where to obtain the result of the computation.

When two or more threads wait for an event to occur, and an event can be virtually anything, this is called synchronization. A construct such as COEND and WAIT performs termination synchronization because the event is the termination of the executing thread(s). Once the thread executing the COEND/WAIT is synchronized with the other thread's termination, it is possible to perform additional operations, such as fetching a result. Notice the synchronization is crucial because it is incorrect to try to obtain the result earlier than the thread's termination. The next few chapters discuss this point in more detail, and show how to synchronize and communicate during execution of two threads, not just when a thread terminates.

5.9 μC++ Threads

Like coroutines (see Sect. 4.1.3, p. 129), μC++ leverages the **class** type generator to access threads. The main benefits of this approach are:

- a thread is contained in an object to leverage all the class features,
- object allocation/deallocation defines a thread's lifetime rather than a control structure.

A μC++ task type has all the properties of a **class**. The general form of the task type is the following:

```
_Task task-name {
  private:
    ...              // these members are not visible externally
  protected:
    ...              // these members are visible to descendants
    void main();     // task main (distinguished member)
  public:
    ...              // these members are visible externally
};
```

A task is an object created from a task type in which a new thread of control starts in its distinguish member routine; this distinguished member is named main and is called the task main. Like a coroutine main, execution of a task main may be suspended as control leaves it, only to carry on from that point when control returns at some later time; however, the mechanism to accomplish this is normally quite different and not discussed until Chap. 10, p. 523. It is distinguished because it has special properties that none of the other member routines have and only the member routine called main in a μC++ task has special properties.

Like a coroutine, a task main has its own execution state, which is the state information needed to retain information while the task main is suspended. In practice, an execution state consists of the data items created by a task, including its local data and routine activations, and a current execution location, which is initialized to a starting point (member main). However, unlike a coroutine, which waits for a thread to resume it, a new thread is implicitly created and begins execution in the task main after a task is instantiated. Instead of allowing direct interaction with main, its visibility is usually **private** or **protected**. The decision to make the task main **private** or **protected** depends solely on whether derived classes can reuse the task main or must supply their own. For example, given the simple task type definition:

```
_Task T {
  void main() { ... }      // distinguished member
  public:
    T() { ... }
};
T t;      // new thread created, which starts execution in T::main
```

the declaration of t can be broken into the following parts:

```
T t;                       // storage allocated
t();                       // implicitly invoke appropriate constructor
START( t.main() );         // start new thread in task main
```

Since declarations can appear anywhere in a C++ block, a new thread can be started anywhere a COBEGIN or START statement can be located.

Termination synchronization is achieved through an indirect mechanism rather than a COEND or WAIT statement. The indirect mechanism is variable deallocation. Since all tasks are created through some form of declaration, they must subsequently be deallocated, at which time their storage is freed. For tasks allocated in a block (i.e., { ... }), the task is implicitly deallocated at the end of the block; for a dynamically allocated task, the task is explicitly deallocated by the **delete** statement. However, it is unreasonable for a task's destructor to deallocate storage if a thread is executing

```
int i;                                          int i;          // return variable
_Task T1 {                                      _Task T1 { void main() { p(5); } };
    void main() { i = 1; ... }                  _Task T2 {
};                                                  int temp;
_Task T2 {                                          void main() { temp = f(8); }
    void main() { p1(5); }                      public:
};                                                  ~T2() { i = temp; }
_Task T3 {                                      };
    void main() { p2(7); }                      void uMain::main() {
};                                                  T1 *tp = new T1;     // start T1
_Task T4 {                                          ... S1 ...
    void main() { p3(9); }                          T2 *tf = new T2;     // start T2
};                                                  ... S2 ...
void uMain::main() {                                delete tp;           // wait for p
    { // COBEGIN                                     ... S3 ...
        T1 t1;  T2 t2;  T3 t3;  T4 t4;              delete tf;           // wait for f
    } // COEND                                      ... S4 ...
}                                               }
```

　　　　(a) COBEGIN/COEND   　　　　(b) START/WAIT

Fig. 5.7 Object format

within it; otherwise, the deallocated storage might be reused for another object but the thread would continue to change it! Therefore, a block cannot end until the threads for all the tasks declared in it have finished execution, and a **delete** statement cannot continue until the thread of the deleted task finishes execution. In both cases, the thread executing the block or **delete** synchronizes with the termination of any threads being deallocated. For example, the deallocation of t can be broken into the following parts:

```
WAIT( t.main );     // wait for thread to terminate, where t is the handle
~t();               // invoke destructor
free( t );          // deallocate storage
```

Fig. 5.7 shows the COBEGIN/COEND example in Fig. 5.5, p. 207 and START/ WAIT example in Fig. 5.6, p. 209 rewritten in an object format. The left COBEGIN/ COEND simulation defines four task types (T1..4), where each main member contains one statements from the original COBEGIN/COEND statement. Then in uMain::main, instances of the four task-types are declared in a block, which subsequently creates threads that execute the task-main routines. (The extra block is unnecessary, but shows how to isolate a group of tasks to simulate a COBEGIN/ COEND at any nesting level.) The thread of uMain::main then immediately attempts to deallocate the 4 tasks but must wait until the threads of these tasks have terminated. Notice, a declaration of the form:

```
{ int i, j, k; }
```

is normally meaningless because the variables are allocated and then immediately deallocated. However, when the objects are tasks, the block provides termination synchronization. Interestingly, a task type can take advantage of all the mechanisms in C++ for instantiating objects, such creating an array of N tasks, as in:

```
{
    T t[N];
} // wait for N tasks to terminate
```

Finally, routine p1 also contained a COBEGIN and might look like this:

```
void p1(...) {
    { // COBEGIN
        T5 t5;  T6 t6;  T7 t7;  T8 t8;
    } // COEND
}
```

The right START/WAIT simulation defines two task types (T1..2), where each main member contains the call from the original START statement. Then in uMain::main, instances of the two task-types are allocated with **new** in the heap at the same locations as the START statements. The thread of uMain::main continues immediately after the task objects are allocated. Eventually, the task objects are deallocated from the heap with **delete** at the same locations as the WAIT statements. The thread of uMain::main blocks at each deallocation until the task object's thread terminates, before deallocating the storage.

By using **new** and **delete** it is possible to obtain the same fine-grain control of thread creation and termination as with START and WAIT. However, the same cannot be said about returning a result. Is the μC++ program the same as the START/WAIT program, with regard to assignment of variable i? The answer is no. In the START/WAIT program, i is updated only after the second WAIT statement; therefore, its value is unaffected in statements S2 or S3, unless it is changed directly in that code. In the μC++ program, i can change at anytime after f1 is assigned because there is no control over the order and speed of execution of tasks. Thus, it is unsafe to use the value of i until after f1's thread has terminated. If i is used, the result of the program is non-deterministic, which means the program may produce different answers each time it is run. This problem is solved by storing the function result in a temporary variable, and only assigning to i in the destructor, after the task's thread has terminated .

In both simulations, it is true that having to start routines embedded in a class-like definition is more complex than for control structures. While creating threads this way may seem awkward, it turns out that this is true only for simple examples; more complex examples (i.e., real life problems) are simpler to specify using a task because of all the power available in the **class** mechanism. It is also shown in Chap. 10, p. 523 that the class-like definition is critical for communication purposes. *For now, all tasks are restricted to having only public constructors and a destructor; all other member routines are* **private** *or* **protected**. Additional **public** member routines are deferred until Chap. 10, p. 523.

5.10   Task Details

The following μC++ task details are presented now to understand subsequent
examples or to help in solving questions at the end of the chapter. More μC++ task
details are presented in Chap. 10, p. 523.

5.10.1   Task Creation and Destruction

A task is the same as a class with respect to creation and destruction, as in:

```
_Task T {
    void main() ...      // task main
};
T *tp;                   // pointer to a T
{ // start a new block
    T t, ta[3];          // local creation
    tp = new T;          // dynamic creation
    ...
} // wait for t, ta[0], ta[1] and ta[2] to terminate and then deallocate
...
delete tp;   // wait for tp' s instance to terminate and then deallocate
```

When a task is created, the appropriate task constructor and any base-class constructors are executed in the normal order by the creating thread. The stack component
of the task's execution-state is created and the starting point (activation point) is
initialized to the task main routine visible by the inheritance scope rules from the task
type. Then a new thread of control is created for the task, which begins execution at
the main routine. From this point, the creating thread executes concurrently with the
new task's thread; main executes until its thread blocks or terminates. The location
of a task's variables–in the task's data area or in member routine main–depends
on whether the variables must be accessed by member routines other than main. A
task main cannot have parameters or return a result, but the same effect can be
accomplished indirectly by passing values through the task's member variables,
called communication variables, which are accessible from both the coroutine's
member and main routines.

A task terminates when its main routine terminates. When a task terminates, so
does the task's thread of control and execution state. A task's destructor is invoked
by the deallocating thread when the block containing the task declaration terminates
or by an explicit delete statement for a dynamically allocated task. Because storage
for a task cannot be deallocated while a thread is executing, a block cannot terminate
until all tasks declared in it terminate. Similarly, deleting a task on the heap must
also wait until the task being deleted has terminated.

While a task that creates another task is conceptually the parent and the created
task its child, μC++ makes no implicit use of this relationship nor does it provide
any facilities based on this relationship. Once a task is declared it has no special
relationship with its declarer other than what results from the normal scope rules.

Like a coroutine, a task can access all the external variables of a C++ program and the heap. However, because tasks execute concurrently, there is the general problem of concurrent access to such shared variables. Furthermore, this problem also arises with **static** member variables within a task instantiated multiple times. Therefore, it is suggested that these kinds of references be used with extreme caution.

5.10.2 Inherited Members

Each task type, if not derived from some other task type, is implicitly derived from the task type uBaseTask, e.g.:

```
_Task task-name : public uBaseTask {
    ...
};
```

where the interface for the base class uBaseTask is:

```
_Task uBaseTask : public uBaseCoroutine { // inherits from coroutine base type
  public:
    uBaseTask();
    uBaseTask( unsigned int stacksize );

    void yield( unsigned int times = 1 );
    enum State { Start, Ready, Running, Blocked, Terminate };
    State getState() const;
};
```

The public member routines from uBaseCoroutine are inherited and have the same functionality.

The overloaded constructor routine uBaseTask has the following forms:

uBaseTask() −creates a task with the default stack size (same as uBaseCoroutine()).

uBaseTask(**int** stackSize) −creates a task with the specified stack size (in bytes) (same as uBaseCoroutine(**int** stackSize)).

Multiple-task execution-states have the same storage management problem as for coroutines (see Sect. 4.7.2, p. 146). Therefore, programmers have to be vigilant to ensure there is sufficient stack space for the calls made by the thread of a task. As for coroutines, this is not usually an issue because call depth is shallow so the default stack is normally adequate. A task type can be designed to allow declarations to specify the stack size by doing the following:

```
_Task T {
  public:
    T() : uBaseTask( 8192 ) {};        // default 8K stack
    T( int s ) : uBaseTask( s ) {};    // user specified stack size
    ...
};
T x, y( 16384 );     // x has an 8K stack, y has a 16K stack
```

The member routine yield gives up control of the CPU to another ready task the specified number of times. For example, the routine call yield(5) ignores the next 5 times the task is scheduled for execution. If there are no other ready tasks, the delaying task is simply delayed and restarted 5 times. Member yield allows a task to relinquish control when it has no current work to do or when it wants other ready tasks to execute before it performs more work. For example, when creating a large number of tasks, it may be important to ensure some of them start execution before all the tasks are created. If after the creation of several tasks the creator yields control, some created tasks then have an opportunity to begin execution before the next group of tasks is created. This facility is not a mechanism to control the exact order of execution of tasks, only to ensure some additional fairness among tasks. Finally, one task *cannot* yield another task; a task can only yield itself. A call such as:

```
x.yield(...)
```

fails, via a dynamic check, if task x is not the same as the currently executing task.

The member routine getState returns the current state of the task, which is one of the enumerated values uBaseTask::Ready, uBaseTask::Running, uBaseTask::Blocked or uBaseTask::Terminate.

The routine:

```
uBaseTask &uThisTask();
```

is used to determine the identity of the task executing this routine. The returned reference to the base-task type, uBaseTask, of the current task can only be used to access the public routines of type uBaseTask and uBaseCoroutine. A routine can verify the stack or yield execution of the calling task by performing the following:

```
uThisTask().verify();
uThisTask().yield();
```

As well, printing a task's address for debugging purposes must be done like this:

```
cout << "task:" << &uThisTask() << endl; // notice the ampersand (&)
```

5.11 Concurrent Propagation

A local exception within a task is the same as for an exception within a routine or class. An exception raised and not handled inside a task performs the C++ default action of calling terminate, which must abort. As mentioned, a nonlocal exception between a task and a coroutine is the same as between coroutines (sequential). An asynchronous exception between tasks is more complex due to the multiple threads.

An asynchronous exception can be handled locally within a task, or nonlocally among coroutines, or concurrently among tasks. All asynchronous exceptions are nonlocal, but nonlocal exceptions can also be sequential. Asynchronous exceptions provide an additional kind of communication over a normal member call. That is, an asynchronous exception can be used to force a communication when an execution state might otherwise be computing instead of accepting calls. For example, two tasks may begin searching for a key in different sets; the first task to find the key needs to inform the other task to stop searching, e.g.:

```
_Task searcher {
    searcher &partner;        // other searching task
    void main() {
        try {
            _Enable {.
                ...           // implicit or explicit polling is occurring
                if ( key == ... )
                    _Resume stop() _At partner;  // inform partner search is finished
            }
        } catch( stop ) { ... }
```

Without this control-flow mechanism, both tasks have to poll for a call from the other task at regular intervals to know if the other task found the key. Asynchronous exceptions handle this case and others.

When a task performs a concurrent raise, it blocks only long enough to deliver the exception to the specified task and then continues. Hence, the communication is asynchronous, whereas member-call communication is synchronous. Once an exception is delivered to a task, the runtime system propagates it at the soonest possible opportunity. If multiple concurrent-exceptions are raised at a task, the exceptions are delivered serially.

5.11.1 Enabling/Disabling Propagation

μC++ allows dynamic enabling and disabling of nonlocal exception-propagation. The constructs for controlling propagation of nonlocal exceptions are the _Enable and the _Disable blocks, e.g.:

```
_Enable <E1> <E2> ... {        _Disable <E1> <E2> ... {
    // code in enable block         // code in disable block
}                              }
```

The arguments in angle brackets for the _Enable or _Disable block specify the exception types allowed to be propagated or postponed, respectively. Specifying no exception types is shorthand for specifying all exception types. Though a nonlocal exception being propagated may match with more than one exception type specified in the _Enable or _Disable block due to exception inheritance (see Sects. 3.13.2, p. 108 and 3.17, p. 115), it is unnecessary to define a precise matching scheme because the exception type is either enabled or disabled regardless of which exception type it matches with.

_Enable and _Disable blocks can be nested, turning propagation on/off on entry and reestablishing the delivery state to its prior value on exit. Upon entry of a _Enable block, exceptions of the specified types can be propagated, even if the exception types were previously disabled. Similarly, upon entry to a _Disable block, exceptions of the specified types become disabled, even if the exception types were previously enabled. Upon exiting a _Enable or _Disable block, the propagation of exceptions of the specified types are restored to their state prior to entering the block.

*Initially, nonlocal propagation is disabled for all exception types in a coroutine
or task*, so handlers can be set up before any nonlocal exceptions can be propagated,
resulting in the following μC++ idiom in a coroutine or task main:

```
void main() {
    // initialization, nonlocal exceptions disabled
    try {                       // setup handlers for nonlocal exceptions
        _Enable {               // enable propagation of all nonlocal exception-types
            // rest of the code for this coroutine or task
        }                       // disable all nonlocal exception-types
    } catch ...                 // catch nonlocal exceptions occurring in enable block
    // finalization, nonlocal exceptions disabled
}
```

Several of the predefined kernel exception-types are implicitly enabled in certain
contexts to ensure their prompt delivery (see the μC++ reference manual).

The μC++ kernel implicitly polls for nonlocal exceptions after a coroutine/
task becomes active, and at the start of a **_Enable** block after enabling nonlocal
exception-propagation. If this level of polling is insufficient, explicit polling is
possible by calling:

```
bool uEHM::poll();
```

For throwable exceptions, the return value from poll is not usable because a
throwable exception unwinds the stack frame containing the call to poll. For
resumable exceptions, poll returns **true** if a nonlocal resumable-exception was
delivered and **false** otherwise. In general, explicit polling is only necessary if pre-
emption is disabled, a large number of nonlocal exception-types are arriving, or
timely propagation is important.

5.12   Divide-and-Conquer

Divide-and-conquer is a technique that can be applied to certain kinds of problems.
These problems are characterized by the ability to subdivide the work across the
data, so that the work can be performed independently on the data. In general, the
work performed on each group of data is identical to the work that is performed on
the data as a whole. In some cases, groups of data must be handled differently, but
each group's work is identical. Taken to the extreme, each data item is processed
independently, but at this stage, the administration of concurrency usually becomes
greater than the cost of the work. What is important is that only termination
synchronization is required to know when the work is done; the partial results can
then be processed further if necessary.

A simple example of divide-and-conquer is adding up the elements of an $N \times N$
matrix. The elements can be added up by row or by column or by blocks of size
$M \times M$, where $M < N$. A task can be created for each row, column or block, and
work independently of the other tasks. Totalling the subtotals is performed after the
tasks terminate; hence, only termination synchronization is needed.

Fig. 5.8 is the control-structure version, which divides a matrix up into rows, and has tasks sum the rows independently. uMain::main creates the matrix of values, and the array where the subtotals generated by the tasks are placed. No code is shown for reading the matrix, just a comment to that effect. (Note, the matrix can be summed during reading, so assume it is modified and summed multiple times in the program.) An extended form of the COBEGIN is used to create a dynamic number of threads. The COFOR statement is like a **for** loop, where the initial thread creates a thread of each iteration of the loop body and then waits for *all* threads executing the loop bodies to terminate. (Explain why this semantics is not the same as putting a COBEGIN statement in a **for** loop.) The loop index row for a particular iteration is available within the loop body; hence, a loop body knows which iteration it is performing, and can use that information to extract appropriate information. The code in the loop body is straightforward, adding up the elements of the row supplied by the COFOR index row, and then terminating. After all of the rows threads terminate, the thread of uMain knows the subtotal array is filled with the summation for each row of the matrix, which are then summed to get the total.

Fig. 5.9 is the explicit task version, which divides a matrix up into rows, and has tasks sum the rows independently. This version puts the code in the COFOR loop body into the main routine of the Adder task. uMain::main first dynamically allocates a task for each row of the matrix, passing to each task the address of the row it is to sum, the number of columns in the row, and the address in the result array to place the total for the row. The next loop immediately deletes each of the newly created tasks, which normally does not make sense, except for the fact that each deleted object is a task. It does not matter what order the Adder tasks are deleted because the loop is restricted by the critical path among Adder tasks, i.e., the slowest executing Adder task. Sometimes the **delete** must wait and other times it can do the deallocation immediately because the task is already finished. After each task deletion, the thread of uMain has completed termination synchronized with that Adder task; hence, the row subtotal for that task must be calculated and the subtotal value stored in its respective location. After all of the rows threads terminate, the thread of uMain knows the subtotal array is filled with the summation for each row of the matrix, which are then summed to get the total.

5.13 Synchronization and Communication During Execution

Up to now tasks only synchronize and communicate when one task terminates. There are many cases where tasks need to synchronize and communicate *during* their lifetime, e.g., in a producer/consumer situation (see Sect. 4.9, p. 156). This section shows that such communication can be done using the facilities discussed so far, although not very well. How to do this properly is discussed in subsequent chapters.

The program in Fig. 5.10, p. 221 shows unidirectional communication between two tasks, prod and cons, during their lifetime. When the producer wants to

```
#include <uCobegin.h>
void uMain::main() {
    const int rows = 10, cols = 10;
    int matrix[rows][cols], subtotals[rows], total = 0;
    // read matrix
    COFOR( row, 0, rows,
    // for ( int row = 0; row < rows; row += 1 )
        subtotals[row] = 0;
        for ( int c = 0; c < cols; c += 1 ) {
            subtotals[row] += matrix[row][c];
        }
    ); // wait for threads
    for ( int r = 0; r < rows; r += 1 ) {
        total += subtotals[r];  // total subtotals
    }
    cout << total << endl;
}
```

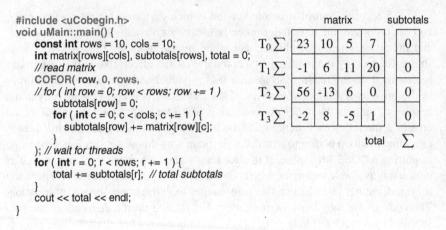

Fig. 5.8 Concurrent summation of matrix elements (COFOR)

```
_Task Adder {
    int *row, cols, &subtotal; // communication
    void main() {
        subtotal = 0;
        for ( int c = 0; c < cols; c += 1 ) {
            subtotal += row[c];
        }
    }
  public:
    Adder( int row[], int cols, int &subtotal ) :
        row( row ), cols( cols ), subtotal( subtotal ) {}
};
void uMain::main() {
    const int rows = 10, cols = 10;
    int matrix[rows][cols], subtotals[rows], total = 0, r;
    // read matrix
    Adder *adders[rows];
    for ( r = 0; r < rows; r += 1 ) { // start threads to sum rows
        adders[r] = new Adder( matrix[r], cols, subtotals[r] );
    }
    for ( r = 0; r < rows; r += 1 ) { // wait for threads to finish
        delete adders[r];
        total += subtotals[r];  // total subtotals
    }
    cout << total << endl;
}
```

Fig. 5.9 Concurrent summation of matrix elements (_Task)

```
enum { Full, Empty } status = Empty;          _Task Cons {
int Data;                                         int N;
                                                  void main() {
_Task Prod {                                          int data;
    int N;                                            for ( int i = 1; i <= N; i += 1 ) {
    void main() {                                         while ( status == Empty ) {} // busy
        for ( int i = 1; i <= N; i += 1 ) {               data = Data; // remove data
            Data = i; // transfer data                    status = Empty;
            status = Full;                            }
            while ( status == Full ) {} // busy   }
        }                                         public:
    }                                             Cons( int N ) : N( N ) {}
    public:                                   };
        Prod( int N ) : N( N ) {}             void uMain::main() {
};                                                Prod prod( 5 ); Cons cons( 5 );
                                              }
```

Fig. 5.10 Synchronization and communication during execution

transfer data, the data is copied into shared storage, i.e., storage visible to both tasks. However, just placing data into the shared variable is insufficient. For communication, one task has to be ready to transmit the information and the other has to be ready to receive it, *simultaneously*. Otherwise data may be transmitted when no one is receiving, or received before it is transmitted. For example, the producer can insert data into the shared storage before the previous data has been copied out by the consumer, or the consumer can copy the same data out of the shared storage multiple times before the next data is inserted by the producer.

To prevent these problems a protocol is established between the producer and consumer. The protocol conceptually has the producer sets a flag *before* data is copied into the shared storage, and the consumer resets the flag *after* the data is removed; thus, by appropriate checking of the flag by the producer and consumer, it is possible to safely transfer data. In the example program, when the producer wants to transmit data, it copies the data into a shared variable and the flag is set by changing status to Full. Then the producer must wait until the consumer receives the data; in this case, the method for waiting is to spin in a loop, called busy waiting, until the consumer removes the data by resetting status to Empty. The consumer, which may have started execution before the producer, does not attempt to remove data until the flag is set, i.e., status is assigned Full; this delay is implemented by busy waiting until the flag is set, i.e., status's value is set to Full. Then the consumer exits its busy loop and copies out the data, after which it resets the flag, i.e., status is assigned Empty. The protocol is repeated for the next transfer of data. The main problem with this approach is the busy waiting by the producer and consumer, which consumes large amounts of CPU time and possibly requires preemptive scheduling; it is never good concurrent programming style to busy wait. Subsequent chapters gradually eliminate explicit busy waiting.

5.14   Summary

Concurrency is inherently complex because of the management of simultaneous actions. All concurrency systems must provide mechanisms to create new threads of control, synchronize execution among threads, and communicate after synchronizing. These mechanisms vary with the particular concurrency systems. In μC++ , instantiating a _Task object implicitly creates a new thread of control and termination of this object forces synchronization, which can be used as a point for communication. While communication among tasks during their lifetime is essential for complex concurrent programs, an efficient mechanism to accomplish this is postponed until later. Temporarily, _Task definitions do not have public members, other than constructors and possibly a destructor, until further material is presented.

5.15   Questions

1. Explain the difference between a *process* and a *task*.
2. Explain the difference between *concurrent* and *parallel* execution.
3. Give three reasons why writing a concurrent program is difficult.
4. Name and explain the three type of concurrent hardware.
5. Concurrent systems can be divided into three major types with respect to how concurrency is introduced into a program. Explain each type.
6. What does it mean for a scheduling strategy to be *preemptive*? *non-preemptive*?
7. Name and explain the five execution states of a thread.
8. A single interrupt (event) occurs in a multitasking system. As a result of this interrupt, one process is moved from the running state to the ready state, and another is moved from the blocked state to the running state. Explain the likely reasons for these two state changes. What can be assumed concerning the task scheduling strategy?
9. Explain why an increment operation (i += 1) is unsafe in a concurrent program.
10. Explain the difference between *user* and *kernel* threads.
11. Can all sequential programs be converted into concurrent programs automatically?
12. List the three major aspects affecting speedup in a concurrent program.
13. State Amdahl's law with respect to speedup of concurrent programs, and explain the variables in the formula.
14. Using Amdahl's law,

    • What is the speedup achieved for a program if 50 % of it can be executed in parallel and there are 2 CPUs to run the parallel portion on?
    • What is the maximum speedup achievable for the program in part a) if an infinite number of CPUs is available to run it?

15. Why does program speedup often not scale linearly with the number of CPUs?

```
#include <iostream>
using namespace std;

volatile int iterations = 10000000,  // ignore volatile, prevent dead-code removal
             shared = 0;

_Task increment {
    void main() {
        for ( int i = 1; i <= iterations; i += 1 ) {
            shared += 1;        // no -O2 to prevent atomic increment instruction
        }
    }
};
void uMain::main() {
    if ( argc == 2 ) iterations = atoi( argv[1] );
#ifdef __U_MULTI__
    uProcessor p;              // create 2nd kernel thread
#endif // __U_MULTI__
    {
        increment t[2];
    } // wait for tasks to finish
    cout << "shared: " << shared << endl;
}
```

Fig. 5.11 Interference

16. A program has 4 sequential stages, where each stage takes the following N units of time to execute: S1 = 5, S2 = 20, S3 = 15, S4 = 60. Stages S2 and S4 are modified to increase their speed (i.e, reduce the time to execute) by 10 and 20 times, respectively. Show the steps in computing the total speedup for the program after the modification.

17. When introducing concurrency into a programming language, what are the basic mechanisms that must be supported?

18. What is a parent-child relationship among tasks and how is it used?

19. Extend the program in Fig. 5.10, p. 221 to perform bidirectional communication between the tasks.

20. Compile the program in Fig. 5.11 using the u++ command, without and with compilation flag -multi and *no optimization*, to generate a uniprocessor and multiprocessor executable. Run both versions of the program 10 times with command line argument 10000000 on a multi-core computer with at least 2 CPUs (cores).

    a. Show the 10 results from each version of the program.
    b. Must all 10 runs for each version produce the same result? Explain your answer.
    c. In theory, what are the smallest and largest values that could be printed out by this program with an argument of 10000000? Explain your answers. (**Hint:** one of the obvious answers is wrong.)
    d. Explain the difference in the size of the values between the uniprocessor and multiprocessor output.

```
volatile int iterations = 100000000;  // ignore volatile, prevent dead-code removal
volatile __int128 shared = 0;     // 128-bit double-word integer

_Task increment {
    void main() {
        for ( int i = 1; i <= iterations; i += 1 ) {
            shared += 3;          // no -O2 to prevent atomic increment instruction
        } // for
    }
};
void uMain::main() {
    if ( argc == 2 ) iterations = atoi( argv[1] );
#ifdef __U_MULTI__
    uProcessor p;                 // create 2nd kernel thread
#endif // __U_MULTI__
    {
        increment t[2];
    } // wait for tasks to finish
    printf( "%lld\n", shared );
}
```

Fig. 5.12 Interference, double word

21. Compile the program in Fig. 5.12 using the u++ command, without and with compilation flag -multi and *no optimization*, to generate a uniprocessor and multiprocessor executable. Run both versions of the program 10 times with command line argument 100000000 on a multi-core computer with at least 2 CPUs (cores).

   a. Show the 10 results from each version of the program.
   b. Must all 10 runs for each version produce the same result? Explain your answer.
   c. In theory, what are the smallest and largest values that could be printed out by this program with an argument of 10000000? Explain your answers. (**Hint:** one of the obvious answers is wrong.)
   d. Explain the difference in the size of the values between the uniprocessor and multiprocessor output.

22. a. Quick sort is one of the best sorting algorithms in terms of execution speed on randomly arranged data. It also lends itself easily to concurrent execution by partitioning the data into those greater than a pivot and those less than a pivot so each partition can be sorted independently and concurrently by another task.

   Write an in-place concurrent quick sort with the following public interface (you may add only a public destructor and private members):

```
template<typename T> _Task Quicksort {
public:
    Quicksort( T values[], unsigned int low, unsigned int high, unsigned int depth );
};
```

   that sorts an array of non-unique values into ascending order. Choose the pivot as follows:

```
pivot = array[low + ( high - low ) / 2];
```

A naïve conversion of a sequential quicksort to a concurrent quicksort partitions the data values as normal, but instead of recursively invoking quicksort on each partition, a new quicksort task is created to handle each partition. (For this discussion, assume no other sorting algorithm is used for small partitions.) However, this approach creates a large number of tasks: approximately $2 \times N$, where N is the number of data values. The number of tasks can be reduced to approximately N by only creating a new quicksort task for one partition and recursively sorting the other partition in the current quicksort task.

In general, creating many more tasks than processors significantly reduces performance (try an example to see the effect) due to contention on accessing the processors versus any contention in the program itself. The only way to achieve good performance for a concurrent quicksort is to significantly reduce the number of quicksort tasks via an additional argument that limits the tree depth of the quicksort tasks (see details below). The depth argument is decremented on each recursive call and tasks are only created while this argument is greater than zero; otherwise sequential recursive-calls are use to sort each partition.

Recursion can overflow a task's stack, since the default task size is only 32K or 64K bytes in μC++. To check for stack overflow, call verify() at the start of the recursive routine, which prints a warning message if the call is close to the task's stack-limit or terminates the program is the stack limit is exceeded. If verify produces a warning or an error, globally increase the stack size for all tasks by adding the following routine to your code:

```
unsigned int uDefaultStackSize() {
    return 512 * 1000;     // set task stack-size to 512K
}
```

which is automatically called by μC++ at task creation to set the stack size. Finally, to maximize efficiency, quicksort tasks must not be created by calls to **new**, i.e., no dynamic allocation is necessary for quicksort tasks.

Add the following declaration to uMain::main after checking command-line arguments but before creating any tasks:

```
uProcessor p[ (1 << depth) - 1 ] __attribute__(( unused )); // 2^depth-1 kernel threads
```

to increase the number of kernel threads to access multiple processors (there is always one existing processor). This declaration must be in the same scope as the declaration of the initial quicksort task for the timing mode.

The executable program is named quicksort and has the following shell interface:

```
quicksort -s unsorted-file [ sorted-file ]
quicksort -t size (>= 0) [ depth (>= 0) ]
```

(Square brackets indicate optional command line parameters, and do not appear on the actual command line.) The type of the input values is provided as a preprocessor variable.

The program has two modes depending on the command option -s or -t (i.e., sort or time):

i. For the sort mode, input number of values, input values, sort using 1 processor, output sorted values. Input and output is specified as follows:

- If the unsorted input file is not specified, print an appropriate usage message and terminate. The input file contains lists of unsorted values. Each list starts with the number of values in that list. For example, the input file:

```
8 25 6 8 -5 99 100 101 7
3 1 -3 5
0
10 9 8 7 6 5 4 3 2 1 0
61 60 59 58 57 56 55 54 53 52 51 50 49 48 47 46 45 44 43 42 41 40 39 38
37 36 35 34 33 32 31 30 29 28 27 26 25 24 23 22 21 20 19 18 17 16 15 14
13 12 11 10 9 8 7 6 5 4 3 2 1 0
```

contains 5 lists with 8, 3, 0, 10 and 61 values in each list. (The line breaks are for readability only; values can be separated by any white-space character and appear across any number of lines.) Since the number of data values can be (very) large, dynamically allocate the array to hold the values, otherwise the array can exceed the stack size of uMain::main.

Assume the first number in the input file is always present and correctly specifies the number of following values; assume all following values are correctly formed so no error checking is required on the input data.

- If no output file name is specified, use standard output. Print the original input list followed by the sorted list, as in:

```
25 6 8 -5 99 100 101 7
-5 6 7 8 25 99 100 101

1 -3 5
-3 1 5
```

blank line from list of length 0 (this line not actually printed)
blank line from list of length 0 (this line not actually printed)

```
9 8 7 6 5 4 3 2 1 0
0 1 2 3 4 5 6 7 8 9

60 59 58 57 56 55 54 53 52 51 50 49 48 47 46 45 44 43 42 41 40 39
  38 37 36 35 34 33 32 31 30 29 28 27 26 25 24 23 22 21 20 19 18 17
  16 15 14 13 12 11 10 9 8 7 6 5 4 3 2 1 0
0 1 2 3 4 5 6 7 8 9 10 11 12 13 14 15 16 17 18 19 20 21
  22 23 24 25 26 27 28 29 30 31 32 33 34 35 36 37 38 39 40 41 42 43
  44 45 46 47 48 49 50 51 52 53 54 55 56 57 58 59 60
```

for the previous input file. End each set of output with a blank line, and start a newline with 2 spaces after printing 22 values from a set of values.

ii. For the time mode, dimension an integer array to size, initialize the array to values size..1 (descending order), sort using $2^{depth} - 1$ processors, and print no values (used for timing experiments). Parameter depth is a non-negative number ($>=$ 0). The default value if unspecified is 0. This mode is used to time the performance of the quicksort over a fixed set of values in descending order using different numbers of processors.

Print an appropriate error message and terminate the program if unable to open the given files. Check command arguments size and depth for correct form (integer) and range; print an appropriate usage message and terminate the program if a value is invalid.

b.   i. Compare the speedup of the quicksort algorithm with respect to performance by doing the following:

- Time the execution using the time command:

```
$ /usr/bin/time -f "%Uu %Ss %E" quicksort -t 100000000 0
14.80u 0.71s 0:15.53
```

(Output from time differs depending on your shell, but all provide user, system and real time.) Compare the *user* (14.8u) and *real* (0:15.53) time among runs, which is the CPU time consumed solely by the execution of user code (versus system) and the total time from the start to the end of the program.

- Adjust the array size to get real time in the range 5 to 20 s. (Timing results below 1 s are inaccurate.) Use the same array size for all experiments.

- After establishing an array size, run 7 experiments varying the value of depth from 0 1 2 3 4 5 6. Include all 7 timing results to validate your experiments.

  ii. State the observed performance difference with respect to scaling when using different numbers of processors to achieve parallelism.

  iii. Very briefly (2-4 sentences) speculate on the program behaviour.

23. a. Merge sort is one of several sorting algorithms that takes optimal time (to within a constant factor) to sort N items. It also lends itself easily to concurrent execution by partitioning the data into two, and each half can be sorted independently and concurrently by another task.

Write a concurrent merge sort with the following public interface (you may add only a public destructor and private members):

```
template<typename T> _Task Mergesort {
  public:
    Mergesort( T values[], unsigned int low, unsigned int high, unsigned int depth );
};
```

that sorts an array of non-unique values into ascending order. A naïve conversion of a sequential mergesort to a concurrent mergesort partitions the data values as normal, but instead of recursively invoking mergesort on each partition, a new mergesort task is created to handle each partition. (For this discussion, assume no other sorting algorithm is used for small partitions.) However, this approach creates a large number of tasks: approximately 2 × N, where N is the number of data values. The number of tasks can be reduced to approximately N by only creating a new mergesort task for one partition and recursively sorting the other partition in the current mergesort task.

In general, creating many more tasks than processors significantly reduces performance (try an example to see the effect) due to contention on accessing the processors versus any contention in the program itself. The only way to achieve good performance for a concurrent mergesort is to significantly reduce the number of mergesort tasks via an additional argument that limits the tree depth of the mergesort tasks. The depth argument is decremented on each recursive call and tasks are only created while this argument is greater than zero; otherwise, sequential recursive-calls are use to sort each partition.

Recursion can overflow a task's stack, since the default task size is only 32K or 64K bytes in μC++. To check for stack overflow, call verify() at the start of the recursive routine, which prints a warning message if the call is close to the task's stack-limit or terminates the program if the stack limit is exceeded. If verify produces a warning or an error, globally increase the stack size for all tasks by adding the following routine to your code before the next test:

```
unsigned int uDefaultStackSize() {
    return 512 * 1000;      // set task stack-size to 512K
}
```

which is automatically called by μC++ at task creation to set the stack size.

To maximize efficiency, mergesort tasks must not be created by calls to **new**, i.e., no dynamic allocation is necessary for mergesort tasks. However, two dynamically sized arrays are required: one to hold the initial unsorted data and one for copying values during a merge. Both of these arrays can be large, so creating them in a task can overflow the task's stack. Hence, the driver dynamically allocates the storage for the unsorted data, and the top-level task of the mergesort allocates the copy array, passing it by reference to its child tasks.

Add the following declaration to uMain::main after checking command-line arguments but before creating any tasks:

```
uProcessor p[ (1 << depth) - 1 ] __attribute__(( unused )); // 2^depth-1 kernel threads
```

to increase the number of kernel threads to access multiple processors (there is always one existing processor). This declaration must be in the same scope as the declaration of the initial mergesort task for the timing mode.

The executable program is named mergesort and has the following shell interface:

```
mergesort -s unsorted-file [ sorted-file ]
mergesort -t size (>= 0) [ depth (>= 0) ]
```

(Square brackets indicate optional command line parameters, and do not appear on the actual command line.) The type of the input values is provided as a preprocessor variable.

The program has two modes depending on the command option -s or -t (i.e., sort or time):

i. For the sort mode, input number of values, input values, sort using 1
processor, output sorted values. Input and output is specified as follows:
- If the unsorted input file is not specified, print an appropriate usage
  message and terminate. The input file contains lists of unsorted
  values. Each list starts with the number of values in that list. For
  example, the input file:

```
8 25 6 8 -5 99 100 101 7
3 1 -3 5
0
10 9 8 7 6 5 4 3 2 1 0
61 60 59 58 57 56 55 54 53 52 51 50 49 48 47 46 45 44 43 42 41 40 39 38
37 36 35 34 33 32 31 30 29 28 27 26 25 24 23 22 21 20 19 18 17 16 15 14
13 12 11 10 9 8 7 6 5 4 3 2 1 0
```

contains 5 lists with 8, 3, 0, 10 and 61 values in each list. (The line
breaks are for readability only; values can be separated by any whitespace character and appear across any number of lines.) Since the
number of data values can be (very) large, dynamically allocate the
array to hold the values, otherwise the array can exceed the stack size
of uMain::main.

Assume the first number in the input file is always present
and correctly specifies the number of following values; assume all
following values are correctly formed so no error checking is required
on the input data.
- If no output file name is specified, use standard output. Print the
  original input list followed by the sorted list, as in:

```
25 6 8 -5 99 100 101 7
-5 6 7 8 25 99 100 101

1 -3 5
-3 1 5

blank line from list of length 0 (this line not actually printed)
blank line from list of length 0 (this line not actually printed)

9 8 7 6 5 4 3 2 1 0
0 1 2 3 4 5 6 7 8 9

60 59 58 57 56 55 54 53 52 51 50 49 48 47 46 45 44 43 42 41 40 39
  38 37 36 35 34 33 32 31 30 29 28 27 26 25 24 23 22 21 20 19 18 17
  16 15 14 13 12 11 10 9 8 7 6 5 4 3 2 1 0
0 1 2 3 4 5 6 7 8 9 10 11 12 13 14 15 16 17 18 19 20 21
  22 23 24 25 26 27 28 29 30 31 32 33 34 35 36 37 38 39 40 41 42 43
  44 45 46 47 48 49 50 51 52 53 54 55 56 57 58 59 60
```

for the previous input file. End each set of output with a blank line,
and start a newline with 2 spaces after printing 22 values from a set
of values.

ii. For the time mode, dimension an integer array to size, initialize the array
to values size..1 (descending order), sort using $2^{depth} - 1$ processors, and
print no values (used for timing experiments). Parameter depth is a non-
negative number ($>= 0$). The default value if unspecified is 0. This

mode is used to time the performance of the mergesort over a fixed set of values in descending order using different numbers of processors.

Print an appropriate error message and terminate the program if unable to open the given files. Check command arguments size and depth for correct form (integer) and range; print an appropriate usage message and terminate the program if a value is invalid.

b.   i.   Compare the speedup of the mergesort algorithm with respect to performance by doing the following:

- Time the execution using the time command:

```
$ /usr/bin/time -f "%Uu %Ss %E" mergesort -t 100000000 0
14.13u 0.59s 0:14.68
```

(Output from time differs depending on the shell, but all provide user, system and real time.) Compare the *user* (14.13u) and *real* (0:14.68) time among runs, which is the CPU time consumed solely by the execution of user code (versus system) and the total time from the start to the end of the program.

- Adjust the array size to get the real time in the range 5 to 20 s. (Timing results below 1 s are inaccurate.) Use the same array size for all experiments.

- After establishing an array size, run 7 experiments varying the value of depth from 0 1 2 3 4 5 6. Include all 7 timing results to validate your experiments.

ii.   State the observed performance difference with respect to scaling when using different numbers of processors to achieve parallelism.

iii. Very briefly (2–4 sentences) speculate on the program behaviour.

24. Multiplying two matrices is a common operations in many numerical algorithms. Matrix multiply lends itself easily to concurrent execution because data can be partitioned, and each partition can be processed concurrently without interfering with tasks working on other partitions (divide and conqueror).

a.   Write a concurrent matrix-multiply with the following interface:

void matrixmultiply(**int** *Z[], **int** *X[], **int** xr, **int** xc, **int** *Y[], **int** yc);

which calculates $Z_{xr,yc} = X_{xr,xcyr} \cdot Y_{xcyr,yc}$, where matrix multiply is defined as:

$$X_{i,j} \cdot Y_{j,k} = \left(\sum_{c=1}^{j} X_{row,c} Y_{c,column} \right)_{i,k}$$

Create a task to calculate each row of the Z matrix from the appropriate X row and Y columns. All matrices in the program are variable sized, and hence, allocated dynamically on the heap.

The executable program is named matrixmultiply and has the following shell interface:

matrixmultiply *xrows xcols-yrows ycols* [*X-matrix-file Y-matrix-file*]

- The first three parameters are the dimensions of the $X_{xr,xcyr}$ and $Y_{xcyr,yc}$ matrices.
- If specified, the next two parameters are the X and Y input files to be multiplied. Each input file contains a matrix with appropriate values based on the dimension parameters; e.g., the input file:

```
1  2  3  4
5  6  7  8
9 10 11 12
```

is a 3×4 matrix. Assume the correct number of input values in each matrix file and all matrix values are correctly formed. After reading in the two matrices, multiply them, and print the product on standard output using this format:

```
$ matrixmultiply 3 4 3 xfile yfile
                                      |      1      2      3
                                      |      4      5      6
                                      |      7      8      9
                                      |     10     11     12
-----------------------------------*-----------------------------
    1       2       3       4     |     70     80     90
    5       6       7       8     |    158    184    210
    9      10      11      12     |    246    288    330
```

Where the matrix on the bottom-left is X, the matrix on the top-right is Y, and the matrix on the bottom-right is Z.

- If no input files are specified, create the appropriate X and Y matrices with each value initialized to 37, multiply them, *but print no output*. This case is used for timing the cost of parallel execution.

Print an appropriate error message and terminate the program if there are an invalid number of arguments, the dimension values are less than one, or unable to open the given input files.

b. i. Test for any benefits of concurrency by running the program in parallel:
- Put the following declaration after the arguments have been analysed:

  uProcessor p[xrows - 1] __attribute__((unused)); // number of CPUs

  This declaration allows the program to access multiple virtual CPUs (cores). One virtual CPU is used for each task calculating a row of the Z matrix. The program starts with one virtual CPU so only xrows - 1 additional CPUs are necessary. Compile the program with the μC++ -multi flag and no optimization.

- Run the program on a multi-core computer with at least 16 or more actual CPUs (cores), with arguments of xrows in the range [1,2,4,8,16] with xcols-yrows of 5000 and ycols of 10000.

- Time each execution using the time command:

  % time ./a.out
  3.21u 0.02s 0:03.32 100.0%

Output from time differs depending on your shell, but all provide user, system and real time. (Increase the number of xcols-yrows and ycols if the timing results are below .1 s.)

* Include all 5 timing results to validate your experiments.

ii. Comment on the user and real times for the experiments.

References

1. Amdahl, G.M.: Validity of the single processor approach to achieving large scale computing capabilities. In: Proceedings of the April 18-20, 1967, Spring Joint Computer Conference, AFIPS '67 (Spring), pp. 483–485. ACM, New York, NY, USA (1967)
2. Andrews, G.R., Schneider, F.B.: Concepts and notations for concurrent programming. ACM Comput. Surv. **15**(1), 3–43 (1983)
3. Bacon, D.F., Graham, S.L., Sharp, O.J.: Compiler transformations for high-performance computing. ACM Comput. Surv. **26**(4), 345–420 (1994)
4. Buhr, P.A., Harji, A.S.: Concurrent urban legends. Concurrency and Computation: Practice and Experience **17**(9), 1133–1172 (2005)
5. Gray, J.: Why do computers stop and what can be done about it? Tech. Rep. 85.7 PN87614, Tandem Computers (1985). http://www.hpl.hp.com/techreports/tandem/TR-85.7.pdf

Chapter 6
Atomicity*

In the previous chapter, the importance of thread synchronization was demonstrated, e.g., before performing communication or data is lost or over written. Notice that synchronization is an action that occurs *among* threads. However, there are situations where a thread may access a non-thread object, e.g., writing to a file or adding a node to a linked-list. In both cases, synchronization is unnecessary with the object because the object is always ready to have an operation applied to it since it has no thread.

However, a complex problem arises if there are multiple threads attempting to operate on the *same* non-thread object simultaneously. Imagine the chaos in a file or linked-list if two threads simultaneously write into a file or add a node to a linked-list. In the case of a file, one thread might write over characters that are being written by the other thread. In the case of a linked-list, one thread might change the link fields at the same time as the other thread, and so, only one of the two nodes is added to the list or the list is left in an inconsistent state.

This problem is solved if the operation on the object is atomic, meaning indivisible.[1] In other words, no other thread can read or modify any partial results during the operation on the object. Note, it is a common mistake to believe atomic operations proceed without interruption. During the atomic operation, a thread's execution may be interrupted by time-slicing or blocking, which makes it appear no thread is using the object. However, atomicity applies to the object not the thread, so even if the thread performing the atomic operation is not executing, no other thread can start a new atomic operation until the current thread restarts and completes the operation. Therefore, each atomic operation executes sequentially (or serially) from the perspective of all threads. The operation performed atomically is called a critical section, and preventing simultaneous execution of a critical section by multiple

---

* This chapter is a revision of "High-Performance N-Thread Software Solutions for Mutual Exclusion" in [6] ©2014 John Wiley & Sons, Ltd. Portions reprinted by permission.
[1]From the Greek $\alpha\tau o\mu o\sigma$ meaning atom (atomic does not mean radioactive).

233
P.A. Buhr, *Understanding Control Flow*, DOI 10.1007/978-3-319-25703-7_6

threads is called mutual exclusion. Therefore, there are two aspects to the problem: knowing which operations must be critical sections and then providing appropriate mutual exclusion for these critical sections.

6.1 Critical Section

A critical section is a pairing: shared data and code manipulating the data executed by multiple threads, where the data can be basic or complex data-types. Collectively, this pairing denotes an instance of a critical section. It is a common mistake to consider only the code as the critical section. Many critical-section instances may exist for a particular block of code with different objects, but an object can only be associated with one critical section at a time; hence, there is a many-to-one, i.e., objects to code, relationship. (Note, a thread can simultaneously access multiple critical sections, and hence, multiple objects, but each object is still only associated with one critical section.) For example, multiple threads may be simultaneously in the file write routine but writing to different files. In this case, the fact that the threads execute the same code, possibly at the same time, does not imply a critical section. Only when threads are in the write routine for the *same* file is a critical section generated.

It is non-trivial to examine a program and detect all the critical sections, particularly because of the pairing necessary to form a critical section. Essentially, a programmer must determine if and when objects are shared by multiple threads and prevent it only if it results in problems. One technique is to detect any sharing and serialize all access. Unfortunately, this approach significantly inhibits concurrency if threads are only reading. It is always the case that multiple threads can simultaneously read data without interfering with one another; only writing causes problems. Therefore, it is reasonable to allow multiple simultaneous readers but writers must be serialized. However, care must be taken. For example, if multiple threads are performing a linear search, they can all be searching the list simultaneously as that only involves reading the shared list. However, if a thread inserts data into the list when the search fails to find a key, there is a problem because the list changes. Clearly, if two threads try to simultaneously update the list, there is a problem. However, there can also be a problem if one thread is updating and another is only reading. The reading thread might start reading the new node before data is inserted or the node is completely linked; either case may cause the reader to fail. One solution is to serialize searching of the list, but that inhibits concurrency because most of the time a key is found and no updating occurs. Therefore, it is wasteful, from a concurrency perspective, to serialize an operation when a write only occurs occasionally. In general, a programmer needs to minimize the amount of mutual exclusion, i.e., make critical sections as short as possible, to maximize concurrency.

However, before rushing ahead on the topic of maximizing concurrency, the fundamental question of how to provide mutual exclusion must be answered. That is, once an operation or part of an operation has been identified as a critical section how is mutual exclusion enforced?

6.2 Mutual Exclusion

The goal of simple mutual exclusion is to ensure only one thread is executing a block of code with respect to a particular object, i.e., a critical section. This capability is accomplished by mutual-exclusion code placed before (entry protocol) and possibly after (exit protocol) the critical section. The entry protocol is divided into two parts:

1. doorway is a prefix in which no waiting (or unbounded looping) occurs.
2. busy waiting is one or more loops causing a delay until it is appropriate to make forward progress.

In general, any number of threads may arrive simultaneously at the entry protocol.

Mutual exclusion solutions can get complex, so it is useful to have an analogy to explain the problems. The analogy used here is a bathroom.[2] Everyone can relate to the fact that a bathroom (the code) is a shared resource that is normally a critical section with respect to each person (object) using it. Therefore, a bathroom requires mutual exclusion to enforce this, and this mutual exclusion is usually put in place at the bathroom door.

6.2.1 Mutual Exclusion Game

By casting the mutual exclusion problem in the form of a game, it makes the discussion more interesting. To preclude trivial solutions to the mutual exclusion game, such as executing each thread to completion before executing another thread, all the following rules are required:

1. Only one thread is in the critical section with respect to a particular object [14].
   The primary requirement and the goal of the game.
2. Threads may run at arbitrary speed and in arbitrary order [14].
   This rule precludes solutions that require one person to start before the other, or that a person can only take a certain amount of time in the bathroom, or a person must be away from the bathroom and not try to enter for a certain amount of time. Therefore, a person can arrive at the bathroom at any time and spend an arbitrary amount of time in the bathroom.

---

[2]The euphemism "bathroom" is not universal; other names include restroom, WC (water closet), washroom, lavatory and just toilet. Choose a euphemism appropriate to your modesty level and cultural background.

3. If a thread is not in the entry or exit code that controls access to the critical section, it may not prevent other threads from entering the critical section [30, p. 318].

   This rule precludes someone from locking the bathroom and taking the key away to guarantee access on their return. Therefore, if someone is not in the bathroom, someone else is always allowed to enter the empty bathroom.

4. In selecting a thread for entry to a critical section, the selection cannot be postponed indefinitely [14]. *Not* satisfying this rule is called indefinite postponement or livelock.

   This rule covers the situation where two people arrive at the bathroom simultaneously and stand at the door saying "You go first", "No, you go first", "No, you go first!!!", "NO, YOU GO FIRST!!!", ... This happens all the time in real life and there is always some way to solve it (this is also true for concurrency). People are never found unconscious outside doorways, collapsed from exhaustion, from yelling "No, you go first". Tasks, on the other hand, do argue back and forth forever! Notice in this case, no one is in the bathroom; the argument is going on *outside* the bathroom. Also, because the people (threads) are arguing, they are taking up resources (CPU time) so they are active or "alive", but indirectly locking each other out of the bathroom, hence the name livelock.

5. After a thread starts entry to the critical section, it must eventually enter [28, p. 321]. *Not* satisfying this rule is called starvation or unfairness.

   When a person arrives at the bathroom, they must be given a guarantee of service. Notice this requirement is not a time guarantee, such as you can go into the bathroom in 5 min. It says that you can get into the bathroom after an unspecified number of people have entered and finished using the bathroom. There is no control on how long a person spends in the bathroom, but when they exit, scheduling of new entrants must ensure everyone waiting eventually gains entry. This rule does not have to be fair, either, as long as there is some way to show eventual entry. For example, the person coming out of the bathroom might be allowed to go right back in again, if they forgot their toothbrush; whereupon, they might decide to take a shower. But when they come out the second time or third time or whatever, someone else waiting is allowed to enter the bathroom. If waiting threads are overtaken by a thread arriving later, there is the notion of barging.

   A stronger notion of eventual entry provides a bound on the number of threads allowed to enter the critical section after a thread has made a request to enter it. For example, *at most* 5 threads execute ahead of an arriving thread. If threads wait in FIFO order, there is a hard waiting bound, e.g., *exactly* 5 threads execute ahead of an arriving thread.

   Some solutions to the mutual exclusion game ignore this rule if it can be shown that the chance for any long-term unfairness is extremely low. That is, the chance that a solution might favour one thread over the other for a long period of time is so small that in practice a thread always gets into the critical section after waiting only a short period of time (where short may be from a human perspective not a computer's perspective). Notice that short periods of unfairness are always tolerated, e.g., one thread might enter the bathroom 20 times in a row before another waiting thread is allowed in. The problem with these kinds of probabilistic solutions is the small chance that one thread may never get into the critical section. In important situations like a rocket ship or nuclear reactor, a probabilistic solution is normally deemed unacceptable because it may result in catastrophic failure.

Indefinite postponement and starvation are related by busy waiting. Unlike synchronization, looping for an event in mutual exclusion *must* prevent unbounded delay. While a large delay still satisfies the theoretical requirement, it is normally impractical and results in failure. Therefore, before a loop starts in mutual exclusion, it must be possible to ensure it stops. It is irrelevant if the loop body is empty, yields or blocks, there must be eventual entry or the loop is busy waiting, which leads to indefinite postponement and starvation.

6.2.2 Self-Checking Critical Section

It is actually very difficult to verify programmatically if an algorithm satisfies all five rules to the mutual exclusion game. In most cases, failure to meet a rule is demonstrated by a counterexample, which is often difficult to construct. However, it is possible to constructively check for violation of rule 1, which is the most important rule of the game, by creating a self-checking bathroom. Upon entering the bathroom, a person writes their name on a chalk board on the *inside* of the bathroom door. A person then starts performing their bathroom chores, but every so often, they look at the chalk board to see if their name is still on the door. If rule 1 is broken, someone has entered the bathroom and changed the name on the back of the door. Notice, the chalk board is essential because just looking around the bathroom is insufficient; e.g., someone could be in the shower and not see someone enter the bathroom. If a person notices the name has changed, does that mean there is someone currently in the bathroom with them?

Fig. 6.1 shows a routine implementing a self-checking critical-section (bathroom). The shared, global variable CurrTid is the chalk board and the assignment at the beginning of CriticalSection initializes it to the address of the current thread executing in the routine. A thread then goes into a loop performing the critical-section operation, but at the end of each iteration, the thread compares its address with the one in CurrTid for any change. If there is a change, rule 1 has been violated and the program is stopped. Is it necessary to check for interference every time through the loop, i.e., what is the minimum amount of checking necessary to detect a violation of the critical section? What advantage is gained by checking in the loop?

Interestingly, there is no perfect mechanism to ensure absolute segregation of the bathroom by the threads. Even if the self-checking bathroom does a check at the end of the routine, there is the potential for a slight overlap between someone

```
uBaseTask *CurrTid;     // shared, current thread in critical section
void CriticalSection() {
    ::CurrTid = &uThisTask();                    // current thread address
    for ( int i = 1; i <= 100; i += 1 ) {        // delay
        // perform critical section operation
        if ( ::CurrTid != &uThisTask() ) {       // check for mutual
            uAbort( "interference" );            // exclusion violation
        }
    }
}
```

```
┌─────────────────┐
│  ┌───────────┐  │
│  │   Peter   │  │
│  └───────────┘  │
│               ● │
│                 │
│     inside      │
└─────────────────┘
```

Fig. 6.1 Self-checking critical-section

entering and someone leaving the bathroom. For example, the thread leaving the critical section could be interrupted *after* the last check but *before* returning from the routine. In essence, there is always the potential for a moment in time when the back foot of someone leaving the bathroom and the front foot of someone entering are both in the bathroom. However, this does not affect the critical section because its work has been completed by the time the apparent violation occurs.

6.3 Software Solution

Is it possible to write (in your favourite programming language) some code that guarantees that a statement (or group of statements) is always serially executed with respect to a particular object? There is no help from the hardware, only the software is used to solve the problem. Basically, this code must create atomicity out of thin air; that is, in a language and on a computer that provides no atomicity, can atomicity be built from basic language and machine capabilities? The answer is yes, but demonstrating it is non-trivial. Initially, solutions for only *two* threads are examined; *N*-thread solutions are examined in Sect. 6.3.8, p. 254.

6.3.1 Lock

The first solution is the obvious one–put a lock on the door of the bathroom. When someone enters the bathroom, they lock the door. While this may work for people, it does not work for computers; in fact, it does not work for people if they behave like computers. Here is a scenario where it fails. Two people walk up to the door, open the door together, enter together and lock the door together. This scenario does not happen normally because people use their sense of sight, hearing and touch to notice there is someone with them. However, computers have none of these senses, and therefore, they cannot use solutions that rely on them.

```
enum Yale { CLOSED, OPEN };
_Task PermissionLock {
    Yale &Lock;
    void main() {
        for ( int i = 1; i <= 1000; i += 1 ) {
            while ( Lock == CLOSED ) {}     // entry protocol
            Lock = CLOSED;
            CriticalSection();              // critical section
            Lock = OPEN;                    // exit protocol
        }
    }
  public:
    PermissionLock( Yale &Lock ) Lock( Lock ) {}
};
void uMain::main() {
    Yale Lock = OPEN;                       // shared
    PermissionLock t0( Lock ), t1( Lock );
}
```

Fig. 6.2 Lock

It is still worth looking at the program that implements a lock (see Fig. 6.2) to see why it fails. The shared variable Yale is either open or closed and is initialized to open; this corresponds to the lock on the bathroom door. Routine uMain::main creates two threads passing a lock reference to each thread. Each thread's constructor stores the lock reference in a class variable so it can be used by the main member, which goes in and out of the self-checking critical-section (bathroom) 1000 times. Having the threads perform 1000 consecutive entries is contrived; in general, a thread goes off to perform some other operation after leaving the critical section, like getting dressed or going to work. Thus, this program should generate many more simultaneous arrives than would occur normally in a concurrent program; nevertheless, it must still handle them.

Note the entry protocol before and the exit protocol after the call to routine CriticalSection, which is trying to ensure mutual exclusion and the other four rules of the mutual exclusion game. The entry protocol must check if the critical section is being used and wait if it is. If it is being used, there is a busy loop that spins around constantly checking the status of the lock. During busy waiting, a thread is using CPU resources but is not accomplishing any useful work. As mentioned in Sect. 5.13, p. 219, busy waiting should be avoided. When the lock is closed, it continues looping because the other thread must be in the critical section (entered the bathroom and locked the door); otherwise, it stops looping, closes the lock and enters the critical section, which happens when no one is in the bathroom at all, or someone in the bathroom unlocks the door and comes out.

Here is the scenario where rule 1 is broken on a multiprocessor. Two threads both execute the test in the entry protocol at the same time. They both see the lock is open, they both close the lock, and they both enter the critical section. On a uniprocessor, it is slightly more complex. The CPU must switch between threads immediately after one thread sees the lock is open and exits the busy wait, but before the lock is closed, i.e., between the two entry protocol statements. The other thread now attempts to enter the critical section, sees the lock is open, closes the lock and enters the critical section. Eventually, the other thread restarts and it does not recheck the lock because it knows it just did that. So it locks the lock (again) and enters the critical section with the other thread. You might think that checking the lock for closed and starting the entry protocol again would fix the problem; however, a thread does not know when it is interrupted, so it cannot know when to check again.

One final point is that even if this could be made to work (and it is in Sect. 6.4, p. 272), it still breaks rule 5. That is, a thread can starve waiting to enter the critical section. In this specific example, there happens to be an eventual entry because each thread only enters the critical section 1000 times. Now consider if the loops are infinite. In theory, one thread could always see the lock closed as the other thread whizzes in and out of the critical section; in practice, it is highly unlikely that this would occur for very long, so this is a probabilistic solution with respect to rule 5.

6.3.2 Alternation

Since the obvious approach does not work, it is necessary to look at alternative approaches. Here is a simple approach that does not work for all rules, but does solve rule 1; the idea is to take turns entering the bathroom. This approach is implemented by putting a chalk board on the *outside* of the bathroom door on which you write your name after *leaving* the bathroom (see right side of Fig. 6.3). This chalk board is different from the one on the *inside* of the bathroom, on which you write your name after *entering* the bathroom for use in checking violation of rule 1. Someone cannot enter the bathroom if their name is on the outside of the door, because it is not their turn; they must wait for the other person to finish their turn in the critical section, leave the bathroom, and change the name. The algorithm begins with either person's name on the chalk board.

The program to implement alternation is on the left side of Fig. 6.3. The shared variable Last, declared in uMain::main indicates which thread was last in the bathroom; this corresponds to the chalk board on the outside of the bathroom door. uMain::main initializes Last to the value 0 or 1. These values are arbitrary names for the two threads; any distinct pair of values works, e.g., thread identifiers. uMain::main then creates two threads passing the names and a reference to the blackboard on the outside of the bathroom door to each thread. Each thread's constructor stores its name and reference to Last in class variables so they can be used by the thread main, which goes in and out of the self-checking critical section (bathroom) 1000 times. Note, one thread's me variable has the value 0 and the other has the value 1 but both threads have a reference to the shared variable Last. The entry protocol is a busy loop waiting until the value of Last is different from the thread's name, which means that it is not the last thread in the critical section. The exit protocol changes Last to the name of the thread last in the critical section.

```
_Task Alternation {
    int me, &Last;
    void main() {
        for ( int i = 1; i <= 1000; i += 1 ) {
            while ( Last == me ) {}          // entry protocol
            CriticalSection();               // critical section
            Last = me;                       // exit protocol
        }
    }
public:
    Alternation( int me, int &Last ) : me( me ), Last( Last ) {}
};
void uMain::main() {
    int Last = rand() % 2;                   // shared, random starter
    Alternation t0( 0, Last ), t1( 1, Last );
}
```

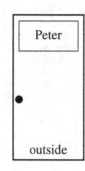

Fig. 6.3 Alternation

Now this approach achieves rule 1 because strict alternation ensures mutual exclusion. Furthermore, alternation does not rely on order or speed of execution (rule 2). However, it does violate rule 3: if a thread is not in the critical section or the entry or exit protocol, it may not prevent other threads from entering the critical section. If one person finishes in the bathroom and goes to work, the other person can enter the bathroom at most once before the other person comes home! So when the person at home leaves the bathroom, they become the last person to use the bathroom and have to wait until the person at work comes home and uses the bathroom. While waiting, the bathroom is empty, yet the algorithm is preventing them from using it. Another example of this kind of failure is if thread 0 only enters the bathroom 500 times while thread 1 wants to enter 1000 times. As soon as thread 0 finishes, there is no partner for the other thread to alternate with, and so it cannot get into the empty bathroom.

While this approach failed, it illustrates an important lesson: a thread must be able to go into the critical section multiple times in succession if the other thread does not want to go in. While direct use of alternation does not work, later algorithms come back to the idea of alternation for secondary purposes.

6.3.3   Declare Intent

While the alternation solution solves rules 1 and 2, it cannot solve rule 3 because there is no information to determine if the other person is *uninterested* in using the critical section, which allow multiple consecutive entries. To solve rule 3, it is necessary to know if a person is *interested* in entering the bathroom [13, § 2.1]. Hence, if one person is uninterested, the other person can make multiple consecutive entries satisfying rule 3. This scheme requires two chalk boards on the outside of the bathroom door (see right side of Fig. 6.4); each is used to indicate intent to

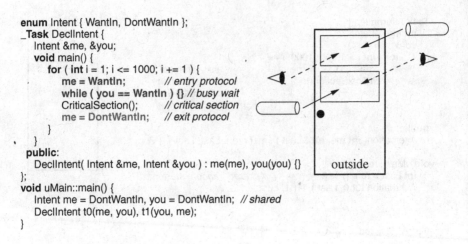

```
enum Intent { WantIn, DontWantIn };
_Task DeclIntent {
    Intent &me, &you;
    void main() {
        for ( int i = 1; i <= 1000; i += 1 ) {
            me = WantIn;              // entry protocol
            while ( you == WantIn ) {} // busy wait
            CriticalSection();         // critical section
            me = DontWantIn;          // exit protocol
        }
    }
  public:
    DeclIntent( Intent &me, Intent &you ) : me(me), you(you) {}
};
void uMain::main() {
    Intent me = DontWantIn, you = DontWantIn;  // shared
    DeclIntent t0(me, you), t1(you, me);
}
```

outside

Fig. 6.4 Declare intent

enter (interest) and erased when leaving the bathroom (uninterested). Each person is assigned one of the chalk boards (top or bottom). A person can only write on their chalk board and look at the other persons. (This approach is expressed in the picture by a piece of chalk to write with, and an eye to look at the other chalk board.) If someone wants to enter the bathroom, they first put a check mark on their chalk board indicating intent to enter and then they look at the other chalk board to see if the other person has indicated intent, i.e., put a check mark on their chalk board. If the other person has indicated intent, it implies one of two cases: the other person is in the bathroom or the other person arrived ahead of you and is just entering the bathroom (you cannot see them standing beside you). In either case, they will eventually exit the bathroom and retract their intent. Since you are watching their chalk board, you will see them exit the bathroom when they erase their chalk board.

The program to implement declare intent is on the left of Fig. 6.4. The shared variables me and you, declared in uMain::main, correspond to the two chalk boards on the outside of the bathroom door; they are both initialized to not intending to enter the critical section. uMain::main then creates two threads passing references to the two shared variables to each thread; however, the variables are reversed for the second thread. This means that thread t0 can see both variables but calls one me and the other you, while thread t1 sees the same two variables but with the names reversed. Each thread's constructor stores these values in class variables so they can be used by the thread main, which goes in and out of the self-checking critical section (bathroom) 1000 times. The entry protocol marks the intent to enter, i.e., that thread's me, and starts a busy loop waiting until the other thread retracts intent, which means it has exited the critical section. The exit protocol retracts intent by changing that thread's me. If one thread does not declare intent, the other thread is free to enter the critical section multiple times in succession, solving rule 3.

This approach satisfies rules 1–3. Mutual exclusion is guaranteed indirectly because the algorithm fails rule 4 (discussed next). There is no code that depends on order and speed of execution (rule 2), and there is no code outside the CS that precludes entry by other threads (rule 3). Rule 4 is violated because in selecting a thread for entry to a CS, the selection *can* be postponed indefinitely. The failure scenario occurs when threads arrive simultaneously. On a multiprocessor, both threads indicate intent to enter at the same time, both notice the other thread wants in, and both wait for the other thread to retract intent on exit from the critical section. However, neither thread can now retract intent because no progress is occurring toward the critical section; both threads are spinning in the empty busy loop, mistakenly thinking the critical section is occupied. On a uniprocessor, the failure scenario is slightly more complex. The CPU must switch between threads immediately after one thread indicates intent but before the other thread's intent is checked, i.e., between the two entry protocol statements. The other thread now attempts to enter the critical section, sets its intent and detects the other thread's intent is set. Both threads now spin in the busy loop, taking turns using the CPU to check the other thread's intent, which never changes, resulting in a livelock. When threads do not arrive simultaneously, each waits as necessary, and if they arrive simultaneously, livelock occurs; hence, mutual exclusion is never violated (rule 1).

6.3.4 Retract Intent

The declare intent solution did solve rules 1–3, so maybe it can be extended to handle rule 4. Notice, the problem *only* occurs on simultaneous arrival, when people say "You go first", "No, you go first", "No, you go first!!!", "NO, YOU GO FIRST!!!", ... As mentioned, livelock problems are always fixable. People solve this problem when one backs down so the other can make progress. This notion of backing down or retracting intent can be incorporated into the previous approach by simply retracting intent in the entry protocol if the other thread has its intent set. The thread that backs down then waits until the other thread exits the bathroom and retracts its intent. At that point, the thread that backed down starts the entire entry protocol again. (This approach is like retesting the lock and trying again as suggested in Sect. 6.3.1, p. 238.) Notice, retracting is a pessimistic action: when one thread sees the other thread's intent is set, it probably means the other thread is in the critical section not the entry protocol, so in many cases, it is unnecessary to back down. But it is impossible to tell if a thread is in the entry protocol or critical section when its intent is set, so simultaneous arrival must be assumed.

The program to implement this is in Fig. 6.5. The only change from the last program is the entry protocol. The entry protocol marks the intent to enter and then checks the other thread's intent. If the other thread's intent is set, intent is retracted and a busy loop is started waiting until the other thread retracts intent. When the other thread retracts its intent, which means it has exited the critical section, the

```
_Task RetractIntent {
    Intent &me, &you;
    void main() {
        for ( int i = 1; i <= 1000; i += 1 ) {
            for ( ;; ) {                        // entry protocol
                me = WantIn;                    // indicate intent
            if ( you == DontWantIn ) break;
                me = DontWantIn;                // retract intent
                while ( you == WantIn ){}       // busy wait
            }
            CriticalSection();                  // critical section
            me = DontWantIn;                    // exit protocol
        }
    }
  public:
    RetractIntent(Intent &me, Intent &you) : me(me), you(you) {}
};
void uMain::main() {
    Intent me = DontWantIn, you = DontWantIn;  // shared
    RetractIntent t0(me, you), t1(you, me);
}
```

Fig. 6.5 Retract intent

entry protocol is started again. As before, if one thread does not declare intent, the other thread is free to enter the critical section multiple times in succession.

Unfortunately, rule 4 is still broken but with a low probability. Again, the problem occurs if threads arrive simultaneously. Here is the scenario where rule 4 is broken on a multiprocessor. The two threads both indicate intent to enter at the same time. They both notice the other thread wants in, and so both retract intent. They both exit the busy loop immediately because neither thread has indicated intent and so both start the protocol over again. If the two threads continue to execute in perfect synchronization, executing the statements of the protocol at the same time, they defer entry forever. However, the chance of staying in perfect synchronization is very low. The moment one thread gets ahead of the other, it enters the critical section because the other thread still has its intent retracted. On a uniprocessor, it is even more complex to produce a failure of rule 4. The CPU must switch back and forth after almost every statement in the entry protocol. Furthermore, this perfect synchronization has to be maintained for the livelock situation. The chances of this occurring in practice is extremely low; nevertheless, it fails in theory.

6.3.5 Prioritized Retract Intent

While the retract intent solution failed to provide a perfect solution to rule 4, it comes probabilistically close. Unfortunately, "close" only counts in the game of horseshoes. Notice the problem only occurs on simultaneous arrival; if there is some way of breaking the tie on simultaneous arrival, the problem is solved. One possible approach is to assign different priorities to the people as a tie-breaking mechanism.

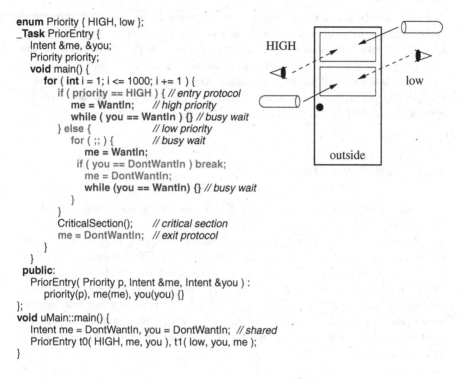

```
enum Priority { HIGH, low };
_Task PriorEntry {
    Intent &me, &you;
    Priority priority;
    void main() {
        for ( int i = 1; i <= 1000; i += 1 ) {
            if ( priority == HIGH ) { // entry protocol
                me = WantIn;        // high priority
                while ( you == WantIn ) {} // busy wait
            } else {                // low priority
                for ( ;; ) {        // busy wait
                    me = WantIn;
                    if ( you == DontWantIn ) break;
                    me = DontWantIn;
                    while (you == WantIn) {} // busy wait
                }
            }
            CriticalSection();      // critical section
            me = DontWantIn;        // exit protocol
        }
    }
  public:
    PriorEntry( Priority p, Intent &me, Intent &you ) :
        priority(p), me(me), you(you) {}
};
void uMain::main() {
    Intent me = DontWantIn, you = DontWantIn;  // shared
    PriorEntry t0( HIGH, me, you ), t1( low, you, me );
}
```

Fig. 6.6 Prioritized retract intent

For example, at one time, it was considered proper etiquette to give a woman higher
priority over a man when simultaneous arrival occurred at a doorway. However,
even if threads had gender, this only solves one of three cases, but the approach can
be adapted simply by giving one person high priority and the other low priority.
When simultaneous arrival occurs, the high-priority person always goes ahead of
the low-priority person.

The program to implement this is in Fig. 6.6. When uMain::main creates the two
threads, it now passes one the value HIGH and the other the value low, in addition to
the other values. The entry protocol is now divided into two parts by the **if** statement:
code for the high-priority thread and code for the low-priority thread. Alternatively,
two different code fragments can be created with the high-priority code executed by
one thread and the low-priority code executed by the other. The code for the high-
priority thread is the declare-intent algorithm (Fig. 6.4, p. 242), and the code for the
low-priority thread is the retract-intent algorithm. Basically, the high-priority thread
never retracts intent; if it detects the other thread has indicated its intent, it just spins
with its intent set until the other thread retracts intent, either in the entry protocol or
by exiting the critical section. The low-priority thread always retracts intent in the
entry protocol, if it detects the high-priority thread wants into or is already in the
critical section. The priorities ensure there is never a livelock.

Unfortunately, this approach violates rule 5: there is no guarantee of eventual entry into the critical section after a thread has made a request to enter it. In theory, the high-priority thread can always *barge* ahead of the low-priority thread by racing out of the critical section and back into it, so the low-priority thread starves, i.e., never enters the critical section; in practice, contention for the critical section is rarely high enough for high-priority threads to cause long-term starvation, so this approach is probabilistically correct for rule 5 in many situations.

6.3.6 Fair Retract Intent

If "close" is not good enough for rule 4, it is also not good enough for rule 5. The problem with the priority scheme is that it is not fair; if it can be made fair, it would solve rule 5. There are two basic approaches for dealing with tie-breaking on simultaneous arrival and ensuring fairness on entry to the CS: alternation and racing. Both approaches alternate entry to the critical section for simultaneous arrivals. While alternation is rejected in Sect. 6.3.2, p. 240, it is now going to be used *but* only for the rare case of simultaneous arrival, when it is known that both threads want to enter the critical section. It is not used in the case when one thread does not want to go into the critical section, and so prevents the other from entering multiple times in succession.

6.3.6.1 Alternation

This scheme is implemented by adding one more chalk board on the outside of the bathroom door, which is used to indicate who was last in the bathroom. Whenever there is a simultaneous arrival, the person who was last in the bathroom has to wait, which seems fair. However, if there is no simultaneous arrival, i.e., the other thread does not want in, the new chalk board is not even used, so a single thread can make multiple entries without the other thread. In fact, the first person to win the mutual exclusion game was the Dutch mathematician Theo J. Dekker, and so this approach is named after him. (The algorithm and credit for its solution are discussed at length by Edsger W. Dijkstra in [13].)

Fig. 6.7 shows a structured implementation of Dekker's algorithm [15, Fig. 1]. (An unstructured version, similar to the original, appears in question 8 at the end of Chap. 2, p. 9.) The program is a modification of combination of the alternation program (Fig. 6.6) but with variable rather than fixed priority assignment. The shared variable Last indicates which thread was last in the bathroom by alternately pointing at the two intent variables in uMain::main; this corresponds to the new chalk board on the outside of the bathroom door. These values are arbitrary names for the two threads; any distinct pair of values works. uMain::main initializes Last to point to one of the intent variables.

```
_Task Dekker {
    Intent &me, &you, *&Last;
    void main() {
        for ( int i = 1; i <= 1000; i += 1 ) {
1           me = WantIn;              // declare intent
2           if ( you == WantIn ) { // other thread want in ?
3               if ( Last == &me ) { // high priority ?
4                   me = DontWantIn; // retract intent
5                   while ( Last == &me ) {}; // low priority
6                   me = WantIn; // re-declare intent
                }
7               while ( you == WantIn ); // high priority
            }
8           CriticalSection( id );
9           Last = &me;            // exit protocol
10          me = DontWantIn;       // retract intent
        }
    }
    public:
    Dekker( Intent &me, Intent &you, Intent *&Last ) :
        me(me), you(you), Last(Last) {}
};
void uMain::main() {
    Intent me = DontWantIn, you = DontWantIn,  // shared
        *Last = rand() % 2 ? &me : &you;
    Dekker t0(me, you, Last), t1(you, me, Last);
}
```

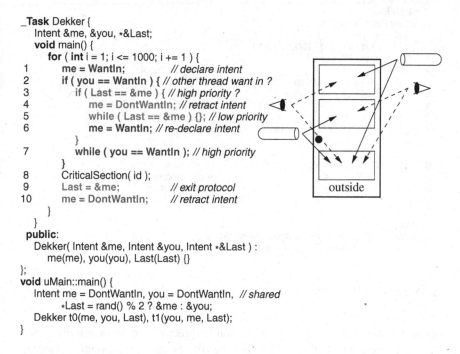

Fig. 6.7 Fair retract intent: Dekker, alternation, linear

The entry protocol sets intent to enter and only does further checking if the other thread also wants to enter. Then the threads divide into the high and low priority threads at line 3, depending on which thread was last in the critical section. The high-priority thread (not last in the bathroom) proceeds to line 7 without retracting its intent and waits for the other thread to retract its intent or exit the critical section. The low-priority thread retracts its intent at line 4 and waits at line 5 for the other thread to exit the critical section. When the high-priority thread exits the critical section, the priority switches (assignment to Last), and the low-priority thread becomes the high-priority thread moving to line 7 and waiting for the other thread to retract its intent or exit the critical section.

Fig. 6.8 shows an alternative implementation of Dekker's algorithm. The outer loop (line 2) is where the high-priority thread busy waits, and the inner loop (line 6) is where the low-priority thread busy waits. The **if** statement (line 4) controls which thread has low or high priority. The low-priority loop is nested in the high-priority loop because of the two steps in the exit protocol: setting Last and retracting intent. The low priority thread in the nested loop of the entry protocol might detect Last having changed, exit the busy loop, but still have to wait for the other thread to complete the exit protocol by retracting its intent. Think of what could go wrong if the low priority thread did not wait for the other thread to complete *all* the exit protocol before preceding into the critical section. In the case of simultaneous

```
_Task Dekker {
    Intent &me, &you, *&Last;
    void main() {
        for ( int i = 1; i <= 1000; i += 1 ) {
1           me = WantIn;
2           for ( ;; ) {                        // entry protocol
3               if ( you == DontWantIn ) break;
4                   if ( Last == &me ) {        // high priority ?
4                       me = DontWantIn;        // retract intent
6                       while ( Last == &me ) {} // low priority
7                       me = WantIn;            // re-declare intent
                    }
            }
8           CriticalSection();                  // critical section
9           Last = &me;                         // exit protocol
10          me = DontWantIn;                    // retract intent
        }
    }
  public:
    Dekker( Intent &me, Intent &you, Intent *&Last ) :
        me(me), you(you), Last(Last) {}
};
```

Fig. 6.8 Fair retract intent: Dekker, alternation, nested

arrival, the thread last in the critical section is directed to the low-priority code, where it retracts intent (line 5), so the other thread can make progress. Hence, livelock is prevented by alternating on simultaneous arrival, and rule 4 is satisfied.

In Dekker's algorithm, the *low-priority thread retracts intent*, so when the high-priority thread exits the critical section and attempts reentry, it does not exclude itself. Now it can take the low priority thread an arbitrary amount of time to restart, exit the low priority busy wait, and set its intent. During this delay, the new low-priority thread (because it was last to enter) can perform an arbitrary number of entries into the critical section. Therefore, unbounded overtaking is allowed by the new low-priority thread. However, *once the new high-priority thread sets its intent*, there is a bound of one as the new low-priority thread cannot enter again unless it is just entering or is already in the critical section. Unbounded overtaking is allowed by rule 3: not preventing entry to the critical section by the delayed thread.

Starvation cannot occur using alternation, because once the low-priority thread sets its intent, it becomes the high-priority thread as last is no longer equal to this thread; hence, the other thread cannot enter again, unless it is just entering or is already in the critical section. Only if the new high-priority thread does not get any CPU time could it starve, but it is assumed all threads eventually execute with some degree of fairness (e.g., because of a preemptive round-robin scheduler).

6.3.6.2 Racing

While alternation uses information set in the exit protocol to prevent livelock and starvation in the entry protocol, racing performs the tie-break in the entry protocol with no additional code in the exit protocol. There are two kinds of races: read and write.

```
int Q[2] = { 0, 0 }, R[2];
#define inv( c ) ((c + 1) % 2)
#define plus( a, b ) ((a + b) % 2)

Q[id] = 1;
R[id] = plus( R[inv(id)], id );
while ( Q[inv(id)] == 1 && R[id] == plus( R[inv(id)], id ) ) {}
CriticalSection();
Q[id] = 0;
```

Fig. 6.9 Fair retract intent: Kessels, read race

Read Race

Peterson-Fischer's 2-thread algorithm [38, p. 92] is the first algorithm to use a read race to prevent livelock and starvation. Fig. 6.9 shows Kessels' simpler version [27, p. 137], which replaces Peterson-Fischer's complex **if** expressions with an arithmetic formula. The mechanism to prevent livelock and starvation is still subtle. Assume threads are 0 and 1. At line 1, a thread races to read the other thread's R state and modify its own. Specifically, T_0 sets its R state to the same as T_1, and T_1 sets its R state to the oppose of T_0. There are two scenarios to consider: sequential and parallel reads. There are eight sequential-read cases: four in which T_0 sets R[0] first, followed by T_1 setting R[1], and T_0 enters the CS; and four cases in which T_1 is first, followed by T_0, and T_1 enters the CS.

	1		2		3		4		5		6		7		8	
	T_0	T_1	T_0	T_1	T_0	T_1	T_0	T_1	T_0	T_1	T_0	T_1	T_0	T_1	T_0	T_1
R[0]/R[1]	0	0	0	1	1	0	1	1	0	0	0	1	1	0	1	1
time 1	0		1		0		1			1		1		0		0
↓ 2		1		0		1		0	1		1		0		0	
	CS	W	CS	W	CS	W	CS	W	W	CS	W	CS	W	CS	W	CS

(Note, the values of the R state variables at the start of the race can be arbitrary and it still works.) In the first column, T_0 sets R[0] = 0 because plus(0, 0) = (0 + 0) % 2 = 0. Then, T_1 sets R[1] = 1 because plus(0, 1) = (0 + 1) % 2 = 1. T_0 was the first to read, and both T_0 and T_1 know this fact because the R states are unequal, and hence, T_0 enters the CS and T_1 waits (W). (Note, the call to plus in line 5 inverts the check so T_0 tests are not equal, while T_1 tests are equal, making one thread wait.) The other three cases are similar, where if T_0 goes first, the values are not equal, and if T_1 goes first, the values are equal. There are four parallel-read cases similar to the sequential case:

	1		2		3		4	
	T_0	T_1	T_0	T_1	T_0	T_1	T_0	T_1
R[0]/R[1]	0	0	1	1	0	1	1	0
1	0	1	1	0	1	1	0	0
	CS	W	CS	W	W	CS	W	CS

```
_Task Peterson {
    Intent &me, &you, *&Last;
    void main() {
        for ( int i = 1; i <= 1000; i += 1 ) {
        •   me = WantIn;                           // entry protocol
            Last = &me;                            // race!
            while ( you == WantIn && ::Last == &me ) {}
            CriticalSection();                     // critical section
            me = DontWantIn;                       // exit protocol
        }
    }
  public:
    Peterson( Intent &me, Intent &you, Intent *&Last ) : me(me), you(you), Last(Last) {}
};
void uMain::main() {
    Intent me = DontWantIn, you = DontWantIn,  // shared
        Intent *Last = rand() % 2 ? &me : &you;
    Peterson t0(me, you, Last), t1(you, me, Last);
}
```

Fig. 6.10   Fair retract intent: Peterson, write race

In the first column, T_0 and T_1 read simultaneously and T_0 sets R[0] = 0 and T_1 sets
R[1] = 1 (same computations as earlier). In all cases, the state toggles (equal ↔ not
equal), and a winner is selected depending on the result state.

Write Race

A write race is another common mechanism used to deal with livelock and starvation
and appeared first in Dijkstra's software solution for N-thread mutual exclusion [14,
p. 569]. However, the most popular occurrence of a write race is Peterson's other
2-thread solution [37, Fig. 1] for mutual exclusion. Like Dekker's algorithm,
Peterson's algorithm uses a third chalk board, but in a slightly different way, to
deal with simultaneous arrivals and fairness. After a person indicates intent on their
own chalk board, they *race* with the other person to put their name on the third
chalk board. The person who wins the race breaks the tie and goes into the critical
section, which handles livelock problems (rule 4). Fairness (rule 5) is provided by
ensuring a person cannot win two races in a row. As with Dekker's algorithm, the
third chalk board is used only for simultaneous arrivals, otherwise a person is free
to enter multiple times in succession.

Fig. 6.10 shows an implementation of Peterson's 2-thread algorithm. The
program looks identical to the declare intent program (Fig. 6.4, p. 242), except for
the entry protocol. If both threads arrive simultaneously, they both indicate their
intent to enter and they both race to put the address of their me variable in Last.
For this race to work, assignment must occur atomically, so one of the values is
overwritten (rather than scrambling the bits during simultaneous assignment). After
the race is over, how do you know which thread won? That is, how does a thread

know which thread put its me variable address in first? In fact, the loser's value is in variable Last, because it wrote over the winner's value! Now each thread enters the busy loop, checking first if the other thread even wants in, and if it does, who won the race. Notice this last check, if the value in Last is that thread's me variable, it lost the race and has to wait. Therefore, livelock cannot occur.

Unlike Dekker's algorithm using alternation, Peterson's algorithm, essentially flips a coin on simultaneous arrival (independent trial). If the coin toss is unfair across many simultaneous arrivals, one thread receives some amount of unfairness. In contrast, alternation retains a history across simultaneous arrival (the thread last in the CS), so threads alternate winning at each simultaneous arrival (dependent trails). Given that simultaneous arrives are rare, this point is unlikely to generate any practical effects.

Starvation cannot occur for the following reason (which also applies to read race). If a thread exits the critical section, and tries to *barge* ahead of a waiting thread, it must first indicate its intent and run a race with itself in the entry protocol (the other thread is still in the busy loop). Interestingly, if you run a race by yourself and you are an optimist, you win the race; if you are a pessimist, you lose the race. In this case, the thread that runs the race by itself loses the race and waits in the busy loop. (Why does it lose the race?) Now the other thread, which is waiting in the busy loop, suddenly notices it has won the previous race because Last has changed, i.e., this thread has now become the high priority thread. Therefore, it makes progress and enters the critical section. Thus, a thread cannot win two races in a row, and so the threads alternate on a particular series of simultaneous arrivals. Since winning a race is random, whoever wins the first race starts the alternation for any series of simultaneous arrivals. Similarly for Dekker's algorithm, whoever was last in the bathroom is random for a simultaneous arrival, but that thread starts the alternation for any series of simultaneous arrivals.

In Peterson's algorithms, *the race loser does not retract intent*, so if the thread in the critical section attempts reentry, it immediately excludes itself from reentering. Therefore, there is bounded overtaking regardless of how long it takes the other thread to complete the entry protocol and enter the critical section. On the surface, this situation seems to violate rule 3, that is, preventing access to the critical section if unoccupied, but the prevention is occurring *in the entry protocol*, which is allowed by rule 3.

6.3.7   Read/Write-Safe

A shared variable is called *atomic* [31, p. 88] if read and write operations on it behave as if they never overlap but always occur in some total order that refines the *precedence* order (i.e., an operation precedes another iff it terminates before the other starts). *Safety* is a weaker property of a shared variable. If, under the assumption that write operations on the variable never overlap, every read operation that does not overlap with any write operation returns the most recently written value, and every read operation that does overlap with some write operation returns an arbitrary value of the correct type. That is, when a write operation on a variable is in progress during a read, the value of the variable is said to *flicker* because reading it çan return an arbitrary value. An even weaker property occurs if write operations are allowed to overlap on a shared variables. When a write operation on the shared variable is in progress during another write, the value of the variable is said to *scramble* because subsequent reading can return an arbitrary value, i.e., not a value written by either write. An algorithm can be R-safe, W-safe, or RW-safe [6], meaning it is immune to flickering or scrambling or both. An algorithm requiring atomic R or W operations is *RW-unsafe*.

Low-cost low-power processors exist with multiple computational-units, e.g., DSPs (digital signal processors), CPUs, and antennas in cell-phones, that can simultaneously read and write to memory. However, to reduce cost/power, atomicity (conflict resolution) may not be provided so simultaneous read/write causes reads to flicker and simultaneous writes cause scrambled bits.

> Multiport memory is widely used in multiprocessor systems because it can provide parallel access to the shared memory. ... Most of these products do not consider the conflicts caused by accessing to the same data, while a few products only provide simple conflict mechanisms, such as busy control scheme [42, p. 251].

In these devices, conflict errors occur infrequently or are not an issue.

Atomicity of memory write can fail on a uniprocessor if assignment is performed in parts. For example, a 32-bit integer constant may be assigned as two 16-bit values because 16-bit values fit in the immediate field of an instruction. Also, larger 64-bit values, e.g. 64-bit address, may be assigned as two 32-bit values by the memory-bus hardware. Hence, simultaneous assignment to the same memory location can result in the bits being scrambled, generating an arbitrary value. Similarly, if a read is performed during a memory write without proper memory-bus arbitration or the assignment is performed in parts, a read sees a flickering value.

Interestingly, a few software mutual-exclusion algorithms are so robust they do not require the hardware to provide an underlying notion of atomicity and can safely work in these devices. Hence, mutual-exclusion algorithms are divided into Read/Write (RW) safe and RW unsafe. In general, RW-unsafe algorithms are simpler as they are not providing pure mutual exclusion but are building on mutual exclusion in the underlying hardware.

> Any (software mutual exclusion) algorithm based upon atomic operations cannot be considered a fundamental solution to the mutual exclusion problem [30, p. 314].

All general-purpose computers provide atomic reads and writes, so for these computers, the distinction is only useful when explaining differences in algorithms that otherwise do the same thing. In some cases, the RW-safety can have an affect on cache behaviour because of different memory accesses.

Peterson's algorithm is RW-unsafe because it relies on atomic assignment (write-write) to decide the winner of the race in the entry protocol. That is, the hardware

```
for ( int i = 0; i < 100; i += 1 ) me = i % 2;      // flicker
me = WantIn;                                          // declare intent
for ( ;; ) {                                          // entry protocol
    if ( you == DontWantIn ) break;
    if ( Last == &me ) {
        for ( int i = 0; i < 100; i += 1 ) me = i % 2; // flicker
        me = DontWantIn;
        while( you == WantIn && Last == &me );         // low priority busy wait
        for ( int i = 0; i < 100; i += 1 ) me = i % 2; // flicker
        me = WantIn;                                   // declare intent
    }
}
CriticalSection();
if ( Last != &me ) {
    for ( int i = id; i < 100; i += 1 ) Last = i % 2 == 0 ? &me : &you; // flicker
    Last = me;
}
for ( int i = 0; i < 100; i += 1 ) me = i % 2;      // flicker
me = DontWantIn;                                     // retract intent
```

Fig. 6.11 Dekker's algorithm with RW-safeness

treats assignment like a critical section and provides mutual exclusion around it rather than scrambling the bits on simultaneous assignment. Dekker's algorithm is W-safe, i.e., the bits are scrambled during simultaneous assignment. This fact is easy to see because the only assignment to the shared variable, Last, occurs in the exit protocol and the other thread cannot make progress out of the entry protocol until both assignments in the exit protocol are finished. Therefore, there are never simultaneous assignments to a shared variable. However Dekker's algorithm is R-unsafe, i.e., the bits flicker during simultaneous assignment. The failure scenario occurs if thread T_0 is exiting the critical section, and its write at line 9 (see Fig. 6.8, p. 248), me = DontWantIn, flickers from WantIn to DontWantIn several times before settling at DontWantIn. Thread T_1 sees DontWantIn at line 3, you == DontWantIn, and enters and exits the critical section, setting Last to T_1. Assume T_1 enters again because there is unbounded overtaking for Dekker, and sees T_0's intent flicker to WantIn, directing T_1 into the low priority code (lines 5-6). T_0's assignment finally finishes, setting its intent DontWantIn and it terminates. Then, T_1 is trapped at line 6 because Last is equal to T_1, which cannot change as T_0 is terminated. The error occurs when T_1 incorrectly sees WantIn when T_0 does not want into the critical section. Finally, both the read-race 2-thread algorithms, Peterson-Fischer and Kessels, are RW-unsafe [6].

Dekker's algorithm can be modified to be RW-safe [7]. Fig. 6.11 shows the RW-safe version of Dekker's algorithm. To give a sense of how robust this version of Dekker's algorithm is in practice, aggressive flickering is added before each assignment to simulate hardware without safeness and the algorithm continues to work. The RW-safe failure for Dekker's algorithm shows that waiting for Last == &me is too rigid. Therefore, the waiting condition is weakened by replacing it with you == WantIn && Last == &me, where the new condition enables progress should the other thread not return. As well, on exit, Last is not changed if a thread makes repeated entries; otherwise, the assignment causes Last to flicker. If the other thread always happens to read the flicker value for itself when the assignment occurs, it can remain trapped in the low-priority busy wait.

6.3.8   N-Thread Mutual Exclusion

Now it is time to increase the complexity of the mutual exclusion game by increasing the number of players from 2 to N. It turns out, even a simple N-thread solution is difficult for most people to grasp from a correctness standpoint.

> Another possible myth is that Dekker's solution can be trivially modified to solve the n process case. The algorithms known to the author (G. L. Peterson) actually require major changes in form that result in entirely new algorithms, even when n is two [37, p. 116].

The history of solutions for N-thread mutual exclusion is as long and complex as that for 2-thread solutions.

6.3.8.1   Prioritized Retract Intent

Edsger W. Dijkstra attempted the first software solution for the N-thread mutual exclusion problem [14, p. 569], but it is fairly complex. However, Donald Knuth subsequently pointed out Dijkstra's algorithm has starvation (breaks rule 5) [28, p. 321]. One of the simplest N-thread algorithms that only cover rules 1–4 was created by Burns and Lynch [9, p. 836], and subsequently modified by Lamport [31, p. 337] (collectively called the B–L algorithms). The B–L algorithm is simpler because it is a straightforward extension of the 2-thread Prioritize Retract Intent (see Fig. 6.6, p. 245), rather than an ad-hoc design. Like the 2-thread version, the N-thread version is based on fixed priorities, and hence, has starvation (breaks rule 5), as a high-priority thread can theoretically preclude a low-priority thread from making progress. Nevertheless, the approach illustrates solving at least rules 1–4. Fig. 6.12 shows a structured version of the B–L algorithm. The algorithm has an array of bytes (but only one bit is used), one per thread, to represent the N blackboards needed on the bathroom door. This array is passed to each thread along with the size of the array and a position/priority value. The position/priority indicates the position in the array of a particular thread's bit and its priority level. For example, thread 5 sets and resets element 5 of the intent array and has lower priority than threads 0–4 and higher priority than threads 6–9, i.e., low subscript values have higher priority.

The entry protocol has two steps. In the first step, a thread begins by setting its intent and then linearly searching in the high-priority direction to see if a thread with higher priority has declared intent. (The direction of the search is immaterial.) If such a thread is found, the searching thread retracts its intent and busy waits until the higher priority thread retracts its intent, and then, the searching thread begins the search over again from its starting position, as in:

```
_Task Worker {
    Intent *intents;
    int N, priority, i, j;

    void main() {
        for ( i = 1; i <= 1000; i += 1 ) {
            // step 1, wait for threads with higher priority
            do {                                            // entry protocol
                intents[priority] = WantIn;
                // check if thread with higher priority wants in
                for ( j = priority - 1; j >= 0; j -= 1 ) {
                    if ( intents[j] == WantIn ) {
                        intents[priority] = DontWantIn;
                        while ( intents[j] == WantIn ) {}
                        break;
                    } // exit
                }
            } while ( intents[priority] == DontWantIn );
            // step 2, wait for threads with lower priority
            for ( j = priority + 1; j < N; j += 1 ) {
                while ( intents[j] == WantIn ) {}
            }
            CriticalSection();                              // critical section
            intents[priority] = DontWantIn;                 // exit protocol
        }
    }
  public:
    Worker( Intent intents[ ], int N, int priority ) :
            intents( intents ), N(N), priority( priority ) {}
};
void uMain::main() {
    const int NoOfTasks = 10;
    Intent intents[NoOfTasks];                              // shared
    Worker *workers[NoOfTasks];
    for ( int i = 0; i < NoOfTasks; i += 1 ) {             // initialize shared data
        intents[i] = DontWantIn;
    }
    for ( int i = 0; i < NoOfTasks; i += 1 ) {
        workers[i] = new Worker( intents, NoOfTasks, i ); // create workers
    }
    for ( int i = 0; i < NoOfTasks; i += 1 ) {             // terminate workers
        delete workers[i];
    }
}
```

Fig. 6.12 N-thread mutual exclusion: prioritize retract intent

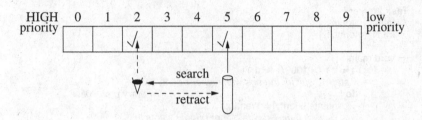

Only after a thread has searched all the way up the high priority direction and found
no thread with higher priority intent, does it move on to the second step. In essence,
a thread sees a moment in time when there are no higher priority threads ahead of it.

In the second step of the entry protocol, a thread searches in the low-priority
direction. However, because all threads in this direction have lower priority, the
searching thread never retracts its intent; it just busy waits until the low-priority
thread retracts its intent either by leaving the critical section or retracting its intent
in the entry protocol and then continues along the list, as in:

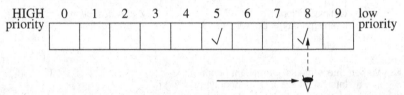

When a thread reaches the end of the list, it sees no lower priority thread in the
critical section and so it can safely enter it.

Since the algorithm is complex, some of the problem cases need to be examined.
First, what happens if a thread is searching in the high-priority direction and a higher
priority thread starts searching *after* its intent has been passed by the lower priority
thread, as in:

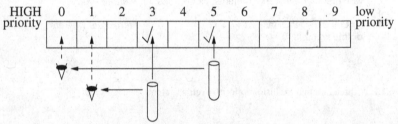

This situation is not a problem because when the higher priority thread starts step 2
of the entry protocol, it waits for the lower priority thread to exit the critical section.
In essence, the lower priority thread started searching *before* the higher priority
thread, and now, the higher priority thread waits for it to complete. In this situation,
the time of arrival affects the priority of a thread. The second case is where a
low-priority thread declares its intent *after* the higher priority thread has started
its search, as in:

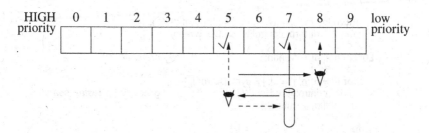

This situation is not a problem because when the lower priority thread finds a high-priority thread's intent, it retracts its intent. Remember, the high priority thread does not retract its intent when performing the low priority search. There are many other cases that need to be examined before this algorithm can be shown to satisfy rules 1–4, but a complete proof is beyond the scope of this book. Suffice it to say, that the algorithm is correct for rules 1–4. The purpose of this discussion is to illustrate the techniques of scanning, retracting, and retrying, and the reasons for them in software solutions.

Notice this solution uses only one bit per thread, indicating the thread's intent to enter the critical section. In fact, any N-thread solution using only atomic read and write has a lower bound of one bit for each thread attempting entry and requires the ability to read the bits of all the threads attempting entry [9]. However, no complete N-thread solution has achieved this lower bound. In effect, dealing with rule 5 (starvation) requires additional information, which correspondingly requires additional bits to represent the information. Furthermore, bits on most computers are not atomically accessible, and it is more efficient to access words (versus bytes) on most architectures. Therefore, minimum storage at the bit/byte level is only of theoretical interest. Finally, B–L is RW-safe requiring no underlying atomicity [24].

6.3.8.2   Knuth/De Bruijn

To prevent starvation, a Dekker-like turn variable needs to be added to a variant of the B–L algorithm. When a thread exits the critical section, it nominates the next thread to enter, and if the nomination is fair, e.g., by cycling among the waiting threads, starvation is eliminated, as in:

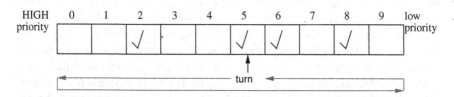

Note, the order of service is not FIFO because the nominated thread may arrive sooner than other waiting threads. For example, threads arrive in the order T_8, T_5, T_2, but are serviced in the order T_5, T_2, T_8 because when T_6 finishes the critical

```
      enum Intent { DontWantIn, WantIn, EnterCS };
      volatile int turn, control[N] = { DontWantIn, ... };

1     L0: control[id] = WantIn;                    // entry protocol
2         Fence();
3     L1: for ( j = turn; j != id; j = cycleDown( j, N ) )
4             if ( control[j] != DontWantIn ) { Pause(); goto L1; } // restart search
5     L2: control[id] = EnterCS;
6         Fence();
7         for ( j = N - 1; j >= 0; j -= 1 )
8             if ( j != id && control[j] == EnterCS ) goto L0;
9         // turn = id;
10        CriticalSection( id );
11        turn = cycleDown( id, N );                // exit protocol
12    L4: control[id] = DontWantIn;
13    L5: ;
```

Fig. 6.13 Knuth

section, it nominates T_5. Nevertheless, each waiting thread eventually gets its *turn*. Complexity occurs because the next nominated thread may not want into the critical section or there may be no waiting threads at all. Essentially, the thread exiting the critical section can move turn, but no matter how hard it tries, it may not find a thread to nominate. Hence, arriving threads still need to determine which one can enter the critical section. For example, turn is set to 0 and threads 2, 5 and 8 arrive simultaneously; these threads need to see each other, and the closest one to turn nominates itself to enter the critical section. Knuth [28, p. 321] used the notion of cyclic scanning (alternation, rather than racing) to generate the first N-thread solution solving all 5 rules. As stated, the scanning in the entry protocol is complex to prevent livelock and ensure the waiting thread closest to turn is nominated. (A simpler version of Knuth's algorithm is discussed in detail.)

What is usual about Knuth's algorithm is how turn is advanced: turn = (id - 1) % N. That is, the next nominated thread is cyclicly beside the thread exiting the critical section, which seems perfectly reasonable as turn should proceed around the intents. However, this approach allows turn to back up. For example, assume three threads.

Knuth's algorithm cycles in descending order, which is different from other algorithms, and needs to be noted during the discussion.

The entry protocol has two steps. In the first step, a thread begins by setting its intent and then scanning in a cycle from turn (one less than the last thread to use the CS in cyclic order) to its id for no threads wanting into the CS (DontWantIn) in that range; otherwise, it restarts the scan. For maximal contention, all intents are set; hence, step 1 (lines 3–4) only allows thread T_{turn} to progress as all other threads starting at position turn see a control value of WantIn for T_{turn} and restart their scan. In this case, threads execute in cyclic order, so the bound on service is $N-1$, that is, the number of threads ahead in the cycle. For less than maximal contention, there is a race (around the cycle) from turn to id, through DontWantIn threads. Therefore, up to $N-1$ threads can proceed to the next step. For example, assume T=4, turn is 3, and all intents are DontWantIn (e.g., a starting scenario):

	intents			exec
T_0	T_1	T_2	T_3	order
D	D	D	D	
W	D	D	D	T_0
W	W	D	D	T_1
W	W	W	D	T_2

T_0 arrives and sets its intent, cycles from element 3 to 1 in control only seeing DontWantIn and enters step 2. T_1 and T_2 follow in that order, cycling from element 3 to id-1 in control only seeing DontWantIn and enter step 2. T_3 does not arrive yet.

As in Dijkstra's algorithm, the second step of the entry protocol provides the mutual exclusion. A thread sets its intent to EnterCS and checks if any thread (excluding self) is also in this step. If so, the entry protocol is restarted, resetting intent from EnterCS to WantIn, which narrows the selection because intents are not retracted (DontWantIn). The selection narrows because on every restart, step 1 only lets one thread continue to step 2 among those returning from the second step. The continuing thread is the one having the minimal distance from turn. For example, T_0 and T_1 see T_2's WantIn after the restart and delay, while T_2 continues to step 2 to compete with any newly arriving threads, such as T_3, that might have gotten through step 1 during this process because turn is still 3. Eventually, a thread is selected and enters the CS. Note, line 9 before entering the CS does not appear to provide any benefits and is commented out. At best, changing turn before the selected thread enters the CS only affects the execution of the waiting threads in the entry protocol as they cannot make progress. All these threads quickly move to step 1 and spin there because T_{turn} has its intent set to EnterCS. For high contention, turn is almost always equal to id at line 9. Finally, the thread exiting the CS resets turn to a different value, so there is little purpose in setting it before entry.

Knuth states the maximum delay-bound for any thread entering the CS is $2^{N-1} - 1$; however, only an informal outline is given for a scenario that generates the bound, from which the reader must infer a proof ('k' is turn):

> For example, if N = 4 suppose computer 4 is at L1 and computers 1, 2, 3 are at L2. Then,
>   (i) computer 1 goes (at high speed) from L2 to L5;
> (ii) computer 2 goes from L2 to L5, then computer 1 goes from L5 to L2;
> (iii) computer 1 goes from L2 to L5;
> (iv) computer 3 goes from L2 to L5, then computer 1 goes from L5 to L2, then computer 2 goes from L5 to L2;
>   (v) (vi), (vii) like (i), (ii), (iii), respectively;
> meanwhile computer 4 has been unfortunate enough to miss the momentary values of k which would enable it to get through to L2 [28, p. 322].

Notice, cycling back at step (v) to restart at (i), computer 3 is still at position L5, and it is impossible for computer 3 to get to position L2 because there is no way for turn to equal 3 without executing computer 4, and there is always a WantIn in intents[4]; hence, computer 3 must wait at step 1. Effectively, computer 3 drops out, and the cycle continues with computers 1 and 2, until 2 drops out, and then

T0 T1 T2 T3
W   D   D   D

T1 L0 to L2 as control[3 cycledown 1] == D (turn == 3)
T2 L0 to L2 as control[3 cycledown 2] == D (turn == 3)
T3 L0 to L2 as control[3 cycledown 3] does not execute (turn == 3)

T1 L2 to L5 to L0 as control[∀ i != E (turn == 0)
T2 L2 to L5 to L0 as control[∀ i != E (turn == 1)
T1 L0 to L5 to L0 as control[1 cycledown 1] does not execute & control[∀ i != E (turn == 0)
T3 L2 to L5 to L0 as control[∀ i != E (turn == 2)
- -
T1 L0 to L2 as control[2 cycledown 1] == D (turn == 2)
T2 L0 to L2 as control[2 cycledown 2] does not execute (turn == 2)

T1 L2 to L5 to L0 as control[∀ i != E (turn == 0)
T2 L2 to L5 to L0 as control[∀ i != E (turn == 1)
T1 L0 to L5 to L0 as control[1 cycledown 1] does not execute & control[∀ i != E (turn == 0)

T3 L0 to L1 and cannot proceed as control[0 cycledown 3] != D (turn == 0)
T2 L0 to L1 and cannot proceed as control[0 cycledown 2] != D (turn == 0)
T1 L0 to L1 and cannot proceed as control[0 cycledown 1] != D (turn == 0)

T0 L1 to L5 as control[0 cycledown 0] does not execute & control[∀ i != E (turn == 1)

Fig. 6.14 Knuth worst-case bound pattern, T=0..3, turn == 3, T0 starts at L1

computer 4 makes progress. Fig. 6.14 shows the complete expansion of Knuth's delay-sequence for 4 threads; the dash line indicates where Knuth's outline stopped. Therefore, T0 enters after threads 1,2,1,3,1,2,1 precede it. In general, the sequence of passing threads is

```
N  passing threads
1  0
2  1 0
3  1 2 1 0
4  1 2 1 3 1 2 1 0
5  1 2 1 3 1 2 1 4 1 2 1 3 1 2 1 0
6  1 2 1 3 1 2 1 4 1 2 1 3 1 2 1 5 1 2 1 3 1 2 1 4 1 2 1 3 1 2 1 0
```

Hence, T_{N-1} passes T0 once, T_{N-2} passes twice, T_{N-1-k} passes 2^k times. Therefore, the bound on the numbers of threads that can pass T0 before it executes can be as great as $\sum_{k=0}^{N-2} 2^k = 2^{N-1} - 1$. Interestingly, the earlier sequence of numbers is the same as the sequence of disk numbers moved in a solution of the classical problem of the towers of Hanoi. Note, substrings of this sequence or the complete sequence are rare, and therefore, even small delays for any thread are unlikely. Because Knuth's algorithm provides a bound, it is the first correct algorithm for N-Thread mutual exclusion.

De Bruijn [5, p. 137] changed Knuth's algorithm by removing line 9 and replacing line 12 with two lines:

if (control[turn] == DontWantIn || turn == id)
    turn = cycleDown(turn, N); // absolute cycle

The key change is from a relative to an absolute cycle, that is, id is changed to turn. As a result, turn cannot *jump around* based on the id of the thread exiting the CS;

instead turn cycles unidirectionally around the intents based on the last id in the CS (like Dekker), which precludes the delay pattern in Knuth's algorithm. As a result, the maximum delay-bound for any thread entering the CS is $N(N-1)/2$.

However, the decrement of turn must be conditional. If it is unconditionally, waiting threads can be skipped during the cycle resulting in starvation. For example, N = 3, turn = 2, and using Fig. 6.13, p. 258 with line 11 changed to turn = cycleDown(turn, N), assume T_0 executes L0 and repeat the sequence:

- T_1 executes lines L0–L2.
- T_2 executes lines L0–L2.
- T_1 executes lines L2–L5, changing turn to 1.
- T_1 executes lines L0–L2.
- T_1 executes lines L2–L5, changing turn to 0.
- T_2 executes lines L2–L5, changing turn to 2.

During this loop, T_0 jumps back to L1 because control[from turn downto 0] != DontWantIn (actually, T_0 may enter the loop at line 7, provided it jumps back to L0 and is not observed by the other threads). The problem is the two threads cycle turn passed the waiting thread T_0.

This scenario is prevented by the **if** statement, which only advances turn if the thread associated with the current turn does not want in. (This includes the thread exiting the CS, which no longer wants in, but it cannot retract its intent until after turn is advanced or there is a race with an entering thread, so there is a special case in the **if** statement.) Hence, T_2 does not advance turn because control[0] wants in, and the cycle earlier is broken. Therefore, starvation cannot occur because the waiting threads are examined in cyclic order, so each thread eventually gets a change to execute but in cyclic order rather than FIFO.

Like Knuth, De Bruijn left the proof that the upper bound $N(N-1)/2$ can actually occur as an exercise for the reader. Therefore, a proof is presented. Assume turn = N - 1 and T_0 executes L0 so control[0] == WantIn:

Repeat
    For id = 1 upto turn (one thread after the other)
        thread$_{id}$ executes lines L0-L2 as control[from turn downto id] == DontWantIn.
    For id = 1 upto turn - 1 (one thread after the other)
        thread$_{id}$ executes lines L2-L5 without decrementing turn as control[turn] == WantIn
        and go back to L0.
    Thread$_{turn}$ executes lines L2-L5, decrements turn, and goes back to L0.
Until turn = 0.

During this loop, T_0 jumps back to L1 because control[from turn downto 1] != DontWant. After the repeat loop, turn == 0 and T_0 executes lines L2–L5, decrements turn back to N - 1, and goes back to L0. In each iteration of the repeat loop, the number of threads entering the CS before T_0 is one less because turn is decremented. Therefore, the total number of threads entering the CS before T_0 is $(N-1)+(N-2)+...+1 = N(N-1)/2$. Both algorithms are RW-unsafe. Assume the assignment intents[id] = WantIn (line 1) flickers to EnterCS, then a winning thread in the second loop (lines 7, 8) can read intents[id] == EnterCS and restart. As a result, progress is no longer guaranteed.[3]

---

[3]If Knuth's algorithm did not combine Dijkstra's b and c into a single array, it may be RW-safe.

Note, both the Knuth and De Bruijn algorithms and their analysis appear in Letters-To-The-Editor and hence are *not* complete refereed papers.

6.3.8.3 Eisenberg and McGuire

The first (almost) complete N-thread solution to the mutual-exclusion game was by Eisenberg and McGuire [16] (see program in Fig. 6.15). This solution is similar to prioritize retract intent (Sect. 6.3.5, p. 244) with a variation on how the priorities work. Instead of having fixed priorities assigned to the array positions, the priorities rotate around the array. The thread currently in or last in the critical section always has the highest priority. The threads waiting to enter, in the clockwise direction from the highest priority, have decreasing priority levels. When the thread in the critical section exits, it rotates the priorities clockwise to the next thread attempting entry, making it the highest priority thread. If no threads are attempting entry, the priorities are not rotated. This algorithm uses three states (DontWantIn, WantIn and EnterCS) to indicate intention (at least 2 bits/intent) and N intents plus an integer variable.

The entry protocol has two steps. In the first step, a thread at position i sets its intent and then linearly searching clockwise from position HIGH, i.e., the position of the current/last user of the critical section, to itself for any thread wanting into the critical section. If such a thread is found, e.g., T_j, that thread has higher priority, so the searching thread restarts the search *but without retracting its intent*, e.g.:

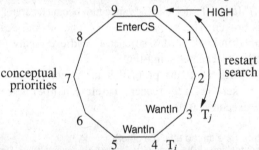

Only after a thread searches from position HIGH to its position and found no thread waiting to enter does it move to the second step. In essence, a thread sees a moment in time when there are no higher priority threads between HIGH and its position.

In the second step of the entry protocol, a thread sets its intent to state EnterCS indicating it has completed the first step of the entry protocol. It then linearly searches all other threads (excluding self) for any that have also reached the second step of the entry protocol and hence have intent set to EnterCS, e.g.:

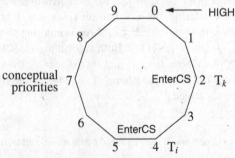

```
enum Intent { WantIn, EnterCS, DontWantIn };

_Task Worker {
    Intent *intents;
    int &HIGH, N, posn;

    void main() {
        int i, j, k;
        for ( i = 0; i < 1000; i += 1 ) {
            for ( ;; ) {                                    // entry protocol
                intents[posn] = WantIn;
                // step 1, wait for threads with higher priority
                for ( j = HIGH; j != posn; )
                    if ( intents[j] != DontWantIn ) j = HIGH; // restart search
                    else j = ( j + 1 ) % N;                 // check next intent
                intents[posn] = EnterCS;
                // step 2, check if any other thread finished step 1
                for ( j = 0; j < N && ( j == posn || intents[j] != EnterCS ); j += 1 ) {}
                if ( j == N && (HIGH == posn || intents[HIGH] == DontWantIn) ) break;
            }
            HIGH = posn;
            CriticalSection();
            for ( j = (HIGH + 1) % N; intents[j] == DontWantIn ; j = (j+1) % N ) {} // exit
            HIGH = j;
            intents[posn] = DontWantIn;
        }
    }
  public:
    Worker( int &HIGH, Intent intents[], int N, int posn ) :
        HIGH( HIGH ), intents( intents ), N( N ), posn( posn ) {}
};
void uMain::main() {
    const int NoOfTasks = 10;
    Worker *workers[NoOfTasks];                    // pointer to an array of workers
    int HIGH;                                      // shared
    Intent intents[NoOfTasks];                     // shared

    HIGH = 0;                                       // initialize shared data
    for ( int i = 0; i < NoOfTasks; i += 1 ) {
        intents[i] = DontWantIn;
    }
    for ( int i = 0; i < NoOfTasks; i += 1 ) {
        workers[i] = new Worker( HIGH, intents, NoOfTasks, i ); // create workers
    }
    for ( int i = 0; i < NoOfTasks; i += 1 ) {      // terminate workers
        delete workers[i];
    }
}
```

Fig. 6.15 N-thread mutual exclusion: Eisenberg and McGuire

Multiple EnterCS states can occur when a higher priority thread arrives after its position has been examined by a lower priority thread in step 1. The second step of the entry protocol succeeds if a thread does not find another thread with an intent of EnterCS, i.e., j == N, and either its position has been designated the highest priority by the thread leaving the critical section or the thread associated with the current highest priority location does not want to enter the critical section. If the appropriate conditions are true, the thread rotates the priorities so that it is now the highest priority thread, i.e., HIGH = posn; otherwise, the entry protocol is repeated.

In the exit protocol, the exiting thread searches in priority order for any thread that wants in other than itself. If a thread is found, that thread is made the highest priority, in affect rotating the priorities; otherwise, HIGH is reset to its previous value. Then the exiting thread retracts its intent. Because HIGH is being read for assignment (versus comparison) in step 1 to restart the search, assignment must be atomic, otherwise writing HIGH could cause incorrect termination of the loop in step 1.

It is easy to see how this algorithm works if there is always a thread in the critical section. Tasks busy wait in step 1 of the entry protocol for the thread currently in the critical section to exit and rotate the priorities by changing HIGH to the waiting thread closest to it in the clock-wise direction. Changing HIGH short-circuits the loop in step 1 of the entry protocol for the thread at that position because j and posn have the value HIGH. All other threads stay in step 1 and the newly assigned high priority thread progresses through step 2 and enters the critical section. The difficult case in this algorithm is when no thread is in the critical section, and HIGH is sitting at an arbitrary location when the threads arrive, e.g., like the initial condition when the threads all start. This situation is the reason for step 2 in the entry protocol.

When there is no thread in the critical section to designate the next thread to enter, the entering threads race to become the next thread to enter, and the previous value of HIGH is used to control the selection. As above, the thread closest to the previous value of HIGH exits step 1 first because it finds no intent set for higher priority threads; the other threads wait for it. However, there can be many false starts by the waiting threads as other threads arrive with different priorities. For example, if threads arrive from low to high priority, all the threads can simultaneously get to step 2 of the algorithm, as the low priority threads miss seeing the later arriving higher-priority threads in step 1. This situation results in *all* of the threads restarting the entry protocol. The arrival of a higher priority thread, including the one at the current HIGH position, can force this cycle to start over again at any time. Hence, the selection process, when there is no thread in the critical section and there are simultaneous arrivals, can be expensive.

The bound on the waiting time is $N - 1$ because a thread may have to wait for all the other threads to enter and leave the critical section before it can proceed. The bound is ensured because rotating the priorities in a fixed direction in the exit protocol eventually services all waiting threads. However, arriving threads are not serviced in FIFO order but in cyclic order. A thread arriving after the current HIGH position is serviced only when threads before the current HIGH position are serviced, even though thread's after the current HIGH position may have arrived prior to thread's before it. Therefore, this algorithm is an example of bounded but non-FIFO selection.

This algorithm introduces a new and crucial concept in its exit protocol: the introduction of cooperation between the acquiring threads and the releasing thread. In all the previous locks, the releasing thread *only* modifies variables associated with itself and possibly a shared variable. All the work in detecting if a lock is open and acquiring the lock is the responsibility of the acquiring threads with no help from the releasing thread. In this solution, the releasing thread must perform additional work on behalf of an acquiring thread. Each acquiring thread relies not only on itself to detect when the lock is released, but also on the releasing thread. This idea of cooperation, where the releaser does more work than just indicating it is finished, forms the basis for advanced lock design.

6.3.8.4 Bakery Algorithm

The second complete N-thread solution to the mutual-exclusion game was by Lamport [29] (see program in Fig. 6.16). This solution introduces a new idea for achieving a bounded waiting time, which appears in different forms in subsequent programs throughout the rest of the book. The new idea is one used by people sharing a resource requiring mutual exclusion, which is to take a ticket on arrival and wait until that ticket is chosen for service. For example, in a bakery, people take a ticket on arrival and then wait for exclusive service. In fact, Lamport's algorithm is often referred to as the bakery algorithm. If the tickets are serviced in increasing order by ticket number, the people are serviced in FIFO order (in contrast to the cyclic order in the previous algorithm). However, Lamport's version of tickets is quite different from that used by people in a store. This algorithm uses M intention states (tickets), needing B bits (usually the size of an integer), and N intents.

The entry protocol has two steps. In the first step, thread$_i$ takes a ticket and stores it at position i in the shared array ticket. The ticket array is initialized to 0, where 0 means a thread has retracted its intent. However, selecting a ticket is done in an unusual manner. Instead of selecting a ticket from a machine that atomically generates monotonically increasing values, a thread computes a unique ticket based on the current ticket values held by any waiting threads. Ticket generation is accomplished by finding the maximum ticket value of the waiting threads and creating a new ticket value one greater, which requires an $O(N)$ search (but could be less, e.g., store the tickets in a binary tree).

Unfortunately, this procedure does not ensure a unique ticket value. Two (or more) threads can simultaneously compute the same maximum ticket value and add one to it, resulting in multiple tickets with the same value. While the chance of this problem occurring is probabilistically low, it still must be dealt with. To deal with this problem, the same technique is used as for the N-thread prioritize-retract-intent solution (see Sect. 6.3.8.1, p. 254), which is to assign a priority to each position in the intent array. When two threads have the same ticket value, their position in the intent array is used to break the tie. As a result, it is possible for thread$_i$ to arrive

```
_Task Worker {
    bool *choosing;
    int *ticket, N, priority;

    void main() {
        int i, j;
        for ( i = 0; i < 1000; i += 1 ) {
            // step 1, compute a ticket
            choosing[priority] = true;           // entry protocol
            int max = 0;                          // O(N) search for largest ticket
            for ( j = 0; j < N; j += 1 )
                if ( max < ticket[j] ) max = ticket[j];
            ticket[priority] = max + 1;           // advance ticket
            choosing[priority] = false;
            // step 2, wait for ticket to be selected
            for ( j = 0; j < N; j += 1 ) {        // check other tickets
                while ( choosing[j] ) {}          // busy wait if thread selecting ticket
                while ( ticket[j] != 0 &&         // busy wait if intent set and
                    ( ticket[j] < ticket[priority] ||   // greater ticket value or subscript
                    ( ticket[j] == ticket[priority] && j < priority ) ) ) {}
            }
            CriticalSection();
            ticket[priority] = 0;                 // exit protocol
        }
    }
  public:
    Worker( bool choosing[ ], int ticket[ ], int N, int priority ) :
        choosing( choosing ), ticket( ticket ), N( N ), priority( priority ) {}
};
void uMain::main() {
    const int NoOfTasks = 10;
    Worker *workers[NoOfTasks];                   // pointer to an array of workers
    bool choosing[NoOfTasks];                     // shared
    int ticket[NoOfTasks];                        // shared
    int i;

    for ( i = 0; i < NoOfTasks; i += 1 ) {        // initialize shared data
        choosing[i] = false;
        ticket[i] = 0;
    }
    for ( i = 0; i < NoOfTasks; i += 1 ) {        // create workers
        workers[i] = new Worker( choosing, ticket, NoOfTasks, i );
    }
    for ( i = 0; i < NoOfTasks; i += 1 ) {        // terminate workers
        delete workers[i];
    }
}
```

Fig. 6.16 *N*-thread mutual exclusion: Lamport (Bakery Algorithm I)

ahead of thread$_j$ and begin computing its ticket but be serviced in non-FIFO order because both threads generate identical tickets due to time-slice interrupts during the ticket computation. This anomaly arises from the non-trivial amount of time required to compute a ticket, which makes it impossible to make the ticket selection atomic.

In the second step of the entry protocol, a thread linearly searches through all the waiting threads (including itself) and waits for any thread with higher priority, because it has a lower ticket value or lower subscript for equal tickets. Remember, a non-waiting thread is identified by a zero ticket value. However, there is a problem if two (or more) threads compute the same ticket value but the lower-priority thread advances to the second step before the higher-priority thread assigns its equal ticket-value into the ticket array, e.g., it is interrupted just before the assignment. When the lower-priority thread checks the ticket array, it finds no thread with an equal ticket-value, as the other thread has not performed its assignment; therefore, it proceeds into the critical section. When the higher-priority thread checks the ticket array, it finds a lower-priority thread with the same ticket value but higher subscript so it proceeds into the critical section, violating the mutual exclusion. To solve this problem, it is crucial to delay checking a thread's ticket value if it is computing a ticket. This information is provided by the choosing array. A thread sets its position in this array before starting to compute a ticket, and resets it only after assigning its new ticket. The search in the second step is now composed of two checks. First, determine if a thread is computing a ticket, and if so, wait for the ticket to be assigned. Second, check if the thread wants in, and if so, is it higher priority. Now a lower-priority thread knows if a higher-priority thread is computing a ticket and waits for the new ticket value to appear. When the ticket value appears, it is either less, equal, or greater than the checking thread's ticket, and it proceeds or waits appropriately. Finally, assignment must be atomic for the bakery algorithm because choosing and ticket values can be read by other threads in step 2 while being written in step 1.

Hehner and Shyamasundar [19] simplified Lamport's algorithm by folding the choosing array into the ticket array (see program fragment in Fig. 6.17). In essence, two ticket values are set aside to indicate that either a thread does not want into the critical section or it is computing a ticket. A non-waiting thread is identified by the maximum possible ticket value, INT_MAX, implying lowest priority, and all elements of the ticket array are initialized to this maximum value. Computing a ticket is identified by the minimum ticket value, 0, implying highest priority.

A thread starts computing its ticket by setting its ticket value to zero, which is the highest-priority ticket-value. No thread can have a ticket value of zero because the maximum value found is always incremented. Notice, during the computation of a thread's ticket-value, the INT_MAX value must be ignored. Now, when a thread is searching in the second step, it cannot proceed if a thread is computing a ticket because of the temporary high-priority value. Only after the new ticket value is assigned does the searching thread make progress. Finally, while busy waiting in the second step, it is unnecessary to explicitly check for non-waiting threads because they all have a priority lower than the searching thread, i.e., INT_MAX.

```
// step 1, select a ticket
ticket[priority] = 0;                         // set highest priority
int max = 0;                                  // O(N) search for largest ticket
for ( int j = 0; j < N; j += 1 ) {
    int v = ticket[j];                        // can change so copy
    if ( v != INT_MAX && max < v ) max = v;
}
max += 1;                                      // advance ticket
ticket[priority] = max;
// step 2, wait for ticket to be selected
for ( j = 0; j < N; j += 1 ) {                // check other tickets
    while ( ticket[j] < max ||                 // busy wait
        ( ticket[j] == max && j < priority ) ) {}
}

CriticalSection();

ticket[priority] = INT_MAX;                   // exit protocol
```

Fig. 6.17 N-thread mutual exclusion: Hehner and Shyamasundar (Bakery Algorithm II)

HIGH priority	0	1	2	3	4	5	6	7	8	9	low priority
ticket	∞	∞	17	∞	∞	18	18	0	20	0	

There is no indefinite postponement (violation of rule 4) for the same reason as in the previous solutions. That is, the priority of the tickets, or alternatively, the priority of a thread's position in the intent array ensures that on simultaneous arrival a tie is always broken. There is no starvation (violation of rule 5) because the ticket values are always increasing as long as there are waiting threads. Hence, if a thread exits the critical section and tries to rush in again ahead of other waiting threads, it *must* generate a ticket value greater than any waiting thread because it examines all their ticket values. Because no thread retracts its intent in the entry protocol, this new maximal ticket value ensures the arriving thread cannot enter before any of the other waiting threads and establishes its bound with respect to any waiting threads.

The problem with this and any other approach based on tickets is that the ticket values cannot increase indefinitely due to the finite size of the integer type, say 2^{32} values. In the worst case, a ticket value overflows back to zero (or a negative value), which results in multiple threads entering the critical section simultaneously, i.e., a violation of the critical section. However, in these bakery algorithms, whenever the critical section becomes unused, i.e., no thread is using it or waiting to use it, the maximal ticket value resets because the next thread selects ticket 0. The ticket values only increase when threads arrive and must wait for entry to the critical section. For example, this failure occurs when 2^{32} threads arrive at the critical section while it is being used, which is highly unlikely. Even two threads can overflow the tickets by perfectly alternating 2^{32} time so one arrives at the critical section while the other is using it; again, this scenario is equally unlikely. Therefore, these algorithms are probabilistically correct because the chance of ticket overflow is extremely small.

6.3.8.5 Tournament

To simplify N-thread solutions and reduce the amount of scanning, a tournament approach is introduced. A tournament uses divide-and-conquer, where only one of every D threads progresses to the next round, and the others busy wait. The approach relies on a simpler mutual-exclusion algorithm for D threads, where D is a small number > 1, usually $D = 2$. Fig. 6.18a shows the maximal binary tree ($D = 2$) approach for N threads by rounding N to the next power of 2, and Fig. 6.18b shows the minimal binary tree. For all trees, threads start at the leaves of the tree, and $\lceil \log_2 N \rceil$ levels of internal nodes are needed to implement the tournament. Each node is a 2-thread solution for mutual exclusion, such as Dekker, Kessels or Peterson. Each thread is assigned to a particular leaf where it begins the mutual exclusion process. At each node, the 2-thread algorithm ensures an arriving thread is guaranteed to make progress (rule 5); i.e., the loser at each node eventually becomes the winner and continues to the next level. Therefore, each thread eventually reaches the root of the tree and enters the critical section. All tournament algorithms allow unbounded overtaking because there is no synchronization among the nodes of the tree. That is, a fast thread can enter the CS arbitrarily often down one branch, while a slow thread is working down another branch. With a minimal binary tree, the tournament approach uses $(N - 1)M$ bits, where $(N - 1)$ is the number of tree nodes and M is the node size (e.g., Dekker's algorithm has a node size involving the variables Last, me, you and the link fields to represent the tree).

Fig. 6.19 shows the basic code for any tournament algorithm. The tree is represented by a triangular matrix, where each row is all the nodes at a specific level of the tree. The thread identifier denotes the leaf node for the starting point of each thread. The entry protocol walks down the tree, competing at each level, and the exit protocol retraces the path retracting intents in reverse order. The thread leaving the CS *must* retract its intents in the reverse order acquired. If intents are not reset in reverse order in the exit protocol, there is a race between released threads and the thread retracting intents that walk the same path in the tree. For example, if T_0 first retracts its intent at node D_1 (rather than the root node), its partner at that level, T_1, can now move down the tree to the next node and set its intent, but that intent can be immediately reset by T_0 as it moves down the tree to the same node as T_1. When intents are retracted in reverse order, released threads move in the opposite direction in the tree from the releasing thread so there is no race.

By this point it should be clear that N-thread solutions to the critical section problem are so complex that only experts can create and validate them. This restricts what can be done by non-experts and requires a high level of trust be placed on their results. Furthermore, all N-thread algorithms require a high degree of communication and cooperation among the participants. Finally, the busy waiting in all the software solutions can be a major source of inefficiency when multiple threads contend for a critical section. Therefore, software solutions are rejected, in general, as a way of providing mutual exclusion for a critical section. However, in certain specialized cases, a software solution may be required and may work effectively and efficiently.

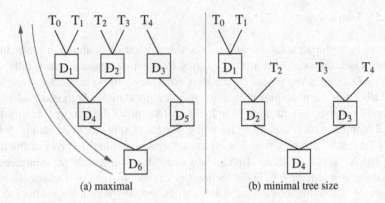

(a) maximal   (b) minimal tree size

Fig. 6.18 N-thread tournament tree, N=5, D=2

```
_Task TournamentMax {
    static Token **tree;              // triangular matrix
    int depth, id;

    void main() {
        unsigned int lid;            // local id at each tree level
        for ( int i = 0; i < 1000; i += 1 ) {
            lid = id;                // entry protocol
            for ( int lv = 0; lv < depth; lv += 1 ) {
                binary_prologue( lid & 1, &tree[lv][lid >> 1] );
                lid >>= 1;           // advance local id for next tree level
            }
            CriticalSection( id );
            for ( int lv = depth - 1; lv >= 0; lv -= 1 ) { // exit protocol
                lid = id >> lv;      // retract reverse order
                binary_epilogue( lid & 1, &tree[lv][lid >> 1] );
            }
        }
    }
  public:
    TournamentMax( struct Token *tree[], int depth, int id ) :
        tree( tree ), depth( depth ), id( id ) {}
};
```

Fig. 6.19 Tournament

6.3.8.6 Arbiter

The final software example is a complete N-thread solution to the mutual-exclusion
game by using a full-time arbitrator thread to control entry to the critical section (see
program in Fig. 6.20). However, this approach changes the definition of the problem
because the N-threads no longer decide among themselves about entry to the critical
section; rather, the N-threads communicate with an arbiter to know when to enter
the critical section. In essence, the mutual exclusion problem among N-threads is
converted into a synchronization problem between the N-threads and the arbiter
(see Sect. 5.13, p. 219).

```
_Task Worker {
    bool *intent, *serving;
    int me, i;

    void main() {
        for ( i = 0; i < 1000; i += 1 ) {
            intent[me] = true;                    // entry protocol
            while ( ! serving[me] ) {}            // wait for turn to start
            CriticalSection();
            intent[me] = false;                   // exit protocol
            while ( serving[me] ) {}              // wait for turn to finish
        }
    }
  public:
    Worker( bool intent[ ], bool serving[ ], int me ) :
        intent( intent ), serving( serving ), me( me ) {}
};
_Task Arbiter {
    bool *intent, *serving, &stop;
    int NoOfTasks;

    void main() {
        int i = 0;
        for ( ;; ) {
            // cycle looking for requests => no starvation
            for ( ; ! intent[i] && ! stop; i = (i + 1) % NoOfTasks ) {}  // anyone want~in ?
            if ( stop ) break;
            serving[i] = true;                    // start turn for worker
            while ( intent[i] ) {}                // wait for worker to exit CS
            serving[i] = false;                   // finish turn for worker
        }
    }
  public:
    Arbiter( bool intent[ ], bool serving[ ], bool &stop, int NoOfTasks ) :
        intent( intent ), serving( serving ), stop( stop ), NoOfTasks( NoOfTasks ) {}
};
void uMain::main() {
    const int NoOfTasks = 10;
    Worker *workers[NoOfTasks];                   // pointer to an array of workers
    bool intent[NoOfTasks], serving[NoOfTasks], stop; // shared

    for ( int i = 0; i < NoOfTasks; i += 1 ) {    // initialize shared data
        intent[i] = serving[i] = false;
    }
    stop = false;

    Arbiter arbiter( intent, serving, stop, NoOfTasks ); // create arbiter
    for ( int i = 0; i < NoOfTasks; i += 1 ) {
        workers[i] = new Worker( intent, serving, i ); // create workers
    }
    for ( int i = 0; i < NoOfTasks; i += 1 ) {    // terminate workers
        delete workers[i];
    }
    stop = true;                                  // stop arbiter
}
```

Fig. 6.20 *N*-thread arbiter

In the entry protocol, a thread indicates its intent to enter and waits until the arbiter indicates the start of this thread's turn. The exit protocol retracts intent after exiting the critical section and waits until the arbiter indicates the finish of the thread's turn. The arbiter cycles around the N intent-flags looking for a thread wanting to enter. Once one is found, the arbiter indicates the start of that thread's turn, and waits for the thread to retract its intent indicating it has exited the critical section. The arbiter then indicates the finish of the thread's turn. Because there are no simultaneous assignments to shared data among the arbiter and N threads, atomic assignment is not required.

There is no indefinite postponement (violation of rule 4) because the arbiter never uses the critical section, it only lets a thread in. There is no starvation (violation of rule 5) because the arbiter cycles through the N intent flags so there are at most $N - 1$ threads ahead of any waiting thread.

Unfortunately, this solution is impractical because the arbiter is continuously busy waiting checking the intent flags even when there is no contention for a critical section. For M critical sections, there are M arbiters spinning constantly, which can consume a substantial amount of the CPU resource. Any attempt to reduce the arbiter spinning, correspondingly slows entry into the critical section. So while the arbiter is largely impractical for software critical sections, the concept of an arbiter is useful and it appears in later approaches.

6.4   Hardware Solutions

Software solutions to the critical section problem cannot be rejected unless there is some alternative. The alternative is to cheat and rely on atomicity provided at the hardware level (as in Peterson's and the N-thread algorithms). At this level, it is possible to make assumptions about execution that are impossible at the software level, e.g., that certain operations are executed atomically, such as assignment, significantly reducing the need for shared information and the checking of this information required in a software solution.

As shown, atomic assignment can be used to simplify mutual exclusion. However, it is straightforward to provide more powerful atomic actions at the hardware level to significantly simplify mutual exclusion. The atomic functionality these instructions provide is the ability to perform an uninterruptable read/write cycle. That is, an instruction reads from memory, possibly performs an action, and then writes to memory guaranteeing that these operations cannot be interrupted; nor can another CPU write to the same memory location during these operations. In the latter case, the memory location is locked during the atomic instruction to other CPUs. Over the years, different computers have provided different atomic instructions. Several of these instructions are examined here, but others exist and each can be used to solve the critical section problem, albeit with varying degrees of complexity and efficiency.

6.4.1   MIPS R4000

An example of a general approach to hardware atomicity is provided on the MIPS R4000 [35] computer and subsequently provided on the Alpha [40], PowerPC [39] and ARM [3] computers. Rather than provide a fixed set of atomic instructions, a general capability exists to build many different atomic operations. This novel approach is used to illustrate several instructions implemented by difference architectures. That is, a multi-line MIPS assembler program is shown that corresponds to single instructions on other architectures; while one instruction may seem better than several instructions, the latter is significantly more general.

The general approach is based on two instructions that capture the necessary requirements of an atomic read/write cycle: LL (load locked) and SC (store conditional). The LL instruction loads (reads) a value from memory into a register, but in addition, it sets a hardware reservation on the memory from which the value is fetched. The reservation granularity varies among the processors from 4 to 2048 bytes. It is then possible to modify the register value through one or more instructions. When the register value is completely modified, it is stored (written) back into the original or another memory location using the SC instruction. However, the store is conditional and occurs only if no interrupt, exception, or interfering write has occurred to the reserved memory location associated with the original LL. If any of these conditions is not met, the store does not occur. Instead, the failure is indicated by setting the register containing the value to be stored to 0.[4]

(The following MIPS assembler programs are simplified by ignoring the delay slots of branch and jump instructions. All the programs require a nop instruction after each branch and jump instruction.)

6.4.2   Test and Set

The test-and-set instruction is the most common atomic instruction. The instruction has one parameter: a pointer to a lock. It is implemented as: read a memory location (possibly into an implicit register), write a fixed value into the memory location (often the value 1), and return the previous value. All these actions are performed as a single atomic operation without interruption and without change by other CPUs to the memory location. It is shown here by a C++ equivalent routine:

```
int testSet( int &lock ) {      // atomic execution
    int temp = lock;            // read
    lock = 1;                   // write
    return temp;                // return previous value
}
```

---

[4] Unfortunately, the register is set to 1 on success, so the value being stored is always destroyed. Setting a condition code would have been better.

The equivalent assembler program written using LL and SC is:

```
testSet:                    // register $4 contains &lock
  ll    $2,($4)             // read and reserve location
  or    $8,$2,1             // set register $8 to 1
  sc    $8,($4)             // attempt to store 1 into lock
  beq $8,$0,testSet         // retry if interference between read and write
  j     $31                 // return previous value in register $2
```

Notice the busy wait around the read/write cycle, via the compare and branch, beq, back to label testSet if the store fails.

How to achieve mutual exclusion using test-and-set is answered by going back to the first attempt at a software solution: locking (see Sect. 6.3.1, p. 238). The problem with the locking solution is the potential for interruption between checking if the lock is open and closing the lock, e.g.:

```
while ( Lock == CLOSED ) {} // entry protocol
// interruption
Lock = CLOSED;
```

This problem can be solved with test-and-set by noticing that after the previous value is returned, the current value is always 1; therefore, the instant the previous value of the lock is returned, the lock is always closed. If the previous value is open, the lock is closed; if the previous value is closed, the lock is closed. In other words, the first thread to test-and-set on an open lock reads the open value and snaps the lock closed, atomically; any other thread simply closes the locks, atomically. Therefore, the entry protocol simply transforms into:

```
int Lock = OPEN;            // shared lock
thread i
while ( testSet( Lock ) == CLOSED ) {} // entry protocol
// critical section
Lock = OPEN;                // exit protocol
```

If the lock is open, the loop stops and the lock is set to closed. If the lock is closed, the loop busy waits until another thread sets the lock to open.

Unlike a software solution, the hardware solution does not depend on any shared information other than the lock. Furthermore, this solution works even for N threads trying to enter a critical section. These observations are very significant because there is a substantial decrease in complexity at the software level with only a marginal increase in complexity at the hardware level. Unfortunately, rule 5 is broken, as there is no bound on service; this problem is addressed in subsequent examples.

The first hardware solution to include a bound was presented by Burns [8] (see Fig. 6.21). Like the software N-thread solution, there is a bit assigned to each thread wanting to enter the critical section; in addition, there is a key used to control the critical section resulting in $N + 1$ bits. Conceptually, the thread in the critical section has the key, and when it leaves, it either hangs it on a hook outside the critical section if no other thread is waiting or passes it directly to a waiting thread.

The entry protocol begins with a thread declaring its intent to enter the critical section. It then busy waits until either:

```
_Task Worker {
    Intent *intents;
    int &Key, N, posn;

    void main() {
        for ( int i = 0; i < 1000; i += 1 ) {
            intents[posn] = WantIn;                      // entry protocol
            // acquire key or selected to enter
            while ( testSet(Key) != 0 && intents[posn] != DontWantIn ); // busy wait

            CriticalSection();

            intents[posn] = DontWantIn;                  // exit protocol
            // locate next thread to enter
            int next;
            for ( next = (posn + 1) % N;                 // search for waiting thread
                  intents[next] != WantIn && next != posn;
                  next = (next + 1) % N ) {}
            if ( next == posn ) {                        // no waiting threads ?
                Key = 0;                                 // return key
            } else {
                intents[next] = DontWantIn;              // stop their busy waiting
            }
        }
    }
  public:
    Worker( int &Key, Intent intents[], int N, int posn ) :
        Key( Key ), intents( intents ), N( N ), posn( posn ) {}
};
void uMain::main() {
    const int NoOfTasks = 10;
    int Key;                                             // shared
    Intent intents[NoOfTasks];                           // shared
    Worker *workers[NoOfTasks];                          // pointer to an array of workers
    int i;

    Key = 0;                                             // initialize shared data
    for ( i = 0; i < NoOfTasks; i += 1 ) {
        intents[i] = DontWantIn;
    }
    for ( i = 0; i < NoOfTasks; i += 1 ) {
        workers[i] = new Worker( Key, intents, NoOfTasks, i ); // create workers
    }
    for ( i = 0; i < NoOfTasks; i += 1 ) {               // terminate workers
        delete workers[i];
    }
}
```

Fig. 6.21 Bounded mutual exclusion with test-and-set

- It acquires the entry key via the test-and-set.

  In this case, the key is hanging outside the critical section and the thread just atomically picks it up. Like the simple test-and-set solution above, if one or more threads simultaneously race to pick up the key, the test-and-set ensures only one wins, so there is no indefinite postponement. Notice, the test-and-set implicitly changes the value of the key to non-zero, so it is only necessary to explicitly reset the key (i.e., set to zero) in the program.

- Or it is told that it has been selected to enter next and is conceptually handed the key by the thread leaving the critical section.

  In this case, the key is not put back on the hook as a thread leaves the critical section, so no other thread can access it. Cooperation is being used by the thread leaving the critical section instead of just putting the key back on the hook and letting the waiting threads race for it, like the simple test-and-set solution. It is through this cooperation that a bound is established.

Interestingly, this algorithm works if assignment is not atomic by coding the busy wait in the entry protocol to compare exact values written in the exit protocol. Hence, even if a value fluctuates during assignment, the busy loop only stops after the final value stabilizes.

The exit protocol begins with a thread retracting its intent to enter the critical section. The exiting thread must now check to see if there are any waiting threads. To do this, it cycles from its position around the array of intent bits until either it finds a thread wanting entry to the critical section or returns back to the starting location of the search (i.e., its intent bit). If another thread is found wanting entry, it is *tricked* into making progress by turning off its intent bit so it terminates its entry-protocol busy-loop (i.e., intents[posn] != DontWantIn is false). Notice, the key is not reset as it is conceptually given to this entering thread; therefore, all other threads continue to see a locked critical section. If no thread is found waiting, the key is reset, which conceptually places it back on the hook outside the critical section.

There are several important points about this algorithm. First, the entry protocol spins executing the test-and-set instruction, which normally causes a problem on most multiprocessor computers. The reason is that any atomic instruction on a multiprocessor is expensive because of the need to ensure mutual exclusion to the particular memory location across all CPUs. This problem is mitigated by performing a test-and-set only after detecting an open lock, as in:

```
while ( lock == CLOSED || testSet( lock ) == CLOSED ) {}   // busy wait until OPEN
```

This busy-waiting approach only does the test-and-set when a thread exits the critical section and resets the lock; otherwise, only a simple read is performed, which is cheaper than an atomic instruction.[5] Second, this hardware solution still requires one bit for each waiting thread, which imposes a maximum on the

---

[5] There is an additional problem with this approach on multiprocessor computers. When the lock is set opened, all waiting threads may simultaneously perform a test-and-set, which causes the hardware problem of invalidating multiple CPU caches; see [1] for solutions to this problem.

number of threads that can wait for entry into the critical section. Furthermore, the cooperation in the exit protocol is $O(N)$ because of the linear search through the list of intent bits. Lastly, the bound on the waiting time is $N-1$ because a thread may have to wait for all the other threads to enter and leave the critical section before it can proceed. The bound is ensured because the linear search always starts from the bit position of the last thread in the critical section. Therefore, in the worst case of all threads waiting, the linear search cycles through all the threads. However, arriving threads are not serviced in FIFO order because the intent bits are serviced in cyclic order not arrival order. A thread arriving behind the current intent bit is serviced only after threads in front of the current intent bit, even though thread's behind the current intent bit may have arrived before thread's in front of it. Therefore, this algorithm is another example of bounded non-FIFO selection.

6.4.3 Fetch and Assign

The fetch-and-assign instruction is the generalization of the test-and-set by atomically assigning *any* value rather than a fixed value to a memory location. The instruction has two parameters: a pointer to a value and a value. It is implemented as: read of a memory location (possibly into an implicit register), write a value into the memory location, and return the previous value. All these actions are performed as a single atomic operation without interruption and without change by other CPUs to the memory location. It is shown here by a C++ equivalent routine:

```
int fetchAssn( int &assn, int val ) { // atomic execution
    int temp = assn;      // read
    assn = val;           // write
    return temp;          // return previous value
}
```

The equivalent assembler program written using LL and SC is:

```
fetchAssn:                 // register $4, $5 contain &assn and val
  ll    $2,($4)            // read and reserve location
  sc    $5,($4)            // attempt to store new val into pointer
  beq $5,$0,fetchAssn      // retry if interference between read and write
  j     $31                // return previous value in register $2
```

Generating mutual exclusion using fetch-and-assign is identical to test-and-set, e.g.:

```
int Lock = 0;              // shared lock
thread i
while ( fetchAssn( Lock, 1 ) != 0 ) {} // entry protocol
// critical section
Lock = 0;                  // exit protocol
```

The generalization of fetch-and-assign makes it slightly more powerful than test-and-set, and this additional capability is used in Sect. 6.4.6, p. 283.

Interestingly, this instruction is often called swap or exchange, and can be using in the following ways:

```
x = fetchAssn( y, x );     // swap x and y
```

Now, if two tasks each performed this swap of x and y with values 3 and 7, respectively, the values become 7 and 3 and then change back to 3 and 7, regardless of order and speed of execution. However, this notion of swap only applies in a sequential domain. In a concurrent domain, where x and y are shared variables, the previous attempt to swap values can fail. The failure occurs if there is an interrupt after the call to fetchAssn, but before the assignment to x:

$$
\begin{array}{ccccc}
T_1 & y & x & T_2 \\
& 7 & 3 \\
FA(y, x) & 3 & \leftarrow 3 \\
\$2:7 \\
& \text{interrupt} \\
& 3 & \leftarrow 3 & FA(y, x) \\
& & & \$2:3 \\
& \text{interrupt} \\
x = \$2 \\
& 3 & 7 \\
& \text{interrupt} \\
& & x = \$2 \\
& 3 & 3
\end{array}
$$

Hence, the result of 3 and 3 is unexpected, and shows that atomicity does not apply to both memory locations. Clearly, an action between register/memory and memory/memory is not equivalent from a concurrency perspective because a register is not shared but both memory locations are shared.

> The memory-to-memory swap should not be confused with the read-modify-write swap; the former exchanges the values of two public registers (memory), while the latter exchanges the value of a public register (memory) with a processor's private register [20, p. 139].

Most programmers think in terms of memory/memory actions because they do not see (use) registers directly. Hence, from a concurrent programmer's perspective, there is no atomic swap, so calling it swap/exchange is confusing; therefore, the name fetch-and-assign is more meaningful as it describes the behaviour from the concurrent programmer's perspective.

6.4.4   Fetch and Increment

The fetch-and-increment instruction is a generalization of fetch-and-assign by performing an increment between the fetch and assignment of a memory location. The instruction has one parameter: a pointer to a value. It is implemented as: read of a memory location (possibly into an implicit register), increment the value, write the value into the memory location, and return the previous value. All these actions are performed as a single atomic operation without interruption and without change by other CPUs to the memory location. It is shown here by a C++ equivalent routine:

```
int fetchInc( int &val ) {      // atomic execution
    int temp = val;             // read
    val += 1;                   // increment and write
    return temp;                // return previous value
}
```

The equivalent assembler program written using LL and SC is:

```
fetchInc:                       // register $4 contains &val
    ll    $2,($4)               // read and reserve location
    add $8,$2,1                 // set register $8 to val + 1
    sc  $8,($4)                 // attempt to store new val into pointer
    beq $8,$0,fetchInc          // retry if interference between read and write
    j     $31                   // return previous value in register $2
```

Often fetch-and-increment is generalized to add any value not just 1, which means it can also decrement with a negative value.

Generating mutual exclusion using atomic increment is similar to test-and-set:

```
int Lock = 0;                   // shared lock
thread i
while ( fetchInc( Lock ) != 0 ) {}  // entry protocol
// critical section
Lock = 0;                       // exit protocol
```

The lock is set to 0, and all threads wanting entry attempt to increment the lock. Because of the atomic increment, only one thread makes the transition from 0 to 1. The thread that makes this transition is returned the value 0, which indicates it can enter the critical section. All other threads busy wait, atomically incrementing the lock. When the thread in the critical section exits, it resets the lock to zero. This assignment must be atomic in case an increment of a partial result causes a problem. Then, one of the busy waiting threads causes the next lock transition from 0 to 1 and enters the critical section.

There are two problems with this solution. First, like test-and-set, this solution has no bound on service. Second, the lock counter can overflow from zero back to zero during the busy waiting, which would allow another thread into the critical section. The time to overflow the lock counter can range from tens of seconds to several minutes depending on the speed of the computer. As long as the time to execute the critical section is less than this amount, including the time a thread might be interrupted by time slicing while in the critical section, the overflow problem can be ignored. Nevertheless, it is a risky solution, especially with the ever increasing speed of modern computers, which shorten the time to overflow, but equally shortens the time to execute the critical section.

A more complex example of how to use atomic increment to solve mutual exclusion is presented that solves rule 5, i.e., no starvation. The algorithm builds a true atomic ticket-dispenser, as opposed to the self-generating tickets for Lamport's algorithm, so each thread simply takes a ticket and waits for its value to appear before entering the critical section. After exiting the critical section, a thread conceptually throws its ticket away (or turns it back in) so it can be reused. Like the previous solutions, there is the potential for ticket overflow. However, this solution allows the tickets to overflow from positive to negative (assuming 2s complement) and back again without problem. The only restriction is that the total number of threads waiting to use a ticket lock is less than the total number of values that can be represented by an integer, e.g., more than 2^{32} values for most 4-byte integers.

This lock solution is presented as a class to encapsulate the two variables needed by each lock, as in:

```
class ticketLock {
    unsigned int tickets, serving;
public:
    ticketLock() : tickets( 0 ), serving( 0 ) {}
    void acquire() {                        // entry protocol
        int ticket = fetchInc( tickets );   // obtain a ticket
        while ( ticket != serving ) {}      // busy wait
    }
    void release() {                        // exit protocol
        serving += 1;
    }
};
```

The acquire member atomically acquires the current ticket and advances the ticket counter so that two threads cannot obtain the same ticket, except in the case of more than 2^{32} threads. Once a ticket is acquired, a thread busy waits until its turn for service. The release member advances the serving counter so the next thread can execute, which is a very simple form of cooperation. Notice, the release member does not use fetchInc to increment serving for the following reasons. First, only one thread can be in the release member incrementing server or the mutual exclusion property has been violated. Second, the next thread wanting entry cannot make progress until the increment has occurred, and even if it continues before the releasing thread exits release, this does not cause a problem because there is no more work performed in release. Finally, this analysis probably requires atomic assignment, even with the inequality check in the busy loop of the entry protocol, because there may be many outstanding ticket values and the server counter could contain several of these values before stabilizing.

This algorithm has many excellent properties. There is no practical limit on the number of waiting threads because it does not require a bit per thread; only $O(1)$ bits are needed (64 bits in this implementation for the two counters). The ticket overflows only if all values are used simultaneously, which is essentially impossible for a 32/64-bit counter. Tasks are serviced in FIFO order of arrival and the cooperation to select the next thread to execute in the critical section is $O(1)$. Only one atomic instruction is executed per entering thread; afterwards, the busy wait only reads, called **local spinning**.

Finally, threads appear to be handled in FIFO order because of the monotonic increasing ticket values due to the atomic increment, which ensures a fair bound on service, the additional busy wait in the implementation of fetchInc using LL and SC, means that a thread, in theory, could spin forever attempting to increment tickets. Is this an artifact of the implementation of atomic increment or it is a general problem? That is, if the architecture implemented a single instruction to perform an atomic increment is this problem solved? In fact, the answer is maybe. On a uniprocessor, a single atomic instruction normally precludes time slicing during its execution, so a thread never waits to do the increment. On a multiprocessor, if the architecture forms a FIFO queue of waiting threads from different CPUs for each memory location involved in an atomic operation, the threads have a bound on service. However, this begs the question of how the threads are added to the hardware waiting queue, because operations on the same end of a queue by multiple threads must be executed atomically. Therefore, there is a recursion that ultimately devolves into a busy wait; thus, there is always a busy wait somewhere in a computer system, in the software or hardware or both. Most multiprocessor computers actually busy wait in the hardware until the memory location becomes unlocked. Therefore, it may be impossible to guarantee a bound in practice. However, the probability of a thread starving is so low that a probabilistic solution at this level is acceptable.

> It is an amusing paradox of critical sections that to implement one, we must appeal to the existence of simpler critical section (called *wait* and *signal*). The implementation of *wait* and *signal* operations, in turn, requires the use of an *arbiter*–a hardware implementation of still simpler critical sections that guarantee exclusive access to a semaphore *(discussed in Chap. 7, p. 313)* by a single processor in a multiprocessor system. This use of nested critical sections continues at all levels of machine design until we reach the atomic level, at which nuclear states are known to be discrete and mutually exclusive [4, p. 241].

6.4.5   Compare and Assign

The compare-and-assign instruction performs an atomic compare and conditional assignment. The instruction has three parameters: a pointer to a value, a comparison value, and a new value for the conditional assignment. It is implemented as: read of a memory location (possibly into an implicit register), compare the value read with the comparison value, and if equal, assign the new value into the memory location. The result of the comparison is returned. All these actions are performed as a single atomic operation without interruption and without change by other CPUs to the memory location. It is shown here by a C++ equivalent routine:

```
bool CAA( int &val, int comp, int nval ) {    // atomic execution
    if ( val == comp ) {        // equal ? assign new value
        val = nval;             // write new value
        return true;            // indicate assignment occurred
    }
    return false;               // indicate assignment did not occur
}
```

The equivalent assembler program written using LL and SC is:

```
CAA:                          // register $4, $5, $6 contain &val, comp, nval
    move $8,$6                // copy nval because destroyed by SC
    ||   $2,($4)              // read and reserve location
    bne $2,$5,notequal        // equal ? try to assign new value
    sc   $8,($4)              // try to write new value
    beq $8,$0,CAA             // retry if interference between read and write
    li   $2,1                 // set $2 to true
    j    $31                  // return result of comparison in register $2
notequal:
    sc   $2,($4)              // write back current value, match for LL
    li   $2,0                 // set $2 to false
    j    $31                  // return result of comparison in register $2
```

Notice the second SC instruction writes back the original value and is required to form a match for the initial LL. No failure check is required because the SC in this case is only used to close the LL. If the second SC is not present, another LL is performed without terminating the first one, which may cause problems on certain architectures. Two of the first computers to have a CAA instruction were the IBM 370 [26] and Motorola MC68000 [36].

An alternative implementation assigns the comparison value with the tested value when unequal.

```
bool CAV( int &val, int &comp, int nval ) {   // atomic execution
    if ( val == comp ) {      // equal ? assign new value
        val = nval;           // write new value
        return true;          // indicate assignment occurred
    }
    comp = val;               // return changed value
    return false;             // indicate assignment did not occur
}
```

The assignment when unequal can be useful as it also returns the current value of the tested variable; however, it requires resetting the compare value before each call.

Here is a simple usage of compare-and-assign to achieve mutual exclusion by simulating test-and-set:

```
int Lock = OPEN;              // shared lock
    thread_i
while ( ! CAA( Lock, OPEN, CLOSED ) ) {}  // entry protocol
// critical section
Lock = OPEN;                  // exit protocol
```

The compare-and-assign compares the lock with OPEN, and if open, assigns it CLOSED, like the test-and-set solution. Also, like the test-and-set solution, this solution has no bound on service.

Interestingly, the SPARC architecture generalizes the fetch-and-assign with the compare, called compare-and-swap:

```
int CAS( int &val, int &comp, int nval ) {    // atomic execution
    int temp = val;           // read
    if ( val == comp ) {      // equal ? assign new value
        val = nval;           // write new value
    }
    return temp;              // return previous value
}
```

which allows:

```
x = CAS( y, y, x );        // swap x and y
```

because y is equal to itself so the assignment always occurs. However, like fetch-and-assign, the programmer does not see an atomic interchanging of values, only an assignment. Other architectures also use the term compare-and-swap for compare-and-assign, which is confusing.

Finally, compare-and-assign is powerful enough to simulate other atomic instructions, like fetch-and-increment (see Sect. 6.4.4, p. 278).

```
int fetchInc( int &val ) {
    int temp;
    for ( ;; ) {
        temp = val;            // copy val
        if ( CAA( val, temp, temp + 1 ) ) break;
    }
    return temp;
}
```

The value of the variable is copied and then an attempt is made to change the value to be one greater. The CAA only assigns the incremented value into the variable if its value has not changed since it was copied, which can only be true if no other thread performed an assignment between the copy and the CAA. Now, the previous ticketLock (see page 280) can be used to establish an ordering.

6.4.6   Mellor-Crummey and Scott

All ticket solutions are only probabilistically correct because of the finite nature of the ticket dispenser, even for 64-bit tickets. For mission-critical situations, like avionics, medical or operating systems, probabilistically correct is insufficient. To provide bounded service without tickets requires a queue to ensure FIFO ordering of waiting threads. John M. Mellor-Crummey and Michael L. Scott [32] created the first queue-based hardware algorithm for mutual exclusion, named after their initials, MCS.

The lock in Fig. 6.22 is used as follows. Each thread creates a node to be added to a queue if it is necessary to wait, e.g.:

```
MCS Lock;                      // shared lock
thread_i
MCS::Node n;                   // thread node for waiting
Lock.acquire( n );             // entry protocol
// critical section
Lock.release( n );             // exit protocol
```

Each thread can allocate the node on its stack as the thread is blocking for the duration of the mutual exclusion and critical section where the node is used; hence, there is no heap allocation. The node contains a pointer to the next waiting thread, possibly null, and a boolean flag for local spinning (busy waiting). As well, the acquire member creates an additional field on the thread's stack; this field is only needed during acquiring so it is separated from the actual node (it could be part of

```
class MCS {
  public:
    struct Node {                                    // queue node
      Node *next;                                    // next waiting thread or NULL
      bool waiting;                                  // spinning
    };
    MCS() : last( NULL ) {}
    void acquire( Node &n ) {
      Node *pred;
      n.next = NULL;
      pred = fetchAssn( &last, &n );  // atomic: pred = last; last = n
      if ( pred != NULL ) {                          // someone on queue ?
        n.waiting = true;                            // mark as waiting
        pred->next = &n;                             // add to queue of waiting threads
        while ( n.waiting ) {}                       // busy wait on private spin variable
      }
    }
    void release( Node &n ) {
      if ( n.next == NULL ) {                        // no one waiting ?
        if ( CAA( &last, &n, NULL ) ) return;  // last == n ? last = NULL
        while ( n.next == NULL ) {}                  // busy wait until node is modified
      }
      n.next->waiting = false;                       // stop their busy wait
    }
  private:
    Node *last;
};
```

Fig. 6.22 MCS list-based queuing lock

the node). Finally, the MCS lock contains a class variable, last, pointing to the last node in the queue of waiting threads or null when the queue is empty. Fig. 6.23 show the storage layout and 3 threads arriving at the lock and attempting to construct a FIFO waiting queue.

Key to the algorithm design is the lazily construct of the waiting queue; i.e., each thread chains its node onto the waiting queue independently so a thread attempting to walk the queue may have to delay until the next node is attached. The acquire member initializes the next field of an acquiring thread's node to NULL. Then the fetchAssn atomically reads the last node in the queue and sets last to the new node. This action ensures each thread sees its unique predecessor node. These steps are shown in Fig. 6.24, p. 286, where step a) shows the initial state when thread T_0 arrives, and steps b), c) and d) show threads T_0, T_1 and T_2 reseting their private pred and global last via the atomic fetchAssn. At this point, thread T_0 does not know the next node in the queue but each thread knows its predecessor node in the queue.

Step e) determines the head of the queue, which is designated by the thread with pred == NULL, which is thread T_0, and it proceeds into the critical section. The remaining threads with pred pointers then connect their nodes into the queue in any order, at any time. For example, thread T_1 sets its waiting flag, the predecessor's node is modified to point at T_1's node, and T_1 busy waits on its waiting flag. Thread T_2 does the same, so both threads are connected into the queue in the order defined

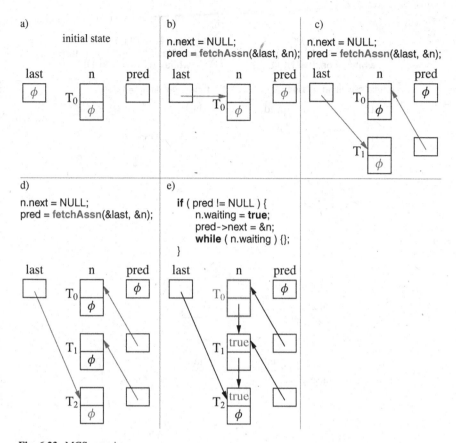

Fig. 6.23 MCS: acquire

from the fetchAssn and busy waiting. Finally, last is pointing at T_2's node for adding new nodes onto the queue.

Fig. 6.24 shows the steps by the release member as threads leave the critical section. If a thread has chained itself onto the releasing thread's node, the releasing thread must perform cooperation to make servicing FIFO. The chained thread must already be busy waiting on its waiting flag because the flag is set before chaining. For example, in step a) T_0 sets T_1's waiting flag to false, so T_1 stops busy waiting and enters the critical section. The same action occurs in step b) when thread T_1 leaves the critical section. Step c) shows thread T_2 leaving the critical section with no thread chained onto its node. Hence, T_2 must be the only node on the queue, and it races to remove itself and set the last null meaning the queue is empty. The problem is that between checking that it is the last node and removing itself, another thread can chain itself onto the queue so this thread's node no longer has a next field that is null. A compare-and-assign is performed to try to set the last pointer to null but only if it is still pointing to T_2's node. Step d) shows if the two values are still equal, last

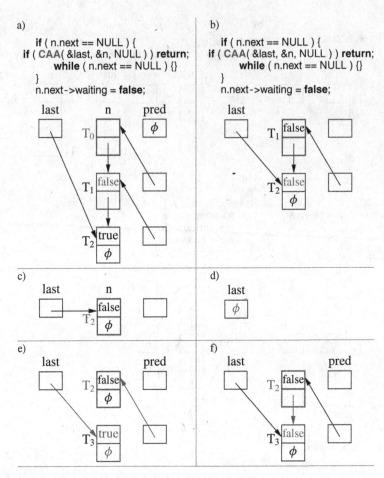

Fig. 6.24 MCS: release

is assigned NULL, and T_2 has successfully removed its node. Step e) shows if the two values are unequal, a thread has linked itself onto the end of the queue. However, while the new thread may have set last, it may not have finished modifying T_2's next to point to its node. Therefore, T_2 must busy wait for the other thread to get from the fetchAssn in acquire to setting this node's next field. Step f) shows that once this is done, T_2's next pointer is set so it proceeds to unblock the new successor node T_3 so it can enter the critical section. Notice how important the ordering of assignments is in acquire. The waiting flag must be set to true *before* setting the next field so that in release it is safe to reset the other thread's waiting flag once the nodes are linked together. Finally, it is unnecessary to have a global front pointer to the queue as the node associated with the thread in the critical section is always at the front of the queue.

6.4.7 Nonreentrant Problem

In sequential programming, there is a concurrency problem introduced by interrupt handling. For example, a sequential program may receive a stop, terminate or timer interrupt. When the interrupt is raised, the operating system stops the program and executes the corresponding interrupt handler installed by the program or the default handler. The handler then executes, returns to the operating system, which may restart or terminate the program depending on the interrupt.

Interrupts introduce a form of concurrency into sequential execution because delivery is nondeterministic between any program instructions; hence, the program may be in an unsafe state when the interrupt is delivered. For example, a program calls the **new** operation to allocate storage, where the **new** operation manages free storage using a list data-structure. Assume that half way through allocating storage, an interrupt is delivered and its interrupt handler runs. Then the handler may also attempt to allocate storage using **new** to leave information about the interrupt; however, the **new** operation cannot be re-entered because its list data-structure is currently in an inconsistent state. Conceptually, the sequential program has become concurrent because the interrupt handler is logically executed by another thread managed by the operating system to execute the interrupt handler, even if the original thread is used by the operating system to perform the handler. That is, the interrupt results in a new (unpredictable) control path through the program that cannot occur by any sequential execution of the program without the interrupt, called the nonreentrant problem. Hence, the **new** operation is conceptually a critical section. However, locking **new** does not help in this case because the handler cannot block; it must execute to completion because logically the handler is being executed by the operating system. Furthermore, masking the interrupt on entry to the handler, which precludes delivery of the same or all interrupts, is too late as the initial interrupt already causes the problem.

Often the inconsistent state can be reduced to just the manipulation of data structures used to manage resources. If these list operations are atomic, it is possible for the interrupt routine to be safe with respect to all of its actions.

6.5 Atomic (Lock-Free) Data-Structure

Adding and removing elements from a list data-structure such as a stack, queue or deque (singly and doubly linked list) are common operations in many problems (see bounded buffer in Sect. 7.5, p. 348), especially in the language runtime-system and within an operating system. These list operations are unsafe with respect to concurrency, i.e., two threads cannot simultaneously modify the link fields of the data structure without corrupting the list integrity. Making list operations like add and remove atomic via a single high-level atomic instruction significantly simplifies the class of problems that rely on list data-structures. The basic approach is to prepare a node, and then with a single atomic operation, add it or remove it from a list to leave information about the interrupt.

Is it possible to build data structures with the basic atomic operations provided by current hardware (and discussed so far)? The answer is yes and no. Yes, it is possible to construct atomic data-structures; but in most cases not solely with the available set of atomic instructions. Hence, it is necessary to augment the hardware instruction with significant software to solve the problem.

As with all locking mechanisms, there is the issue of starvation (rule 5). Correspondingly, atomic data-structures are classified as lock free if there is potential for starvation (unfairness), and wait free if there is no starvation. As it is true for all locks, achieving wait free is more complex because of the need to generate a service bound as well as mutual exclusion. While MCS (see Fig. 6.22, p. 284) constructs a queue data-structure, the CAA instruction is used to allow multiple threads to simultaneously add to one end of a stack, but only one thread is removing from the queue, i.e., the thread exiting the critical section. This restricted form of access to the data structure is sufficient for the problem of building mutual exclusion.

6.5.1 Stack

The simplest data structure is a stack, so that is the starting point for creating a lock-free date-structure, but with the more complex requirement of multiple threads simultaneously adding and removing. For example, a set of resources, e.g., a group of printers, can have multiple threads attempting to remove a resource from the set to use it, and subsequently, adding the resource back to the set once used. Fig. 6.25 shows the stack data structure at lines 1–6. The stack nodes have data and a link field that points to the next node on the stack, where the last node has a null link-field. The stack itself is just pointer to the top first node in the stack or null if the stack is empty. Using the CAA instruction it is possible to write the push (lines 8–13) and pop (lines 14–21) routines to add and remove nodes to/from a stack.

To add a node to the stack, the caller first creates a node (see Fig. 6.26, p. 290a), then calls push passing the node. The busy loop copies the stack top pointer into the next field of the new node to be added to the top of the stack (see Fig. 6.26, p. 290b). Then a CAA operation is performed on the stack top pointer, top, and the new top pointer in n.next (see Fig. 6.26, p. 290c). If the top pointer in the header has changed since its value was copied into n.next, the address of the new node is *not* copied into top (see Fig. 6.26, p. 290d). Hence, an intervening push (or pop) occurred after the top pointer was copied into n.next, changing the stack. Therefore, the thread has to try again by updating n.next to the new top (see Fig. 6.27, p. 291a), and attempt to atomically set the top pointer (see Fig. 6.27, p. 291b). Eventually, the CAA is successful (see Fig. 6.27, p. 291c) and the top pointer is atomically set to the new node.

To remove a node from the stack, the pop routine copies the stack top pointer t (see Fig. 6.28, p. 292a), within the busy loop. Then a check is made for popping

```
1    class Stack {
2    public:
3        struct Node {
4            // resource data
5            Node *next;                    // pointer to next node (resource)
6        };
7        void push( Node &n ) {
8            for ( ;; ) {                   // busy wait
9                n.next = top;              // link new node to top node
10                if ( CAA( top, n.next, &n ) ) break; // attempt to update top node
11            }
12        }
13        Node *pop() {
14            Node *t;
15            for ( ;; ) {                   // busy wait
16                t = top;                   // copy top node
17                if ( t == NULL ) return NULL;   // empty stack ?
18                if ( CAA( top, t, t->next ) ) return t; // attempt to update top node
19            }
20        }
21        Stack() : top( NULL ) {}
22    private:
23        Node *top;                         // pointer to stack top
24    };
```

Fig. 6.25   Lock-free stack, ABA problem

from an empty stack, which results in returning NULL. If the stack is not empty, a CAA operation is performed on the stack top-pointer, top, and the new top pointer in t (see Fig. 6.28, p. 292b). If the top pointer in the header has changed since its value was copied into t, the address of the second node, t->next, is *not* copied into top (see Fig. 6.28, p. 292c). Hence, an intervening pop (or push) occurred after the top pointer was copied into t, changing the stack. Therefore, the thread has to try again by updating t to the new top, and attempt to atomically set the top pointer (see Fig. 6.29, p. 292b). Eventually, the CAA is successful (see Fig. 6.29, p. 292c) and the top pointer is set to the second node on the stack, atomically removing the first node.

If CAV is used (see Fig. 6.30, p. 294), the initialization of n.next and t are moved outside the busy loops in push and pop, respectively, because the CAV resets the compare value with the stack top when the compare fails.

Notice, in the pop operation the node pointed to by t may have been removed between copying top to t and computing t->next, resulting in random data being generated by t->next. In general, this is not a problem because the CAA does not assign the invalid data into the stack header because top is unequal to t. (A problem might occur if the reference t->next addresses outside of the program's memory, resulting in an address fault.) However, there is a problem causing failure for a particular series of pops and pushes, called the ABA problem. For example, given a stack with three nodes:

$$top \rightarrow x \rightarrow y \rightarrow z$$

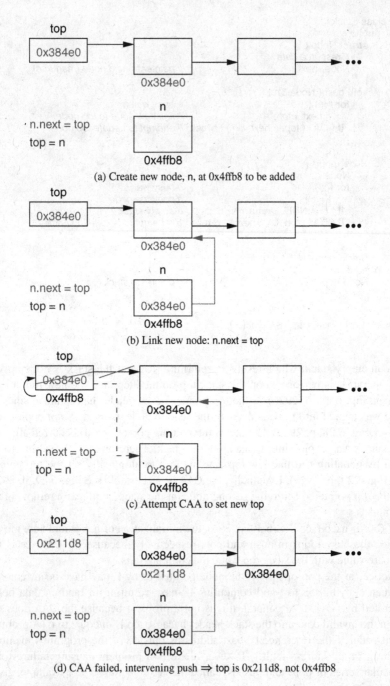

(a) Create new node, n, at 0x4ffb8 to be added

(b) Link new node: n.next = top

(c) Attempt CAA to set new top

(d) CAA failed, intervening push ⟹ top is 0x211d8, not 0x4ffb8

Fig. 6.26 Failed push attempt

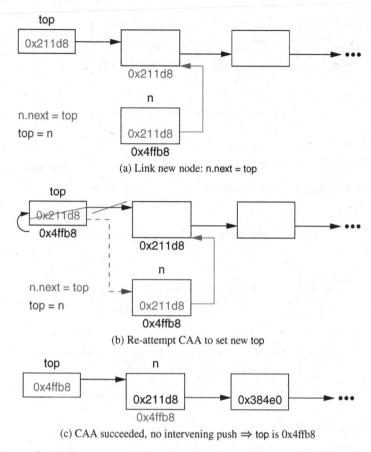

(a) Link new node: n.next = top

(b) Re-attempt CAA to set new top

(c) CAA succeeded, no intervening push ⇒ top is 0x4ffb8

Fig. 6.27 Successful push attempt

and a popping thread, T_i, has t set to node x and dereferenced t->next to get the local value of y for its argument to CAA. T_i is now time-sliced **before the CAA**, and while blocked, nodes x and y are popped, and x is pushed again:

   top → x → z

Now, when T_i unblocks and performs the CAA, it successfully removes x because it is the same header before the time-slice, but incorrectly sets top to its local value of node y, giving:

   top → y → ???

where the next pointer of y may have any value, as it could have been added to other lists or the storage freed and reused. The stack data is now lost and the stack is left in an inconsistent state.

   Interestingly, there is no ABA problem if pop is implemented directly using LL/SC:

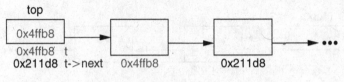

t = top

(a) Copy top node, 0x4ffb8, to t for removal

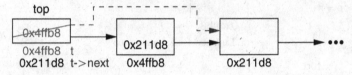

t = top

(b) Not empty, attempt CAA to set new top to next node

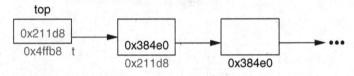

t = top

(c) CAA failed, intervening pop ⟹ update failed top is not t, so no
assignment

Fig. 6.28   Failed pop attempt

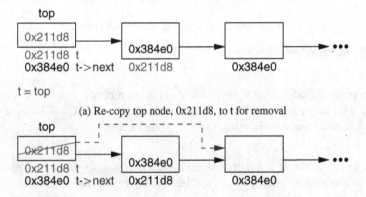

t = top

(a) Re-copy top node, 0x211d8, to t for removal

t = top

(b) Not empty, attempt CAA to set new top to next node

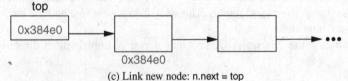

(c) Link new node: n.next = top

Fig. 6.29   Successful pop attempt

```
Pop:                    // register $4 contains &top
  ll    $2,($4)         // read top and reserve location: t = top
  bne $2,$0,null        // empty stack ?
  lw  $8,8($2)          // load next pointer: t->next
  sc  $8,($4)           // attempt to store t->next into top
  beq $8,$0,Pop         // retry if interference between read and write
  j     $31             // return
null:
  sc  $2,($4)           // write back current value, match for LL
  j     $31             // return
```

The reason is that a reservation is more powerful than an instantaneous atomic instruction. That is, SC directly detects *change* at any time independent of values rather than indirectly checking if a value changes. Hence, SC is not tricked by adding, removing, and re-adding the same values because it detects top has changed over that time period. Unfortunately, few computers have LL/SC, and supporting architectures have restricted LL/SC, which do not work in all cases.

Fig. 6.30 shows a probabilistic solution to this problem using a counter (ticket) and a double-wide compare and assign instruction CAAD. The solution increments a counter in the stack header every time a node is pushed. As a result, a removing thread can detect if a node has been removed and re-added to the list because the counter in the header node is increased on the second push. To make this work, the CAAD instruction is used to atomically read and write both fields of the header node (double wide). In practice, a 32-bit counter is considered insufficient for ABA protection, as the counter can roll over in a year, assuming a push operation every nanoseconds; however, a 64-bit counter exceeds 500 years before roll-over at the same rate. The two 64-bit fields are in a structure combined with the 128-bit integer, atom, via a **union**. The integer atom has the correct type for the CAAD routine.

In the push routine, the busy loop copies the top of the stack, link, to the next field of the new node to be pushed on the top of the stack. Because the header contains two fields, normal assignment cannot be assumed to be atomic as the values may be copied in two steps; in general, structure assignment is non-atomic. However, it is unnecessary to use the CAAD to atomically perform the assignment because the subsequent CAAD would fail if the assignment is corrupted and reload a valid value. Then, like the algorithm in Fig. 6.25, p. 289, a CAAD operation is performed on the stack top pointer, via link, and the new top pointer in n.next. If the top pointer in the header has changed since its value was copied into n.next, the address of the new node is *not* copied into top nor is the counter updated. otherwise, the CAAD is successful and the top pointer is set to the new node *and* the counter in the stack header is incremented, counting this push operation.

In the pop routine, the busy loop copies the top of the stack, link, to the temporary t using the same technique as in push. Then, like the algorithm in Fig. 6.25, p. 289, a check is first made for popping from an empty stack, and NULL is returned. If the stack is not empty, a CAAD operation is performed on both fields of the stack header. If the top pointer in the header has changed since its value was copied into t, the address of the second node, t.top->next, is *not* copied into top nor is the counter updated. otherwise, the CAAD is successful and the top pointer is set to the

```
class Stack {
public:
    struct Node;                        // forward declaration
private:
    union Link {
        struct {                        // 64-bit x 2
            Node *top;                  // pointer to stack top
            uintptr_t count;            // count each push
        };
        __int128 atom;                  // gcc, 128-bit integer
    } link;
public:
    struct Node {
        // resource data
        Link next;                      // pointer to next node/count (resource)
    };
    void push( Node &n ) {
        n.next = link;                  // atomic assignment unnecessary, fixed by CAA
        for ( ;; ) {                    // busy wait
            if ( CAVD( link.atom, n.next.atom, (Link){ &n, n.next.count + 1 }.atom ) ) break;
        }
    }
    Node *pop() {
        Link t = link;                  // atomic assignment unnecessary, fixed by CAA
        for ( ;; ) {                    // busy wait
            if ( t.top == NULL ) return NULL;   // empty stack ?
            if ( CAVD( link.atom, t.atom,
                 (Link){ t.top->next.top, t.count }.atom ) ) return t.top;
        }
    }
    Stack() { link.atom = 0; }
};
```

Fig. 6.30 Lock-free stack, no ABA, probabilistic

second node on the stack, atomically removing the first node, *but leaving the counter unchanged by using the original counter value from the copied header*. Because the counter value is also checked implicitly by the CAAD, it ensures a failed assignment for an intervening pop/push.

Specifically, the problem scenario is fixed, e.g., a stack with the basic structure:

top,3 → x → y → z

and a popping thread, T_i, has t set to node x,3 and dereferenced t.top->next to get the local value of y for its argument to CAAD. T_i is now time-sliced before the CAA, and while blocked, nodes x and y are popped, and x is pushed again:

top,4 → x → z

because the adding of x back onto the stack increments the counter. Now, when T_i unblocks and performs the CAAD, it is unsuccessful because its header x,3 does not match the current stack header, x,4.

As mentioned this solution is only probabilistic because the counter is finite in size (as for a ticket counter). The failure situation occurs if thread T_i is time-sliced as above and then sufficient pushes occur to cause the counter to wrap around to the value stored in T_i's header *and* node x just happens to be at the top of the stack when T_i unblocks. Given a 32/64-bit counter, and the incredibly unlikely circumstance that must occur, it is doubtful if this failure situation could arise in practice.

Finally, none of the algorithms using CAA and CAAD have a bound on the busy waiting; therefore, rule 5 is broken. Herlihy [20] shows no wait-free solutions are possible using existing hardware instructions. Furthermore, there are no known lock-free direct-solutions using existing hardware instructions for a data structure more complex than the stack solution shown here. Hence, without more sophisticated atomic instructions, there are no simple solutions for lock-free data-structures.

6.5.2   Generalizing Lock-Free

Building lock-free data-structures more complex than a stack using only CAA/V and without ABA issues is significantly more complex [23]. The naïve approach to implement a lock-free data-structure is for a writer thread to copy the data structure, allowing reader threads to continue reading old data, and then atomically update the top pointer to the modified data structure for all new readers. The problem occurs for the writer because it must dispose of the old data structure returned by the atomic operation. Unfortunately, the writer cannot immediately delete this data because there may be outstanding readers still accessing it.

When the size of data structure and the number of writers is small, a simple approach of allowing a memory leak is possible by not freeing the storage. Hence, readers can continue to access their particular version of the data structure for as long as the program runs. Clearly, the leaked storage builds up over time. In programming languages with garbage collection, the freeing problem is implicitly solved because the old storage is collected periodically when there are no reader threads referencing it. Fig. 6.31 shows a Java lock-free stack without ABA, but each node pushed onto the stack is copied, and the copies are returned. The copy must be dynamically allocated, where the heap is a shared resource requiring mutual exclusion; hence, some form of locking is required or another lock-free data structure is required for the lock-free operation. There cannot be an ABA problem because the same node is never pushed onto the stack, only new nodes. The copies are freed implicit by the garbage collector when they are no longer referenced. In programming languages without garbage collection, freeing the storage must be accomplished by different *cooperative techniques*, and these techniques differentiate lock-free algorithms. It is easy to see why programmers can convert Java lock-free solutions into C/C++ and unknowingly be exposed to ABA problems.

Furthermore, this lock-free scheme can be applied at a finer granularity, such as each node in the structure. Now a writer thread only copies a node, updates it, and snaps the modified node back into the list, which can be complex when there are multiple pointers, as in a doubly linked list (use double-wide CAA/V to update both

```
class Stack {
    private AtomicReference<Node> top = new AtomicReference<Node>(); // stack top

    public void push( Node n ) {
        Node newn = new Node( n );                  // COPY
        for ( ;; ) {                                // busy wait
            newn.next = top.get();                  // link new node to top node
            if ( top.compareAndSet( newn.next, newn ) ) break; // attempt to update top node
        }
    }
    public Node pop() {
        Node t;
        for ( ;; ) {                                // busy wait
            t = top.get();                          // copy top node
            if ( t == null ) return null;           // empty stack ?
            if ( top.compareAndSet( t, t.next ) ) return t; // attempt to update top node
        }
    }
    public Stack() {}
}
```

Fig. 6.31 Java: lock-free stack, no ABA

the forward/backward pointers atomically). Still each old node has to persist until there are no more threads reading it.

Unfortunately, the storage reclamation problem is often neglected in lock-free algorithms. For example, one of the first lock-free queue algorithms, MS queue [34, Fig. 1], appears to be easily convertible into any programming language. However, the free head.prt) (see line D19) does not mean the storage can be reused, as is the case when a normal free occurs. Instead, the free means the storage can be used *only* after there are no outstanding references by reader threads. Hence, the algorithm is only directly convertible into a managed language with garbage collection. A consequence of the need for the delayed free is the need to dynamically allocate the node at the start of the enqueue routine, at least from the pool of nodes managed for the data structure. However, there are many situations where the caller of enqueue wants to supply the storage for a node that is added to a list because the node is cheaply allocated on the stack or reused for other purposes. As well, the allocator must be equally lock-free or the data structure is not lock-free.

One example for managing storage, when there is no garbage collection, is hazard pointers [33]. For simplicity, assume a single writer and multiple readers threads are accessing a lock-free data-structure. Each reader has a shared pointer, which is its hazard pointer. A reader sets its hazard pointer to any entity (data structure or component thereof) it is accessing, and the duration the pointer is set indicates the duration of access. The writer must keep a list of the old entities it has replaced with modified ones, which is a superset of the hazard pointers. Periodically, the writer scans the reader hazard pointers and deletes unreferenced entities in its old-entity list.

Generalizing hazard pointers to multiple writers and multiple lock-free data-structures adds significant complexity [21]. Furthermore, at least one thread must always be designated for hazard duty and terminating readers must be handled. In general, these approaches to do not scale, and hence, are useful only in restricted scenarios. Interestingly, these specialized scenarios may have no lock-based solution (e.g., non-reentrant problem).

6.5.3   Lock Versus Lock-Free

- The class of problems that can be solved by lock-free approaches is limited. Furthermore, lock-free approaches can require restructuring a problem. As soon as multiple shared data-structures are modified simultaneously, the only practical approach is to use a lock.
- All lock-free *dynamic-size* data-structures using only CAA/V require some form of garbage collector to lazily delete storage when it is no longer referenced. (Solutions without garbage collection are possible for a fixed-sized array of nodes or where small localized memory-leaks are possible.) In languages with garbage collection, this capability comes for free (at the cost of garbage collection). For languages without garbage collection, the code is complex and error prone in comparison with locks, requiring epoch-based reclamation, read-copy-update (RCU), or hazard pointers.
- While better performance is claimed for lock-free data-structures, there is no long-term evidence to support this claim. Many high-performance locking situations, e.g., operating system kernels and databases, continue to use locking in various forms, even though there are a broad class of lock-free data-structure readily available.
- While lock-free data-structures cannot have deadlock (see Sect. 8.2.3, p. 399), there is seldom deadlock using locks for the simple class of problems solvable using lock-free approaches. For example, protecting basic data-structure operations with locks is usually very straightforward. Normally deadlock occurs when accessing multiple resources simultaneously, which is not a class of problems dealt with by lock-free approaches. Furthermore, disciplined lock usage, such as ranking locks to avoid deadlock (see Sect. 8.4, p. 407), works well in practice and is not onerous for the programmer. Finally, some static analysis tools are helpful for detecting deadlock scenarios.
- Lock-free approaches have thread-kill tolerance, meaning no thread owns a lock, so any thread can terminate at an arbitrary point without leaving a lock in the closed state. However, within an application, thread kill is an unusual operation and thread failure means an unrecoverable error or major reset.
- A lock-free approach always allows progress of other threads, whereas locks can cause delays if the lock owner is preempted. However, this issue is a foundational aspect of preemptive concurrency. And there are ways to mitigate this issue for locks using scheduler-activation techniques [2]. However, lock-free is not immune to delays. If a page is evicted containing part of the lock-based or lock-free data, there is a delay. Hence, lock free is no better than lock based if the page

fault occurs on frequently accessed shared data. Given the increasing number of processors and large amount of memory on modern computers, neither of these delays should occur often.

- Lock-free approaches are reentrant, and hence, can be used in signal handlers, which are implicitly concurrent. Locking approaches cannot deal with this issue.
- Lock-free approaches are claimed not to have priority inversion. However, inversion can occur because of the spinning required with atomic instructions, like CAA, as the hardware does not provide a bound for spinning threads. Hence, a low-priority thread can barge head of a high-priority thread because the low-priority thread just happens to win the race at the CAA instruction. Essentially, priority inversion is a foundational aspect of preemptive concurrency and can only be mitigated.

The conclusion is that for unmanaged programming-language (i.e., no garbage collection), using classical locks is simple, efficient, general, and causes issues only when the problem scales to multiple locks. For managed programming-languages, lock-free data-structures are easier to implement, but only handle a specific set of problems, and the programmer must accept other idiosyncrasies, like pauses in execution for garbage collection.

6.6 Exotic Atomic Instructions

Since lock-free data-structures are important but somewhat difficult to implement, why not augment the hardware to better support them by providing more powerful atomic mechanisms? This section examines a few approaches that illustrate some attempts, past and present, to provide additional atomic mechanisms.

The swap instruction performs an atomic interchange of two values in memory (versus a register and memory). The instruction has two parameters: two pointers to the values to be interchanged. It is implemented as: two reads from the memory locations (possibly into implicit registers), and two assignments of the values back into each other's memory locations. All these actions are performed as a single atomic operation without interruption and without change by other CPUs to the memory location. It is shown here by a C++ equivalent routine:

```
void Swap( int &val1, int &val2 ) {   // atomic execution
    int temp = val1;        // read
    val1 = val2;            // read and write
    val2 = temp;            // write
}
```

The equivalent assembler program written using LL and SC is:

```
Swap:                    // registers $4 and $5 contain *val1, *val2
  ll  $2,($4)            // read and reserve location
  ll  $3,($5)            // read and reserve location
  sc  $3,($4)            // attempt to store
  sc  $2,($5)            // attempt to store
  beq $3,$0,Swap         // retry if interference between read and write
  beq $2,$0,Swap         // retry if interference between read and write
  j   $31
```

Notice that it is necessary to lock two memory locations to implement this atomic instruction. Unfortunately, current computers only allow one memory location to be locked, so this assembler program cannot work. Furthermore, even the ability to lock two memory locations is insufficient because, if the first store is successful and the second store fails, information has been changed before it is correct. In this case, the memory locations cannot be reserved independently, but must be tied together so that a change to one causes a failure during a store to the other.

Here is how a swap instruction can be used to achieve mutual exclusion:

```
int Lock = OPEN;          // shared lock
thread i
int dummy = CLOSED;       // entry protocol, local thread variable
for ( ;; ) {
    Swap( Lock, dummy );
    if ( dummy == OPEN ) break;
}
// critical section
Lock = OPEN;              // exit protocol
```

A thread specific memory location, dummy, is initialized with the CLOSED value for each thread attempting entry to the critical section. Then a busy loop is started swapping dummy and Lock. If Lock has the value OPEN, that value is atomically swapped with dummy. After the swap, dummy has the value OPEN and Lock is CLOSED. Hence, Lock is snapped closed at the same instance that its value is copied into dummy, like in the test-and-set solution. Since each thread has its own dummy variable, only one thread obtains the lock. The other threads keep swapping the value CLOSED between Lock and dummy, until a thread exits the critical section and sets the Lock to OPEN. Whereupon, one of the other threads swaps CLOSED into Lock and OPEN into its dummy. Also like the test-and-set solution, this solution has no bound on service.

Suggestions have been made to extend the power of LL and SC to deal with multiple memory locations instead of just one, e.g., adding two instructions [18, p. 129]:

1. LLP (load-linked-pipelined): load and link to a second address after an LL. This load is linked to the following SCP.
2. SCP (store-conditional-pipelined): Store to the specified location provided that no modifications have occurred to either of the memory cells designated by *either* of the most recent LL and LLP instructions.

It is now possible to implement an atomic swap:

```
Swap:                          // registers $4 and $5 contain *val1, *val2
    ll   $2,($4)               // read and reserve location
    llp  $3,($5)               // read and reserve location
    scp $3,($4)                // attempt to store
    sc  $2,($5)                // attempt to store
    beq $2,$0,Swap             // retry if interference between read and write
    j    $31
```

The SCP store is buffered pending a successful SC, at which time registers $2 and $3 are written atomically to locations ($5) and ($4), respectively. The number of levels of nested LLP and SCP instructions would depend on the particular hardware architecture. One level is needed for atomic swap, and levels of 3 and 4 are needed to implement some of the following exotic atomic instructions.

Advanced **hardware transactional memory** has been proposed that allows up to N (4,6,8) reservations, e.g, the advanced synchronization facility (ASF) proposal for the AMD64 [10] and hardware transactional memory (HTM) for the Sun Rock [12]. Similar to a database **transaction**, these approaches optimistically execute changes, and either commits all the changes, or rolls back the changes and restarts if reservations are violated. Given these more powerful hardware capabilities, it is possible to implement several data structures without an ABA problem. For example, adding a node to a singly linked-list with a head and tail pointer:

```
newnode.link = 0;
Enqueue:
    SPECULATE head, tail           // 2 memory reservations
    if ( head == 0 && tail == 0 ) {  // list empty ?
        head = tail = newnode;       // first node
    } else {
        SPECULATE tail.link          // now 3 memory reservations
        tail.link = newnode;         // chain to end
        tail = newnode;              // update new list end
    }
    COMMIT Enqueue                   // restart if reservations violated
```

SPECULATE sets the reservation points for the specified variables and (reads) makes local copies of these variables. The operation proceeds using the local copies until the COMMIT, which writes the local copies to the reserved locations only if no changes have occurred. Otherwise, the operation is restarted with new reservations and local copies.

Software transactional memory [22] provides an unlimited number of reservations, so that after a set of operations, it is possible to check for any change, rollback and restart the operation. For example, inserting a new node into a doubly linked-list (ignoring special cases for inserting at the beginning or end of the list):

```
void insertBefore( Node &newnode, Node &before ) {
    atomic {          // SPECULATE
        newNode.prev = before;
        newNode.next = before.next;
        before.next.prev = newNode;
        before.next = newNode;
    }                 // COMMIT OR RESTART
}
```

Like hardware transactions reservations are implicitly generated for before, before.next, and before.next.prev, and private versions of these variables are generated for computation purposes. After the computation is complete, the reservations are checked for interference. If no interference, the values are atomically updated; otherwise, the reservations are reestablished and computation is restarted. Clearly, bookkeeping costs and rollbacks typically result in significant performance degradation, even with hardware support.

In the 1980s, the VAX [41] computer dealt with the problem directly by providing instructions to atomically insert and remove a node to/from the head or tail of a circular doubly linked list, illustrated approximately by the following C routines:

```
struct links {
    links *front, *back;
}
bool INSQUE( links &entry, links &pred ) {    // atomic execution
    entry.front = pred.front; entry.back = pred;  // insert entry following pred
    pred.front.back = entry; pred.front = entry;
    return entry.front == entry.back;         // circular queue previously empty ?
}
bool REMQUE( links &entry ) {
    entry.back.front = entry.front;
    entry.front.back = entry.back.front;
    return entry.front == entry.back;         // circular queue now empty ?
}
```

While these instructions can insert and remove anywhere in a doubly linked list, the operations are restricted to the list head and tail for multiprocessor usage.

If atomic list operations are so useful, why are they missing in modern computers? The answer is that these instructions require many hardware cycles to execute and must reserve from 2 to 6 memory locations. Furthermore, during the execution of these large atomic instructions (critical sections), no interrupts can be delivered to the processor, so it is not *listening* to external events (affecting order and speed of execution). Hence, there is a trade off between software and hardware designers: software designers want to simplify and make efficient the most important low-level atomic operations, while hardware designers want to maximize efficiency of all operations. Unfortunately, large atomic instructions can have a global effect on performance, and hence, slow down sequential programs not using concurrency features. Hence, an open question remains: what is the smallest large atomic instruction that can build the most important class of basic atomic operations? The problem is that as soon as a more powerful atomic instruction is introduced, software developers will add another *important* basic operation that it cannot solve. Nevertheless, targeting basic list-operations is a laudable goal being examined in new processors.

6.7   Uniprocessor Tricks

A few *tricks* were developed on uniprocessors computers for dealing with non-determinism and are interesting to know. However, none of these approaches scale to multiprocessor systems because two or more processors can simultaneously access the shared data.

One simple approach for small embedded systems, like a music player, is to set/reset a global flag on entering and leaving a critical section. When a timer interrupt occurs, the flag is checked, and if set, the interrupt handler returns, ignoring the time slice, and returning to the task in the critical section. This forces the task through the critical section, but gives the task another time slice of execution; hence, other tasks may not get a chance to execute. The next time slice can be shortened to mitigate the lost time-slice, or another flag can be set to indicate the time slice was missed, and the exit protocol checks and resets this flag and then yields voluntarily. A similar approach is to turn off interrupts, e.g., timer interrupts, around critical sections to provide mutual exclusion. However, toggling interrupts can be an expensive operation.

An alternate approach is to tag critical sections (start and end points), and check at the start of an interrupt if any execution is in one of the tagged zones. If so, execution is forced out of the critical section by either undoing execution back to the start of the critical section, called **roll backward** (like transactional memory), or by doing the remainder of the critical section, called **roll forward**. In either case, the lock for the critical section is not released to prevent another thread from acquiring it. After the roll backward/forward, there is logically no thread in the critical section, so the interrupt handler can safely enter it, if necessary. When control returns to the interrupted thread, it releases the lock for the critical section.

Some of these approaches are used in multiprocessor runtime-systems, where each kernel thread is managed by a runtime kernel with thread-local storage. That is, each kernel thread has non-shared flags it can set/reset as above to deal with certain special critical sections associated with the runtime kernel. Hence, each kernel thread is managed like a uniprocessor and can use some of these simple approaches.

6.8   Summary

Software solutions can generate mutual exclusion out of thin air, that is, mutual exclusion can be constructed without extending a programming language or the hardware it executes on. However, all software solutions are complex and require at least one bit of information be shared among all threads attempting entry to a critical section. Hardware solutions generate mutual exclusion by providing atomicity at the instruction execution level by restricting interrupts and controlling access to memory. Certain atomic hardware instructions are more powerful than others.

Compare-and-assign is considered a reasonably powerful, yet simple to implement, atomic instruction. The more general LL/SC instructions allow a variety of atomic operations to be built. However, the ability to only lock one address is insufficient to build operations like atomic swap or a compare-and-swap that actually *swaps*, not just assigns. There is a strong argument for a few exotic atomic instructions to simplify mutual exclusion and build lock-free data-structures in both programming-language runtime systems and in the operating system. Future work is being done on both hardware and software transactional memory, but the question of cost must be addressed.

6.9 Questions

1. Define the terms: *synchronization, critical section* and *mutual exclusion.*
2. Explain the difference between *synchronization* and *mutual exclusion.*
3. Explain the relationship between a *critical section* and *mutual exclusion.*
4. Give the 5 rules of the mutual-exclusion game.
5. Explain how the self-checking critical section (see Sect. 6.2.2, p. 237) detects a thread has violated mutual exclusion.
6. While people use locks on doors to proved privacy (mutual exclusion), explain briefly why this does not work for threads (or even for people).
7. What rule of the mutual-exclusion games is *not* satisfied when using a door-style lock to protect a critical section? Explain.
8. Taking turns using a critical section is fair, but what rule of the mutual-exclusion games is *not* satisfied. Explain.
9. Explain what it means for a thread to *declare intent.*
10. What rule of the mutual-exclusion games is *not* satisfied if threads only declare intent? Explain.
11. What action do people and threads do to prevent livelock when declaring intent? Explain.
12. For the retract intent solution (see Fig. 6.5, p. 244):

    - Explain which rules of the mutual-exclusion game this solution does **NOT** satisfy.
    - Explain why this solution works almost all the time.

13. The following is the entry protocol code for the prioritized entry algorithm for mutual exclusion.

```
if ( priority == HIGH ) {
    me = WantIn;
    while( you == WantIn ) {}
} else {
    while( true ) {
        me = WantIn;
        if ( you == DontWantIn ) break;
        me = DontWantIn;
        while( you == WantIn ) {}
    }
}
```

```
bool intent[2] = { false, false };          // shared between tasks
int turn = 0;

_Task Hyman {
    int me, you;
    void main() {
        for ( int i = 1; i <= 1000; i += 1 ) {
            intent[me] = true;              // entry protocol
            while ( turn != me ) {
                while ( intent[you] ) {}
                turn = me;
            }
            CriticalSection();
            intent[me] = false;             // exit protocol
        }
    }
  public:
    Hyman( int me, int you ) : me(me), you(you) {}
};
void uMain::main() {
    Hyman h0( 0, 1 ), h1( 1, 0 );
}
```

Fig. 6.32 Hyman mutual exclusion

    a. Why is it necessary to prioritize threads when retracting intent?
    b. What is the problem with the protocol?
    c. Referring to the code, explain how the problem can arise.

14. Explain how Dekker's algorithm uses alternation to prevent indefinite postponement and starvation.

15. Explain why there is a bound on Dekker's algorithm and state the bound. That is, if one task has just completed the entry protocol (and is about to enter the critical section) and another arrives, what is the maximum number of times the first task can enter the critical section before the second task may enter. This bound prevents starvation while the critical section is being used. (Not to be confused with indefinite postponement where tasks are attempting entry and no task is using the critical section.)

16. Figure 6.32 shows a solution to the mutual-exclusion problem by Harris Hyman that appeared in a letter (i.e., a non-refereed article) to the Communications of the ACM [25]. Unfortunately it does not work. Explain which rule(s) of the critical-section game is broken and the pathological situation where it does not work.

17. Figure 6.33 shows a Dekker-like solution to the mutual exclusion problem, where line 14 of the original Dekker algorithm has been changed from **while**(Last == &me) to **while** (you == WantIn). Unfortunately it does not work.

    a. Explain which rule(s) of the critical-section game is broken and the pathological situation where it does not work.
    b. Explain why it never failed during a test of 100,000 tries.

18. Explain the difference between Dekker's and Peterson's algorithm with respect to execution assumptions.

```
enum Intent {WantIn, DontWantIn};
Intent *Last;

_Task DekkerLike {
    Intent &me, &you;

    void main() {
        for ( int i = 1; i <= 1000; i += 1 ) {
            for ( ;; ) {                       // entry protocol, high priority busy wait
                me = WantIn;
                if ( you == DontWantIn ) break;
                if ( Last == &me ) {
                    me = DontWantIn;
                    while ( you == WantIn ){}   // versus while( Last == &me ){}
                }
            }
            CriticalSection();                 // critical section
            Last = &me;                        // exit protocol
            me = DontWantIn;
        }
    }
  public:
    Dekker( Intent &me, Intent &you, Intent *&Last ) : me(me), you(you), Last(Last) {}
};
void uMain::main() {
    Intent me = DontWantIn, you = DontWantIn, *Last = rand() % 2 ? &me : &you;
    Dekker t0(me, you, Last), t1(you, me, Last);
}
```

Fig. 6.33 Dekker-like 2-thread mutual exclusion

19. How does Peterson's algorithm prevent a fast thread from starving a slow thread?

20. Figure 6.34 shows a Peterson solution to the mutual exclusion problem. Does this solution work if lines 8 and 9 are interchanged? If the solution does not work, explain a pathological situation that results in failure of one rule of the critical-section game. Be sure to clearly specify which rule is broken and why.

21. Peterson's algorithm uses a write race to prevent livelock and starvation; Fig. 6.35 shows Kessels' use of a read race to achieve the same goal [27, p. 137].

    a. Explain, briefly, how this algorithm works.
    b. Explain what initial values are required for Last1 and Last2.
    c. Show informally that Kessels' algorithm satisfies rules 3, 4 and 5 of the critical-section game. (You should be able to accomplish this in a single page of text.)

22. a. When solving an N-thread software solution to the critical section problem, what information must each thread indicate about itself and what must it know about the other $N-1$ threads?
    b. What are the minimum number of bits needed to generate an N-thread solution for mutual exclusion that allows starvation?
    c. Why are more bits needed to eliminate starvation for an N-thread solution?

```
1    enum Intent {WantIn, DontWantIn};
2    Intent *Last;
3
4    _Task Peterson {
5        Intent &me, &you;
6        void main() {
7            for ( int i = 1; i <= 1000; i += 1 ) {
8                me = WantIn;                    // entry protocol
9                ::Last = &me;
10               while ( you == WantIn && ::Last == &me ) {}
11               CriticalSection();              // critical section
12               me = DontWantIn;                // exit protocol
13           }
14       }
15   public:
16       Peterson( Intent &me, Intent &you ) : me(me), you(you) {}
17   };
18   void uMain::main() {
19       Intent me = DontWantIn, you = DontWantIn;
20       Peterson t0(me, you), t1(you, me);
21   }
```

Fig. 6.34 Peterson-like 2-thread mutual exclusion

```
enum Intent { WantIn, DontWantIn };

_Task Kessels {
    int who;
    Intent &me, &you;
    int &Last1, &Last2;
    void main() {
        for ( int i = 1; i <= 10000; i += 1 ) {
            me = WantIn;                        // entry protocol
            Last1 = ( Last2 + who ) % 2;        // race
            while ( you == WantIn && Last1 == ( Last2 + who ) % 2 ) {}
            CriticalSection();                  // critical section
            me = DontWantIn;                    // exit protocol
        }
    }
public:
    Kessels( int who, Intent &me, Intent &you, int &Last1, int &Last2 ) :
        who(who), me(me), you(you), Last1(Last1), Last2(Last2) {}
};
void uMain::main() {
    Intent me = DontWantIn, you = DontWantIn; // shared
    int Last1, Last2;
    Kessels t0( 0, me, you, Last1, Last2), t1(1, you, me, Last2, Last1 );
}
```

Fig. 6.35 Kessels 2-thread mutual exclusion

23. All software solutions for the mutual-exclusion problem have two major drawbacks; explain each drawbacks.

24. When write is not atomic, different assumptions are possible for simultaneous write to the same memory location; Sect. 6.3.7, p. 251 assumes the bits are scrambled. Corman et al. [11, p. 690] suggest other assumptions:

    * arbitrary: any value from among those written is stored (but not scrambled);
    * priority: the value written by the lowest-indexed CPU is stored;
    * combining: the value stored is a combination of the values written, e.g., sum, max.

    Discuss the effect of these alternate write assumptions with respect to correct execution of the Dekker and Peterson algorithms.

25. The *B–L N-Task Prioritized Retract Intent* algorithm is subject to starvation (see Sect. 6.3.8.1, p. 254). One possible way to deal with this is to rotate the threads' priorities after each access to the critical section. Explain how this can prevent starvation.

26. a. Does the Bakery algorithm (see Fig. 6.16, p. 266) solve all 5 rules of the mutual-exclusion game perfectly?

    b. What are the tickets for in the bakery algorithm and why is the algorithm only probabilistically correct?

    c. Explain the problem in ticket selection for the N-thread Bakery algorithm. How does the algorithm deal with this problem?

    d. Part of the Bakery algorithm uses static priorities to decide which thread can enter the critical section. Why do these static priorities not lead to starvation?

27. In a tournament algorithm for software mutual-exclusion, the exit protocol after the critical section must release the tree nodes in *reverse* order (from root to leaf). If the nodes are released in normal order (from leaf to root), there is a failure scenario. Using the tournament tree in Fig. 6.18, p. 270a, illustrate this failure scenario for thread T_0, assuming it has just exited the critical section and releases the nodes in normal order.

28. In the *Arbiter* algorithm for mutual exclusion, how is fairness (rule 5) guaranteed?

29. What is the primary mechanism used by atomic hardware-instructions to simplify construction of mutual exclusion?

30. a. Write a C++ routine that performs the steps of a test-and-set instruction. Indicate with a comment(s) the code representing the atomically operation performed by the instruction.

    b. Show how this instruction can be used to solve the N-thread mutual-exclusion problem for rules 1–4.

31. a. Write a C++ routine that performs the steps of a fetch-and-increment instruction. Indicate with a comment(s) the code representing the atomically operation performed by the instruction.

    b. Show how this atomic instruction can be used to build mutual exclusion by completing a class with the following public interface (only add a public destructor and private members):

```
class Lock {
    . . .                            // YOU ADD HERE
  public:
    Lock();                          // YOU WRITE THESE ROUTINES
    void entryProtocol();
    void exitProtocol();
};
```

which is used as follows:

```
Lock l;

l.entryProtocol();
// critical section
l.exitProtocol();
```

The solution may use busy waiting, must deal with starvation, and **assume assignment is not atomic**. State any assumptions or limitations of the solution.

c. The fetch-and-increment instruction provides the old value of a counter before incrementing it. Imagine just an atomic increment instruction that does not return the old value. Is it possible to construct mutual exclusion with this instruction? If so, is it possible to construct a solution that has a bound on service?

32. a. Write a C++ routine that performs the steps of an atomic swap instruction. Indicate with a comment(s) the code representing the atomically operation performed by the instruction.

b. Use this swap routine to show an atomic swap instruction can be used to solve the N-thread mutual exclusion problem. The answer does NOT have to deal with starvation and assume assignment is atomic.

c. Does this solution work for N threads? Which rule of the mutual-exclusion game does this solution break?

33. Write a function with the following interface:

```
int transfer( int &account1, int &account2, int amount);
```

such that, in a system with only two bank accounts, two or more threads transferring money between them never destroy money (i.e., account1 + account2 should be the same before all the transfers start, and after all the transfers end). Use the CAV instruction directly to solve this problem. Do not use CAV to create a lock. CAV is defined as:

```
bool CAV(int &val, int &comp, int nval) { // atomic execution
  if ( val == comp ) {                    // equal ?
    val = nval;                           // assign
    return true;                          // indicate new assign occurred
  }
  comp = val;                             // return val read via comp
  return false;                           // indicate new assign did not occur
}
```

34. How does the Mellor-Crummey and Scott (MCS) algorithm provide a bound, i.e., prevent starvation, for waiting threads entering a critical section?

35. What does it mean for a data structure to be *lock free* or *wait free*?

36. Give an advantage and disadvantage of a lock-free data-structure.

37. Given an atomic compare/swap instruction which conditionally interchanges two values atomically, shown by the C++ equivalent routine:

```
// need address of node pointer, and "*&" automatically references the Node argument
bool CS( Node *&a, Node *&b, Node *&c ) {  // atomic execution
    if ( a == b ) {                        // equal ?
        Node *temp = b;                    // swap b and c
        b = c;
        c = temp;
        return true;                       // indicate swap occurred
    }
    return false;                          // indicate swap did not occur
}
```

Assume the following data structures:

```
struct Node {      // nodes for each element on the stack
    // data
    Node *next;    // pointer to next node
};
Node *stack;       // global pointer to top of stack
```

which generate a stack data structure implemented using a linked list, as in:

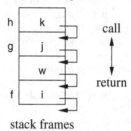

stack frames

Use the C routine version of the compare-and-swap given above to write an insertion routine:

```
void push( Node *&top, Node *&newNode ) {
    // YOU WRITE THIS CODE
}
```

which performs an atomic insertion of a new stack node onto the top of the stack.

38. a. Write a C++ routine that performs the steps of an atomic compare/assignment instruction. Indicate with a comment(s) the code representing the atomically operation performed by the instruction.

   b. Assume the following data structures:

```
struct Node {      // nodes for each element on the stack
    // data
    Node *next;    // pointer to next node
};
Node *stack;       // global pointer to top of stack
```

   build a lock-free push operation for the stack:

```
void push( Stack &h, Node &n ) {
    // YOU WRITE THIS CODE
}
```

The solution may use busy waiting and does not have to deal with starvation.
39. Use the CAAD instruction as defined in Sect. 6.6, p. 298 to build routines front
    and back, which remove a node from the front and add a node to the back of a
    singly lined list, respectively.

References

1. Anderson, T.E.: The performance of spin lock alternatives for shared-memory multiprocessors. IEEE Trans. Parallel Distrib. Syst. **1**(1), 6–16 (1990)
2. Anderson, T.E., Bershad, B.N., Lazowska, E.D., Levy, H.M.: Scheduler activations: Effective kernel support for the user-level management of parallelism. ACM Trans. Comput. Syst. **10**(1), 53–79 (1992)
3. ARM Architecture Reference Manual, vol. ARM DDI 0406C.b (ID072512). ARM (2012)
4. Brinch Hansen, P.: Concurrent programming concepts. Softw. Pract. Exp. **5**(4), 223–245 (1973)
5. de Bruijn, N.G.: Additional comments on a problem in concurrent programming control. Commun. ACM **10**(3), 137–138 (1967). Letter to the Editor
6. Buhr, P.A., Dice, D., Hesselink, W.H.: High-performance N-thread software solutions for mutual exclusion. Concurrency Comput. Pract. Exp. **27**(3), 651–701 (2015)
7. Buhr, P.A., Dice, D., Hesselink, W.H.: Dekker's mutual exclusion algorithm made rw-safe. Concurrency Comput. Pract. Exp. **28**(1), 144–165 (2016)
8. Burns, J.E.: Mutual exclusion with linear waiting using binary shared variables. SIGACT News **10**(2), 42–47 (1978)
9. Burns, J.E., Lynch, N.A.: Mutual exclusion using indivisible reads and writes. In: Proceedings of the 18th Annual Allerton Conference on Communications, Control and Computing, Monticello, Illinois, USA, pp. 833–842 (1980). http://groups.csail.mit.edu/tds/papers/Lynch/-allertonconf.pdf [Accessed on March 2014]
10. Chung, J., Yen, L., Diestelhorst, S., Pohlack, M., Hohmuth, M., Christie, D., Grossman, D.: Asf: Amd64 extension for lock-free data structures and transactional memory. In: Proceedings of the 2010 43rd Annual IEEE/ACM International Symposium on Microarchitecture, MICRO '43, pp. 39–50. IEEE Computer Society, Washington, DC, USA (2010)
11. Cormen, T.H., Leiserson, C.E., Rivest, R.L.: Introduction to Algorithms. Electrical Engineering and Computer Science Series. MIT Press/McGraw-Hill, Cambridge (1992)
12. Dice, D., Lev, Y., Marathe, V.J., Moir, M., Nussbaum, D., Olszewski, M.: Simplifying concurrent algorithms by exploiting hardware transactional memory. In: Proceedings of the Twenty-second Annual ACM Symposium on Parallelism in Algorithms and Architectures, SPAA'10, pp. 325–334. ACM, New York, NY, USA (2010)
13. Dijkstra, E.W.: Cooperating sequential processes. Tech. rep., Technological University, Eindhoven, Netherlands (1965). Reprinted in [17] pp. 43–112.
14. Dijkstra, E.W.: Solution of a problem in concurrent programming control. Commun. ACM **8**(9), 569 (1965)
15. Doran, R.W., Thomas, L.K.: Variants of the software solution to mutual exclusion. Inf. Process. Lett. **10**(4/5), 206–208 (1980)
16. Eisenberg, M.A., McGuire, M.R.: Further comments on Dijkstra's concurrent programming control problem. Commun. ACM **15**(11), 999 (1972)
17. Genuys, F. (ed.): Programming Languages. Academic Press, London, New York (1968). NATO Advanced Study Institute, Villard-de-Lans, 1966
18. Greenwald, M., Cheriton, D.: The synergy between non-blocking synchronization and operating system structure. In: Proceedings of the Second USENIX Symposium on Operating Systems Design and Implementation, pp. 123–136. USENIX Association, Seattle, Washington, U.S.A. (1996)
19. Hehner, E.C.R., Shyamasundar, R.K.: An implementation of P and V. Inf. Process. Lett. **12**(4), 196–198 (1981)

20. Herlihy, M.: Wait-free synchronization. ACM Trans. Progr. Lang. Syst. **13**(1), 124–149 (1991)
21. Herlihy, M., Luchangco, V., Martin, P., Moir, M.: Nonblocking memory management support for dynamic-sized data structures. ACM Trans. Comput. Syst. **23**(2), 146–196 (2005)
22. Herlihy, M., Luchangco, V., Moir, M., Scherer III, W.N.: Software transactional memory for dynamic-sized data structures. In: Proceedings of the Twenty-second Annual Symposium on Principles of Distributed Computing, PODC '03, pp. 92–101. ACM, New York, NY, USA (2003)
23. Herlihy, M., Shavit, N.: The Art of Multiprocessor Programming. Morgan Kaufmann Publishers, San Francisco (2008)
24. Hesselink, W.H.: Verifying a simplification of mutual exclusion by Lycklama–Hadzilacos. Acta Informatica **50**(3), 199–228 (2013)
25. Hyman, H.: Comments on a problem in concurrent programming control. Commun. ACM **9**(1), 45 (1966). Letter to the Editor
26. IBM System/370 Principles of Operation, 9th edn. GA22-7000-8. IBM (1981)
27. Kessels, J.L.W.: Arbitration without common modifiable variables. Acta Inf. **17**(2), 135–141 (1982)
28. Knuth, D.E.: Additional comments on a problem in concurrent programming control. Commun. ACM **9**(5), 321–322 (1966). Letter to the Editor
29. Lamport, L.: A new solution of dijkstra's concurrent programming problem. Commun. ACM **17**(8), 453–455 (1974)
30. Lamport, L.: The mutual exclusion problem: Part I–a theory of interprocess communication. J. ACM **33**(2), 313–326 (1986)
31. Lamport, L.: The mutual exclusion problem: Part II–statement and solutions. J. ACM **33**(2), 327–348 (1986)
32. Mellor-Crummey, J.M., Scott, M.L.: Algorithm for scalable synchronization on shared-memory multiprocessors. ACM Trans. Comput. Syst. **9**(1), 21–65 (1991)
33. Michael, M.M.: Hazard pointers: Safe memory reclamation for lock-free objects. IEEE Trans. Parallel Distrib. Syst. **15**(6), 491–504 (2004)
34. Michael, M.M., Scott, M.L.: Simple, fast, and practical non-blocking and blocking concurrent queue algorithms. In: Proceedings of the Fifteenth Annual ACM Symposium on Principles of Distributed Computing, PODC'96, pp. 267–275. ACM, New York, NY, USA (1996)
35. MIPS R4000 Microprocessor User's Manual. MIPS Computer Systems Inc (1991)
36. M68000 Family Programmer's Reference Manual. Motorola (1992)
37. Peterson, G.L.: Myths about the mutual exclusion problem. Inf. Process. Lett. **12**(3), 115–116 (1981)
38. Peterson, G.L., Fischer, M.J.: Economical solutions for the critical section problem in a distributed system (extended abstract). In: Proceedings of the Ninth Annual ACM Symposium on Theory of Computing, STOC '77, pp. 91–97. ACM, New York, NY, USA (1977)
39. Programming Environments Manual for 32-Bit Implementations of the PowerPC Architec-tureARM Architecture, vol. MPCFPE32B, rev. 3rd edn. Freescale Semiconductor (2005)
40. Sites, R.L. (ed.): Alpha Architecture Reference Manual. Digital Press, One Burlington Woods Drive, Burlington (1992)
41. VAX-11 Architecture Reference Manual. Digital Press, Bedford (1982)
42. Zuo, W., Zuo, W., Jiaxing, L.: An intelligent multi-port memory. In: Symposium on Intelligent Information Technology Application Workshops, Shanghai, China, pp. 251–254. IEEE Computer Society, Los Alamitos, CA, USA (2008)

Chapter 7
Locks

The previous two chapters (Chaps. 5, p. 191 and 6, p. 233) introduce the notions of synchronization and mutual exclusion. Understanding the difference between these crucial concepts is a significant step in designing and building concurrent programs. In general, *synchronization* defines a timing relationship among tasks and *mutual exclusion* defines a restriction on access to shared resources. While both synchronization and mutual exclusion share the notion of constraining operations in time, the practical temporal differences are so profound they should always be considered as independent concepts.

Synchronization is concerned with maintaining a timing relationship, which includes actions happening at the same time, e.g. synchronized swimming, or happening at the same relative rate, e.g. synchronizing video/audio signals, or simply some action having to occur before another (precedence relationship), e.g. synchronizing manufacturing operations. Synchronization is accomplished using a variety of concurrent techniques, such as latches, barriers, rendezvous, etc., and often its main purpose is for communication of data. The key point is that synchronization always requires two or more tasks because a single task is self-synchronized, i.e., a single task does not require any concurrent techniques to interact with itself.

Simple mutual exclusion ensures only one task is in a critical section at a time. Complex mutual exclusion may allow multiple tasks in a critical section but with some "complex" restriction among tasks, such as allowing multiple readers to share a resource simultaneously but writers must be serialized. Any solution to mutual exclusion (simple or complex) must provide appropriate access restrictions, assume that order and speed of task execution is arbitrary, that tasks not in the critical section cannot prevent other tasks from entering, that tasks do not postpone indefinitely when deciding to enter the critical section, and finally, there is often some notion of fairness (guarantee) on entry so no task starves (short or long term). These rules (see Sect. 8.2.3.2, p. 400 for details) are significantly more complex than those for establishing a timing relationship with synchronization.

© Springer International Publishing Switzerland 2016
P.A. Buhr, *Understanding Control Flow*, DOI 10.1007/978-3-319-25703-7_7

Specifically, the differences between synchronization and mutual exclusion are as follows:

1. Mutual exclusion does not require an interaction among tasks when entering a critical section. That is, when there is no simultaneous arrival at a critical section or no task is in the critical section, a task may enter the critical section without interacting with another task. For a lightly accessed critical section, a task may seldom encounter another task; nevertheless, the mutual exclusion is still required. Conversely, synchronization mandates an interaction (rendezvous) with another task before one or more tasks can make progress. Fundamentally, synchronization of a task with itself is meaningless, because a task is always synchronized with itself.

2. Mutual exclusion forbids assuming any specific timing relationship among tasks; synchronization enforces a timing relationship. If two (or more) tasks arrive simultaneously at a critical section, this is a random occurrence, not synchronization between the tasks. Therefore, just because a task blocks (spins) as part of mutual exclusion, the delay does not imply any synchronization between a delayed task(s) and the task(s) using the critical section. For mutual exclusion, such a delay is arbitrary, and therefore, cannot be used for any kind of synchronization notification or communication.

3. Mutual exclusion must not prevent entry to an inactive critical section; synchronization must prevent progress until a partner arrives.

4. Mutual exclusion always protects shared resources, while synchronization does not require any sharing.

Hence, these two concepts are neither similar nor a subset of one another. Furthermore, synchronization and mutual exclusion mistakes result in completely different kinds of errors (see Chap. 8, p. 395).

Because synchronization and mutual exclusion are so different, it is reasonable to imagine that very different mechanisms are needed to implement them. However, it is sometimes possible to use a single lock to perform both functions. Given a general software/hardware lock described in Chap. 6, p. 233, it is possible to construct mutual exclusion in the following way:

```
lock = OPEN;
     task₁                      task₂
     ...                        ...
     lock entry code            lock entry code
     critical section           critical section
     lock exit code             lock exit code
     ...                        ...
```

The lock starts unlocked (open) so a task may enter the critical section, and the entry/exit code provides the necessary mutual exclusion. Now using the same lock, it may be possible to construct synchronization in the following way:

```
lock = CLOSED;
    task₁                        task₂
    ...                          ...
    S1                           lock entry code
    lock exit code               S2
    ...                          ...
```

Here, the lock starts locked (closed) instead of unlocked (opened), which seems peculiar. Also, the entry and exit code no longer bracket a critical section; instead, the protocol is asymmetric between the synchronizing tasks. The trivial case is when task₁ executes S1 before task₂ tries to execute S2, and thus, task₁ executes the exit code that opens the lock; when task₂ reaches the entry code, no waiting is necessary. In the opposite situation, task₂ reaches the entry code before task₁ gets to or finishes execution of S1. The trick here is that the lock is initially closed, therefore task₂ waits for the lock to be opened. Only after task₁ completes S1 and the lock exit-code is the lock opened so that task₂ can make progress. In fact, this approach is similar to the technique used in the communication program in Fig. 5.13, p. 219. Thus, some locks can be used to control synchronization *and* provide mutual exclusion, allowing tasks to communicate during execution and access shared resources using a single mechanism.

This chapter focuses on abstracting the detailed, low-level mechanisms for constructing synchronization and mutual exclusion into different kinds of high-level locks, and then how to use these locks to write concurrent programs that require synchronization and mutual exclusion.

7.1 Lock Taxonomy

Locks can be divided into two general categories: spinning and blocking:

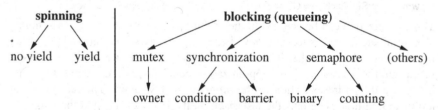

Spinning locks continuously check (busy wait) for an event to occur, implying the waiting task is solely responsible for detecting when the event happens. (While checking, a task oscillates between ready and running states due to either time slicing or yielding.) Blocking locks do not busy wait, but rather block until an event occurs, implying some *other* mechanism must unblock the waiting task when the event happens. Within each of the general categories, there are different kinds of spinning and blocking locks, which are discussed in detail.

7.2 Spin Lock

A spin lock is the general abstraction for a lock built from a software approach (e.g., Dekker) or hardware instruction (e.g., test-and-set). As the name suggests, a spin lock loops (spins) continuously checking for an event to occur, which is busy waiting.

```
while( TestSet( Lock ) == CLOSED ); // use up time-slice (no yield)
```

Unfortunately, busy waiting makes a spin lock impractical for providing *general* synchronization or mutual exclusion, for the following reason. In all the examples so far, if a task is busy waiting, it loops until:

1. a critical section becomes unlocked or an event happens,
2. or the waiting task is pre-empted at the end of its time-slice and put back on the ready queue.

On a multiprocessor, a waiting task may consume substantial amounts of CPU time spinning until another task indicates an event has occurred. A uniprocessor has the same problem, and it is exacerbated by the fact that all checking after the first check is superfluous because the event cannot occur until another task is scheduled, completes its action, and indicates the event, as there is only one CPU. Thus, any further spinning to check for the event by the waiting task during its time-slice is futile. In fact, a waiting task may experience multiple periods of futile spinning, until another task eventually indicates the occurrence of an event. To increase efficiency in the uniprocessor case, a task could explicitly terminate its time-slice and move back to the ready state after the first event check fails. For example, in any of the software solutions presented in Chap. 6, p. 233, placing a call to yield() (see Sect. 5.10.2, p. 215) in the body of the entry-protocol busy-loops can decrease the execution time by up to two orders of magnitude on a uniprocessor!

```
while( TestSet( Lock ) == CLOSED ) { yield(); } // relinquish time-slice (yield)
```

This optimization can be adapted to the multiprocessor case by having a spinning task terminate its time-slice and move back to the ready state after N checks have failed; other tasks would then have an opportunity to execute on that CPU. However, in the multiprocessor case, this optimization could produce the opposite effect, i.e., cause the entire execution of the program to slow down. The reason is that terminating a time-slice puts the task back on the ready queue, and the length of the ready queue could be long if there are a large number of tasks. Thus, even if the multiprocessor has several CPUs, a task might still have to wait a substantial period of time to get to the front of the ready queue to run. Alternatively, if the task just remains spinning, it might detect the event much earlier assuming the task making the change is already scheduled on another CPU. In essence, it is a gamble by the spinning task to remain spinning to obtain quick response or yield its time-slice to better utilize the CPU overall. Some systems, like μC++, allow the duration of spinning to be adjusted so an application can find a balance between these conflicting goals, called an adaptive lock. Finally, depending on how the spin lock is implemented, it may break rule 5, i.e., no bound on service, possibly resulting in starvation of one or more tasks.

Nevertheless, the spin lock is appropriate and necessary in situations where there is no other work to do. For example, in the μC++ multiprocessor kernel, a spin lock is used to protect access to the ready queue to ensure safety when multiple CPUs are adding and removing tasks from this queue. If a CPU cannot acquire the ready-queue spin-lock, it *must* spin because there is no other work it can do until it acquires the spin lock because all work comes from ready tasks on this queue. Furthermore, a CPU cannot block because it is always running (except for the special case where the CPU powers down to save electricity). Therefore, a spin lock is necessary in a concurrent system but not necessarily at the user level.

7.2.1 Spin Lock Details

μC++ provides a non-yielding spin lock, uSpinLock, and a yielding spin lock, uLock. Both locks are built directly from an atomic instruction; the particular atomic instruction depends on the architecture on which μC++ is running. These locks are either closed (0) or opened (1), and waiting tasks compete to acquire the lock after it is released. The competition means waiting tasks can be selected in any order. In theory, arbitrary selection order could result in starvation if tasks are constantly contending for the lock and one unlucky task never acquires it; in practice, this scenario seldom occurs.

The specific lock details are:

```
class uSpinLock {                 class uLock {
  public:                           public:
    uSpinLock(); // open              uLock( unsigned int value = 1 ); // default open
    void acquire();                   void acquire();
    bool tryacquire();                bool tryacquire();
    void release();                   void release();
};                                };
uSpinLock x, y, *z;               uLock x, y, *z;
z = new uSpinLock();              z = new uLock( 0 ); // closed
```

The declarations create six lock variables, all initialized to open, except the last uLock variable, which is explicitly set closed.

uSpinLock in μC++ is non-preemptive, meaning once a task acquires the lock on a particular CPU, no other task may execute on that CPU, which allows performance optimizations and additional error checking in the μC++ kernel, where uSpinLock is used extensively. A consequence of the non-preemptive restriction is that uSpinLock can only be used for mutual exclusion because the task acquiring the lock must be the task releasing it, and hence, its constructor does not take a starting state and instances are initialized to open. Because uSpinLock is non-preemptive, it is only used internally in the μC++ runtime.

The constructor routine uLock has the following form:

uLock(**unsigned int** value = 1) – this form specifies an initialization value for the lock. Appropriate values are 0 and 1. The default value is 1.

The following discussion applies to both uSpinLock and uLock. The member routines acquire and release are used to atomically acquire and release the lock, closing and opening it, respectively. acquire acquires the lock if it is open, otherwise the calling task spins waiting until it can acquire the lock. The member routine tryacquire makes one attempt to acquire the lock, i.e., it does not wait. tryacquire returns **true** if the lock is acquired and **false** otherwise. This method allows a thread to check if an event has occurred without blocking when it has other work to do; the thread rechecks for the event after the work is completed. release releases the lock, which allows any waiting tasks to compete to acquire the lock. Any number of releases can be performed on a lock as a release only (re)sets the lock to open (1).

It is *not* meaningful to read or to assign to a lock variable, or copy a lock variable, e.g., pass it as a value parameter. Why is this true? Copying a lock would, in essence, provide another way to open the door (like copying the key for a real lock). Hence, copying must be prevented to ensure mutual exclusion.

7.2.2 Synchronization

In synchronization, two or more tasks must execute a section of code in a particular order, e.g., a block of code S2 must be executed only after S1 has completed. In Fig. 7.1a, two tasks are created in uMain::main and each is passed a reference to an instance of uLock. As in previous synchronization examples, the lock starts closed instead of open so if task t2 reaches S2 first, it waits until the lock is released by task t1. As well, the synchronization protocol is separated between the tasks instead of surrounding a critical section.

7.2.3 Mutual Exclusion

In simple mutual exclusion, two or more tasks execute a section of code one at a time, e.g., a block of code S1 and S2 must be executed by only one task at a time. In Fig. 7.1b, two tasks are created in uMain::main and each is passed a reference to an instance of uLock. Each task uses the lock to provide mutual exclusion for two critical sections in their main routine by acquiring and releasing the lock before and after the critical section code. When one task's thread is in a critical section, the other task's thread can execute outside the critical sections but must wait to gain entry to the critical section.

Does this solution afford maximum concurrency, that is, are tasks waiting unnecessarily to enter a critical section? The answer depends on the critical sections. (Remember, a critical section is a pairing of data and code.) If the critical sections

```
_Task T1 {                    _Task T2 {                    _Task T {
   uLock &lk;                    uLock &lk;                    uLock &lk;
   void main() {                 void main() {                 void main() {
      ...                           ...                           ...
      S1                           lk.acquire();                 lk.acquire();
      lk.release();                S2                            // critical section
      ...                           ...                          lk.release();
   }                             }                                ...
 public:                        public:                          lk.acquire();
   T1( uLock &lk ) : lk(lk) {}     T2( uLock &lk ) : lk(lk) {}    // critical section
};                             };                               lk.release();
void uMain::main() {                                             ...
   uLock lock( 0 );  // closed
   T1 t1( lock );                                              }
   T2 t2( lock );                                            public:
}                                                              T( uLock &lk ) : lk(lk) {}
                                                             };
                                                             void uMain::main() {
                                                                uLock lock( 1 );  // open
                                                                T t0( lock ), t1( lock );
                                                             }

              (a) Synchronization
                                                                (b) Mutual exclusion
```

Fig. 7.1 Spin lock

are disjoint, that is, they operate on an independent set of variables, one task can be in one critical section while the other task is in the other critical section. If the critical sections are not disjoint, i.e., they operate on one or more common variables, only one task can be in either critical section at a time. To prevent inhibiting concurrency if the critical sections are disjoint, a separate lock is needed for each critical section. In the example program, if the critical sections are independent, two locks can be created in uMain::main and passed to the tasks so maximum concurrency can be achieved.

7.3 Blocking Locks

As pointed out in Sect. 7.2, p. 316, a spin lock has poor performance because of busy waiting. Can anything be done to remove the busy wait? The answer is (mostly) yes, but only if the task releasing the lock is willing to do some additional work. This work is the cooperation mentioned at the end of Sect. 6.3.8.3, p. 262. That is, the responsibility for detecting when a lock is open is not borne solely by the waiting tasks attempting to acquire the lock, but also shared with the task releasing the lock. For example, when a person leaves the bathroom, if they tell the next person waiting that the bathroom is empty, that is cooperation. What advantage does the releasing task gain in doing this extra work, which has no immediate benefit to it? The answer is that in the long run each task has to wait to use the bathroom, so cooperating benefits both (all) people using the bathroom. In general, each task does a little extra work so that all tasks perform better.

Hence, for blocking locks, an arriving task only gets *one* check to test if the lock is open, and then blocks. Once blocked, the task is completely dependent on the exiting task to unblock it, otherwise it waits forever. In contrast, for spinning locks, an arriving task could miss seeing the exiting task reset the lock, but eventually rechecks the lock and finds it open. Hence, the ability to have multiple checks makes the lock less complex at the cost of poorer performance.

Therefore, all blocking locks have state to facilitate lock semantics and a list of blocked acquirers.

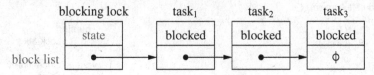

Which task is scheduled next from the list of blocked tasks? The intuitive answer is that the waiting tasks are serviced in FIFO order to ensure a bound on waiting time. However, the only requirement is eventual progress for each task. For example, tasks may have execution priorities, and these priorities are factored into the selection of which task executes next, while still ensuring a bound via aging the priorities.

7.3.1 Mutex Lock

A **mutex lock** is used only for mutual exclusion, and tasks waiting on these locks block rather than spin when the critical section is occupied. Restricting a lock to just mutual exclusion is usually done to help programmers clearly separate lock usage between synchronization and mutual exclusion, and possibly to allow special optimizations and checks as the lock only provides one specialized function. Mutex locks are divided into two kinds: single and multiple acquisition. Single acquisition is non-reentrant, meaning the task that acquires the lock (lock owner) cannot acquire it again, while multiple acquisition is reentrant, meaning the lock owner can acquire it multiple times, called an **owner lock**.

Single-acquisition locks have appeared in all previous examples of mutual exclusion. However, single acquisition cannot handle looping or recursion involving the same lock, e.g.:

```
void f() {
    ...
    lock.acquire();
    ... f();                    // recursive call within critical section
    lock.release;
    ...
}
```

The recursive call within the critical section fails after the first recursion because the lock is already acquired, which prevents further entry into the critical section by the lock owner. (This situation is called a deadlock and is discussed in Chap. 8, p. 395.) Using the bathroom analogy, this situation corresponds to a person acquiring mutual exclusion to the bathroom, and then needing to momentarily step out of the bathroom because there is no soap. Clearly, the person using the bathroom does not want to release the bathroom lock because someone could then enter the bathroom. Hence, the lock must stay locked to other tasks but allow the task that has currently acquired the lock to step out and back into the bathroom to get some soap. While in theory it is possible to restructure a program to eliminate this situation (e.g., always bring extra soap into bathroom just in case there is none); in practice, the restructuring is difficult and in some case impossible if code is inaccessible (e.g., library code).

Multiple-acquisition locks solve this problem by allowing the lock owner to reenter the critical section multiple times. Using the bathroom analogy, once a person has acquired the bathroom lock, they should be able to enter and leave the bathroom as many times as they want before releasing the lock for someone else. To allow multiple acquisition, the lock remembers the task that has acquired the lock (owner), and that task is allowed to acquire the lock again without blocking. The number of lock releases depends on the particular implementation of the owner lock. Some implementations may require only one release, regardless of the number of acquires, while other implementations may require the same number of releases as acquires.

Fig. 7.2a presents an outline for the implementation of a mutex (owner) lock. The blocking aspect of a mutex lock requires two changes: a waiting task blocks when it cannot acquire the lock and cooperation occurs at release to unblock a waiting task, if one is present. A task blocks by linking itself onto a list, marking itself blocked, and yielding its time-slice, *without putting itself on the ready queue*. Since this task is not on the ready queue, it is ineligible for execution until the task releasing the lock transfers it from the blocked list to the ready queue. Because changing variables and adding and removing a node to/from a list is not atomic, mutex locking is necessary to protect the critical section within the implementation of the blocking mutex-lock. The only mechanism available to provide the locking is the nonblocking spin-lock or a wait-free mechanism, which is used to provide the necessary mutual exclusion. Finally, the lock has auxiliary variables inUse flag and an optional owner indicator, if it is a multiple-acquisition lock. The inUse flag indicates if the lock is acquired, and it is set and reset by the task that currently owns the lock. The flag is tested by an acquiring task, and if set, the task blocks on the lock's blocking list, unless it is the lock owner. Adding the owner-lock feature requires remembering which task currently has the lock acquired, and checking during a lock acquire so the lock owner does not block.

Clearly, it is necessary for the blocking task to release the spin lock before blocking otherwise the lock owner cannot acquire the spin lock to perform the unblocking action (cooperation). Unfortunately, there is a fundamental problem. The obvious way to perform this step is:

```
// add self to blocked list of lock
lock.release();        // allow lock owner to release and unblock next waiting task
// PREEMPTION
yieldNoSchedule(); // yield CPU but do not reschedule onto ready queue
```

```
class MutexLock {
    queue<Task> blocked;      // blocked tasks
    spinlock lock;            // nonblocking lock
    bool inUse;               // resource in use ?
    Task *owner               // optional, lock owner
public:
    MutexLock() : inUse(false), owner(NULL) {}
```

```
    void acquire() {                          void acquire() {
        lock.acquire();                           lock.acquire();
        while ( inUse                             if ( inUse
            && owner != thistask() ) {                && owner != thistask() ) {
            // add self to blocked list              // add self to blocked list
            yieldNoSchedule( lock );                 yieldNoSchedule( lock );
            lock.acquire(); // re-acquire            lock.acquire(); // re-acquire
        }                                         }
        inUse = true;                             inUse = true;
        owner = thistask(); // new owner          owner = thistask(); // new owner
        lock.release();                           lock.release();
    }                                         }
    void release() {                          void release() {
        lock.acquire();                           lock.acquire();
        owner = NULL; // no owner                 owner = NULL; // no owner
        if ( ! blocked.empty() ) {                if ( ! blocked.empty() ) {
            // remove task from blocked list          // remove task from blocked list
            // and make ready                         // and make ready
                                              } else {
                                                  inUse = false;
        }                                         }
        inUse = false;
        lock.release(); // always                 lock.release(); // always
    }                                         }
};                                        };
```

| (a) Barging, starvation | (b) No barging or starvation |

Fig. 7.2 Mutex-lock implementation

However, there is a race between the blocking and unblocking tasks. The blocking task can release the spin lock but be preempted *before* the yield and put onto the ready queue. Because the spin lock is released, an unblocking task can see the blocking task on the lock's blocked list. The unblocking task now attempts to take this blocked task from the lock waiting list and put it onto the ready queue, but the task is already on the ready queue because of the preemption. A task cannot be no more than one scheduling list.

As a result, *magic* is necessary to atomically yield without scheduling *and* release the spin lock. This ensures a releasing task cannot start the release routine until the blocking task is on the lock's blocking list and not executing on a CPU. The magic is often accomplished with more cooperation:

yieldNoSchedule(lock);   // yield CPU but do not reschedule onto ready queue

Here, the spin lock is passed to the runtime system, which does the yield without schedule and then, on behalf of the user, unlocks the lock. Note, the runtime system cannot be preempted between these operations because it cannot put itself onto the ready queue or there is nothing to schedule the other tasks. Hence, the runtime violates order and speed of execution by being non-preemptable (see Sect. 6.7, p. 302).

A releasing task checks for blocked tasks and schedules one if available, and then resets the inUse flag and owner. Notice, the inUse is necessary because the blocked list may now be empty after scheduling a blocked task. Hence, an acquiring task cannot determine the status of the lock from the blocking list because there may be an invisible unblocked task, restarted by the releasing task, on the ready queue.

After a blocked task restarts, it must reacquire the spin lock because there are additional operations needing mutual exclusion. However, there is a race between the blocked task and new arriving tasks, either of which may acquire the lock's spin lock. If the restarted blocked task loses the race, it must block again and wait to be restarted again, and the newly arriving task has barged ahead of the task that has waited longer. Hence, there is the potential for unbounded waiting of a blocked task resulting in short- or long-term starvation. However, in circumstances where any task may service an action, it does not matter if some wait while others work, as long as the work gets done. (The issues of barging tasks, starvation and work sharing are discussed further in this and other chapters.)

Fig. 7.2b removes barging, and hence starvation, by conditionally resetting inUse only when there are no blocked tasks. Hence, all acquiring tasks see the lock as acquired and block. When the unblocked task restarts, it progresses without further checking because it is granted acquisition directly from the releasing task. The unblocking task *still* reacquires the spin lock because it updates variables before leaving the entry protocol. Otherwise, multiple tasks can be in the entry protocol simultaneously, both the released task and bargers, where bargers are directed to block because the inUse is set. If the entry code is restructured to conditionally release the lock:

```
if ( inUse
        && owner != thistask() ) {
    // add self to blocked list
    yieldNoSchedule( lock );
} else {
    inUse = true;
    lock.release();
}
owner = thistask(); // new owner
```

there is still potential for simultaneous access to variable owner for the multiple-acquisition version, which requires atomic read and write operations; otherwise, owner could flicker to a barging task as the releasing task is assigning it, and both tasks enter the critical section.

Fig. 7.3a presents a safer and slightly more efficient solution without any simultaneous variable access and the unnecessary release/acquire of the spin lock to transfer the mutual exclusion. After the releasing task acquires the spin lock and decides to unblock a task, *it does not release the spin lock* (baton passing, see Sect. 7.6.1, p. 356), which is accomplished by moving the spin-lock release into the **else** clause in member release. The releasing task may not access any of the shared

```
void acquire() {                          void acquire() {
    lock.acquire();                            lock.acquire();
    if ( inUse                                 if ( blocked.empty() ) { // waiting ?
         && owner != thistask() ) {                // add self to blocked list
        // add self to blocked list               lock.release();
        yieldNoSchedule( lock );               } else if ( blocked.head() == thistask() ) {
        // UNBLOCK HOLDING LOCK                     lock.release();
    }                                          } else {
    inUse = true;                                  // add self to blocked list
    owner = thistask(); // new owner              yieldNoSchedule( lock );
    lock.release();                                // DO NOT REACQUIRE LOCK
}                                              }
                                           }
void release() {                          void release() {
    lock.acquire();                            lock.acquire();
    owner = NULL; // no owner                  // remove task from head of blocked list
    if ( ! blocked.empty() ) {                 if ( ! blocked.empty() ) {
        // remove task from blocked list           // make task at front ready
        // and make ready                          // but do not remove
        // DO NOT RELEASE LOCK                 }
    } else {
        inUse = false; // conditional
        lock.release(); // NO RACE            lock.release(); // always release lock
    }
}                                         }
```

| (a) No lock reacquire | (b) No auxiliary variables |

Fig. 7.3 Mutex-lock implementation

data associated with the lock after restarting a blocked task because it may start execution immediately. When the blocked task restarts in member acquire, the spin-lock acquire after the yield is removed because the spin lock has not been released, so the unblocked task can safely perform any additional operations needing mutual exclusion. In effect, the mutual exclusion provided by the spin lock is transferred directly from the releasing task to the unblocking task. Here, the critical section is not bracketed by the spin lock; instead, the acquire and release are performed in separate blocks of code, similar to lock usage for synchronization.

Finally, Fig. 7.3b shows a further simplification by removing variables inUse and owner. This approach leaves the lock owner at the front of the blocked list while in the critical section to act as the flag and owner variables. In the release routine, the lock owner removes its own node from the blocked list rather removing the next owner. Therefore, while the critical section is being used, the blocked list always has a node on it, which can be checked for in-use and owner. Any acquiring task now sees the blocked list is not empty and waits. Note, the unblocking task in the acquire routine does not need to reacquire the spin lock because no lock variables are accessed before entering the critical section.

The primary purpose of the blocking lock is to eliminate busy waiting. Has the busy wait been removed? No, it still exists because the spin lock is necessary and the spin lock has busy waiting. So has any benefit been achieve? Yes, instead of busy waiting for the large user critical-section (100s or 1000s of instructions), the busy wait is only for the short time to conditionally set state variables and possibly block (10s of instructions). The short busy wait gives a probabilistically smaller chance of starvation. As stated previously, concurrent systems all have one or more busy waits and rely on some probabilistic argument concerning starvation. So the trick is to keep making the probability smaller and smaller.

7.3.1.1 Owner Lock Details

μC++ only provides a multiple-acquisition lock (owner lock) because it subsumes the notion of a single-acquisition mutex lock; i.e., if a task only acquires an owner lock once before a release, the lock behaves as a single-acquisition lock. The type uOwnerLock defines an owner lock:

```
class uOwnerLock {
  public:
    uOwnerLock();
    unsigned int times() const;
    ubaseTask *owner() const;
    void acquire();
    bool tryacquire();
    void release();
};
uOwnerLock x, y, *z;
z = new uOwnerLock;
```

The declarations create three owner-lock variables and initialize them to open. An owner lock is owned by the task that acquires it; all other tasks attempting to acquire the lock block until the owner releases it. The owner of an owner lock can acquire the lock multiple times, but a matching number of releases must occur or the lock remains in the owner's possession and other tasks cannot acquire it.

The member routine times returns the number of times the lock has been acquired by the lock owner. The member routine owner returns the task owning the lock or NULL if there is no owner. The member routine acquire acquires the lock if it is open, otherwise the calling task blocks until it can acquire the lock. The member routine tryacquire makes one attempt to try to acquire the lock, i.e., it does not block; the value **true** is returned if the lock is acquired and **false** otherwise. The member routine release releases the lock, and if there are waiting tasks, one is restarted; waiting tasks are released in FIFO order.

It is *not* meaningful to read or to assign to an owner lock variable, or copy an owner lock variable (e.g., pass it as a value parameter).

7.3.1.2 Mutual Exclusion

A mutex lock is used exactly the same way as a spin lock to construct mutual exclusion (see Fig. 7.1, p. 319b). The lock is passed by reference to the participating tasks, which bracket one or more critical sections by acquiring and releasing the lock. When one task's thread is in a critical section, the other task's thread can execute outside the critical sections but must wait to gain entry to the critical section. If the mutex lock is an owner lock, a lock owner may enter the critical section multiple times.

7.3.1.3 Lock-Release Pattern

Because locking requires a two-step protocol, i.e., acquire and release, there is the potential for mistakes, in particular, forgetting the lock release. In many cases, a programmer correctly includes the lock release but there is some non-obvious control path that misses the release. This problem occurs when a **break** or **return** is added to a loop or routine, providing an alternate exit that misses the release, or an unexpected exception is raised at a lower level terminating a block with a lock release that does have a cleanup handler. There are a few programming-language patterns that can be used to mitigate this problem.

- executable statement–finally clause

```
uOwnerLock lock;
lock.acquire();
try {
    ...                    // protected by lock
} _Finally {
    lock.release();
}
```

Both Java and μC++ support a **_Finally** clause on the **try** statement. A finally clause is always executed regardless of how the **try** block terminates. Putting the lock release into the **_Finally** clause ensures any form of block exit (normal, **break**, **return**, exception), always releases the lock.

- allocation/deallocation (RAII–Resource Acquisition Is Initialization)

```
class RAII {                    // create once
    uOwnerLock &lock;
  public:
    RAII( uOwnerLock &lock ) : lock( lock ) { lock.acquire(); }
    ~RAII() { lock.release(); }
};
uOwnerLock lock;
{
    RAII raii( lock );         // lock acquired by constructor
    ...                        // protected by lock
}                              // lock release by destructor
```

The C++ constructor/destructor mechanism can be used to capture the entire mutex-lock pattern, i.e., both acquire and release. The idiom is called RAII,[1] and it ties resource usage, e.g., the lock, to object lifetime. The RAII class has a reference to a mutex lock and its constructor acquires the lock and its destructor releases the lock. By declaring an instance of this class in a block that brackets a critical section, the lifetime of the RAII object is now the same as the duration

---

[1]The term was coined by Bjarne Stroustrup [11, p. 389], and is not particularly meaningful.

of the locking. The lock is automatically acquired at the start of the block via the object's constructor, and automatically released regardless of how the block terminates because a destructor for a local object is always executed.

Both approaches provide a strong safety guarantee for mutex-lock usage, and should be used when the language supports one of these features. Of the two approaches, the _Finally clause clearly shows the lock usage, while RAII hides the lock usage via an indirect mechanism.

7.3.1.4 Stream Lock

One example of owner-lock usage in μC++ is controlling I/O to a C++ stream. Because a stream may be shared by multiple tasks, characters generated by the insertion operator (<<) and/or the extraction operator >> in different tasks may be intermixed. For example, if two tasks execute the following:

```
task₁ : cout << "abc " << "def " << endl;
task₂ : cout << "uvw " << "xyz " << endl;
```

some of the different outputs that can appear are:

abc def	abc uvw xyz	uvw abc xyz def	abuvwc dexf	uvw abc def
uvw xyz	def		yz	xyz

In fact, concurrent operations can even corrupt the internal state of the stream, resulting in failure. As a result, some form of mutual exclusion is required for concurrent stream access. A coarse-grained solution is to perform all stream operations (e.g., I/O) via a single task, providing the necessary mutual exclusion for the stream. A fine-grained solution is to have a lock for each stream, which is acquired and released around stream operations by each task.

μC++ provides a fine-grained solution where an owner lock is acquired and released indirectly by instantiating a type that is specific to the kind stream: type isacquire for input streams and type osacquire for output streams. For the duration of objects of these types on an appropriate stream, that stream's owner lock is held so I/O for that stream occurs with mutual exclusion within and across I/O operations performed on the stream. The lock acquire is performed in the object's constructor and the release is performed in the destructor. The most common usage is to create an anonymous object to lock the stream during a single cascaded I/O expression, e.g.:

```
task₁ : osacquire( cout ) << "abc " << "def " << endl; // anonymous locking object
task₂ : osacquire( cout ) << "uvw " << "xyz " << endl; // anonymous locking object
```

constraining the output to two different lines in any order:

abc def	uvw xyz
uvw xyz	abc def

The anonymous locking object is only deallocated after the entire cascaded I/O expression is completed, and it then implicitly releases the stream's owner lock in its destructor.

Because of the properties of an owner lock, a task can allocate multiple locking objects for a specified stream, and the stream's owner lock is only released when the topmost locking object is deallocated. Therefore, multiple I/O statements can be protected atomically using normal block structure, e.g.:

```
{    // acquire the lock for stream cout for block duration
     osacquire acq( cout ); // named stream lock
     cout << "abc";
     osacquire( cout ) << "uvw " << "xyz " << endl; // ok to acquire and release again
     cout << "def";
}    // implicitly release the lock when "acq" is deallocated
```

This handles complex cases of nesting and recursion with respect to reading or printing:

```
int f( int i ) {
    if ( i > 0 ) osacquire( cout ) << g( i - rand() % 2 ) << endl;
    return i;
}
int g( int i ) {
    if ( i > 0 ) osacquire( cout ) << f( i - rand() % 2 ) << endl;
    return i;
}
```

Here, the mutually recursive routines both print and so they both want to acquire mutual exclusion at the start of printing. (Inserting debugging print statements often results in nested output calls.) Hence, once a task acquires the I/O owner lock for a stream, it owns the stream until it unlocks it, and it can acquire the lock as many times as is necessary after the first acquisition. Therefore, the previous example does not cause a problem even though a single task acquires and releases the I/O owner lock many times. However, it is poor concurrency practice to hold a lock longer than necessary, as might occur during the mutually recursive calls.

7.3.2 Synchronization Lock

In contrast to a mutex lock, a **synchronization lock** is the weakest form of lock and used solely for synchronization. Restricting a lock to just synchronization is usually done to help programmers clearly separate lock usage between synchronization and mutual exclusion, and possibly to allow special optimizations and checks as the lock only provides one specialized function. A synchronization lock is often called a **condition lock**, with wait/signal(notify) for acquire/release. While a synchronization lock has internal state to manage tasks blocked waiting for an event, it does not retain state about the status of the event it may be associated with. That is, a synchronization lock does not know if the event has or has not occurred; its sole purpose is to block and unblock tasks from a list, usually in FIFO order.

Like the implementation of a mutex lock, the blocking aspect of a synchronization lock requires two changes: a waiting task needs to block when the event has not occurred, and cooperation occurs at release to unblock a waiting task, if one is present. A task blocks by linking itself onto a list, marking itself blocked, and yielding its time-slice, *without putting itself on the ready queue*. Since this task is not on the ready queue, it is ineligible for execution until the task releasing the lock transfers it from the blocked list to the ready queue. Again, the adding and removing operations of a node to/from a list are not atomic; hence, mutex locking is necessary to protect the critical section within the implementation of a blocking synchronization-lock.

Synchronization locks are divided into two kinds, external or internal locking, depending on how the mutex locking is provided. External means the synchronization lock uses an external mutex lock to protect its state, while internal means the synchronization lock uses an internal mutex lock to protect its state.

The form of the external locking for a synchronization lock can vary. Fig. 7.4(a) presents an outline for the implementation of an unprotected synchronization lock, meaning the programmer must use a programming convention of externally bracketing all usages of the synchronization lock with mutual exclusion provided via a mutex lock. To accomplish this, it is often necessary to pass the mutex lock to the acquire routine because this routine *must both block and release the mutex lock* otherwise a releasing task cannot acquire the (external) mutex lock to perform the unblocking action (cooperation). When a task is unblocked, it may have to reacquire the lock or the lock must already be acquired. It is also the programmer's responsibly to use the same mutex lock for a particular usage of the synchronization lock. While different mutex locks can be used to protect the synchronization lock at different times, great care must be exercised to ensure no overlapping use of a synchronization lock among multiple mutex locks. The alternative is to have another task release the mutex lock after a task has blocked. Hence, there are two acquire routines in the synchronization lock to handle either scenario.

An alternate implementation binds a specific mutex lock to a synchronization lock, via the constructor, for the lifetime of the synchronization lock.

```
class SyncLock {
    ...
    MutexLock &mutexlock;
public:
    SyncLock( MutexLock &mutexlock ) : list( NULL ), mutexlock( mutexlock ) {}
```

which potentially reduces the chance for errors in usage. Because the mutex lock is fixed, it is no longer passed as a parameter to member acquire.

The following usage pattern illustrates how an internal synchronization-lock is used.

```
class SyncLock {                        class SyncLock {
    queue<Task> blocked;  // blocked tasks     queue<Task> blocked;  // blocked tasks
                                                spinlock lock;
public:                                  public:
    SyncLock() : list( NULL ) {}            SyncLock() : list( NULL ) {}
    void acquire( MutexLock &mutexlock ) {  void acquire( MutexLock &mutexlock ) {
                                                lock.acquire();
        // add self to blocked list             // add self to blocked task list
                                                mutexlock.release();
        yieldNoSchedule( mutexlock );          yieldNoSchedule( lock );
        // possibly reacquire mutexlock        // lock is already held on restart
                                            }
    }                                       void acquire() {
    void acquire() {                            lock.acquire();
                                                // add self to blocked task list
        // add self to blocked task list        yieldNoSchedule( lock );
        yieldNoSchedule();                  }
    }                                       void release() {
    void release() {                            lock.acquire();
                                                if ( list != NULL ) {
        if ( list != NULL ) {                      // remove task from blocked list
            // remove task from blocked list       //   and make ready
            //   and make ready                    // do not release lock
                                                } else {
                                                    lock.release();
        }                                       }
    }                                       }
}                                       };
};
                                                (b) Internal locking
        (a) External locking
```

Fig. 7.4 Synchronization-lock implementation

```
// shared variables
    MutexLock m;                    // external mutex lock
    SyncLock s;                     // synchronization lock
    bool flag = false;             // indicate if event has occurred
// acquiring task
    m.acquire();                   // mutual exclusion to examine state & possibly block
    if ( ! flag ) {                // event not occurred ?
        s.acquire();               // block for event
    }
// releasing task
    m.acquire();                   // mutual exclusion to examine state
    flag = true;                   // raise flag
    s.release();                   // possibly unblock waiting task
    m.release();                   // release mutual exclusion
```

However, there is a problem: the acquiring task blocked holding the external mutual-exclusion lock! This problem is fixable by altering the acquiring pattern.

```
// acquiring task
    m.acquire();                   // mutual exclusion to examine state & possibly block
    if ( ! flag ) {                // event not occurred ?
        m.release();               // release external mutex-lock
        CAN BE INTERRUPTED HERE
        s.acquire();               // block for event
    }
```

However, there is now the race problem of releasing the mutual-exclusion lock and blocking on synchronization lock. The releasing task can proceed as soon as the mutex lock is released but before the acquiring task has blocked on the synchronization lock. Now the release of the synchronization lock is lost because a synchronization lock does not remember state about the event. To prevent the race, the other form of acquire is used to release lock using the first usage pattern.

```
// acquiring task
    m.acquire();              // mutual exclusion to examine state & possibly block
    if ( ! flag ) {           // event not occurred ?
        s.acquire( m );       // block for event and release mutex lock
    }
```

Has the race been prevented? Yes, because of the magic in yieldNoSchedule, which blocks and releases the mutex lock atomically (see page 322).

Fig. 7.4b presents an outline for the implementation of an internal synchronization lock, which provides its own internal mutual exclusion. The additional state necessary is a lock for mutual exclusion (usually a spin lock, as in the mutex lock). This form of synchronization lock is more robust in usage because of the internal locking. The usage pattern for acquire is still the same as for an external synchronization-lock because the flag indicating the event status must be tested with mutual exclusion or its status could change. In theory, the release pattern can be relaxed.

```
// releasing task
    flag = true;              // raise flag
    s.release();              // possibly unblock waiting task
```

The external mutex lock is not required because the internal lock in sufficient to unblock the next waiting task. Even if a time-slice occurs between the mutex-lock and synchronization-lock release in acquire, no arriving task can make progress until the synchronization-lock is released by yieldNoSchedule. However, in most cases, it is still necessary to use the previous release pattern, because there is a race that can lose the signal, which is discussed next.

7.3.2.1 Condition Lock Details

The type uCondLock defines a internal synchronization-lock:

```
class uCondLock {
  public:
    uCondLock();
    bool empty();
    void wait( uOwnerLock &lock );
    void signal();
    void broadcast();
};
uCondLock x, y, *z;
z = new uCondLock;
```

(Note the name change: wait $\Rightarrow$ acquire and signal $\Rightarrow$ release.) The declarations create three condition locks and initializes them to closed (i.e., always block).

The member routine empty returns **false** if there are tasks blocked on the queue and **true** otherwise. The routines wait and signal are used to block a thread on and unblock a thread from the queue of a condition, respectively. The wait routine atomically blocks the calling task and releases the argument owner-lock; in addition, the wait routine *re-acquires its argument owner-lock before returning*. The signal routine checks if there is a waiting task, and if so, unblocks a waiting task from the queue of the condition lock; waiting tasks are released in FIFO order. The signal routine can be safely called without acquiring any owner lock associated with tasks waiting on the condition. The broadcast routine is the same as the signal routine, except all waiting tasks are unblocked.

It is *not* meaningful to read or to assign to a lock variable, or copy a lock variable (e.g., pass it as a value parameter).

7.3.2.2 Synchronization

In synchronization, two or more tasks must execute a section of code in a particular order, e.g., a block of code S2 must be executed only after S1 has completed. In Fig. 7.5, two tasks are created in uMain::main and each is passed a reference to an instance of uCondLock because a lock cannot be copied, i.e., passed by value. As in previous synchronization examples, the lock starts closed instead of open so if task t2 reaches S2 first, it waits until the lock is released by task t1. As well, the synchronization protocol is separated between the tasks instead of surrounding a critical section.

The issue in this example is the conditional race by task t1. It must *not* block if task t2 has already performed S1, which requires communication between the tasks. The communication is accomplished using global-variable done to indicate if S1 has or has not occurred. But setting and testing this variable has to occur with mutual exclusion or there is race between checking and setting. That is, task t1 determines S1 has not occurred but is interrupted before it can block; then task t2 completes S1 but its signal on the condition lock is *lost* because t1 has not blocked yet. Remember, there is no state in a condition lock to remember if a signal has occurred. Hence, an external mutex-lock is necessary to protect the state variable done and this lock must correspondingly be passed to the condition lock to be released if task t1 blocks. Similarly, task t2 has to use the mutex lock to ensure t1 does not check the flag just before it is set to true and make the wrong assumption about S1; but t2 does *not* need this lock to safely unblock (signal) task t1 because the condition lock has internal locking. As this example illustrates, it is common to need an external lock in scenarios like this. Correspondingly, this external lock can often be used to provide the protection for the condition lock, which is why external synchronization-locks can be more efficient than internal synchronization-locks by eliminating the unnecessary internal locking.

```
bool done = false;

_Task T1 {                                      _Task T2 {
  uOwnerLock &mlk;                                uOwnerLock &mlk;
  uCondLock &clk;                                 uCondLock &clk;

  void main() {                                   void main() {
    ...                                             ...
    mlk.acquire(); // prevent lost signal           S1;
    if ( ! done )   // signal occurred ?            mlk.acquire(); // prevent lost signal
    // signal not occurred                          done = true;   // remember signal
      clk.wait( mlk ); // atomic wait/release       clk.signal();  // potential signal lost
    // mutex lock re-acquired after wait            mlk.release();
    mlk.release(); // release either way            ...
    S2;                                           }
    ...                                           public:
  }                                                 T2( uOwnerLock &mlk, uCondLock &clk ):
  public:                                             mlk(mlk), clk(clk) {}
    T1( uOwnerLock &mlk, uCondLock &clk ) :       };
      mlk(mlk), clk(clk) {}
};

void uMain::main() {
  uOwnerLock mlk;
  uCondLock clk;
  T1 t1( mlk, clk );
  T2 t2( mlk, clk );
}
```

Fig. 7.5 Condition lock: synchronization

7.3.3 Barrier

A barrier is used to coordinate a group of tasks before and after performing a concurrent operation. A single barrier provides a one-shot stop and start point, while multiple barriers can be combined into a cycle with multiple stop and start points and repeated interactions.

one shot   cyclic

Hence, a barrier is specifically for synchronization and cannot be used to build mutual exclusion. Unlike previous synchronization locks, a barrier retains state about the events it manages, specifically the number of tasks blocked on the barrier. Since manipulation of this state requires mutual exclusion, most barriers use internal locking. For example, three processes must execute a section of code in a particular order: S1, S2 and S3 must *all* execute before S5, S6 and S7 are executed.

```
T1::main() {        T2::main() {        T3::main() {
   ...                 ...                 ...
   S1                  S2                  S3
   b.block();          b.block();          b.block();
   S5                  S6                  S7
   ...                 ...                 ...
}                   }                   }
void uMain::main() {
   uBarrier b( 3 );
   T1 x( b );
   T2 y( b );
   T3 z( b );
}
```

The barrier is initialized to control 3 tasks and passed to each task by reference
(not copied). The barrier works by blocking each task at the call to block until
all 3 tasks have reached their call to block on barrier b. The last task to call block
detects that all the tasks have arrived at the barrier, so rather than blocking, it
releases all the tasks (cooperation). Hence, all 3 tasks leave the barrier together
(synchronized) after arriving at the barrier. Note, must know in advance the total
number of block operations executed before the tasks are released. Why not use
termination synchronization and create new tasks for each computation? The reason
is that the creation and deletion of computation tasks may be an unnecessary expense
that can be eliminated by using a barrier. More importantly, it may be necessary to
retain information about prior computations by the tasks using the barrier.

In general, a barrier computation is composed of multiple worker tasks controlled
by one or more barriers. Each barrier has the following basic structure:

1. initialization: prepare work for the computation phase
2. release: tell worker tasks (simultaneously) to perform their computation
3. computation: each worker task performs a portion of the total computation, in
   arbitrary order and speed
4. synchronization: the workers report completion of their computation
5. summary: compile the individual computations into a final result

Control can cycle through these steps multiple times so the worker tasks perform
computations multiple times *during* their lifetime. Before a task starts its next
computation, it is essential to wait for the previous computations to complete, which
is why a barrier is needed. Imagine the situation where a fast task completes its
second computation before a slow task has completed its first, so now the tasks are
no longer in synchronization with respect to the computations. In general, the fast
task cannot begin the second computation because it is sharing resources with the
slow task still performing its first computation. In this case, the tasks interfere with
one another without proper synchronization.

There are several ways to use a barrier lock. One approach is to have a
coordinator task, which performs the sequential initialization and summary work,
and have worker tasks perform the concurrent computation. However, this approach
results in an additional task, the coordinator, and a synchronization at both the
start and end of the work, instead of just at the end. The reason for the additional
synchronization at the start is that the coordinator must wait on the barrier along

with the workers to know when the work is complete, so it can summarize and re-initialize. However, when the last worker arrives at the barrier, *all* the tasks are restarted, but only the coordinator can execute at this time to do the summary on the just completed computation, and then perform the initialization for the next computation. To prevent the worker tasks from rushing ahead and destroying the results of the previous computation and/or starting to compute again with uninitialized data, the workers must block on another barrier at the start of the computation until the coordinator also blocks on the same barrier. Only then is it known that the summary and re-initialization are complete, and all the worker tasks are ready to begin the next round of computation. Therefore, the basic structure of a worker task's main routine in this approach is:

```
for ( ;; ) {
    start.block();          // synchronize
    // compute
    end.block();            // synchronize
}
```

It is possible to eliminate both the coordinator task and the start synchronization simply by using cooperation among the worker tasks. The cooperation has the last worker synchronizing at the barrier, i.e., the task that ends the computation phase does the necessary summary work plus the initialization to begin the next computation, and finally, releases the other worker tasks. This action is done implicitly by the barrier, which knows when the last task arrives and uses that task's thread to execute some cooperation code on behalf of all the tasks. Therefore, the last task does the work, but the code to do it is part of the barrier not the task's main. Hence, the basic structure of a worker task's main routine is simplified to:

```
for ( ;; ) {
    // compute
    end.block();            // synchronize with implicit cooperation by the last task
}
```

The following discussion shows how the μC++ barrier can be used to implement this simpler and more efficient approach.

In μC++, the type uBarrier defines a barrier, and a barrier is a special kind of coroutine called a _Cormonitor:

```
_Cormonitor uBarrier {
    protected:
        void main() {
            for ( ;; ) { suspend(); }
        }
    public:
        uBarrier( unsigned int total );
        _Nomutex unsigned int total() const;
        _Nomutex unsigned int waiters() const;
        void reset( unsigned int total );
        void block();
        virtual void last() { resume(); }
};
uBarrier x(10), *y;
y = new uBarrier( 20 );
```

(The details of a _Cormonitor are discussed in Sect. 9.10, p. 472. Also, see Sect. 9.10.2, p. 473 for a complete implementation of uBarrier.) The declarations create two barrier variables and initialize the first to work with 10 tasks and the second to work with 20 tasks. For now, assume it is safe for a barrier coroutine to be accessed by multiple tasks, i.e., only one task is allowed in the barrier at a time.

The constructor routine uBarrier has the following form:

uBarrier(**unsigned int** total) – this form specifies the total number of tasks participating in the synchronization. Appropriate values are ≥ 0. A 0 initialization value implies the barrier does not cause any task to wait, but each calling task runs member routine last.

The member routines total and waiters return the total number of tasks participating in the synchronization and the total number of tasks currently waiting at the barrier, respectively. The member routine reset changes the total number of tasks participating in the synchronization; no tasks may be waiting in the barrier when the total is changed. block is called to synchronize with total tasks; tasks block until any total tasks have called block.

The virtual member routine last is called by the last task to synchronize at the barrier. It can be replaced by subclassing from uBarrier to provide a specific action to be executed when synchronization is complete. This capability is often used to reset a computation before releasing the tasks from the barrier to start the next computation. The default code for last is to resume the coroutine main. Like last, the coroutine main is usually replaced by subclassing to supply the code to be executed before and after tasks synchronize. The general form for a barrier main routine is:

```
void main() {
    for ( ;; ) {
        // code executed before synchronization (initialization)
        suspend();
        // code executed after synchronization (finalization)
    }
}
```

Normally, the last operation of the constructor for the subclass is a resume to the coroutine main to prime the barrier's initialization. When main suspends back to the constructor, the barrier is initialized and ready to synchronize the first set of tasks.

It is *not* meaningful to read or to assign to a barrier variable, or copy a barrier variable (e.g., pass it as a value parameter).

Fig. 7.6a shows the simplest use of barriers segmenting a pipeline of computations, where all worker tasks are in a particular segment at any time. (Each numbered vertical line in the diagram matches with a corresponding suspend in the barrier::main code.) Fig. 7.6b shows that arbitrarily complex topologies are possible, where tasks branch down different paths or loop around a section each controlled by the barrier. Note, only one group of worker tasks can be in particular segment at a time, but multiple groups can proceed simultaneously through segments of the barrier. Hence, each group of tasks perform a series of concurrent computations requiring synchronization after each step. As in previous situations, the coroutine allows this complex series to be written in a form that follows directly from the

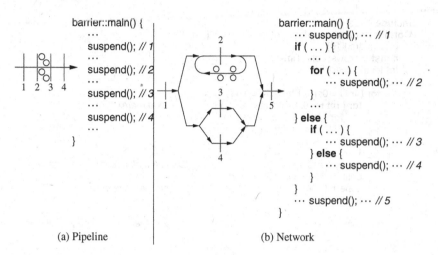

(a) Pipeline   (b) Network

Fig. 7.6   Barrier structure

algorithm, rather than flattening the code and maintaining explicit execution-state information.

Fig. 7.7 shows the matrix summation example from Sect. 5.12, p. 218 extended to read in multiple matrices and sum the elements of each matrix. (Some of the variables have been made global to simplify the example.) The program uses an extension of the basic uBarrier to control the synchronization of the Adder tasks for summing each matrix. The extension is accomplished by subclassing from type uBarrier, generating a new barrier type called Accumulator, replacing the main and block members, and adding the member eod. The coroutine main is the control point of the barrier. It is a simple loop with a one-stage pipeline, where the initialization reads a matrix and then suspends back to the priming constructor or the last task to arrive completing a barrier group. After being resumed by this last task, the total of the matrix is added to super total of all matrices, and the total is printed and reset to zero. The constructor for Accumulator is passed the matrix storage and dimensions, the number of matrices, and it does a resume to prime the coroutine to read the first matrix. The destructor for Accumulator prints out the super total of *all* the matrices summed. The member block is called by the Adder tasks to accumulate the row subtotals of a matrix and block waiting for all subtotals to be generated.

An Adder task computes the sum of a row in the matrix. The constructor for Adder is passed a row of the matrix, the number of columns in the row, the location to place the subtotal, and a Accumulator barrier on which to synchronize. The task main of Adder loops while the barrier indicates there is a matrix to sum, computes the sum of its row of the matrix, and blocks on the barrier transmitting its subtotal. If it is the last adder to arrive at the barrier, instead of blocking, the default member last in subclass uBarrier is called implicitly, which resumes the coroutine main of the Accumulator. In general, the Accumulator's coroutine main restarts at the first suspend in the middle of the outer **for** loop, sums the subtotals and prints the total, loops back to read the next matrix, and if data is present, suspends back to the last worker task, which then releases the other worker tasks to start the cycle again. (Notice, the use of the μC++ labelled break to implement a multi-level exit.) If no data is present, the

```
#include <uBarrier.h>
_Cormonitor Accumulator : public uBarrier {
    int (*matrix)[10];
    const int rows, cols, Times;
    int total, supertotal;
    void main() {
        for ( int i = 0; i < Times; i += 1 ) {
            for ( int r = 0; r < rows; r += 1 ) {          // read matrix
                for ( int c = 0; c < cols; c += 1 ) {
                    cin >> matrix[r][c];
                }
            }
            suspend();                                     // last task to barrier restarts here
            cout << "T: " << total << endl;
            supertotal += total;                           // sum ALL matrices
            total = 0;
        }
        suspend();                                         // must return to last resumer
    }
  public:
    Accumulator( int matrix[ ][10], int rows, int cols, int Times ) : matrix( matrix ),
        rows(rows), cols(cols), Times(Times), uBarrier(rows), total(0), supertotal(0) {
        resume();                                          // prime barrier
    }
    ~Accumulator() { cout << "S: " << supertotal << endl; }
    void block( int subtotal ) { total += subtotal; uBarrier::block(); }
};
_Task Adder {
    const int size, Times;
    int *row;
    Accumulator &acc;
    void main() {
        for ( int i = 0; i < Times; i += 1 ) {             // process each matrix
            int subtotal = 0;
            for ( int r = 0; r < size; r += 1 ) subtotal += row[r];
            acc.block( subtotal );                         // provide subtotal; wait for next row
        }
    }
  public:
    Adder( int row[ ], int size, int Times, Accumulator &acc ) :
        row( row ), size( size ), Times( Times ), acc( acc ) {}
};
```

Fig. 7.7 Matrix summation with barrier

outer loop is terminated, the done flag is set to indicate completion of the barrier, and control suspends back to the last adder task, causing the release of the other worker tasks, which immediately terminate their task main. (Notice, running off the end of the barrier's coroutine main would be incorrect because control would transfer to the barrier's starter task not the last resumer.)

The only problem with this technique is that the resume in the constructor of Accumulator precludes further inheritance. If another task inherits from Accumulator, Accumulator's constructor starts the coroutine main before all the constructors have completed, which in most cases is not what the programmer wants. Unfortunately, this is a general problem in C++ and can only be solved by using a programming convention or a language extension.

7.3.4 Binary Semaphore

A semaphore is the blocking equivalent to a yielding spin-lock (see Sect. 7.1, p. 319), providing both synchronization and mutual exclusion. The interface for semaphores, including its name, is from Edsger W. Dijkstra [4]. Historically, a "semaphore" is a system of visual signalling by positioning movable arms or flags to encode letters and numbers [10]. In concurrent programming, tasks signal one another using shared variables instead of flags, as in the communication between tasks in Sect. 5.13, p. 219 but without the busy wait. Two kinds of semaphores are discussed: binary semaphore and general or counting semaphore. The binary semaphore is a lock with two values: open and closed; the general semaphore or counting semaphore has multiple values.

A semaphore has two parts: a counter and a list of waiting tasks; both are managed by the semaphore. Like the barrier, a semaphore retains state and uses its counter to "remember" releases. In the case of the binary semaphore, the counter has a maximum value of one. After a semaphore is initialized, there are only two operations that affect the value of the semaphore: acquire (entry protocol) and release (exit protocol). The names of the acquire and release routine for a semaphore are P and V, respectively. Initially, Dijkstra stated these names have no direct meaning and are used "for historical reasons" [5, p. 345], but subsequently gave a more detailed explanation:

> P is the first letter of the Dutch word "passeren", which means "to pass"; V is the first letter of "vrijgeven", the Dutch word for "to release". Reflecting on the definitions of P and V, Dijkstra and his group observed the P might better stand for "prolagen" formed from the Dutch word "proberen" (meaning "to try") and "verlagen" (meaning "to decrease") and V for the Dutch word "verhogen" meaning "to increase" [2, p. 12].

In English, remember P is for pause (wait) and V is for vacate (release).

The semaphore counter keeps track of the number of tasks that can make progress, i.e., do not have to wait. A list of waiting tasks forms only when the counter is 0. The list is the basis of cooperation between acquiring and releasing tasks, allowing the V operation to find a waiting task to restart. In the semaphore case, a waiting task does not spin; it moves itself directly to the blocked state when it finds the semaphore counter is 0. Therefore, each waiting task *relies* on a corresponding releasing task to wake it up; this is in contrast to a spin lock where the releaser only marks the lock open, and it is the waiting task's responsibility to notice the change. Cooperation does mean the individual cost of releasing a semaphore is greater but there is a global reduction in wasted time because of the elimination of unnecessary spinning by waiting tasks.

7.3.4.1 Synchronization

In synchronization, two tasks must execute a section of code in a particular order, e.g., a block of code S2 must be executed only after S1 has completed. In Fig. 7.8a,

```
_Task T1 {                  _Task T2 {                  _Task T {
  BinarySem &lk;              BinarySem &lk;              BinarySem &lk;
  void main() {              void main() {              void main() {
    ...                        ...                        ...
    S1                         lk.P();                    lk.P();
    lk.V();                    S2                         // critical section
    ...                        ...                        lk.V();
                                                          ...
  }                          }
public:                    public:                      lk.P();
  T1( BinarySem &lk ) :      T2( BinarySem &lk ) :      // critical section
       lk(lk) {}                  lk(lk) {}              lk.V();
};                         };                            ...
void uMain::main() {
  BinarySem lock( 0 );                                 }
  T1 t1( lock );                                      public:
  T2 t2( lock );                                        T( BinarySem &lk ) : lk(lk) {}
}                                                      };
                                                       void uMain::main() {
                                                         BinarySem lock( 1 );
                                                         T t0( lock ), t1( lock );
                                                       }
```

| (a) Synchronization | (b) Mutual exclusion |

Fig. 7.8 Binary semaphore lock

two tasks are created in uMain::main and each is passed a reference to an instance of BinarySem because a lock cannot be copied, i.e., passed by value. As in previous synchronization examples, the lock starts closed instead of open so if task t2 reaches S2 first, it waits until the lock is released by task t1. As well, the synchronization protocol is separated between the tasks instead of surrounding a critical section.

7.3.4.2 Mutual Exclusion

Mutual exclusion is constructed in the obvious way using a BinarySem. In Fig. 7.8b, two tasks are created in uMain::main and each is passed a reference to an instance of BinarySem. Each task uses the lock to provide mutual exclusion for two critical sections in their main routine by acquiring and releasing the lock before and after the critical section code. When one task's thread is in a critical section, the other task's thread can execute outside the critical sections but must wait to gain entry to the critical section.

Does this solution afford maximum concurrency, that is, are tasks waiting unnecessarily to enter a critical section? Again, the answer depends on the critical sections. If the critical sections are disjoint, two semaphores are needed; if the critical sections are not disjoint, one semaphore is sufficient.

```
class BinarySem {
    queue<Task> blocked;   // blocked tasks
    spinlock lock;         // nonblocking lock
    int inUse;             // resource in use ?
public:
    BinarySem( int start = 1 ) : inUse( start ) {}
    void P() { see acquire in Fig. 7.3, p. 324 without owner }
    void V() { see release in Fig. 7.3, p. 324 without owner }
};
```

Fig. 7.9 Semaphore implementation

7.3.4.3 Implementation

Fig. 7.9 presents an outline for the implementation of a binary semaphore. The implementation can use either implementation from Fig. 7.3, p. 324, with the simple extension of making inUse a counter that can be initialized to 0 or 1 via the constructor. The different initialization values toggle the semaphore from a mutual exclusion to a synchronization lock.

One implementation question for a binary semaphore, where the counter logically only goes between 0–1, is what does the V operation do in the case where a user attempts to increment the counter above the value of 1, e.g., by executing two consecutive V operations on the same semaphore when there are no blocked tasks? (If there are N blocked tasks, it is possible to V $N + 1$ times, unblocking all the tasks and leaving the counter at 1, without causing a problem.) Two possible answers are to ignore the second V and leave the counter at 1, or generate an error message and terminate the program. There is no fixed rule for handling this scenario, and a semaphore implementor may choose any appropriate action so long as the semantics of the semaphore are preserved. In general, a user should not rely on any particular semantics for this situation, and should write programs so that the situation does not occur.

7.3.5 Counting (General) Semaphore

All uses of semaphores thus far have been binary semaphores, i.e., the value of the semaphore counter is either 0 or 1. Binary semaphores are sufficient for mutual exclusion and simple synchronization. However, there is nothing that *precludes* the value of the semaphore from increasing above 1. Edsger W. Dijkstra gives credit to:

> the Dutch physicist and computer designer C. S. Scholten to have shown a considerable field of applicability for semaphores that can also take on larger values *(values greater than 1)* [4, p. 67].

As well, Dijkstra presented a weak equivalence between binary and counting semaphores [4, pp. 72–76]. The difficult question is defining a meaning for a multi-valued semaphore. In the case of mutual exclusion, what is a multi-valued lock? How can a multi-valued semaphore help with synchronization?

To understand multi-valued mutual exclusion, it is necessary to expand the meaning of a critical section from simple (1 thread) to complex (N threads). What does it mean to have N threads in a critical section? Imagine a bar with a sign restricting the maximum number of people to N for fire regulations. The bouncer proves the mutual exclusion by allowing only N people in the bar at any time. The bar is a complex multi-valued critical-section with appropriate mutual exclusion. The bouncer implements the mutual exclusion by a small counter they click up when people enter the bar and click down when people leave the bar. When the counter hits N, the bouncer stops entry, and people queue up outside the bar or go to another bar.

To understand multi-valued synchronization, it is necessary to expand the meaning of synchronization from simple (2 threads) to complex (N threads). What does it mean to have N thread synchronization? Imagine pouring beer into glasses for N friends in a bar. No one should drink from their glass until the pouring is over so all the glasses get an equal amount of beer, but more importantly, so none of the beer gets poured onto the table because a glass is moved. Hence, there is a synchronization point after the pouring is complete (Cheers, Santé, Prost), so everyone knows it is safe to take their drink, i.e., the pouring is complete.

7.3.5.1 Synchronization

In synchronization, two or more tasks must execute a section of code in a particular order, e.g., a block of code S2 must be executed only after S1 has completed. In Fig. 7.10a, three tasks must execute a section of code in a particular order. S2 and S3 only execute after S1 has completed. Similar to previous synchronization examples, the semaphore starts at 0 (closed) so if task T1 or T2 reaches S2 or S3 first, they wait until the lock is released by task T3. The difference is task T3 Vs the semaphore twice to ensure both T1 and T2 can make progress, which may raise the semaphore as high as two. Try to construct a scenario where the semaphore does not reach two. Notice, it does not matter if T3 is interrupted between the calls to V or which of T1 or T2 makes progress first, the requirement that S1 be executed before S2 and S3 is still achieved.

7.3.5.2 Mutual Exclusion

A multi-valued lock allows more than one task to end a block of code, but restricts the total number that can enter. (The block of code is no longer a critical section because a critical section is defined to only allow a single task in it.) Going back to the bathroom example, imagine a public bathroom with multiple toilets. A counting semaphore can be used to restrict the number of people that enter the bathroom to the number of toilets. In Fig. 7.10b, the counting semaphore is initialized to 3,

```
T1::main() {    T2::main() {    T3::main() {        void T::main() {
   ...             ...             S1                    ...
   lk.P();         lk.P();         lk.V(); // lk.V(2)    lk.P();
   S2              S3              lk.V();               // up t0 tasks in
   ...             ...             ...                   // critical section
}               }               }                        lk.V();
                                                         ...
void uMain::main() {
   CntSem lock( 0 ); // closed                         }
   T1 x( lock );
   T2 y( lock );                                       void uMain::main() {
   T3 z( lock );                                          CntSem lock( 3 ); // allow 3
}                                                         T t0( lock ), t1( lock ), t2( lock );
                                                       }

        (a) Synchronization                                  (b) Mutual exclusion
```

Fig. 7.10 Counting semaphore lock

the number of toilets, and each P operation decreases the semaphore counter until it is 0, after which any additional tasks attempting entry are blocked. As each task leaves, the counting semaphore is increased up to the maximum of 3. The semaphore counter oscillates between 0 and 3, as tasks enter and exit, without causing any task to block. Therefore, a counting semaphore is used to control access to a resource with multiple instances.

If a counting semaphore is used to control entry to a public bathroom, do the toilets still need locks? Clearly, the answer is yes! In fact, it is often the case that one or more binary semaphores are used in conjunction with a counting semaphore. For example, a computer may have 3 identical tape drives, and allocation of the drives is controlled by a counting semaphore initialized to 3. If all the drives are used, the counting semaphore causes allocating tasks to block. However, it is still necessary to use a binary semaphore to ensure mutual exclusion for adding and removing the nodes that represent the tape drives from the list protected by the counting semaphore. For example, three tasks might arrive simultaneously and all try to use the first tape drive.

7.3.5.3 Implementation

Fig. 7.11 presents an outline for the implementation of a counting semaphore. The semaphore has a counter and pointer to a linked list of waiting tasks. A task is added to the linked list in the P routine, if it cannot make progress, and made ready in the V routine. In this implementation, the semaphore counter goes negative when tasks are blocked waiting, and the absolute value of a negative counter value is the number of waiting tasks. Knowing how many tasks are waiting on a semaphore might be useful, but is not a requirement of a semaphore implementation. Nevertheless, a semaphore user cannot determine that the implementation allows the counter to go negative; a user only sees the logical behaviour of the semaphore through its interface, which is a counter going from 0–1 or 0–N, depending on the kind of semaphore. Notice,

```
class CntSem {
    queue<Task> blocked;   // blocked tasks
    spinlock lock;         // nonblocking lock
    int cnt;               // resource in use ?
public:
    CntSem( int start = 1 ) : inUse( start ) {}
    void P() {
        lock.acquire();
        cnt -= 1;
        if ( cnt < 0 ) {
            // add self to blocked list
            yieldNoSchedule( lock );
            // UNBLOCK HOLDING LOCK
        }
        lock.release();
    }
    void V() {
        lock.acquire();
        cnt += 1;
        if ( cnt <= 0 ) {
            // remove task from blocked list and
            //   and make ready
            // DO NOT RELEASE LOCK
        } else {
            lock.release(); // NO RACE
        }
    }
};
```

Fig. 7.11 Counting semaphore implementation

when a releasing task restarts a waiting task, it passes control of the semaphore to that waiting task. All other tasks trying to access the semaphore are either blocked waiting or are in the process of blocking. The task released by the V operation knows that it is the only task restarted, and therefore, when it eventually moves to the running state, it can exit the P routine without further checks. In essence, the cooperation ensures a task is not made ready unless the condition it is waiting for is true.

7.3.6   Semaphore Details

The μC++ semaphore provides a counting semaphore, which can be used as a binary semaphore, by following a convention of only having values 0 and 1. The specific lock details are:

```
class uSemaphore {
  public:
    uSemaphore( unsigned int cnt = 1 );
    void P();
    void P( uSemaphore &s );
    void V( unsigned int times = 1 );
    bool empty();
};
uSemaphore x, y(0), *z;
z = new uSemaphore(4);
```

The declarations create three semaphore variables and initialize them to the value 1, 0 and 4, respectively.

The constructor routine uSemaphore has the following form:

uSemaphore(**unsigned int** cnt) – this form specifies an initialization value for the semaphore counter. Appropriate count values are ≥ 0. The default value is 1.

The member routines P and V are used to perform the counting semaphore operations. P decrements the semaphore counter if the value of the semaphore counter is greater than zero and continues; if the semaphore counter is equal to zero, the calling task blocks. The second form of P is discussed in Sect. 7.6.6, p. 370. V wakes up the task blocked for the longest time (FIFO service) if there are tasks blocked on the semaphore and increments the semaphore counter. If V is passed a positive integer value, the semaphore is Ved that many times. The member routine empty() returns false if there are tasks blocked on the semaphore and true otherwise.

It is *not* meaningful to read or to assign to a semaphore variable, or copy a semaphore variable (e.g., pass it as a value parameter).

7.4   Lock and COBEGIN

As was mentioned in Sect. 5.8.3, p. 207, COBEGIN/COEND can only generate trees of tasks, while FORK/JOIN can generate an arbitrary graph of tasks. The following discussion shows that locks in conjunction with COBEGIN/COEND are strongly equivalent to FORK/JOIN. The locks used are semaphores to eliminate busy waiting, but spin locks can be used instead. The approach is straightforward, use the lock to control synchronization of the statements in the COBEGIN.

For example, given the following series of statements:

$$S_1 \quad : \quad a \leftarrow 1$$
$$S_2 \quad : \quad b \leftarrow 2$$
$$S_3 \quad : \quad c \leftarrow a + b$$
$$S_4 \quad : \quad d \leftarrow 2 * a$$
$$S_5 \quad : \quad e \leftarrow c + d$$
$$S_6 \quad : \quad f \leftarrow c + e$$

what is the maximum concurrency that generates the same result as sequential execution of the statements? To determine maximum concurrency requires analysing which data and code depend on each other. For example, statements S_1 and S_2 are independent; they can be executed in either order or at the same time, and not interfere with each other. However, statement S_3 depends on both S_1 and S_2 because it uses the results of the assignments to variables a and b. If statement S_3 executes before or between or during the execution of S_1 and S_2, the value of c might not be the same as for sequential execution because old values of a and b are used in the calculation of c.

Dependencies among statements can be shown graphically in a precedence graph. A precedence graph is different from a thread graph (see Sect. 5.8.2, p. 206). A precedence graph shows when tasks must start to ensure dependences among data and code for correct execution; a thread graph shows when tasks start and end but no order of execution is specified to produce consistent results.

Fig. 7.12a shows the precedence graph for the above series of statements. Relative time runs down the graph showing when statements execute. The graph on the left shows sequential execution of the statements; the graph on the right shows maximum concurrent execution. The dashed lines separate levels where statements execute concurrently because they are independent. The time between dashed lines is the time to execute all the statements at that level; if the statements are executed in parallel at each level, the total time to execute the program decreases. Look through the statements and precedence graph to see why each statement appears at its particular level in the graph.

It is impossible to achieve the concurrency indicated in the precedence graph with only COBEGIN because the join points overlap, forming a network rather than a tree structure. However, with the addition of locks, it is possible to precisely control the execution of the threads executing the statements of the COBEGIN. The statements can be written using COBEGIN and semaphores to stop and start (synchronize) execution appropriately, as in the following pseudo code:

```
VAR L1, L2, L3, L4, L5 : SEMAPHORE := 0;
COBEGIN
    BEGIN            a := 1;         V(L1);  END;   // S1
    BEGIN            b := 2;         V(L2);  END;   // S2
    BEGIN P(L1); P(L2); c := a + b; V(L3);  END;   // S3
    BEGIN P(L1);     d := 2 * a;    V(L4);  END;   // S4
    BEGIN P(L3); P(L4); e := c + d; V(L5);  END;   // S5
    BEGIN P(L3); P(L5); f := c + e;         END;   // S6
COEND
```

Fig. 7.12b shows the process graph for the above series of statements. The approach is to create a semaphore for each statement, except the last statement, and V each statement's semaphore once the statement has completed execution. Each statement with a dependency starts with a P operation for each statement it depends on. The P operations cause a statement to "wait" until its dependent statements have completed execution, including their V operation. This approach is nothing more than a complex version of the synchronization shown in Sect. 7.3.4.1, p. 339, which states code S2 cannot be executed before code S1. Finally, the thread graph for

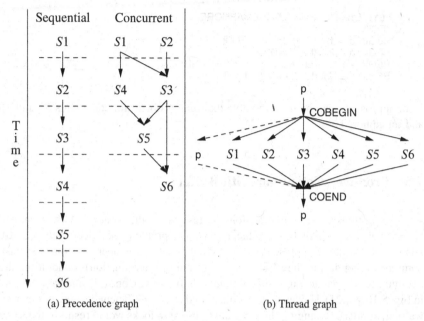

(a) Precedence graph   (b) Thread graph

Fig. 7.12 Precedence versus thread

this program is a simple tree that branches six ways and joins at the COEND, which is quite different from the precedence graph, which expresses the notion of dependency among the threads *after* they are created.

Does this solution work? In fact, it does not work. Notice that statements $S3$ and $S4$ both depend on $S1$, however there is only one V at the end of $S1$ on semaphore L1 but two Ps at the start of $S3$ and $S4$. Now remember, V opens the semaphore, and P closes the semaphore. The problem is that the first P closes L1 so the second P never finds the lock open, independent of the order of execution of the three statements. The same problem occurs with statements $S5$ and $S6$ and semaphore L3.

There are several ways to fix this problem; two are discussed here and another in the next section. One fix is to V the semaphore L1 after it is Ped so that the semaphore is open for the other thread, as in:

```
COBEGIN
  ...
  BEGIN P(L1); V(L1); P(L2); c := a + b; V(L3); END;
  BEGIN P(L1); V(L1); d := 2 * a; V(L4); END;
  ...
```

However, this solution leaves the semaphore L1 open after execution of the COBEGIN because the number of Vs and Ps does not balance, which may or may not be a problem, but should be noted. Another fix is to introduce another semaphore, as in:

```
VAR L11, L12, L2, L3, L4, L5 : SEMAPHORE := 0;
COBEGIN
    BEGIN a := 1; V(L11); V(L12); END;
    BEGIN b := 2; V(L2); END;
    BEGIN P(L11); P(L2); c := a + b; V(L3); END;
    BEGIN P(L12); d := 2 * a; V(L4); END;
    ...
```

Both approaches can be used to solve the same problem for statements $S5$ and $S6$ and semaphore L3.

7.5   Producer-Consumer with Buffer

As for coroutines, it is common for one task to produce data that is consumed by another task, which is a producer-consumer problem (see Sect. 4.9, p. 156). Also, Sect. 5.13, p. 219 presented the first attempt at a producer and consumer task communicating during their lifetime (not just at task termination). In addition, the communication was accomplished through a buffer of size one (i.e., the data variable in Fig. 5.10, p. 221). However, it was dismissed as too inefficient because of the busy waiting; similarly, changing the program to use spin locks would result in the same problem. This problem can be fixed by using semaphores.

Now, because tasks execute at different speed and in different order, the producer or consumer may temporarily speed up or slow down. Sometimes it is useful to smooth out differences in speed by increasing the size of the buffer used for communication. A larger buffer allows the producer task to continue producing elements even if the consumer is blocked temporarily, and the consumer task to continue consuming elements even if the producer is blocked temporarily.

In detail, the producer-consumer problem with tasks using a buffer is defined as follows. Two tasks are communicating unidirectionally through a buffer. The producer puts elements at the end of a buffer, and the consumer takes these elements from the front of the buffer. The buffer is shared between the producer and the consumer. There are restrictions placed on the producer and consumer depending on the size of the buffer, which are discussed in the next two sections.

7.5.1   Unbounded Buffer

In this fictitious situation, the buffer is of unbounded or infinite length:

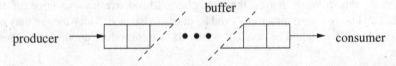

Because the buffer is infinitely long, the producer never has to wait. However, the consumer may have to wait when the buffer is empty for a producer to insert an element. As a result, service between the producer and consumer may not be in

```
const int QueueSize = ∞                    const int QueueSize = 10
int front = 0, back = 0;                   int front = 0, back = 0;
int elements[QueueSize];                   int elements[QueueSize];
uSemaphore full( 0 );                      uSemaphore full(0), empty(QueueSize);

_Task Producer {                           _Task Producer {
    void main() {                              void main() {
        for ( ;; ) {                               for ( ;; ) {
            // produce an element                      // produce an element
                                                       empty.P();
            // add to back of buffer                   // add to back of buffer
            full.V();                                  full.V();
        }                                          }
        // produce a stopping value                // produce a stopping value
    }                                          }
};                                         };
_Task Consumer {                           _Task Consumer {
    void main() {                              void main() {
        for ( ;; ) {                               for ( ;; ) {
            full.P();                                  full.P();
            // remove element from buffer              // remove element from buffer
            if ( stopping value ? ) break;             if ( stopping value ? ) break;
            // consume element                         // consume element
                                                       empty.V();
        }                                          }
    }                                          }
};                                         };

    (a) Unbounded buffer                       (b) Bounded buffer
```

Fig. 7.13   Producer-consumer simple

the order that requests are made to access the buffer, i.e., service is non-FIFO
with respect to the buffer. In this situation, accommodating non-FIFO service is
essential. Fig. 7.13a shows the major components of the producer-consumer using
an unbounded buffer. The shared declarations are divided into two components:
communication and task management. The variables front, back and elements are
an array implementation of an infinite buffer, with indices to the front and back
of the buffer, respectively, used for communication. The variable full is a counting
semaphore that indicates how many full slots are in the buffer; the semaphore is
initialized to 0 indicating the buffer is initially empty. Notice the producer Vs the
semaphore *after* an element is inserted into the buffer so it counts up with each
element inserted; the consumer Ps the semaphore *before* an element is removed so
the semaphore counts down with each element removed. If the semaphore counter
drops to 0, indicating no elements in the buffer, the consumer blocks until the
producer inserts an element and Vs the semaphore (non-FIFO order).

Is there a problem adding and removing elements from this (fictitious) shared
buffer? When the buffer has multiple elements in it, the producer and consumer
are separated by these elements, and hence, do not interfere with one another
(depending on the buffer implementation, which is discussed shortly). Clearly, a
problem can arise when the buffer is empty and the producer starts to insert an
element while at the same time the consumer tries to remove it. In this case, the

consumer removes a partially inserted element from the buffer, which contains incomplete (erroneous) data. Fortunately, the semaphore full ensures that there are no simultaneous operations on the shared buffer for this boundary case. The consumer cannot attempt to remove an element until the producer has completely inserted it. In effect, the producer never tells the consumer something has occurred, until it is done.

Is this a synchronization problem or a mutual exclusion problem? All the signs indicate that this is a synchronization problem. Look at how the semaphore full is used. First, it is initialized to closed instead of open. Second, the V is in one task and the P is in another task instead of bracketing a block of code. Therefore, semaphore full is used for synchronization.

7.5.2 Bounded Buffer

An unbounded buffer cannot exist, but it is a simple starting point for introducing the problems associated with a concurrently accessed buffer. In this realistic situation, the buffer is of bounded or finite length:

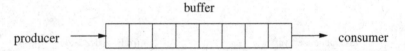

Because the buffer is finite in length, the producer may have to wait for the consumer to remove an element. As for the unbounded buffer, the consumer may have to wait until elements are produced. Again, service between producer and consumer is non-FIFO depending on the state of the buffer. Fig. 7.13b shows the major components of the producer-consumer using a bounded buffer. The only change from the unbounded buffer program is the additional counting-semaphore empty, which indicates the number of empty slots in the buffer. The producer now has to contend with the possibility that the buffer has no empty slots for it to fill. To accomplish this, semaphore empty is used in the reverse way to semaphore full; empty is initialized to the buffer size, indicating that initially all buffer slots are empty, and it counts down as each empty slot is filled. Notice the producer Ps the semaphore *before* inserting an element into the buffer, so it counts down with each element inserted; the consumer Vs the semaphore *after* an element is removed so the semaphore counts up with each element removed. The sum of the semaphore counters for full and empty is always the buffer size; that is, the number of full and empty slots in the buffer always equals the buffer size. The use of two counting semaphores to control access to the bounded buffer is a powerful example of synchronization. The program has no if statements to check the status of the buffer; all checking occurs within the semaphore abstraction. However, notice that the semaphore empty starts at the buffer size and not 0, which is slightly unusual for a synchronization semaphore, but consistent with a counting semaphore managing a resource with multiple instances (see Sect. 7.3.5.2, p. 342).

Does this solution produce maximum concurrency? In fact, it may not. Look at the code for the bounded-buffer consumer. Notice that the semaphore empty is Ved *after* the element is consumed. When the buffer is full, should the producer have to wait for the consumer to process an element before it can insert another into the buffer? The answer depends on where the element is consumed. In some situations, the consumer may not copy the element out of the buffer because the element is large, making copying expensive, or copying may not be allowed; therefore, the element must be consumed in place. Hence, the producer must wait until the buffer slot becomes free. Alternatively, the consumer may copy an element out of the buffer and consume the copy. In this case, the consumer should let the producer know that a slot is empty immediately after the element is removed (copied). To accomplish this, the statement empty.V() needs to be moved after the remove from the buffer to achieve maximum concurrency. A similar situation is possible for the producer; the producer may produce elements directly in a buffer slot or produce them elsewhere and copy them into a buffer slot when complete.

Does this solution handle multiple producers and consumers? It is reasonable to imagine multiple producers inserting elements into the buffer, and correspondingly, multiple consumers taking elements out of the buffer. If the producer is much faster than the consumer, multiple consumers may be needed to keep pace with the producer; the reverse may also be true. Does the current solution properly handle this situation? In fact, the two semaphores, full and empty, ensure *multiple* producers or consumers block if the buffer is full or empty. A semaphore does not know or care if it is decremented or incremented by a single or multiple tasks; once the semaphore is at 0, it blocks any number of tasks. However, the problem of simultaneous access to the buffer occurs again. In this case, the problem is not between operations occurring at opposite ends of the buffer, but operations occurring on the same end of the buffer. The semaphore empty does not prevent multiple producers from simultaneously attempting to insert elements into the same empty buffer slot; similarly, the semaphore full does not prevent multiple consumers from simultaneously attempting to remove elements from the same full buffer slot. This situation is the same as that discussed in Sect. 7.3.5.2, p. 342: locks are still needed on the toilet doors of a public bathroom protected with a counting semaphore. Thus, the buffer itself must be protected with a binary semaphore so that insertions and removals are serialized. How many binary semaphores are needed to ensure maximum concurrency? The answer depends on the buffer implementation. If insert and removal are independent, other than at the boundary case of an empty buffer, then separate semaphores can protect each end of the buffer to allow insertion by a producer at the same time as removal by a consumer; otherwise, a single semaphore must protect both insertion and removal. For example, if the buffer is implemented as a queue, the queue implementation must not access any common data between the add and remove operations, except in the case of an empty buffer. It can be difficult to ensure this requirement in the queue implementation.

Fig. 7.14, p. 353 shows a complete producer-consumer program using a bounded buffer that supports multiple producers and consumers. The bounded buffer is generic in the type of the elements stored in the buffer. An array implementation is used for the buffer, with two subscripts that move around the buffer in a cycle. The buffer size is specified when the buffer is created, so individual buffer instances can be different sizes, but the size does not change after creation. There are 4 semaphores: full and empty ensure producers and consumers delay if the buffer fills or empties, respectively, and ilock and rlock ensure the buffer insert and remove operations are atomic with regard to multiple producers and consumers, respectively. The buffer declares a null copy constructor and assignment operator to preclude any form of copying because its local semaphores cannot be copied. This requirement is a logical consequence of the restriction that an object cannot be copied unless all of its members can be copied.

The producer and consumer tasks communicate integer values in the range 1–100 inclusive using an instance of the buffer. uMain::main creates the buffer, and then dynamically creates an array of N producers and another array of M consumers, each element of both arrays is passed a reference to the buffer. Then uMain's thread deletes the producers, which cause it to wait for those threads to terminate (i.e., termination synchronization). After the producers have finished, enough stopping values are inserted in the buffer to cause all the consumers to terminate. Then uMain's thread deletes the consumers, which cause it to wait for those threads to terminate (i.e., termination synchronization).

7.6 Readers and Writer

The next important standard problem in concurrency is the readers and writer problem. This problem stems from the observation made in Sect. 6.1, p. 234 that multiple tasks can simultaneously read data without interfering with one another; only writing cause problems. This capability is possible because reading does not change the resource, and so, one reader does not affect another. However, writing tasks must have mutual exclusion to a resource before changing it. The mutual exclusion ensures that readers do not read partial results that could cause the reader to subsequently fail. As well, it ensures writers do not interfere with each other by writing over each others partial calculations.

This observation is important because most of the operations performed on shared resources are reading and only a small amount is writing. For example, most files or linked lists are read for searching reasons, rather than update reasons. Therefore, there is significant potential for increasing concurrency by differentiating between reading and writing, since it is possible to have multiple concurrent readers. As mentioned in Sect. 7.3.5.2, p. 342, a new kind of critical section needs to be defined: one where multiple tasks can be in it if they are only reading, but only one writer task can be in the critical section at a time.

While the statement of the readers and writer problem seems straightforward, the solution is not. Solving the readers and writer problem is like solving the N-task mutual exclusion game, with the added complexity that multiple readers can be in the critical section but only one writer. However, unlike the original

```
#include <uSemaphore.h>

template<typename ELEMTYPE>
class Buffer {
    const int size;
    int front, back;
    uSemaphore full, empty;
    uSemaphore ilock, rlock;
    ELEMTYPE *Elements;

    Buffer( Buffer & );  // no copy/assignment
    Buffer &operator=( Buffer & );
  public:
    Buffer( const int size = 10 ) :
        size( size ), full( 0 ), empty( size ) {
        front = back = 0;
        Elements = new ELEMTYPE[size];
    }
    ~Buffer() {
        delete Elements;
    }
    void insert( ELEMTYPE elem ) {
        empty.P();  // wait if buffer is full

        ilock.P();   // serialize insertion
        Elements[back] = elem;
        back = ( back + 1 ) % size;
        ilock.V();

        full.V();    // signal a full buffer slot
    }
    ELEMTYPE remove() {
        ELEMTYPE elem;

        full.P();    // wait if buffer is empty

        rlock.P();  // serialize removal
        elem = Elements[front];
        front = ( front + 1 ) % size;
        rlock.V();

        empty.V();  // signal empty buffer slot
        return elem;
    }
};
```

(a) Bounded buffer

```
_Task producer {
    Buffer<int> &buf;
    void main() {
        const int NoOfElems = rand() % 20;
        int elem;

        for ( int i=1; i <= NoOfElems; i+=1 ) {
            yield( rand() % 20 );  // produce
            elem = rand() % 100 + 1;
            buf.insert( elem );
        }
    }
  public:
    producer( Buffer<int> &buf ) : buf( buf ) {}
};
_Task consumer {
    Buffer<int> &buf;
    void main() {
        int elem;

        for ( ;; ) {
            elem = buf.remove();
            if ( elem == -1 ) break;  // stop ?
            yield( rand() % 20 );  // consume
        }
    }
  public:
    consumer( Buffer<int> &buf ) : buf( buf ) {}
};
void uMain::main() {
    const int NoOfCons = 3, NoOfProds = 4;
    Buffer<int> buf;  // create shared buffer
    producer *prods[NoOfProds];
    consumer *cons[NoOfCons];

    // create produces and consumers
    for ( int i = 0; i < NoOfCons; i += 1 )
        cons[i] = new consumer( buf );
    for ( int i = 0; i < NoOfProds; i += 1 )
        prods[i] = new producer( buf );

    for ( int i = 0; i < NoOfProds; i += 1 )
        delete prods[i];  // wait producers

    // terminate each consumer
    for ( int i = 0; i < NoOfCons; i += 1 )
        buf.insert( -1 );
    for ( int i = 0; i < NoOfCons; i += 1 )
        delete cons[i];  // wait consumers
}
```

(b) Producer consumer

Fig. 7.14 Producer-consumer complex

mutual exclusion game, which was strictly a software solution, the readers and writer solution can use hardware locks. Still, the structure of the solution is very similar: construct some entry and exit code before and after the read and the write operation(s) that ensures the correct access to the critical section.

Like the original mutual exclusion problem, it is useful to have an analogy to explain the problems. The analogy is that readers and writers arrive at the entrance to a room in which there is a blackboard and chalk (see Fig. 7.15). The reader tasks read the data on the black board, and the writer tasks may read the data on the black board and use the chalk to write new data. The readers and writers queue outside the room, and some appropriate entry and exit protocol ensures the readers and writer mutual exclusion.

Like software solutions to mutual exclusion, there is a history of attempts at solving this problem. Probably the most well-known pair of solutions using semaphores were given by Courtois et al. [3]; both solutions are examined (see Fig. 7.16). The general outline is as follows. A reader task calls the routine reader to perform a read and a writer task calls writer to write. The protocol must allow multiple readers but serialize writers. Normally, each routine would have the values to be read or written passed as arguments, but that is superfluous for this discussion.

Fig. 7.16a is the simpler solution. It has a counter, rdcnt, to count the number of simultaneous reader tasks using a resource; a semaphore, e, to provide mutual exclusion for modifying rdcnt and examining its value; and a semaphore, rw, to block the first reader of a group of readers, as well as writers waiting entry.

The reader entry protocol acquires mutual exclusion to safely modify and check the reader counter. After acquiring mutual exclusion, the reader counter is incremented and a check is made for the first reader. The first reader of a group P's on semaphore rw, which is 1 if there is no writer, so the reader does not wait, or which is 0 if there is a writer, so the reader waits while holding the entry semaphore, e. If no writer task is using the resource, the first reader task exits the entry protocol, releasing the semaphore e, and starts to read. Any additional readers that come along acquire the entry semaphore, determine they are not the first reader and start reading. If a writer task is using the resource, holding the semaphore e, prevents other reader tasks from attempting entry; these readers block outside the critical section on semaphore e.

As readers finish reading, they execute the reader exit protocol. Note, readers can finish reading in any order. As for the entry protocol, the exit protocol acquires the entry semaphore to modify and examine the reader counter. After acquiring mutual exclusion, the reader counter is decremented and a check is made for the last reader. The last reader of a group, V's on semaphore rw to start any writer that might be waiting (cooperation) or to leave the semaphore with a value of 1 for the next group of reader tasks.

The writer entry protocol acquires semaphore rw, which is 1 if there are no readers, so the writer does not wait, or which is 0 if there is at least one reader, so the writer waits. After acquiring mutual exclusion, writing begins. When the writer finishes writing, the write exit protocol V's on semaphore rw to restart either the first

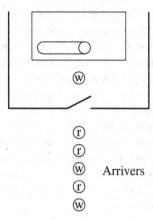

Arrivers

Fig. 7.15 Readers and writer

```
int rdcnt = 0;
uSemaphore e(1), rw(1);

void reader() {
    e.P();              // entry protocol
        rdcnt += 1;
        if ( rdcnt == 1 ) rw.P();
    e.V();



    // READ

    e.P();              // exit protocol
        rdcnt -= 1;
        if ( rdcnt == 0 ) rw.V();
    e.V();
}
void writer() {
    rw.P();             // entry protocol



    // WRITE

    rw.V();             // exit protocol
}
```

(a) Solution 1

```
int rdcnt = 0, wrtcnt = 0;
uSemaphore e1(1), e2(1), e3(1), r(1), rw(1);

void reader() {
    e3.P();             // entry protocol
      r.P();
        e1.P();
          rdcnt += 1;
          if ( rdcnt == 1 ) rw.P();
        e1.V();
      r.V();
    e3.V();

    // READ

    e1.P();             // exit protocol
        rdcnt -= 1;
        if ( rdcnt == 0 ) rw.V();
    e1.V();
}
void writer() {
    e2.P();             // entry protocol
        wrtcnt += 1;
        if ( wrtcnt == 1 ) r.P();
    e2.V();
    rw.P();

    // WRITE

    rw.V();             // exit protocol
    e2.V();
        wrtcnt -= 1;
        if ( wrtcnt == 0 ) r.V();
    e2.V();
}
```

(b) Solution 2

Fig. 7.16 Courtois et al: readers and writer solutions

reader of group of readers, a writer, or leave the semaphore with a value of 1 to prepare for the next group of reader tasks or a writer.

Unfortunately, this solution breaks rule 5: starvation. The problem is that an infinite stream of readers causes writers to starve, which occurs because a reader never checks in its entry protocol for a waiting writer if there are readers already reading. The next solution attempts to correct this problem.

Fig. 7.16b is very complicated. In fact, it is so complex it is not worth struggling through a detailed explanation. (Some of the complexity results from not making any assumptions about the order tasks are released after a V operation, i.e., they do not assume FIFO release of tasks.) Furthermore, this solution still allows starvation, but it is the readers that can starve if there is an infinite stream of writers. This problem occurs because a writer never checks in its entry protocol for a waiting reader if there is a writer already writing.

There is also a peculiar problem with non-FIFO order of writers, i.e., one writer can arrive at its entry protocol *before* another writer but execute *after* it. This phenomenon occurs if the first writer is pre-empted or the two writers race between the statements at the end of the writer entry protocol:

```
e2.V();
// pre-emption on uniprocessor or race on multiprocessor
rw.P();
```

The second writer can execute its entry protocol, find wrtcnt is 1, acquire semaphore rw, change the resource, and execute its exit protocol, before the first writer executes, even though the first writer executed the entry protocol *ahead* of the second! Having values written out of order is unacceptable for many problems. All these problems and additional ones are addressed in subsequent solutions.

7.6.1 Split Binary Semaphores and Baton Passing

Neither of the previous two solutions solves the readers and writer problem because both suffer from starvation. Furthermore, the second solution it too complex to understand and prove correct. To deal with the complexity problem, techniques are needed to help program complex semaphore solutions. Two techniques are introduced to provide a methodology for writing complex semaphore programs: split-binary semaphore [7], developed by Edsger W. Dijkstra, and baton passing [1], developed by Gregory R. Andrews; these techniques can be used separately or together.

A split-binary semaphore is a technique (coding convention) for collectively ensuring that a group of critical sections, possibly protected with different semaphores, execute as one critical section; i.e., only one of the critical sections executes at a time. The reason one semaphore cannot be used to protect all the critical sections is:

- Complex protocol code must be executed atomically either before continuing or blocking, e.g., managing the reader counter in the previous example requires atomicity.
- Specific tasks must wait together on separate queues, e.g., reader and writer tasks wait on different semaphores. If different kinds of tasks wait together on the same semaphore, it becomes difficult to ensure a particular kind of task restarts after the next V operation. That is, it is usually impossible to search down the list of blocked tasks for a particular kind of task and unblock it.

Thus, a split-binary semaphore is a collection of semaphores where at most one of the collection has the value 1. Formally, the sum of all semaphore counters used in the entry and exit code is always less than or equal to one (assuming the semaphore counters do not go negative, see Sect. 7.3.5.3, p. 343). Therefore, when one task is in a critical section protected by the split-binary semaphore, no other task can be in a critical section protected with the split-binary semaphore, even though different semaphores are used to protect the critical sections. The term "split" comes from the fact that the action of a single binary semaphore is divided among a group of binary semaphores. The notion of splitting can be further applied to construct a weak equivalence between binary and counting semaphores. The multiple states of the counting semaphore are split into binary semaphores and explicit counters [8].

Fig. 7.17 illustrates split-binary semaphores by transforming the producer-consumer problem from counting semaphores (see Sect. 7.5.2, p. 350) to split-binary semaphores. The original solution has two counting semaphores, full and empty, which are each replaced by *splitting* them into two binary semaphores, and an explicit counter. For example, the counting semaphore full is replaced by the binary semaphores e1 and full and the counter fullcnt. Thus, there are *two* split-binary semaphores. The binary semaphores e1 and e2 control all protocol operations that require mutual exclusion; each of these semaphores starts open (i.e., with the value 1). The counting nature of the counting semaphore is mimicked in the protocol via the two counter variables emptycnt and fullcnt, respectively. Finally, the binary semaphores full and empty are where tasks block if they cannot proceed.

The counting semaphore P operation is transformed into a critical section protected by an entry semaphore, which decrements the associated counter variable and checks if the current task should block or continue. If the counter is negative, the task blocks on the appropriate waiting semaphore, but first the entry semaphore is released so another task can enter the critical section as for the case when the task does not block. In the former case, the entry semaphore must be released *before* blocking on the appropriate waiting semaphore, otherwise the task blocks first and never releases the entry semaphore so tasks cannot enter the critical section. The counting semaphore V operation is also transformed into a critical section protected by an entry semaphore, which checks for waiting tasks. If the counter is negative, a blocked task must be present, and it is made ready by Ving the appropriate (binary) waiting semaphore, and then the associated counter variable is incremented and the entry semaphore is released. Restarting a blocked task is the cooperation that removes the busy wait.

```
int front = 0, back = 0;                  int front = 0, back = 0;
int elements[10];                         int elements[10];
uSemaphore full(0), empty(10);            uSemaphore e1(1), full(0), e2(1), empty(0);
                                          int fullcnt = 0, emptycnt = 10;

_Task Producer {                          _Task Producer {
    void main() {                             void main() {
        for ( ;; ) {                              for ( ;; ) {
            // produce an element                     // produce an element
            empty.P();                                e2.P();        // simulate general P
                                                      emptycnt -= 1;
                                                      if ( emptycnt < 0 ) {
                                                          e2.V(); empty.P();
                                                      } else
                                                          e2.V();

            // add queue element                      // add queue element

            full.V();                                 e1.P();        // simulate general V
                                                      if ( fullcnt < 0 )
                                                          full.V();
                                                      fullcnt += 1;
                                                      e1.V();
        }                                         }
        // produce a stopping value               // produce a stopping value
    }                                         }
};                                        };
_Task Consumer {                          _Task Consumer {
    void main() {                             void main() {
        for ( ;; ) {                              for ( ;; ) {
            full.P();                                 e1.P();        // simulate general P
                                                      fullcnt -= 1;
                                                      if ( fullcnt < 0 ) {
                                                          e1.V(); full.P();
                                                      } else
                                                          e1.V();

            // remove queue element                   // remove queue element

            empty.V();                                e2.P();        // simulate general V
                                                      if ( emptycnt < 0 )
                                                          empty.V();
                                                      emptycnt += 1;
                                                      e2.V();
            if ( stopping value ? ) break;            if ( stopping value ? ) break;
            // consume element                        // consume element
        }                                         }
    }                                         }
};                                        };

        (a) General semaphore                     (b) Split binary semaphore
```

Fig. 7.17 Split binary semaphore

Baton passing is a technique (coding convention) for precisely controlling the cooperation between a releasing and a blocked task. Note that there is no actual baton; the baton is a conceptual metaphor to help understand and explain the complexity of the problem, just as there is no split-binary semaphore. The rules of baton passing are:

- there is exactly one baton,
- no task makes progress unless it has the baton,
- once the baton is given up, a task cannot change variables in the entry or exit protocol.

Examples of baton passing are presented in solutions to the readers and writer problem.

Six solutions to the readers and writer problem using split-binary semaphores and baton passing are analysed. The first two solutions have the same problems as the previous solutions but illustrate the techniques of split-binary semaphores with baton passing. The next three solutions remove problems associated with the first two solutions, in particular, starvation and a new phenomenon called staleness. The last solution deals with the peculiar problem of non-FIFO order of writers.

7.6.2 Solution 1

The analogy presented at the start of Sect. 7.6, p. 352 is extended to handle split-binary semaphores and baton passing. In Fig. 7.18, a table is placed at the entrance to the room and a baton is placed on the table. Readers and writers initially approach the front of the table in a queue and use the baton to determine if they have to wait or can enter the room. If they have to wait, they do so in the appropriate queue on the left (readers) or right (writers) of the table.

Fig. 7.19, p. 361 shows the program that implements this model. Notice, the baton never enters the room; it is used solely to manage cooperation among arriving, waiting and leaving tasks. The program contains three semaphores, all of which compose a single split-binary semaphore, and four counters used in the protocol. The semaphores are discussed first. entry is used to provide mutual exclusion for the entry and exit protocols. The other two semaphores are used to block readers or writers that must wait to enter the room. This split-binary semaphore not only protects multiple critical sections (all the entry and exit protocols) but also the two waiting semaphores containing different kinds of tasks (readers and writers). Again, the readers and writers wait on different semaphores so it is possible to restart an appropriate kind of task. The first two counters, rdelay and wdelay, keep track of the number of delayed readers and writers that cannot enter the room, and so, are blocked on semaphores rwait and wwait, respectively. The last two counters keep track of the number of readers and writers in the room, rcnt and wcnt, respectively. wcnt never increases above one because of the serial nature of writing.

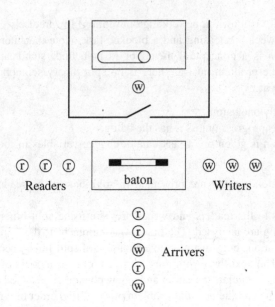

Fig. 7.18 Readers and writer

To explain the algorithm, assume that the room is currently occupied by a writer and a reader arrives. The reader conceptually picks up the baton by Ping on the entry semaphore, which decrements to zero. (Now all semaphores have a zero value.) The reader now has mutual exclusion and can examine all the protocol variables knowing no other task can read or modify them. The reader first checks if there is a writer in the room. If there is a writer, the reader increments the number of delayed readers, puts down the baton by Ving on entry and waits by Ping on rwait. A reader assumes it will be restarted eventually via cooperation when the writer, currently in the room, leaves. If there is no writer, or the reader is restarted after waiting, the reader first increments the number of concurrent readers and then checks if there are any other readers that it can read with. If the number of delayed readers in greater than zero, it is decremented and a waiting reader is Ved from semaphore rwait. As a result, a group of waiting readers take turns unblocking each other, one after the other, which is referred to as **daisy-chain unblocking**, and the readers begin reading in FIFO order. Otherwise, the baton is put back on the table for any new arrivers and the reader starts reading.

Notice, the baton is not put back on the table when the next waiting reader is Ved. Conceptually, the baton is passed directly from the current reader to the waiting reader. When the waiting reader wakes up, it does so holding the conceptual baton, which means it has mutual exclusion over the entry protocol when it restarts execution after rwait.P() and decrements the number of delayed readers. The notion of passing the baton forms the basis of cooperation among tasks entering and leaving the room. It ensures that when an appropriate task is woken up, that task is the only one that can legitimately continue execution with respect to the resource.

```
uSemaphore entry(1), rwait(0), wwait(0);
int rdelay = 0, wdelay = 0, rcnt = 0, wcnt = 0;

void Read() {
    entry.P();                          // entry protocol
    if ( wcnt > 0 ) {                   // resource in use ?
        rdelay += 1; entry.V(); rwait.P(); rdelay -= 1;
    }
    rcnt += 1;
    if ( rdelay > 0 )                   // more readers ?
        rwait.V();                      // pass baton
    else
        entry.V();                      // put baton down

    // READ

    entry.P();                          // exit protocol
    rcnt -= 1;
    if ( rcnt == 0 && wdelay > 0 )      // last reader ?
        wwait.V();                      // pass baton
    else
        entry.V();                      // put baton down
}
void Write() {
    entry.P();                          // entry protocol
    if ( rcnt > 0 || wcnt > 0 ) {       // resource in use ?
        wdelay += 1; entry.V(); wwait.P(); wdelay -= 1;
    }
    wcnt += 1;
    entry.V();                          // put baton down

    // WRITE

    entry.P();                          // exit protocol
    wcnt -= 1;
    if ( rdelay > 0 )                   // waiting readers ?
        rwait.V();                      // pass baton
    else if ( wdelay > 0 )              // waiting writers ?
        wwait.V();                      // pass baton
    else
        entry.V();                      // put baton down
}
```

Fig. 7.19 Readers and writer: solution 1

When a reader finishes reading it must pick up the baton because the exit protocol examines shared variables. Note, readers can finish reading in any order. The exiting reader can then safely decrement the number of concurrent readers, and if it is the last reader of the current group, it must perform the necessary cooperation by checking if there is a writer waiting. If the number of delayed writers is greater than zero, a waiting writer is Ved from semaphore wwait. Otherwise the baton is put back on the table for any new arrivers and the reader leaves. A reader does not check for any delayed readers because newly arriving readers immediately enter the room if there are readers already in the room. Again, notice the baton is not put back on the table if a waiting writer is Ved. The baton is conceptually passed directly from the last reader to the waiting writer. When the waiting writer wakes up, it does so holding the conceptual baton, which means it has mutual exclusion over the entry protocol when it restarts execution after wwait.P() and decrements the number of delayed writers.

Now assume that the room is currently occupied by a writer and another writer arrives. The arriving writer picks up the baton and checks if there are readers or a writer in the room. If there is a group of readers or a writer, the writer increments the number of delayed writers, puts down the baton, and waits. A writer assumes it will be restarted eventually via cooperation when the last reader of a group or a writer leaves the room. If there is neither a group of readers nor a writer, or the writer is restarted after waiting, the writer increments the number of writers (it could just set wdelay to 1), puts down the baton and starts writing.

When a writer finishes writing it must pick up the baton because the exit protocol examines shared variables. The exiting writer can then safely decrement the number of writers, and check for any delayed readers or writers. If the number of delayed readers or writers in greater than zero, a waiting reader or writer is Ved from the appropriate semaphore. Otherwise the baton is put back on the table for any new arrivers and the writer leaves.

One interesting situation needs to be examined. Assume a reader has started the entry protocol but detected a writer in the room. The reader increments rdelay, Vs semaphore entry and then is interrupted by a time-slice *before* it can block on rwait. The writer in the room now continues execution and leaves the room. Since the reader has conceptually put down the baton, the exiting writer can pick it up and enter its exit protocol. It detects the waiting reader because the reader incremented rdelay *before* putting the baton down, and Vs semaphore rwait; however, the reader is not blocked on the semaphore, yet. Is this a problem? The answer is no because the V increments rwait to 1 so whenever the reader restarts execution it will not block but continue execution, and decrement rwait back to 0. Therefore, the order and speed of execution among the readers and writers does not affect the entry and exit protocol, which is as it should be. Essentially, the counting property of the semaphore remembers the V occurring *before* its matching P.

An interesting consequence of this situation is that the counters rdelay and wdelay are essential and cannot be replaced given additional semaphore information. For example, uSemaphore provides a member empty indicating if there are tasks blocked on the semaphore. It would appear the counters rdelay and wdelay could be eliminated and replaced with tests for non-empty reader or writer semaphores indicating delayed reader and writer tasks, respectively, i.e., a test like rdelay > 0 becomes !rwait.empty(). However, this simplification does not work because of the possibility of interruption between putting the baton down and blocking, e.g., the test !rwait.empty() returning false when in fact there is a reader task just about to wait. Hence, the delay counters not only indicate how many tasks are delayed on a semaphore but also provide additional temporal information about *wanting* to block (i.e., declaring intent in Sect. 6.3.3, p. 241) and *actually* being blocked.

Unfortunately, there are two problems with this solution: one major and one minor. The major problem is discussed now and the minor problem is postponed to a subsequent solution. The major problem is that as long as readers keep coming along, no writer can make progress, resulting in starvation of the writers. This problem can be seen by looking at the reader's entry protocol. A reader only checks for a writer in the room; it does not check for any waiting writers, so effectively readers have higher priority than writers (as in the prioritize retract entry solution to mutual exclusion in Sect. 6.3.5, p. 244).

7.6.3 Solution 2

One way to alleviate, but not eliminate, the starvation problem is to switch the priority of the readers and writers so a writer has the highest priority. This approach is reasonable because on most computer systems approximately 80 % of operations are reads and 20 % writes; therefore, there are many more readers than writers in a normal concurrent system. Thus, the probability of a continuous stream of writers is extremely rare because there are not that many writers in a system, making starvation of readers very unlikely (i.e., a probabilistic solution).

Switching priority between readers and writers in very simple. The second line of the entry protocol for a reader is changed to the following:

Old	New
...	...
if (wcnt > 0) {	if (wcnt > 0 || wdelay > 0) {
...	...

A reader now checks for both a writer using the resource *and* for waiting writers, and waits appropriately. Hence, a reader defers access to the resource to any writer.

The other change starts at the third line of a writer's exit protocol. The two **if** statements are interchanged so that delayed writers are serviced ahead of delayed readers:

Old	New
...	...
if (rdelay > 0)	if (wdelay > 0)
rwait.V();	wwait.V();
else if (wdelay > 0)	**else if** (rdelay > 0)
wwait.V();	rwait.V();
...	...

Now when a writer leaves, it first checks for waiting writers and servers them before checking for waiting readers.

7.6.4 Solution 3

Probabilistic solutions, like the previous one, are usually unacceptable. In fact, this starvation problem can be solved using a technique from Dekker's algorithm (see

Sect. 6.3.6.1, p. 246). Dekker's algorithm alternates between tasks for simultaneous arrivals, which can be transformed into alternating between a delayed group of readers and a delayed writer for the readers and writer problem. In other words, when there are both delayed readers and writers, alternate service to them to ensure both make progress.

The only change necessary to implement the alternation is to reverse the order of the **if** statements in the writer's exit protocol in the previous solution (i.e., put the code back to the same order as the first solution):

Old	New
...	...
if (wdelay > 0)	**if** (rdelay > 0)
wwait.V();	rwait.V();
else if (rdelay > 0)	**else if** (wdelay > 0)
rwait.V();	wwait.V();
...	...

Now readers check for writers first on leaving and writers check for readers first on leaving, which results in alternation when there are tasks waiting on both semaphores. As well, readers cannot barge ahead of waiting writers in entry the protocol because of the modified condition, and writers cannot barge ahead of readers in the entry protocol because an exiting writer gives priority to readers. Thus, there is no starvation problem.

However, there is another new problem that exists with these three solutions, which was mentioned as a minor problem at the end of Sect. 7.6.2, p. 359. The problem is that a reader task may read information out of temporal order with writer tasks, and therefore, read information that is older than the value should be, called staleness. For example, a reader task arrives at 1:00 but cannot read because at 12:30 a writer arrived and is still writing. Another writer now arrives at 1:30 and then another reader arrives at 2:00; both wait for the current writer to finish, giving:

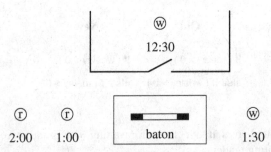

Assuming the current writer finally finishes at 2:30, and the current group of readers is restarted, i.e., the reader that arrived at 1:00 and the reader that arrived at 2:00. Unfortunately, the reader that arrived at 2:00 now reads the value written from 12:30 to 2:30, however it really wants to read the new value from the writer that arrived at 1:30, not the old value that was written starting at 12:30. The problem occurs because *all* readers in a waiting group are restarted regardless of their order of arrival with respect to waiting writers.[2] For some situations, staleness is not a problem; for other situations, staleness can result in logical inconsistencies, e.g., stock trading, or in catastrophic failure, e.g., air-traffic control.

For writer tasks, there is a similar problem with respect to readers, called freshness, if multiple writers are serviced before readers. (This situation happens if there is a temporary starvation scenario where writers are serviced ahead of waiting readers.) In this case, reader tasks always read the freshest data, but may miss reading older, possibly important, values written over by other writers. For some situations, freshness is not a problem; for other situations, freshness can result in problems, e.g., if a reader task is waiting for a particular data value, it may never see it because it is overwritten.

While solutions 1 and 3 suffer from staleness, solution 2 suffers from freshness. This situation occurs because writers have higher priority in solution 2 so many writes may occur while readers are waiting. Therefore, when readers eventually restart, they miss reading older, possibly important, values that have been written over by other writers.

7.6.5   Solutions 4 and 5

The problem with reading data out of order in the previous solutions comes from separating the waiting readers and writers into two queues. For example, at one time banks and airports used a separate line of waiting customers for each bank teller. The problem is that you can arrive ahead of someone else but receive service *after* them because your line is delayed by a long transaction between a customer and the teller. In effect, you are receiving "stale" service (but there is a bound on service: the number of people ahead of you in your line). Stale service can result in real problems not just angry customers. Imagine writing a cheque without sufficient funds to cover the cheque. You rush to the bank to deposit enough money to cover the cheque, but the cheque casher also appears at the bank to cash the cheque. This situation is not a problem because you arrived ahead of them; however, you receive service *after* the cheque casher, and as a result, the cheque bounces (i.e., is not cashed due to insufficient funds). Most banks now use a single line; when a teller becomes free, the person at the head of the line is serviced next. This approach precludes stale service because the single line provides a relative temporal ordering of customers. Notice it is sufficient to know that everyone ahead of you arrived before you and everyone after you arrived after you; it is unnecessary to know the absolute time of arrive of any customer for the scheme to work, and therefore, a clock is unnecessary.

---

[2]This situation is analogous to entering a bank with multiple service queues and tellers, and receiving service after people that arrived later than you, i.e., stale service. The reason for this anomaly is that you selected the queue for a teller that is slow or who must service a client with a large request. This situation is normally solved by using a single service queue with multiple tellers.

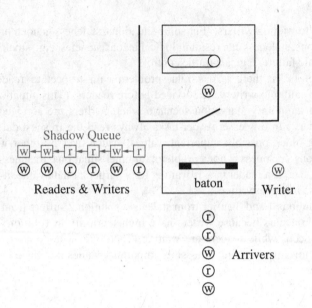

Fig. 7.20 Readers and writer

To mimic this solution in the readers and writer program both readers and writers must block on the same semaphore, which ensures a relative temporal ordering (see Fig. 7.20). Unfortunately, information is lost when readers and writers wait on the same semaphore: it is no longer possible to distinguish whether a waiting task is a reader or writer task. The loss of this information means a reader cannot tell if the next waiting task is a reader or a writer so it does not know if it should wake up the next task. If the reader wakes up a writer, there is no way that the writer can wait again at the *front* of the semaphore because semaphores are usually implemented with FIFO waiting. This point was made with regard to split-binary semaphores in Sect. 7.6.1, p. 356. Two possible solutions are discussed to recover the lost information. Both solutions use a single semaphore to block both readers and writers to maintain relative order of arrival, and hence, prevent stale readers, but each solution uses a different technique to deal with the lack of knowledge about the kind of blocked tasks.

In the first approach (see Fig. 7.21), a reader assumes the next task on the waiting semaphore is a reader and wakes it up. Because of the potential for inadvertently waking a writer, each writer must recheck if it can use the resource. If it cannot use the resource because there are readers still using it, the writer waits again on a special semaphore that has at most one writer task waiting on it (see right side of Fig. 7.20). The special semaphore is given the highest priority whenever the baton is passed so a writer that was inadvertently restarted is always serviced next. Notice, this approach is not busy waiting because there is a bound of at most two checks and blocks for any writer. While viable, this solution requires additional complexity to manage the special semaphore, and additional execution time to block and unblock a writer task if it is inadvertently awakened.

```
uSemaphore entry(1), rwwait(0), wwait(0);
int rwdelay = 0, wdelay = 0, rcnt = 0, wcnt = 0;

void Read() {
    entry.P();                                    // entry protocol
    if ( wcnt > 0 || wdelay > 0 || rwdelay > 0 ) {  // resource in use ?
        rwdelay += 1; entry.V(); rwwait.P(); rwdelay -= 1;
    }
    rcnt += 1;
    if ( rwdelay > 0 )                            // more readers ?
        rwwait.V();                               // pass baton
    else
        entry.V();                                // put baton down

    // READ

    entry.P();                                    // exit protocol
    rcnt -= 1;
    if ( rcnt == 0 ) {                            // last reader ?
        if ( wdelay != 0 )                        // writer waiting ?
            wwait.V();                            // pass baton
        else if ( rwdelay > 0 )                   // anyone waiting ?
            rwwait.V();                           // pass baton
        else
            entry.V();                            // put baton down
    } else
        entry.V();                                // put baton down
}
void Write() {
    entry.P();                                    // entry protocol
    if ( rcnt > 0 || wcnt > 0 ) {                 // resource in use ?
        rwdelay += 1; entry.V(); rwwait.P(); rwdelay -= 1;
        if ( rcnt > 0 ) {                         // wait once more ?
            wdelay += 1; entry.V(); wwait.P(); wdelay -= 1;
        }
    }
    wcnt += 1;
    entry.V();                                    // put baton down

    // WRITE

    entry.P();                                    // exit protocol
    wcnt -= 1;
    if ( rwdelay > 0 )                            // anyone waiting ?
        rwwait.V();                               // pass baton
    else
        entry.V();                                // put baton down
}
```

Fig. 7.21 Readers and writer: solution 4

```
uSemaphore entry(1), rwwait(0);
int rwdelay = 0, rcnt = 0, wcnt = 0;

enum RW { READER, WRITER };        // kinds of tasks
struct RWnode : public uColable {
    RW rw;                          // kind of task
    RWnode( RW rw ) : rw(rw) {}
};
uQueue<RWnode> rwid;                // queue of RWnodes

void Read() {
    entry.P();                      // entry protocol
    if ( wcnt > 0 || rwdelay > 0 ) {    // resource in use ?
        RWnode r( READER );
        rwid.add( &r );             // remember kind of task
        rwdelay += 1; entry.V(); rwwait.P(); rwdelay -= 1;
        rwid.drop();
    }
    rcnt += 1;
    if ( rwdelay > 0 && rwid.head()->rw == READER ) // more readers ?
        rwwait.V();                 // pass baton
    else
        entry.V();                  // put baton down

    // READ

    entry.P();                      // exit protocol
    rcnt -= 1;
    if ( rcnt == 0 && rwdelay > 0 )     // last reader ?
        rwwait.V();                 // pass baton
    else
        entry.V();                  // put baton down
}
void Write() {
    entry.P();                      // entry protocol
    if ( rcnt > 0 || wcnt > 0 ) {       // resource in use ?
        RWnode w( WRITER );
        rwid.add( &w );             // remember kind of task
        rwdelay += 1; entry.V(); rwwait.P(); rwdelay -= 1;
        rwid.drop();
    }
    wcnt += 1;
    entry.V();                      // put baton down

    // WRITE

    entry.P();                      // exit protocol
    wcnt -= 1;
    if ( rwdelay > 0 )              // anyone waiting ?
        rwwait.V();                 // pass baton
    else
        entry.V();                  // put baton down
}
```

Fig. 7.22 Readers and writer: solution 5

The next solution (see Fig. 7.22) is the same as solution 3, but gets back the
lost information when both readers and writers wait on the same semaphore queue
by maintaining an additional *shadow* queue (see left side of Fig. 7.20, p. 366),
which is always the same length as the semaphore queue, and each node of the
additional queue indicates if the corresponding task blocked on the semaphore is
a reader or writer. Maintaining the additional queue can be seen in the program in
both locations where tasks block. A node is created and initialized to the particular
kind of task, and then it is put on the back of the additional queue before the baton
is put down and the task waits on the semaphore. When a waiting task is restarted,
it immediately takes its node off the front of the additional queue. Notice that each
node is not dynamically allocated; it is automatically allocated at the top of the
task's stack before blocking, which is very efficient. The reader entry protocol can
now determine if the task blocked at the front of the semaphore queue is a reader or
writer by examining the value in the node at the front of the additional queue. Note,
it is necessary to check for the existence of a delayed task, i.e., non-empty queue,
before checking the node at the head of the queue or an invalid pointer dereference
occurs. Clearly, this solution only works if the semaphore uses FIFO scheduling of
blocked tasks; if the semaphores used some other scheduling scheme for selecting
tasks from the blocked list (while still maintaining a bound), it would have to be
mimicked precisely otherwise the two lists would get out of synchronization.

Finally, a variation on this solution is for the writer to awaken the next group of
readers to use the resource when it exits the resource rather than have the readers
awaken each other, which is referred to as **multiple unblocking**. The cooperation
for starting multiple readers is moved from the reader's entry protocol:

Old	New
...	...
if (rwdelay > 0 && rwid.head()->rw == READER)	
rwwait.V();	
else	
entry.V();	entry.V();
...	...

to the writer's exit protocol:

Old	New
...	...
if (rwdelay > 0)	**if** (rwdelay > 0)
	while (rwdelay > 0 && rwid.head()->rw == READER)
rwwait.V();	rwwait.V();
else	**else**
entry.V();	entry.V();
...	

While the total work done by each variation is the same, the difference is which
task does the work. The writer task now does more than its share of the cooperation
work, making the latter variation less fair. However, the issue of fairness is always
difficult to judge. Further discussion on this issue appears at the end of Sect. 9.7.2,
p. 464.

7.6.6 Solution 6

Unfortunately, solution 5 does not work. The problem was mentioned earlier in the discussion of the Courtois et al solution; that is, the peculiar problem with non-FIFO order of writers, i.e., one writer can arrive at its entry protocol before another writer but execute *after* it. As a result, writers may execute in a very bizarre sequence, which makes reasoning about the values read by the reader tasks impossible. In all the solutions so far, both the reader and writer entry protocols have a code sequence like the following:

    entry.V(); Xwait.P();

Assume a writer picks up the baton and there are readers currently using the shared resource, so it puts the baton down, entry.V(), but is time-sliced before it can wait, Xwait.P(). Another writer does the same thing, and this can occur to any depth. Now the writers may not restart execution in the same order that they were interrupted, even in a system that places time-sliced tasks at the end of a FIFO ready queue because a double time-slice of the same task can occur before it eventually waits, which means writer tasks may not execute in FIFO order of arrival. This case is *also* a problem for the readers because, even after all the work done in the previous solutions, readers may still read stale information. Assume a reader picks up the baton and there is a writer currently using the shared resource, so it puts the baton down, entry.V(), but is time-sliced before it can wait, Xwait.P(). A writer can then arrive and block on the waiting semaphore ahead of the reader even though the writer arrived at the entry protocol after the reader. This behaviour causes the failure of solution 5 because it is impossible to keep the explicit list of task-kinds, i.e., reader or writer, consistent with the implicit list of blocked tasks on the semaphore rwwait. After a node is added to the explicit list, there is no guarantee the task adding the node is the next to block on the semaphore.

The failure to maintain a temporal ordering of arriving reader and writer tasks is significant. As mentioned, incrementing the rwdelay counter before releasing the protocol semaphore ensures an exiting reader or writer never misses waking up a waiting task. However, the rwdelay counter *does not* control the order tasks wait on Xwait, only that *some* waiting task is awakened. In fact, it is impossible to ensure waiting order with only two semaphores, like entry and Xwait. The proof is straightforward. Semaphore entry must be released (Ved) before waiting on Xwait; reversing the order of these operations does block the waiting task but leaves the entry and exit protocol locked so new tasks cannot enter the system nor can tasks leave the system. Because entry must be released before waiting on Xwait, and there is no control over order or speed of execution, it is always possible for a blocking task to be prevented from blocking for an arbitrary time period, allowing other tasks to barge ahead of it on the waiting queue.

What is needed is a way to atomically block and release the entry lock. The μC++ type uSemaphore provides this capability through an extended P member (see Sect. 7.3.6, p. 344):

    Xwait.P(entry);

which atomically Vs the argument semaphore, entry, and then blocks the calling task if necessary. The implementation of the extended P member is simply:

```
void uSemaphore::P( uSemaphore &s ) { // executed atomically
    s.V();
    P();
}
```

Notice that the task executing the extended P can still be interrupted between the V and P operations. However, any new task that acquires the entry semaphore and rushes to block on the waiting semaphore cannot acquire the waiting semaphore until after the task using it has blocked. By replacing all sequences of the form entry.V(); Xwait.P(); in Fig. 7.21, p. 367 with the form Xwait.P(entry), the problem of stale readers and writers is finally eliminated. Furthermore, it is possible to remove the delay counters and replace them with tests of non-empty semaphores queues (see the discussion at the end of Sect. 7.6.2, p. 359). Unfortunately, most semaphores do not provide such an extended P operation; therefore, it is important to find a solution using only the traditional semaphore operations.

One possible, but very inefficient, solution is to have the reader and writer tasks take a ticket before putting the baton down (like the hardware solution in Sect. 6.4.4, p. 278). To pass the baton, a serving counter is first incremented and then all tasks blocked on the semaphore are woken up. Each task then compares its ticket value with the serving value, and proceeds if the values are equal and blocks otherwise. Starvation is not an issue because the waiting queue is a bounded length. This approach uses the fact that a task establishes its FIFO position as soon as it takes a ticket, which is independent of when the task tries to block on the waiting semaphore; even if a task is time-sliced multiple times before it can block on the waiting semaphore, no other tasks can make progress because their ticket value is not being served. Unfortunately, the cost of waking up all waiting tasks for each baton pass is prohibitively expensive. In fact, this is largely the solution that people use with tickets and a server in a store. When the server increments the server counter, everyone checks their ticket, but only the person with the matching ticket goes to the counter for service. Notice, each person must be vigilant, otherwise they will be skipped over, and therefore, it is difficult to do other work, such as reading a book, while waiting. (How could cooperation be used to allow waiting people to read their books without missing their turn?)

An efficient solution is possible by introducing a **private semaphore** for each task instead of having one semaphore on which the readers and writers wait (see Fig. 7.23). (This approach is similar to the private busy waiting flag in the MCS hardware solution in Sect. 6.4.5, p. 281.) Initially, this seems wrong because stale readers occurred in previous solutions using separate waiting semaphores for the readers and writers. To ensure FIFO service, the queue indicating the kind of waiting task, i.e., reader or writer, is used like the ticket in the previous solution but with cooperation. Before putting the baton down, a reader or writer creates a node containing the kind of task and a private semaphore on which it waits, and puts the node on the tail of the queue. The task then attempts to block on its private semaphore. To pass the baton, the private semaphore at the head of the queue is Ved,

```
uSemaphore entry(1);
int rcnt = 0, wcnt = 0;

enum RW { READER, WRITER };        // kinds of tasks
struct RWnode : public uColable {
    RW rw;                          // kind of task
    uSemaphore sem;                 // private semaphore
    RWnode( RW rw ) : rw(rw), sem(0) {}
};
uQueue<RWnode> rwid;               // queue of RWnodes

void Read() {
    entry.P();                      // entry protocol
    if ( wcnt > 0 || ! rwid.empty() ) {   // resource in use ?
        RWnode r( READER );
        rwid.add( &r );             // remember kind of task
        entry.V(); r.sem.P();
        rwid.drop();
    }
    rcnt += 1;
    if ( ! rwid.empty() && rwid.head()->rw == READER ) // more readers ?
        rwid.head()->sem.V();       // pass baton
    else
        entry.V();                  // put baton down

    // READ

    entry.P();                      // exit protocol
    rcnt -= 1;
    if ( rcnt == 0 && ! rwid.empty() )    // last reader ?
        rwid.head()->sem.V();       // pass baton
    else
        entry.V();                  // put baton down
}
void Write() {
    entry.P();                      // entry protocol
    if ( rcnt > 0 || wcnt > 0 ) {   // resource in use ?
        RWnode w( WRITER );
        rwid.add( &w );             // remember kind of task
        entry.V(); w.sem.P();
        rwid.drop();
    }
    wcnt += 1;
    entry.V();                      // put baton down

    // WRITE

    entry.P();                      // exit protocol
    wcnt -= 1;
    if ( ! rwid.empty() )           // anyone waiting ?
        rwid.head()->sem.V();       // pass baton
    else
        entry.V();                  // put baton down
}
```

Fig. 7.23 Readers and writer: solution 6

if present. If the task associated with the private semaphore is blocked, it is woken up. If the task is not blocked yet because of a time-slice, the V is remembered by the semaphore and the task does not need to block when it eventually executes the P. Notice that it no longer matters if a task is time-sliced (one or more times) between putting the baton down and waiting. Once a task puts its node on the list it establishes its FIFO position in the queue (like taking a ticket), which is independent of when the task tries to block on its private semaphore, and only one task attempts to block on each private semaphore so it is immaterial whether the semaphore implementation unblocks task in FIFO or non-FIFO order. The cooperation comes from the fact that the exiting task (server) knows who has the next ticket (i.e., the task at the front of the queue) and can wake them directly.

Clearly, the cost of creating and deleting the private semaphore is greater than having an extended P that atomically blocks and releases another semaphore. Subsequent discussion comes back to this special form of P to generate an efficient solution. Nevertheless, it is possible to construct a correct readers and writer solution using only a traditional semaphore.

7.6.7 Solution 7

Fig. 7.24 shows an ad-hoc solution with little or no use of split-binary semaphores and baton-passing. That is, the solution is specialized to the readers/writer problem and the technique is unlikely to work with other problems. The key observation is that the entry semaphore already blocks the threads in temporal order, and hence, there is no need to shift them onto a reader/writer queue in the same order. Like solution 4, one writer waits on a special semaphore until readers leave the resource. *The waiting writer blocks holding the baton to force other arriving tasks to wait on entry, which violates normal baton rules, but forces arriving threads to queue onto the* entry *semaphore.* The semaphore lock is used only for mutual exclusion to adjust the counters. Both entry and lock start open, which violates the split-binary semaphore rule as the sum of the counters is greater than 1. Note, the locks are always released in the reverse order of acquisition. Is temporal order preserved? Yes, there is no moving of tasks from one blocking list to another except for the special case of one writer moving to high-priority writer queue (private semaphore). While this solution is the shortest, it is harder to reason about correctness because there is no pattern in the solution.

7.7 Summary

A spin lock is an abstraction for some hardware-level mutual-exclusion facility. The difference between a spinning and blocking lock occurs when a task cannot acquire the lock: the task's state remains running/ready versus blocked. Many different kinds

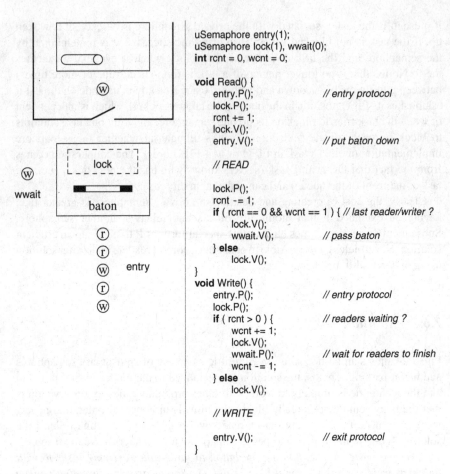

```
uSemaphore entry(1);
uSemaphore lock(1), wwait(0);
int rcnt = 0, wcnt = 0;

void Read() {
    entry.P();                      // entry protocol
    lock.P();
    rcnt += 1;
    lock.V();
    entry.V();                      // put baton down

    // READ

    lock.P();
    rcnt -= 1;
    if ( rcnt == 0 && wcnt == 1 ) {  // last reader/writer ?
        lock.V();
        wwait.V();                  // pass baton
    } else
        lock.V();
}
void Write() {
    entry.P();                      // entry protocol
    lock.P();
    if ( rcnt > 0 ) {               // readers waiting ?
        wcnt += 1;
        lock.V();
        wwait.P();                  // wait for readers to finish
        wcnt -= 1;
    } else
        lock.V();

    // WRITE

    entry.V();                      // exit protocol
}
```

Fig. 7.24 Readers and writer: solution 7

of locks have been built, each providing more functionality to support complex synchronization and mutual exclusion. Regardless of the sophistication of a lock, they all begin to reach their complexity limit fairly quickly. For example, using a counting semaphore produces an efficient solution for communication among tasks through a buffer, but still not a particularly elegant one because of all the globally shared information. The semaphore solutions for the readers and writer problem are complex enough that reasoning about their correctness is difficult. Also, some of these solutions assume that tasks blocked on a semaphore are released in FIFO order, which may not be true in all concurrent systems. Therefore, it is necessary to examine other approaches that can simplify some of the complexity. However, there are cases where efficiency is paramount so that spinning and blocking locks provide the best solutions, but in general, this is infrequent.

7.8   Questions

1. What is a spinlock and what does it mean for it to be yielding or non-yielding?
2. What is busy waiting and why is it a particularly bad way of waiting in a single-processor multi-threading environment?
3. Explain, in general, two ways of reducing busy waiting.
4. Use the fetchInc instruction as defined in Sect. 6.4.4, p. 278 to build a barrier lock with the following public interface (you may only add a public destructor and private members). The solution may use busy waiting and must deal with starvation.

   ```
   class Barrier {
       Barrier( unsigned int total );
       void block();
   };
   ```

   which is used as follows:

   ```
   Barrier b( 3 );
   b.block(); // synchronize with other tasks
   ```

5. The following is a collection of assignments:

$$S_1 \; : \; B \leftarrow A$$
$$S_2 \; : \; C \leftarrow B$$
$$S_3 \; : \; A \leftarrow A + 1$$
$$S_4 \; : \; D \leftarrow C + 1$$
$$S_5 \; : \; E \leftarrow B + D$$
$$S_6 \; : \; F \leftarrow D + A$$
$$S_7 \; : \; G \leftarrow E + F$$

Thus the environment consists of seven variables. Initially, the environment is in the following state:

$$A = 1, B = 2, C = 3, D = 4, E = 5, F = 6, G = 7$$

Throughout the following questions, assume that each of the statements is executed atomically; that is, once a statement begins executing, it finishes without interference from other statements.

- If statements 1 through 7 above are executed sequentially, what is the final state of the environment?
- Draw a precedence graph for the statements, showing the maximum amount of parallelism that can be obtained in executing these statements while obtaining the same results as sequential execution.
- Suppose that the assignments are grouped into two processes: one process consists of statements 1 through 6, in that order, while the other consists of statement 7. The two processes execute concurrently (but remember that each statement executes atomically). What are the possible final states of the environment?

6. Assume a concurrency system that has only a binary semaphore, bSem, with member routines P and V, respectively. Use the binary semaphore to build a counting semaphore, cSem, with member routines P and V, respectively. Efficiency is not an issue, i.e., busy waiting is allowed.

7. The following code sequence exists in the entry protocols for readers/writer implementations, where the baton is put down and a thread blocks:

    entry.V(); X.P(); // X is some semaphore

    Explain, in general, how this code sequence may result in staleness or freshness.

8. A PRAM (pronounced "pee-ram") is one mathematical model that is used to design algorithms for computers that use massive parallelism. Massively parallel computers have not just dozens of processors, but thousands. The difficulty is to figure out how these thousands of processors can most efficiently be used to solve problems. In this question, you are to simulate a PRAM running an algorithm for finding the maximum of n distinct integers.

    A good (fast) PRAM algorithm for finding the maximum of n distinct integers x_1, x_2, ..., x_n is as follows. Initialize an array of flags NotMax[] with n entries to FALSE. Assume the PRAM has enough processors that it can assign one to each distinct pair of integers. Let $P(i,j)$ be the processor assigned to the pair (x_i, x_j) where $1 \le i < j \le n$. $P(i,j)$ compares x_i to x_j. After this comparison, $P(i,j)$ knows which one of the two could not be the maximum, for example, if $x_j < x_i$ then x_j could not be the maximum. After determining which of the two could not be the maximum, $P(i,j)$ writes a TRUE to the NotMax flag for that integer, for example, if $x_j < x_i$ then set NotMax[j] to TRUE.

    After each processor has done this, all but one of the NotMax[] flags will be TRUE. The one that is FALSE tells which integer is the maximum. To find which flag is FALSE, assign one processor to each flag in NotMax[]. Exactly one of these processors will find that its flag is FALSE, and that processor can write the maximum integer into some chosen location.

    You are to implement this algorithm as follows:

    - Input a list of numbers x_1 to x_n from standard input. The list is terminated with a -1 value. Assume that n is not known in advance.
    - Create the PRAM. This means that you generate as many processes as you will need to run the algorithm. Do not allow any process to start its PRAM algorithm until all processes are created.
    - Run the PRAM algorithm to find the maximum. Let each process die after completing its algorithm.
    - Return to Step 1 again, until the end of file is reached.

    Things to Note: Use as much parallelism as possible! For each set of integers, create an appropriate number of processes. Do not create any more than you actually use. Create the processes in an efficient way. Do not let any process start its PRAM algorithm until all needed processes are created, i.e., have a synchronized start. A correct program will end up having at least two synchronization points (three if you are smart). Handling the synchronization is the interesting part of this question, the rest is fairly easy. If every process writing to a shared variable is trying to write the same thing, then you do not have to worry about mutual exclusion among the writers. You may use only semaphores to solve this question.

9. This is a modified version of the Cigarette Smokers Problem[3] [Patil71]. There are N smokers; each smoker repeatedly makes a cigarette and smokes it. To smoke a cigarette, 3 ingredients are needed: paper, tobacco and a match. Interestingly, smokers are divided into three kinds:

   a) one has an infinite supply of papers and matches,
   b) another an infinite supply of tobacco and matches,
   c) and finally an infinite supply of tobacco and papers.

   On a table accessible to all the smokers is a tobacco pouch with an infinite amount of tobacco, a package of cigarette papers with an infinite number of papers, and a box of matches with an infinite number of matches. A smoker goes to the table and chooses the ingredient needed to smoke a cigarette (depending on which kind of smoker it is), takes the ingredient off the table, uses it to make and light a cigarette, puts the ingredient back on the table, and finally smokes the cigarette. If a smoker arrives at the table and the ingredient needed is unavailable, they must wait (i.e., block) at the table until the ingredient is returned (busy-waiting is not allowed).

   Each smoker has the following interface (you may add only a public destructor and private members):

```
_Task Smoker {
  public:
    enum States { Needs, Blocking, Smoking };
    Smoker( Table<NoOfKinds> &table,     // shared table, NoOfKinds is number of kinds
            const unsigned int Id,        // smoker identifier, value between 0 and N-1
            Printer &printer              // OPTIONAL, depends on printing location
    );
};
```

   A smoker begins by randomly choosing which kind of smoker it will be for its lifetime (one of the 3 kinds above); a value from 0–2. Next, the smoker randomly chooses the number of cigarettes it will smoke during its lifetime; a value between 0–19. Then the smoker begins obtaining ingredients to make and smoke the specified number of cigarettes, which involves the following conceptual steps for each cigarette:

   a) obtain the package with the necessary ingredient from the table
   b) removed the ingredient from the package (randomly yield between 0–2 times)
   c) return the package to the table
   d) make and smoke the cigarette (randomly yield between 0–9 times)

   (Yielding multiple times is performed by calling task member yield(N).)

---

[3]Now politically incorrect.

The interface for the table is (you may add only a public destructor and private members):

```
template<unsigned int kinds> class Table {
  public:
    Table( Printer &printer );
    void acquire( unsigned int Id, unsigned int kind );
    void release( unsigned int Id, unsigned int kind );
};
```

The number of kinds of smokers is passed to the table via the template parameter. (Essentially, the table does not need to know about the meaning of the different kinds of tasks.) A smoker calls the acquire member, passing its identification and kind of smoker, to obtain the package containing the missing ingredient needed to smoke a cigarette. The acquire member blocks the smoker if the particular package is currently unavailable. After conceptually removing the needed ingredient from the package, the smoker calls the release member to return the package to the table, and then pretends to smoke a cigarette. Verify the kind argument to acquire and release is in the range 0 to kinds-1; if it is invalid, print an appropriate message and exit the program. Use semaphores (uSemaphore) to provide synchronization and mutual exclusion; all of the uSemaphore member routines are allowed except lock1.P(lock2).

All output from the program is generated by calls to a printer, excluding error messages. The interface for the printer is (you may add only a public destructor and private members):

```
_Monitor / _Cormonitor Printer {
  public:
    Printer( unsigned int NoOfTasks );
    void print( unsigned int Id, Smoker::States state, unsigned int kind );
};
```

(You do not need to know the details of a _Monitor or _Cormonitor; treat it as either a class or coroutine with the magic property that only one task can execute it at a time. Choose between them based on whether you need coroutine properties to implement the printer. Note, the coroutine main of a _Cormonitor *must* be a **private** member.) The printer attempts to reduce output by storing information for each smoker until one of the stored elements is overwritten. When information is going to be overwritten, all the stored information is flushed and storing starts again. Output should look similar to the following:

line no	output		
	S0	S1	S2
1	N P	N T	N T*
2	S P*		B
3	N P*	S T	
4	S P		
5	N P		
6	S P	N T*	S T
7	N P*	S T	
8	S P		
9	N P		
10	S P		
11	N P		
12	S P		

Each column is assigned to a smoker with an appropriate title, e.g., "S0". A column entry is the state transition for that smoker, containing one of the following states:

State	Meaning
N k	need resource k, where k is T (tobacco), M (matches), P (paper)
B	blocking for a resource
S k	smoking, acquired a k resource from the table to start

The asterisk * marks the prior buffer information for the task causing the buffered data to be flushed. That is, the * on line i appears above the value on line $i + 1$ that caused the buffer to be flushed. The buffer is cleared by a flush so previously stored values do not appear when the next task flushes the buffer and an empty column is printed. For example, in the first line of the above output, S2 has the value "N T" in its buffer slot, and all the other buffer slots are full. When S2 attempts to print "B", which overwrites its current buffer value of "N T", the buffer must be flushed and a * is placed beside its "N T" to indicate that S2 caused the flush. S2's new value of "B" appears on the next line. Note, a * is **NOT** printed again for consecutive state transitions by the same task causing a flush (see lines 4–5 and 8–12). In the second line of the example, the buffer begins filling with values, until S0 needs to overwrite its value of "S P" with "N P"; the buffer is flushed with an * beside the "S P" value for S0, and S0's new value of "N P" is placed in the buffer. Then S1 places a new value of "S T" into the buffer. S0's next value of "S P" causes a flush *and* a * because there was an intervening insertion by S1. All output spacing can be accomplished using the standard 8-space tabbing, so it is unnecessary to build and store strings of text for output. Calls to perform printing may be performed from the table and/or a smoker task (you decide where to print).

The executable program is named smokers and has the following shell interface:

smokers [*no-of-smokers (1-10)*]

(Square brackets indicate optional command line parameters, and do not appear on the actual command line.) if no value is given for the number of smokers, assume 5. Assume the value is a valid integer, but check if it is in the range 1–10, and print an appropriate usage message and exit the program if outside the range.

10. The sleeping barber is a problem proposed by E. W. Dijkstra. A barber shop has a cutting room with one chair and a waiting room with N chairs. The waiting room has an entrance, and next to the entrance is the cutting room with the barber's chair; the entrances to the waiting and cutting room share the same sliding door, which always closes one of them. The sliding door ensures that when the barber opens the door to see if anyone is waiting, a new customer cannot simultaneously enter the room and not be seen.

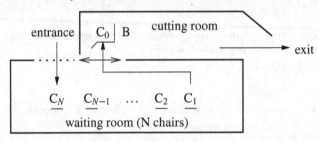

When the barber arrives or finishes a haircut, he opens the door to the waiting room and checks for waiting customers. If the waiting room is not empty, he invites the next customer (first-in first-out (FIFO) service order) for a haircut, otherwise he goes to sleep in the barber's chair.

Customers enter the waiting room one at a time if space is available; otherwise, they go to another shop (called balking). If a customer finds the waiting room is not empty, they wait their turn in the waiting room; if the waiting room is empty, the customer opens the door to the cutting room to see if the barber is there but sleeping. If the barber is not there, the customer closes the door and sits down in the waiting room to wait for the barber to appear; otherwise, the customer leaves the cutting-room door open, wakes the barber, and sits down in the waiting room waiting for the barber to wakeup and get ready.

Implement the barber shop using μC++ semaphores to provide mutual exclusion and synchronization. The implementation may not use busy waiting. The interface for the barber shop is (you may add only a public destructor and private members):

```
class BarberShop {
  public:
    BarberShop( Printer &prt, const unsigned int MaxWaitingCust );
    void hairCut( int id );                  // called by customer
    int startCut();                          // called by barber
    void endCut();                           // called by barber
};
```

A customer calls the hairCut member to enter the barber shop. The barber calls the startCut member to obtain the next customer; if there are no customers, the barber goes to sleep (blocks). startCut returns the customer identifier for a waiting customer. The barber calls endCut after completing the haircut.

The interface for the barber is (you may add only a public destructor and private members):

```
_Task Barber {
    void main();
  public:
    Barber( Printer &prt, BarberShop &bs, unsigned int cutDelay );
};
```

The barber begins by randomly (use rand) yielding between [0-cutDelay) times so it may not arrive before the first customers start entering the barber shop. (Yielding is performed by calling task member yield(N).) The barber repeats the following steps: call startCut in the barber shop to get customer, randomly yield between [0-cutDelay) times to simulate the haircut, call endCut in the barber shop to indicate ending of haircut. The barber terminates when he receives a customer identifier of -1 from startCut.

The interface for a customer is (you may add only a public destructor and private members):

```
_Task Customer {
    void main();
  public:
    Customer( Printer &prt, BarberShop &bs, unsigned int id, unsigned int custDelay );
};
```

A customer begins by randomly yielding between [0-custDelay) times so the customers arrive at the barber shop at random times. A customer makes a single call to hairCut in the barber shop to get a haircut. A customer does not restart until the barber has completed their haircut, i.e., only restarts after the barber calls endCut for the customer.

All output from the program is generated by calls to a printer, excluding error messages. The interface for the printer is (you may add only a public destructor and private members):

```
_Monitor / _Cormonitor Printer {
    void main();
  public:
    Printer( const unsigned int MaxWaitingCust );
    void barber( char status );          // called by barber
    void customer( int id );             // called by customer
};
```

(You do not need to know the details of a _Cormonitor; treat it solely as a coroutine with the magic property that only task can execute it at a time. Note, the coroutine main of a _Cormonitor *must* be a private member.) Figure 7.25 shows two example outputs from different runs of the program. The output consists of four columns:

Barber	Cutting	Balked	Waiting
AGS			
			3
C	3		
			0
GC	0		
			7
			7 17
			7 17 14
G			
		2	
C	7		17 14
			17 14 13
GC	17		14 13
			14 13 8
		10	
		15	
GC	14		13 8
GC	13		8
			8 6
			8 6 9
GC	8		6 9
			6 9 16
GC	6		9 16
			9 16 18
		11	
GC	9		16 18
GC	16		18
			18 5
GC	18		5
GC	5		
			4
			4 12
			4 12 19
GC	4		12 19
GC	12		19
			19 1
GC	19		1
GC	1		
GS			
			-1
C	-1		
F			

% sleepingbarber 3 20 5 100

Barber	Cutting	Balked	Waiting
			6
			6 12
AGC	6		12
GC	12		
			7
			7 15
			7 15 10
GC	7		15 10
			15 10 1
GC	15		10 1
GC	10		1
			1 19
G			
			1 19 14
C	1		19 14
			19 14 4
GC	19		14 4
			14 4 8
GC	14		4 8
GC	4		8
			8 5
			8 5 13
		17	
		3	
G			
		16	
		2	
C	8		5 13
			5 13 0
GC	5		13 0
GC	13		0
GC	0		
GS			
			18
C	18		
			11
GC	11		
			9
GC	9		
GS			
			-1
C	-1		
F			

Fig. 7.25 Sleeping barber: example output

a. barber states
A   arrival at the barber shop (after initial yields)
G   attempting to get a customer from the waiting room
S   going to sleep in the barber chair waiting for a customer
C   cutting a customer's hair
F   leaving the barber shop
The printer reduces output by condensing *consecutive* barber state-changes along a single line.

b. customer having haircut
c. customer balked because waiting room is full
d. list of customers in the waiting room

All printing must occur in the coroutine main, i.e., no printing can occur in the coroutine's member routines. All output spacing can be accomplished using the standard 8-space tabbing, so it is unnecessary to build and store strings of text for output. Calls to perform printing may be performed in the barber-shop members or in the barber/customer tasks (you decide where to print).

The shell interface to the sleepingbarber program is as follows:

sleepingbarber [MaxWaitingCust [NoOfCusts [CutDelay [CustDelay [RandomSeed]]]]]

(Square brackets indicate optional command line parameters, and do not appear on the actual command line.) Where the meaning of each parameter is:

MaxWaitingCust: maximum number of customers that can wait in the barber shop waiting room, i.e., MaxWaitingCust equals N chairs. The default value if unspecified is 5.

NoOfCusts: number of customers attempting to obtain a haircut during a run of the program. The default value if unspecified is 20.

CutDelay: number of times the barber yields to simulate the time required to cut a customer's hair. The default value if unspecified is 2.

CustDelay: number of times a customer yields *before* attempting entry to the barber shop. The default value if unspecified is 40.

RandomSeed: initial seed value for the random number generator set using routine srand. When given a specific seed value, the program must generate the same results for each invocation. You must also make the following call uThisProcessor().setPreemption(0) to turn off preemptive timeslicing. If the seed is unspecified, use a random value like the process identifier (getpid) or current time (time), so each run of the program generates different output.

Assume all arguments are valid positive integer values, i.e., no error checking is required.

uMain::main creates the printer, barber shop, barber and NoOfCusts customer tasks. After all the customer tasks have terminated, uMain::main calls hairCut with a customer identifier of −1.

11. a. Implement a generalized FIFO bounded-buffer for a producer/consumer problem with the following interface (you may add only a public destructor and private members):

```
template<typename T> class BoundedBuffer {
  public:
    BoundedBuffer( const unsigned int size = 10 );
    void insert( T elem );
    T remove();
};
```

which creates a bounded buffer of size size, and supports multiple producers and consumers. You may *only* use uCondLock and uOwnerLock to implement the necessary synchronization and mutual exclusion needed by the bounded buffer.

Implement the BoundedBuffer in the following ways:

i. Use busy waiting when waiting for buffer entries to become free or empty. In this approach, new tasks may barge into the buffer taking free or empty entries from tasks that have been signalled to access these entries. This implementation uses one owner and two condition locks, where the waiting producer and consumer tasks block on the separate condition locks. (If necessary, you may add more locks.) The reason there is barging in this solution is that uCondLock::wait re-acquires its argument owner-lock before returning. Now once the owner-lock is released by a task exiting insert or remove, there is a race to acquire the lock by a new task calling insert/remove and by a signalled task. If the calling task wins the race, it barges ahead of any signalled task. So the state of the buffer at the time of the signal is not the same as the time the signalled task re-acquires the argument owner-lock, because the barging task changes the buffer. Hence, the signalled task may have to wait again (looping), and there is no guarantee of eventual progress (long-term starvation).

ii. Use *no* busy waiting when waiting for buffer entries to become free or empty; in this approach, new (barging) tasks must be prevented from taking free or empty entries if tasks have been unblocked to access these entries. This implementation uses one owner and three condition locks, where the waiting producer, consumer, and barging tasks block on the separate condition locks, and (*has no looping*). (If necessary, you may add more locks.) Hint, one way to prevent barging is to use a flag variable to indicate when signalling is occurring; entering tasks test the flag to know if they are barging and wait on the barging condition-lock. When signalling is finished, barging tasks are unblocked. (Other solutions to prevent barging are allowed but loops are not allowed.)

Before inserting or removing an item to/from the buffer, perform an assert that checks if the buffer is not full or not empty, respectively. Both buffer implementations are defined in a single .h file separated in the following way:

```
#ifdef BUSY                    // busy waiting implementation
// implementation
#endif // BUSY

#ifdef NOBUSY                  // no busy waiting implementation
// implementation
#endif // NOBUSY
```

Test the bounded buffer with a number of producers and consumers. The producer interface is:

```
_Task Producer {
    void main();
  public:
    Producer( BoundedBuffer<BTYPE> &buffer, const int Produce,
              const int Delay );
};
```

The producer generates Produce integers, from 1 to Produce inclusive, and inserts them into buffer. Before producing an item, a producer randomly yields between 0 and Delay-1 times. Yielding is accomplished by calling yield(times) to give up a task's CPU time-slice a number of times. The consumer interface is:

```
_Task Consumer {
    void main();
  public:
    Consumer( BoundedBuffer<BTYPE> &buffer, const int Delay,
              const BTYPE Sentinel, BTYPE &sum );
};
```

The consumer removes items from buffer, and terminates when it removes a Sentinel value from the buffer. A consumer sums all the values it removes from buffer (excluding the Sentinel value) and returns this value through the reference variable sum. Before removing an item, a consumer randomly yields between 0 and Delay-1 times.

uMain::main creates the bounded buffer, the producer and consumer tasks. Use a buffer-element type, BTYPE, of int and a sentinel value of -1 for testing. After all the producer tasks have terminated, uMain::main inserts an appropriate number of sentinel values (the default sentinel value is -1) into the buffer to terminate the consumers. The partial sums from each consumer are totalled to produce the sum of all values generated by the producers. Print this total in the following way:

```
total: ddddd
```

The sum must be the same regardless of the order or speed of execution of the producer and consumer tasks.

The shell interface for the boundedBuffer program is:

```
boundedBuffer [ Cons [ Prods [ Produce [ BufferSize [ Delays ] ] ] ] ]
```

(Square brackets indicate optional command line parameters, and do not appear on the actual command line.) Where the meaning of each parameter is:

Cons: positive number of consumers to create. The default value if unspec-
           ified is 5.

Prods: positive number of producers to create. The default value if unspec-
           ified is 3.

Produce: positive number of items generated by each producer. The default
           value if unspecified is 10.

BufferSize: positive number of elements in (size of) the bounder buffer. The
           default value if unspecified is 10.

Delays: positive number of times a producer/consumer yields *before* insert-
ing/removing an item into/from the buffer. The default value if unspecified is Cons + Prods.

Use the following monitor to safely generate random values (monitors will
be discussed shortly):

```
_Monitor MPRNG {
public:
    MPRNG( unsigned int seed = 1009 ) { srand( seed ); }       // set seed
    void seed( unsigned int seed ) { srand( seed ); }          // set seed
    unsigned int operator()() { return rand(); }               // [0,UINT_MAX]
    unsigned int operator()( unsigned int u ) { return operator()()%(u+1); } // [0,u]
    unsigned int operator()( unsigned int l, unsigned int u ) {
                        return operator()( u - l ) + l; } // [l,u]
};
```

Check all command arguments for correct form (integers) and range; print an
appropriate usage message and terminate the program if a value is missing
or invalid.

b. i. Compare the busy and non-busy waiting versions of the program with
    respect to performance by doing the following:

    • Time the execution using the time command:

    ```
    % time ./a.out
    3.21u 0.02s 0:03.32 100.0%
    ```

    (Output from time differs depending on your shell, but all provide user,
    system and real time.) Compare the *user* time (3.21u) only, which is
    the CPU time consumed solely by the execution of user code (versus
    system and real time).

    • Use the program command-line arguments 50 55 10000 30 10 and
    adjust the Produce amount (if necessary) to get execution times in
    the range 0.1 to 100 s. (Timing results below 0.1 s are inaccurate.)
    Use the same command-line values for all experiments.

    • Run both the experiments again after recompiling the programs with
    compiler optimization turned on (i.e., compiler flag -O2). Include all
    4 timing results to validate your experiments.

    ii. State the observed performance difference between busy and nobusy
    waiting execution, without and with optimization.

    iii. Speculate as to the reason for the performance difference between busy
    and nobusy waiting execution.

    iv. Add the following declaration to uMain::main after checking command-
    line arguments but before creating any tasks:

    ```
    #ifdef __U_MULTI__
    uProcessor p[3] __attribute__(( unused )); // create 3 kernel thread for total of 4
    #endif // __U_MULTI__
    ```

    to increase the number of kernel threads to access multiple processors.
    This declaration must be in the same scope as the declaration of the
    producer and consumer tasks. Compile the program with the -multi flag
    and no optimization on a multi-core computer with at least 4 CPUs

(cores), and run the same experiment as above. Include timing results to validate your experiment.

v. State the observed performance difference between uniprocessor and multiprocessor execution.

vi. Speculate as to the reason for the performance difference between uniprocessor and multiprocessor execution.

12. There are n children, all of whom eat Sema Four Grain Cereal, each box of which contains a plastic toy. The toys come in j styles and each style comes in k colours. Since it cannot be determined without opening the package (and removing most of the cereal) what style/colour combination is in a given box, and equal numbers of the $j * k$ style/colour combinations were produced, the effect of buying a box of cereal is to make a uniform random selection among $j * k$ alternatives. Even for quite small values of j and k, it can take rather a long time to accumulate a complete set (and, of course, before long the cereal manufacturer will switch to a completely different kind of toy). Therefore, the n children trade the toys among themselves in order to get a complete set sooner. (Each child starts with two toys, whose styles and colours are randomly determined.)

You are to simulate this trading activity. The simulation has one task for each child and at least two additional tasks as specified below; additional tasks may be used if you wish. The interface for the child task is:

```
_Task Child {
  public:
    Child( int whoami, ToyBox &toybox );
    ~Child();
};
```

Restrict the trading so that each child offers at most one toy for trading at a time, though multiple independent trades must be capable of being conducted simultaneously. All communication among tasks is done through a shared data-area. The interface for the shared data-area is:

```
class ToyBox {
  public:
    ToyBox( const int nChildren, const int nStyles, const int nColours );
    ~ToyBox();
    void wakeChildren();                      // Toymaker signals toy creation complete
    void wakeEverybody();                     // Wakes sleeping tasks when game is over
    void putChildToSleep( int who );          // Child calls to block until gets toy
    void putToyMakerToSleep();                // Toymaker calls to block
    void wakeToyMaker();                      // Timer wakes up toymaker
    void receiveToy( int who, Toy newToy );   // Toymaker gives toy to someone from toybox
    Toy  findTradeToy( int who );             // Child finds trade toy
    void tradeToy( int who, Toy newToy );     // Child trades toy or blocks if no trade partner
    int  isWinnerYet();                       // Has a winner been declared yet?
};
```

If you wish, a toy may be offered for trade for "any other" or for a more restricted possible set of exchanges, but the information given (at least on any single trade offer) must not reveal the current holdings of the trader, i.e., the other children should not be assumed to be completely co-operative. The tasks interact through shared storage protected by semaphores. Thus, you will likely have a storage area for each "child" task indicating whether that child is currently offering a toy for trading, what that toy is, and what restrictions have been put on the toy to be traded for it. An associated semaphore is used to protect access and modification of the area. Similarly, semaphores are used to block tasks, notably child tasks that are waiting for a suitable trade to be offered.

Another per-child storage area within the ToyBox, protected by a semaphore, is used to pass new toys to a child. It is possible that a child fails to pick up a toy from this area before the next toy arrives. (This is likely to be a bug, but it could be the result of unfortunate parameter settings and an overload of trading activity.) In such a case, it is legitimate for the toy-generation task to discard the new toy. In designing the use of shared storage and semaphores in your program, be sure to use the class mechanism of C++ appropriately, rather than using an arbitrary collection of global variables.

The ToyMaker task creates new toys (i.e., finding the toy in the cereal box). It periodically generates a new toy for each child. The new toys can be for all children simultaneously or a toy may be generated for child 1, followed by a delay, then a toy for child 2, a delay, and so on, provided each child gets toys at approximately the same rate. A pseudo-random number generator is used to determine the style and colour of the new toy. If a child task is blocked waiting for a trade when a new toy is generated, the toy-generation task must unblock it to accept the new toy. The interface for the toy maker is:

```
_Task ToyMaker {
  public:
    ~ToyMaker();
    ToyMaker( ToyBox &toybox, const int nChildren, const int nStyles,
              const int nColours );
};
```

Every time it wakes, or every mth times it wakes for some m you select, it generates a new toy or set of toys.

One additional task provides a simulated timing facility. It is used to implement the "periodic" aspect of the ToyMaker task. The interface for the timer task is:

```
_Task Timer {
  public:
    Timer( const int delay, ToyBox &toybox );          // Constructor
    ~Timer();
};
```

The timing task contains a loop with a yield(newdelay) followed by a call to wakeToyMaker to "wakes up" the toy-generation task. You do not need to use the timing task for any other purpose, but you are required to implement it separately from the toy-generation task to keep open the possibility of using it for other purposes. For example, you could use it to unblock child tasks that have been blocked for rather a long time, allowing the child to select an alternative toy to offer for trading. Note that such unblocking is not a requirement of the assignment, although unblocking on arrival of a new toy is required.

Stop the simulation as soon as any child obtains a complete set of toys. Print out the identity of the child that has a complete set, the exact holdings of each child, and the total number of toys held by all. Note that you need to shut down all tasks to terminate your program cleanly. This requirement means each child task must be informed a complete set has been obtained, unblocking it if it is currently blocked, and the timing and toy-generation tasks must also be told to terminate. You are to decide the most appropriate means to use in informing your various tasks that they should terminate. You must provide appropriate trace output showing the arrival of new toys and all trading activity, so that the actions of the program can be followed. The precise form of the trace output is not specified here; designing good trace output is part of the assignment. Note that thoroughness and conciseness are both desirable properties of trace output. You should provide a trace that contains substantial information that is genuinely useful, but not excessive information or information presented in an unnecessarily verbose fashion.

Name your program toys. The number of children may be compiled into your program, but must be easy to change. Use the value $n = 4$ for testing. Other parameters are specified on the command line:

toys j k [seed]

The parameters j and k are as specified above; each must be a positive integer. The parameter seed specifies the seed value for the random-number generator. The last parameter is optional, the other two are required. You may assume that the syntax of the command line is correct in that the appropriate number of integer values will be present. If the seed parameter is omitted, a value is generated in the program. (Check the documentation for the random-number generator you choose to determine whether there are restrictions on seed values.)

Test your program using reasonably small parameter values, for example $j = 2$ and $k = 3$, to avoid excessive execution and trace output before a complete set of toys is achieved by some child. A program such as this one is extremely difficult to test thoroughly because you cannot directly control which parts of the algorithm are executed. Instead, you must inspect trace output to determine what was exercised on a particular execution. Make sure that you have dealt with all potential race conditions.

This program is significantly more complex than preceding ones. Be sure to begin by implementing the simplest possible version of the program. For example, begin by making all offers to trade for "any other" and only add more complex trading restrictions if (a) you have the simple program working and (b) you really want to.

13. A group of N (N > 1) philosophers plans to spend an evening together eating and thinking [6, p. 131]. Unfortunately, the host philosopher has only N forks and is serving a special spaghetti that requires 2 forks to eat. Luckily for the host, philosophers (like university students) are interested more in knowledge than food; after eating a few bites of spaghetti, a philosopher is apt to drop her

forks and contemplate the oneness of the universe for a while, until her stomach begins to growl, when she again goes back to eating. So the table is set with N plates of spaghetti with one fork between adjacent plates. For example, the table would look like this for N=4:

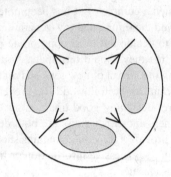

Consequently there is one fork on either side of a plate. Before eating, a philosopher must obtain the two forks on either side of the plate; hence, two adjacent philosophers cannot eat simultaneously. The host reasons that, when a philosopher's stomach begins to growl, she can simply wait until the two philosophers on either side begin thinking, then *simultaneously pick up the two forks on either side of her plate* and begin eating. (Note, once a fork is *picked up*, it is temporarily owned by a philosopher and unavailable to any other philosopher.) If a philosopher cannot pick up both forks immediately, then she must wait until both are free. (Imagine what would happen if all the philosophers simultaneously picked up their right forks and then waited until their left forks were available.)

The table manages the forks and must be written as a class using μC++ semaphores to provide mutual exclusion and synchronization. The table implementation has the following interface (you may add only a public destructor and private members):

```
class Table {
    // private declarations for this kind of table
  public:
    Table( const unsigned int NoOfPhil, Printer &prt );
    void pickup( unsigned int id );
    void putdown( unsigned int id );
};
```

Member routines pickup and putdown are called by each philosopher, passing the philosopher's identifier (value between 0 and $N-1$), to pick up and put down both forks, respectively. Member routine pickup does not return until both forks can be picked up. To simultaneously pick up and put down both forks may require locking the entire table for short periods of time. No busy waiting is allowed; use cooperation among philosophers putting down forks and philosophers waiting to pick up forks. Your cooperation solution does *not* have to deal with starvation among philosophers waiting at the table; i.e., two or more philosophers may prevent another philosopher from getting an opportunity to eat. For example, with 3 philosophers, one philosopher might check its left than its right and another its right and left, and hence, alternate use of the forks, while the third philosopher is never checked. Guaranteeing global fairness of cooperation, in general, is complex. However, any mechanism to handle barging must prevented starvation among the barging and signalled philosophers (versus global starvation among all philosophers). That is, barging and signalled philosophers must eventually make progress assuming the cooperation scheme is fair. As a result, any loops used to deal with barging must ensure one (or more) waiting philosopher makes progress; hence, there should never be a case where all waiting philosophers unblock and then reblock (which is busy waiting).

A philosopher eating at the table is simulated by a task, which has the following interface (you may add only a public destructor and private members):

```
_Task Philosopher {
  public:
    enum States { Thinking = 'T', Hungry = 'H', Eating ='E',
                  Waiting = 'W', Finished = 'F' };
    Philosopher( unsigned int id, unsigned int noodles, Table &table, Printer &prt );
};
```

Each philosopher loops performing the following actions:

- hungry message
- yield a random number of times, between 0 and 4 inclusive, to simulate the time to get hungry
- pickup forks
- pretend to eat a random number of noodles, between 1 and 5 inclusive
  if there are less noodles than the number chosen, the philosopher eats all remaining noodles
- eating message
- yield a random number of times, between 0 and 4 inclusive, to simulate the time to eat the noodles
- put down forks
- if eaten all the noodles, stop looping
- thinking message
- yield a random number of times, between 0 and 19 inclusive, to simulate the time to think

Yielding is accomplished by calling yield(times) to give up a task's CPU timeslice a number of times.

All output from the program is generated by calls to a printer, excluding error messages. The interface for the printer is (you may add only a public destructor and private members):

```
_Monitor / _Cormonitor Printer {        // choose one of the two kinds of type constructor
  public:
    Printer( unsigned int NoOfPhil );
    void print( unsigned int id, Philosopher::States state );
    void print( unsigned int id, Philosopher::States state, unsigned int bite,
                unsigned int noodles );
};
```

A philosopher calls the print member when it enters states: thinking, hungry, eating, finished. The table calls the print member *before* it blocks a philosopher that must wait for its forks to become available. The printer attempts to reduce output by storing information for each philosopher until one of the stored elements is overwritten. When information is going to be overwritten, all the stored information is flushed and storing starts again. Output must look like that in Fig. 7.26.

Each column is assigned to a philosopher with an appropriate title, e.g., "Phil0", and a column entry indicates its current status:

State	Meaning
H	hungry
T	thinking
W l,r	waiting for the left fork l and the right fork r to become free
E n,r	eating n noodles, leaving r noodles on plate
F	finished eating all noodles

Identify the right fork of philosopher$_i$ with number i and the left fork with number $i + 1$. For example, W2,3 means forks 2 and/or 3 are unavailable, so philosopher 2 must wait, and E3,29 means philosopher 1 is eating 3 noodles, leaving 29 noodles on their plate to eat later. When a philosopher finishes, the state for that philosopher is marked with F and all other philosophers are marked with " . . .".

Information is buffered until a column is overwritten for a particular entry, which causes the buffered data to be flushed. If there is no new stored information for a column since the last buffer flush, an empty column is printed. When a task finishes, the buffer is flushed immediately, the state for that object is marked with F, and all other objects are marked with "...". After a task has finished, no further output appears in that column. All output spacing can be accomplished using the standard 8-space tabbing. Buffer any information necessary for printing in internal representation; **do not build and store strings of text for output.**

In addition, you are to devise and include a way to test your program for erroneous behaviour. This testing should be similar to the check performed in the routine CriticalSection, from software solutions for mutual exclusion, in that it should, with high probability, detect errors. Use an assert or tests that call μC++'s uAbort routine to halt the program with an appropriate message. (HINT: once a philosopher has a pair of forks, what must be true about the philosophers on either side?)

The executable program is named phil and has the following shell interface:

phil [P [N [S]]]

P is the number of philosophers and must be greater than 1; if P is not present, assume a value of 5. N is the number of noodles per plate and must be greater than 0; if N is not present, assume a value of 30. S is the seed for the random-number generator and must be greater than 0. If the seed is unspecified, use a

```
$ phil 5 20 56083
Phil0   Phil1   Phil2   Phil3   Phil4
******  ******  ******  ******  ******
H
E1,19   H
T       W2,1    H       H       H
        E4,16   W3,2    W4,3    E4,16
        T       E4,16   E4,16   T
                T       T
                E4,16   H
                T
                H
        H       E2,14
H       W2,1    T       W4,3
W1,0    E1,15           E3,13
                        T
                        H       H
                                E3,13
                                T
                        E5,8    H
E3,16   T                       W0,4
T                       T       E4,9
H                       H
W1,0            H               T
E2,14           E4,10   W4,3
T       H       T               H
        E3,12           E5,3    W0,4
H       T               T       E4,5
W1,0                            T
E5,9
T       H       H               H
        E5,7                    E3,2
        T       E3,7    H       T
        H       T
H       E2,5            E3,0
        T
...     ...     ...     F       ...
        H                       H
        E1,4
E2,7    T
T               H               E1,1
                E2,5            T
        H       T
        E1,3    H
        T       E4,1
H               T               H
                H
        H       E1,0
E3,4    W2,1
T
...     ...     F       ...     ...
        E1,2                    E1,0
        T
...     ...     ...     ...     F
H
E4,0
F       ...     ...     ...     ...
        H
        E2,0
...     F       ...     ...     ...
************************
Philosophers terminated
```

Fig. 7.26 Output for 5 philosophers, each with 20 noodles

random value like the process identifier (getpid) or current time (time), so each run of the program generates different output. Check all command arguments for correct form (integers) and range; print an appropriate usage message and terminate the program if a value is missing or invalid. The driver must handle an arbitrary number of philosophers and noodles, but only tests with values less than 100 for the two parameters will be made, so the output columns line up correctly.

Use the following monitor to safely generate random values (monitors will be discussed shortly):

```
_Monitor MPRNG {
  public:
    MPRNG( unsigned int seed = 1009 ) { srand( seed ); }              // set seed
    void seed( unsigned int seed ) { srand( seed ); }                 // set seed
    unsigned int operator()() { return rand(); }                      // [0,UINT_MAX]
    unsigned int operator()( unsigned int u ) { return operator()()%(u+1); } // [0,u]
    unsigned int operator()( unsigned int l, unsigned int u ) {
                    return operator()( u - l ) + l; } // [l,u]
};
```

Note, because of the non-deterministic execution of concurrent programs, multiple runs with a common seed may not generate the same output. Nevertheless, shorts runs are often the same so the seed can be useful for testing. Check all command arguments for correct form (integers) and range; print an appropriate usage message and terminate the program if a value is missing or invalid.

(**WARNING: in GNU C, -1 % 5 != 4, and on UNIX, the name fork is reserved.**)

References

1. Andrews, G.R.: A method for solving synronization problems. Sci. Comput. Program. **13**(4), 1–21 (1989)
2. Andrews, G.R., Schneider, F.B.: Concepts and notations for concurrent programming. ACM Comput. Surv. **15**(1), 3–43 (1983)
3. Courtois, P.J., Heymans, F., Parnas, D.L.: Concurrent control with readers and writers. Commun. ACM **14**(10), 667–668 (1971)
4. Dijkstra, E.W.: Cooperating sequential processes. Tech. rep., Technological University, Eindhoven, Netherlands (1965). Reprinted in [9] pp. 43–112.
5. Dijkstra, E.W.: The structure of the "THE"–multiprogramming system. Commun. ACM **11**(5), 341–346 (1968)
6. Dijkstra, E.W.: Hierarchical ordering of sequential processes. Acta Inf. **1**, 115–138 (1971)
7. Dijkstra, E.W.: A tutorial on the split binary semaphore. Tech. Rep. EWD703, Nuenen, Netherlands (1979)
8. Dijkstra, E.W.: The superfluity of the general semaphore. Tech. Rep. EWD734, Nuenen, Netherlands (1980)
9. Genuys, F. (ed.): Programming Languages. Academic Press, London, New York (1968). NATO Advanced Study Institute, Villard-de-Lans, 1966
10. Holzmann, G.J., Pehrson, B.: The first data networks. Sci. Am. **12**(1), 124–129 (1994)
11. Stroustrup, B.: The Design and Evolution of C++. Addison-Wesley, Boston (1994)

Chapter 8
Concurrency Errors

The introduction of threads and locks into a programming language introduces new kinds of errors not present in sequential programming; several of these errors have been mentioned in previous chapters. When writing concurrent programs, it is important to understand the new kinds of errors so they can be avoided or debugged when they occur. Therefore, it is appropriate to take a short diversion from the discussion of specifying concurrency to explain these new programming problems.

As mentioned at the end of Sect. 5.2, p. 192, the temporal nature of concurrent programs makes avoiding and debugging errors extremely complex and very frustrating. The following discussion revisits some of the problems already discussed and introduces several new ones in an attempt to give a deeper understanding of the issues.

8.1 Race Error

A race condition occurs when two or more tasks share a resource without synchronization or mutual exclusion. As a result, the shared resource can change (be written to) by one task while another task is reading or writing it. A race condition does not imply an error, e.g., a race condition is used in Peterson's algorithm (see Sect. 6.3.6.2, p. 250) to break ties for simultaneous arrivals. In general, a race condition is used to generate some form of non-determinism among tasks, which can be used in various ways, such as a random-number generator or making an arbitrary decision.

A race error occurs when a race condition is inadvertently created by a programmer by failing to synchronize before performing some action on a shared resource or provide mutual exclusion for a critical section using the shared resource. As a result, two or more tasks race along erroneously assuming that some action has occurred or race simultaneously into a critical section. In both cases, the tasks eventually corrupt the shared data (and possibly the non-shared data indirectly

© Springer International Publishing Switzerland 2016

P.A. Buhr, *Understanding Control Flow*, DOI 10.1007/978-3-319-25703-7_8

through the shared data), i.e., variables become incorrect in any number of ways. A race error is the most insidious error in concurrent programming and the most difficult to debug.

There are many issues in locating a race error. The first issue goes back to the basics of concurrent programming: identifying shared variables and ensuring proper synchronization of and mutual exclusion for these variables by multiple tasks. Sometimes subtle interactions occur that the programmer is unaware of, e.g., unknowingly calling a library routine using shared variables but having no mutual exclusion. (This situation occurs frequently in UNIX systems that are not thread-safe.) However, imagining all the possible interactions among tasks and shared data in a concurrent program can be extremely difficult, so it is possible in a complex concurrent system for a synchronization point or mutual exclusion to be missed. The next chapter begins the discussion of high-level concurrency constructs, combined with software engineering techniques, to help localize access to shared data, and hence, mitigate both of these problems.

The second issue in locating a race error is that the program becomes corrupted because of incorrect access to shared data, but the corruption does not occur all the time nor does it cause immediate failure. A program might run for years before a particular execution sequence results in a race that corrupts shared data. Furthermore, once the shared data is corrupted, the program might continue for a significant time before the corruption cascades sufficiently to cause an actual failure. In this case, the error occurs at a substantial distance, both in time and location, from the original problem. While this situation occurs even in sequential programs, multiple threads make it more pronounced.

All of these issues conspire to make locating the original problem extremely difficult, because to a large extent there is no pointer back to the problem area. Some systems provide the ability to generate information events for certain kinds of changes and/or interactions in a concurrent program. This stream of events can be analysed to look for situations that might represent missing synchronization or mutual exclusion. However, in many cases, generating the event stream perturbs the program sufficiently to change its behaviour so the race error does not occur. Such a perturbation is called the probe effect, i.e., connecting a probe to the program for examination changes its behaviour resulting in a "Heisenbug" (see page 195). In this case, the only way to locate a race error is by examination of the program code and performing thought experiments about what might happen with respect to different execution sequences.

However, there is often sufficient latitude to insert some checking code without causing the problem to vanish. One simple way to check for violations of mutual exclusion is by using a trap, like the technique shown in the self-checking bathroom (see Sect. 6.2.2, p. 237). Traps can be placed at various locations in a program validating mutual exclusion at very low cost, and hence, having little probe effect. A similar trap can be constructed for synchronization by setting a shared variable indicating work completed by one task and checking the variable before continuing in another task.

8.2   No Progress

The next group of errors are all similar in one respect: each results in one or more tasks ceasing to make forward progress with respect to its computation. That is, a task stops performing its specified computation and appears to do nothing. While all the following errors share this common symptom, each has a subtly different way of manifesting itself, and hence, a correspondingly different kind of solution to solve the problem. Understanding each form of no-progress error is crucial to knowing how to fix it.

8.2.1   Livelock

Livelock was introduced and defined in Sect. 6.2.1, p. 235. In general, it occurs when a selection algorithm, e.g., mutual exclusion, can postpone indefinitely, i.e., the "You go first" problem. All livelock problems occur on simultaneous arrival, and all can be solved given a good tie breaking rule. Notice, there is no requirement to be fair in breaking the tie; fairness is a separate issue. The goal is to make a selection as quickly as possible on simultaneous arrival, e.g., to get a task into a critical region as fast as possible.

An excellent example of livelock is a traffic intersection with a 4-way stop. In general, when cars arrive simultaneously at a 4-way stop, the rule to break the tie is the car on the right[1] has the right of way and goes first. However, what about the situation where 4 cars arrive simultaneously (see Fig. 8.1a)? This situation results in a livelock because each driver is deferring to the car on the right. As a result, the cars sit at the intersection forever! (It is humorous to note this potentially life threatening situation should be added to the many others that occur when driving a car.) The problem is that the tie breaking rule is simply insufficient to handle all the simultaneous arrival cases. Augmenting the rule to say the driver with the largest license plate number goes first would solve the problem (and there are other possible solutions, too). In fact, any system in which the components can be uniquely numbered, e.g., unique task identifiers, can solve the livelock problem by devising a tie breaking rule using this value for all simultaneous arrival situations.

Livelock problems are usually easy to find in a concurrent program either with a concurrent debugger or using print statements. The usual symptom for livelock is a non-terminating application using large amounts of CPU time. The reason for this symptom is that two or more tasks are spinning in a livelock. By attaching a concurrent debugger to the program, stopping all execution, and examining the execution locations of the tasks, it is usually possible to quickly spot the spinning tasks and where they are spinning. Using print statements is not as good because it

---

[1]The car on the left if you drive on the other side of the road.

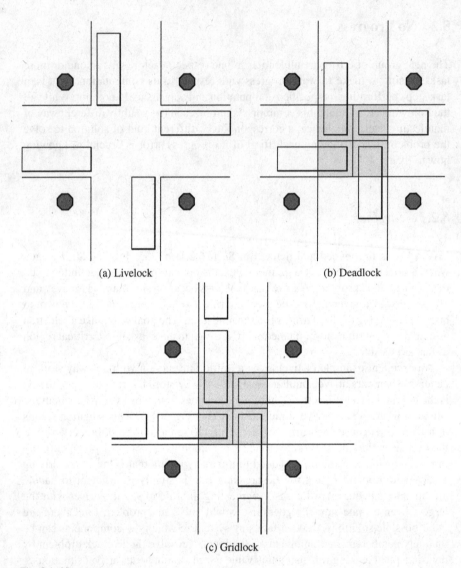

(a) Livelock   (b) Deadlock

(c) Gridlock

Fig. 8.1 No progress

may perturb execution sufficiently so the simultaneous arrival does not occur often
or at all. Furthermore, it can generate a huge amount of output before a livelock
occurs.

What is unusual about livelock is that a task is not making progress yet it is
conceptually ready at any time, switching between the active and ready states, so it
is consuming CPU resources but accomplishing nothing.

8.2.2   Starvation

Starvation was introduced and defined in Sect. 6.2.1, p. 235. In general, it occurs when a selection algorithm, e.g., mutual exclusion, allows one or more tasks to make progress while ignoring a particular task or set of tasks so they are never given an opportunity to make progress. (In livelock, no task is making progress.) All starvation problems occur when there is a persistent lack of fairness in task selection; temporary unfairness is acceptable as long as there is a bound on the length of the wait. Hence, starvation requires some notion of high and low priority, where the priority can be based on anything. For true starvation to occur, a low priority task must never be selected, which requires that a high priority task always be available for selection over the low priority task. In practice, there is usually some window where no high priority task is available for selection and so a low priority task makes progress. Hence, starvation usually requires an extremely busy system, often so busy that starvation is the least of the problems. Therefore, starvation is more a theoretical problem than a practical one.

However, just hoping that a concurrent system does not have starvation is asking for trouble. It is always better if an algorithm can be designed to be free of starvation. The reason is that it may appear a particular selection algorithm, with respect to a set of tasks and resources, seems fine, but in conjunction with another selection algorithm, problems may arise. Even though there is no true starvation in finite programs, there may be unwanted periods of unfairness, which result in the short-term delay of tasks. The short-term delay may not cause an error but may produce a behaviour that was neither anticipated nor desired by the programmer. In the case of real-time programs even a short-term delay can result in catastrophic errors. Finding short-term unfairness usually requires a trace of task scheduling to reveal the order tasks were delayed and made ready. Often this is sufficient information to locate where and why tasks were scheduled in that order.

Like livelock, a starving task is not making progress yet it is conceptually ready at any time, switching between the active, ready and possibly blocked (depending on the implementation) states, so it is possibly consuming CPU resources but accomplishing nothing.

8.2.3   Deadlock

This error has been mentioned but not discussed before and is associated with the phenomenon of tasks blocking for either synchronization or mutual exclusion. It is possible for one or more tasks to get into a state where no progress is possible because the tasks become blocked forever, called deadlock. This state is in contrast to livelock or starvation where the tasks are conceptually ready but cannot get scheduled; in deadlock, tasks are actually blocked. In this discussion, traditional deadlock is divided into two forms. The reason for the subdivision is that traditional deadlock encompasses two quite different problems, each with its own particular kind of solution. The two different problems are associated with synchronization and mutual exclusion, respectively. Systems that report deadlock usually do not state which kind of deadlock has occurred. Using different terms more precisely identifies the problem, which correspondingly defines the potential solutions, because synchronization deadlock is usually a trivial mistake in cooperation, while mutual-exclusion deadlock is usually a complex mistake in resource allocation.

8.2.3.1 Synchronization Deadlock

When there is a failure in cooperation, so a task blocks but is never unblocked by a cooperating task, it is called synchronization deadlock (sometimes called stuck waiting). The simplest example of synchronization deadlock is the following:

```
void uMain::main() {
    uSemaphore s(0);   // lock is closed
    s.P();             // wait for lock to open
}
```

In this program, task uMain blocks on semaphore s but there is no other task to subsequently unblock it. Clearly, there is a failure in cooperation when a task waits for some event that never happens. Alternatively, the semaphore is incorrectly initialized to 0 instead of 1. Notice, this is not the same as a race error where a task forgets to wait; in this case, the task waits but no other task restarts it.

Synchronization deadlock problems are usually simple mistakes in cooperation. The usual symptom for synchronization deadlock is application termination with a deadlock message or a non-terminating application using no CPU time. The reason for this latter symptom is that one or more tasks are blocked in a synchronization deadlock, preventing the program from terminating. By attaching a concurrent debugger to the program, and examining the execution locations of the tasks, it is usually possible to quickly spot the blocked task and on which lock it is blocked.

8.2.3.2 Mutual Exclusion Deadlock

When a task blocks while attempting to acquire mutual exclusion for a shared resource, but is never unblocked because the resource never becomes free, it is called mutual-exclusion deadlock. An example of mutual-exclusion deadlock can be constructed using the previous traffic intersection with a 4-way stop. After the 4 drivers sit for a few minutes deferring to the car on the right, they all simultaneously decide to break the law (i.e., not defer to the driver on the right) and proceed through the intersection (see Fig. 8.1, p. 398b). In addition, all 4 cars have no reverse gear so they cannot back up! At this point, absolutely nothing can be done by the drivers to fix the situation; they are trapped forever in the intersection with no mechanism for escape. Dijkstra referred to this situation as a "deadly embrace" [2, p. 105] because the only solution is to terminate one of the participants associated with the deadlock. In this case, one or more of the cars has to be towed out of the intersection to terminate the deadlock and allow further progress.

While it is highly unlikely that all 4 cars are without reverse gear, what if the cars behind move forward (see Fig. 8.1, p. 398c). This situation is called gridlock and happens in large cities during rush hour. In general, there is a traffic law which states it is illegal to enter an intersection unless the entire car has the opportunity to proceed completely through it. This law ensures gridlock cannot occur; unfortunately, people do not always obey this law! (Notice, this law still does not prevent deadlock in the previous case, because at the moment each driver decides not to defer to the driver on the right, it appeared safe to enter the intersection. Therefore, even if a law is created that prevents livelock, the drivers could be fast enough to all enter the intersection and form a deadlock.)

Mutual exclusion deadlock can occur in many ways in a concurrent program. One of the simplest ways is by nesting acquisition of locks for acquiring resources, as in:

```
uSemaphore L1(1), L2(1);
```

task$_1$		task$_2$	
L1.P()		L2.P()	// acquire opposite lock
R1		R2	// access resource
L2.P()		L1.P()	// acquire opposite lock
R2		R1	// access resource

In this example, task$_1$ acquires lock L1 to access resource R1 and then attempts to acquire lock L2 to access resource R2. At the same time, task$_2$ acquires lock L2 to access resource R2 and then attempts to acquire lock L1 to access resource R1. The result is that both task$_1$ and task$_2$ block on the inner P operation because they cannot acquire the other lock as it is held by the other task. When the tasks block, there is a deadlock because task$_1$ is holding lock L1 and waiting for lock L2, while task$_2$ is holding lock L2 and waiting for lock L1. Hence, both tasks are waiting for a resource that will not be freed, and since both tasks have blocked, neither can give up their resource so the other can make progress. Notice, the two tasks must conceptually acquire and then wait *simultaneously* (on a single CPU, the execution switching must occur such that it appears simultaneous). This code might run without problem for years until one day an execution sequence occurs that produces this particular scenario. Furthermore, these two code fragments can be located in different parts of the program where each is correct on its own.

The preceding explanation for mutual-exclusion deadlock only gives an ad hoc definition; the formal definition is as follows. There are 4 conditions [1, p. 70] that must be true *simultaneously* for a set of tasks to achieve a mutual-exclusion deadlock. Each of these conditions is demonstrated through the traffic intersection with a 4-way stop.

1. There exists more than one shared resource (critical section) requiring mutual exclusion.

A traffic intersection has essentially four shared resources, corresponding to the quadrant of the intersection in front of each traffic lane. These quadrants must interact in complex ways to safely allow traffic through the intersection. For example, what is the maximum number of cars that can be simultaneously in an intersection without causing an accident? The answer is 4, because 4 cars can be simultaneously turning right without interfering with each other. Depending on the action performed by a car, it may require mutual exclusion on 1, 2 or 3 quadrants simultaneously to safely proceed. Therefore, an intersection clearly has multiple shared components requiring mutual exclusion because two cars cannot occupy the same space at the same time.

2. A task holds a resource while waiting for access to a resource held by another task (hold and wait).

   In the deadlock picture above, each car is holding the portion of road it is sitting on (the gray area in the picture). As well, each car is waiting for the portion of the road directly in front of it. Therefore, each car is holding a resource, part of the traffic intersection, and waiting for another resource, another part of the traffic intersection.

3. There exists a circular wait of tasks on resources (circular wait).

   In the deadlock picture, it is easy to see the cycle among the cars; each car is holding a resource that is being waited for by the car to the left of it.

4. Once a task has acquired a resource, it cannot be taken back (no pre-emption).

   Because the cars have no reverse gear, or more realistically the cars behind move forward, the resource being held (part of the traffic intersection) cannot be given back by the drivers. For tasks, this problem manifests itself because they block, and hence, cannot perform any work, such as giving up a held resource.

For example, if all 4 drivers advance halfway into the intersection, each of the previous conditions occurs, and hence, a mutual-exclusion deadlock occurs. However, if one of the drivers proceeds through the intersection before the others start, livelock is broken, and even though 2 cars can get into a hold and wait, a deadlock cannot occur because the third car can proceed so no cycle can form. Hence, the 4 conditions, plus the simultaneous requirement, must exist for mutual-exclusion deadlock.

Why is synchronization deadlock not mutual-exclusion deadlock? This question can be answered by showing that synchronization deadlock does not satisfy any of the deadlock conditions required for mutual-exclusion deadlock. Is there a critical section requiring mutual exclusion? For synchronization deadlock, the lock a task acquires is being used for synchronization not protecting a critical section. Is the task holding a shared resource and waiting for another such resource? For synchronization deadlock, the task has neither acquired a resource (not even the lock) nor is it waiting for another resource. Can the acquired resource be given back through some form of pre-emption? Since no resource is acquired, there is nothing that can be given back. Is there a circular wait among tasks holding and waiting on resources? Since there are no resources and there is only one task, there cannot be a circular wait. Finally, there is no set of circumstances or conditions that must occur simultaneously to produce a synchronization deadlock.

Mutual exclusion deadlock problems are more complex mistakes involving multiple tasks accessing multiple resources. The usual symptom for mutual-exclusion deadlock is termination of the application with some form of deadlock message, or the application does not terminate and is using no CPU time. The reason for this latter symptom is that one or more tasks is blocked in a mutual-exclusion deadlock, preventing the program from terminating. (Because this symptom is the same as for synchronization deadlock, it is common to refer to both kinds of errors with the generic term deadlock.) By attaching a concurrent debugger to the program, and examining the execution locations of the tasks, it is usually possible to determine which tasks have resources allocated and which resources tasks are blocked on. However, this information only indicates the deadly embrace, not how the embrace formed; therefore, it is necessary to work backwards to some point during the execution of the tasks to determine why the embrace formed, which can be a complex analysis. Trace events showing the execution and allocation ordering may be necessary to locate the reason for a complex deadlock. If the concurrent system does not provide a tracing facility, it can be mimicked with debug print statements, albeit with substantial work on the part of the programmer.

8.3 Deadlock Prevention

Is it possible to eliminate deadlock from a concurrent algorithm? Yes, but only if some conditions that lead to the deadlock can be eliminated. Notice, prevention occurs during the static design of an algorithm not when the algorithm is running, which means the program using a prevention algorithm cannot deadlock no matter what order or speed the tasks execute. Since the requirements are different for synchronization and mutual-exclusion deadlock, each is discussed separately.

8.3.1 Synchronization Deadlock Prevention

To prevent synchronization deadlock all synchronization must be eliminated from a concurrent program. Without synchronization, no task waits for an event to occur, and hence, there is no opportunity to miss an uncommunicated event from a cooperating task. However, without synchronization, tasks cannot communicate as it is impossible to establish safe points for transferring data, which means the only programs that can be written are ones where tasks run independently, possibly causing a side effect, such as a clock task managing a clock on the terminal screen. Notice, this restriction even eliminates divide-and-conquer algorithms (see Sect. 5.12, p. 218) because they require termination synchronization. Therefore, preventing synchronization deadlock severely limits the class of problems that can be solved, making it largely impractical for almost all concurrent programming.

8.3.2 Mutual Exclusion Deadlock Prevention

When designing a concurrent algorithm, it may be possible to statically ensure that one or more of the conditions for mutual-exclusion deadlock cannot occur. Each of the conditions is examined as to the feasibility of removing it from a concurrent algorithm.

1. No mutual exclusion
   If a concurrent algorithm requires no mutual exclusion, there can be no mutual-exclusion deadlock. For example, divide-and-conquer algorithms require only synchronization but no mutual exclusion, and therefore, cannot encounter mutual-exclusion deadlock. However, no mutual exclusion means virtually no shared resources, which significantly limits the class of problems that can be solved, but still allows many reasonable programs.

2. No hold and wait
   To eliminate hold and wait requires no shared resource be given to a task unless all shared resources it requests can be supplied so the task never waits for a resource. In general, this requirement means that before a concurrent program begins execution it must identify its worst case allocation to the runtime system. Based on this information, a scheduling scheme is statically developed that precludes deadlock.

   While this restriction does preclude mutual-exclusion deadlock, it has unfortunate side-effects. First, identifying worst-case resource requirements may be impossible because resource needs may depend on dynamic information, like an input value. Second, even if worst case resource requirements can be identified statically, they may never be reached during execution nor all needed at the start of the program. As a result, there is poor resource utilization because more resources are allocated than actually needed to handle a situation that rarely occurs, and these resources may be held longer than is necessary, e.g., from start to end of program execution. For certain programs with high worst case resource requirements, there is the further problem of a long delay or possible starvation because the necessary set of resources is difficult or impossible to accumulate while other programs are running on the system.

   For example, in the previous traffic intersection problem, the law that a car must not proceed into an intersection unless it can proceed completely through the intersection imposes a control on hold and wait. A driver must have sufficient space on one of the 3 exit roads before being allocated any space in the intersection, i.e., 1 square to turn right, 2 squares to drive straight through, and 3 squares to turn left. By ensuring that all drivers follow this policy, gridlock cannot occur.

3. Allow pre-emption
   Interestingly, pre-emption is a dynamic phenomenon, i.e., the runtime system makes a dynamic decision at some arbitrary time, from the perspective of the executing tasks, to take back some resource(s) given out earlier. Therefore, a programmer cannot know statically which resource(s) or when or how often the request to return one might occur. Hence, statically, the programmer must

assume any or all resources can be pre-empted at any time and must attempt to compose an algorithm given this severe requirement. In general, it is impossible to compose reasonable algorithms given such a requirement.

It is possible to show that pre-emption is unnecessary in a system by doing the following. When a task holding resources attempts to acquire another resource that is currently unavailable, the task does not block but is required to give up all the resources it has acquired and start again. In effect, this approach is a form of self-pre-emption. Again, this is largely impractical, except in very unusual circumstances, where the number of acquired resources is small and/or the chance of a resource being unavailable is extremely low. As well, the problem of restarting some or all of the program's execution may require undoing changes made to the environment. (This point is discussed further.)

4. No circular wait

If it is possible to show a circular wait cannot occur, then mutual-exclusion deadlock cannot occur. For many specific situations it is possible to eliminate the potential for circular wait by controlling the order that resources are acquired by tasks. In the previous example of nested acquisition of locks, it is possible to prevent deadlock by ensuring both tasks allocate the resources in the same order, as in:

```
uSemaphore L1(1), L2(1);
```

```
task₁                 task₂

L1.P()      L1.P()    // acquire same lock
   R1          R1     // access resource
L2.P()      L2.P()    // acquire same lock
   R2          R2     // access resource
```

Since only one task can acquire L1, the other task cannot make progress toward acquiring L2, so it cannot hold the other resource; therefore, the task holding L1 never has to wait to acquire L2. While this order of resource allocation precludes mutual-exclusion deadlock, it has the drawback that $task_2$ is now allocating resources in the reverse order it needs them, which may result in poor resource utilization. In fact, virtually all resource allocation ordering schemes have a side-effect of either inhibiting concurrency and/or reducing resource utilization, in exchange for providing mutual-exclusion deadlock free execution. Therefore, the choice is between performance versus robustness.

Controlling the order that resources are allocated can be specific or general. Many concurrent algorithms can be subtly modified to control allocation ordering, while limiting negative side-effects. Clearly, the more known about an algorithm, the more specific the control ordering can be made to optimize for the algorithm's particular behaviour. For example, if tasks are organized in a ring with a shared resource between each (see questions 13, p. 389 and 9, p. 496), as in:

$$R_5 \qquad T_1$$

$$T_5 \qquad R_1$$

$$R_4 \qquad\qquad T_2$$

$$T_4 \qquad R_2$$

$$R_3 \qquad T_3$$

and each task needs *both* the resource on the left and right occasionally, there is the potential for mutual-exclusion deadlock if each task acquires the right resource and then tries to acquire the left resource because of the hold and wait cycle. However, there are many control orderings (schedulings) that can be applied in this specific scenario to prevent mutual-exclusion deadlock. One example is that a task cannot acquire a resource unless it can acquire both of them. Alternatively, have each task acquire the right resource first and then the left, except for one task, which acquires the left resource first and then the right. This control ordering ensures the task on the right of the special task can always acquire both resources and make progress. The negative side-effect, in both cases, is inhibiting some concurrency and under utilizing the resources. Concurrency is inhibited because a task may be able to make some progress with only one of the two resources, and resources are underutilized because of the required order of allocation.

While many algorithm specific schemes exist for controlling resource allocation ordering, there are also several general approaches, such as the ordered resource policy (ORP) [4, p. 78]. These control ordering schemes work for different kinds of algorithms, but must assume worst case situations because of a lack of detailed knowledge of the algorithms; therefore, they are not as efficient as specific control schemes. The ORP approach is similar to the N-task software solution presented in Sect. 6.3.8, p. 254, in that a task acquires resources from lowest priority to highest. Formally, the ORP approach is as follows:

- Divide all resources into classes: R_1, R_2, R_3, etc.
  This rule creates logical classes and assigns monotonically increasing priorities to each class (i.e., the resource class subscript is the priority, where a larger subscript number represents a higher priority). A class can contain multiple instances, which might be identical or different.
- Tasks can only request a resource from class R_i if holding no resources from any class R_j such that $j \geq i$
  This rule requires resources to be allocated strictly from lowest priority class to highest.
- If a resource contains multiple instances, requesting several instances must occur simultaneously

This rule follows from the fact that an allocated resource must be from a class with higher priority than the currently held maximum priority for a task. Hence, a task cannot acquire one R_i, and then attempt to acquire another. To get N instances of a particular resource requires all N be obtained in a single request. If this rule is relaxed to allow an equality, $i = j$, two tasks could both be holding an instance of R_i and request another that is unavailable, resulting in a mutual-exclusion deadlock.

Because the preceding inequality is strict, a circular wait is impossible. The proof is straightforward.

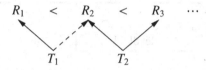

Denote the highest class number for which task T holds a resource by $h(T)$. If task T_1 requests a resource of class k and is blocked because that resource is held by task T_2, then it follows $h(T_1) < k \le h(T_2)$. Allowing T_1 to block cannot affect T_2 because T_2 has already acquired all resources greater than or equal to k that it needs, and hence, T_1 cannot be holding resources needed by T_2. Therefore, there can be no hold and wait cycle.

In some cases there is a natural division of resources into classes, making the ORP work nicely. In other cases, some tasks are forced to acquire resources in an unnatural sequence, complicating their code, inhibiting concurrency, and producing poor resource utilization.

For the traffic intersection, preventing mutual-exclusion deadlock through no circular wait would involve rules that allow cars into the intersection, e.g., to start a left turn, but ensure the car can ultimately clear the intersection. Traffic lights (as opposed to a 4-way stop) provide additional control to preclude some circular waits from forming, such as a left turning car.

Finally, there may be programs where each of the four conditions may hold among tasks at different times, but it is possible to demonstrate there is no point during execution when all four conditions are true at the same time so deadlock cannot occur.

8.4 Deadlock Avoidance

Deadlock prevention is achieved by a programmer constructing a concurrent program using carefully designed algorithms. Prevention ensures an algorithm is deadlock free *before* it is executed by a concurrent program, establishing a level of robustness that may be crucial for certain applications. The drawback of deadlock prevention is that certain algorithms are not amenable (e.g., dynamic resource requirements), and resources may be underutilized or concurrency inhibited or both.

For certain situations, these drawbacks are not as important as the robustness. For example, NASA is happy to buy more powerful computers and add more resources if it means the software in a rocket ship's computer is deadlock free. The last problem NASA needs is a deadlock occurring during lift off.

However, when the restrictions imposed by deadlock prevention are unacceptable, it is necessary to switch to a dynamic approach where algorithms essentially take risks, moving from a guaranteed safe status to a potentially unsafe status to achieve better performance and utilization, but are prevented from actually entering deadlock during execution by the runtime system.

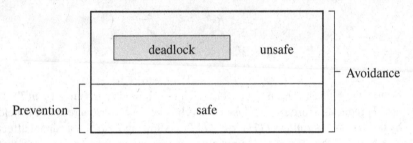

While deadlock prevention is an active approach with respect to the programmer, i.e., building deadlock free algorithms, deadlock avoidance is a passive approach where the runtime system does all the work. However, there is an administrative cost for avoiding deadlock at runtime: the runtime system must monitor execution at varying levels of detail depending on the particular technique used. This monitoring consumes both memory and CPU resources.

If the runtime system detects a deadlock would occur when a task is about to block on a lock for synchronization or mutual exclusion reasons, the system basically has two options with respect to the blocking task:

1. Terminate the blocking task or program containing it
   In many situations this is the only option, regardless of the severity of the option. However, it gives the programmer no possibility to deal with the problem programmatically.
2. Return immediately from the lock request indicating a refusal to allow the task to acquire the lock and spin or block waiting for it to become free.
   In this option, the task must not spin or block waiting for the resource to become free. The task can only come back later and try again or release some held resources to ultimately acquire the resource associated with the lock. However, there is a significant design cost for programmers as a program must be written to deal with the potential of lock refusal. A programmer may have to add substantial code to deal with this new situation during runtime, which may have little or nothing to do with the algorithm performed in the program.

The following discussion explains how the runtime system can detect an approaching deadlock when a task is about to block.

8.4.1 Synchronization Deadlock Avoidance

Avoiding synchronization deadlock involves detecting when a blocking task will not be subsequently unblocked; this requires a crystal ball to look into the future. In general, it is impossible to tell at the time a task blocks on a lock if another task will eventually unblock it. Essentially, only if the last task in the system is about to block on a lock and all the other tasks are blocked on locks, is it possible to conclude that synchronization deadlock is about to occur, and this task should not be allowed to block. (This technique is used in μC++ to know when to print the deadlock error-message and terminate execution.) At all intermediate system states, it is always possible that some task, with visibility to the lock(s), could unblock a task from it. Extensive static analysis might determine that some or all tasks cannot see every lock, or that each task cannot lock and unlock every lock, and hence, the tasks and locks could be formed into logical groups, and a synchronization deadlock only occurs if all tasks in the logical group block. However, the existence of pointers to locks makes such analysis extremely difficult, if not impossible, in many cases. Therefore, without extensive static analysis, avoidance of synchronization deadlock can only be accomplished by checking for the last running task of a program attempting to block, and avoiding this block.

8.4.2 Mutual-Exclusion Deadlock Avoidance

Avoiding mutual-exclusion deadlock requires the ability to dynamically track all resource allocation and ownership by tasks, which usually requires a single resource allocator managing all resource allocation and free requests. The resource allocator gives out available resources, and blocks tasks if a resource is unavailable, unless blocking might lead to deadlock. The question the resource allocator must answer is: will blocking a task lead to deadlock? Therefore, it must maintain sufficient information about what is occurring in the system to decide how to respond to each resource request. The decision regarding a request does not have to be absolutely accurate. In other words, denying a request does not imply that blocking the requester would produce a deadlock. The decision can be conservative, meaning a request maybe denied even though it does not lead directly to deadlock but could be too close to deadlock for the allocator to allow blocking. For resource allocation, there are criteria on which such a decision can be made.

Two resource allocation schemes are examined. The first scheme is historical and not precise in that it might deny a request which would not lead to deadlock. The second scheme is precise by maintaining sufficient information to know for each request whether it will cause a mutual-exclusion deadlock. While neither scheme allows a request that leads to deadlock, both have a high runtime cost. These two schemes represent two ends of a spectrum for resource allocation schemes. Many different schemes exist along the spectrum, each trading off precision of detection with cost of detection.

8.4.2.1   Banker's Algorithm

The Banker's algorithm [2, pp. 105-110] was suggested by Dijkstra, and was the first attempt to construct an algorithm for a runtime system to detect pending deadlock. The algorithm checks for a safe execution sequence that precludes hold and wait. As mentioned, precluding hold and wait means not starting execution unless all needed shared resources are available. This scheme ensures that sufficient resources are always available for a task to obtain its worst case resource allocation but performs the check incrementally rather than statically. The main requirement of this approach is that each task know its maximum resource requirements before starting execution, and not exceed the maximum during execution. As mentioned, this is impractical in many cases, as tasks may not know the maximum resource requirements before starting execution nor does the maximum represent the average allocation needs. Another drawback of the algorithm is that it is conservative (i.e., not precise) with respect to avoiding deadlock, but it never allows a request that does lead to deadlock.

The Banker's algorithm is best explained through an example. Imagine a system with 3 tasks and 4 kinds of resources. The number of total instances of each kind of resource is:

Total available resources (TR)

R_1	R_2	R_3	R_4
6	12	4	2

i.e., there are 6 R_1 instances available for allocation by tasks, 12 R_2 available for allocation, and so on. As well, each task has the following maximum resource needs and cannot exceed them during execution:

	R_1	R_2	R_3	R_4	
T_1	4	10	1	1	maximum (M)
T_2	2	4	1	2	needed for
T_3	5	9	0	1	execution

Here, task T_1 requires, in its worst case scenario, 4 R_1, 10 R_2, 1 R_3, 1 R_4. In general, it may never come close to this worst case scenario during execution, but in rare circumstances it could reach these levels. Also, this matrix is usually sparse because, unlike this example, few tasks use all the different resources in a system.

Now pretend the system has been running for a while and some resources have already been given out, so the resource allocator has the following table of currently allocated resources:

	R_1	R_2	R_3	R_4	
T_1	2	5	1	0	currently (C)
T_2	1	2	1	0	allocated
T_3	1	2	0	0	

Here, task T_1 is currently allocated (holding), 2 R_1, 5 R_2, 1 R_3, 0 R_4. As can be seen, none of the tasks are close to their worst case scenario in *all* resource categories.

Now a resource request is made by T_1 for another R_1, attempting to increase the number of R_1 resources it is holding from 2 to 3. The resource allocator must decide if granting this request is safe for the entire system with respect to deadlock. Therefore, before it gives out the resource, the resource allocator must ensure no hold and wait can occur for all or a subset(s) of tasks assuming each jumps to its worst case allocation. To accomplish this check, the resource allocator performs a forward simulation, *pretending* to execute the tasks to completion (at which point the task would release its allocated resources) and *pretending* each jumps to its worst case allocation during the execution. It starts by changing the number of R_1s allocated to T_1 from 2 to 3 in matrix C; all the following calculations assume this change. If it can be shown each task can successfully execute to completion with its worst case allocation, then there is a safe execution sequence that ensures no hold and wait. But if no such sequence can be constructed, it does not imply the system will deadlock for the resource request because the calculated worst case scenario will probably not occur. Therefore, the Banker's algorithm is conservative as it might deny the resource request even though deadlock would not result from granting the request; on the other hand, it never grants a request that results in deadlock.

To simplify the calculation, the resource allocator builds or maintains a matrix that is the amount each task would need to increase from its current allocated resources to its maximum.

	R_1	R_2	R_3	R_4	
T_1	1	5	0	1	needed (N) to
T_2	1	2	0	2	achieve maximum
T_3	4	7	0	1	(N = M - C)

Here, task T_1 needs 1 R_1, 5 R_2, 0 R_3, 1 R_4 to jump from its current allocation to its worst case scenario. (Remember, the number of currently allocated R_1 resources has been increased to 3.) This matrix is just the difference between the maximum matrix (M) and the current allocation matrix (C).

To determine if there is a safe sequence of execution, a series of pretend allocations, executions and frees are performed. Starting with the total resources, the first step is to subtract the currently allocated resources to find the currently available resources. This step is accomplished by adding the columns of the currently allocated matrix, C, and subtracting from the total available resources:

$$\text{current available resources (AR)}$$
$$1 \quad 3 \quad 2 \quad 2 \quad (AR = TR - \sum C_{cols})$$

Given the available resources, AR, look through the rows of the need matrix, N, to determine if there are sufficient resources for any task to achieve its worst case allocation. Only task T_2 (row 2 of N) has values in each column less than or equal to the available resources. Therefore, it is the only task that could be started and allowed to jump to its worst case scenario without possibly encountering a hold and wait. Now pretend to run task T_2, and assume it does jump to its worst case scenario, so the available resources drop by the amount in the row of matrix N for

T_2. Then pretend T_2 completes execution, at which time it releases all the resources it is holding so the available resources increase by the amount in the row of matrix M for T_2. These two steps occur as follows:

$$T_2 \quad \frac{0 \quad 1 \quad 2 \quad 0}{2 \quad 5 \quad 3 \quad 2} \quad \begin{array}{l} (AR = AR - N_{T_2}) \\ (AR = AR + M_{T_2}) \end{array}$$

where the first line is the decrease in available resources when T_2 jumps to its maximum, and the second line is the increase after T_2 terminates and releases its held resources. This step is now repeated, except T_2 is finished so its row is ignored in any of the matrices.

Given the newly available resources, look through the rows of the need matrix, N, (excluding row 2) to determine if there are sufficient resources for any task to achieve its worst case allocation. Only task T_1 has values in each column less than or equal to the available resources. Therefore, it is the only task that could be started and allowed to jump to its worst case scenario without possibly encountering a hold and wait. Now pretend to run task T_1, and assume it does jump to its worst case scenario, so the available resources drop by the amount in the row of matrix N for T_1. Then pretend T_1 completes execution, at which time it releases all the resources it is holding so the available resources increase by the amount in the row of matrix M for T_1. These two steps occur as follows:

$$T_1 \quad \frac{1 \quad 0 \quad 3 \quad 1}{5 \quad 10 \quad 4 \quad 2} \quad \begin{array}{l} (AR = AR - N_{T_1}) \\ (AR = AR + M_{T_1}) \end{array}$$

where the first line is the decrease in available resources when T_1 jumps to its maximum, and the second line is the increase after T_1 terminates and releases its held resources.

Repeating this step for the remaining task, T_3, shows it could be started and allowed to jump to its worst case scenario without possibly encountering a hold and wait. Pretending to run task T_3, assuming it jumps to its worst case scenario, and releasing its held resources on completion generates:

$$T_3 \quad \frac{1 \quad 3 \quad 4 \quad 1}{6 \quad 12 \quad 4 \quad 2} \quad \begin{array}{l} (AR = AR - N_{T_3}) \\ (AR = AR + M_{T_3}) \end{array}$$

The check for correct execution of the Banker's algorithm is that AR is now equal to TR, which follows from the fact that there are no tasks executing so all the resources are available. (If AR does not equal TR, one (or more) of the tasks has walked off with some resources.) Therefore, the Banker's algorithm has demonstrated a safe execution order exists, T_2, T_1, T_3, where giving a new resource R_1 to T_1 does not result in a hold and wait even in the worst case scenario for all tasks in the system.

This particular example behaved nicely because at each step there is only one task that could be allowed to jump to its worst case scenario without performing a hold and wait. What if there is a choice of tasks for execution? It turns out it does not matter which task is selected as all possible selections produce the same result. For example, if T1 or T3 could go to their maximum with the current resources, then choose either as a safe order exists starting with T1 if and only if a safe order exists starting with T3. The proof is intuitive because no matter which task goes first, the other task subsequently starts it turn with the same or more resources available never less, and both tasks can execute with the current available resources.

If a safe ordering is found, does that imply task scheduling is adjusted to the safe order sequence discovered by the algorithm? No, tasks can continue to execute in arbitrary order and speed because the safe ordering implies there cannot be a hold and wait resulting in deadlock with the currently allocated resources. Furthermore, if the next allocation request is from the starting task specified by the previous safe order sequence, the resource can be granted without computing a new sequence because the previous calculation already showed this task can reach its worst case without problems. If any other task requests a resource, the banker's algorithm must be performed again to determine if a safe execution sequence exists. Therefore, the safe execution ordering generated by the Banker's algorithm does not imply tasks must subsequently execute in that order.

The execution cost of the Banker's algorithm is somewhat high. For each task, $O(RT)$ comparisons are required to find the next task in the safe execution order, where R is the number of resources and T is the number of tasks; therefore, $O(RT^2)$ comparisons are needed for all T tasks to be safely scheduled. $O(R)$ arithmetic operations are needed to update vector AR for each task chosen, for a total of $O(RT)$; another $O(RT)$ operations are needed to compute the initial state of AR. The storage cost is $O(RT)$ for matrices M, C and N, which dominates the additional cost of vector AR.

8.4.2.2   Allocation Graph

The allocation graph was suggested by Ric Holt [5] and involves graphing task and resource usage at each resource allocation. This graph is an exact representation of the system resource allocations, and therefore, is an exact model of the system. With this model, it is possible to determine precisely if an allocation request results in deadlock, by checking for cycles in the graph.

The allocation graph is defined with the following nodes and arcs:

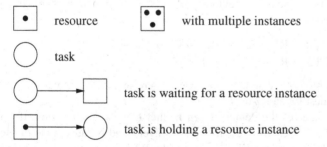

A resource is denoted by a square; each instance of the resource is represented by a dot in the square. A task is represented by a circle. A directed arc from a task (circle) to a resource (square) indicates that the task is waiting for the resource to become free. A directed arc from a resource instance (dot in a square) to a task (circle) indicates the resource instance is being held (used) by the task.

The reason a resource may have multiple instances, e.g., a tape drive resource might have 3 drives, is so a task can request a generic tape drive when the drives provide identical capabilities. A generic request for a tape drive, instead of a specific request for a particular tape drive, prevents waiting if the specific drive is in use but other equally usable drives are available; hence, a generic request enhances concurrency and the program is simplified.

The following allocation graph shows an instant in time during the execution of a system:

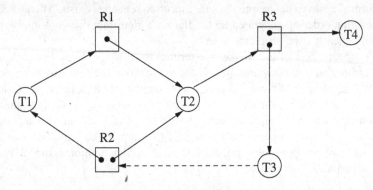

There are 4 tasks and 3 resources. T1 is holding an R2 and waiting for an R1. T2 is holding an R1 and R2, and waiting for an R3. T3 is holding an R3 and attempting to acquire an R2 (dashed line). T4 is holding an R3. For the moment, ignore T4 and the resource it is holding.

The resource allocator must decide if the request by T3 for an R2 will result in deadlock. To do this, it *pretends* to let T3 block waiting for an R2, because both instances are currently in use, by drawing the dashed line into the graph. The resource allocator now looks for cycles in the graph; if the graph (excluding T4) contains no cycles, the system is not deadlocked. This result follows from the 5 conditions for deadlock discussed previously. A cursory examination of the graph results in two cycles:

$$T1 \to R1 \to T2 \to R3 \to T3 \to R2 \to T1$$
$$T2 \to R3 \to T3 \to R2 \to T2$$

Trace through the graph to locate the two cycles. Therefore, the resource allocator would deny the request for an R2 by T3.

Note, when T3 receives the denial, it can neither busy wait nor block. If T3 busy waits for an R2 to become free, it becomes livelocked because none of the other tasks can make progress until T3 releases the R3 it is holding, but T3 will never release the R3 because the event it is spinning for cannot occur. Therefore, the system is in an undetectable mutual-exclusion deadlock because a cycle has logically been created by the live-blocking (spinning) of T3. It is undetectable because the system cannot determine that T3 is not making progress as it appears to be using CPU time (busy waiting). If T3 blocks for an R2 to become free, e.g., on a separate semaphore, it becomes synchronization deadlocked because none of the other tasks can make progress until T3 releases the R3 it is holding so none of these tasks can unblock the waiting T3. Therefore, the system is in a mutual-exclusion deadlock because a cycle has logically been created by the blocking of T3. Notice that different kinds of concurrency errors are occurring in this discussion depending on the perspective of task T3 or of the system.

Now re-introduce T4 and its resource into the graph. With this arc in the graph, there is no longer a deadlock, even with the cycles in the graph, because T4 eventually releases the R3 it is holding, which breaks the cycles because the arc between T2 and R3 changes direction. The reason the graph indicated a false deadlock is because the resources have multiple instances. If an isomorphic graph is created, where each resource has only one instance, as in:

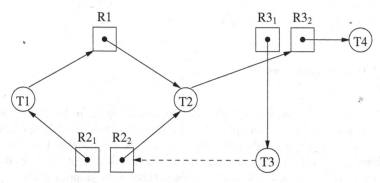

both cycles can be made to disappear by having T2 wait for $R3_2$, and hence, it is possible to allow T3 to block waiting for an R2. However, building this isomorphic graph is non-trivial; the decision to have T2 wait on $R3_2$, instead of $R3_1$ to break the cycle, is a difficult selection. Basically for each resource with multiple instances, the instances are separated, and for each task waiting for these resources, it can now wait for any of the separated instances; an edge from a process to a resource now has multiple vertices it can point to, and each arrangement of edges must be examined for cycles. Regardless of how the isomorphic graph is generated, a cycle now implies a deadlock; if a graph is found without a cycle, there is no deadlock. General cycle detection involves a depth-first search, which is $O(N+M)$ where N is the number of nodes and M is the number of edges. For the deadlock graphs, the number of nodes is $R+T$ and the number of edges is RT if each task is waiting for each resource and one task has all the resources. Therefore, cycle detection for the isomorphic graph is dominated by the $O(RT)$ term. One way to construct the isomorphic graph is to restrict allocation of resources to one unit at a time, which has the property of at most one request edge from any task node. This restriction can be imposed on the user or implemented implicitly by the resource allocator, i.e., a request for N resources is processed as N separate requests. To check for deadlock, cycle detection has to be performed for each allocated unit of resource versus an allocation of multiple units by a single request and then performing a single deadlock check.

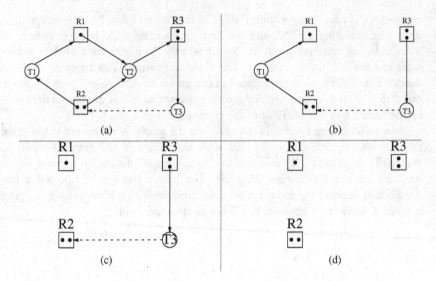

Fig. 8.2 Deadlock graph reduction

An alternative approach to locating deadlocks directly from the original allocation graph and handling multiple units in a single request is a technique called
graph reduction [5, pp. 188–189]. The approach is the same as the Banker's
algorithm, where the resource allocator performs a forward simulation, *pretending*
to execute and free resources to eliminate those parts of the graph where tasks are
clearly not deadlocked (see Fig. 8.2); if any tasks remain after all non-deadlock
ones are removed, there must be a deadlock. Starting with the graph on page 414
with the request by T3 for an R2, the algorithm searches the graph for a task that
is not blocked, such as T4 (it has no directed arc from itself to a resource). Like
the Banker's algorithm, the graph reduction algorithm pretends T4 completes and
releases its resources, producing Fig. 8.2a. Because there is now a free R3, it is
possible to grant the allocation request of T2 for an R3, which unblocks T2. It is now
possible to pretend T2 completes and releases its resources, producing Fig. 8.2b.
There is now a choice of unblocked tasks as either T1 or T3 can acquire resources R1
and R2, respectively. Like the Banker's algorithm, when there is a choice, it does not
matter which is chosen as the algorithm produces the same reduced graph. Choosing
task T1, it is now possible to pretend T1 completes and releases its resources,
producing Fig. 8.2c. Finally, it is now possible to pretend T3 completes and releases
its resources, producing Fig. 8.2d. As can be seen, there are no remaining tasks in
the reduced graph, which implies there is no deadlock. Furthermore, like the check
for correct execution of the Banker's algorithm, all the resources are now available.

The straightforward algorithm for graph reduction is similar in cost to the Banker's algorithm. Depending on the implementation approach, e.g., an adjacency matrix or adjacency lists, there are $O(RT)$ or $O(T)$ comparison operations to find an unblocked task, respectively. Once an unblocked task is located, it requires $O(R)$ list operations (assuming a task is waiting for every resource) to release its resources and assign them to any task waiting on each released resource (assuming there are links from resources to waiting tasks). Since there are T tasks, the total is $O(R^2T^2)$ or $O(RT^2)$ operations depending on the implementation approach; the cost increases by another search (at least $O(R)$) if there are no links from resources to waiting tasks. The storage cost is $O(RT)$.

Holt [5, pp. 193–194] showed it is possible to reduce the computation cost to $O(RT)$ comparisons and arithmetic operations, if care is taken in the implementation. For each process, a count is maintained of the resources it is waiting for; for each resource, a list of requesting processes is maintained in order by amount requested. Finally, a list of unblocked tasks is maintained. When a reduction occurs (the pretend execution of a task and release of its allocated resources), the wait counts and resource lists are updated; if a wait count reaches zero, the task is added to the unblocked list, which eliminates the search for an unblocked task. Each edge in the graph is examined at most once in updating wait counts, and there are at most $O(RT)$ edges. The amount of other work required to do a single reduction is $O(R)$, and thus $O(RT)$ overall. The amount of space required to store the graph is $O(RT)$, which dominates the cost of the other lists.

8.5 Deadlock Detection and Recovery

The final approach for dealing with deadlock is to just let it happen, check for it occasionally, and use pre-emption to recover resources to break the deadlock(s). Clearly, this is a dynamic approach, and it requires the ability to detect deadlock and preempt resources.

As seen in the previous discussion, discovering deadlock is not easy, has a non-trivial administration cost and requires a reasonable amount of cooperation among all executing tasks so the resource allocator always knows which tasks own what resources (imagine a task giving an allocated resource to another task and not telling the resource allocator). In effect, detecting deadlock requires constructing an allocation graph and performing a graph reduction. How does this differ from deadlock avoidance? Instead of checking for deadlock on each resource allocation, it is possible to check for deadlock much less frequently. For example, only check for deadlock(s) every T seconds or every time a resource cannot be immediately allocated. The latter choice is reasonable because most resources can be granted immediately, and hence, do not involve a blocking wait. If a resource cannot be granted immediately, either the system is busy or a deadlock has occurred and tasks are holding resources. In this situation, the system (or part of it) may lock up for T seconds until the deadlock is discovered and dealt with. For people, this kind of delay in discovering deadlock is usually not a problem if it occurs infrequently. However, for time-critical situations, such a delay may be unacceptable.

Finally, assuming the deadlock can be detected with reasonable administrative cost, how does the system recover? Clearly, recovery involves pre-emption of one or more tasks in each deadlock cycle. However, the pre-emption decision is not easy and should prevent starvation by not preempting the same task multiple times. First, given a set of tasks in a deadlock, which and how many of the tasks must be pre-empted? Second, given a selected task(s) to preempt, what form of pre-emption is performed? The form of pre-emption can be kind, by unblocking a task and informing it to release some held resource, or cruel, by killing the task and recovering all of its held resources, and possibly restarting it again at some time in the future. The former requires cooperation by the task to release a held resource (and how does the task decide which resource to release?). The latter has problems because the task may have changed the environment so it is now incorrect or incomplete. For example, the killed task may have gotten half way through updating a file. If the file is left updated, it contains erroneous information; if the task is restarted, it may start updating the file from the beginning instead of the pre-emption point, possibly corrupting the data in the first half of the file. While some resources like a printer cannot be easily pre-empted and subsequently returned, some resources can be pre-empted and returned without affecting the task holding the resource. For example, memory is a resource that can be pre-empted from a task by writing the task's memory out to disk and reading it back in again at a later time. While the task is on disk, the memory can be used by another task; when the task is read back in, it continues execution as if nothing happened. However, even this situation may not always work if the task has time critical components, like periodic reading from a device.

8.6   Summary

Finding and fixing errors in a concurrent program can be a daunting task. The temporal nature of a concurrent program, the non-determinism during execution, the need to synchronize threads, and the requirement for atomic access to shared data introduces concurrency specific errors: race error, livelock, starvation, and synchronization and mutual-exclusion deadlock. Unlike sequential programming, where most debugging occurs by inserting print statements to determine execution order and data values, concurrent programming cannot always use this technique because the print statements cause probe effects and the amount of output may be enormous due to the rarity of an error. The best approach is always prevention, so algorithms can statically eliminate concurrency errors. However, there is a price to be paid for prevention, either in inhibiting concurrency or under utilizing resources. For specific cases, prevention is a viable approach for reducing or eliminating concurrency errors. For the general case, the cost of prevention is usually unacceptable. The general case, which includes a mixture of different kinds of concurrent programs, is best handled by avoidance, if there is sufficient space and time, or recovery, if the cost of error detection must be kept low. Unfortunately, most concurrent systems provide little or no support for detecting errors nor aid in the debugging process; capabilities like deadlock avoidance or concurrent profilers, event traces, and debuggers are still the exception rather than the rule. The most common solution for most concurrent problems is for the computer operator to monitor the system and kill processes that might be causing problems or reboot the system when that fails. Clearly, rebooting the system is the ultimate pre-emption.

8.7 Questions

1. a. Define the terms:
      i. race condition
      ii. livelock
      iii. starvation
      iv. deadlock (name and define both kinds)
   b. Can any of these situations occur in a sequential program?
2. a. What concurrency properties are violated by a race condition?
   b. Why are race conditions hard to detect?
   c. What are possible consequences of race conditions in a concurrent program?
   d. What is the *probe effect* and why does it happen?
3. What does *no progress* mean with respect to a concurrent program?
4. Name 3 kinds of concurrent errors that result in *no progress*.
5. a. What is *live* about livelock?
   b. What execution states can a livelocked thread occupy?
   c. Can a livelock always be broken?
   d. Suggest ways to break a livelock.
   e. Give two examples where livelock situations occur in real life.
6. a. Why is starvation often ignored?
   b. Does starvation apply to only one thread or to multiple threads.
   c. What is *short-term* starvation?
7. Explain the difference between *livelock* and *starvation*.
8. Assume a program is not making progress. Give a simple test to determine if the program has a *livelock* or *deadlock*.
9. What are the five conditions for a mutual-exclusion deadlock?
10. Explain the problem and implication associated with attempting to prevent *synchronization deadlock*.
11. Explain the problem and implications associated with attempting to prevent *mutual-exclusion deadlock*. For each of the five conditions, discuss problems with attempting to prevent it.
12. With respect to preventing conditions for mutual-exclusion deadlock, which one has the most practical value.

13. Consider the 4-way stop situation in Fig. 8.1, p. 398c. What is the traffic law that attempts to prevent this situation from occurring.

14. The ordered resource policy (ORP) divides resources into groups where a resource can be requested from group i if the requester is not holding a resource from group j where $j \geq i$.

    a. Explain how ORP prevents deadlock.
    b. Is this policy for deadlock prevention or avoidance? Explain.
    c. Explain how ORP leads to inefficient resource utilization for a simple example with two tasks, T1 and T2, and two resources, R1 and R2.

15. The Dining Philosopher algorithm page 389 had philosophers pick up both forks at the same time. Is this an example of deadlock prevention or avoidance? Explain.

16. If tasks are organized in a ring with a shared resource between each, as in:

$$R_5 \qquad T_1$$

$$T_5 \qquad\qquad R_1$$

$$R_4 \qquad\qquad T_2$$

$$T_4 \qquad\qquad R_2$$

$$R_3 \qquad T_3$$

and each task needs *both* the resource on the left and right occasionally, there is the potential for mutual-exclusion deadlock if each task acquires the right resource and then tries to acquire the left resource because of a hold and wait cycle. Suggest a resource allocation policy (ordering/scheduling) that can be applied in this specific scenario to prevent mutual-exclusion deadlock.

17. Given the following code fragment:

```
uSemaphore L1(1), L2(1); // open
task1          task2
L1.P()         L2.P()
  R1             R2
  L2.P()         L1.P()
    R2             R1
```

Explain the following:

    a. Explain how deadlock can occur.
    b. What *kind* of deadlock is it?
    c. Change the example so the deadlock cannot occur.
    d. Give one negative side-effect of the change.
    e. Name and explain one of the five deadlock conditions your solution precludes.

18. Consider a system in which there is a single resource with 11 identical units. The system uses the banker's algorithm to avoid deadlock. Suppose there are four processes P_1, P_2, P_3, P_4 with maximum resource requirements $P_{max} = (m_1\ m_2\ m_3\ m_4)$ units held by P_i, respectively. A system state is denoted by $P_{held} = (h_1\ h_2\ h_3\ h_4)$, where h_i is the number of resource units held by P_i, respectively. Which of the following states are safe? Use the banker's algorithm to justify your answers.

   a. $P_{max} = (2\ 7\ 5\ 8)$
      i. $P_{held} = (2\ 2\ 0\ 7)$
      ii. $P_{held} = (2\ 4\ 1\ 4)$
      iii. $P_{held} = (2\ 4\ 4\ 1)$
   b. $P_{max} = (2\ 5\ 8\ 8)$
      i. $P_{held} = (1\ 1\ 4\ 4)$
      ii. $P_{held} = (0\ 1\ 2\ 7)$
      iii. $P_{held} = (1\ 2\ 4\ 2)$
   c. $P_{max} = (2\ 7\ 4\ 9)$
      i. $P_{held} = (1\ 3\ 1\ 5)$
      ii. $P_{held} = (1\ 2\ 3\ 4)$
      iii. $P_{held} = (1\ 3\ 2\ 4)$

19. Consider a system with four resources and processes. The system uses the banker's algorithm to avoid deadlock. Given the following maximum resource requirements and currently allocated resources, show the *need* matrix, and for each step in the banker's algorithm, show the remaining amount of each available resource both after theoretically granting them to a task and after the task has theoretically finished with them. Finally, state if the system is safe or not.

a.

Task	Resource 1 Alloc.	Max.	Resource 2 Alloc.	Max.	Resource 3 Alloc.	Max.	Resource 4 Alloc.	Max.
T1	0	1	2	2	1	3	1	1
T2	4	5	2	5	1	2	1	1
T3	1	7	0	2	1	2	1	1
T4	2	4	1	1	0	1	0	0
Total units	9		5		5		4	

b.

Task	Resource 1 Alloc.	Max.	Resource 2 Alloc.	Max.	Resource 3 Alloc.	Max.	Resource 4 Alloc.	Max.
T1	0	1	2	3	1	3	1	1
T2	4	5	2	5	1	2	1	1
T3	1	7	0	2	1	2	1	1
T4	2	4	1	1	0	1	0	0
Total units	9		5		5		5	

20. Why is it always safe to give a process the last unit it needs to reach its maximum needed amount?

21. Consider the following situation. A set of N tasks shares M identical resources. Resources may be acquired and released strictly one at a time. Each task uses at least one resource but no task ever needs more than M resources. The sum of the maximum needs for all tasks is strictly less than $N + M$. Show that deadlock cannot occur in this system.

22. If the banker's algorithm finds there is a choice among tasks that can execute, what does this imply and how should the algorithm proceed? Explain.

23. If the banker's algorithm finds that a particular state is unsafe, does this guarantee that this particular state deadlocks should execution be allowed to proceed? Explain.

24. Explain briefly how process allocation graphs can be used to detect deadlock (do not explain what a process allocation graph is, just explain how) and why are they not commonly used in operating systems.

25. Is a resource-allocation graph an example of deadlock prevention or avoidance? Explain.

26. For each of the resource-allocation graphs in Fig. 8.3, determine if the system is in deadlock by using graph reduction.

27. Explain the difference between deadlock *prevention*, *avoidance* and *recovery*.

28. a. Name a technique that could be used to *prevent* mutual-exclusion deadlock due to hold and wait cycles.

    b. Name a technique that could be used to *avoid* mutual-exclusion deadlock.

29. In deadlock detection-and-recovery, why is *preemption* of a deadlocked task difficult?

30. Explain how *nested monitor calls* can result in deadlock (see Sect. 9.9, p. 471).

    Suggest a resource allocation policy (ordering/scheduling) that can be applied in this specific scenario to prevent mutual-exclusion deadlock.

References

1. Coffman, Jr., E.G., Elphick, M.J., Shoshani, A.: System deadlocks. ACM Comput. Surv. 3(2), 67–78 (1971). DOI http://doi.acm.org/10.1145/356586.356588
2. Dijkstra, E.W.: Cooperating sequential processes. Tech. rep., Technological University, Eindhoven, Netherlands (1965). Reprinted in [3] pp. 43–112.
3. Genuys, F. (ed.): Programming Languages. Academic Press, London, New York (1968). NATO Advanced Study Institute, Villard-de-Lans, 1966
4. Havender, J.W.: Avoiding deadlock in multitasking systems. IBM Syst. J. 7(2), 74–84 (1968)
5. Holt, R.C.: Some deadlock properties of computer systems. ACM Comput. Surv. 4(3), 179–196 (1972)

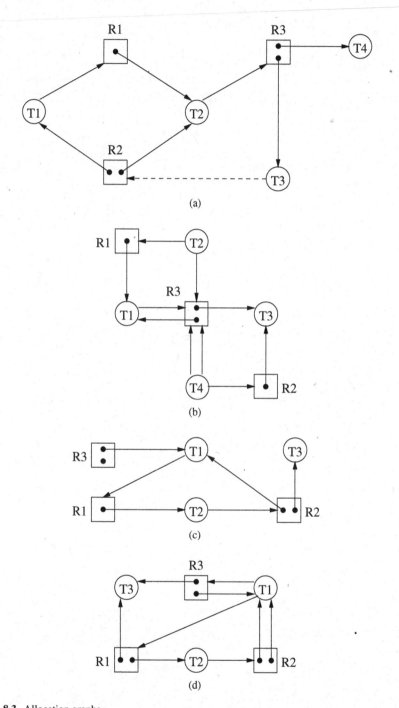

Fig. 8.3 Allocation graphs

Chapter 9
High-Level Concurrency Constructs

Chapter 7, p. 313 on threads and locks ended with the readers and writer problem, which is an important concurrent problem. However, it is clear that the solutions to the readers and writer problem were becoming complex; too complex to feel comfortable about the correctness of the solution without extensive analysis. While coding conventions like split-binary semaphores and baton passing give a formal design approach, the resulting programs are still complex, both to manage and maintain; basically, relying on programmers following coding conventions to assure correctness is a poor approach. As well, there is the subtle problem of properly handling staleness and writing because of the "window" for interruption between releasing the entry semaphore and blocking. In essence, we have arrived at the same impasse that occurred with software solutions for mutual exclusion, that is, the complexity and inefficiency of the locking solution is increasing for more complex critical-section. Therefore, it is worthwhile to search for a different approach to reduce the complexity, as for hardware solutions for mutual exclusion. However, in this case, the programming language, not the hardware, provides the mechanism to simplify the solution.

The conclusion is that explicit locks, such as semaphores, are too low level for concurrent programming.

We must therefore conclude that semaphores do not enable a compiler to give a programmer the effective assistance in error detection that he should expect from an implementation of a high-level language [4, p. 239].

Essentially, using explicit locks is the concurrent equivalent of assembler programming. Just as most assembler programming is replaced with programming in a high-level language, explicit locks can be replaced with high-level concurrency constructs in a programming language. The goal is to get the compiler to check for correct usage and follow any complex coding conventions implicitly. The drawback is that language constructs may preclude certain specialized techniques, therefore introducing inefficiency or inhibiting concurrency. For most concurrent programs, these drawbacks are insignificant in comparison with the speed of composition, and subsequent reliability and maintainability of the high-level concurrent program.

© Springer International Publishing Switzerland 2016
P.A. Buhr, *Understanding Control Flow*, DOI 10.1007/978-3-319-25703-7_9

(The same is true for high-level programming versus assembler programming.) Only very rarely should it be necessary to drop down to explicit locks to apply a specialized technique to achieve maximum speed or concurrency.

As well, concurrency constructs are essential for sound and efficient code generation by a compiler [7]. If a compiler is unaware of concurrency in a program, it may perform valid sequential code optimizations that *invalidate* the concurrent program. For example, in the code fragment:

```
P( sem );
i += 1;
V( sem );
```

a compiler might move the call to V *before* the increment because the variables i and sem appear to be independent. While this optimization is valid for a sequential program, it clearly invalidates a concurrent program. If this optimization is turned off to prevent this problem, many valid optimizations do not occur, reducing the overall efficiency of the program because of a small number of problem situations. High-level constructs delineate all the cases where a compiler can or cannot perform particular optimizations.

This chapter begins to examine high-level concurrent program concepts to help simplify the complexity of writing a concurrent program, and provide for sound and efficient implementation. Subsequent chapters examine more complex concurrent constructs.

9.1   Critical Region

One of the first high-level constructs to be proposed was the **critical region**. It was first suggested and discussed by C. A. R. Hoare [11], and subsequently extended by Per Brinch Hansen [3, 4]; the extended form of Per Brinch Hansen is presented. Two new features were proposed: a declaration qualifier, **shared**, and a new control structure, **region**. The declaration qualifier is used to indicate variables accessed by multiple threads of control, which are shared resources, as in:

```
shared int v;
```

The variable v is an integer accessible by multiple threads of control. Now, all access to a **shared** variable *must* occur in a **region** statement, and within the region, mutual exclusion is guaranteed, as in:

```
// access to v disallowed
region v {
    // access to v allowed
}
// access to v disallowed
```

A simple implementation would be nothing more than creating an implicit lock for each **shared** variable, and acquiring and releasing the lock at the start and end of the **region** statement, as in:

```
shared int v;     MutexLock v_lock;
region v {        v_lock.acquire();
     ...
}                 v_lock.release();
```

One additional extension to the critical region is allowing reading of a shared variable *outside* the critical region and modification only *within* a region, e.g.:

```
shared int v;
int i = v;        // reading allowed outside a region
region v {
    v = i;        // writing allowed only in a region
    i = v;        // reading still allowed in a region
}
```

The compiler can easily check this particular semantics, and enforce it. (Notice, this capability is already possible when working with mutex locks.) However, it is unclear if this extension provides any significant new capability. In particular, there is the potential problem of reading partially updated information while a task is modifying a shared variable in a region, which can result in obtaining inconsistent values (e.g., a negative bank account balance because the balance temporarily goes negative at one point during updating). Even if the values are consistent, reading a shared variable outside a region is speculative, as the value may change immediately. However, this capability might provide a low-cost mechanism, for example, to statistically chart a shared variable over time, where the chart is a representative sample of the data values. Not having to acquire mutual exclusion to sample (read) the shared variable reduces execution cost and does not inhibit concurrency for other tasks modifying the variable.

While not a significant step forward over mutex locks, the critical region does have one compelling advantage: it enforces the entry and exit protocol through the syntax. Forgetting either of the braces for the **region** block results in a compilation error, i.e., syntax error; forgetting either a P or V results in a runtime error, which is much harder to detect, e.g., the race error. Furthermore, the critical region delineates the boundary for certain compiler optimizations, e.g., code cannot be moved into or out of the region block. Thus, the **region** statement is a simple example of a higher-level concurrency construct, and it illustrates the important idea of telling the compiler that the program is, in fact, a concurrent program.

Nesting of critical regions is also possible, as in:

```
shared int x, y;
region x {
    ...
    region y {
        ...
    }
    ...
}
```

where mutually exclusive access is acquired for shared variable x, and subsequently, acquired for shared variable y. The inner critical region could be in a conditional statement, e.g., an **if** statement, and hence, not always executed. Nesting allows acquiring shared resources only when needed, which maximizes the potential for concurrency. However, nested acquisitions of locks have the potential for deadlock, as in:

```
shared int x, y;

    task₁            task₂
    region x {       region y {
       ...              ...
       region y {       region x {
          ...              ...
       }                }
       ...              ...
    }                }
```

While the identical problem can be constructed with a mutex lock, it is (usually) impossible for the compiler to detect the situation and issue a warning or error. On the other hand, the critical region statement gives the compiler the potential to statically check for this deadlock situation if it can examine all code that composes a program.[1]

Even though the critical region has advantages over a mutex lock, it only handles critical sections; no support is available for synchronization, and hence, communication. Using critical regions for mutual exclusion and some synchronization lock for synchronization is not ideal; these two concepts need to be integrated.

9.2   Conditional Critical Region

To deal with the lack of synchronization capability, the critical region is augmented with a conditional delay capability involving the shared variable. The first form of the conditional critical-region was devised by C. A. R. Hoare [11], and only implemented in a restricted form[2] in the programming language Edison [6, p. 371]:

```
region shared-variable {
    await ( conditional-expression );
    ...
}
```

To enter a conditional critical-region, it must be simultaneously true that no task is in any critical region for the specified shared variable and the value of the **await** expression for the particular critical region is true. If the **await** expression is false, the task attempting entry is blocked (busy waiting is unacceptable) and the region lock is implicitly released so that other tasks can continue to access the shared variable (otherwise there is synchronization deadlock). A crucial point is that the block and release occur atomically, as for the extended P operation in Sect. 7.6.6, p. 370, so there is no possibility for staleness problems associated with interruption between these operations.

---

[1] Aliasing problems may preclude complete checking for nested deadlock situations.

[2] No shared variables were supported; hence, the **region** statement had only a conditional expression so only one critical region could be active in a program.

A good way to illustrate the conditional critical-region is through the bounded buffer example, which requires both mutual exclusion and synchronization.

```
shared queue<int> q; // shared queue of integers
```

producer task	consumer task

```
region q {                      region q {
    await ( ! q.full() );           await ( ! q.empty() );
    // add element to queue         // remove element from queue
}                               }
```

The left conditional critical-region can only be entered by a producer if there is no other task in either critical region for q, and the queue is not full. The right conditional critical-region can only be entered by a consumer if there is no other task in either critical region for q, and the queue is not empty. As a result, the producer cannot attempt to insert elements into a full buffer, nor can the consumer attempt to remove elements from an empty buffer. Hence, the conditional critical-region supports the necessary non-FIFO servicing of producer and consumer when the buffer is empty or full.

Does this solution handle multiple producers and multiple consumers using the shared queue q? The answer is yes, but it does inhibit concurrency slightly. Recall that the bounded buffer in Sect. 7.5.2, p. 350 uses different locks to protect simultaneous insertion or removal by producers and consumers, respectively. Therefore, a producer can be inserting at the same time as a consumer is removing, except when the list is empty. However, the critical region ensures that only one task is using the shared queue at a time; therefore, there can never be simultaneous insertions and removals at either ends of the queue. Is this loss of concurrency justified? It largely depends on the problem, but, in general, the loss is justified because of the other gains associated with using high-level constructs. In particular, the time to insert or remove is short so the chance of a simultaneous insert and remove occurring is relatively small, and hence, any delay is very short.

What about more complex problems, like the readers and writer problem? While it is possible to build an atomic increment or a binary/general semaphore using a critical region (see Fig. 9.1), and hence construct a solution to the readers and writer problem using the previous solutions, this defeats the purpose of having high-level concurrency constructs. However, the obvious solution for the readers and writer problem using conditional critical-regions does not work:

```
shared struct {
    int rcnt, wcnt;
} rw = { 0, 0 };
```

reader task	writer task

```
region rw {                     region rw {
    await ( wcnt == 0 );            await ( rcnt == 0 );
    rcnt += 1;                      wcnt += 1;
    // read                         // write
    rcnt -= 1;                      wcnt -= 1;
}                               }
```

Here, a reader task waits until there is no writer ($wcnt = 0$), and a writer task waits until there is no reader ($rcnt = 0$). Furthermore, only one writer can be in the critical

```
int atomicInc( shared int &val ) {        shared struct semaphore {
    int temp;                                 int cnt;
    region val {                          };
        temp = val;                       void P( shared semaphore &s ) {
        val += 1;                             region s {
    }                                             await ( s.cnt > 0 );
    return temp;                                  s.cnt -= 1;
}                                             }

                                          }
                                          void V( shared semaphore &s ) {
                                              region s {
                                                  s.cnt += 1;
                                              }

                                          }
```

        (a) Atomic increment   (b) General semaphore

Fig. 9.1 Low-level concurrency primitives using critical region

region for shared variable rw at a time so writing is serialized. However, the problem is reading the resource in the critical region, because that prevents simultaneous readers; i.e., only one reader can be in the critical region for shared variable rw at a time.

This problem can be solved by moving the reading of the resource operation *outside* the reader critical region by dividing it into two:

```
region rw {            // entry protocol
    await ( wcnt == 0 );
    rcnt += 1;
}
// read
region rw {            // exit protocol
    rcnt -= 1;
}
```

Now a reader only establishes mutual exclusion while manipulating the shared counters, not while reading the resource. This structure is unnecessary for writing because there is at most one writer and that writer can be the only task with mutual exclusion in the critical region. It is assumed there is no potential for starvation of readers, because when a writer leaves the critical region some fair choice must be made by the critical region implementation between a reader or writer task as both counters wcnt and rcnt are 0. However, this solution has the potential for starvation of writers; a continuous stream of readers keeps rcnt > 0, and hence wcnt == 0, so no writer can enter the writer critical region.

Per Brinch Hansen made a subtle but important modification to the conditional critical-region to solve this problem: allow placement of the synchronization condition anywhere within the critical region. (This modification is similar to the notion of an exit in the middle of a loop.) For example, in:

```
region v {
    s1
    await ( ... );             // condition in middle of critical region
    s2
}
```

mutual exclusion for v is acquired at the start of the region and *s1* is executed. If the condition of the **await** is true, *s2* is executed and mutual exclusion is released on exit from the region. If the condition of the **await** is false, the task blocks at the **await** and releases mutual exclusion (atomically) so other tasks may enter regions for the shared variable. Only when the condition is made true by another task does the blocked task continue execution; it does so *after* the **await**, executes *s2*, and mutual exclusion is released on exit from the region. Notice, a task does not *restart* the region statement when the **await** condition becomes true, it continues from the **await** clause where it blocked (like continuing after a P operation on a semaphore after it is Ved).

Brinch Hansen then presented the following writer code:

```
region rw {
    wcnt += 1;
    await ( rcnt == 0 );        // condition in middle of critical region
    // write
    wcnt -= 1;
}
```

(Actually, the writer code in [3, p. 577] is more complex and the reason is discussed shortly.) This subtle change allows each writer task to acquire unconditional mutual exclusion up to the point of the condition before possibly blocking, allowing an arriving writer to set the writer counter so that readers know if there are waiting writers. In essence, the code before the condition of the critical region is equivalent to part of the code in the entry protocol of the split-binary semaphore solutions where the entry semaphore allows incrementing counters before blocking. Unfortunately, this writer code gives priority to writer tasks, and hence, can cause starvation of reader tasks, e.g., a continuous stream of writers keeps wcnt > 0, and hence rcnt == 0, so no reader can enter its critical region. It turns out that Brinch Hansen *wanted* this semantics; but it is not what we want.

To build a solution with no starvation and no staleness using conditional critical-regions is more complicated, and requires using tickets, as in Sect. 6.4.4, p. 278 and suggested again in Sect. 7.6.6, p. 370. The basic approach is for each reader and writer task to first take a ticket to define arrival order, and then conditionally check if it can proceed by comparing the ticket with a serving value, as in:

```
shared struct {
    int rcnt, wcnt, tickets, serving;
} rw = { 0, 0, 0, 0 };
```

reader task	**writer task**

```
region rw {                // entry protocol      region rw {
    int ticket = tickets;                              int ticket = tickets;
    tickets += 1;                                      tickets += 1;
    await ( ticket == serving && wcnt == 0 );          await ( ticket == serving && rcnt == 0 );
    rcnt += 1;                                         wcnt += 1;
    serving += 1;                                      serving += 1;
}                                                  }
// read                                            // write
region rw {                // exit protocol
    rcnt -= 1;                                         wcnt -= 1;
}                                                  }
```

The conditions for the reader and writer task are the conjunction of whether it is their turn and a task of the other kind is not using the resource. Only when both are true can a task proceed. Notice the reader entry protocol increments the serving counter *before* exiting the first **region** so that another reader task may enter. If a writer task has the next ticket, it remains blocked because rcnt > 0, as do all subsequent readers because their ticket values are greater than the writer's. While the writer protocol appears to do the same, mutual exclusion is not released from the **await** until the end of the **region**, so no task accessing the same shared variable may enter the critical region. As a result, once a writer task's condition becomes true, neither a reader nor a writer task can take a ticket nor have its condition become true because of the mutual-exclusion property of a region.

A consequence of this particular solution is that there may be a significant delay before any task may enter the critical region because writing the resource is done with mutual exclusion. Therefore, newly arriving reader and writer tasks must block *outside* the critical region waiting to obtain a ticket. Now if the internal implementation of a critical region does not maintain and service these tasks in FIFO order, there is the potential for staleness and freshness. If there is no FIFO ordering, it is possible to compensate by modifying the writer protocol so writing the resource is not done in the critical region (like reading), as in:

```
region rw {              // entry protocol
    int ticket = tickets;
    tickets += 1;
  await ( ticket == serving && rcnt == 0 );
    wcnt += 1;
}
// write
region rw {              // exit protocol
    wcnt -= 1;
    serving += 1;
}
```

It is now possible for reader and writer tasks to obtain a ticket while writing is occurring; the expectation is that tasks will only block inside the entry protocol on the await condition because the unconditional code at the start of the entry protocol is so short. Clearly, there is no guarantee this is always true, but it may be as probabilistically correct as such a system can come. (Brinch Hansen used this form for his writer protocol in [3, p. 577] for the same reason.) Notice that it is necessary to move the increment of the serving counter to the writer exit protocol, otherwise if a writer task has the next ticket, it could violate the mutual exclusion because rcnt == 0. By incrementing the serving counter *after* the current write is complete, no progress can be made by the next writer in this scenario even though rcnt == 0.

9.2.1   Implementation

While the conditional critical-region is appealing, it virtually precludes any form of direct cooperation between the releaser of the mutual exclusion and the next task to acquire mutual exclusion. Since there are no explicit queues a task can block on, it is impossible for an exiting task to directly select the next task to execute in the critical region. Thus, an exiting task may know precisely which task is next to use the resource, however, it cannot express this information to the implementation of the critical region. At best, cooperation can be accomplished indirectly through a mechanism like a ticket; unfortunately, managing tickets is additional complexity, which, in turn, raises the complexity of the solution. Therefore, for problems like the readers and writer, where service order is crucial, the conditional critical-region provides no direct help, which negates the reason of using a high-level concurrency construct.

In addition to this lack of expressibility, the implementation of the conditional critical-region is expensive.

The main difficulty of achieving an efficient implementation is the reevaluation of synchronizing conditions each time a critical region is completed [4, p. 243].

The basic implementation of a conditional critical-region is illustrated in Fig. 9.2. Each shared variable has associated with it two queues: an entry queue for tasks waiting to enter the region for the shared variable and a conditional queue for tasks having entered the region but unable to execute because of a false condition. All tasks with a false condition wait on the same conditional queue independent of the conditional expression, i.e., there is only one conditional queue for all the different conditionals for a particular shared variable. When a task leaves the region, either because of a false condition for an **await** or completion of the region code, it may have changed the state associated with the shared variable so that one or more of the conditions for the waiting tasks are now true. Therefore, all tasks on the conditional queue are transferred to the entry queue, and some task on the entry queue (usually the front one) is moved to the ready state to attempt execution of the region. Specifically, each **await**(cond) is translated into:

```
if ( ! cond ) {
    // move all tasks from conditional to entry queue
    do {
        // block on conditional queue
    } while ( ! cond );
}
```

and on exit from the region, all tasks are moved from the conditional to entry queue. Notice, a task waiting on an **await** only moves tasks from the conditional to entry queue once; thereafter, it wakes up inside a repeat loop, checks its condition, and either proceeds or blocks again, otherwise tasks would endlessly cycle between the two queues. (Think about this last point and make sure you understand it before proceeding.)

An alternative implementation, involving cooperation, has the task blocking or leaving the region reevaluate the conditional expressions on behalf of the waiting tasks on the conditional queue to see if any task can enter the region. While this latter approach seems reasonable, it imposes limitations on the form of the conditional expression; in particular, the conditional may only involve the shared variable and constants, otherwise the state of the waiting tasks has to be accessed

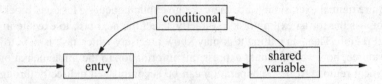

Fig. 9.2 Implementation of conditional critical region

for local variables. This particular implementation restriction is discussed further in this chapter.

While neither of these implementations are busy waiting, because there is always a bound on the number of tasks to be tested, i.e., the number of tasks on the conditional queue, both are clearly expensive, especially if there are a large number of tasks accessing the critical regions for a particular shared variable, and the conditions are complex. Furthermore, there must be some level of fairness to ensure starvation and possibly staleness cannot occur. For example, after a task leaves a region, tasks waiting on the conditional queue might be moved to the entry queue in FIFO order and *before* tasks that are waiting on the entry queue, so tasks waiting the longest have a greater opportunity of executing first. In all cases, the underlying reason for the complexity, and hence, inefficiency of the conditional critical-region is the lack of direct cooperation; this issue is developed further in this chapter.

9.3   Monitor

While the conditional critical-region was an important first step towards moving concurrency into a programming language to provide a high-level concurrency construct, it fails to provide simple, efficient solutions for medium difficulty concurrent problems, like readers and writer. This point was identified very quickly after introducing the conditional critical-region by its initial creators. As a result, they went back to the drawing board and created the next level of high-level concurrency constructs, this time dealing with the shortcomings of the conditional critical-region.

Interestingly, at the same time work was occurring on the development of high-level concurrency language constructs, the initial work on object-oriented programming was occurring. It was inevitable that interaction occur, and the result was the first object-oriented concurrency construct, called a **monitor**. Again, it was C. A. R. Hoare and Per Brinch Hansen who did the initial work on the development of the monitor:

> The main problem is that the use of critical regions scattered throughout a program makes it difficult to keep track of how a shared variable is used by concurrent processes. It has therefore recently been suggested that one should combine a shared variable and the possible operations on it in a single, syntactic construct called a *monitor* [4, p. 244].

Such a collection of associated data and procedures is known as a *monitor*; and a suitable notation can be based on the *class* notation of SIMULA67[3] [12, p. 549].

Hence, the basic monitor is an abstract data type combining shared data with serialization of its modification through the operations on it. In μC++, a monitor is an object with mutual exclusion defined by a monitor type that has all the properties of a **class**. The general form of the monitor type is the following:

```
_Monitor monitor-name {
  private:
    ...              // these members are not visible externally
  protected:
    ...              // these members are visible to descendants
  public:
    ...              // these members are visible externally
};
```

In addition, it has an implicit mutual-exclusion property, like a critical region, i.e., only one task at a time can be executing a monitor operation on the shared data. The monitor shared data is normally **private** so the abstraction and mutual-exclusion property ensure serial access to it. However, this simple description does not illustrate the additional synchronization capabilities of the monitor, which are discussed shortly. A consequence of the mutual-exclusion property is that only one member routine can be *active* at a time because that member can read and write the shared data. Therefore, a call to a member of a monitor may block the calling task if there is already a task executing a member of the monitor. Only after the task in the monitor returns from the member routine can the next call occur. μC++ defines a member with this implicit mutual-exclusion property as a **mutex member** (short for mutual-exclusion member), and the public members of a monitor are normally mutex members (exceptions are discussed shortly). Similar to coroutines (see Sect. 4.1.3, p. 129), a monitor is either **active** or **inactive**, depending on whether or not a task is executing a mutex member (versus a task executing a coroutine main). The monitor mutual exclusion is enforced by **locking** the monitor when execution of a mutex member begins and **unlocking** it when the active task voluntarily gives up control of the monitor. In essence, the fields of a shared record have become the member variables of a monitor, and a region statement has become a mutex member, with the addition of parameters.

The following example compares an atomic counter written as a critical region and as a monitor:

---

[3]SIMULA67 [9] was the first object-oriented programming language.

Critical Region	Monitor
| ```
void inc( shared int &counter ) {
    region counter {
        counter += 1;
    }
}
shared int cnt = 0;
inc( cnt );   // atomically increment counter
``` | ```
_Monitor atomicCnt {
    int counter;
  public:
    atomicCnt( int start ) : counter(start) {}
    void inc() {
        counter += 1;
    }
};
atomicCnt cnt(0);
cnt.inc();   // atomically increment counter
``` |

(In both cases, additional routines are necessary to read the counter and provide other operations.) Notice, a monitor type can generate multiple monitor objects (called monitors) through declarations, just like a coroutine type can generate multiple coroutines. Similarly, it is possible to create multiple instances of a shared type with associated critical regions.

As for a critical region, each monitor has a lock, which is basically Ped on entry to a mutex member and Ved on exit, as in:

```
_Monitor atomicCnt {
    MutexLock m_Lock;              // implicit code
    int counter;
  public:
    ...
    void inc(...) {
        m_Lock.acquire();         // implicit code
        counter += 1;
        m_Lock.release();         // implicit code
    }
}
```

Because a monitor is like a shared variable, each monitor must have an implicit entry queue on which calling tasks block if the monitor is active (busy waiting is unacceptable). In μC++, arriving tasks wait to enter the monitor on the entry queue, and this queue is maintained in order of arrival of tasks to the monitor (see top of Fig. 9.3). When a task exits a mutex member, the next task waiting on the entry queue is made ready so tasks are serviced in FIFO order, and the monitor mutual exclusion is implicitly passed to this task (i.e., the baton is passed) so when it restarts no further checking is necessary.

At this stage, the main difference between the critical region and monitor is strictly software engineering with respect to localizing the code manipulating the shared data. However, if this was the only difference between the critical region and the monitor, there would be little improvement in *expressing* complex concurrency problems. The major advancement of the monitor is the conditional blocking capabilities for synchronization over those of the conditional critical-region so that simple solutions can be constructed for problems like the readers and writer. Most of the remainder of this chapter is devoted to explaining these advanced conditional blocking capabilities.

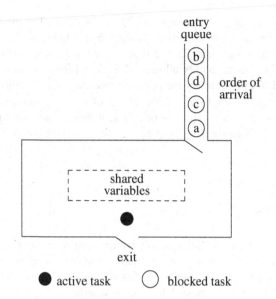

Fig. 9.3 Entry queue

9.3.1 Mutex Calling Mutex

One property that varies among different kinds of monitors is the ability of a mutex member to call another mutex member. In the simple monitor implementation given above using a mutex lock, the first call to the mutex member acquires the lock and a second call by the same task to the same or different mutex member results in mutual-exclusion deadlock of the task with itself. (Why is this not a synchronization deadlock?) Hence, one mutex member cannot call another. However, this restriction can be dealt with by moving the shared code into a no-mutex member and having the mutex members call the no-mutex member, as in:

Mutex calling Mutex	Mutex calling No-Mutex

_Monitor M {
 	
public:
  mem1(...) { s1 }
  mem2(...) { mem1(); ... }
}
	_Monitor M {
	  mem3(..) { s1 } // no-mutex, shared code
	public:
	  mem1(...) { mem3(...) } // mutex
	  mem2(...) { mem3(...); ... } // mutex
	}

Here, mutex member mem2 is calling mutex member mem1 and then performing some additional work. To prevent a deadlock, the code for mem1 is factored into a no-mutex routine, mem3, and mem3 is called from mutex members mem1 and mem2. This restructuring ensures that only one attempt is made to acquire the monitor lock.

While the restructured monitor is strongly equivalent to the original monitor, it introduces additional complexity having nothing to do with the monitor's actual implementation. Therefore, it is more convenient for programmers if the language

allows calls from one mutex member to another. μC++ *does* allow the active task in
a monitor to call among mutex members without deadlocking. In effect, once a task
acquires the monitor lock it can acquire it again, like the owner lock discussed in
Sect. 7.3.1, p. 320. This capability allows a task to call into the mutex member of
one monitor, and from that mutex member call into the mutex member of another
monitor, and then call back to a mutex member of the first monitor, i.e., form a
cycle of calls among mutex members of different monitors. Therefore, in μC++,
once a task acquires a monitor, there is no restriction on the use of the monitor's
functionality.

9.4   Scheduling

The conditional blocking capabilities of a monitor are referred to as scheduling,
where tasks schedule themselves by explicitly blocking when execution cannot
continue and explicitly unblocking tasks that can execute when the state of the
monitor changes (i.e., cooperation). The type of scheduling capability differs with
the kind of monitor, and the kind of monitor controls how much and how easy it is
to build cooperation. (This issue is discussed in detail in Sect. 9.11, p. 474.) Notice,
scheduling in this context does not imply that tasks are made running; it means a task
waits on a queue until it can continue execution and then is made ready. Only when
a task waits on the ready queue is it finally scheduled by the CPU and made running.
Hence, there can be multiple levels of scheduling occurring in a system, and a task
may have to wait at each level before making progress. As a concurrent programmer,
it is necessary to write complex scheduling schemes for different shared resources
to achieve various effects. For example, for a file containing shared information,
access to the file by multiple tasks may be scheduled using the readers and writer
algorithm to achieve maximum concurrency among readers and writers of the file.
A file can be implemented as a monitor with a simple interface called by tasks for
reading and writing data from the file, and within the monitor, the calling tasks are
scheduling for reading and writing. More complex scheduling occurs for certain
disk scheduling algorithms, where multiple task requests for I/O to different files on
a particular disk are ordered from highest to lowest by track number, and serviced
in that order. A disk can be implemented as a monitor with a simple interface called
by tasks for I/O of data on the disk, and within the monitor, the calling tasks are
scheduled from highest to lowest by track number. Notice, there are three levels
of scheduling occurring: first, a task is scheduled for reading or writing on the
file by the file monitor, then scheduled for I/O on the disk containing the file by
the device monitor, and finally, scheduled for access to a CPU to interact with the
disk device performing the data transfer by the operating system. Such complex
scheduling patterns are common in computer systems.

Two basic techniques for performing scheduling are introduced and discussed in
detail: external and internal scheduling. Most high-level concurrency systems support at least one of these techniques, and μC++ supports both. External scheduling
schedules tasks outside the monitor and is accomplished with the accept statement.

```
template<typename ELEMTYPE> _Monitor BoundedBuffer {
    int front, back, count;
    ELEMTYPE Elements[20];
  public:
    BoundedBuffer() : front(0), back(0), count(0) {}
    _Nomutex int query() { return count; }

    void insert( ELEMTYPE elem ) {
        if ( count == 20 ) _Accept( remove );  // hold calls
        Elements[back] = elem;
        back = ( back + 1 ) % 20;
        count += 1;                  ·
    }
    ELEMTYPE remove() {
        if ( count == 0 ) _Accept( insert );   // hold calls
        ELEMTYPE elem = Elements[front];
        front = ( front + 1 ) % 20;
        count -= 1;
        return elem;
    }
};
```

Fig. 9.4 Monitor bounded buffer: external scheduling

Internal scheduling schedules tasks inside the monitor and is accomplished using wait and signal. A system can exist with only one of the two scheduling schemes, but it will be shown there is only a weak equivalence between the schemes.

9.4.1 External Scheduling

To illustrate external monitor scheduling, a μC++ generic bounded buffer example is presented in Fig. 9.4. The basic monitor definition given thus far is sufficient to understand the example; a detailed description of a μC++ monitor is presented later in Sect. 9.6, p. 455. The buffer implementation is a fixed sized array with front and back pointers cycling around the array, as in Sect. 7.5.2, p. 350, with an additional counter in this implementation for the number of full slots in the buffer. The BoundedBuffer interface has four members: the constructor, query, insert and remove. In general, public members of a μC++ monitor are mutex members, and hence, execute mutually exclusively with one another; however, some exceptions are shown.

A monitor's construction appears not to require mutual exclusion. The reason is that, until the monitor is initialized, its declaration is incomplete; only after completion of the declaration can tasks reference the monitor, and hence, make calls to it. Since tasks cannot call the monitor until its declaration is complete, there can be no concurrency during its construction so no mutual exclusion is required. Unfortunately, there is a flaw in this argument. It is possible for a monitor constructor to place the monitor's address into a shared variable *before* its declaration is complete. Hence, a task polling the shared variable could use the address to make a call during construction. (While this is extremely poor programming style, it is possible.) Therefore, μC++ provides mutual exclusion during the initialization phase of a monitor so calls to a monitor's mutex members block until the monitor's declaration is complete.

There is a true exception for providing mutual exclusion to a monitor's public members. The query member for the bounded buffer has the declaration qualifier _Nomutex, which explicitly states there is no mutual exclusion on calls to this public member. Therefore, a monitor may be inactive, i.e., no mutex member is executing, but still have tasks executing no-mutex members. Clearly, this capability must be used judiciously to prevent violation of the shared data, and hence, possible race errors. On the other hand, it is useful for enhancing concurrency and other software engineering aspects of a monitor (discussed later). In the case of the bounded buffer, the no-mutex member query only reads the shared data, i.e., the number of elements in the buffer, so it cannot violate the shared data. This same capability was suggested for the critical region (see page 427), where the shared variable can be read outside of the critical region. However, is the value read meaningful? Because there is no mutual exclusion on the call to query, another task can be in the monitor incrementing or decrementing the value of count. Assuming atomic assignment, as for Peterson's algorithm, query always returns a consistent value, either the previous value or the current value of count; hence, query always returns a value in the range 0–20 (buffer size), never a value like -37. However, since the value returned by query can change immediately after it is read, is such a no-mutex member useful? For example, the following code:

```
if ( m.query() < 20 ) m.insert(...);
```

does not guarantee the calling task will not block on the call to insert because the value returned by query may change before the call to insert occurs. However, making query a mutex member does not solve this problem; exactly the same problem can occur because there is still a window for another task to race into the monitor between the mutex calls query and insert (albeit a smaller window). Therefore, there is no advantage to making query a mutex member, and doing so only inhibits concurrency to the insert and remove members, which can execute concurrently with query. What good is the query member? As suggested for reading a shared variable outside a critical region, it can be used to statistically sample the state of the buffer and print a graph. If the graph indicates the buffer is constantly empty or full, the buffer can be made smaller or larger, respectively. In other words, exact data is unnecessary to determine trends in behaviour.

The insert and remove members not only require mutual exclusion, but synchronization through conditional mutual exclusion. That is, when the buffer is empty or full, consumer and producer tasks must block, and cooperation should be used to unblock them when the buffer changes. Examine the code for mutex members insert and remove in Fig. 9.4. Both start by checking the buffer state to determine if progress can be made, like the await statement for the critical region. However, the mechanism to control progress is more direct and allows cooperation. The _Accept statement indicates which call is acceptable given the current state of the monitor.

If the buffer is full, the only acceptable call is to remove, which frees a buffer slot; all calls to insert, *including* the insert call executing the **_Accept** statement, are held (blocked) until a call to remove occurs. Similarly, if the buffer is empty, the only acceptable call is to insert, which fills a buffer slot; all calls to remove, *including* the remove call executing the **_Accept** statement, are held (blocked) until a call to insert occurs. Unlike the conditional critical-region, when a task in a monitor knows it cannot execute, it does not passively wait for its condition to become true, it actively indicates that its condition can only become true after a call occurs to a particular mutex member, which is a very precise statement about what should happen next in the monitor, and hence, a very precise form of cooperation.

Notice, the **_Accept** statement does not specify the next task to enter the monitor, only the next mutex member to execute when calls occur. Hence, a task is selected indirectly through the mutex member it calls. Notice, also, the **_Accept** statement allows tasks to use the monitor in non-FIFO order, like the conditional of the conditional critical-region. That is, the entry queue may have several producer tasks blocked on it because the buffer is full, but when a consumer arrives its call to remove is accepted ahead of the waiting producers. In the case where a consumer is already waiting on the entry queue when a producer accepts remove, the waiting consumer is immediately removed from the entry queue (regardless of its position in the queue) and allowed direct entry to the monitor. Hence, when the buffer is full, a waiting consumer is processed immediately or a delay occurs until a consumer calls the monitor. Therefore, the monitor implementation for **_Accept** must check if there is any task waiting on the entry queue for the accepted member, which may require a linear search of the entry queue. If no appropriate task is found, the monitor is set up to only accept a call to the accepted member. Because linear search is slow, the monitor implementation usually puts a calling task on two queues: the entry queue, in order of arrival, and a mutex queue for the called member, also in order of arrival. These queues are illustrated at the top of Fig. 9.5, where each task appears on two queues (duplicates are shaded). Hence, it is possible to know without a search if there are tasks waiting to call any particular mutex member. Notice, the entry queue is always necessary for selecting the next task in FIFO order when a task exits the monitor, i.e., returns from a mutex member, but the mutex queues are optional, only enhancing the efficiency of the implementation over searching the entry queue for an accepted caller.

As mentioned, the task executing the **_Accept** blocks, which implicitly releases mutual exclusion on the monitor so a call can proceed to the accepted mutex member. Like the extended P operation in Sect. 7.6.6, p. 370 and the conditional critical-region, the block and release occur atomically so there is no possibility for staleness problems associated with interruption between these operations. However, where does the accepting task block, i.e., on what queue does it block? In the case of a conditional critical-region, a task executing an **await** statement with a false condition blocks on the shared variable's implicit conditional queue (see Sect. 9.2.1, p. 432). In the case of a task executing a **_Accept** statement, the task blocks on an implicit stack associated with the monitor, called the acceptor/signalled stack (see right side of Fig. 9.5). Why a stack rather than a queue? The reason is that

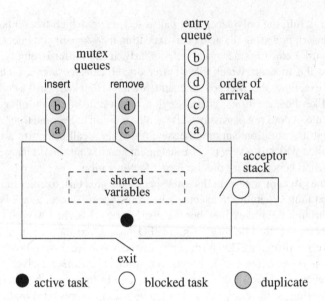

Fig. 9.5 External scheduling: implicit queues

accepts can be nested, i.e., one task can accept member X, which when called can accept member Y, which when called can accept member Z. When mutex member Z exits, which task should execute next in the monitor? This question can be answered by thinking about cooperation. An accepted task (normally) changes the monitor so the blocked acceptor waiting for this change can continue. If an inappropriate task is scheduled next, the cooperation may be invalidated. Therefore, the most sensible task to execute next is the acceptor, which unblocks knowing that the monitor is in a validate state for it to continue (assuming the accepted member is written correctly with respect to cooperation). Hence, when mutex member Z exits, the task accepting it is unblocked, and when it exits member Y, the task accepting it is unblocked, in member X. This sequence is like routine call/return, where X calls Y calls Z, returning from Z to Y to X. In the case of the routine call sequence, the calls are performed by a single task; in the case of the accept call sequence, the calls are performed by different tasks. To implement this accept/call/unblock sequence requires a stack instead of queue to manage the blocked accepting tasks. In the above scenario, the task performing an accept in X and then the task performing an accept in Y are pushed onto the acceptor stack, and subsequently, popped off in LIFO order. Unless the task performing Z does a further accept, it never blocks on the acceptor stack, but may have blocked on the entry queue waiting for its call to be accepted.

Finally, notice that the bodies of members insert and remove are defined *outside* of the monitor type. This code organization results from the mutually recursive references in the accept statements between these two members and the C++ *definition before use rule*. If both members are defined in the monitor, one accept statement references the other before it is defined, generating a compile-time error.

Hence, the member prototypes are defined in the monitor, and the member bodies are defined afterwards, allowing them to reference any of the monitor members.

Several advanced features relating to accepting mutex members such as accepting multiple mutex-members and private mutex-members are postponed until later.

9.4.2 Internal Scheduling

A complementary approach to external scheduling is internal scheduling. Essentially, external scheduling controls state changes to the monitor by scheduling calls to specified mutex members, which indirectly schedule tasks calling from *outside* the monitor. External scheduling takes advantage of the entry queue to block tasks unconditionally when the monitor is active (i.e., block outside the monitor) and of the acceptor stack to block tasks conditionally that have entered the monitor (i.e., block inside the monitor). Most of the scheduling that occurs and the programmer thinks about is the outside scheduling from the entry queue rather than the internal scheduling on the acceptor stack, which occurs implicitly as part of the accept statement semantics. Internal scheduling turns this around, where most of the scheduling occurs inside the monitor instead of from the entry queue (the entry queue must still exist). To do scheduling *inside* the monitor requires additional queues *inside* the monitor on which tasks can block and subsequently be unblocked by other tasks. In fact, this kind of scheduling is very similar to the synchronization capabilities provided by synchronization locks.

To illustrate internal monitor scheduling, a μC++ generic bounded buffer example is presented in Fig. 9.6. The bounded buffer is essentially the same as the external scheduling version in Fig. 9.4, p. 439, except for the mechanism for conditional blocking. Notice the declaration of the two uCondition variables at the top of the bounded buffer. A condition variable is an external synchronization lock (see Sect. 7.3.2, p. 328) protected by the implicit monitor mutex-lock. It is common to associate with each condition variable an assertion about the state of the mutex object. For example, in the bounded buffer, a condition variable might be associated with the assertion "waiting for an empty buffer slot". Blocking on that condition variable corresponds to blocking until the condition is satisfied, that is, until an empty buffer slot appears. Correspondingly, a task unblocks a task blocked on that condition variable only when there is an empty buffer slot. However, the association between assertion and condition variable is implicit and not part of the language; assertions are often used to reason about correctness of cooperation.

Nevertheless, assertions often affect the name given to a condition variable, where naming usually falls into these categories:

1. The condition name identifies a precise event that must be true to fulfill the cooperation of a waiter, e.g.:

   ```
   uCondition empty;
   ```

```
template<typename ELEMTYPE> _Monitor BoundedBuffer {
    int front, back, count;
    ELEMTYPE Elements[20];
    uCondition full, empty;                    // waiting consumers & producers
public:
    BoundedBuffer() : front(0), back(0), count(0) {}
    _Nomutex int query() { return count; }

    void insert( ELEMTYPE elem ) {
        if ( count == 20 ) empty.wait();       // block producer
        Elements[back] = elem;
        back = ( back + 1 ) % 20;
        count += 1;
        full.signal();                         // unblock consumer
    }
    ELEMTYPE remove() {
        if ( count == 0 ) full.wait();         // block consumer
        ELEMTYPE elem = Elements[front];
        front = ( front + 1 ) % 20;
        count -= 1;
        empty.signal();                        // unblock producer
        return elem;
    }
};
```

Fig. 9.6 Bounded buffer: internal scheduling

so empty.wait() means "wait for an empty buffer slot" and empty.signal() means "there is now an empty buffer slot".

2. Alternatively, the condition name identifies a property of the shared resource that must be true before waiters can continue execution, e.g.:

    uCondition nonFull;

so nonFull.wait() means "wait until the buffer is not full" and nonFull.signal() means "the buffer is not full".

The difference is subtle and largely depends on the perspective of the programmer writing the solution. That is, the programmer thinks from the perspective of the tasks using the resource, or from the perspective of the resource about how tasks use it.

Now examine the start of mutex members insert and remove in Fig. 9.6. Both begin by checking the buffer state to determine if progress can be made, like the accept version. However, the mechanism to control progress is even more explicit for internal scheduling. In fact, it is very similar to the semaphore version (see right example of Fig. 7.13, p. 349), except the monitor version has an explicit counter, count, because a condition variable has no counter.[4] The lack of an implicit counter also necessitates explicit checking of the counter, which is done implicitly for a semaphore. If progress cannot be made, i.e., the buffer is full or empty, the task in the

---

[4] In fact, a counter is unnecessary because the state of the buffer, i.e., full or empty, can be determined by appropriate comparisons between front and back. However, these comparisons can be subtle, whereas the counter is straightforward.

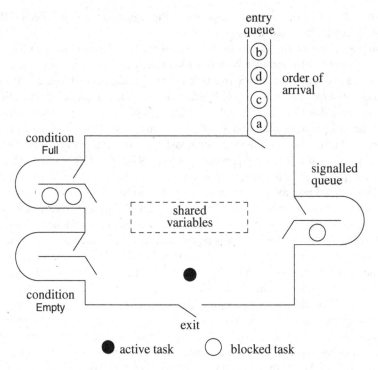

entry
queue

order of
arrival

condition
Full

signalled
queue

shared
variables

condition
Empty

exit

● active task   ○ blocked task

Fig. 9.7 Internal scheduling: implicit queues

monitor explicitly executes a wait to block its execution at this time (like a P), which implicitly unlocks the monitor so another task can enter and change the monitor state. Again, the block and unlock are performed atomically. However, unlike the P operation, which may not block if the semaphore counter is greater than 0, a wait *always* blocks the task executing it. The blocked task relies on cooperation to unblock it at some appropriate time. If a task can make progress, an element is added or removed from the buffer, respectively.

Cooperation occurs as a task exits either mutex member insert or remove. Both routines attempt to wake up a task that is waiting for a specific event to occur. For example, if a producer task has blocked itself on condition empty waiting for an empty buffer slot, cooperation suggests the next consumer task wake a waiting producer because it has created an empty slot in the buffer. The reverse situation exists when the buffer is empty and a consumer task is waiting for a full buffer slot; the next producer should wake a waiting consumer because it has created a full slot in the buffer. Restarting a blocked task is done with a signal on the specified condition variable, which restarts one (and only one) waiting task (like a V), and both insert and remove end by unconditionally signalling the appropriate condition variable. The signals can be unconditional because of the lack of an implicit counter for condition variables; hence, if the condition has no waiting tasks, the signal does nothing. If the speed of the producer and consumer tasks are reasonably balanced, the buffer is seldom full or empty, and hence, the signals do nothing because tasks are not blocked. (The ideal scenario.)

However, occasionally the buffer fills or empties and tasks must wait. Fig. 9.7 shows a snapshot of a monitor with tasks waiting. First, tasks are waiting on the entry queue because there is an active task in the monitor. Second, some tasks have previously entered the monitor and blocked on a condition queue by executing a wait (see left side of Fig. 9.7). Finally, the active task in the monitor has signalled one of the tasks from a condition queue. The semantics of the μC++ signal is that the signalled task waits until the signalling task exits the monitor or waits. (Details of other possible semantics are presented in Sect. 9.11, p. 474.) Interestingly, this semantics appears to be the exact opposite of the accept, which blocks the acceptor until the accepted task exits the monitor or waits. However, an accept is more than than a signal, it is a combination of a wait and signal. The wait component of an accept occurs implicitly and blocks the acceptor on the top of the acceptor stack. The signal component of an accept is performed implicitly when the accepted task finishes a mutex member or waits, i.e., there is an implicit signal of the acceptor task from the top of the acceptor stack. The effect is that the acceptor task waits until the accepted task exits the monitor or waits.

As a result of the signal semantics, the signalled task is removed from the condition queue and must be temporarily stored (like an acceptor) until the signalling task exits or waits, which is accomplished by moving the signalled task to an implicit queue associated with the monitor, called the signalled queue (see right side of Fig. 9.7). When the signalling task exits or waits, the task at the front of the signalled queue becomes the active task in the monitor (i.e., the baton is passed from the signaller to the signalled task). Notice, the signalled queue serves a similar purpose to the acceptor stack, i.e., to facilitate the implicit management of tasks in the monitor. If the signalling task does multiple signals, multiple tasks are moved to the signalled queue, and when the signaller exits or waits, the front signalled task becomes the active monitor task, and when it exits or waits, the next signalled task becomes the active monitor task, and so on. When there are no tasks on the signalled queue, a task at the front of the entry queue is selected if one is present. Processing the signalled queue before the entry queue ensures an external task cannot barge ahead of an internal task, which has already waited its turn in the monitor.

As can be seen, internal scheduling is slightly more complex than external scheduling, but simpler than semaphores. It is simpler than semaphores because the monitor implicitly handles all the baton passing necessary when a task waits or exits the monitor to implicitly schedule the next task to enter the monitor. *Finally, there is no legitimate circumstance where a mutex, synchronization, or semaphore lock should be used in a monitor.* If a task blocks on a lock inside a monitor, no task can enter the monitor because the task blocks holding the implicit monitor-lock. Therefore, unless some task has access to the lock from outside the monitor, the monitor is locked forever. Having external access to the lock used in the monitor clearly violates the abstraction of the monitor. Only condition variables should be used in a monitor for synchronization because blocking on a condition variable implicitly releases the monitor lock.

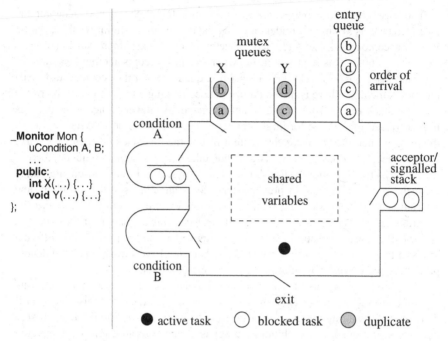

Fig. 9.8 μC++ mutex object

9.5 External and Internal Scheduling

As mentioned, external and internal scheduling are complementary techniques, and therefore, can appear together in the same monitor. This section discusses what it means to combine the two techniques, followed by the appropriateness of each technique.

9.5.1 Combining Scheduling Techniques

Combining external and internal scheduling implies controlling some tasks outside the monitor and others inside the monitor, which means the monitor uses both accept and signal/wait. While the concept seems straightforward, it has ramifications on the way the monitor behaves. Fig. 9.8 shows the general structure of a μC++ monitor using a combination of external and internal scheduling. Looking around the figure, there are the external entry queue and mutex queues (top), as well as the internal condition queues (left). However, there is only an acceptor stack (right), not an acceptor stack *and* a signalled queue.

The reason for having only one implicit location for managing both acceptor and signalled tasks is to simplify understanding, and hence, programming of the monitor. If both acceptor stack and signalled queue exist, complexity increases when tasks appeared on both. This scenario occurs when one task accepts another task, and the accepted task signals a task from a condition queue. When the accepted task exits the mutex member, there is now a choice between taking a task from the top of the acceptor stack or the front of the signalled queue. Whatever choice is made, it is implicitly part of the monitor implementation, and therefore, beyond the control of the programmer. If tasks were chosen first from either the stack or queue, e.g., take from the acceptor stack until empty and then take from the signalled queue, there is the potential for starvation and/or staleness problems. If tasks are chosen alternately from the stack and queue to prevent starvation, staleness is still a problem, and internal scheduling within the monitor becomes extremely complex because the programmer must compensate if the monitor selects from an inappropriate structure. As noted in earlier discussions, using a single data structure for two different kinds of tasks (e.g., reader and writer tasks) does not have starvation and staleness problems, and makes programming in the monitor simpler.

Therefore, it is appropriate to place acceptor and signalled tasks on a single data structure, and when a task exits or waits, select an element from this structure, if there are tasks waiting, otherwise select from the entry queue. Should this structure be a stack or a queue? The obvious answer is a queue because temporal ordering is preserved, which ensures no starvation or staleness. Nevertheless, the choice in μC++ is a stack, called the **acceptor/signalled stack**. The reason is to preserve the semantics of the accept statement, which services calls to mutex members in LIFO order. Otherwise, nested accepts restart in reverse order from normal routine calls, which most programmers would find counter intuitive, leading to mistakes. The problem with a stack is the potential for starvation and staleness because tasks can be pushed on the stack and never popped, and temporal order is not maintained. However, unlike the situation where the monitor implementation is implicitly selecting from a stack or a queue and the programmer has no control, here the programmer has complete control and can easily compensate for any problems associated with the implicit acceptor/signalled stack. In fact, the only anomaly occurs during multiple signalling, where multiple signalled tasks are pushed onto the implicit stack and subsequently restarted (popped off) in reverse order from their waiting time on the condition queue. If this semantics is incorrect for an application, it is usually possible to convert multiple signalling to daisy-chain signalling, where each restarted task signals the next task to be restarted. (Both daisy-chain signalling and multiple signalling are discussed shortly). Resolving the conflict between the semantics of accept and signal/wait is an example of a design trade off between interacting language constructs.

In summary, there are two kinds of scheduling: external and internal. External scheduling blocks the acceptor and other inappropriate tasks by only accepting calls from tasks that can legitimately execute given the current state of the monitor. When the active monitor task blocks on an accept statement, the next active task is chosen from the specified mutex queue. Because nested accepts are possible, acceptors block on an implicit stack associated with each monitor until the accepted call completes; therefore, nested accept calls behave like nested routine calls, except the calls are executed by different threads. Internal scheduling blocks tasks on explicit condition queues internal to the monitor, when the state of the monitor is inappropriate. Specifically, when the active monitor task blocks on a wait or exits the monitor, the next active task is selected first from the acceptor/signalled stack and then from the entry queue. Unlike blocked acceptor tasks, which are implicitly restarted, tasks blocked on condition variables are explicitly restarted via signalling. A signalled task does not restart until *after* the signaller task exits or waits. Both acceptor and signalled tasks block on the same implicit stack in the monitor. Because a stack is necessary to preserve accept semantics, care must be taken with multiple signalling to prevent starvation and/or staleness.

9.5.2   Scheduling Selection

Given the two approaches to scheduling, external and internal, what guidelines can a programmer use to select the most appropriate approach? It turns out there is only a weak equivalence between the two scheduling schemes. As a result, there are situations where only one scheduling approach is appropriate.

In general, external scheduling is easier to understand and code because it is only necessary to specify the next mutex member to execute and the monitor implicitly handles all the details. Specifying the next mutex member to execute is a reasonably direct and powerful way to control synchronization among tasks using a monitor. From an implementation standpoint, external scheduling can be more efficient in specialized circumstances, e.g., when the monitor is heavily used. During heavy usage, tasks block on the entry queue because the monitor is active. With internal scheduling, tasks must unblock from the entry queue and possibly block again on a condition queue because the monitor state is currently inappropriate. In this case, a task blocks and unblocks twice (double blocking) before completion of a mutex member. With external scheduling, it may be possible for some tasks to block only on the entry queue, and hence, save some overhead costs. An example where double blocking is not eliminated is the bounded buffer using external scheduling (see Fig. 9.4, p. 439). When the buffer is full, a perfect interleaving of producers and consumers can result in producers waiting on the entry queue and then on the acceptor stack until the next consumer removes an element. Hence, double blocking can occur with both external and internal scheduling; however, in some situations external scheduling experiences less double blocking than internal scheduling.

If external scheduling is simpler than internal scheduling, why not use it all the time? Unfortunately, the following situations cannot be handled adequately by external scheduling:

9.5.2.1   Member Parameter Scheduling

The best way to understand this situation is to note that in a normal routine call, the calling arguments are inaccessible until *after* the routine begins execution. Only in the special case of a call to a mutex member, which may block the caller, is it reasonable for a task in the monitor to consider examining the calling arguments of the tasks blocked on a mutex queue. Since the calling tasks are blocked, it is safe to read the arguments as they cannot change. Why is this capability desirable? Imagine servicing monitor requests in decreasing order of the argument value, e.g., if the argument is age, service the youngest person first. (The issue of starvation is ignored to simplify the discussion, but it only increases the complexity of these kinds of scheduling schemes.) To provide such a capability requires adding a new feature to the accept statement to search a mutex queue and examine the arguments of tasks blocked on the queue, e.g.:

   _**Accept**(mem(age) *where age is the smallest*);

This capability is clearly peculiar to mutex members and is not an intuitive extension of the normal routine call mechanism. Nor is it clear how to specify the conditional selection, e.g., determining which age is the smallest. (Attempts at providing this form of conditional selection are presented in Sect. 13.4.2, p. 690.) One possible solution to this problem, without extending the accept statement, is to have a public member for each age (0–130), and the requester must call the appropriate member. (To accomplish this requires using a more advanced feature of the accept statement, e.g., accepting multiple mutex members, which is discussed shortly.) However, enumerating the necessary members, selecting the members, and making the appropriate call, is unacceptable because the amount of program text is proportional to the range of the parameter value. For example, a parameter range of 1,000,000 requires 1,000,000 members and possibly corresponding accept clauses, and in most cases, the range is only sparsely populated. Furthermore, this situation is exacerbated if the criteria for scheduling depends on the arguments from two or more different mutex queues. Imagine a situation where two different kinds of tasks call two different mutex members both passing an argument used in scheduling. To decide which task to select requires searching both mutex queues, and it is unclear how such a complex mechanism can be provided.

Internal scheduling provides a solution to this scenario without requiring language extensions. Instead of the active task attempting to access task arguments outside the monitor on the mutex queues, internal scheduling has each task begin its mutex member, where the parameters now represent the calling arguments, and now the decision to block or not block on a condition variable can be made by examining both the parameters and the monitor state using standard language control structures. Clearly, the style of cooperation may change significantly between these alternatives.

Fig. 9.9 shows two versions of an interesting problem illustrating the need to access parameter information from multiple mutex queues. The problem is a simple dating service, where girls and boys call a corresponding mutex member with a

```
_Monitor DatingService {
   uCondition Girls[20], Boys[20], Exch;
   int GirlPhoneNo, BoyPhoneNo;
public:
   int Girl( int PhoneNo, int ccode ) {
      if ( Boys[ccode].empty() ) {
         Girls[ccode].wait();
         GirlPhoneNo = PhoneNo;
         Exch.signal();
      } else {
         GirlPhoneNo = PhoneNo;
         Boys[ccode].signal();
         Exch.wait();
      }
      return BoyPhoneNo;
   }
   int Boy( int PhoneNo, int ccode ) {
      if ( Girls[ccode].empty() ) {
         Boys[ccode].wait();
         BoyPhoneNo = PhoneNo;
         Exch.signal();
      } else {
         BoyPhoneNo = PhoneNo;
         Girls[ccode].signal();
         Exch.wait();
      }
      return GirlPhoneNo;
   }
};
```

(a) Using exchange condition

```
_Monitor DatingService {
   uCondition Girls[20], Boys[20];
   int GirlPhoneNo, BoyPhoneNo;
public:
   int Girl( int PhoneNo, int ccode ) {
      if ( Boys[ccode].empty() ) {
         Girls[ccode].wait( PhoneNo );
      } else {
         GirlPhoneNo = PhoneNo;
         BoyPhoneNo = Boys[ccode].front();
         Boys[ccode].signal();
      }
      return BoyPhoneNo;
   }
   int Boy( int PhoneNo, int ccode ) {
      if ( Girls[ccode].empty() ) {
         Boys[ccode].wait( PhoneNo );
      } else {
         BoyPhoneNo = PhoneNo;
         GirlPhoneNo = Girls[ccode].front();
         Girls[ccode].signal();
      }
      return GirlPhoneNo;
   }
};
```

(b) Using condition-queue node

Fig. 9.9 Scheduling using parameter information: solution 1

phone number and a compatibility code (0–19). When a client calls with a matching compatibility code, the phone numbers of the pair are exchanged so they can arrange a date. A girl or boy blocks in the monitor until a matching date appears. Parameter information is needed from both the Boy and Girl mutex queues to construct a match *and* to return the phone numbers. With internal scheduling, the parameter information is received and stored in the monitor where it can be manipulated as necessary to solve the problem.

The left version in Fig. 9.9 is discussed first. An array of conditions is used for blocking clients of the same gender with the same compatibility until a date arrives. Since there are 20 compatibility codes, the array of conditions is dimensioned to 20. When a client arrives, it checks the opposite array at the position with the same compatibility code, and if that condition queue is empty, it blocks on its gender array at the position denoted by its compatibility code. If there is a date waiting on the appropriate condition queue, the phone number is copied into a global monitor communication variable, and the date is signalled. However, there is a problem because the signaller needs to wait for the date to unblock and copy its phone number from a local variable into a global monitor communication variable to get the date's phone number. The problem is that the signaller continues to execute after the signal, and the signalled task only unblocks *after* the signaller exits or waits. Since the signaller cannot exit without a phone number, it has to wait. (If it does exit immediately, the phone number from the previous date is erroneously returned.) Therefore, there is an additional condition variable, Exch, used just for the necessary communication in the monitor to exchange phone numbers (see page 460 for a mechanism to eliminate condition Exch). The task blocks on the exchange condition, and the next task to become active in the monitor is at the top of the acceptor/signalled stack, which is the signalled date. The signalled date unblocks after the wait on the array of conditions, copies its phone number into the appropriate global monitor communication variable, signals its date on the Exch condition, and exits with the appropriate date's phone number. The next task to become active in the monitor is the one at the top of the acceptor/signaller stack, which is the signalled date. It unblocks after the wait on Exch, and exits with the appropriate date's phone number.

An alternative approach, which reduces the amount of internal blocking for exchanging phone numbers, is to store the compatibility codes for all the blocked tasks in a global monitor data structure. Then the task that finds a date can signal the date, copy their phone number from the global data structure, and return, without having to wait for the date to unblock to obtain their phone number from a local variable. However, the data structure to store the compatibility codes is reasonably complex, i.e., an array of queues, because there may be many tasks waiting on each compatibility condition queue. Furthermore, data must be synchronized between the compatibility data structure and the condition queues at all times to correctly reflect the necessary information for each blocked task.

μC++ provides a language feature that simplifies this approach by folding the scheduling data structure into the condition queue (see right version in Fig. 9.9). Since a condition queue already builds a queue data structure, it seems wasteful to build another complete queue to store the additional compatibility code information. As well, nodes must be added and removed from both data structures at exactly the same times and in the same order (e.g., non-FIFO scheduling of tasks from a condition variable). Therefore, μC++ allows a single integer value to be stored with each blocked task on a condition queue by passing the value to wait (see details in Sect. 9.6.3, p. 459). This capability can be seen in the right example of Fig. 9.9 where each call to wait has the form:

gender[ccode].wait(PhoneNo);

When each task blocks, the value stored in each condition node of the condition queue is a phone number. When a task finds a date, it is sufficient to examine the information stored with the blocked task at the front of the condition queue to obtain a date's phone number, which is accomplished with the statement:

*gender*PhoneNo = *gender*[ccode].front();

which returns the phone number stored with the blocked task on the front of the condition queue (or stored with the next task to be unblocked if non-FIFO scheduling is used). Notice, the date is signalled *after* the phone number is copied from the condition queue, because a signal moves the blocked task from the condition queue to the acceptor/signalled stack, which is inaccessible in a monitor.

Unfortunately, both of the previous solutions make unrealistic assumptions about the compatibility code. The previous approaches are reasonable only when the range of the scheduling values is small, as the storage usage is proportional to the value range. As mentioned, the range of the compatibility code may be large and sparse, which means an array of condition variables the size of the compatibility code is inappropriate in general. Furthermore, the compatibility code may not be a single value but a table of values (e.g., answers to a questionnaire), and only a single integer value can be stored in a μC++ condition-queue node.

Fig. 9.10 shows a monitor that deals with both these problems using a list data structure and the notion of a *private condition*, similar to a private semaphore approach suggested in Sect. 7.6.6, p. 370. A list is constructed with nodes containing a task's compatibility code information (or a pointer to it) and a private condition variable. When a task must wait, it blocks on the private condition variable and is the only task to block on that condition variable. This approach uses storage proportional to the number of blocked tasks, which in many cases is significantly less than the range of the scheduling values. Also, the scheduling value can be arbitrarily complex, and the insert and search can also be arbitrarily complex.

Both Girl and Boy members start by searching the opposite list for a compatible date. The search returns a pointer to a Node data structure, which should be a compatible date, or NULL, which means there is no compatible date. If there is no compatible date, the task creates a Node on its execution stack, initialized with its compatibility information, inserts the node on the appropriate waiting list, and blocks on its private condition variable in the node. When a task unblocks, it removes its node from the list, and the remainder of the code is the same as the left example in Fig. 9.9, p. 451, except a date is signalled from the private condition of the found node. A solution based on private conditions (like the private semaphore approach in Sect. 7.6.6, p. 370) can be constructed for the right example in Fig. 9.9, p. 451, by storing the phone number in the list node along with the compatibility code and a private condition variable.

It might be argued that this problem can be restructured so that tasks call a single member, passing information identifying the kind of task (i.e., girl or boy). However, restructuring is not always possible because of other factors, such as legacy issues. Therefore, concurrency constructs must be able to handle this level of scheduling, and internal scheduling provides the necessary flexibility.

9.5.2.2 Delay Scheduling

This situation arises when a request may need to block (delay) during its execution. Delay scheduling *does not* occur in the external-scheduling bounded-buffer (see Fig. 9.4, p. 439), as the cooperation ensures that once a call to insert or remove begins, it can always execute to completion. In contrast, calls to the DatingService may have to block because a partner is unavailable. The delay scheduling could

```
_Monitor DatingService {
    struct Node : public uSeqable {
        int ccode;
        uCondition block;                              // private condition
        Node( int ccode ) : ccode( ccode ) {}
    };
    Node *Search( uSequence<Node> &gender, int ccode ) {
        // return node with matching compatibility code or NULL
    }
    uSequence<Node> Girls, Boys;
    uCondition Exch;
    int GirlPhoneNo, BoyPhoneNo;
  public:
    int Girl( int PhoneNo, int ccode ) {
        Node *boy = Search( Boys, ccode );            // check for match
        if ( boy == NULL ) {                          // no match ?
            Node n( ccode );                          // create and add node
            Girls.uAdd( &n );
            n.block.wait();                           // block on private condition
            Girls.remove( &n );
            GirlPhoneNo = PhoneNo;                    // set communication variable
            Exch.signal();                            // restart date
        } else {
            GirlPhoneNo = PhoneNo;                    // set communication variable
            boy->block.signal();                      // unblock date
            Exch.wait();                              // wait for date phone number
        }
        return BoyPhoneNo;                            // return date phone number
    }
    int Boy( int PhoneNo, int ccode ) {
        Node *girl = Search( Girls, ccode );          // check for match
        if ( girl == NULL ) {                         // no match ?
            Node n( ccode );                          // create and add node
            Boys.uAdd( &n );
            n.block.wait();                           // block on private condition
            Boys.remove( &n );
            BoyPhoneNo = PhoneNo;                     // set communication variable
            Exch.signal();                            // restart date
        } else {
            BoyPhoneNo = PhoneNo;                     // set communication variable
            girl->block.signal();                     // unblock date
            Exch.wait();                              // wait for date phone number
        }
        return GirlPhoneNo;                           // return date phone number
    }
};
```

Fig. 9.10 Scheduling using parameter information: solution 2

be removed by immediately returning a -1 to indicate no compatible partner is available. However, this approach presents a significant problem to the caller if it must achieve a successful call as its only approach is to busy wait making repeated calls, which is execution-time expensive and can result in starvation. To provide delay scheduling using external scheduling requires a calling task to perform member-parameter scheduling of the opposite gender with a particular compatibility code. For example, if a Boy task calls into the DatingService, it must execute an accept statement like:

_Accept(Girl *with same ccode*);

but this prevents other exchanges from occurring until the appropriate call occurs. Hence, delaying until an appropriate event occurs while continuing to service requests cannot be done solely with external scheduling.

The issue forcing internal scheduling when delay scheduling is needed is that a task can only block once on the entry queue, i.e., it is impossible to go back out of the monitor and wait again on the entry queue. Hence, after a task enters a monitor, any further blocking can only occur with nested accepts, which forces a stack ordering on request processing. While most concurrent languages disallow scheduling from inside a mutex object back outside onto the entry queue, it is possible. This capability might be provided by a statement of the form:

requeue *mutex-member-name*

which blocks the executing task, places it back on the specified mutex queue and schedules the next task for the monitor. In effect, the original call has been transformed into a new call to the same or another mutex member with possibly different arguments. This requeued call is then accepted again, when the monitor state is appropriate for the call to proceed.

Requeueing appears equivalent to internal scheduling, but this is not the case. A mutex member working on a request may accumulate complex execution and data state. To requeue a request, the work accomplished thus far and temporary results must be bundled and forwarded to the requeue mutex member handling the next step of the processing, usually by placing this information into global task variables; alternatively, the work is re-computed at the start of the requeue mutex member, if possible. In contrast, waiting on a condition variable automatically saves the execution location and any partially computed state. In fact, simulating internal scheduling with requeue is similar to simulating a coroutine using a routine or class, where the programmer must explicitly handle the execution and/or data state, possibly using global variables. Therefore, there is only a weak equivalence between requeueing and internal scheduling.

9.6 Monitor Details

The following μC++ monitor details are presented to understand subsequent examples or to help in solving questions at the end of the chapter.

While there is a **_Nomutex** qualifier, which implies no mutual exclusion, there is also a **_Mutex** qualifier, which implies mutual exclusion. Both qualifiers can qualify **private**, **protected** and **public** member routines. As well, both qualifiers can also qualify a **class** definition:

_Mutex class M1 { ... **_Nomutex class** M2 { ...

When the _Mutex qualifier is placed on a **class** definition, it indicates all public member routines have the mutual-exclusion property, unless overridden on specific member routines with the _Nomutex qualifier. When the _Nomutex qualifier is placed on a **class** definition, it indicates all public member routines have the no-mutual-exclusion property, which is the same as a **class**, unless overridden on specific member routines with the _Mutex qualifier. The default qualifier for a class, i.e., if no qualifier is specified, is _Nomutex because the mutual-exclusion property for public members is not needed. Therefore, a **class** creates a monitor if and only if it has at least one _Mutex member routine, and that _Mutex member routine can have any visibility, i.e., **private**, **protected** or **public**. As well, the destructor of a monitor is always mutex, regardless of where it is defined or if it makes no references to the monitor's shared variables. The reason for this requirement is same as that for a task, i.e., the storage for the monitor cannot be deallocated if the monitor is active (a task's thread is executing in the monitor). Hence, a monitor always has one mutex member, its destructor, and a monitor's destructor cannot be qualified with _Nomutex, e.g., the following is the monitor with minimum number of mutex members:

```
class M {
  public:
    _Mutex ~M() {}      // only mutex member
};
```

(However, it is doubtful if this trivial case is useful.) The following examples illustrate most of the different possible combinations for implicit and explicit creation of mutex members of a mutex object:

```
_Mutex class M1 { // publics implicitly mutex      _Nomutex class M2 { // publics implicitly
  private:                                            private:            //   no mutex
    _Mutex int m1();    // explicit mutex               _Mutex int m1();    // explicit mutex
    int m2();           // implicit no mutex            int m2();           // implicit no mutex
  public:                                             public:
    ~M1();              // implicit mutex               ~M1();              // implicit mutex
    int m3();           // implicit mutex               int m3();           // implicit no mutex
    _Nomutex int m4();  // explicit no mutex            _Mutex int m4();    // explicit mutex
}                                                   }
```

In fact, the name _Monitor used so far is just a preprocessor macro for "_Mutex class" defined in include file uC++.h.

9.6.1 Monitor Creation and Destruction

A monitor is the same as a class with respect to creation and destruction, except for a possible delay for the destructing task, as in:

```
_Mutex class M {
   public:
      void r( ... ) ...        // mutex member
};
M *mp;                        // pointer to a M
{ // start a new block
      M m, ma[3];             // local creation
      mp = new M;             // dynamic creation
      ...
} // wait for m, ma[0], ma[1] and ma[2] to terminate and then deallocate
...
delete mp;  // wait for mp's instance to terminate and then deallocate
```

When a monitor is created, the appropriate monitor constructor and any base-class constructors are executed in the normal order by the creating thread. Because a monitor is a mutex object, the execution of its destructor waits until it can gain access to the monitor, just like the other mutex members of the monitor, which can delay the termination of the block containing a monitor or the deletion of a dynamically allocated monitor.

9.6.2 Accept Statement

A _Accept statement dynamically chooses the mutex member(s) that executes next, which indirectly controls the next accepted caller, that is, the next caller to the accepted mutex member. The simplest form of the _Accept statement is:

```
_Accept( mutex-member-name );
```

with the restriction that constructors, new, delete, and _Nomutex members are excluded from being accepted. The first three member routines are excluded because these routines are essentially part of the implicit memory-management runtime support. _Nomutex members are excluded because they contain no code affecting the caller or acceptor with respect to mutual exclusion. The syntax for accepting a mutex operator member, such as operator =, is:

```
_Accept( operator = );
```

Currently, there is no way to accept a particular overloaded member. Instead, when an overloaded member name appears in a _Accept statement, calls to any member with that name are accepted. A consequence of this design decision is that once one routine of a set of overloaded routines becomes mutex, all the overloaded routines in that set become mutex members. The rationale is that members with the same name should perform essentially the same function, and therefore, they all should be eligible to accept a call.

When a _Accept statement is executed, the acceptor is blocked and pushed on the top of the implicit acceptor/signalled stack and a task is scheduled from the mutex queue for the specified mutex member. If there is no outstanding call to that mutex member, the acceptor is accept-blocked until a call is made. The accepted member is then executed like a member routine of a conventional class by the caller's thread.

If the caller is expecting a return value, this value is returned using the **return** statement in the member routine. *Notice, an accept statement accepts only one call, regardless of the number of mutex members listed in the statement.* When the caller's thread exits the mutex member or waits, further implicit scheduling occurs. First, a task is unblocked from the acceptor/signalled stack if present, and then from the entry queue. Therefore, in the case of nested accept calls, the execution order between acceptor and caller is stack order, as for a traditional routine call. If there are no waiting tasks present on either data structure, *the next call to any mutex member is implicitly accepted.*

The extended form of the **_Accept** statement is used to accept one of a group of mutex members using a list of mutex member names and/or multiple accept clauses, as in:

```
_Accept( mutex-member-name-list )
        statement                               // optional statement
or _Accept( mutex-member-name )
        statement                               // optional statement
...
    ...
```

A list of mutex members in an **_Accept** clause, e.g.:

```
_Accept( insert, remove );
```

it is equivalent to:

```
_Accept( insert ) or _Accept( remove );
```

Before a **_Accept** clause is executed, an outstanding call to the corresponding member must exist. If there are several mutex members that can be accepted, the **_Accept** clause nearest the beginning of the statement is executed. Hence, the order of the **_Accept**s indicates their relative priority for selection if several accept clauses can execute. Once the accepted call has completed *or the caller waits*, the statement after the accepting **_Accept** clause is executed and the accept statement is complete. If there are no outstanding calls to these members, the task is accept-blocked until a call to one of these members is made.

Note, when there are multiple **_Accept** clauses in the accept statement, *only one call is accepted* ("or" not "and"). This semantics is often confusing when using an accept statement and it may be helpful to draw an analogue between an accept statement with multiple accept clauses and an **if** statement with multiple **else if** clauses, as in:

```
if ( C1 ) {                    _Accept( M1 ) {
    S1                             S1
} else if ( C2 ) {             } or _Accept( M2 ) {
    S2                             S2
} else if ( C3 ) {             } or _Accept( M3 ) {
    S3                             S3
}                              }
```

The **if** statement only executes one of S1, S2, S3; it does not execute them all. The reason is that the first conditional to evaluate to true executes its corresponding "then" clause (S1, S2, or S3), and the **if** statement terminates. Similarly, the accept statement accepts the first call to one of mutex members M1, M2, or M3, then executes the corresponding "then" clause (S1, S2, or S3) and the _**Accept** statement terminates. The analogue also holds when there is a list of mutex member names in an accept clause, as in:

```
if ( C1 || C2 ) {          _Accept( M1, M2 ) {
    S1                          S1
} else if ( C3 ) {         } or _Accept( M3 ) {
    S2                          S2
}                          }
```

The analogy differs when all the conditions are false for the **if** statement and no outstanding calls exist for the accept statement. For the **if** case, control continues without executing any of the "then" clauses; for the _**Accept** case, control *blocks* until a call to one of the accepted members occurs and then the corresponding "then" clause is executed. Hence, an accept statement accepts only one call, regardless of the number of mutex member names specified in the accept clauses forming the statement, and then any code associated with accepting that mutex member is executed. (See Sect. 10.8.1, p. 545 for further extensions to the _**Accept** statement, including how to accept no calls.) To accept multiple calls requires executing multiple accept *statements*, not multiple accept *clauses*.

9.6.3   Condition Variables and Wait/Signal Statements

In μC++, the type uCondition creates a queue object on which tasks can be blocked and reactivated in FIFO order, and is defined:

```
class uCondition {
  public:
    bool empty() const;
    long int front() const;
};
uCondition a, *b, c[5];
```

A condition variable is owned by the mutex object that performs the first wait on it; subsequently, only the owner can wait and signal that condition variable. The member routine empty() returns **false** if there are tasks blocked on the queue and **true** otherwise. The member routine front returns an integer value stored with the waiting task at the front of the condition queue. It is an error to examine the front of an empty condition queue. (front is used again on page 467.)

It is *not* meaningful to read or to assign to a condition variable, or copy a condition variable (e.g., pass it as a value parameter), or use a condition variable if not its owner.

To join such a condition queue, the active task calls member wait of the condition variable, e.g.,

```
empty.wait();
```

which causes the active task to block on condition empty, which causes further implicit scheduling. First, a task is unblocked from the acceptor/signalled stack if present, and then from the entry queue. If there are no waiting tasks present on either data structure, *the next call to any mutex member is implicitly accepted.*

When waiting, it is possible to optionally store an integer value with a waiting task on a condition queue by passing an argument to wait, e.g.:

empty.wait(3);

If no value is specified in a call to wait, the value for that blocked task is undefined. The integer value can be accessed by other tasks through the uCondition member routine front. This value can be used to provide more precise information about a waiting task than can be inferred from its presence on a particular condition variable. The value stored with a waiting task and examined by a signaller should not be construed as a message between tasks. The information stored with the waiting task is not meant for a particular task nor is it received by a particular task. Any task in the monitor can examine it. Also, the value stored with each task is *not* a priority for use in the subsequent selection of a task when the monitor is unlocked.

A task is reactivated from a condition variable when another (active) task executes a signal. There are two forms of signal. The first form is the signal, e.g.:

Full.signal();

The effect of a call to member signal is to remove one task from the specified condition variable and push it onto the acceptor/signalled stack. The signaller continues execution and the signalled task is unblocked when it is next popped off the acceptor/signalled stack. The second form is the signalBlock, e.g.:

Full.signalBlock();

The effect of a call to member signalBlock is to remove one task from the specified condition variable and make it the active task, and push the signaller onto the acceptor/signalled stack, like an accept. The signalled task continues execution and the signaller is unblocked when it is next popped off the acceptor/signalled stack.

Fig. 9.11 shows how the signalBlock can be used to remove the Exch condition from the left example in Fig. 9.9, p. 451. By replacing the calls to signal on the gender condition variables with a calls to signalBlock, the signaller now waits for its date to unblock and copy its phone number from a local variable into a global monitor communication variable, and exit with the signaller's phone number. When the date exits its mutex member, the signaller unblocks and exits with the date's phone number from the global monitor communication variable. Notice, the total amount of blocking and unblocking is identical in both versions of the program.

9.7   Readers and Writer Problem

It is now time to go back to the problem that caused the move to high-level concurrency constructs: the readers and writer problem. A series of solutions are presented that correspond to semaphore solutions 3–6 in Sect. 7.6, p. 352. However,

```
_Monitor DatingService {
    uCondition Girls[20], Boys[20];
    int GirlPhoneNo, BoyPhoneNo;
public:
    int Girl( int PhoneNo, int ccode ) {
        if ( Boys[ccode].empty() ) {
            Girls[ccode].wait();
            GirlPhoneNo = PhoneNo;
        } else {
            GirlPhoneNo = PhoneNo;
            Boys[ccode].signalBlock();  // wait for date to copy phone number
        }
        return BoyPhoneNo;
    }
    int Boy( int PhoneNo, int ccode ) {
        if ( Girls[ccode].empty() ) {
            Boys[ccode].wait();
            BoyPhoneNo = PhoneNo;
        } else {
            BoyPhoneNo = PhoneNo;
            Girls[ccode].signalBlock();  // wait for date to copy phone number
        }
        return GirlPhoneNo;
    }
};
```

Fig. 9.11 Scheduling using parameter information: solution 3

before examining the monitor solutions, the basic structure of each solution is examined from a software engineering perspective.

Stepping back to the conditional critical-region solution for the readers and writer problem, the solution is structured as an entry and exit protocol for the reader and possibly for the writer (see page 431). As for locks (see start of Chap. 7, p. 313), the entry and exit protocol for readers and writers needs to be abstracted into routines so it is not duplicated and the implementation is independent of the interface. For conditional critical-region, the protocol can be encapsulated into four routines, used as follows:

```
shared struct rw { ... }
```

reader	writer
StartRead(rw);	StartWrite(rw);
// read	// write
EndRead(rw);	EndWrite(rw);

However, this style of coding is exactly the same as bracketing a critical section with P and V, with the same potential for mistakes, e.g., forgetting an EndRead or EndWrite call. A better structure is to encapsulate both the protocol and the operation into two routines, as in:

reader	writer
Read(rw, ...);	Write(rw, ...); ·

```
class ReadersWriter {
    _Mutex void StartRead();
    _Mutex void EndRead();
    _Mutex void StartWrite();
    _Mutex void EndWrite();
public:
    void Read( ... ) {
        StartRead();
        // read
        EndRead();
    }
    void Write( ... ) {
        StartWrite();
        // write
        EndWrite();
    }
};
```

Fig. 9.12 Basic structure for readers/writer solutions

where "..." are arguments passed to the read or write operation within the protocol routines, respectively. The object-oriented form makes rw into a monitor type with mutex members Read and Write, as follows:

    reader   writer

    rw.Read(...);   rw.Write(...);

Unfortunately, for reading, this organization presents exactly the same problem as putting both the read protocol and read operation together in a single critical region, i.e., only one reader can be in the monitor (critical region) at a time, and hence, there are no simultaneous readers. Therefore, it is necessary to put the reader entry and exit protocol back into separate mutex members, which is back to the initial structure. The answer is to put the protocol and operation into a **_Nomutex** interface member of the monitor, which the user calls. This structure is identical to the above conditional critical-region example but retains the object-oriented style by using member routines instead of normal routines. Therefore, the basic structure of all the following monitor solutions for the readers and writer problem is shown in Fig. 9.12:

There are two interface routines, Read and Write, both of which have no mutual exclusion (i.e., **_Nomutex** members); both interface routines make calls to private mutual exclusion routines. (Remember, the presence of a single mutex member makes a type a mutex type.) Notice, like the conditional critical-region case, the Write routine can have the protocol and operation together because there is at most one writer and that writer can be the only task with mutual exclusion in the monitor. However, for consistency, both Reader and Writer members are structured the same way. This situation illustrates how a complex protocol can be enforced through no mutex members, even when the protocol requires multiple mutex calls. The Mesa programming language provides exactly the same capability:

> For example, a public external procedure *(no mutex member)* might do some preliminary processing and then make repeated calls into the monitor proper before returning to its client [17, p. 157].

```
class ReadersWriter {
    uCondition rwait, wwait;
    int rcnt, wcnt;

    _Mutex void StartRead() {
        if ( wcnt > 0 || ! wwait.empty() ) { rwait.wait(); }
        rcnt += 1;
        rwait.signal();
    }
    _Mutex void EndRead() {
        rcnt -= 1;
        if ( rcnt == 0 ) { wwait.signal(); }          // last reader ?
    }
    _Mutex void StartWrite() {
        if ( rcnt > 0 || wcnt > 0 ) { wwait.wait(); }
        wcnt += 1;
    }
    _Mutex void EndWrite() {
        wcnt -= 1;
        if ( ! rwait.empty() ) { rwait.signal(); }     // anyone waiting ?
        else wwait.signal();
    }
  public:
    ReadersWriter() : rcnt(0), wcnt(0) {}
    _Nomutex int readers() { return rcnt; }
    ...
};
```

Fig. 9.13 Readers and writer: solution 3

9.7.1   Solution 3

The first solution examined is solution 3, which is the first semaphore solution to deal with no starvation of readers or writers, but still allows staleness. The monitor version is presented in Fig. 9.13.

Notice the delay counters from the semaphore solution are gone. Instead, these counters have been replaced by checks for non-empty condition queues. As pointed out at the end of Sect. 7.6.2, p. 359, it is impossible to do this for a semaphore solution without a special P routine, which atomically Vs the parameter semaphore and then blocks the calling task if necessary (see end of Sect. 7.6.6, p. 370). It is possible for a monitor solution because of the ability to atomically release the monitor lock and wait on a condition variable.

The algorithm in the monitor is basically the same as its semaphore counterpart. The reader entry protocol checks if there is a writer using the resource or waiting writers, and if so, waits. Otherwise, the reader increments the read counter and signals another waiting reader. As a result, a group of waiting readers take turns unblocking each other, one after the other, called daisy-chain signalling, and the readers begin reading in FIFO order. Notice the signal is unconditional, unlike the semaphore version, because signalling an empty condition variable does not affect future waits. The reader exit protocol decrements the read counter, and the last reader of a group signals a waiting writer. Again, the signal is unconditional, unlike the semaphore version, for the same reason. The writer entry protocol checks if there are reader(s) or a writer using the resource, and if so, waits. Otherwise, the writer simply increments the write counter. The writer exit protocol decrements the write counter, and a check is made for a waiting reader, and if none, a waiting writer.

In all the mutex members, the notion of a baton is implicitly managed by the monitor. In effect, the additional support provided by the monitor mitigates the need to use an analogy like baton passing to cope with complexity. As well, the delay counters are superfluous and temporal anomalies between unlocking the monitor and waiting on a condition do not exist. However, there is still staleness because of the use of two waiting queues for the readers and writers.

9.7.2   Solutions 4 and 5

To eliminate staleness requires delaying both readers and writers on a single waiting queue to preserve temporal order of arrival. The monitor solutions in Figs. 9.14 and 9.15, p. 466 present two alternatives for eliminating staleness, and both alternatives were discussed in Sect. 7.6.5, p. 365 using semaphores. Solution 4 has readers about to enter the resource assume the next task on the combined waiting condition (where both readers and writers wait in temporal order) is a reader and wake it up. Because of the potential for inadvertently waking a writer, each writer must recheck if it can use the resource. If the writer cannot use the resource because there are readers using it, the writer waits again on a special condition, which has at most one writer task waiting on it. The special condition is given the highest priority so a writer inadvertently restarted is always serviced next. Notice, this potential double blocking *in the monitor* by a writer requires internal scheduling (see Sect. 9.5.2, p. 449) because of the delay scheduling.

The reader entry protocol checks if there is a writer using the resource or a waiting high-priority writer or any waiting readers or writers, and if so, waits. Otherwise, the reader increments the read counter and unconditionally signals another waiting reader or writer; it is this signal that may inadvertently wake a writer, which must then be treated as having the highest priority. Again, daisy-chain signalling is used to restart the reader tasks. The reader exit protocol decrements the read counter, and the last reader of a group checks first for a high-priority writer and signals it if present, otherwise it unconditionally signals any waiting reader or writer. The writer entry protocol checks if there are readers or a writer using the resource, and if so, waits. When the writer wakes up, it must check again if there are any readers because it could have been inadvertently woken; if there are readers, the writer waits again on the high-priority condition. Otherwise, the writer simply increments the write counter. The writer exit protocol decrements the write counter, and unconditionally signals any waiting reader or writer.

The next solution (see Fig. 9.15, p. 466) is the same as solution 3, but gets back the lost information when both readers and writers wait on the same condition queue by maintaining a separate queue, which is always the same length as the condition

```
class ReadersWriter {
    uCondition rwwait, wwait;
    int rcnt, wcnt;

    _Mutex void StartRead() {
        if ( wcnt > 0 || ! wwait.empty() || ! rwwait.empty() ) { rwwait.wait(); }
        rcnt += 1;
        rwwait.signal();
    }
    _Mutex void EndRead() {
        rcnt -= 1;
        if ( rcnt == 0 ) {                              // last reader ?
            if ( ! wwait.empty() ) { wwait.signal(); }  // writer waiting ?
            else { rwwait.signal(); }                   // anyone waiting ?
        }
    }
    _Mutex void StartWrite() {
        if ( rcnt > 0 || wcnt > 0 ) {
            rwwait.wait();                              // wait once
            if ( rcnt > 0 ) { wwait.wait(); }          // wait once more ?
        }
        wcnt += 1;
    }
    _Mutex void EndWrite() {
        wcnt -= 1;
        rwwait.signal();                               // anyone waiting ?
    }
  public:
    . . .
};
```

Fig. 9.14 Readers and write: solution 4

queue, and each node of the separate queue indicates if the corresponding task blocked on the condition is a reader or writer. Maintaining the additional queue can be seen in the program in both locations where tasks block. A node is created and initialized to the particular kind of task, and then it is put on the back of the separate queue and the task waits on the condition. When a waiting task is restarted, the cooperation ensures it can immediately take its node off the front of the additional queue. Notice that a queue node is not dynamically allocated; it is allocated at the top of the task's stack before blocking, which is very efficient. The reader entry protocol can now determine if the task blocked at the front of the condition queue is a reader or writer by examining the value in the node at the front of the separate queue. Note, it is necessary to check for the existence of a blocked task (or non-empty queue) before checking the node at the head of the queue or an invalid pointer dereference occurs. This solution is important because its corresponding semaphore solution (see Fig. 7.22, p. 368) did not work. The reason the monitor solution works is the atomic unlocking of the monitor and blocking of a task by the wait. Hence, there is no possibility for the explicit list of task-kinds and the implicit list of blocked tasks on the condition variable to get out of synchronization.

Like the DatingService monitor on page 451, it is possible to simplify the previous solution by folding the separate queue of reader/writer information into

```
class ReadersWriter {
    uCondition rwwait;
    int rcnt, wcnt;

    enum RW { READER, WRITER };
    struct RWnode : public uColable {
        RW rw;                                    // kind of task
        RWnode( RW rw ) : rw(rw) {}
    };
    uQueue<RWnode> rwid;                          // queue of kinds

    _Mutex void StartRead() {
        if ( wcnt > 0 || ! rwwait.empty() ) {
            RWnode r( READER );
            rwid.uAdd( &r );                      // remember kind of task
            rwwait.wait();
            rwid.uDrop();
        }
        rcnt += 1;
        if ( ! rwwait.empty() && rwid.head()->rw == READER ) { // more readers ?
            rwwait.signal();
        }
    }
    _Mutex void EndRead() {
        rcnt -= 1;
        if ( rcnt == 0 ) { rwwait.signal(); }     // last reader ?
    }
    _Mutex void StartWrite() {
        if ( rcnt > 0 || wcnt > 0 ) {
            RWnode w( WRITER );
            rwid.uAdd( &w );                      // remember kind of task
            rwwait.wait();
            rwid.uDrop();
        }
        wcnt += 1;
    }
    _Mutex void EndWrite() {
        wcnt -= 1;
        rwwait.signal();                          // anyone waiting ?
    }
  public:
    ...
};
```

Fig. 9.15 Readers and write: solution 5(a)

the condition queue by storing the reader/writer information for each task in the condition-queue node. In this case, the value is the kind of task, i.e., reader or writer, which is stored in each condition node (see Fig. 9.16, p. 468). It is sufficient for a reader task to examine the kind of task at the front of the queue to know when to stop unblocking reader tasks. This solution is the same as solution 5(a), except the explicit queue is gone and replaced by storing a value with a blocked task at both calls to wait (one in StartRead and one in StartWrite). As well, the condition member front is used in StartRead to examine the user value stored with the task blocked at the front of the condition queue to determine if it should be signalled, but only after checking that there is a node to examine.

A variation on this solution is for the writer to awaken the next group of readers to use the resource when it exits the resource rather than have the readers awaken each other (see Fig. 9.17). Instead of daisy-chain signalling the waiting readers in StartRead, the readers are multiply signalled in EndWrite. Here, the cooperation for signalling a group of readers has been moved from the reader tasks to the writer, so when a reader task restarts after waiting it only has to increment the read counter. Now each signal moves a reader from the condition queue onto the acceptor/signalled stack. Because μC++ uses a stack for storing signalled tasks, the readers exit in LIFO order. Fortunately, LIFO restarting of readers does not cause problems with respect to correctness or staleness.

The final solutions show how external scheduling can be used instead of internal scheduling to provide the simplest solutions. These solutions work because the monitor's entry queue maintains calls in FIFO order (maintaining temporal order of arrival), and tasks are selected from this queue when the monitor is inactive. Two solutions are shown because one is significantly better than the other. The obvious solution, in Fig. 9.18, p. 469(a), works as follows. A reader calling StartRead, checks for a writer using the resource, and if so, accepts a call to EndWrite, which blocks it on the acceptor/signalled stack and allows *only* a call to EndWrite. All other calls block outside of the monitor. After the writer using the resource calls EndWrite and decrements the write counter, the reader is restarted in the monitor, increments the reader counter, and can return to read the resource. The monitor is now inactive, and the next task to enter is the one at the head of the entry queue, i.e., the task waiting the longest, which might be either a reader or a writer task.

A writer calling StartWrite checks for either a writer or reader using the resource. If there is a writer using the resource, the writer in the monitor accepts a call to EndWrite, which blocks it on the acceptor/signalled stack and blocks all other calls outside the monitor until the writer using the resource calls EndWrite. If there are readers using the resource, the writer in the monitor accepts a call to EndRead, which blocks it on the acceptor/signalled stack and blocks all other calls outside the monitor, effectively marking the end for any new reader tasks joining this group (i.e., no more calls to StartRead are allowed).

In either case, there is no starvation possible by a continuous stream of readers or writers because tasks are always removed from the front of the FIFO entry queue, and the reader or writer wanting entry to the resource blocks other tasks outside the monitor. The first reader to finish calls EndRead, which is accepted by a waiting writer, if there is one, or the call is implicitly accepted because the monitor is inactive as there are no calling tasks. This reader and subsequent readers each decrement the read counter and accept the next finishing reader's call to EndRead, except the next exiting reader, resulting in nested accepts. As a writer finishes, its call to EndWrite is accepted by either an accepting reader or writer, if there is one, or the call is implicitly accepted because the monitor is inactive as there are no calling tasks. The writer then decrements the write counter. Thus, all the accepts match with appropriate routine calls.

```
class ReadersWriter {
    uCondition rwwait;
    int rcnt, wcnt;
    enum RW { READER, WRITER };

    _Mutex void StartRead() {
        if ( wcnt > 0 || ! rwwait.empty() ) { rwwait.wait( READER ); }
        rcnt += 1;
        if ( ! rwwait.empty() && rwwait.front() == READER ) { rwwait.signal(); }
    }
    _Mutex void EndRead() {
        rcnt -= 1;
        if ( rcnt == 0 ) { rwwait.signal(); }              // last reader ?
    }
    _Mutex void StartWrite() {
        if ( rcnt > 0 || wcnt > 0 ) { rwwait.wait( WRITER ); }
        wcnt += 1;
    }
    _Mutex void EndWrite() {
        wcnt -= 1;
        rwwait.signal();                                    // anyone waiting ?
    }
  public:
    ...
};
```

Fig. 9.16 Readers and write: solution 5(b)

```
class ReadersWriter {
    uCondition rwwait;
    int rcnt, wcnt;
    enum RW { READER, WRITER };

    _Mutex void StartRead() {
        if ( wcnt > 0 || ! rwwait.empty() ) { rwwait.wait( READER ); }
        rcnt += 1;
    }
    _Mutex void EndRead() {
        rcnt -= 1;
        if ( rcnt == 0 ) { rwwait.signal(); }              // last reader ? \
    }
    _Mutex void StartWrite() {
        if ( rcnt > 0 || wcnt > 0 ) { rwwait.wait( WRITER ); }
        wcnt += 1;
    }
    _Mutex void EndWrite() {
        wcnt -= 1;
        if ( ! rwwait.empty() && rwwait.front() == WRITER ) {
            rwwait.signal();                                // unblock writer
        } else {                                            // multiple signalling
            while ( ! rwwait.empty() && rwwait.front() == READER ) {
                rwwait.signal();                            // unblock reader
            }
        }
    }
  public:
    ...
};
```

Fig. 9.17 Readers and write: solution 5(c)

```
class ReadersWriter {
    int rcnt, wcnt;

    _Mutex void EndRead() {
        rcnt -= 1;
        if ( rcnt > 0 ) { _Accept( EndRead ); }
    }
    _Mutex void EndWrite() {
        wcnt = 0;
    }
    _Mutex void StartRead() {
        if ( wcnt > 0 ) { _Accept( EndWrite ); }
        rcnt += 1;
    }
    _Mutex void StartWrite() {
        if ( wcnt > 0 ) { _Accept( EndWrite ); }
        else if (rcnt > 0) {_Accept( EndRead );}

        wcnt = 1;
    }
  public:
    ...
};
```

(a) Daisy-chaining accepting

```
class ReadersWriter {
    int rcnt, wcnt;

    _Mutex void EndRead() {
        rcnt -= 1;

    }
    _Mutex void EndWrite() {
        wcnt = 0;
    }
    _Mutex void StartRead() {
        if (wcnt > 0) {_Accept( EndWrite );}
        rcnt += 1;
    }
    _Mutex void StartWrite() {
        if (wcnt > 0) {_Accept( EndWrite );}
        else while ( rcnt > 0 ) {
            _Accept( EndRead ); }
        wcnt = 1;
    }
  public:
    ...
};
```

(b) Multiple accepting

Fig. 9.18 Readers and write: solution 5 (d & e)

The problem with this solution is that it inhibits concurrency in two ways. First, concurrency is inhibited by making each exiting reader task from a group, except the last reader, wait for *all* reader tasks in that group to exit. This problem results from the nested accepts, which stack up the exiting readers as they try to leave EndRead. Hence, there is a long delay before any reader in that group can exit the monitor and continue performing new work. Second, when an exiting reader is waiting for the next reader to exit, no new readers can enter the monitor because only EndRead calls are accepted. Hence, there is a long delay before a new reader can enter the monitor and subsequently read the resource.

To prevent these problems, it is clear that neither EndRead nor EndWrite can do an accept because that blocks the exiting task, which wants to leave immediately, and new reader tasks, which want to read simultaneously with the current group of readers. However, the accept cannot be removed; it must be relocated, and there is only one place it can be moved to. The solution in Fig. 9.18b moves the accepts of the completing readers into a loop in StartWrite. In the daisy-chain solution, the writer only accepts the next exiting reader of a group; in the multiple-accept solution, the writer accepts all the exiting readers of the current reader group. The longest delay an exiting reader experiences is the time to restart the writer and for it to cycle through the loop. Notice, the technique used to solve this problem is to switch from daisy-chain accepting to multiple accepting. Does this solution inhibit concurrency for the writer task performing the accepts of the readers? No, because that writer cannot enter the resource until the current group of readers completes, so it would otherwise be blocked. Clearly, a writer is doing a little more of the cooperation work over the previous solution, which amortized the cooperation work

```
_Monitor uSemaphore {                          _Monitor uSemaphore {
    int cnt;                                       int cnt;
                                                   uCondition cntPos;
  public:                                        public:
    uSemaphore( int cnt = 1 ) : cnt(cnt) {}        uSemaphore( int cnt = 1 ) : cnt(cnt) {}
    void V() {                                     void V() {
        cnt += 1;                                      cnt += 1;
                                                       cntPos.signal();
    }                                              }
    void P() {                                     void P() {
        if ( cnt == 0 ) _Accept( V );                  if ( cnt == 0 ) cntPos.wait();
        cnt -= 1;                                      cnt -= 1;
    }                                              }
};                                             };
```

| (a) External scheduling | (b) Internal scheduling |

Fig. 9.19 Mimic Semaphore with monitor

evenly across all the tasks. This scheme might be a problem if each task is charged separately for performing its work because a writer does the additional cooperation work. In general, the extra work is extremely small, unless there are hundreds or thousands of reader tasks in a group.

9.7.3   Solution 6

There is no need for an equivalent to semaphore solution 6 because a monitor's wait atomically unlocks the monitor and blocks the current task on an exit, wait, or signal so using a private condition is unnecessary. Interestingly, it is still possible to construct a monitor solution using private conditions, which mimics the corresponding semaphore solution exactly.

9.8   Condition, Wait, Signal vs. Counting Semaphore, P, V

As mentioned, the wait and signal operations on condition variables in a monitor are similar to P and V operations on counting semaphores. The wait can block a task's execution, while a signal can cause another task to be unblocked. In fact, it is easy to construct a semaphore with operations P and V using a monitor (see Fig. 9.19). Semaphores can also be used to build monitors, although any solution requires following complex coding conventions, which the compiler cannot check. As well, other important criteria, such as ease of use in programming complex concurrent problems, like the readers and writer problem, must be considered. Therefore, there is only a weak equivalence between the two mechanisms.

Other specific differences between condition variables and semaphores are as follows. When a task executes a P operation, it does not necessarily block since the semaphore counter may be greater than zero. In contrast, when a task executes a wait it always blocks. As a consequence, a condition can only be used for synchronization not mutual exclusion. When a task executes a V operation on a semaphore it either unblocks a task waiting on that semaphore or, if there is no task to unblock, increments the semaphore counter. In contrast, if a task executes a signal when there is no task to unblock, there is no effect on the condition variable; hence, signals may be lost so the order of executing wait and signals in a monitor is critical. Another difference between semaphores and monitors is that tasks awakened by a V can resume execution without delay. In contrast, because tasks execute with mutual exclusion within a monitor, tasks awakened from a condition variable are restarted only when the monitor is next unlocked. Finally, monitors may inhibit some concurrency because there is only one monitor lock, e.g., simultaneously inserting and removing from a bounded buffer (see the discussion in Sect. 9.2, p. 428). Essentially, the semaphore can provide finer grain concurrency than a monitor, but at a high cost in complexity.

9.9 Monitor Errors

As mentioned previously in Sect. 9.3.1, p. 437, some monitor implementations result in deadlock if the active monitor task calls a mutex member, which can be solved with code restructuring. While code restructuring can avoid this particular error, there are other problems when using monitors.

One problem that has been studied extensively is nested monitor call. When a task blocks in a monitor, either through _Accept or wait, other tasks can enter the monitor so that progress can be made. However, when a task, T1, calls from one monitor, M1, to another monitor, M2, and blocks in M2, M2 can continue to process requests but not M1. The reason M1 cannot process requests is that task T1 still has M1 locked and blocking in M2 only releases M2's monitor lock. Therefore, acquiring one monitor and blocking in another monitor results in a hold and wait situation, which may reduce concurrency in most cases and may result in a synchronization deadlock in others.

In some situations, holding all the monitor resources except the last is exactly the desired semantics; in other cases, it is not the desired semantics. Suggestions have been made for special monitor semantics to handle this situation, e.g., when a task blocks in a monitor, all the monitor locks it is currently holding are released. Clearly, neither approach is perfect for all circumstances, and hence, both or more semantics would need to be supported, further increasing the complexity of the monitor. In μC++, there is no special semantics for the nested monitor situation; monitor locks are held if a task holding them blocks. Therefore, this situation must be considered when designing complex resource allocation schemes, otherwise it might lead to deadlock.

9.10   Coroutine-Monitor

The coroutine-monitor is a coroutine with mutual exclusion and so it can be accessed simultaneously by multiple tasks. A coroutine-monitor type has a combination of the properties of a coroutine and a monitor, and can be used where a combination of these properties are needed, such as a finite automata that is used by multiple tasks.

A coroutine-monitor type has all the properties of a **_Coroutine** and a **_Mutex class**. The general form of the coroutine-monitor type is the following:

```
_Mutex _Coroutine coroutine-name {
private:
    ...            // these members are not visible externally
protected:
    ...            // these members are visible to descendants
    void main();   // starting member
public:
    ...            // these members are visible externally
};
```

Like the **_Mutex** qualifier on a **class**, the **_Mutex** qualifier on a **_Coroutine** means all public member routines of the coroutine have the mutual-exclusion property, unless overridden on specific member routines with the **_Nomutex** qualifier. When the **_Nomutex** qualifier is placed on a **_Coroutine** definition, it indicates all public member routines have the no-mutual-exclusion property, which is the same as a **_Coroutine**, unless overridden on specific member routines with the **_Mutex** qualifier. The default for a coroutine if no qualifier is specified is **_Nomutex** because the mutual-exclusion property for public members is typically not needed.

```
_Mutex _Coroutine MC1 {                 _Nomutex _Coroutine MC2 {
    ...                                     ...
public:                                 public:
    mem1() ...          // mutex            mem1() ...          // no mutex
    _Nomutex mem2()... // no mutex         _Mutex mem2() ... // mutex
    ~MC1() ...          // mutex           ~MC2() ...          // mutex
}                                       }
```

Therefore, a **_Coroutine** creates a coroutine-monitor if and only if it has at least one **_Mutex** member routine, and that **_Mutex** member routine can have any visibility, i.e., **private, protected** or **public**. As well, the destructor of a coroutine-monitor is always mutex, regardless of where it is defined or if it makes no references to the coroutine-monitor's shared variables. Hence, a coroutine-monitor always has one mutex member, its destructor, and a coroutine-monitor's destructor cannot be qualified with **_Nomutex**. For convenience, the preprocessor macro name **_Cormonitor** is defined to be "**_Mutex _Coroutine**" in uC++.h.

9.10.1   Coroutine-Monitor Creation and Destruction

A coroutine-monitor is the same as a monitor with respect to creation and destruction.

```
_Mutex _Coroutine uBarrier {
    uCondition Waiters;
    unsigned int Total, Count;

    void init( unsigned int total ) {
        Count = 0;
        Total = total;
    }
  protected:
    void main() {
        for ( ;; ) {
            suspend();
        }
    }
  public:
    uBarrier( unsigned int total ) {
        init( total );
    }
    _Nomutex unsigned int total() const {       // total participants in the barrier
        return Total;
    }
    _Nomutex unsigned int waiters() const { // number of waiting tasks
        return Count;
    }
    void reset( unsigned int total ) {
        init( total );
    }
    void block() {
        Count += 1;
        if ( Count < Total ) {                  // all tasks arrived ?
            Waiters.wait();
        } else {
            last();                             // call the last routine
            Count = 0;
            for ( ; ! Waiters.empty(); ) {      // restart all waiting tasks
                Waiters.signal();
            }
        }
    }
    virtual void last() {                       // called by last task to reach the barrier
        resume();
    }
};
```

Fig. 9.20 Barrier implementation

9.10.2 Coroutine-Monitor Control and Communication

A coroutine monitor can make use of suspend, resume, _Accept and uCondition variables, wait, signal and signalBlock to move a task among execution states and to block and restart tasks that enter it. As for monitors, when creating a cyclic call-graph (i.e., full coroutines) using coroutine-monitors and multiple threads, it is the programmer's responsibility to ensure the cycle does not result in deadlock, often by having at least one of the members in the cycle be a _Nomutex member.

Fig. 9.20 shows the implementation of the coroutine-monitor uBarrier discussed in Sect. 7.3.3, p. 333. This example illustrates how all of the ideas presented so far are combined. First, because a barrier is accessed by multiple tasks, it must have mutual exclusion; as well, because a barrier needs to retain state between calls to last, it should be a coroutine. The constructor initializes the total number of tasks using the barrier and other internal counters. The two public _Nomutex members, total and waiters, return barrier state information, i.e., the total number of tasks using the barrier and the number of tasks currently waiting on the barrier, respectively. Even though both members are _Nomutex, consistent values are always returned. The public member reset changes the total number of tasks using the barrier. No tasks may be waiting on the barrier when this total is changed. The public member block counts the tasks as they arrive at the barrier and blocks all but the last one. The last task invokes the member last to reset the barrier and unblocks any waiting tasks using multiple signalling. (Member last is made **virtual** so it can be overridden by subclasses and work correctly with subtype polymorphism.) The default last member resumes the default virtual coroutine main, which simply suspends back. Normally, a user supplies more complex versions of these two members through inheritance (see Fig. 7.7, p. 338), which manipulates complex state. Notice the use of resume, suspend, wait and signal in this coroutine-monitor, illustrating the combination of capabilities from the coroutine and the monitor.

9.11   Monitor Taxonomy

Interestingly, the term "monitor" does not denote a single language construct with fixed semantics. While all monitors imply some form of implicit mutual exclusion to ensure data associated with the monitor is accessed serially, it is the scheduling aspect that varies greatly among monitors. Without a clear and precise understanding of these variations it is extremely difficult to write correct concurrent programs using monitors. Therefore, understanding the differences is essential when trying to select the best monitor to solve a problem, or when confronted with a specific monitor, knowing how to use this monitor to solve a problem.

9.11.1   Explicit and Implicit Signal Monitor

The monitors discussed thus far all use explicit synchronization mechanisms, such as accepting or signal/wait. This form of monitor is referred to as an **explicit signal monitor** because a programmer explicitly performs the synchronization, usually using some form of cooperation. The alternative to explicit synchronization is conditional delay, similar to the **await** of the conditional critical-region, but for monitors. In this kind of monitor, the synchronization is implicitly performed by the implementation, and hence, is referred to as an **implicit signal monitor** or

```
monitor BoundedBuffer {
    int front, back, count;
    int Elements[20];
public:
    BoundedBuffer() : front(0), back(0), count(0) {}

    void insert( int elem ) {
        waituntil count != 20;              // buffer full ?
        Elements[back] = elem;
        back = ( back + 1 ) % 20;
        count += 1;
    }
    int remove() {
        waituntil count != 0;               // buffer empty ?
        int elem = Elements[front];
        front = ( front + 1 ) % 20;
        count -= 1;
        return elem;
    }
};
```

Fig. 9.21 Bounded buffer: implicit synchronization

automatic-signal monitor because the unblocking (signalling) of waiting tasks is done automatically. The implicit/automatic-signal monitor was proposed by Hoare [12, p. 556].

An implicit/automatic-signal monitor has the unconditional wait on a condition variable changed to use a wait on a conditional expression, e.g.:

waituntil *conditional_expression*

If the conditional expression is false, a task blocks and the monitor automatically checks for a task with a true condition or selects the next task from the entry queue. A waiting task is only unblocked when the expression it is waiting on becomes true. A consequence of this change is the elimination of condition variables and signals, which simplifies the monitor. However, conditional delays cannot express direct cooperation and can be runtime expensive (see Sect. 9.2.1, p. 432). Fig. 9.21 illustrates a fictitious automatic-signal monitor (i.e., not supported in μC++) for a bounded buffer.

9.11.2 Implicit Monitor Scheduling

Previous discussion has centred on how a programmer can schedule tasks in a monitor, either internally or externally. However, a monitor has a small amount of implicit scheduling, which attempts to keep the monitor as busy as possible if there are waiting tasks. For example, in μC++, when a task exits the monitor, implicit scheduling occurs to restart the next blocked task on the acceptor/signalled stack or entry queue. A programmer cannot change this implicit scheduling; it is part of the

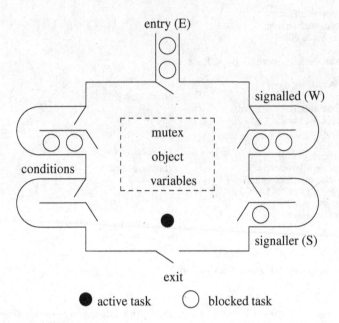

entry (E)

signalled (W)

mutex
object
variables

conditions

signaller (S)

exit

● active task   ○ blocked task

Fig. 9.22 General mutex object

internal implementation of the monitor. However, the particular implicit scheduling for μC++ is not the only approach; other implicit scheduling schemes are valid.

In general, implicit scheduling can sensibly be applied in the following three situations: when a task executes a wait, an accept/signal or exits from a mutex member. In these three situations, the monitor can become inactive, and hence, implicit scheduling occurs to make the monitor active again if tasks are waiting. As well, the implicit scheduler must know where to look for waiting tasks so one can be scheduled to use the monitor. Waiting tasks are normally blocked on a number of queues internal to the monitor (e.g., the entry queue). Fig. 9.22 shows the general form of a monitor with a set of tasks using, or waiting to use, the monitor. The entry, signalled, and condition queues have been discussed previously. (It is sufficient for this general discussion to use queues; the stack in μC++ is a special case related to a different issue.) The new queue in the diagram is the signaller queue, which is used for signal-block scheduling, where the signaller task must wait for the signalled task to execute. For accepting, it is possible to consider the mutex queues like condition queues and the signaller queue as the acceptor stack; accepting is then like signal-block, where the acceptor waits for the signalled task, on one of the specified mutex queues, to execute. (The difference is that signal-block on an empty condition does not block, whereas an accept on an empty mutex queue(s) blocks.) For this discussion, it is assumed that any signal moves the signalled task to the signalled queue and the signaller task to the signaller queue, before implicit scheduling occurs. In this way, the implicit scheduler has a complete and simple picture of all the tasks waiting to use the monitor. In the case of an automatic-signal monitor, there are no condition queues and only one queue is needed to manage the tasks with false conditional expressions (similar to the implementation of conditional critical-region); the tasks with false conditional expressions can be put on the signalled queue because each waiting task is effectively eligible to run when the monitor is unlocked so that it can recheck its conditional expression. Thus, the diagram in Fig. 9.22 can be used to locate all waiting tasks for both explicit and implicit signal monitors. The implicit scheduler can now select a task from any of the entry, signalled, or signaller queues. In certain situations, one or more of these queues can be empty. Depending on the kind of monitor, a particular choice is made. All other tasks must wait until the next implicit scheduling point is reached by the active monitor task.

9.11.3   Monitor Classification*

To understand the differences among monitors, it is necessary to have a classification scheme that clearly delineates the differences in a meaningful way. The classification must provide a criteria for identifying any differences among monitors. The criteria should generate some form of taxonomy, in which all extant monitors should appear; the taxonomy may be general enough to suggest forms for which there are no existing monitors.

The following monitor taxonomy covers all extant monitors and uncovers several new ones. Initially, the monitors are divided into two groups based on whether the signal operation is explicit or implicit; within these two broad categories, several additional sub-categories are developed based on the semantics of the signal operation.

9.11.3.1   Explicit-Signal Monitors

The classification scheme for explicit-signal monitors is based on an exhaustive case analysis of the scheduling possibilities for the three internal monitor queues–the entry, signalled and signaller queues–when an implicit scheduling point is reached by the active monitor task. The different kinds of monitors are classified based on the relative priorities associated with these three queues. Each queue has a specific static priority, referred to as entry priority (E_p), signalled (waiting) priority (W_p), and signaller priority (S_p), respectively. The relative orderings of these three priorities yields 13 different possibilities, which are given in Table 9.1. There is one case in which the 3 priorities are equal. There are $\binom{3}{2} = 3$ cases in which exactly two priorities are equal, and each equal pair can be either greater than or less than the

---

* This section is a revision of "Monitor Classification" in [8] ©1995 ACM. Portions reprinted by permission.

Table 9.1 Relative priorities for internal monitor queues

	Relative priority	
1	$E_p = W_p = S_p$	
2	$E_p = W_p < S_p$	
3	$E_p = S_p < W_p$	
4	$E_p < W_p = S_p$	
5	$E_p < W_p < S_p$	
6	$E_p < S_p < W_p$	
7	$S_p = W_p < E_p$	Rejected
8	$W_p < S_p = E_p$	
9	$W_p < E_p < S_p$	
10	$S_p < W_p = E_p$	
11	$S_p < E_p < W_p$	
12	$W_p < S_p < E_p$	
13	$S_p < W_p < E_p$	

third priority, hence $\binom{3}{2} \times 2 = 6$ cases. Finally, there are $3! = 6$ cases in which the priorities are all different.

Cases 7–13 are rejected because the entry queue has priority over an internal queue. Giving the entry queue this level of priority has several severe disadvantages. First, it inhibits concurrency: it blocks tasks that could otherwise exit the monitor and continue their normal execution. Second, it creates the potential for unbounded waiting if there is a steady stream of tasks entering the monitor. Moreover, there are few, if any, compensating advantages to giving the entry queue such priority. Therefore, only cases 1–6 of Table 9.1 are examined.

If two or more queues have equal priority, the scheduler chooses one arbitrarily. Notice, it is acceptable for the entry queue to have equal priority with the other queues. In these cases, the arbitrary choice for selection ensures some bound on waiting among the queues so a continuous stream of calling tasks does not preclude tasks from being scheduled from other queues. Finally, if the highest-priority queue is an internel queue can have at most one task waiting on it because after a task blocks on the highest priority queue, it is immediately restarted. As a result, most implementations optimize out the queue associated with the highest priority task, which is why μC++ has only a single queue (stack). Nevertheless, for purposes of understanding the classification scheme, all queues need to be identified and understood, even though some queues may not appear in the implementation.

9.11.3.2 Immediate-Return Monitor

One additional explicit signal monitor needs mentioning for completeness, and because it identifies an interesting property of monitors that is important in later discussions. The interesting property is that most signals occur directly or indirectly before a return statement.

Table 9.2 Relative priorities for extended immediate-return & automatic-signal monitor

	Relative priority
1	$E_p = W_p$
2	$E_p < W_p$
3	$W_p < E_p$

The question whether the signal should always be the last operation of a monitor procedure is still open [12, p. 557].

This property is true for all the monitors in this chapter, except two versions of the dating service monitor, which have a signal before a wait. In Brinch-Hansen's Concurrent Pascal [5, p. 205] this property was enforced by having the signal also return the signaller from the mutex member. This kind of monitor is called an **immediate return monitor** because the signal implicitly does a return. Since the signaller leaves the monitor, the next task to enter the monitor is the signalled task, if there is one. Such a monitor precludes a task from multiple signalling or executing code after the signal with the monitor lock.

While this property occurs frequently in monitors, it is not true for all monitors. In fact, as has been pointed out by Howard [13, p. 51] and Andrews [1, p. 312], some monitor programs that can be written with ordinary explicit-signal monitors cannot be written with immediate-return monitors unless the interface to the monitor is changed. As a result, there is only a weak equivalence between the immediate-return monitor and other explicit-signal monitors. Howard proposed an **extended immediate-return monitor** [13, p. 51] allowing a signal to also precede a wait; in this case, the signaller does not leave the monitor because it blocks immediately on the specified condition queue for the wait after the signal. Again, the signalled task, if there is one, enters the monitor next. The extended immediate-return monitor has been shown to be as general as the other explicit-signal monitors.

However, there are still useful situations where a signaller may continue executing in a monitor immediately after a signal, i.e., not return or block. For example, Fig. 9.17, p. 468 shows a solution for the readers and writer problem where the finishing writer task does all of the signalling for the next task(s) to use the resource, i.e., it signals the next writer or the next group of reader tasks using multiple signalling rather than daisy-chain signalling. While it might appear that the finishing writer does more than its fair share of work with respect to the cooperation, there are cases where it is more efficient to localize the cooperation rather than spread it out [8, p. 101].

The monitor categorization-scheme is applicable to both the immediate-return and extended immediate-return monitors; however, there is no signaller queue because either the signaller task leaves the monitor immediately or it is put on a condition queue. Therefore, the next active task is either a calling or a signalled task. Table 9.2 shows these possibilities. Again, the case where the entry queue has priority over an internal queue is rejected.

9.11.3.3 Automatic-Signal Monitors

It is possible to further classify the implicit/automatic-signal monitor based on the kinds of variables allowed in the conditional expression. If both monitor variables and local variables of a mutex member may appear in the conditional expression, the monitor is called a general automatic-signal monitor. If only monitor (global) variables are allowed in the conditional expression, the monitor is called a restricted automatic-signal monitor.

General automatic-signal monitors require an expensive implementation, as for conditional critical-region (see page 433), because, in the worst case, it involves re-evaluating the conditional expressions of all waiting tasks. Since a conditional expression can potentially depend on local variables of a task, including parameters of a mutex member, the local context of a task must be accessed to evaluate its conditional expression. The simplest way to accomplish this is to awaken tasks from the signalled queue one at a time so each can re-evaluate its conditional expression. If a task evaluates its condition and finds the condition true, it proceeds; otherwise, it again blocks on the signalled queue and allows another task to try. The problem with this approach is that many context switches may occur before some task can proceed.

Restricted automatic-signal monitors have a much more efficient implementation. Since all variables in the conditional expressions are monitor variables, and hence do not depend on the context of individual tasks, the conditional expressions can be evaluated efficiently by the task that is about to unlock the monitor. The efficiency can be further improved by noting which conditional expressions represent distinct conditions; if two or more tasks are waiting for the same condition, it need only be evaluated once. Kessels [14] proposed a notation that both restricts conditional expressions to use only monitor variables and also allows the programmer to specify which conditional expressions represent distinct conditions. His notation moves the conditional expressions from the wait into the monitor declarations and gives each a name; these names are then used in the wait instead of an expression, e.g.:

```
monitor M {
    int a, b;
    condexpr(a > b) c;    // only monitor variables allowed in the expression
    int r(...) {
        ... waituntil c; ...    // wait until the conditional expression, c, is true
```

Since only monitor variables are allowed in a conditional expression, the time it takes to find the next task to execute is determined by the cost of re-evaluating the conditional expressions. Thus, compared to general automatic-signal monitors, there is the potential for significant execution time saving in determining the next task to execute. The drawback is that local mutex member information, including parameters, cannot be used in a conditional expression of a restricted automatic-signal wait, which precludes solutions to certain problems, like the dating service.

The monitor-categorization scheme is applicable to either kind of automatic-signal monitors; however, there are no condition queues and no signaller queue.

Table 9.3 Useful monitors

Signal Property	Priority	No priority
Blocking	$E_p < S_p < W_p$ Priority Blocking (PB)	$E_p = S_p < W_p$ No Priority Blocking (NPB)
NonBlocking	$E_p < W_p < S_p$ Priority Non-Blocking (PNB)	$E_p = W_p < S_p$ No-Priority Non-Blocking (NPNB)
Quasi-Blocking	$E_p < W_p = S_p$ Priority Quasi-Blocking (PQB)	$E_p = W_p = S_p$ No-Priority Quasi-Blocking (NPQB)
Extended Immediate Return	$E_p < W_p$ Priority Immediate Return (PRET)	$E_p = W_p$ No-Priority Immediate Return (NPRET)
Automatic Signal	$E_p < W_p$ Priority Automatic Signal (PAS)	$E_p = W_p$ No-Priority Automatic Signal (NPAS)

Therefore, the next active monitor task is either a calling task or a task on the signalled queue waiting for its conditional expression to evaluate to true. Table 9.2, p. 479 shows these possibilities. Again, the case where the entry queue has priority over an internal queue is rejected.

9.11.3.4 Simplified Classification

The remaining "useful" monitors are now organized along the following lines (see Table 9.3). First, the monitors are divided into two groups (the columns) based on the priority of the entry queue. This division is useful because when the priority of the calling tasks is equal to either the signaller tasks or signalled tasks, it may make writing a monitor more complex. (This complexity is discussed further in Sect. 9.13.1, p. 490.) These two groups are called the priority monitor and no-priority monitor, respectively. In priority monitors, tasks already in the monitor have priority over calling tasks; in no-priority monitors, they do not. The importance of this crucial property has often been highly underrated and even ignored in the explanation of a monitor's semantics behaviour.

Within the two groups, it is possible to pair the monitors based on aspects of the signal (the rows). In the blocking monitor, the signaller task blocks on the signaller queue while the signalled task re-enters the monitor. In contrast, in the non-blocking monitor, the signaller task continues execution in the monitor and the signalled task can re-enter the monitor only when the monitor is unlocked. In the quasi-blocking monitor, either signaller or signalled tasks continue execution in the monitor and the other blocks. Finally, the extended immediate return and automatic-signal monitors form the last two pairs of monitors. This organization makes it easy to remember and understand the different kinds of monitors. Interestingly, there are four new kinds of monitors identified by the classification scheme over those discussed in the past: PQB, NPQB, NPRET and NPAS.

μC++ only supports priority monitors, and there is a choice between blocking or non-blocking signal with signalBlock and signal, respectively.

9.12   Monitor Equivalence

All monitors are equivalent in a very weak sense by noting that any kind of monitor can be implemented with semaphores and can in turn be used to implement semaphores. Thus any monitor program for one kind of monitor can be mechanically translated into a program for any other kind of monitor by "compiling" the monitor program into code that synchronizes using semaphore operations and then using the other kind of monitor to implement the semaphore operations. However, this transformation is unsatisfying because it yields a much lower level program than the original. (This kind of very weak equivalence between language features has been called the "Turing tar pit" by Howard [13, p. 49].) Only with transformations preserving the basic structure of the monitor program, i.e., transformations that do not introduce any new types, nor change the monitor interface or its overall structure, can monitor kinds be considered strongly equivalent. These transformations are amenable to programmers and language translators when converting from one kind of monitor in one language to a different kind of monitor in another language.

Because there are 10 kinds of monitors, there are $\binom{10}{2}$ different transformations. In fact, all transformations are possible [8], so any monitor can be transformed into another, while preserving the basic structure of the monitor program. However, many of the transformations are complex, illustrating a weak equivalence between certain kinds of monitors, although still structure preserving. The only transformations examined here are the ones from explicit signal monitors to automatic signal. The reason these transformation are especially interesting is because many languages with monitors do not support automatic signalling, and automatic signalling is a useful technique for quick prototyping of a monitor, where speed of software development overrides execution performance. After a concurrent system is working, any performance bottleneck resulting from an automatic-signal monitor can be converted to an explicit-signal monitor.

9.12.1   Non-FIFO Simulations

Two non-FIFO simulations are presented for PB and PNB explicit-signal monitors to a PAS monitor. These simulations illustrate the techniques needed to construct an automatic-signal monitor. Both simulations use an additional condition variable. However, these non-FIFO simulations suffer from starvation and staleness/freshness, which are both dealt with in Sect. 9.12.2, p. 487. The basic approach in these transformations is to have each task check its own conditional expression. If the condition is true, the task proceeds to use the monitor; if it is false, the task wakes up the next waiting task in the monitor so it can check its condition. This approach results in repeatedly waking all waiting tasks to let them recheck their conditions.

In general, a simulation involves changes in three or four locations of the automatic-signal monitor to convert to an explicit-signal monitor:

1. monitor-variable declarations: these are additional definitions and declarations added solely for the simulation and not part of the original automatic-signal monitor.

2. monitor-routine entry: this is additional definitions, declarations, and code involving signal/wait inserted at the start of each monitor routine in preparation for using the automatic-signal monitor by a particular task. This section may be empty in a simulation, i.e., no code is required.

3. waituntil statement: this statement is transformed into declarations and code, involving signal/wait, mimicking the waituntil statement.

4. monitor-routine exit: this is additional declarations and code, involving signal/wait, inserted before the return of each monitor routine usually to complete the current predicate checking-cycle and/or initiate the next one. This section may be empty in a simulation, i.e., no code is required.

Each simulation is shown as a table with a line for each of the change points and one column containing the automatic-signal code and the other column the equivalent explicit-signal code.

The transformation from a priority automatic-signal (PAS) monitor to a priority nonblocking (PNB) monitor is shown in Table 9.4. This transformation declares a condition variable, named IS, on which tasks with false predicates wait. There is an initial check if the predicate expression is true, and if so, continue. Otherwise, all tasks blocked on condition IS are signalled, which is an example of multiple signalling (see Sect. 9.5.1, p. 447), to recheck their predicate expressions because the monitor state may have changed. The current task then blocks in a loop rechecking its predicate expression each time it is signalled. On return from a monitor routine, all tasks on condition IS are signalled (using multiple signalling) so they can recheck their predicate expressions because the monitor state may have changed. Notice, when a task finds its predicate is true and continues to use the monitor, there may be tasks blocked on the signalled (W) queue. These tasks form the front of the next checking cycle started by a return or a rewait by the task using the monitor.

The transformation is straightforward, except to ensure the loop signalling all tasks on condition IS terminates. Using the nonblocking signal, all tasks on condition IS are moved to the signaller queue before another task can execute. Therefore, condition IS always empties and the loop terminates. Interestingly, this transformation does not work if the nonblocking signal is changed to a blocking signal. The problem occurs while attempting to signal all the tasks blocked on condition IS. Because the signalled task executes first, it can find its condition false and block again on condition IS. Hence, when the signaller task restarts, it always finds condition IS non-empty, so it loops forever checking predicates. Finally, the multiple signalling in this algorithm is performed with a loop, which is $O(n)$; if a signalAll (broadcast) is available, the entire condition list can be moved by a single linked-list operation, which is $O(1)$. Nevertheless, there are always $O(n)$ predicate checks.

The transformation from a priority general-automatic-signal monitor to a priority-blocking (PB) monitor is shown in Table 9.4. As before, a condition variable

Table 9.4 Transform PAS monitor to PNB monitor

PAS	PNB
declarations	condition IS;

waituntil C_i;	**if** (! C_i) {
	    while (! IS.empty()) signal IS;
	    do {
	        wait IS;
	    } **while** (! C_i);
	}

return $expr_{opt}$;	**while** (! IS.empty()) signal IS; **return** $expr_{opt}$;

Table 9.5 Transform PAS monitor to PB monitor

PAS	PB
declarations	condition IS;

waituntil C_i;	**for** (; ! C_i;) { // optional check
	    signalblock IS;
	    if (C_i) **break**;
	    wait IS;
	}

return $expr_{opt}$;	signalblock IS; **return** $expr_{opt}$;

is declared, named IS, on which tasks with false predicates wait. As well, the waituntil of the automatic-signal monitor can begin with or without an initial predicate check, i.e., the predicate check can be removed from the top of the **for** loop, in an attempt to deal with starvation and staleness/freshness. Otherwise, the first task on condition IS is signalled, which starts daisy-chain signalling (see Sect. 9.7.1, p. 463), to recheck its predicate expression because the monitor state may have changed. Because the signaller blocks for this signal, it must again recheck its predicate expression when it restarts because the monitor state may have changed. Only if the predicate expression is still false does the task block on condition IS. When a task is signalled, it loops back (and possibly rechecks its predicate expression, and if still false) signals the first task on condition IS. On return from a monitor routine, the first task on condition IS is signalled, which starts daisy-chain signalling, so it can recheck its predicate expressions because the monitor state may have changed. Notice, when a task finds its predicate is true and continues to use the monitor, there may be tasks blocked on the signaller queue. These tasks form the front of the next checking cycle started by a return or a rewait by the task using the monitor.

Section 9.13.2, p. 491 points out that a returning task with a blocking signal can have its exit delayed, possibly significantly, because of the blocking-signal semantics. With respect to the transformation, there can be an $O(n)$ delay if multiple waiting tasks have a true predicate as a result of changes from a returning task. As a result, tasks may not exit the monitor in FIFO order. Since this is a fundamental problem of blocking signal, no simulation using blocking signal can completely prevent its occurrence.

The transformation is straightforward, except to ensure the loop signalling all tasks on condition IS terminates. With the blocking signal, the signaller is moved to the signaller queue *before* another task can execute. Because the signalled task cannot wait again on condition IS without first doing a blocking signal on condition IS, which puts it on the signaller queue, eventually condition IS becomes empty. Interestingly, this transformation does not work if the blocking signal is changed to a nonblocking signal. Again, the problem occurs while attempting to signal all the tasks blocked on condition IS. Because the signaller task executes first, it blocks immediately on condition IS at the wait. Hence, when a signalled task restarts, it always finds condition IS non-empty, so it loops forever checking predicates.

9.12.1.1 Problems

Unfortunately, these transformations do not deal with starvation and/or staleness/ freshness. The problem with the transformations is that some notion of fairness, like FIFO ordering, of task condition-checking is not ensured. Fig. 9.23 shows one possible starvation/staleness/freshness scenario for the PNB simulation.[5] The failing PNB scenario requires a task to enter the monitor with waiting tasks (false predicates), and the entering task's predicate is also false. The entering task then moves all the tasks to the signaller queue (multiple signalling) so these tasks can recheck their predicates, as the monitor state may have changed. However, after the waiting tasks are moved, the entering task waits on the empty IS condition variable, putting it at the head of the queue. As the waiting tasks unblock, test and wait again, they line up behind the entering task, e.g. (and see line 8 in Fig. 9.23):

	IS	monitor	signaller	
1	A B	C		enter; C_i false
2		C	A B	signal all IS
3	C	A	B	wait IS
4	C	A	B	unblock; C_i false
5	C A	B		wait IS
6	C A	B		unblock; C_i false
7	C A B			wait IS

Hence, the entering task checks its predicate first on the next checking cycle. In Fig. 9.23, task TW_2 acquires the resource ahead of task TW_1. If task TW_4 arrives and steps 4–14 are repeated, task TW_1 is in a starvation scenario.

Fig. 9.24, p. 487 shows one possible starvation/staleness/freshness scenario for the PB simulation. The failing PB scenario is more complex, requiring two tasks to enter and wait before the problem occurs. As above, the entering task does not end up at the end of the waiting condition IS nor at the head; instead, it appears second

---

[5] For all tables of this form, the queue head is on the left. Also, for a line with a "wait" comment, the wait operation has already been performed by the task in the monitor on the previous line, and the "wait" line shows that task already blocked on the specified condition variable.

	IS	monitor	signaller	
1		TW_1		enter; C_i false
2		TW_1		signal all IS
3	TW_1			wait IS
4	TW_1	TW_2		enter; C_i false
5		TW_2	TW_1	signal all IS
6	TW_2	TW_1		wait IS;
7	TW_2	TW_1		unblock; C_i false
8	TW_2 TW_1			wait IS
9	TW_2 TW_1	TS_3		enter; make C_i true
10		TS_3	TW_2 TW_1	signal all; return
11		TW_2	TW_1	unblock; C_i true; make C_i false
12		TW_2	TW_1	signal all; return
13		TW_1		unblock; C_i false
14	TW_1			wait IS

Fig. 9.23 Starvation/staleness PNB

from the head, and the task previously at the tail is at the head. The entering task gets into the wrong position because the blocking signal puts it at the head of the signaller queue list, and similarly, the other waiting tasks block behind it if their predicates are false or there is no predicate check before signalling. As a result, the entering task is unblocked first from the signaller queue, and hence, performs its predicate check ahead of the other waiting tasks for the next predicate check. The last waiting task gets into the wrong position because it signals an empty condition (IS), which does nothing, and hence, it is the first to wait on IS, e.g. (see also lines 11–21 in Fig. 9.24):

	IS	monitor	signaller	
1	A B C	D		enter; C_i false
2	A B C	D		signalblock IS
3	B C	A	D	unblock; signalblock IS
4	C	B	D A	unblock; signalblock IS
5		C	D A B	unblock; signalblock IS
6	C	D	A B	C_i false; wait IS
7	C D	A	B	C_i false; wait IS
8	C D A	B		C_i false; wait IS
9	C D A B			

Hence, the previous tail of the waiting tasks checks its predicate first on the next checking cycle. In Fig. 9.24, task TW_2 acquires the resource ahead of task TW_1. If task TW_5 arrives and steps 11–34 are repeated, task TW_1 is in a starvation scenario.

Hence, for these simulations, staleness and/or freshness could occur for different applications because the tasks do not recheck their conditions in FIFO order. These simulation algorithms, which on the surface seem to provide the desired semantics, may fail because of subtle execution behaviour of the explicit-signal monitor used for the implementation or because of small deficiencies in the simulation algorithm itself.

	IS	monitor	signaller	
1		TW_1		enter; C_i false
2		TW_1		signalblock IS
3	TW_1			wait IS
4	TW_1	TW_2		enter; C_i false
5	TW_1	TW_2		signalblock IS
6		TW_1	TW_2	unblock; C_i false
7		TW_1	TW_2	signalblock IS;
8	TW_1	TW_2		wait IS
9	TW_1	TW_2		unblock; C_i false
10	$TW_1 \, TW_2$			wait IS
11	$TW_1 \, TW_2$	TW_3		enter; C_i false
12	$TW_1 \, TW_2$	TW_3		signalblock IS
13	TW_2	TW_1	TW_3	unblock; C_i false
14	TW_2	TW_1	TW_3	signalblock IS
15		TW_2	$TW_3 \, TW_1$	unblock; C_i false
16		TW_2	$TW_3 \, TW_1$	signalblock IS
17	TW_2	TW_3	TW_1	wait IS
18	TW_2	TW_3	TW_1	unblock; C_i false
19	$TW_2 \, TW_3$	TW_1		wait IS
20	$TW_2 \, TW_3$	TW_1		unblock; C_i false
21	$TW_2 \, TW_3 \, TW_1$			wait IS
22	$TW_2 \, TW_3 \, TW_1$	TS_4		enter; make C_i true
23	$TW_2 \, TW_3 \, TW_1$	TS_4		signalblock IS (begin return)
24	$TW_3 \, TW_1$	TW_2	TS_4	unblock; C_i true; make C_i false
25	$TW_3 \, TW_1$	TW_2	TS_4	signalblock IS (begin return)
26	TW_1	TW_3	$TS_4 \, TW_2$	unblock; C_i false
27	TW_1	TW_3	$TS_4 \, TW_2$	signalblock IS
28		TW_1	$TS_4 \, TW_2 \, TW_3$	unblock; C_i false
29		TW_1	$TS_4 \, TW_2 \, TW_3$	signalblock IS
30	TW_1	TS_4	$TW_2 \, TW_3$	wait IS
31	TW_1	TS_4	$TW_2 \, TW_3$	return
32	TW_1	TW_2	TW_3	return
33	TW_1	TW_3		unblock; C_i false
34	$TW_1 \, TW_3$			wait IS

Fig. 9.24 Starvation/staleness PB

9.12.2 FIFO Simulation

If FIFO testing of predicates is unimportant, the previous simulations are sufficient. However, many programmers assume (rightly or wrongly) that FIFO testing occurs, and in some cases, FIFO testing is required for correctness. It is often argued that if FIFO ordering is required, it is the programmer's responsibility to code it. However, adding FIFO ordering on top of an existing automatic-signal implementation may be difficult or impossible because of the need to control ordering sufficiently to ensure correctness.

The following simulation guarantees waiting tasks have their predicates checked in FIFO order for each particular waituntil. That is, ordering is not FIFO with respect to calling the monitor but *with respect to each execution of a* waituntil *statement during a single access to a monitor*. This definition requires a task with a true predicate to first check other waiting tasks, which handles the case where two or more tasks wait on the same or equivalent predicates multiple times during a single monitor access, as in:

```
waituntil( x == y ); // first wait
waituntil( x == z ); // second wait
```

Assume a task sets y and z to the value of x, exits the monitor, and there are two tasks waiting on the first waituntil. FIFO order selects the longest waiting task to check its predicate; this task restarts and immediately checks the second equivalent predicate, which is true. However, the other task waiting for the first equivalent predicate is now waiting longer by the FIFO definition, so even though the checking task has a true predicate, it must be placed on the end of the FIFO queue to allow the other task to discover its first predicate is true. Only if all waiting tasks have false predicates can the task with the true predicate continue. This case is subtle but important; however, it has a performance impact. Finally, for languages that allow side-effects in expressions, such as C++ and Java, it is important to only evaluate predicates when necessary in a simulation. The presented simulation performs the minimal number of predicate evaluations.

Table 9.6 is the transformation from a priority general-automatic-signal monitor to a priority nonblocking monitor using a linked list of condition variables, and any number of counters and flag variables. Each waiting task blocks on its own condition; hence, there is only one task blocked on each condition variable. The list order defines the FIFO relationship among waiting tasks.

The waituntil of the automatic-signal monitor is transformed into a check if no waiting tasks and the predicate expression is true, and if so, continue. Otherwise, a cursor used to traverse the FIFO linked-list is set to the head of the list, and a node with a condition variable is created and inserted at the end of the FIFO linked-list. The order of these two operations is important because the next operation needs to know if the list was empty before the new node was added.[6] Also, the list node is allocated each time a task waits, which could be done once on entry. On return from a monitor routine, if the list of waiting tasks is not empty, the cursor used to traverse the FIFO linked-list is set to the head of the list, one waiting task is signalled to start a daisy-chain checking-cycle, and the returning task exits directly. The check for an empty list is necessary because the signal accesses the list through the cursor, which is NULL for an empty list.

---

[6] Again, no dynamic allocation is performed by this algorithm, as the list node is created as a local variable on the task's stack, which eliminates the need for dynamic storage-allocation.

Table 9.6 Transform PAS monitor to PNB monitor: N queue

PAS	PNB: N queue

declarations	**struct** IS_NODE_T : **public** seqable {
	    condition cond;
	};
	struct IS_T {
	    sequence<IS_NODE_T> waiting;
	    IS_NODE_T *cursor;
	} IS

waituntil C_i;	**if** (! IS.waiting.empty() || ! C_i) {
	    IS.cursor = IS.waiting.head();
	    IS_NODE_T IS_node;
	    IS.waiting.addTail(&IS_node);
	    for (;;) { // checking cycle
	        if (IS.cursor != 0) signal IS.cursor->cond;
	        wait IS_node.cond;
	        if (C_i) **break**;
	        IS.cursor = IS.waiting.succ(&IS_node);
	    }
	    IS.waiting.remove(&IS_node);
	}

return $expr_{opt}$;	**if** (! IS.waiting.empty()) {
	    IS.cursor = IS.waiting.head();
	    signal IS.cursor->cond;
	}
	return $expr_{opt}$;

The main body of the waituntil code is a loop performing the checking cycle. A waiting task executes this loop until its predicate is true. The first action in the loop is to check if the cursor is not NULL (0), which implies there are other tasks to signal in this checking cycle so the next task on the FIFO list of conditions is signalled (via cursor) to continue the daisy-chain signalling. Now the task waits on the condition in its node until it is signalled to recheck its predicate. When a task unblocks to perform a check, it checks its predicate. If its predicate is true, the task exits the checking loop and proceeds to use the monitor. Otherwise, the cursor is moved to the next node of the linked-list, the next waiting task is signalled, and this task waits again.

The predicate check at the start of the waituntil simulation ensures a task with a true predicate cannot proceed if there are any waiting tasks. In this case, the task with the true predicate places itself at the back of the waiting list, and a complete check is performed (as for a false predicate). If no other task has a true predicate, the original task with the true predicate is guaranteed to unblock as it is the last node on the list. Whereupon, it rechecks its true predicate and continues.

During the checking cycle, each task moves the cursor if its predicate is false, and this process continues through all nodes of the FIFO list, ensuring every waiting task checks its predicate and the predicates are checked in FIFO order. Because the last task on the linked-list does *not* signal a task before waiting, the checking cycle is guaranteed to stop as there can be no task on the signaller queue to continue further checking. Because daisy-chain signalling is used, at most one task appears on the signaller queue. This can be seen by observing that signals appear directly or indirectly before a **return** or wait, hence no other signal can occur before the signalled task restarts. Hence, during the checking cycle when a task finds its predicate is true, it proceeds to use the monitor with a guarantee of an empty signaller-queue due to the daisy-chain signalling. Therefore, at the next unlocking point, all waiting tasks are blocked on their specific condition variable in the FIFO queue before starting the checking cycle. The algorithm is $O(n)$ because for each of the n tasks on the linked-list, only one predicate check is performed. Also, this simulation is optimal with respect to minimizing context switching, as no additional searching is required to process waiting tasks in FIFO order, and no reordering is required to maintain FIFO order, both of which introduce additional context switching for the waiting tasks.

9.13   Monitor Comparison

The following is a summation of the criteria a programmer can use in selecting a particular kind of monitor to solve a concurrency problem. (Although, in most cases, the language designer has already selected the kind of monitor(s), and a programmer must conform to it.)

9.13.1   Priority/No-Priority

When a condition is signalled in a priority monitor, control transfers directly or indirectly to a task waiting for the condition to occur (unless the condition variable is empty). In either case, this transfer allows the signaller and signalled tasks to establish an internal protocol for synchronization and communication through monitor variables (i.e., cooperation). In contrast, a signal in a no-priority monitor, as in the programming languages Mesa, Modula-2+, Modula-3[7] and Java, act as a "hint" to a waiting task to resume execution at some convenient future time [15, p. 111][2, p. 102][16, p. 93]. In this approach, a task may signal a condition whenever it *might* be true; the signalled task is responsible for checking whether it actually *is* true. This style is a cautious approach to concurrency control, where the signalled and signaller tasks can make no assumptions about order of execution, even within the monitor. Hence, for no-priority monitors, the assertion for the condition that is signalled may no longer hold by the time the signalled task gains

---

[7] Modula-3 takes this one step further by defining the signal routine to wake up at least one task, which implies that it may wake up more than one task. This semantics is modelled in the taxonomy as a no-priority non-blocking monitor with a loop around each signal that executes a random number of times.

control of the monitor, making cooperation difficult or impossible. Thus, when a waiting task restarts, it must determine if the monitor state it was waiting for is true instead of assuming it is true because it was signalled. This lack of guarantee often results in a wait being enclosed in a **while** loop so a task rechecks if the event for which it was waiting has occurred (as is done implicitly in the automatic-signal monitor). This coding style is busy waiting as there is no bound on the number of times a tasks may awake, only to wait again.

As well, it is difficult to implement certain scheduling schemes using no-priority monitors because a calling task can *barge* ahead of tasks that have already been waiting in the monitor. Unless special care is taken by including extra code to deal with this situation, it is impossible to guarantee FIFO scheduling, which may be critical to a particular problem (e.g., readers and writer problem). In such cases, it is necessary to simulate a priority monitor to prevent barging, which increases both the complexity of the solution and the execution cost.

Finally, there is the potential for unbounded waiting in no-priority monitors. If the implementation chooses randomly among internal queues of the same priority, there is no bound on the number of tasks that are serviced before a task is selected from a particular queue. In practice, however, this problem is usually solved by the implementation, which combines queues with the same priority so that tasks placed on them have a bounded number of tasks ahead of them. Thus, the only advantage of a no-priority monitor is that a task does not have to wait as long on average before entering the monitor.

9.13.2 Blocking/Non-blocking

A blocking signal guarantees control goes immediately to the signalled task. This direct transfer is conceptually appealing because control transfers to a task waiting for a particular assertion to become true; thus, the signaller does not have an opportunity to inadvertently falsify the assertion that was true at the time of the signal. Conversely, it is possible for the signalled task to incorrectly alter the monitor state prior to resumption of the signaller. This kind of signal is used when the task fulfilling some cooperation arrives *before* the task needing the cooperation, and hence, must be restarted (signalled) to perform the cooperation before the signaller task can continue.

A non-blocking signal guarantees control continues with the signaller task. This non-transfer is conceptually appealing because it is what most programmers naturally think of; thus, the signaller is obligated to establish the proper monitor state only when the monitor is unlocked as the monitor state at the time of the signal is irrelevant. Conversely, it is possible with multiple signalling for one of the signalled tasks to incorrectly alter the monitor state for the other signalled tasks. This kind of signal is used when the task fulfilling cooperation arrives *after* the task needing the cooperation, and hence, must be restarted (eventually) to use the cooperation.

The main differences between the two kinds of monitors are performance and coding problems. A major performance issue stems from the fact that signals are often the last operation of a mutex member. In this case, it is important for the signaller to exit the monitor immediately so it can continue concurrently outside the monitor with the signalled task inside the monitor, which is exactly the behaviour of the non-blocking monitor. However, it is impossible to simulate this behaviour with a blocking signal because the signaller blocks before the return can occur, which results in the unnecessary cost of blocking the signaller and the inhibited concurrency while the signaller needlessly waits for the signalled task to run. This situation is exacerbated by daisy-chain signalling because no task leaves the monitor until the last task in the chain is signalled and leaves the monitor. Hence, the blocking signal makes inefficient the most common monitor idiom, which is poor design. It might be possible to mitigate the problem of a blocking signal before a return by having the compiler optimize that signal into a non-blocking signal, but this changes the semantics of the monitor.

Two coding problems between non-blocking and blocking signal have already been illustrated in the previous monitor transformations. The transformations show how subtle issues in the signalling semantics can result in an infinite loop. The following are additional examples of coding problems between blocking and non-blocking kinds of monitors. In the blocking case, the signalled task cannot restart the signaller task from a condition on which it will eventually wait because the signaller is currently on the signaller queue. For example, the straightforward approach to communicating data to and from task A and B in a monitor:

Task A	Task B
msg = . . .	**wait** MsgAvail
signal MsgAvail	print msg
wait ReplyAvail	reply = . . .
print reply	**signal** ReplyAvail

fails for a blocking monitor because task B's signal of condition ReplyAvail is lost because task A has not yet blocked on condition ReplyAvail because it is on the acceptor/signalled stack. In the non-blocking case, the signaller blocks on the condition *before* the signalled task starts so the signalled task knows that it can restart its signaller if that is appropriate. The opposite problem occurred in the dating service solution:

Boy Task	Girl Task
boyPhoneNo = phoneNo	**wait** Girl
signal Girl	girlPhoneNo = phoneNo
print girlPhoneNo	print boyPhoneNo

where the straightforward solution fails for a non-blocking monitor because the Boy task does not wait for the Girl task to restart and copy her phone number into the communication variable. In the blocking case, the signaller blocks on the acceptor/signalled stack *before* accessing the communication variable that is set by the signalled task.

9.13.3 Quasi-blocking

Because the order of execution of the signaller and signalled tasks is unknown, cooperation among tasks can be difficult to establish. Therefore, this kind of monitor is not particularly useful, even though it appears implicitly in some situations such as an operating system kernel.

9.13.4 Extended Immediate Return

The immediate-return monitor was invented to optimize the signal-return case that occurs frequently in monitors at the cost of restricting the ability to write certain monitor algorithms. The extended immediate-return monitor allows any monitor to be written, with the restriction that a signal must appear before a wait or return. The restrictions on signal placement allow efficient implementation of a monitor. However, the restrictions also mandate a particular coding style, signals before waits and returns, which may unnecessarily complicate the coding of a monitor and obscure its algorithm.

9.13.5 Automatic Signal

Unfortunately, the general automatic-signal monitor becomes expensive when the number of tasks in the monitor is large. However, restricted automatic-signal monitors are competitive with explicit-signal monitors, especially when there are only a few condition variables, because they depend only on the number of conditional expressions and not the number of tasks in the monitor. Yet, the restricted automatic-signal monitor's conditional expressions cannot involve local variables or parameters of a request, e.g., a disk-scheduling algorithm where requests are serviced in track number rather than request arrival order. Hence, there is a class of important problems that cannot be handled by a restricted automatic-signal monitor.

Where the automatic-signal monitor excels is in prototyping a concurrent system. It is usually simpler to ignore cooperation during the initial stages of development and concentrate on the logical properties necessary for correctness. The conditional expressions of an automatic-signal monitor capture these logical properties. After the system is functioning, performance problems can be addressed by converting those monitors involved in bottlenecks into explicit-signal monitors, using appropriate cooperation.

9.14   Summary

Concurrency constructs are crucial to sound and efficient concurrency because the compiler is aware the program is concurrent. Furthermore, high-level concurrency constructs can substantially reduce the complexity of solving a concurrent problem, e.g., readers and writer. The first concurrency construct was the critical region for handling mutual exclusion, followed immediately by the conditional critical-region for handling both synchronization and mutual exclusion. While primitive, these constructs paved the way for the first successful (and object-oriented) concurrency construct, the monitor. A monitor combines concurrency capabilities, such as mutual exclusion and synchronization, along with software engineering capabilities, such as abstraction and encapsulation. Since its inception, several different kinds of monitors have been suggested and implemented in different programming languages. The fundamental difference among the kinds of monitors is directly related to the form of signalling used in synchronization, be it implicit or explicit. Priority monitors are demonstrably better than no-priority monitors for constructing complex cooperation among tasks. Both non-blocking and blocking signal are useful, but non-blocking is more powerful because it efficiently handles the common case of a signal as the last action of a mutex member. Without a clear understanding of the signalling differences among monitors, it is very easy to make errors using them.

9.15   Questions

1. Some programming language systems have only a P and V operation while others have only a monitor construct. Yet either system can be used to solve the same problems in essentially the same way. How do we know this is true?
2. Fig. 9.19, p. 470 shows a semaphore written using a monitor, with either external or internal scheduling. If the semaphore is extended with member P(s), which atomically Vs the argument semaphore, s, and then blocks the calling task if necessary (see page 370 for details), show it cannot be written with external scheduling.
3. Explain why the "wait *condition–variable*" of a monitor cannot be implemented with just a P(*condition–variable*) and V(*monitor–lock*) operation?
4. Consider the Hoare monitor in Fig. 9.25.

   - which task(s) is running?
   - which task(s) is ready to enter the monitor?
   - which task(s) is blocked?
   - which task(s) has executed a WAIT? On what condition variable?
   - If task e becomes blocked on the acceptor/signalled stack, does this imply that task d immediately enters the monitor? Explain.
   - Suppose tasks d and e complete. Which task next enters the monitor?

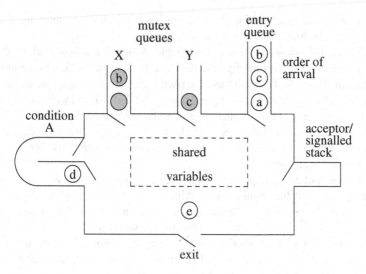

Fig. 9.25   Hoare monitor

5. Explain the difference between external and internal scheduling, and give two situations that preclude using external scheduling.

6. Explain why automatic-signal monitors are easier to use than explicit signal monitors but more expensive in terms of execution time.

7. Write a monitor (semaphores are not allowed) that implements the following kind of access to a resource. There are two kinds of tasks, B and G, which are trying to get access to a resource. To get access to the resource, each task must call the StartDating routine in the monitor, passing it an appropriate value for a B task and an appropriate value for a G task. When a task is finished with the resource, it must call EndDating to release the resource. The monitor must guarantee that a single B task and a single G task start sharing the resource together (but not necessarily at the exact same instant). No other pair of B-G tasks can start sharing the resource until the previous pair has finished. Either partner of the pair using the resource can leave at any time after they have started together. That is, if the B task leaves, do not start another B; wait for the partner G to leave and then start a new pair. You must guarantee that starvation of a particular B or G task does not occur assuming that an appropriate partner will always appear.

   To test the monitor, write two tasks, called Boy and Girl, that each start dating and then delay for a random number of times between 1–5 inclusive (use yield()). The body of these task's main member looks like:

```
StartDating();
// verify that the monitor is working correctly
// delay for a random period
// verify that the monitor is working correctly
EndDating();
```

The check may require using shared variables between the monitor and the Boy and Girl tasks. Start 30 of the Girl and Boy tasks.

Notice the following scenario is possible. A Boy task is signalled, it charges out of the monitor, flys through the resource and charges back into the monitor before the Girl task of the pair has even been signalled. Nevertheless, the monitor must fulfill its mandate of pairing and release the Girl task and wait for it to finish with the resource before another pair of tasks is released. So the Girl task may get to the resource and discover that she has been stood up for the date (sigh), even though the matching-making monitor arranged a date. This scenario is not the monitor's problem.

Before and after a process delays, see if you can devise some check that verifies that the monitor is working correctly (e.g., similar to the check performed in the routine CriticalSection). You are allowed to use a global variable(s) in this check since it is strictly for verifying the correctness of the monitor, and would be removed after testing. It is possible to do the testing without globals by passing the address of the test variables but since they will ultimately be removed, the global variables is the cleanest testing facility.

8. Write a simple "alarm clock" monitor that tasks use to put themselves to sleep until a certain time. The monitor measures time in arbitrary time units called "ticks". The alarm clock should be initialized to 0 ticks. Figure 9.26 shows the structure of the clock monitor and ticker task. Complete the four entry routines of the clock monitor. The monitor should be designed to be used in a situation where there is no limit on the number of sleeping tasks. The monitor can use any data structure appropriate to handle any number of sleeping tasks.

   In a real system, clock hardware might generate an interrupt that would be used to call tick(). In your program, start a task that calls tick() at regular intervals, similar to the one in Fig. 9.26.

   Use the Clock monitor in a program that creates tasks that sleep for varying amounts of time. The output of the program should show the tasks wake up at the right times.

9. A group of N (N > 1) philosophers plans to spend an evening together eating and thinking [10, p. 131]. Unfortunately, the host philosopher has only N forks and is serving a special spaghetti that requires 2 forks to eat. Luckily for the host, philosophers (like university students) are interested more in knowledge than food; after eating a few bites of spaghetti, a philosopher is apt to drop her forks and contemplate the oneness of the universe for a while, until her stomach begins to growl, when she again goes back to eating. So the table is set with N plates of spaghetti with one fork between adjacent plates. For example, the table would look like this for N=4:

```
_Monitor Clock {
  friend class ticker;
  void tick() {
    // Used only by a clock task to tell the monitor that a tick has elapsed.
  }
public:
  int ctime() {
    // This routine returns the current time in ticks.
  }
  void sleep_until( int t ) {
    // This routine causes the calling task to sleep until time t is
    // reached. If time t is already passed, the task does not sleep.
  }
  void sleep_for( int n ) {
    // This routine causes the calling task to sleep for n ticks.
    // If n < 0, the task does not sleep.
  }
};

_Task ticker {
  Clock &clock;

  void main() {
    for ( ;; ) {
      _Accept( ~ticker ) {
        break;
      } _Else {
        _Timeout( uDuration( 0, 1000 ) );
        clock.tick();
      } // _Accept
    } // for
  }
public:
  ticker( Clock &clock ) : clock(clock) {}
};
```

Fig. 9.26 Clock and ticker

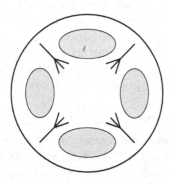

Consequently there is one fork on either side of a plate. Before eating, a philosopher must obtain the two forks on either side of the plate; hence, two adjacent philosophers cannot eat simultaneously. The host reasons that, when a philosopher's stomach begins to growl, she can simply wait until the two philosophers on either side begin thinking, then *simultaneously pick up the*

two forks on either side of her plate and begin eating. (Note, once a fork is *picked up*, it is temporarily owned by a philosopher and unavailable to any other philosopher.) If a philosopher cannot pick up both forks immediately, then she must wait until both are free. (Imagine what would happen if all the philosophers simultaneously picked up their right forks and then waited until their left forks were available.)

Implement a table to manage the forks as a:

a. class using only μC++ semaphores to provide mutual exclusion and synchronization. You are not allowed to use member lock1.P(lock2).

b. μC++ monitor using only internal scheduling.

c. μC++ monitor using only internal scheduling but simulates a Java monitor. In a Java monitor, there is only one condition variable and calling tasks can barge into the monitor ahead of signalled tasks. To simulate barging use the following routine in place of normal calls to a condition-variable wait:

```
void Table::wait() {
    noforks.wait();                          // wait until signalled
    while ( rand() % 5 == 0 ) {              // multiple bargers allowed
        _Accept( pickup, putdown ) {         // accept barging callers
        } _Else {                            // do not wait if no callers
        } // _Accept
    } // while
}

void Table::signalAll() {
    while ( ! noforks.empty() ) noforks.signal(); // drain the condition
}
```

This code randomly accepts calls to the interface routines, if a caller exists. Hint, to prevent barging, use tickets to control barging in pickup.

d. Explain why this problem cannot be solved with a μC++ monitor using only external scheduling.

Figure 9.27 shows the different forms for each μC++ table implementation (you may add only a public destructor and private members), where the preprocessor is used to conditionally compile a specific interface. This form of header file removes duplicate code by using the preprocessor to conditionally compile a specific interface. A preprocessor variable is defined on the compilation command to select a particular type of monitor implementation using the following syntax:

```
u++ -DTABLETYPE_INT -c TableINT.cc
```

Member routines pickup and putdown are called by each philosopher, passing the philosopher's identifier (value between 0 and $N - 1$), to pick up and put down both forks, respectively. Member routine pickup does not return until both forks can be picked up. To simultaneously pick up and put down both forks may require locking the entire table for short periods of time. No busy waiting is allowed; use cooperation among philosophers putting down forks and philosophers waiting to pick up forks. Your cooperation solution does *not* have to deal with starvation among philosophers waiting at the table; i.e.,

```
#if defined( TABLETYPE_SEM )        // semaphore solution
// includes for this kind of table
class Table {
    // private declarations for this kind of table
#elif defined( TABLETYPE_INT )       // internal scheduling monitor solution
// includes for this kind of table
_Monitor Table {
    // private declarations for this kind of table
#elif defined( TABLETYPE_INTB )     // internal scheduling monitor solution with barging
// includes for this kind of table
_Monitor Table {
    // private declarations for this kind of table
    uCondition noforks;             // only one condition variable
    void wait();                    // barging version of wait
    void signalAll();               // unblock all waiting tasks
#else
    #error unsupported table
#endif
    // common declarations
    public:                         // common interface
    Table( const unsigned int NoOfPhil, Printer &prt );
    void pickup( unsigned int id );
    void putdown( unsigned int id );
};
```

Fig. 9.27 Table interfaces

two or more philosophers may prevent another philosopher from getting an opportunity to eat. For example, with 3 philosophers, one philosopher might check its left than its right and another its right and left, and hence, alternate use of the forks, while the third philosopher is never checked. Guaranteeing global fairness of cooperation, in general, is complex. However, for each kind of table, you must prevent barging philosophers, and your mechanism to handle barging must prevented starvation among the barging and signalled philosophers (versus global starvation among all philosophers). That is, barging and signalled philosophers must eventually make progress assuming the cooperation scheme is fair. As result, any loops used to deal with barging must ensure one (or more) waiting philosopher makes progress; hence, there should never be a case where all waiting philosopher unblock and then reblock (which is busy waiting).

A philosopher eating at the table is simulated by a task, which has the following interface (you may add only a public destructor and private members):

```
_Task Philosopher {
public:
    enum States { Thinking = 'T', Hungry = 'H', Eating = 'E',
                  Waiting = 'W', Barging = 'B', Finished = 'F' };
    Philosopher( unsigned int id, unsigned int noodles, Table &table, Printer &prt );
};
```

Each philosopher loops performing the following actions:

- hungry message
- yield a random number of times, between 0 and 4 inclusive, to simulate the time to get hungry

- pickup forks
- pretend to eat a random number of noodles, between 1 and 5 inclusive
  if there are less noodles than the number chosen, the philosopher eats all remaining noodles
- eating message
- yield a random number of times, between 0 and 4 inclusive, to simulate the time to eat the noodles
- put down forks
- if eaten all the noodles, stop looping
- thinking message
- yield a random number of times, between 0 and 19 inclusive, to simulate the time to think

Yielding is accomplished by calling yield(times) to give up a task's CPU time-slice a number of times.

All output from the program is generated by calls to a printer, excluding error messages. The interface for the printer is (you may add only a public destructor and private members):

```
_Monitor / _Cormonitor Printer {        // choose one of the two kinds of type constructor
public:
    Printer( unsigned int NoOfPhil );
    void print( unsigned int id, Philosopher::States state );
    void print( unsigned int id, Philosopher::States state, unsigned int bite,
                unsigned int noodles );
};
```

A philosopher calls the print member when it enters states: thinking, hungry, eating, finished. The table calls the print member *before* it blocks a philosopher that must wait for its forks to become available. The printer attempts to reduce output by storing information for each philosopher until one of the stored elements is overwritten. When information is going to be overwritten, all the stored information is flushed and storing starts again. Output must look like that in Fig. 9.28.

Each column is assigned to a philosopher with an appropriate title, e.g., "Phil0", and a column entry indicates its current status:

State	Meaning
H	hungry
T	thinking
W *l,r*	waiting for the left fork *l* and the right fork *r* to become free
E *n,r*	eating *n* noodles, leaving *r* noodles on plate
B	barging into the monitor and having to wait for signalled tasks
F	finished eating all noodles

Identify the right fork of philosopher$_i$ with number i and the left fork with number $i + 1$. For example, W3,2 means forks 3 and/or 2 are unavailable, so philosopher 2 must wait, and E3,29 means philosopher 1 is eating 3 noodles, leaving 29 noodles on their plate to eat later. When a philosopher finishes, the

```
$ phil 5 20 56083
Phil0  Phil1  Phil2  Phil3  Phil4
****** ****** ****** ****** ******
H
E1,19 H
T      W2,1  H      H      H
       E4,16 W3,2   W4,3   E4,16
       T     E4,16         T
             T      E4,16
             H      T
H                   H
E2,17               E4,12  H
             E3,13  T      W0,4
T            T
             H             E3,13
             E1,12         T
       H     T
       E3,13
       T
       H     H      H
       E1,12        E5,7
H      T                   H
E4,13
T            E1,11  T      E5,8
       H     T             T
       E5,7                H
H      T            H      E2,6
E5,8         H      E1,6   T
T      H            T
H      E4,3  W3,2
E4,4   T     E2,9   H      H
             T      E1,5   W0,4
T                   T      E2,4
       H.                  T
       E3,0
...    F     ...    ...    ...
                    H
H                   E3,2
E1,3         H      T
T            E2,7   H
H            T      W4,3   H
E1,2                E2,0   W0,4
T
...    ...   ...    F      ...
                           E4,0
...    ...   ...    ...    F
H            H
E2,0
F      ...   ...    ...    ...
             E1,6
             T
             H
             E5,1
             T
             H
             E1,0
...    ...   F      ...    ...
************************
Philosophers terminated
```

Fig. 9.28 Output for internal-scheduling monitor, 5 philosophers, each with 20 noodles

state for that philosopher is marked with F and all other philosophers are marked with `` . . .".

Information is buffered until a column is overwritten for a particular entry, which causes the buffered data to be flushed. If there is no new stored information for a column since the last buffer flush, an empty column is printed. When a task finishes, the buffer is flushed immediately, the state for that object is marked with F, and all other objects are marked with "...". After a task has finished, no further output appears in that column. All output spacing can be accomplished using the standard 8-space tabbing. Buffer any information necessary for printing in internal representation; **do not build and store strings of text for output.**

In addition, you are to devise and include a way to test your program for erroneous behaviour. This testing should be similar to the check performed in the routine CriticalSection, from software solutions for mutual exclusion, in that it should, with high probability, detect errors. Use an assert or tests that call μC++'s uAbort routine to halt the program with an appropriate message. (HINT: once a philosopher has a pair of forks, what must be true about the philosophers on either side?)

The executable program is named phil and has the following shell interface:

phil [P [N [S]]]

P is the number of philosophers and must be greater than 1; if P is not present, assume a value of 5. N is the number of noodles per plate and must be greater than 0; if N is not present, assume a value of 30. S is the seed for the random-number generator and must be greater than 0. If the seed is unspecified, use a random value like the process identifier (getpid) or current time (time), so each run of the program generates different output. Check all command arguments for correct form (integers) and range; print an appropriate usage message and terminate the program if a value is missing or invalid. The driver must handle an arbitrary number of philosophers and noodles, but only tests with values less than 100 for the two parameters will be made, so the output columns line up correctly.

Use the following monitor to safely generate random values:

```
_Monitor MPRNG {
  public:
    MPRNG( unsigned int seed = 1009 ) { srand( seed ); }  // set seed
    void seed( unsigned int seed ) { srand( seed ); }      // set seed
    unsigned int operator()() { return rand(); }           // [0,UINT_MAX]
    unsigned int operator()( unsigned int u ) { return operator()()%(u+1); } // [0,u]
    unsigned int operator()( unsigned int l, unsigned int u ) {
                      return operator()( u - l ) + l; } // [l,u]
};
```

Note, because of the non-deterministic execution of concurrent programs, multiple runs with a common seed may not generate the same output. Nevertheless, shorts runs are often the same so the seed can be useful for testing. Check all command arguments for correct form (integers) and range; print an appropriate usage message and terminate the program if a value is missing or invalid.

(WARNING: in GNU C, -1 % 5 != 4, and on UNIX, the name fork is reserved.)

10. The sleeping barber is a problem proposed by E. W. Dijkstra. A barber shop has a cutting room with one chair and a waiting room with N chairs. The waiting room has an entrance, and next to the entrance is the cutting room with the barber's chair; the entrances to the waiting and cutting room share the same sliding door, which always closes one of them. The sliding door ensures that when the barber opens the door to see if anyone is waiting, a new customer cannot simultaneously enter the room and not be seen.

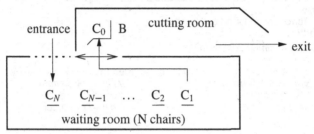

When the barber arrives or finishes a haircut, he opens the door to the waiting room and checks for waiting customers. If the waiting room is not empty, he invites the next customer (first-in first-out (FIFO) service order) for a haircut, otherwise he goes to sleep in the barber's chair.

   Customers enter the waiting room one at a time if space is available; otherwise, they go to another shop (called balking). If a customer finds the waiting room is not empty, they wait their turn in the waiting room; if the waiting room is empty, the customer opens the door to the cutting room to see if the barber is there but sleeping. If the barber is not there, the customer closes the door and sits down in the waiting room to wait for the barber to appear; otherwise, the customer leaves the cutting-room door open, wakes the barber, and sits down in the waiting room waiting for the barber to wakeup and get ready.

   Implement the barber shop as a:

   a. class using μC++ semaphores to provide mutual exclusion and synchronization.

   b. μC++ monitor using internal scheduling.

   c. μC++ monitor that simulates a general automatic (implicit) signal monitor.

   The implementations may not use busy waiting. The μC++ semaphore, external and internal scheduling implementations must service waiting customers in FIFO order. The μC++ automatic-signal monitor does not have to service waiting customers in FIFO order. The interface for the barber shop is (you may add only a public destructor and private members):

```
#if defined( IMPLTYPE_SEM )                    // semaphore solution
// includes for this kind of barber shop
class BarberShop {
    // private declarations for this kind of barber shop
#elif defined( IMPLTYPE_INT )                  // internal scheduling monitor solution
// includes for this kind of barber shop
_Monitor BarberShop {
    // private declarations for this kind of barber shop
#elif defined( IMPLTYPE_AUTO )                 // automatic-signal monitor solution
// includes for this kind of barber shop
_Monitor BarberShop {
    // private declarations for this kind of barber shop
#else
    #error unsupported barber shop
#endif
    // all common declarations
  public:
    BarberShop( Printer &prt, const unsigned int MaxWaitingCust );
    void hairCut( int id );                    // called by customer
    int startCut();                            // called by barber
    void endCut();                             // called by barber
};
```

where the preprocessor is used to conditionally compile a specific interface. You
can define the appropriate preprocessor variable on the compilation command
using the following syntax:

```
u++ -DIMPLTYPE_INT -c BarberShopINT.cc
```

A customer calls the hairCut member to enter the barber shop. The barber calls
the startCut member to obtain the next customer; if there are no customers,
the barber goes to sleep (blocks). startCut returns the customer identifier for
a waiting customer. The barber calls endCut after completing the haircut. The
automatic-signal implementation should be slightly different from the explicit
signal because there is no (or little) cooperation.

μC++ does not provide an automatic-signal monitor so it must be simulated
using the explicit-signal mechanisms. For the simulation, create an include file,
called AutomaticSignal.h, which defines the following preprocessor macros:

```
#define AUTOMATIC_SIGNAL ...
#define WAITUNTIL( pred, before, after ) ...
#define RETURN( expr... ) ...  // gcc variable number of parameters
```

These macros must provide a *general* simulation of automatic-signalling, i.e.,
the simulation cannot be specific to this question. Macro AUTOMATIC_SIGNAL
is placed only once in an automatic-signal monitor as a private member,
and contains any private variables needed to implement the automatic-signal
monitor. Macro WAITUNTIL is used to wait until the pred evaluates to true. If a
task must block waiting, the expression before is executed before the wait and
the expression after is executed after the wait. Macro RETURN is used to return
from a public routine of an automatic-signal monitor, where expr is optionally
used for returning a value. Figure 9.29 shows a bounded buffer implemented as
an automatic-signal monitor.

```
Monitor BoundedBuffer {
    AUTOMATIC_SIGNAL;
    int front, back, count;
    int Elements[20];
public:
    BoundedBuffer() : front(0), back(0), count(0) {}
    _Nomutex int query() { return count; }

    void insert( int elem ) {
        WAITUNTIL( count < 20, , );      // empty before/after
        Elements[back] = elem;
        back = ( back + 1 ) % 20;
        count += 1;
        RETURN();
    }

    int remove() {
        WAITUNTIL( count > 0, , );       // empty before/after
        int elem = Elements[front];
        front = ( front + 1 ) % 20;
        count -= 1;
        RETURN( elem );
    }
};
```

Fig. 9.29 Automatic signal monitor

Make absolutely sure to *always* have a RETURN() macro at the end of each mutex member. As well, the macros must be self-contained, i.e., no direct manipulation of variables created in AUTOMATIC_SIGNAL is allowed from within the monitor.

The interface for the barber is (you may add only a public destructor and private members):

```
_Task Barber {
    void main();
public:
    Barber( Printer &prt, BarberShop &bs, unsigned int cutDelay );
};
```

The barber begins by randomly (use rand) yielding between [0-cutDelay) times so it may not arrive before the first customers start entering the barber shop. (Yielding is performed by calling task member yield(N).) The barber repeats the following steps: call startCut in the barber shop to get customer, randomly yield between [0-cutDelay) times to simulate the haircut, call endCut in the barber shop to indicate ending of haircut. The barber terminates when he receives a customer identifier of −1 from startCut.

The interface for a customer is (you may add only a public destructor and private members):

```
_Task Customer {
    void main();
public:
    Customer( Printer &prt, BarberShop &bs, unsigned int id, unsigned int custDelay );
};
```

A customer begins by randomly yielding between [0-custDelay) times so the customers arrive at the barber shop at random times. A customer makes a single call to hairCut in the barber shop to get a haircut. A customer does not restart until the barber has completed their haircut, i.e., only restarts after the barber calls endCut for the customer.

All output from the program is generated by calls to a printer, excluding error messages. The interface for the printer is (you may add only a public destructor and private members):

```
_Monitor / _Cormonitor Printer {
    void main();
public:
    Printer( const unsigned int MaxWaitingCust );
    void barber( char status );              // called by barber
    void customer( int id );                 // called by customer
};
```

Figure 9.30 shows two example outputs from different runs of the program. The output consists of four columns:

a. barber states

   A   arrival at the barber shop (after initial yields)

   G   attempting to get a customer from the waiting room

   S   going to sleep in the barber chair waiting for a customer

   C   cutting a customer's hair

   F   leaving the barber shop

   The printer reduces output by condensing *consecutive* barber state-changes along a single line.

b. customer having haircut

c. customer balked because waiting room is full

d. list of customers in the waiting room

All printing must occur in the coroutine main, i.e., no printing can occur in the coroutine's member routines. All output spacing can be accomplished using the standard 8-space tabbing, so it is unnecessary to build and store strings of text for output. Calls to perform printing may be performed in the barber-shop members or in the barber/customer tasks (you decide where to print).

The shell interface to the sleepingbarber program is as follows:

sleepingbarber [MaxWaitingCust [NoOfCusts [CutDelay [CustDelay [RandomSeed]]]]]

(Square brackets indicate optional command line parameters, and do not appear on the actual command line.) Where the meaning of each parameter is:

MaxWaitingCust: maximum number of customers that can wait in the barber shop waiting room, i.e., MaxWaitingCust equals N chairs. The default value if unspecified is 5.

NoOfCusts: number of customers attempting to obtain a haircut during a run of the program. The default value if unspecified is 20.

CutDelay: number of times the barber yields to simulate the time required to cut a customer's hair. The default value if unspecified is 2.

% sleepingbarber 3 20 5 100

Barber	Cutting	Balked	Waiting
AGS			
			3
C	3		
			0
GC	0		
			7
			7 17
			7 17 14
G			
		2	
C	7		
			17 14
			17 14 13
GC	17		14 13
			14 13 8
		10	
		15	
GC	14		13 8
GC	13		8
			8 6
			8 6 9
GC	8		6 9
			6 9 16
GC	6		9 16
			9 16 18
		11	
GC	9		16 18
GC	16		18
			18 5
GC	18		5
GC	5		
			4
			4 12
			4 12 19
GC	4		12 19
GC	12		19
			19 1
GC	19		1
GC	1		
GS			
			-1
C	-1		
F			

% sleepingbarber 3 20 5 100

Barber	Cutting	Balked	Waiting
			6
			6 12
AGC	6		12
GC	12		
			7
			7 15
			7 15 10
GC	7		15 10
			15 10 1
GC	15		10 1
GC	10		1
			1 19
G			
			1 19 14
C	1		19 14
			19 14 4
GC	19		14 4
			14 4 8
GC	14		4 8
GC	4		8
			8 5
			8 5 13
		17	
		3	
G			
		16	
		2	
C	8		5 13
			5 13 0
GC	5		13 0
GC	13		0
GC	0		
GS			
			18
C	18		
			11
GC	11		
			9
GC	9		
GS			
			-1
C	-1		
F			

Fig. 9.30 Sleeping barber: example output

CustDelay: number of times a customer yields *before* attempting entry to the barber shop. The default value if unspecified is 40.

RandomSeed: initial seed value for the random number generator set using routine srand. When given a specific seed value, the program must generate the same results for each invocation. You must also make the following call uThisProcessor().setPreemption(0) to turn off preemptive timeslicing. If the seed is unspecified, use a random value like the process identifier (getpid) or current time (time), so each run of the program generates different output.

Assume all arguments are valid positive integer values, i.e., no error checking is required.

uMain::main creates the printer, barber shop, barber and NoOfCusts customer tasks. After all the customer tasks have terminated, uMain::main calls hairCut with a customer identifier of −1.

11. A small optical disk drive can be modelled by the following monitor.

```
_Monitor DiskDrive {
    const char *data;
    int currentTrack;
    int tracksMoved;
  public:
    static const int NoOfTracks = 100, TrackSize = 20;
    DiskDrive() : data( "abcdefghijklmnopqrs" ) {
        currentTrack = 0;
        tracksMoved = 0;
    }
    void Seek( int track ) {
        int distance = abs( currentTrack - track );
        uBaseTask::yield( distance );
        tracksMoved += distance;
        currentTrack = track;
    }
    void Read( char *buffer ) {
        strcpy( buffer, data );
    }
    int Distance() {
        return tracksMoved;
    }
};
```

This disk drive is read-only and has one hundred tracks, numbered 0 through 99, each of which stores only twenty characters (which, in this simulation, are always the same 20 characters). For your convenience, the last character on each track has the ' \0 ' character.

The user interface consists of three members. Seek moves the read-head to a specified track and records the distance moved. Read copies the current track into a buffer. Distance returns the total distance that the head has traveled since the disk drive has been created.

Disk *access time* is the sum of the time to move the disk head to the requested track, the time for the disk to rotate to the desired sector on the track, and the time to transfer data to/from the sector. These times are named the *seek time*, *rotation delay* and *data transfer*, respectively. Because the time to move the head is proportional to the distance between tracks, and the rotation and transfer time combined is often less than the time to move the head just one track, the best way to reduce the average disk access time is to shorten the seek time by minimizing the head movement.

Write a monitor to **efficiently** schedule disk seek-time using the shortest seek time first (SSTF) algorithm. The SSTF algorithm picks, from all pending requests, the sequence of requests that are closest to the current head position in either direction. If the closest two requests in either direction are equal distance from the current position, the scheduler must pick the lower numbered track.

The user interface for the disk scheduler is:

```
_Monitor DiskScheduler {
  public:
    DiskScheduler( DiskDrive &disk );
    _Nomutex void ScheduleTrack( int track );
    void Done();
};
```

The disk parameter to the constructor is used to seek to the appropriate track before returning from ScheduleTrack. ScheduleTrack is *not* a mutex member so that the disk seek can be performed without locking the scheduler; otherwise, new requests cannot be scheduled while the seek is occurring.

To read a track, a client executes the following protocol:

```
scheduler.ScheduleTrack( track );
disk.Read( buf );
scheduler.Done();
```

Note, the ScheduleTrack entry must block the invoking task until it is that task's turn to read. The Done entry is invoked to inform the disk scheduler that the read operation completed and the disk drive is now free.

Your main program creates the scheduler, reads in a series of track numbers from cin, and for each track number, start a disk client task. The series of track numbers are terminated by end of file and are error free (i.e., assume all values are numeric and in the specified range). Each client initially yields a random number of times from 0 to M, inclusive, and then reads its track so that all clients do not attempt to read the disk simultaneously.

The output from the program should show clearly the order in which tracks are requested, the order in which clients are serviced, and how these events are interleaved. Also, when all the requests have been serviced, the program should print the average distance the disk head has moved per request (i.e., the total distance moved divided by the number of requests). **NOTE:** the routine names read and write are used by the UNIX operating system and **cannot** be used as routine names in the program.

The shell interface to the diskscheduler program is as follows:

```
diskscheduler [ M ]
```

(Square brackets indicate optional command line parameters.) if M is missing, assume 0. Assume the value M is a valid integer value, i.e., no error checking is required.

12. There are a number of locks that provide both synchronization and mutual exclusion. For example, a sequence/event-counter mechanism is based on two objects: a **sequencer** and an **event counter**. The metaphor for this mechanism is the ticket machine used to control the order of service at a store. A sequencer,

S, corresponds to the numbered tags that are obtained from a ticket dispenser by arriving customers. An event counter, E, corresponds to the sign labeled "now serving", which is controlled by the servers. (As with all metaphors, its purpose is to understand a mechanism not to appear in the solution.)

The interface for the sequencer is (you may add only a public destructor and private members):

```
#if defined( IMPLTYPE_SEM )                    // semaphore solution
// includes for this kind of buffer
class Sequencer {
    // private declarations for this kind of buffer
#elif defined( IMPLTYPE_INT )                  // internal scheduling monitor solution
// includes for this kind of buffer
_Monitor Sequencer {
    // private declarations for this kind of buffer
#elif defined( IMPLTYPE_AUTO )                 // automatic-signal monitor solution
// includes for this kind of buffer
_Monitor Sequencer {
    // private declarations for this kind of buffer
#else
    #error unsupported sequencer type
#endif
    // all common declarations
  public:
    Sequencer();
    unsigned int ticket();
    _Nomutex unsigned int check();
};
```

The value of a sequencer is, in effect, the value of the last numbered ticket to be taken. The first ticket is numbered 1, so the initial value of a sequencer is 0. The mutex member, ticket, atomically advances the sequencer by one and returns the sequencer's value. Hence, a sequencer yields a non-negative, increasing, contiguous sequence of integers. A ticket operation corresponds to a newly arriving customer taking a unique numbered tag. The non-mutex member, check, returns the last ticket value taken.

The interface for the event counter is (you may add only a public destructor and private members):

```
#if defined( IMPLTYPE_SEM )                    // semaphore solution
// includes for this kind of buffer
class EventCounter {
    // private declarations for this kind of buffer
#elif defined( IMPLTYPE_INT )                  // internal scheduling monitor solution
// includes for this kind of buffer
_Monitor EventCounter {
    // private declarations for this kind of buffer
#elif defined( IMPLTYPE_AUTO )                 // automatic-signal monitor solution
// includes for this kind of buffer
_Monitor EventCounter {
    // private declarations for this kind of buffer
#else
    #error unsupported event-counter type
#endif
  public:
    EventCounter( unsigned int event = 0 );
    void await( unsigned int ticket );
    void advance();
    _Nomutex unsigned int check();
};
```

The event counter, in effect, holds the highest ticket number of any customer being served. The constructor parameter event specifies the initial number of events that can be handled before blocking, with the default being 0. For example, if a store has 3 sales people, the event counter is initialized to 3 so that the first 3 customers, all having tickets less than or equal to the counter, do not block. The await member corresponds to a customer beginning to wait for service. A lock is simulated through the following usage of a Sequencer and an Event Counter:

```
E.await( S.ticket() );
```

which causes a task (customer) to take a ticket and wait until E reaches the ticket value. That is, an E.await(v) suspends the calling task if the value in E < v; otherwise, the task proceeds. The advance member, executed by a server, corresponds to starting service with a new customer. The event counter is incremented and the next task (customer) is admitted for service. (This corresponds to incrementing the "now serving" sign and calling out the new number.) Hence, an E.advance() operation reawakens a task waiting for the event counter to reach its ticket value. Multiple tasks are reawakened when multiple servers simultaneously become free. The member check returns the highest ticket being served.

Tickets may not be serviced in order because they may not be presented in order due to the non-atomic steps of taking a ticket and waiting. When a lower numbered ticket eventually appears, it is always serviced *before* any higher numbered tickets that are waiting. In essence, if you miss seeing your ticket number appear on the serving sign, your ticket is still valid and can be presented for service at any time. The non-mutex check member, returns the current event value for the event counter. For example, assume an event counter starts at 3 representing 3 servers. The first 3 customers arrive and take tickets 1–3. Customer 3 presents its ticket first and is allowed to proceed. Customer 4 arrives and takes ticket 4. Customer 3 completes, and advances the service counter to 4. Now any customer with ticket $\leq$ 4 can obtain service but there are at most 3 of them. Customer 5 arrives, takes ticket 5 and presents its ticket for service but must block because the service counter is only 4. Customers 1 and 4 present their tickets and are allowed to proceed. Customer 6 arrives, takes ticket 6 and presents its ticket for service but must block because the service counter is only 4. Customer 1 completes, and advances the service counter to 5. Now any customer with ticket $\leq$ 5 can obtain service but there are at most 3 of them. And so on. Hence, there are never more than 3 customers with the potential to obtain service at any time, which is crucial because there are only 3 servers able to process requests. There is a small inhibiting of concurrency because a server is prevented from servicing a large waiting ticket-value until all the lower ones are presented. This issue is part of this design for an event counter; in general, the delay is usually extremely short because the ticket is taken and immediately presented for service. Note, all of these actions rely on the programmer using the sequencer and event counter correctly. All the customers *must* perform the necessary cooperation in the correct order or the process fails.

Implement the Sequencer and EventCounter as a:

a. class using μC++ semaphores to provide mutual exclusion and synchronization, tion,
b. μC++ monitor using internal scheduling,
c. μC++ monitor that simulates a general automatic-signal monitor. For this solution, it is not required to service a lower numbered ticket *before* any higher numbered tickets that are waiting.

The kind of implementation is specified by a preprocessor variable on the compilation command using the following syntax:

u++ -DIMPLTYPE_INT -c EventCounter.cc

μC++ does not provide an automatic-signal monitor so it must be simulated using the explicit-signal mechanisms. For the simulation, create an include file, called AutomaticSignal.h, which defines the following preprocessor macros:

```
#define AUTOMATIC_SIGNAL ...
#define WAITUNTIL( pred, before, after ) ...
#define RETURN( expr, .. ) ...  // gcc variable number of parameters
```

These macros must provide a *general* simulation of automatic-signalling, i.e., the simulation cannot be specific to this question. Macro AUTOMATIC_SIGNAL is placed only once in an automatic-signal monitor as a private member, and contains any private variables needed to implement the automatic-signal monitor. Macro WAITUNTIL is used to wait until the pred evaluates to true. If a task must block waiting, the expression before is executed before the wait and the expression after is executed after the wait. Macro RETURN is used to return from a public routine of an automatic-signal monitor, where expr is optionally used for returning a value. Figure 9.29, p. 505 shows a bounded buffer implemented as an automatic-signal monitor.

Make absolutely sure to *always* have a RETURN() macro at the end of each mutex member. As well, the macros must be self-contained, i.e., no direct manipulation of variables created in AUTOMATIC_SIGNAL is allowed from within the monitor.

Use only the sequence/event-counter mechanism to construct a generalized FIFO bounded-buffer for a producer/consumer problem with the following interface:

```
template<typename T> class BoundedBuffer {
  public:
    BoundedBuffer( Printer<T> &prt, const int size = 10 );
    void insert( const int Id, T elem );
    T remove( const int Id );
};
```

which creates a bounded buffer of size BufferSize, and supports multiple producers and consumers. The insert and remove members are passed the Id of the calling producer/consumer, respectively. You must devise a way to use the sequencer/event-counter to implement the necessary synchronization and mutual exclusion needed by the bounded buffer.

Test the bounded buffer and its use of the sequencer/event-counter with a number of producers and consumers. The interface for a producer is (you may add only a public destructor and private members):

```
_Task Producer {
    void main();
  public:
    Producer( Printer<T> &prt, BoundedBuffer<T> &buffer,
              const int Id, const int Produce, const int Delay );
};
```

The producer generates Produce random integers from [32,100] inclusive and inserts them into buffer. (Assume the buffer-element type, T, can accept a value from 32–100 inclusive.) Immediately after starting and before producing an item, a producer randomly yields between 0 and Delay-1 times.

The interface for a consumer is (you may add only a public destructor and private members):

```
_Task Consumer {
    void main();
  public:
    Consumer( Printer<T> &prt, BoundedBuffer<T> &buffer,
              const int Id, const int Delay, const T Sentinel );
};
```

The consumer removes items from buffer, and terminates when it removes a Sentinel value from the buffer. Immediately after starting and before removing an item, a consumer randomly yields between 0 and Delay-1 times.

All output from the program is generated by calls to a printer, excluding error messages. The interface for the printer is (you may add only a public destructor and private members):

```
template<typename T> _Monitor / _Cormonitor Printer {// choose monitor or cormonitor
    void main();
  public:
    Printer( const unsigned int NoOfProd, const unsigned int NoOfCons );
    void change( const unsigned int Id, const char state );
    void change( const unsigned int Id, const char state, const unsigned int ticket );
    void changeval( const unsigned int Id, const char state, const T value );
};
```

The printer generates output like that in Fig. 9.31. Each column is assigned to a consumer (C) or producer (P), and a column entry indicates its current status:

State	Meaning	Additional Information
S	starting (C/P)	
F	finished (C/P)	
G	getting value (C)	
I	inserting (P)	value
R	removing (C)	value
Y	before acquiring synchronization (C/P)	ticket
M	before acquiring mutual exclusion (C/P)	ticket

Information is buffered until a column is overwritten for a particular entry, which causes the buffered data to be flushed. The asterisk * marks the information to be overwritten that caused the buffered data to be flushed. If there is no new stored information for a consumer/producer since the last buffer flush, an empty column is printed. Note, a * is *not* printed again for state transitions causing flushing for the same task causing an initial flush. In general, the * on line i appears above the value on line $i + 1$ that caused the buffer to be flushed. There is one special case for the "F x" state of the final voter to receive a result. That state transition must appear on a separate line with "..." appearing in all the other voter columns to indicate that a subgroup has completed voting. All output spacing can be accomplished using the standard 8-space tabbing, so it is unnecessary to build and store strings of text for output. Calls to perform printing may be performed in the buffer or in the consumer/producer tasks (you decide where to print).

uMain::main creates the printer, bounded buffer, the producer and consumer tasks. After all the producer tasks have terminated, uMain::main inserts an appropriate number of sentinel values into the buffer to terminate the consumers.

The shell interface for the eventcounter program is:

eventcounter [Cons [Prods [Produce [BufferSize [Delays]]]]]

(Square brackets indicate optional command line parameters, and do not appear on the actual command line.) Where the meaning of each parameter is:

Cons: number of consumers to create. The default value if unspecified is 5.

Prods: positive number of producers to create. The default value if unspecified is 3.

Produce: positive number of items generated by each producer. The default value if unspecified is 10.

BufferSize: positive number of elements in (size of) the bounder buffer. The default value if unspecified is 10.

Delays: positive number of times a producer/consumer yields *before* inserting/removing an item into/from the buffer. The default value if unspecified is Cons + Prods.

Check all command arguments for correct form (integers) and range; print an appropriate usage message and terminate the program if a value is missing or invalid.

13. The Santa Claus problem [18] is an interesting locking problem. Santa Claus sleeps in his shop at the North Pole until he is woken. In order to wake him, one of two conditions must occur:

    a. All five of the reindeer used to deliver toys have returned from their year-long holiday.

    b. Three of the E elves have a problem that need Santa's help to solve. (One elf's problem is not serious enough to require Santa's attention; otherwise, he would never get any sleep.)

```
% eventcounter 3 2 2 2 1                              Y:8
Cons:0 Cons:1 Prod:0 Prod:1              M:6*  M:8
****** ****** ****** ******              R:89
S                                        G
G                                        Y:8         I:75*
Y:1   S*                                             Y:9
      G                                  M:7*        M:9
      Y:2   S*                           R:85
            I:14                         G
            Y:1                          Y:9
            M:1                          ...   ...   F     ...
            I:73                         M:8*
            Y:2                          R:52
            M:2   S*                     G
                  I:23                   Y:10        I:95*
                  Y:3                                Y:10
M:1*              M:3                     M:9*        M:10
R:14                                     R:75
G                                        G
Y:3         I:96*                        Y:11        I:40*
            Y:4                                      Y:11
      M:2*  M:4                           M:10*      M:11
      R:73                               R:95
      G                                  G
      Y:4         I:59*                   Y:12
                  Y:5                     ...   ...   ...   F
M:3*              M:5                     M:11*
R:23                                     R:40
G                                        G
Y:5         I:89*                        Y:13        I:-1*
            Y:6                                      Y:12
      M:4*  M:6                                      M:12
      R:96                                           I:-1
      G                                              Y:13
      Y:6         I:85*                   M:12* M:13
                  Y:7                     R:-1
M:5*              M:7                     ...   F     ...   ...
R:59                                     M:13*
G                                        R:-1
Y:7         I:52*                         F     ...   ...   ...
                                         ***********************
```

Fig. 9.31 Event counter: example output

If Santa is woken by all five reindeer, it must be Christmas, so he hitches them to the sleigh, delivers toys to all the girls and boys, and then unhitches them once they have returned. The reindeer go back on vacation until next year, while Santa goes back to sleep. If Santa is woken by three elves needing to consult him, he ushers them into his office where they consult on toy research and development, and then he ushers them out. The elves go back to work, and Santa goes back to sleep. Once Santa is awake, if he discovers that both conditions are true, priority is given to the reindeer since any problems the elves have can wait until after Christmas. Note that if Santa is consulting with one group of elves, any other elves that arrive desiring to consult must wait until Santa is ready to consult with the next group.

To prevent the reindeer from perpetually preventing the elves from getting Santa's help, there is a bound of N on the number of times the reindeer can be served before a group of elves is served when there are 3 elves waiting.

All synchronization is performed by the monitor Workshop. The interface for Workshop is (you may add only a public destructor and private members):

```
_Monitor Workshop {
    // private members go here
public:
    enum Status { Consulting, Delivery, Done };
                // printer,      bound,        elves,      reindeer delivery
    Workshop( Printer &prt, unsigned int N, unsigned int E, unsigned int D );
    Status sleep();              // santa calls to nap; when Santa wakes status of next action
    void deliver( unsigned int id );          // reindeer call to deliver toys
    bool consult( unsigned int id );          // elves call to consult Santa,
                // true => consultation successful, false => consultation failed
    void doneConsulting( unsigned int id );   // block Santa/elves until meeting over
    void doneDelivering( unsigned int id );   // block Santa/reindeer until toys are delivered
    void termination( unsigned int id );      // elves call to indicate termination, optional
};
```

The interface for Santa is (you may add only a public destructor and private members):

```
_Task Santa {
    // private members go here
public:
    Santa( Workshop &wrk, Printer &prt );
};
```

Santa executes until sleep returns status Done indicating the elves and reindeer are finished. The task main of the Santa task looks like:

• yield a random number of times between 0 and 10 inclusive so all tasks do not start simultaneously
• start message
• loop
  – yield a random number of times between 0 and 3 inclusive so that messages are not consecutive
  – napping message
  – block in workshop if nothing to do
  – awake message
  – if done consulting/deliveries, stop looping
  – if delivering toys, yield between 0 and 5 times inclusive to simulate delivery time, indicate delivery done, and then deliver-done message
  – if consulting, yield between 0 and 3 times inclusive to simulate consultation time, indicate consultation done, and then consultation-done message
• finished message

Yielding is accomplished by calling yield(times) to give up a task's CPU time-slice a number of times.

The interface for Elf is (you may add only a public destructor and private members):

```
_Task Elf {
    // private members go here
  public:
    enum { CONSULTING_GROUP_SIZE = 3 }; // number of elves consulting with Santa
    Elf( unsigned int id, Workshop &wrk, Printer &prt, unsigned int numConsultations );
};
```

Note, numConsultations is either C or 3. The task main of the Elf task looks like:

- yield a random number of times between 0 and 10 inclusive so all tasks do not start simultaneously
- start message
- loop until done number of consultations
  - yield a random number of times between 0 and 3 inclusive so that messages are not consecutive
  - working message
  - yield a random number of times between 0 and 5 times inclusive to simulate time working
  - help message
  - wait for consultation
  - if consultation failed, consulting-failed message, stop looping
  - consulting-succeeded message
  - yield a random number of times between 0 and 3 times inclusive to simulate consultation time
  - indicate consultation done
  - consultation-done message
- indicate termination
- finished message

A consultation with Santa can fail because the number of elves may not be a multiple of the group size (3). So when elves finish, there comes a point when there are not enough elves to form a group and a consultation cannot occur. Interestingly, this problem can occur even when the number of elves is a multiple of the group size. For example, if there are 6 elves, numbered 1..6, and each does 2 consultations, there are 4 consultations. However, if elf 6 is delayed, i.e., does not participate in the initial consultations, then one possible failure scenario is:

	consultations		
	1	2	3
elves	3*	4	5
	1*	2*	4*
	5	6	

Elves 1, 2, 3 and 4 perform their 2 consultations and terminate, leaving elf 5, who has done 1 consultation and elf 6 who has done 0 consultations; since there are only two elves remaining, the final consultation cannot occur.

The interface for Reindeer is (you may add only a public destructor and private members):

```
_Task Reindeer {
    // private members go here
  public:
    enum { MAX_NUM_REINDEER = 5 };   // number of reindeer for delivering toys
    Reindeer( unsigned int id, Workshop &wrk, Printer &prt, unsigned int numDeliveries );
};
```

Note, numDeliveries is either D or 3. The task main of the Reindeer task looks like:

- yield a random number of times between 0 and 10 inclusive so all tasks do not start simultaneously
- start message
- loop until done number of deliveries
  - yield a random number of times between 0 and 3 inclusive so that messages are not consecutive
  - vacation message
  - yield a random number of times between 0 and 5 inclusive to simulate vacation time
  - checking-in message
  - wait for delivery
  - delivering-toys message
  - yield a random number of times between 0 and 5 inclusive to simulate toy-delivery time
  - indicate delivery done
  - delivery-done message
- finished message

All output from the program is generated by calls to a printer, excluding error messages. The interface for the printer is (you may add only a public destructor and private members):

```
_Monitor / _Cormonitor Printer {                     // choose monitor or cormonitor
  public:
    enum States {
        Starting = 'S', Blocked = 'B', Unblocked = 'U', Finished = 'F', // general
        Napping = 'N', Awake = 'A',                    // Santa
        Working = 'W', NeedHelp = 'H',                 // elf
        OnVacation = 'V', CheckingIn = 'I',            // reindeer
        DeliveringToys = 'D', DoneDelivering = 'd',    // Santa, reindeer
        Consulting = 'C', DoneConsulting = 'c',        // Santa, elf
        ConsultingFailed = 'X',                        // elf
    };
    Printer( const unsigned int MAX_NUM_ELVES );
    void print( unsigned int id, States state );
    void print( unsigned int id, States state, unsigned int numBlocked );
};
```

The printer attempts to reduce output by storing information for each task until one of the stored elements is overwritten. When information is going to be overwritten, all the stored information is flushed and storing starts again. Output

State	Meaning
S	Santa/Elf/Reindeer is starting
N	Santa is about to try and nap
A	Santa is awake from his nap
W	Elf is working
H	Elf needs to consult with Santa
V	Reindeer is on vacation
I	Reindeer is back from vacation and checking in
D	Santa/Reindeer is delivering toys
d	Santa/Reindeer is done delivering toys
C	Santa/Elf is consulting
X	Elf failed to consult
c	Santa/Elf is done consulting
B	Santa blocks going to sleep[a]
B n	Elves blocked (including self) for consultation
B n	Reindeers blocked (including self) for Christmas
B n	Elves + Santa blocked at end of consultation
B n	Reindeer + Santa blocked at end of delivery
U [n]	Santa/Elf/Reindeer unblock, n value see B
F	Santa/Elf/Reindeer is finished

[a]Santa does not specify n when blocking/unblocking in sleep because no choice has been made between working with the elves or reindeer.

Fig. 9.32 Task states

should look similar to that in Fig. 9.33. Each column is assigned to a task with an appropriate title, e.g., "E1", and a column entry indicates its current state (see Fig. 9.32): Information is buffered until a column is overwritten for a particular entry, which causes the buffered data to be flushed. If there is no new stored information for a column since the last buffer flush, an empty column is printed. When a task finishes, the buffer is flushed immediately, the state for that object is marked with F, and all other objects are marked with "...". After a task has finished, no further output appears in that column. All output spacing can be accomplished using the standard 8-space tabbing. Buffer any information necessary for printing in internal representation; **do not build and store strings of text for output.** Calls to perform printing may be performed from the tasks and/or the workshop (you decide where to print).

For example, in line 9 of Fig. 9.33, tasks R7 and R10 have the values "B 1" and "V" in their buffer slots and the other buffer slots are empty. When R10 attempts to print "I", which overwrites its current buffer value of "V", the buffer must be flushed generating line 9. R10's new value of "I" is then inserted into its buffer slot. When R10 attempts to print "B 2", which overwrites its current buffer value of "I", the buffer must be flushed generating line 10 and no other values are printed on the line because the print is consecutive (i.e., no intervening call from another object).

Fig. 9.33 output trace:

#	Sa	E1	E2	E3	E4	E5	R6	R7	R8	R9	R10
1	$ northpole 1 5 1003 1 1										
2	Sa	E1	E2	E3	E4	E5	R6	R7	R8	R9	R10
3	--	--	--	--	--	--	--	--	--	--	--
4	S							S			
5	N							V			
6	B		S		S						
7		S			W						
8		W	W				S	I			S
9								B 1			V
10											I
11			H								B 2
12			B 1		H						
13		H			B 2				S		
14		B 3		S							
15	U			W		V					
16	A										
17	C		U 3	H			I		V		
18			C		U 2	S					S
19		U 1			C						V
20	B 1	C	B 2	B 1	B 3	W	B 3		I	I	
21	U 3	c			H				B 4	B 5	
22	c		U 2								
23	N		c		U 1						
24					c	B 2					
25	...	F	...	...	...	...	...	...	...	...	...
26	...	...	F	...	...	...	...	...	...	...	...
27	A										
28	D							U 5			
29								D			U 4
30							U 3				D
31							D		U 2		
32									D	U 1	
33										D	
34	...	...	...	...	F	...	...	...	...	...	...
35				U 2							
36				X	U 1						
37	B 3				X			B 1	B 2	B 4	B 5
38	...	...	...	F	...	...	...	...	...	...	...
39							d				
40	...	...	...	...	...	...	F	...	...	...	...
41								U 5			
42								d			
43	...	...	...	...	...	...	...	F	...	...	...
44									U 4		
45									d		
46	...	...	...	...	...	...	...	...	F	...	...
47	U 3										
48	d									U 2	
49										d	
50	...	...	...	...	...	...	...	...	...	F	...
51	N										U 1
52											d
53	...	...	...	...	...	...	...	...	...	...	F
54	...	...	...	...	F	...	...	...	...	...	...
55	A										
56	F	...	...	...	...	...	...	...	...	...	...
57	Workshop closed										

Fig. 9.33 Northpole: example output

The executable program is named northpole and has the following shell interface:

northpole [N [E [Seed [C [D]]]]]

N is the bound on the number of times the reindeer get served ahead of the elves and must be greater than 0. If unspecified, use a default value of 3. E is the number of elves and must be greater than 0. If unspecified, use a default value of 3. Seed is the seed for the random-number generator and must be greater than 0. If the seed is unspecified, use a random value like the process identifier (getpid) or current time (time), so each run of the program generates different output. Use the following monitor to safely generate random values:

```
_Monitor PRNG {
  public:
    PRNG( unsigned int seed = 1009 ) { srand( seed ); } // set seed
    void seed( unsigned int seed ) { srand( seed ); }   // set seed
    unsigned int operator()() { return rand(); }        // [0,UINT_MAX]
    unsigned int operator()( unsigned int u ) { return operator()() % (u + 1); } // [0,u]
    unsigned int operator()( unsigned int l, unsigned int u ) {
        return operator()( u - l ) + l; } // [l,u]
};
```

Note, because of the non-deterministic execution of concurrent programs, multiple runs with a common seed may not generate the same output. Nevertheless, shorts runs are often the same so the seed can be useful for testing. C is the number of times each elf wants to consult with Santa and must be greater than or equal to 0. If unspecified, use a default value of 3. (All elves use the same value.) D is the number of times each reindeer wants to deliver toys with Santa and must be greater than or equal to 0. If unspecified, use a default value of 3. (All reindeer use the same value.) Check all command arguments for correct form (integers) and range; print an appropriate usage message and terminate the program if a value is missing or invalid.

References

1. Andrews, G.R.: Concurrent Programming: Principles and Practice. Benjamin/Cummings Publishing, Redwood City (1991)
2. Birrell, A., Brown, M.R., Cardelli, L., Donahue, J., Glassman, L., Gutag, J., Harning, J., Kalsow, B., Levin, R., Nelson, G.: Systems Programming with Modula-3. Prentice Hall Series in Innovative Technology. Prentice-Hall, Englewood Cliffs (1991)
3. Brinch Hansen, P.: Structured multiprogramming. Commun. ACM **15**(7), 574–578 (1972)
4. Brinch Hansen, P.: Concurrent programming concepts. Softw. Pract. Exp. **5**(4), 223–245 (1973)
5. Brinch Hansen, P.: The programming language concurrent pascal. IEEE Trans. Softw. Eng. **2**, 199–206 (1975)
6. Brinch Hansen, P.: The design of Edison. Softw. Pract. Exp. **11**(4), 363–396 (1981)
7. Buhr, P.A.: Are safe concurrency libraries possible? Commun. ACM **38**(2), 117–120 (1995)
8. Buhr, P.A., Fortier, M., Coffin, M.H.: Monitor classification. ACM Comput. Surv. **27**(1), 63–107 (1995)

9. Dahl, O.J., Myhrhaug, B., Nygaard, K.: Simula67 Common Base Language. Norwegian Computing Center, Oslo Norway (1970)
10. Dijkstra, E.W.: Hierarchical ordering of sequential processes. Acta Inf. **1**, 115–138 (1971)
11. Hoare, C.A.R.: Towards a theory of parallel programming. In: Hoare, C.A.R., Perott, R.H. (eds.) Operating Systems Techniques, pp. 61–71. Academic Press, New York (1972)
12. Hoare, C.A.R.: Monitors: An operating system structuring concept. Commun. ACM **17**(10), 549–557 (1974)
13. Howard, J.H.: Signaling in monitors. In: Proceedings Second International Conference Software Engineering, pp. 47–52. IEEE Computer Society, San Francisco, U.S.A (1976)
14. Kessels, J.L.W.: An alternative to event queues for synchronization in monitors. Commun. ACM **20**(7), 500–503 (1977)
15. Lampson, B.W., Redell, D.D.: Experience with processes and monitors in mesa. Commun. ACM **23**(2), 105–117 (1980)
16. Lea, D.: Concurrent Programming in Java: Design Principles and Patterns, 1st edn. Addison-Wesley, Boston (1997)
17. Mitchell, J.G., Maybury, W., Sweet, R.: Mesa language manual. Tech. Rep. CSL–79–3, Xerox Palo Alto Research Center (1979)
18. Trono, J.A.: A new exercise in concurrency. SIGCSE Bull. **26**(3), 8–10 (1994)

Chapter 10
Active Objects

Up to this point, tasks have been used solely to create a new thread of control and provide termination synchronization. In this role, such tasks are called an **active object**. Hence, the only member routines in a task type have been public constructors and possibly a destructor. This chapter expands on the capabilities of these active objects by introducing uses for other public members, called by other tasks.

Since a task type is like a class, it might seem obvious that it can have public members, which could be called by other tasks; however, there is a problem. When a task is created, it has a thread executing in its task main, and the scope of the task main allows the task's thread to access all the task's variables. If other tasks call public members of a task, these public members *also* have access to all the task's variables. Unless the calling threads are restricted to reading data, there is the potential for interference (i.e., race error). Even reading can result in problems because inconsistent values can be read when the task's thread is updating its variables. In essence, there are multiple threads accessing the same shared data without any mutual exclusion. While it is conceivable to use explicit locks in the member routines and task main to control access, this defeats the purpose of using a high-level language construct. Therefore, a task needs the mutual-exclusion property, like a monitor, if it is going to have public members called by other tasks.

10.1 Execution Properties

At this juncture, it is reasonable to review the basic properties of execution discussed so far to see how these properties relate to the language constructs in μC++. Three new execution properties have been introduced and discussed: execution state (Sect. 4.1.3, p. 129), thread (Chap. 5, p. 191) and mutual exclusion (Chap. 6, p. 233). An execution state is necessary so each coroutine and task has its own stack on which it can suspend (block) and subsequently resume (unblock), implicitly

© Springer International Publishing Switzerland 2016

P.A. Buhr, *Understanding Control Flow*, DOI 10.1007/978-3-319-25703-7_10

saving all necessary state during the suspension and reestablishing it on resumption. A thread is necessary to create a concurrent program with multiple execution points. Remember, an execution state and thread are the minimum properties required for independent execution. Finally, mutual exclusion is necessary to protect shared data accessed by multiple threads.

The first two properties are fundamental, i.e., it is impossible to create them from simpler constructs in a programming language. No amount of effort using basic control structures and variables can create new execution stacks and have the program context switch among them, nor is it possible to create a new thread of control that executes concurrently with other threads. Only mutual exclusion can be generated using basic control structures and variables (see Chap. 6, p. 233), but these software algorithms are complex and inefficient to the point of being impractical in all but a few special circumstances. For example, without atomic hardware instructions, N-task mutual exclusion is impractical, and atomic read/ write instructions are not accessible through any of the basic language constructs. Therefore, all 3 of the new execution properties must be built into new language constructs tailored to achieve practical concurrent execution. Only the language compiler knows what constitutes an execution state and what has to be saved and restored for a context switch, and only it knows what atomic hardware instructions are available on the target architecture and where it is safe to perform certain optimizations during code generation. Finally, only the language runtime system knows how to manage and schedule multiple tasks. Language designers incorporate some or all of these three properties in different ways into a programming language (see Chap. 13, p. 637).

One factor affecting language design is the orthogonality of the three execution properties, resulting in 8 potential language constructs. However, in general, not all of the combinations are useful, so it is worth examining all the combinations. In object-oriented languages, the three execution properties should be properties of an object. (In non-object-oriented languages, associating the three execution properties with language features is more difficult.) Therefore, an object may or may not have an execution state, may or may not have a thread, and may or may not have mutual exclusion. In the situation where an object does not have the minimum properties required for execution, i.e., execution state and thread, those of its caller must be used.

Table 10.1 shows the different high-level constructs possible when an object possesses different execution properties. Case 1 is a basic object, with calls to its member routines, which has none of the execution properties. In this case, the caller's execution-state and thread are used to perform the execution and there is no mutual exclusion. The lack of mutual exclusion means access must be serialized among threads or controlled through some explicit locking mechanism. Case 2 is like Case 1 but deals with the concurrent access problem by implicitly ensuring mutual exclusion for the duration of each computation by a member routine. This construct is a monitor. Case 3 is an object that has its own execution-state but no thread or mutual exclusion. Such an object uses its caller's thread to advance its own execution-state and usually, but not always, returns the thread back to the caller

Table 10.1 Language constructs from execution properties

Object properties		Object's member-routine properties	
Thread	Execution state	No mutual exclusion	Mutual exclusion
No	No	1 Class-object	2 Monitor
No	Yes	3 Coroutine	4 Coroutine-monitor
Yes	No	5 (Rejected)	6 (Rejected)
Yes	Yes	7 (Rejected?)	8 Task

(semi- and full coroutining, respectively). This construct is a coroutine. Case 4 is like Case 3 but deals with the concurrent access problem by implicitly ensuring mutual exclusion. This construct is a coroutine-monitor. Cases 5 and 6 are objects with a thread but no execution state. Both cases are rejected because the thread cannot be used to provide additional concurrency. First, the object's thread cannot execute on its own since it does not have an execution state, so it cannot perform any independent actions. Second, if the caller's execution-state is used, assuming the caller's thread can be blocked to ensure mutual exclusion of the execution state, the effect is to have two threads serially executing portions of a single computation, which does not provide additional concurrency. Case 7 is an object that has its own thread and execution state. Because it has both a thread and execution state it is capable of executing on its own; however, it lacks mutual exclusion. Without mutual exclusion, access to the object's data is unsafe; therefore, having public members in such an object would, in general, require explicit locking, which is too low-level. Furthermore, there is no significant performance advantage over case 8. For these reasons, this case is rejected. Case 8 is like Case 7 but deals with the concurrent access problem by implicitly ensuring mutual exclusion. This construct is a task.

It is interesting that Table 10.1 generates all of the higher-level language constructs present in existing languages, but the constructs are derived from fundamental properties of execution not ad hoc decisions of a programming-language designer. As mentioned previously, if one of these constructs is not present, a programmer may be forced to contrive a solution that violates abstraction or is inefficient. Therefore, when trying to decide which construct to use to solve a problem in μC++ , start by asking which of the fundamental execution properties does an object need. If an object needs to suspend/resume (wait/signal) and retain state during this period, the execution-state property is needed. If an object needs its own thread of control to execute concurrently, the thread property is needed. If an object is accessed by multiple threads, the mutual-exclusion property is needed. The answers to these 3 questions define precisely which μC++ construct to select for a solution. Therefore, execution state, thread and mutual exclusion are the three building blocks for all advanced program construction.

10.2   Indirect/Direct Communication

Why have public members in a task, especially since none have been required up to
this point? The answer follows from the fact that there are two fundamental forms
of communication: indirect communication and direct communication. Indirect
communication is where two active objects communicate through a third party
(usually an inactive object), e.g., when people communicate via writing, possibly
through a letter or electronic mail, communication is indirect. In essence, indirect
communication implies a station-to-station communication and neither party is
immediately available during the dialogue. Direct communication is where two
active objects communicate directly with one another, e.g., when people communicate via talking, possibly over a telephone or electronic chat, that communication
is direct. In essence, direct communication implies a point-to-point communication
channel and both parties are immediately available to participate in the dialogue.

Each form of communication is important, providing capabilities unavailable by
the other. Indirect communication provides delayed response but does not require
either party to be constantly synchronized or available. Direct communication provides immediate response in a conversation but requires both parties be constantly
synchronized and available. Imagine if people could only communicate by writing
letters (email or by talking (chat). Neither form of communication is sufficient to
satisfy all the basic communication requirements. While one form can simulate the
other in a very weak sense (i.e., weak equivalence), both are needed to deal with
quite different communication needs. Hence, the two kinds of communication are
complementary, and both are needed in a concurrent system. Up to now, all forms of
communication among tasks have been indirect. That is, tasks communicate through
some shared data, protected by explicit locks (e.g., semaphores) or implicit locks
(e.g., monitors).

10.2.1   Indirect Communication

The bounded buffer is a common example of a third party object through which
tasks communicate information indirectly. Fig. 10.1 illustrates the usage of a buffer
by a producer and a consumer task with a timing graph, where time advances
from top to bottom. Figs. 10.1a and b illustrate the ideal cases where a producer
or consumer can find the buffer neither full or empty, and so they can insert and
remove data from the buffer without synchronization blocking (mutual exclusion
blocking is only necessary for multiple producers and consumers). Figs. 10.1c and d
illustrate the cases where a producer or consumer has to wait for data to be inserted
or removed. (The waiting time of a task is indicated in the timing graph by a dashed
line.) Notice, the consumer has to wait when the buffer is empty for a producer
to insert an element, and then the consumer is unblocked via cooperation as the
producer exits the buffer. Similarly, the producer has to wait when the buffer is
full for a consumer to remove an element, and then the producer is unblocked via

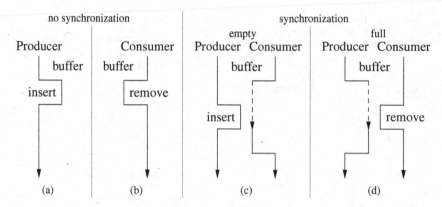

Fig. 10.1 Indirect communication, unidirectional

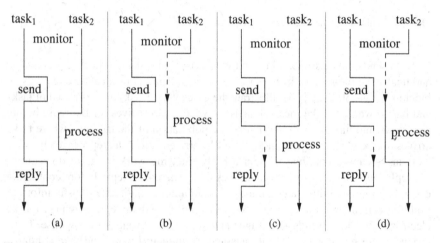

Fig. 10.2 Indirect communication, bidirectional

cooperation as the consumer exits the buffer. What is important in this example is that the ideal case involves no blocking (the minimum synchronization time), which is possible only with indirect communication. Blocking is eliminated via the buffer between the producer and consumer, which keeps the two tasks largely independent. Only boundary conditions on the buffer, e.g., full or empty, cause a blocking situation.

In the bounded buffer example, the data transfer is unidirectional, i.e., the data flows in one direction between producer and consumer, and hence, the producer does not obtain a response after inserting data in the buffer. Fig. 10.2 illustrates the usage of a monitor to indirectly transfer information *bidirectionally* between two tasks. Like sending email, $task_1$ sends a message in the monitor and returns at some time to check for a response. $Task_2$ arrives at the monitor to read the message, formulate a reply, and then continue. Fig. 10.2a illustrates the ideal case where $task_1$ arrives

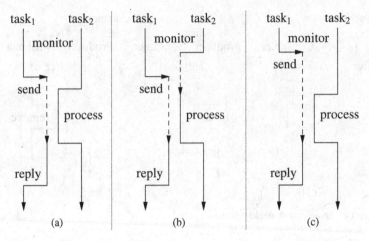

Fig. 10.3 Indirect communication, reply required

first and sends the message, followed by the arrival of task$_2$ to process the message, and finally the return of task$_1$ to retrieve the reply. Again, this ideal case requires no blocking. Figs. 10.2b, c and d illustrate the cases where task$_2$ arrives ahead of task$_1$ and has to wait until the message arrives, where task$_1$ arrives for the reply before it is ready and has to wait, and finally, a combination of the last two, where task$_2$ arrives before the message is ready and task$_1$ arrives before the reply is ready.

If task$_1$ cannot continue without a reply (i.e., the work it has to do requires the reply), it must wait until task$_2$ arrives and generates a reply before continuing execution. Fig. 10.3 illustrates the usage of a monitor to indirectly transfer information bidirectionally between two tasks, where an immediate reply is required. Like electronic chat, task$_1$ sends a message in the monitor and waits for a response. Task$_2$ arrives at the monitor to read the message, formulate a reply, and then continue. Fig. 10.3a illustrates the ideal case where task$_1$ arrives first with the message and waits, followed by the immediate arrival of task$_2$ to process the message, and finally the unblocking of task$_1$ to retrieve the reply. Here, even the ideal case requires blocking. Fig. 10.3b and c illustrate the cases where task$_2$ arrives ahead of task$_1$ and has to wait until the message arrives, and task$_1$ arrives ahead of task$_2$ and has to wait for the reply, respectively.

In these 3 scenarios, observe that the first scenario has a buffer of size N, and in the last two cases a buffer of size 1. As well, in the first two cases, both synchronization and mutual exclusion are necessary for the buffer (supplied by the monitor). The buffer reduces the amount of blocking by eliminating the need for the tasks to interact directly. In the last case, only synchronization is necessary; mutual exclusion is not required (although the monitor still provides mutual exclusion). In other words, blocking is always required for the immediate reply case, which correspondingly implies synchronization always occurs.

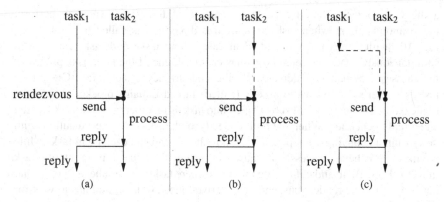

Fig. 10.4 Direct communication

Finally, these scenarios can be made more complex when multiple producers and consumers are introduced. The complexity occurs because processing the message and/or reply in the monitor precludes other tasks from entering the monitor because of the mutual-exclusion property, so unless the processing is very short, the data should be dealt with outside the monitor so concurrency is not inhibited for other communicating tasks (see Chap. 11, p. 563 for techniques to accomplish this). For $task_1$, the solution is to simply copy the reply out of the monitor and then processes it. For $task_2$, the solution is to copy the message out of the monitor, and subsequently reenter the monitor once it has processed the message and generated a reply. The reply must be copied and stored in the monitor, and cooperation requires the matching receiver for a reply be unblocked, if waiting in the monitor. It may also be necessary to have an additional buffer for the replies as well as the messages.

In summation, indirect communication takes advantage of the fact that blocking is often unnecessary because an immediate response to a message is not required. Blocking is eliminated by using buffers to temporarily store information until the other party in the communication appears. If an immediate response is required, blocking is always required, which eliminates the need for a buffer.

10.2.2 Direct Communication

The last scenario of indirect communication mimics direct communication. The key point is that the monitor provides no shared data (i.e., no buffer), and hence, is only used for synchronization. Direct communication optimizes this particular scenario by providing the necessary synchronization *without* the need to create and manage an additional indirect object (which has no data anyway).

Fig. 10.4 illustrates the direct transfer of information bidirectionally between two tasks, where an immediate reply is required. In this scenario, $task_1$ sends a message to $task_2$ directly. The two tasks must first synchronize to perform the communication; when tasks synchronize directly it is called a rendezvous. Fig. 10.4a illustrates the rare but ideal case where $task_1$ and $task_2$ rendezvous simultaneously. Once the rendezvous has occurred, one of the two tasks processes the message. Which one depends on the concurrency system: in μC++ , it is $task_1$'s (caller's) thread while $task_2$'s (called) thread remains blocked during the rendezvous. The message must be copied into $task_2$'s member, where it is processed and a reply generated. When the reply is ready, both tasks continue execution, with $task_1$'s thread copying the reply. Notice, no other thread can execute in $task_2$ while the message is being processed because of the mutual exclusion property of a task in μC++. Figs. 10.4b and c illustrate the cases where $task_2$ arrives ahead of $task_1$ and has to wait for the rendezvous, and $task_1$ arrives ahead of $task_2$ and has to wait for the rendezvous, respectively.

While the message itself has to be processed in $task_2$'s member, the reply could also be processed in $task_2$'s member instead of being copied out for processing by $task_1$. However, processing the reply in $task_2$'s member precludes other tasks from entering it because of the mutual-exclusion property, so unless the processing is very short, the reply should be dealt with outside the called task.

As mentioned, at the point of the rendezvous, either thread could be used to process the message. Noticing which thread reaches the rendezvous first suggests which thread should execute the member routine processing the message. Fig. 10.4a is simultaneous arrival, which occurs rarely; in this case, either task could process the message. In Fig. 10.4b, $task_2$ arrives at the rendezvous first and blocks. If this case is common, using $task_2$'s thread is inefficient because $task_1$'s thread must block and $task_2$'s thread unblock. It is more efficient to leave $task_2$'s thread blocked and allow $task_1$'s thread to execute $task_2$'s member. In Fig. 10.4c, $task_1$ arrives at the rendezvous first and blocks. If this case is common, using $task_1$'s thread is inefficient because $task_2$'s thread must block and $task_1$'s thread unblock. It is more efficient to leave $task_1$'s thread blocked and allow $task_2$'s thread to execute its member. It is possible to dynamically decide which task to block and continue, by checking if the rendezvous partner is or is not available. If the rendezvous partner is not available, the task blocks; if the rendezvous partner is available, the task executes the member. However, making the decision as to which thread blocks or continues adds to the complexity of the implementation. In fact, after experimentation, the most common case in most programs is where the caller task finds the called task blocked, i.e., Fig. 10.4d. (Why this case is the most common is discussed in Chap. 11, p. 563.) Therefore, the best average performance is obtained by having the caller's thread execute a task's mutex member, which is what is done in μC++. As well, having the caller's thread execute the member in μC++ is consistent with how coroutine and monitor members are executed; for both, the caller's thread and execution-state are used. Therefore, when routines uThisCoroutine or uThisTask are invoked in a public member, they return the coroutine or task identifier associated with the caller object, rather than the one associated with the called object, which reflects the fact that the caller's execution-state is being used for the execution because no context switch has occurred to the other coroutine or task at this point.

10.3 Task

The basic features of à task are discussed in Sect. 5.10, p. 214: task main, creation and destruction, and inherited members. Similar to a monitor (see Sect. 9.3, p. 434) a task is **active** if a thread is executing a mutex member or the task main, otherwise it is **inactive**. The task's mutual exclusion is enforced by locking the task when executing a mutex member or the task main, and unlocking it when the active thread voluntarily gives up control of the task. As for monitors, public members of a task are mutex by default, and a thread executing a task's mutex member is allowed to call another mutex member of that task without generating mutual-exclusion deadlock (see Sect. 9.3.1, p. 437).

10.4 Scheduling

Scheduling for a task is similar to that of a monitor except the programmer must be aware of the additional thread associated with the task. Unlike a monitor, when a task is created it starts *active*, i.e., with a thread running in it. Therefore, no calls to mutex members can occur until the initial thread either accepts a mutex member or waits; in both cases, the initial task thread blocks, allowing another thread to acquire mutual exclusion of the task and begin execution of a mutex member. As for monitors, there are two scheduling techniques: external and internal scheduling. Finally, because the mutex property is the same for all mutex types, the implicit scheduling mechanism and data structures for a task are the same as for a monitor (see Fig. 10.5 as a reminder, which is the same as Fig. 9.8, p. 447).

10.4.1 External Scheduling

External scheduling uses the accept statement to schedule tasks waiting on the implicit mutex queues (these tasks called a mutex member and blocked). To illustrate external task scheduling, a generic μC++ bounded buffer example is presented in Fig. 10.6, p. 533, built using a task rather than a monitor. In this case, using a task is unnecessary and inefficient; a monitor is clearly the best construct because of the indirect communication. Nevertheless, it is illustrative to see how easy it is to convert a monitor to a task to solve this problem.

The buffer implementation is the same as that in Sect. 9.4.1, p. 439 (see Fig. 9.4, p. 439), i.e., a fixed sized array with front and back pointers cycling around the array, with an additional counter in this implementation for the number of full slots in the buffer. The interface has four members: the constructor, query, insert and remove. The only difference in the code from the external monitor solution is that the synchronization is moved from routines insert and remove into the task main.

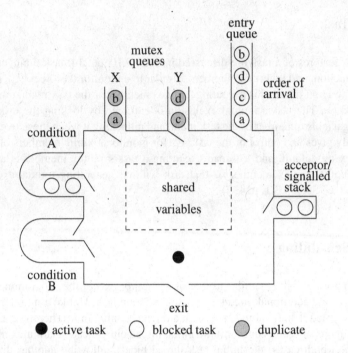

Fig. 10.5 μC++ mutex object

The task main loops forever (stopping it is discussed shortly) accepting calls to either insert or remove. This accept statement introduces the ability to accept a call to one of a number of mutex members using the **or** clause. (The **or** clause is discussed in detail in Sect. 9.6.2, p. 457.)

As calls are made to members insert and remove, the task main accepts each one, which causes its thread to block on the acceptor/signalled stack and unblocks a waiting caller from the appropriate mutex queue closest to the start of the accept statement, or if no waiting caller, for a call to one of the specified mutex member(s) to occur. When the caller eventually exits the mutex member, the task's thread is popped off the acceptor/signalled stack and continues execution *after* the accept statement (remember, only one call is accepted). The thread of the task main then loops around to accept the next caller. Notice, the task's thread must alternate its execution in the task main with the callers to members insert and remove, otherwise the task's thread would prevent the callers from entering the mutex members. (Therefore, there is no advantage in having a thread to accept the calls; a monitor implicitly accepts all the mutex members when inactive without the need of an additional thread.) In addition, some other mechanism is needed to provide synchronization when the buffer is full or empty.

To provide the necessary synchronization, the task's thread must conditionally accept the mutex members; otherwise, a caller has to block in the insert or remove routines, which requires internal scheduling (discussed next). Moving the

```
template<typename ELEMTYPE> _Task BoundedBuffer {
    enum { Size = 20 };
    int front, back, count;
    ELEMTYPE Elements[Size];
  public:
    BoundedBuffer() : front(0), back(0), count(0) {}
    _Nomutex int query() { return count; }

    void insert( ELEMTYPE elem ) {
        Elements[back] = elem;
        back = (back + 1) % Size;
        count += 1;
    }
    ELEMTYPE remove() {
        ELEMTYPE elem = Elements[front];
        front = (front + 1) % Size;
        count -= 1;
        return elem;
    }
  protected:
    void main() {
        for ( ;; ) {
            _When (count != Size) _Accept( insert );
            or _When (count != 0) _Accept( remove );
        }
    }
};
```

Fig. 10.6 Task bounded buffer: external scheduling

conditional control from the external monitor solution into the task main's loop does not work:

```
for ( ;; ) {
    if ( count == 0  ) _Accept( insert );
    else if ( count == Size ) _Accept( remove );
}
```

This approach fails because the task's thread only accepts members when the buffer is full or empty, not at any intermediate buffer state. To deal with this case requires augmenting the conditional control:

```
for ( ;; ) {
    if ( 0 < count && count < Size ) _Accept( insert, remove );
    else if ( count < Size ) _Accept( insert );
    else /* if ( 0 < count ) */ _Accept( remove );
}
```

The first **if** statement checks if both conditions are true, i.e., the buffer is neither empty nor full, and if so, accepts both members. If the first condition is false, either the buffer is full or empty. The next **if** statement determines which of these cases is true and accepts the appropriate member. (Notice the optimization of eliminating the last check because it must be true given the other checks.)

While this conditional control now works, it points out a major problem with this approach to conditionally accepting mutex members. Generalizing the conditional control based on the first failing buffer example results in:

```
if ( C1 ) _Accept( M1 );
else if ( C2 ) _Accept( M2 );
```

However, this does not result in either M1 or M2 being accepted if both conditions are true. The order imposed by the **if** statements together with the meaning of **_Accept** results in a something weaker. It says accept M1 when C1 is true, accept M2 when C1 is false and C2 is true, and *only* accept M1 when C1 and C2 are true instead of accepting both M1 and M2. Therefore, this approach results in starvation of callers to M2 if condition C1 is always true even when there are no calls to M1. For this reason, the first buffer example failed.

Now generalize the second working buffer example but extend it from 2 to 3 conditionals:

```
if        ( C1 && C2 && C3 ) _Accept( M1, M2, M3 );
else if   ( C1 && C2 ) _Accept( M1, M2 );
else if   ( C1 && C3 ) _Accept( M1, M3 );
else if   ( C2 && C3 ) _Accept( M2, M3 );
else if   ( C1 ) _Accept( M1 );
else if   ( C2 ) _Accept( M2 );
else if   ( C3 ) _Accept( M3 );
```

This form is necessary to ensure that for every true conditional, only the corresponding members are accepted. The general pattern for N conditionals is:

$$\binom{N}{N} + \binom{N}{N-1} + \ldots + \binom{N}{1} = (1+1)^N - 1 \quad \text{from the binomial theorem.}$$

Having to write an exponential number of statements, i.e., $2^N - 1$, to handle this case is clearly unsatisfactory, both from a textual and performance standpoint, and is an example of weak equivalence with the following language construct.

To prevent the exponential growth for conditional accepting, μC++ provides a **_When** clause. The two **_When** clauses in the task main of Fig. 10.6 make the accept clause conditional on the condition specified in the **_When**. A condition must be true (or omitted) before a member is accepted. If the condition is false, the accept does not occur even if there is a calling task waiting on the mutex queue of the specified member. In the bounded buffer example, the first **_When** clause only accepts calls to insert if the buffer has empty slots (count < Size), and the second **_When** clause only accepts calls to remove if the buffer has non-empty slots (count > 0). Notice only one of the two conditionals can be false simultaneously, so the accept statement always accepts either one or both of the two members. If either or both of conditionals are true, but there are no outstanding calls, the acceptor is blocked until a call to an appropriate member is made. The exponential number of statements are eliminated because the **_When** and the **_Accept** clauses are checked *simultaneously* during execution of the accept statement instead of having to first check the conditionals and then perform the appropriate accept clauses in an accept statement.

While conceptually the **_Accept** clauses are checked *simultaneously*, an implementation must provide some ordering. If a random checking-ordering is used, then calls to each mutex member have some probability of being accepted, and hence, no starvation can occur. However, this approach precludes a programmer from prioritizing the order of selection, which can be useful. If a specific checking-ordering is used, the programmer has fine-grain control on the order of selection but must ensure that all calls are eventually selected to preclude starvation. In either case, there is no requirement for all the C_i to be executed. As soon as a true C_i is found with callers to a specified mutex member, it is possible to short-circuit the evaluation of the accept testing and proceed with the call. Therefore, if the C_i have side-effects, not all are executed.

While the **_When** clause is the same as the conditional of a conditional critical-region (see Sect. 9.2, p. 428), the **_When** clause does not result in busy waiting; the busy wait is eliminated by the cooperation in the task solution for the bounded buffer. Instead of having each producer and consumer constantly check if the buffer is accessible, they block outside the buffer (external scheduling) until accepted when the buffer is in an appropriate state. Hence, conditional control does not imply busy waiting, it is lack of cooperation that implies busy waiting.

One outstanding issue is the case when all the conditionals are false, which means no call is accepted. There are two options available, both problematic. The first option is to block at the end of the accept waiting for a call, which is the normal semantics for an accept statement. However, the task is now in a synchronization deadlock because it is waiting for an event that cannot occur, i.e., a call when no call is accepted. The second option is to continue execution after the accept without accepting a call. However, after the accept statement, the task must reevaluate all the conditionals to know if a call was accepted or use a flag variable, as in:

```
flag = false;
_When ( C1 ) _Accept( M1 ) {
    flag = true;
} or _When ( C2 ) _Accept( M2 ) {
    flag = true;
}
if ( flag ) {
    // an accept occurred
} else {
    // all conditionals are false
}
```

This second option could easily result in a mistake if appropriate checking is not made, as the acceptor incorrectly assumes some cooperation has occurred by an accepted call, when in fact no call may be accepted because all the conditionals are false. This situation can lead to an infinite loop around an accept statement accepting no calls.

μC++ deals with both these situations. The default action for the case when all the accepts are conditional (as in the bounded buffer example) and all the **_When** conditions are false is to do nothing (like a **switch** statement with no matching **case** clauses). This semantics prevents the synchronization deadlock. As a result, it is

possible to substitute the **if** statement with a **_When** clause in the external monitor
solution for the bounded buffer (see page 439), as in:

```
void BoundedBuffer::insert( int elem ) {
    _When ( count == Size ) _Accept( remove ); // hold calls to insert
    . . .
int BoundedBuffer::remove() {
    _When ( count == 0 ) _Accept( insert );      // hold calls to remove
    . . .
```

In both cases, the monitor solution results in the accept statements not being
executed when the buffer is neither full nor empty. (Note, directly substituting a **if** by
an **_When** is only possible for the trivial situation of an accept statement with single
_When clause.) In the situation where a programmer needs to know if no accept
clause is executed, a terminating **_Else** clause can be used on the accept statement.
If no call is accepted for an accept statement because all **_When** conditions are false
or no callers, the terminating **_Else** clause is executed instead of blocking, as in:

```
void BoundedBuffer::insert( int elem ) {
    _When ( count == Size ) _Accept( remove );
    _Else { // terminating else
        // call to remove did not occur but buffer may be full
    }
```

Therefore, a terminating **_Else** allows the programmer to know the accept statement
did not accept a call without having to reevaluate the conditions or use a flag
variable. Nevertheless, care must be taken in using the **_Else** clause as it can easily
lead to busy waiting or possibly an infinite loop.

Now look back at Fig. 10.6, p. 533 with the following question: why is
BoundedBuffer::main defined at the end of the task? The reason is the *definition before
use rule* in C++ (see Sect. 9.4.1, p. 439 for a similar situation). Since the accept
statement references members insert and remove, both must be defined *before* the
accept statement refers to them. It is a common mistake to put the accept statement
before the routine it is accepting, and get an error from μC++ that one or more
members are not mutex (only mutex members can be accepted). The reason for this
error is that μC++ has not seen the routine definition so it assumes the routine is
no-mutex.

One final point about potential starvation when using the **_Accept** statement.
When several members are accepted and outstanding calls exist to some subset of
these members, a call is selected based on the order of appearance of the **_Accept**
clauses in the accept statement. Hence, the order of the accept clauses indicates
the relative priority for selection if there are several outstanding calls. As will be
shown in future examples, this is an important feature. In the bounded-buffer task,
calls to insert and remove require equal priority when the buffer is neither full nor
empty for fairness; however, priority is given to producers over consumers because
member insert is accepted first. This priority can lead to short-term unfairness for
the consumers, but the bound on the length of the buffer (specified through the
_When clause) ensures consumers eventually make progress (i.e., when the buffer
is full). However, imagine an infinite sized buffer; in this case, the **_When** clause is
removed from the **_Accept**(insert). Now if a continuous supply of producer calls

occurs, it could prevent a consumer from ever removing an element from the buffer, and hence, result in consumer starvation.

One simple way of dealing with this problem is to use the Dekker solution of alternation, as in:

```
void BoundedBuffer::main() {
    for ( ;; ) {
        _When ( count < Size ) _Accept( insert );    // "insert" has highest priority
        or _When ( count > 0 ) _Accept( remove );

        _When ( count > 0 ) _Accept( remove ); // "remove" has highest priority
        or _When ( count < Size ) _Accept( insert );
    }
}
```

Here the accept statement has been duplicated in the **for** loop but with the order of accept clauses reversed in the second accept statement. Each time through the loop, each of the two mutex members is treated as the highest priority in the accept statements. Hence, when there are simultaneous calls from both producers and consumers, the calls are handled alternately, resulting in fairness. Notice, this situation is largely fictitious because it requires an infinite sized buffer and a continuous stream of producer calls to produce starvation. For normal finite resource situations, temporary periods of unfairness occurring in a few rare situations from the priority associated with the order of the accept clauses do not cause problems. Therefore, duplicating the accept clauses in this way is largely unnecessary, except in a few rare situations.

10.4.2 Internal Scheduling

The complementary approach to external scheduling is internal scheduling, where calling tasks are largely scheduled inside a task from explicit condition variables rather than from outside the task from implicit mutex queues. As for monitors, internal scheduling is accomplished using condition variables, and signal/wait. To illustrate internal scheduling, a generic μC++ bounded buffer example is presented in Fig. 10.7, built using a task rather than a monitor. Again, using a task is unnecessary and inefficient, but it illustrates how easy it is to convert a monitor to a task to solve this problem.

The first point to note is that, except for the existence of the task main, the code is identical to the monitor solution in Fig. 9.6, p. 444. The second point to note is that the conditional control is removed from the accept statement in the task main. The last point to note is that even though this is internal scheduling, there is still an accept statement in the task main performing external scheduling.

This example illustrates even more why using a task for this problem is inappropriate. When the buffer task is created, no producer or consumer can get in to use the buffer because of the task's thread. The accepts in the buffer's task main are necessary to ensure the buffer's thread blocks so the producer and consumer can

```
template<typename ELEMTYPE> _Task BoundedBuffer {
    uCondition full, empty;
    int front, back, count;
    ELEMTYPE queue[Size];
public:
    BoundedBuffer() : front(0), back(0), count(0) {}
    _Nomutex int query() { return count; }
    void insert( ELEMTYPE elem ) {
        if ( count == Size ) empty.wait();
        queue[back] = elem;
        back = (back + 1) % Size;
        count += 1;
        full.signal();
    }
    ELEMTYPE remove() {
        if ( count == 0 ) full.wait();
        ELEMTYPE elem = queue[front];
        front = (front + 1) % Size;
        count -= 1;
        empty.signal();
        return elem;
    }
protected:
    void main() {
        for ( ;; ) {
            _Accept( insert, remove );
        }
    }
};
```

Fig. 10.7 Task bounded buffer: internal scheduling

access the buffer. However, the conditional control is now performed by cooperation
between the producer and consumer, without help from the buffer task. Remember,
the caller's thread is used to execute the member routines, so it is the producer
and consumer executing the waits and signals in the members insert and remove.
If either a producer or consumer finds the buffer full or empty, respectively, they
block on the appropriate condition, and that condition is subsequently signalled by
the opposite kind of task on exit from the member routine. When the buffer is not
full or empty, the buffer task unblocks and does another iteration of the loop in its
task main between each producer and consumer call. When the buffer is either full
or empty, the buffer task is still unblocked because it is at the top of the acceptor/
signalled stack after a task waits on a condition variable.

So in this particular example, the buffer's thread does absolutely nothing to help
solve the problem, but it does slow down the entire process by constantly blocking
and unblocking between calls to insert and remove.

10.5 External and Internal Scheduling

The last example illustrates the use of both internal and external scheduling by a task. In most tasks, some external scheduling is always required, and in addition some internal scheduling may be required. So the two common forms are strictly external or a combination of external and internal; it is rare for a task to only use internal scheduling. The reason is that the task's thread must block for other tasks to interact, and the management of the task's thread to achieve this effect requires that it accept calls to the interacting tasks.

10.6 Accepting the Destructor

As mentioned, the destructor of a mutex object is always mutex and the accept statement accepts any mutex member; therefore, the destructor is eligible to be accepted in an accept statement like any other mutex member. But why accept the destructor of a mutex object, especially a task?

The answer to this question starts with another question: who calls the destructor of an object? The compiler implicitly inserts calls to the destructor before storage is deallocated (at the end of a block for a local variable or as part of the **delete** for a dynamically allocated variable). An executing thread then makes the destructor calls via the implicitly inserted calls; when a thread invokes an implicit destructor call for a mutex object, it must block until the destructor is accepted (all calls to mutex members must be accepted). However, up to this point, no explicit accepting of a mutex object's destructor has occurred in any monitor, coroutine-monitor or task (i.e., all the kinds of mutex types). How then has the call to the destructor been accepted?

In the case of a monitor or coroutine-monitor, the destructor is implicitly accepted by the implicit scheduling when a task exits a mutex object and there is no task on the acceptor/signalled stack. In this case, the next task from the entry queue (C) is implicitly accepted, and if that call happens to be to the destructor, it is accepted. The destructor is then executed and the object deallocated by the calling task's thread. If there are tasks blocked on the entry queue or condition variables associated with the mutex object, the destructor cannot complete so the program terminates with an error. For implicit acceptance of the destructor, there can never be tasks blocked on the acceptor/signaller stack as it must be empty before the implicit scheduling selects a task from the entry queue (C < W < S). Thus, in all the previous programs using monitors, code has been set up so the call to the destructor is the last call made to the monitor:

```
{
    BoundedBuffer buf;
    {
        Consumer cons( buf );        // pass buffer to consumer task
        Producer prod( buf );        // pass buffer to producer task
    } // implicit call to consumer and producer destructor (wait for termination)
} // implicit call to buffer destructor (no tasks using the buffer now)
```

The inner block cannot terminate until both the consumer and producer tasks
have terminated. Once the inner block has terminated, the outer block terminates
and implicitly calls the destructor of the bounded buffer, buf. Since the consumer
and producer have terminated, there are no tasks either calling or in the buffer.
Therefore, the call to the destructor by the deleting task (most likely uMain) is
implicitly accepted from the entry queue, the destructor is executed, and the storage
deallocated (from the stack). (In fact, the nested blocks are unnecessary in this
example because deallocation is defined in C++ to occur in the reverse order to
allocation.)

What about the producer and consumer tasks in the previous example as both
their destructors are implicitly called at the end of the inner block? As noted,
the destructor call to a task must wait for the task's thread to terminate before
it can execute, but up to this point, no explicit acceptance of a task's destructor
has occurred in any task so how does the call get accepted? The mechanism
follows from the fact that after a task's thread terminates, the task becomes a
monitor (see Sect. 10.7, p. 544). Hence, when the task's thread exits the mutex
object (by termination), the implicit scheduling first checks the acceptor/signalled
stack (which is empty) and then checks the entry queue (which has the call to
the destructor). Thus, the last action done by the terminating task is to implicitly
schedule the call to its destructor (cooperation). If there are other outstanding calls
ahead of the destructor call, it is responsibility of the task designer to ensure the call
to the destructor is eventually implicitly accepted, which can be accomplished by
having the other tasks immediately exit the monitor.

With this deeper understanding of how implicit scheduling accepts the destructor,
it is now possible to examine explicit scheduling of the destructor. Which leads back
to the original question: why accept the destructor of a mutex object, especially a
task? The answer is to provide a mechanism for determining when to terminate
a task's thread. Up to now, tasks have been self-terminating, i.e., they perform a
set piece of work, and once completed, they terminate, which through a series of
circumstances (see above) causes the destructor to be implicitly accepted. What if a
task needs to terminate because of an external event? That is, one task tells another
it is time to stop execution and terminate. The only mechanism to accomplish this is
with indirect communication by using a shared variable that is set by one task and
polled for change by the other; but polling is unacceptable. It is now possible to use
direct communication using a public member like the stop member in the consumer
coroutine of Fig. 4.17, p. 158, which sets a flag to stop the loop in the task's main
member. Hence, it is possible to stop the infinite loop in the task main of the bounded
buffer task by augmenting it to:

```
template<typename ELEMTYPE> _Task BoundedBuffer {
    ...
    bool done;                          // indicates if task should terminate
  public:
    BoundedBuffer() : ..., done( false ) {}
    ...
    void stop() { done = true; }
  protected:
    void main() {
        for ( ; ! done; ) {
            _Accept( stop );
            or _When ( count < Size ) _Accept( insert );
            or _When ( count > 0 ) _Accept( remove );
            ...
```

Now, another task can call the stop member at any time, as in the following:

```
{
    BoundedBuffer buf;
    {
        Consumer cons( buf );      .// pass buffer to consumer task
        Producer prod( buf );       // pass buffer to producer task
    } // implicit call to consumer and producer destructor (wait for termination)
    buf.stop();
} // implicit call to buffer destructor (no tasks using the buffer now)
```

Finally, as mentioned in Sect. 2.2, p. 10, flag variables can normally be eliminated by using advanced control-flow; hence, it should be possible to remove the done flag in the previous example. However, to remove the flag variable requires a control-flow extension to the accept statement:

```
_Accept( ... ) statement            // action
```

The addition is a statement after an _Accept clause, which is executed only if that accept clause is triggered by a call. Hence, control flow waits for a call, executes the call, and then executes the statement associated with accept for the called member. Each _Accept clause can have a statement, so each one can detect if it triggers the call. Given this new capability, it is possible to exit the infinite loop with a **break** statement when the stop member is called rather than when a flag is set:

```
    ...
    void stop() {}
  protected:
    void main() {
        for ( ;; ) {
            _Accept( stop ) { break; } // terminate loop on call
            or _When ( count < Size ) _Accept( insert );
            or _When ( count > 0 ) _Accept( remove );
            ...
```

While this approach works, and is essential in certain circumstances (see Sect. 10.10, p. 548), notice that the explicit call to stop occurs immediately before the implicit call to the destructor, which is an unfortunate duplication as both calls are involved in the termination and deallocation of the buffer task. Therefore, the stop routine and destructor are merged with single accept of the destructor:

```
void main() {
    for ( ;; ) {
        _Accept ( ~BoundedBuffer ) { break; }
        or _When (count != Size) _Accept( insert );
        or _When (count != 0) _Accept( remove );
    }
    // clean up code
}
```

Now when the implicit call occurs to the destructor, it is detected by the buffer task and the loop can be exited, the task can clean up (e.g., free storage or close files), and finally the task's thread terminates by returning from the task main. What is happening here is the task calling the destructor and the task accepting the destructor are synchronizing without communicating (i.e., neither stop nor the destructor have parameters nor return a result). The synchronization is sufficient for the called task to know it must terminate.

While accepting the destructor appears to provide a convenient mechanism of informing a task to terminate, there is a problem: the semantics of accepting a mutex member cause the acceptor to block and the caller to execute. Now if the call to the destructor is executed, the destructor completes and the object is deallocated. Hence, the task's thread does not restart to finish the accept statement nor the task main because the task object is deallocated. (This behaviour is similar to deallocating a coroutine that has not terminated.) Therefore, with the current semantics for the accept statement it is impossible for the task's thread to restart and perform clean up in the task main because it is deallocated immediately after accepting the destructor. As a result, all clean up is forced into the destructor. However, this restriction may force variables that logically belong in the task's main into the task, making these variables have a greater visibility than is necessary from a software engineering standpoint. Furthermore, the fact that control does not return to the _Accept statement when the destructor is accepted seems confusing, as that is what occurs in all other cases.

To solve this problem, the semantics for accepting a destructor are different from accepting a normal mutex member. When the destructor is accepted, the caller is blocked and pushed onto the acceptor/signalled stack instead of the acceptor. Therefore, control restarts at the accept statement *without* executing the destructor, which allows a task to clean up before it terminates. When it terminates, the call to the destructor is popped off the acceptor/signalled stack (remember it is at the top of the stack) by the implicit scheduling and the destructor executes followed by the deallocation of the storage. Interestingly, the semantics for accepting the destructor are the same as for a signal (see page 460), where the acceptor task is the signaller task and the task calling the destructor is the signalled task.

One common error made with task termination is for a destructor call, intended as a signal to stop a task, to occur too early in a computation. Once accepted, the task's thread can terminate and then the task is deallocated, all before the computation is complete, which almost always results in an error. This problem is demonstrated by modifying the example using the stop routine to:

```
{
    BoundedBuffer buf;
    Consumer cons( buf );      // pass buffer to consumer task
    Producer prod( buf );      // pass buffer to producer task
    buf.stop();                // call too early: cons and prod tasks still executing
} // implicit calls to destructor for prod, cons, and buf (in this order)
```

The previous inner block seems superfluous because deallocation occurs in reverse order to allocation. However, the call to buf.stop() now occurs *before* the calls to the destructor for prod and cons because these calls now occur at the end of the outer block instead of in the middle due to the previous inner block. As a result, the call to the buffer's destructor can occur while the producer and consumer tasks are using the buffer, which results in the buffer terminating and cleaning up, becoming a monitor, and most likely failing thereafter when used again by a producer or consumer. (In fact, the bounded-buffer task using internal scheduling does work correctly in this scenario but the external scheduling version does not. Why does one work and the other not work?) Interestingly, the previous example does work correctly if the bounded-buffer task accepts its destructor instead of using the stop member, as in:

```
{
    BoundedBuffer buf;
    Consumer cons( buf );      // pass buffer to consumer task
    Producer prod( buf );      // pass buffer to producer task
} // implicit calls to destructor for prod, cons, and buf
```

The reason is the destructor for the bounder-buffer task is called last on block exit so it cannot be deallocated until after the producer and consumer have finished using it.

However, it is still possible to generate a problem scenario when accepting the destructor. One common mistake is to have the consumer and/or producer task accept its destructor in order to know when to stop production and/or consumption. Again, the problem is that the call to the destructor occurs immediately at the end of the block in which the producer and consumer are declared, possibly before the task's main starts execution. As a result, the first call accepted is the destructor call, so the tasks terminate without having done any work. Only if there is a delay *before* the end of the block can the producer and consumer make progress, as in:

```
{
    BoundedBuffer buf;
    Consumer cons( buf );      // pass buffer to consumer task
    Producer prod( buf );      // pass buffer to producer task
    // delay for some period of time
} // implicit calls to destructor for prod, cons, and buf
```

The problem with this approach is that after the time delay, both the producer and consumer may accept their destructors immediately, and as a result, the consumer does not have the opportunity to clean out all the elements in the buffer before it is deleted, which may result in an error. To ensure the buffer is emptied, the consumer has to check the buffer state in its clean up code at the end of its task main, and continue processing data until the buffer state becomes empty.

Another way to generate a problem scenario is with dynamic allocation, as in:

```
{
    BoundedBuffer *buf = new BoundedBuffer;
    Consumer *cons = new Consumer( buf );
    Producer *prod = new Producer( buf );
    delete buf;
    delete cons;
    delete prod;
}
```

Here the order of deallocation is the same at the order of allocation, instead of the reverse order (as at the end of a block). As a result, the destructor for the buffer is called immediately, and it terminates without having been used or in the middle of usage by the producer and consumer.

10.7   When a Task Becomes a Monitor

As discussed in Sect. 10.1, p. 523, the mutual-exclusion property of a type is independent of whether the type has an associated thread. Interestingly, if a task's thread waits or terminates, the task can continue to be used. When the task's thread is blocked or terminated, the object still exists with the mutex property but no associated thread, so it becomes a monitor. (In a similar way, when a coroutine terminates it becomes a class-object because the execution state is no longer accessible.) Now when the task's thread blocks or terminates, the object is inactive and its implicit scheduling attempts to first start a task on the acceptor/signaller stack and then from the entry queue. As mentioned, the destructor of a mutex object is always mutex; so an implicit call to the destructor can be waiting on the entry queue. As for a monitor, if there are tasks blocked on conditions, or the acceptor/signaller stack, or the entry queue, the destructor can still be invoked if the task's thread waits. However, since the task's thread must be blocked on a condition queue associated with the task, an error is generated because the destructor cannot complete while threads are blocked in the task. The destructor can use blocking signals to wake the blocked threads, and hence, deal with this case.

As mentioned, it is rare for a task to only use internal scheduling, but it is possible by cheating: let the task's thread terminate or block so the task becomes a monitor, then use monitor internal scheduling techniques. The following are modifications to the bounder-buffer task in Fig. 10.7, p. 538 so only internal scheduling is used:

```
... _Task BoundedBuffer {          ... _Task BoundedBuffer {
    ...                                ...
                                       uCondition cheating;
  public:                            public:
    ...                                ...
                                       ~BoundedBuffer() { cheating.signalBlock(); }
  protected:                         protected:
    void main() {                      void main() {
        // no code                         cheating.wait();
    }                                  }
};                                 };
```

In the left program, the accept statement has been removed from the task main so when the thread starts, it immediately terminates, changing the task into a monitor. This solution is now identical to the monitor solution using internal scheduling except for the unnecessary expense of creating an execution state and starting and terminating a thread, neither of which are used. In the right program, the accept statement has been replaced with a wait, so when the thread starts, it immediately blocks changing the task into a monitor. The solution is now identical to the monitor solution using internal scheduling, except the bounded-buffer's thread must be restarted in the destructor so that it can terminate before the destructor can complete. This unblocking is accomplished using a signalBlock because the task executing the destructor must wait until the signalled task completes (and terminates). Both cases cheat because they convert the task to a monitor for its entire lifetime, which begs the question of why use a task in the first place.

10.8 Task Details

Like a class and coroutine, the qualifiers **_Mutex** and **_Nomutex** can qualify the **_Task** definition, as well as the **private, protected** and **public** member routines. When the **_Mutex** qualifier is placed on a **_Task** definition, it indicates all public member routines have the mutual-exclusion property, unless overridden on specific member routines with the **_Nomutex** qualifier. When the **_Nomutex** qualifier is placed on a **_Task** definition, it indicates all public member routines have the no-mutual-exclusion property, unless overridden on specific member routines with the **_Mutex** qualifier. The default for a task if no qualifier is specified is **_Mutex** because the mutual-exclusion property for public members is typically needed.

```
_Mutex _Task T1 {                       _Nomutex class T2 {
    ...                                     ...
  public:                                 public:
    void mem1() ...      // mutex           void mem1() ...      // no mutex
    _Nomutex void mem2() ... // no mutex    _Mutex void mem2() ... // mutex
    ~T1() ...            // mutex           ~T2() ...            // mutex
}                                       }
```

Since a task always has the mutual-exclusion property, it means, like a monitor, a task always has one mutex member, its destructor, and a task's destructor cannot be qualified with **_Nomutex**.

10.8.1 Accept Statement

The basic structure of the accept statement is presented in Sect. 9.6.2, p. 457. The following are additional capabilities.

The simple form of the **_Accept** statement is:

```
_When ( conditional-expression )                // optional guard
    _Accept( mutex-member-name-list );
```

with the restriction that constructors, **new, delete** and **_Nomutex** members are excluded from being accepted. The first three member routines are excluded because these routines are essentially part of the implicit memory-management runtime support. That is, the object does not exist until after the **new** routine is completed and a constructor starts; similarly, the object does not exist after **delete** is called. In all these cases, member routines cannot be called, and hence accepted, because the object does not exist or is not initialized. **_Nomutex** members are excluded because they contain no code affecting the caller or acceptor with respect to mutual exclusion.

A **_When** guard is considered true if it is omitted or if its *conditional-expression* evaluates to non-zero. The *conditional-expression* of a **_When** may call a routine, *but the routine must not block or context switch.* The guard must be true and an outstanding call to the specified mutex member(s) must exist for a call to be accepted. If there are several mutex members that can be accepted, selection priority is established by the left-to-right placement of the mutex members in the **_Accept** clause of the statement. Hence, the order of the mutex members in the **_Accept** clause indicates their relative priority for selection if there are several outstanding calls. If the guard is true and there is no outstanding call to the specified member(s), the acceptor is accept-blocked until a call to the appropriate member(s) is made. If the guard is false, execution continues without accepting any call; in this case, the guard is the same as an **if** statement, e.g.:

```
_When ( count == 0 ) _Accept( mem );   ≡  if ( count == 0 ) _Accept( mem );
```

Note, an accept statement with a true guard accepts only one call, regardless of the number of mutex members listed in the **_Accept** clause.

The extended form of the **_Accept** statement conditionally accepts one of a group of mutex members and then allows a specific action to be performed *after* the mutex member is called, e.g.:

```
_When ( conditional-expression )                // optional guard
    _Accept( mutex-member-name-list )
        statement                                // action
or _When ( conditional-expression )             // optional guard
    _Accept( mutex-member-name-list )
        statement                                // action
or
    ...
    ...
_When ( conditional-expression )                // optional guard
    else                                         // optional terminating clause
        statement
```

Before an **_Accept** clause is executed, its guard must be true and an outstanding call to its corresponding member(s) must exist. If there are several mutex members that can be accepted, selection priority is established by the left-to-right, then top-to-bottom placement of the mutex members in the **_Accept** clauses of the statement. If some accept guards are true and there are no outstanding calls to these members, the task is accept-blocked until a call to one of these members is made. If all the accept guards are false, the statement does nothing, unless there is a terminating _Else clause with a true guard, which is executed instead. Hence, the terminating _Else clause allows a conditional attempt to accept a call without the acceptor blocking. Again, a group of _Accept clauses is not the same as a group of if statements, e.g.:

```
if ( Ci ) _Accept( Mi );              _When ( Ci ) _Accept( Mi );
else if ( Cj ) _Accept( Mj );         or _When ( Cj ) _Accept( Mj );
```

The left example accepts only M_i if C_i is true or only M_j if C_i is false and C_j is true. The right example accepts either M_i or M_j if C_i and C_j are true. Once the accepted call has completed *or the caller waits*, the statement after the accepting _Accept clause is executed and the accept statement is complete.

10.9 When to Create a Task

While the example of the bounded-buffer task allowed many of the "dos and don'ts" of a task with public members to be illustrated, it is not a good example of when to use a task. A task is largely inappropriate for a bounded-buffer because the thread of the bounded-buffer task has no work to do with respect to management of the buffer. In fact, the task thread slows down the entire process by alternating execution between calling tasks, and yet does nothing when it restarts.

Fig. 10.8 shows that it is possible to move some of the buffer administration from the member routines into the task main. Notice members insert and remove now contain the absolute minimum of code needed to deliver or retrieve an element to/from the buffer. Therefore, the producer and consumer now do less work in the buffer, and hence, can spend more time producing or consuming elements, respectively. However, the buffer management work has not disappeared; it has been moved into the accept statement in the buffer's task main. When the buffer's thread restarts after accepting a call, it performs the appropriate buffer management work for the particular call that was accepted. Now the buffer is actually doing some useful work each time through the loop. Thus, on a multiprocessor computer, there would be a slight speedup because there is now additional concurrency in the program resulting in increased parallelism, i.e., the production and consumption of elements overlaps with the buffer management.

Unfortunately, the amount of additional concurrency generated by executing two lines of buffer management by another task is insufficient to cover the cost of the blocking and unblocking of the buffer's thread for each call to the buffer. In other words, the administrative cost is greater than the cost of having the tasks do the work themselves. People constantly have to perform this kind of cost-benefit analysis in their lives: do you hire someone to get work done faster, or is it faster to work a little more and do the work yourself? The next chapter explores this question in detail.

```
template<typename ELEMTYPE> _Task BoundedBuffer {
    ...
public:
    ...
    void insert( ELEMTYPE elem ) {
        Elements[back] = elem;
    }
    ELEMTYPE remove() {
        return Elements[front];
    }
protected:
    void main() {
        for ( ;; ) {
            _When ( count < Size ) _Accept( insert ) {
                back = (back + 1) % Size;
                count += 1;
            } or _When ( count > 0 ) _Accept( remove ) {
                front = (front + 1) % Size;
                count -= 1;
            }
        }
    }
};
```

Fig. 10.8   Task bounded buffer: performing work

10.10   Producer-Consumer Problem

Fig. 10.9 shows a task based solution for the producer-consumer problem derived
from the full-coroutine version in Fig. 4.18, p. 160. Because information flows bidirectionally between the producer and consumer, a communication cycle is required,
which necessitates mutual references. The mutual reference is accomplished using
the approach mentioned in Sect. 4.8.2, p. 152, that is, pass the final partner after the
other task is instantiated, which is accomplished through the Prod::start member.

Both producer and consumer tasks start execution after their declaration. The
producer task's main immediately accepts its start member to obtain the number of
elements it is to produce and its consumer partner. The main member executes N
iterations of generating two random integer values between 0–99, printing the two
values, calling the consumer to deliver the two values, accepting the payment, and
printing the status returned from the consumer.

The call from the producer to the consumer's delivery routine transfers the
generated values. When a call to delivery is accepted, it is the producer task,
prod, executing the member. The values delivered by the producer are copied into
communication variables in the consumer and the producer blocks on a conditional
variable (internal scheduling). The blocking restarts cons where it accepts delivery
so it can examine the transferred values and prepare a status value to be returned.

The consumer task's main member iterates accepting calls to either its stop
or delivery members. The stop member is used solely for synchronization so it
contains no code. After accepting a call to the stop member, the loop terminates.
After accepting a call to the delivery member, the delivered values are printed,

```
_Task Cons {                              _Task Prod {
    uCondition check;                         Cons *cons;        // communication
    Prod &prod;        // communication       int N, money, receipt;
    int p1, p2, status;                       void main() {
    void main() {                                 int i, p1, p2, status;
        int money = 1, receipt;                   _Accept( start );
        for ( ;; ) {                              for ( i = 1; i <= N; i += 1 ) {
            _Accept( stop ) {                         p1 = rand() % 100;
                break;                                p2 = rand() % 100;
            } or _Accept( delivery ) {                cout << "prod delivers: " <<
                cout << "cons receives: " <<              p1 << ", " << p2 << endl;
                    p1 << ", " << p2;                 status = cons->delivery( p1, p2 );
                status += 1;                          _Accept( payment );
                check.signalBlock();                  cout << "prod status: " <<
                cout << " and pays $" <<                  status << endl;
                    money << endl;                }
                receipt = prod.payment( money );  cons->stop();
                cout << "cons receipt #" <<        cout << "prod stops" << endl;
                    receipt << endl;          }
                money += 1;                   public:
            }                                     Prod() : receipt(0) {}
        }                                         int payment( int money ) {
        cout << "cons stops" << endl;                 Prod::money = money;
    }                                                 cout << "prod payment of $" <<
    public:                                               money << endl;
    Cons( Prod &p ) : prod(p), status(0) {}           receipt += 1;
    int Cons::delivery( int p1, int p2 ) {            return receipt;
        Cons::p1 = p1; Cons::p2 = p2;             }
        check.wait(); // let cons check elements  void start( int N, Cons &c ) {
        return status;                                Prod::N = N; cons = &c;
    }                                             }
    void stop() {}                            };
};                                            void uMain::main() {
                                                  Prod prod;
                                                  Cons cons( prod );
                                                  prod.start( 5, cons );
                                              }
```

Fig. 10.9 Bidirectional task: producer-consumer

the return status is incremented, and the consumer task signals the producer to restart so the producer can return the status. A signalBlock is used to ensure the producer is restarted immediately. The consumer restarts after the producer exits the delivery member, prints the amount it pays for the values, calls back to the producer's payment member with the money, prints the receipt from the producer and increments the amount of money for the next payment.

The delivery member returns the status value to the call in prod's main member, where the status is printed. The loop then repeats calling delivery, where each call is accepted by the consumer task. When the consumer restarts, it continues in the statement after **_Accept**(delivery). The consumer restarts the producer and calls prod's payment, where these calls only restart the producer after the member exits, not during the member, as for delivery. These operations must be done in this order, otherwise the call to payment results in a mutual-exclusion deadlock as prod's thread is blocked on condition check preventing calls to prod.

After iterating N times, the producer calls the stop member in cons. Notice, member stop is being accepted along with delivery each time through the loop in Cons::main. When the call is accepted, the producer exits immediately. The consumer then continues terminating its loop, prints a termination message and exits the main member terminating the consumer's thread, which makes it a monitor so its destructor is now accepted. The producer also continues, prints a termination message and exits its main member terminating the producer's thread, which makes it a monitor so its destructor is now accepted. Task uMain is restarted as it was previously blocked on calls to the destructors of the producer and consumer, which are now accepted. uMain then deallocates the producer and consumer, and exits its main member.

The consumer uses a stop member instead of accepting its destructor because the call to its destructor occurs too early (in uMain). Accepting the destructor could have been used if the producer created the consumer instead of uMain; however, such restructuring is not always possible. The producer does not need a stop member or to accept its destructor because it is self-terminating.

10.11   Tasks and Coroutines

It is a common mistake to assume a coroutine created by a task is owned by it and only that task can use it. In fact, any coroutine can be "passed off" to another task. The only requirement is that only one task use the coroutine at a time. To ensure mutual execution of coroutine execution, the passing around of a coroutine must involve some form of cooperation such that only one task uses the coroutine at a time. Alternatively, the coroutine can be made a coroutine-monitor to provide mutual exclusion. However, the cost in locking and unlocking the coroutine-monitor may be unnecessary if serial usage cooperation can be established.

In Chap. 4, p. 125, a weak equivalence is demonstrated between a coroutine and a routine or class. There is also a weak equivalence between a coroutine and a task, because both have a separate execution state for their distinguished member. However, simulating a coroutine with a task is non-trivial because the organizational structure of a coroutine and a task are different. Furthermore, simulating full coroutines that form a cyclic call-graph may be impossible with tasks because a task's mutual exclusion may disallow multiple entries by the same task causing deadlock. Finally, a task is inefficient for this purpose because of the higher cost of switching both a thread and execution state as opposed to just an execution state. In μC++ , the cost of communication with a coroutine is, in general, less than half the cost of communication with a task, unless the communication is dominated by transferring large amounts of data.

```
_Task Base {                          _Task Derived {
    ...                                   ...
    void main() {                         void main() {
        ...                                   ...
        _Accept( m1 ) s1;                     _Accept( m1 ) s1'; // different s1
        or _When( c1 ) _Accept( m2 ) s2;      or _When( c1 ) _Accept( m2 ) s2;
        ...                                   or _Accept( m3 ) s3;
                                              ...
    }                                     }
public:                               public:
    void m1(...) {...}                    void m2(...) {...}   // override
    void m2(...) {...}                    void m3(...) {...}   // add
};                                    };
```

Fig. 10.10   Inheritance anomaly

10.12   Inheritance Anomaly Problem

For class, coroutine, monitor and coroutine-monitor it is possible to inherit from one another to establish different kinds of reuse, i.e., subtyping and implementation. When monitors and tasks inherit from one another there is a problem, called the inheritance anomaly.

> Inheritance anomaly arises when additional methods of a subclass cause undesirable re-definitions of the methods in the superclass. Instead of being able to incrementally add code in a subclass the programmer may be required to re-define some inherited code, thus the benefits of inheritance are lost [3, p. 571].

Matsuoka and Yonezawa [4] present the first major discussion on the inheritance anomaly with respect to concurrency. The anomaly often refers to problems reusing synchronization control between a base (super) class and an inheriting derived (sub) class. As members are replaced or added, it is crucial they be correctly synchronized with respect to existing concurrent behaviour. The inheritance anomaly does exist and hinders reuse. Finally, the inheritance anomaly problem is similar to the lock composability problem where locks are nested because of subroutine calls, e.g., the nested monitor problem (see Sect. 9.9, p. 471).

In μC++, this problem results from the need to add control actions in constructors and/or main member, which precludes actions in the subclass or causes duplication of code in the subclass's main member. Fig. 10.10 shows a basic inheritance anomaly and illustrates how synchronization code must be copies. The derived class overrides member m2 and adds member m3. The derived task main must override the task main of the base class because it does not accept the new member m3. Hence, the synchronization component of the base task's main must be copied into the derived task's main so it can be augmented and extended. Any unnecessary code duplication is always a maintenance problem. The base class can mitigate the problem by making the _When conditions into boolean members and the statements after the _Accept clauses into members, so the derived class can reuse these routine in its _Accept clauses. However, this refactoring is very fine grain.

Note, the inheritance anomaly occurs in any inheritance system, and is not specific to concurrency [1, § 7]. When a base-class's member routine is overridden, it is impossible for the derived class to reuse the base-class's code unless it is only wrapping the code. For example, a change to internal code requires copying:

```
void base::m2(...) {
    ...
    if ( j > 5 ) ...
    ...
}
```

If the derived class needs to adjust the **if** statement to

```
    if ( j > 5 && k < 20 ) ..
```

it must copy all the code.

It is important to put the inheritance anomaly into perspective. It has been noted (see [2] and others) that only about 20–30 % of all classes are ever inherited from, that the depth of inheritance is usually quite shallow (e.g. two to three levels), and that the need for multiple inheritance is at the interface (type) level. That is to say, most software systems are composed of many private classes used for implementation purposes, and only a small number of public classes are used by clients. Furthermore, most clients only use the public classes directly rather than extending them for specialization purposes. This observation mitigates to some extent the scale of the inheritance anomaly by limiting the amount of re-specification by inheriting classes. Nevertheless, there is a real problem, and it does preclude reuse.

In summary, the inheritance anomaly is a reuse problem, which is practically insolvable. Next, the inheritance anomaly is not specifically a concurrency problem, it just happens to occur when attempting to reuse synchronization. Any attempt at a complete solution to the inheritance anomaly requires the ability to replace virtually any component along the inheritance chain, as well as storing and restoring inherited state. Such generality may require all accesses to occur through pointers, which quickly becomes runtime expensive, and that all storage be accessible, which may violate abstraction. While a reasonable effort should be made to mitigate the inheritance anomaly, the problem will always remain. Nevertheless, it is a problem people feel compelled to solve, especially with respect to concurrency, and it is often incorrectly used as the sole criterion to judge the quality of a synchronization mechanism in a concurrent programming language.

10.13   Summary

A concurrent system needs two forms of communication, indirect and direct, to handle two different kinds of interactions among tasks. In direct communication, a task calls another task's member routine, which implies a task needs the mutex property to prevent simultaneous access of its data by the calling thread and the task's thread. Because a task has the mutex property, it also has the capability to schedule calls to it using external scheduling and calling tasks within it using internal scheduling. Accepting the destructor of a task is a useful mechanism for knowing when a task should stop executing.

10.14 Questions

1. What is an *active object*?
2. What are the three basic execution properties?
3. Fill in each of the entries with the different kinds of object type available in μC++. Put "N/A" in any box that does not have an associated kind of object type in μC++.

	No Mutual Exclusion / No Synchronization	Mutual Exclusion / Synchronization
No Stack / No Thread	**class**	
Stack / No Thread		
Stack / Thread		

4. In Table 10.1, p. 525, explain why cases 5 and 6 are rejected, and case 7 is potentially rejected.
5. Explain the difference between *indirect* and *direct* communication among tasks, and explain why both are necessary.
6. Why is blocking often unnecessary for indirect communication?
7. For a monitor and task, after creation, what is the status of the mutex members (i.e., open or closed)?
8. What is a *rendezvous* in direct communication?
9. In μC++, which thread processes the message for a rendezvous and why?
10. What purpose does the _**When** clause provide on an _**Accept** clause?
11. The following _**Accept** statement is used by a task implementing a bounded buffer:

```
_When ( count != Size ) _Accept( insert );
or _When ( count != 0 ) _Accept( remove );
```

Explain in detail how this statement works and what it does.
12. What would happen in the previous _**Accept** statement if both _**When** clauses could be false?
13. Why can only _**Mutex** members be accepted?
14. Are the following two statements equivalent to each other?

```
_When ( a > b ) _Accept( mem );
if ( a > b ) _Accept( mem );
```

15. Remove the _**When** clauses from this single _**Accept** statement by transforming it into multiple **if/else** and _**Accept** statements, while retaining the same execution behaviour:

```
    _When ( C1 ) _Accept( A );
    or _When ( C2 ) _Accept( B );
    or _When ( C3 ) _Accept( C );
```

16. Given the following accept statement:

    ```
    _Accept( A );
    or _Accept( B );
    _Else ...;
    ```

    a. What priority is implied, with respect to accepting calls?
    b. Is there a way to recode this as to make it fair?
    c. If the **or** is removed, explain the behaviour of the statements.
    d. When should the **_Else** clause be present?
    e. Why is the **_Else** clause potentially dangerous?

17. μC++ implicitly starts a task's thread after its constructors are executed. Java requires explicit starting of a task's thread after its constructors are executed by calling the start member.

μC++	Java
Tasktype t;	Tasktype t;
// thread starts implicitly	t.start(); *// thread starts explicitly*

    Show how to mimic the Java behaviour in μC++.

18. Explain two ways a task can become a monitor during execution.
19. Explain why accepting a task's destructor is a useful capability.
20. What is unusual about accepting the destructor in μC++?
21. Consider the following code fragment. How can it be changed to improve concurrency?

    ```
    _Task BoundedBuffer {
        void main() {
            ... _Accept( insert ); ...
        }
      public:
        void insert( int elem ) {
            buffer[pos] = elem;
            count += 1;
            pos = (pos + 1) % size;
        }
    };
    ```

22. Assume a series of nested accepts has occurred in a task so there are several tasks blocked on the acceptor/signalled stack. Now the task accepts the destructor. Show how tasks below the task accepting the destructor on the acceptor/signalled stack can be released so the task's destructor terminates without error.
23. If a task creates a coroutine, does it own that coroutine object, i.e., does the creating task have mutually exclusive access to the coroutine?
24. Write a program that plays the following simple card game. Each player takes a number of cards from a deck of cards and passes the deck to the player on the left. A player must take at least one card and no more than a certain maximum. The player who takes the last card wins.

Each player is a task with the following interface (you may add only a public destructor and private members):

```
_Task player {
. public:
    player();
    void start( player &partner );
    void play( int deck );
};
```

Member start is called after creation to supply the player on the left. Member play is called by a player's partner to pass on the remaining deck of cards after a play has made a play. Task uMain starts the game by passing the deck of cards to one of the players, and that player begins the game.

Write a program that plays 3 games sequentially (i.e., one game after the other, not 3 concurrent games). For each game, generate a random number of players in the range from 2 to 8 inclusive, and a random number of cards in the deck in the range from 20 to 52 inclusive. Have each player follow the simple strategy of taking a random number of cards in the range from 1 to 5 (i.e., do not get fancy).

The output should show a dynamic display of the game in progress. That is, which task is taking its turn, how many cards it received from the player on the right and how many cards it took. At the end of each game, make sure that all tasks terminate.

Use only direct communication among the players for task communication, i.e., no monitors or semaphores.

25. Consider a vault protected by three locks A, B and C, each operated by its own unique key. Suppose there are the same number of guards as keys, and each guard carries a single key for the corresponding lock A, B and C, respectively. Each of the guards must periodically enter the vault alone to verify that nothing has been stolen. A supervisor possesses one copy of each key, but never leaves her office.

To enter the vault, each guard must request from the supervisor each of the two additional keys needed to enter the vault, but may request only one key at a time. The supervisor replies to a key request when that key is available. Once in possession of all three keys, a guard checks the vault and returns the two borrowed keys one at a time. The supervisor only receives requests for keys, and each guard only makes requests to the supervisor for keys.

Write a μC++ program that simulates the above scenario. The supervisor has the following user interface:

```
_Task Supervisor {
    public:
    void get( int who, int key );
    void put( int who, int key );
};
```

A guard calls member get, passing who they are (a value in the range 0 to $(N - 1)$, where N is the number of keys to open the vault), and the value of the key they are trying to get from the supervisor (a value in the range 0 to

($N-1$), where N is the number of keys to open the vault). A guard calls member put, passing who they are and the value of the key they are returning to the supervisor. The guard has the following user interface:

```
_Task Guard {
    int who;
    Supervisor &super;

    void CheckVault() {
        yield( rand() % 20 );
    }
    void CoffeeBreak() {
        yield( rand() % 20 );
    }
public:
    Guard( int who, Supervisor &super ) : who(who), super(super) {}
};
```

Each guard is started with the value of who they are (a value in the range 0 to ($N-1$), where N is the number of keys to open the vault), and a reference to the supervisor. A guard enters the vault 10 times, each time acquiring the necessary $N-1$ keys. When a guard has the keys needed to check the vault, the routine CheckVault() is called. After checking the vault, the guard returns the $N-1$ keys and calls CoffeeBreak().

You must devise a solution that the guards follow so they do not deadlock (any solution is allowed as long as it is not grossly inefficient). (Hint: use a simple solution discussed in the notes.) Explain why your solution is deadlock free.

26. Willy, Wally, Wesley and Warren are four workers on an assembly line. Each has their own position on the line and each does one step in the assembly of some product. Sally is the supervisor of the assembly line, and her responsibility is to move the assembly line forward one position when all of the workers are finished with the work that is currently at their position. Willy, Wally, Wesley and Warren each (independently) tell Sally when they are finished with their work (ready for the line to move).

Ian is a roving inspector who checks to see if the workers are doing their work properly. When Ian wishes to do an inspection, he sends a message to Sally and gets back a list of workers who are finished with the work at their station. (If no workers are finished at the time Ian wants to inspect them, then Sally waits until at least two are finished before responding to Ian's message.) Then Ian randomly chooses one of these finished workers, goes to their position and inspects their work. NOTE: During an inspection, the line is NOT allowed to move. After the inspection, Ian reports his findings to Sally. If Ian is unsatisfied with the work, Sally must inform the appropriate worker to re-do the job before allowing the assembly line to move.

As a real-world analogue, think of a car assembly line with 4 workers installing 4 doors on a car. A car appears in front of Willy, Wally, Wesley and Warren at essentially the same time and they start installing the doors. The car cannot move until the doors are all on the car and Sally is told this. As soon as

Sally moves the car forward, a new car appears in front of Willy, Wally, Wesley and Warren for them to work on. You may assume that Willy, Wally, Wesley and Warren never have to wait for doors after a car appears in front of them. Ian is walking up and down the car assembly line, stopping at different stations to inspect the work.

Simulate the assembly line. Willy, Wally, Wesley, Warren, Sally and Ian are all tasks. All communication between tasks must be direct. To simulate the time required by a worker to do his work, have the worker pick a random N between 10 and 15, and then yield(N). To simulate the time required by Ian to do his work, have him pick a random M between 5 and 10, and then yield(M). Assume that in each inspection, there is a 75 % chance that Ian will be satisfied with the work. Note that if Ian is not satisfied, he demands that the work be re-done but does not re-check it afterwards. After each inspection, Ian takes a coffee break before doing the next inspection. Simulate the coffee break by having Ian pick a random B between 30 and 50 and then yield(B). The simulation ends after the assembly line has moved forward some given number of times, say 50.

Test your simulation thoroughly and explain your tests. Feel free to change the parameters (e.g., coffee break delay time) to aid in your testing.

NOTE: Do not generate large amounts of output. Part of your job is to produce concise test cases and present them in a nice way. This means every task cannot just print what it is doing.

27. Define a *polynomial* with integer coefficients as the infinite sequence

$$(a_0, a_1, a_2, \ldots)$$

where $a_i \in \mathcal{Z}$ and only a finite number of the a_i are not zero, i.e. the degree is finite.

Equality and addition are defined for polynomials as follows:

$$(a_0, a_1, a_2, \ldots) = (b_0, b_1, b_2, \ldots) \Leftrightarrow a_i = b_i \ \forall i \geq 0$$

$$(a_0, a_1, a_2, \ldots) \oplus (b_0, b_1, b_2, \ldots) = (a_0 + b_0, a_1 + b_1, a_2 + b_2, \ldots)$$

Multiplication is defined by the rule:

$$(a_0, a_1, a_2, \ldots) \otimes (b_0, b_1, b_2, \ldots) = (c_0, c_1, c_2, \ldots)$$

where

$$c_0 = a_0 b_0$$
$$c_1 = a_0 b_1 + a_1 b_0$$
$$c_2 = a_0 b_2 + a_1 b_1 + a_2 b_0$$
$$\vdots$$
$$c_n = a_0 b_n + a_1 b_{n-1} + a_2 b_{n-2} + \cdots + a_{n-1} b_1 + a_n b_0$$

a. Expressing c_n using summation notation aids in program design.
b. Write a concurrent program named polyp to calculate the product, $A \otimes B$, of two polynomials, using a task for each c_n calculation. The public task interface is:

```
_Task Coeff {
  public:
    Coeff( int polyA[ ], int polyB[ ], int n, int sizeA,
           int sizeB, int &Cn ); // Cn is nth coefficient of product AB
};
```

The shell interface of the program is

```
polyp [-c] fileA fileB
```

Each of the two file arguments contains a sequence of integers for the polynomial coefficients, separated by whitespace (i.e., blanks, tabs or newlines). The sequence starts with the total number of integers in the file, followed by integers for the coefficients, ordered by increasing subscript index (i.e., n a_0 a_1 etc.).

uMain of polyp writes the product polynomial to standard output using the same sequence format, i.e., number of coefficients followed by the coefficient numbers (i.e., m c_0 c_1 etc). Use a single blank character to separate numbers.

The option -c writes all the polynomials, operands and product, to standard output in three columns:

$$a_0 \; b_0 \; c_0$$
$$a_1 \; b_1 \; c_1$$
$$\cdot \quad \cdot \quad \cdot$$

Assume there are no errors in the input files (files are not empty and the number of coefficients is correct and at least one) and all command line information is error free (files exist and are readable or writable).

28. Sequentially searching an array A of N unique integer elements for the minimum value takes time $O(N)$. When there are N^2 processors available, the search time can be reduced to $O(1)$, not counting I/O or processor start-up time. This reduction is accomplished by using N "teams" of N processors and a strike-out array, S, of size N initialized to contain ones. $team_i$ is responsible for crossing-out element A_i as a candidate for the minimum. Within $team_i$, processor $p_{i,j}$ for $1 <= j <= N$, compares A_j to A_i. If A_j is smaller, A_i is crossed out by placing a zero in S_i. Assume the parallel hardware allows concurrent writes to the same memory location. The values are output by having N of the processors, $p_{i,1}$ for $1 <= i <= N$, examine S_i and A_i. If $S_i = 1$, then $p_{i,1}$ outputs A_i. Hence, the minimum value is output in time $O(1)$.

a. Even if processors are cheap, this approach is neither algorithmically nor processor efficient. Examine the algorithm and explain why it is inefficient.

Then, describe a more efficient algorithm, explaining why it is more efficient, how many processors it uses and what each processor does.

b. Write a concurrent μC++ program which implements your improved algorithm from a..

The cross-out task has the following public interface (you may add only a public destructor and private members):

```
_Task CrossOut {
  public:
    CrossOut( choose suitable parameters );
};
```

The executable program is to be named minimum and has the following shell interface:

```
minimum input-file [output-file]
```

- If the input file is not specified, print an appropriate usage message and terminate. The input file contains lists of integer values where each list contains unique elements. Each list starts with the number of values in that list. For example, the input file:

```
8 25 6 8 -5 99 100 101 7
3 1 -3 5
0
10 9 3 7 6 0 4 8 1 2 5
```

contains 4 lists with 8, 3, 0 and 10 values in each list. (The line breaks are for readability only; values can be separated by any white-space character.) Read a list of values into an array (only one list at a time should be read in). You must handle an arbitrary number of values in a list. (HINT: GNU C++ allows arrays to be dynamically dimensioned.)

You may assume there are no errors in the input file and a file always contains at least one number.

- If no output file name is specified, use standard output. Print the original input list followed by the minimum value in the list, as in:

```
25 6 8 -5 99 100 101 7
Minimum is: -5

1 -3 5
Minimum is: -3

Warning! No minimum. List of length 0.

9 3 7 6 0 4 8 1 2 5
Minimum is: 0
```

for the previous input file.

Assume all command line information is error free, e.g., files exist and are readable/writable.

The entire program can be written in approximately 100 lines.

c. Do duplicate input values cause any trouble in achieving the stated timing for finding and printing a single minimum number? If so, can the algorithm be fixed? Explain both replies.

d. The "cross-out" approach can also be used to solve the problem of searching an array of N elements in parallel for a particular value and printing its location. If the array contains duplicate values, what problem has just been introduced? Explain one way to solve this problem.

All written answers require only brief explanations.

29. Searching can lend itself easily to concurrent execution by partitioning the search data so each partition can be searched independently and concurrently by a task. For example, a search engine may use worker tasks to search a set of text files for a user-specified text string (key). The value returned to the user is the line and column number of the key in the file associated with the worker task(s) that locate the string; other worker tasks should stop searching as quickly as possible once the string is found. It is possible for multiple tasks to simultaneously find the string.

Write a concurrent search with the following public interface (you may add only a public destructor and private members):

```
_Task Searcher {
    _Event Stop {};                        // used to stop other searcher tasks
    ...                                    // YOU WRITE THIS CODE
    void main() {
        _Accept( start );                  // wait to be started
        ...                                // YOU WRITE THIS CODE
    }
  public:
    Searcher( const char key[], const char fileName[],
            Searcher *const searchers[], const unsigned int noOfSearchers );
    void start() {};
    void join() {};
};
```

A searcher task is passed a search key and a fileName to search for the presence of the key. In addition, an array containing all the searcher tasks, searchers, and its size, noOfSearchers, is passed.

Each searcher task opens the given file. If the open fails, print an appropriate message and terminate the program; otherwise, read a line of text from the file and check the line for the key text. If the key is not found within a line of text, yield a random number of times between [0–5) before reading and checking the next line to allow progress of other tasks and delivery of nonlocal exceptions. If the key is found, notify the other searching tasks by raising the exception, Stop, at each searcher task. Note, this mechanism to short-circuit the search cannot preclude multiple tasks from finding the key simultaneously and sending duplicate Stop exceptions. The Searcher task should have no dynamic allocation, i.e., no **new**s, and the first line of Searcher::main, i.e., the **_Accept**, is explained later in the course.

The driver creates *all* the searcher tasks, one per search file, and then calls the start member for each task. The driver then calls the join member for each searcher task to wait for their main members to finish searching. Only after *all* calls to the join members have returned, may the searcher tasks be deleted. This two-step protocol ensures a task cannot start before all the tasks are created nor be deleted before an exception is raised at it. (The mechanism that makes this work is explained later in the course.)

The executable program is named searcher and has the following shell interface:

searcher "search-text" file-name1 [file-name2 ...]

Where search-text is the search key followed by a list of file names with a minimum of one name. The search text must be surrounded by quotation marks if it contains whitespace or special characters. The search text may be arbitrarily long, there may be an arbitrarily number of file names, and the lines of text within a file may be arbitrarily long. If no search text and file name is specified, print an appropriate usage message and terminate. The program prints the search results to standard output.

The output must have the form:

% searcher science Alexandre_Dumas Babylon_5 Leonardo_da_Vinci
task 0xa1e70 found string "science" at line 3 column 8 of file Babylon_5
task 0x98c60 stopping search at line 6 of file Leonardo_da_Vinci
task 0xaa070 failed to find string "science" in file Alexandre_Dumas

where the first task found the string, the second task is stopped during its search, and the last task completed its search without finding the string. The line and column numbers start at 1, not 0. You may use different names to identify the tasks.

References

1. Buhr, P.A., Harji, A.S.: Concurrent urban legends. Concurrency Comput. Pract. Exp. **17**(9), 1133–1172 (2005)
2. Cargill, T.A.: Does C++ really need multiple inheritance? In: USENIX C++ Conference Proceedings, pp. 315–323. USENIX Association, San Francisco, California, U.S.A. (1990)
3. Crnogorac, L., Rao, A.S., Ramamohanarao, K.: Classifying inheritance mechanisms in concurrent object-oriented programming. In: Jul, E. (ed.) ECOOP '98–Object-Oriented Programming, *Lecture Notes in Computer Science*, vol. 1445, pp. 571–601. Springer, New York (1998)
4. Matsuoka, S., Yonezawa, A.: Analysis of inheritance anomaly in object-oriented concurrent programming languages. In: Agha, G., Wegner, P., Yonezawa, A. (eds.) Research Directions in Concurrent Object-Oriented Programming, pp. 107–150. MIT Press, New York (1993)

Chapter 11
Enhancing Concurrency

Parallelism occurs when multiple threads execute simultaneously to decrease a program's execution, i.e., the program takes less real (wall-clock) time to complete a computation. The computation must be divided along dimension(s) and these subdivisions are executed asynchronously by the threads. The decrease in execution time is limited by the number of these subdivisions that can be executed simultaneously (see Amdahl's law page 203).

There are many concurrent design patterns that aid in subdividing an algorithm so it can be implemented by multiple threads. Up to this point, many basic patterns have been presented, e.g., locks, barrier, read/write lock, monitor, etc. However, the concurrency discussion has been at the level of programming in the small. That is, how to write small concurrent programs involving a few tasks or how to write fragments of larger concurrency programs. It is now time to examine techniques that are used to construct large concurrent programs.

Every practical concurrent program involves some communication among threads. One thread communicates with another in order to provide inputs (arguments), and/or to receive the output (results) produced by the other thread. If the thread providing the inputs is the same thread that later receives the output, then the communication pattern is analogous to a sequential routine-call, where one routine provides arguments to another and receives the result. A rendezvous call by one thread to a **_Mutex** member of a task is an example of this communication pattern. Such a call is known as a synchronous call because the two tasks must synchronize in order to pass the arguments from caller to callee, and because the caller remains blocked until the callee returns the result.

While a synchronous call is simple and useful, it may limit parallelism because the caller task is forced to block until the result is returned. In some cases there is a subdivision of the computation that the caller task can perform while the callee task is computing the caller's result. In such a case, it is more appropriate to use an asynchronous call. An asynchronous call can be thought of as two synchronous calls, one to provide the inputs and a second one to receive the output, e.g.:

© Springer International Publishing Switzerland 2016   563
P.A. Buhr, *Understanding Control Flow*, DOI 10.1007/978-3-319-25703-7_11

```
callee.start( arg );            // provide arguments
// caller performs other work asynchronously
result = callee.finish();       // obtain result
```

Here, the call to start returns as soon as the arguments are transferred from caller to callee. Computation then proceeds for both the caller and callee, concurrently. In an asynchronous call, the caller and callee are known as the client and server, respectively. Note, the client may still have to block (or poll) at the call to finish, if the server has not yet finished the client's computation. The amount of parallelism that can be obtained in this way depends on the amount of concurrent computation that can be done by the client and server. If there is little concurrency possible, then the overhead of two synchronous calls and creating the server outweighs the benefits gained by any potential parallelism, and a single synchronous call is sufficient.

A client may also have to block when calling the start method to transmit arguments, if the server is performing some other operation at the time of the call. If the server only handles one outstanding asynchronous call at a time from one client task it should always be ready to receive and respond to the start method immediately, minimizing blocking time for the client. Depending on the application it may be necessary to have a more complicated server, one that can manage multiple outstanding asynchronous calls from multiple clients simultaneously. Constructing a server that can handle calls efficiently while minimizing blocking time for clients generally requires additional buffering of arguments and results.

The previous chapter introduced active objects with direct communication, which forms the foundation for high-level concurrent programming in the large. As mentioned, the foundational pattern for active objects is the client/server pattern, where client tasks request a service from a server task. Hence, a concurrent system is divided into those tasks creating/needing work (clients) and those tasks doing the work (servers). A client can be its own server (and vice versa), i.e., the client/server creates some work and then executes the work, or does some work and gives itself the result. However, partitioning tasks allows specialized/secure work generators and work executors. Finally, a client and server can switch roles. For example, a server performing work may need some resource to complete the work, which it requests from another server, and hence, this work request turns the server into a client.

While there are several ways to structure active objects [4], the primary pattern used in this chapter is the *administrator*, based on an anthropomorphic view of process structuring.

> Although some have argued against a strongly anthropomorphic view of process structuring, we think it is essential in the initial stages of problem decomposition and structuring for concurrency or parallelism. There is ample opportunity for establishing mathematical properties and proofs after the structure is chosen. All branches of science and engineering rely heavily on analogies and visualization to prompt insight and intuition, and the closest experience most of us have with collections of asynchronous processes is the organizations of people. Moreover, organizations of people function effectively (through perhaps not ideally) with a much higher degree of parallelism than programs anyone has yet been

able to build. ...The human organization analogy is of considerable help in choosing what processes should be used, what their responsibilities should be, and how they should interact. It even helps in suggesting what information should be communicated between processes, and when they need to synchronize [2, p. 445].

The discussion in this chapter shows how to increase concurrency on both the server and client side of direct communication. The goal is to be able to construct a high-performance concurrent-system that scales to large numbers of tasks for use on many processors.

11.1 Server Side

The reason a client calls a server is to have it perform work. For example, to get a hair cut, the customer brings their hair (client), and the stylist does the specialized work of cutting the hair (server), while the client remains blocked.

```
_Task Customer {                _Task Stylist {
    public:                         public:
                                        void haircut(...) { /* cut hair */ }
        void main() {                   void main() {
            stylist.haircut();              for ( ;; ) _Accept( haircut );
        }                               }
}                               }
```

However, there is no concurrency here because the customer cannot go anywhere or do anything (except chit-chat) during the hair cut. To get concurrency, the customer needs to leave their hair (wig) for the stylist to cut so the customer can do other work asynchronously.

```
_Task Customer {                _Task Stylist {
    public:                         public:
        void main() {                   void haircut(...) { /* drop off wig */ }
            stylist.haircut();          void main() {
            /* do other work */             for ( ;; ) _Accept( haircut ) { /* cut wig */ }
        }                               }
}                               }
```

Notice, this same technique is used in the bounded buffer (see Fig. 10.8, p. 548) to move work done by the producer/consumer tasks into work done by the bounded-buffer task, which allows the buffer clients to return quickly and do other asynchronous work.

Hence, the general server pattern is to take the code in a member routine called by a client and refactor it into two parts: copy in and performing work.

| **No Concurrency** | **Refactor, Some Concurrency** |

```
_Task Server {                  _Task Server {
    public:                         public:
        void mem1(...) { S1 }            void mem1(...) { S1.copy-in }
        void mem2(...) { S2 }            void mem2(...) { S2.copy-in }
        void main() {                   void main() {
            _Accept( mem1 );                _Accept( mem1 ) { S1.work }
            or _Accept( mem2 );             or _Accept( mem2 ) { S2.work };
        }                               }
}                               }
```

There is no concurrency in the left example as the server is blocked while the client does the work. Alternatively, the client can block on a condition variable in the member, which switches back to the server so it can do the work, and then the server unblocks the client. In either case, there is no concurrency, only synchronization because one of the two threads is blocked for the duration of the rendezvous. Some concurrency is possible in the right example if the work can be refactored into administrative (S1.copy-in) and work (S1.work) code, i.e., move code from the member to the statement executed after the accepted member. Now there is a small overlap between client and server because a client gets away earlier, i.e., does not have to wait for the server to complete work, which increases concurrency.

11.1.1 Buffers

The previous technique achieves concurrency by providing a buffer of size one between the client and server where the data is copied in. If a call is made when the buffer is empty, the client and server tasks can execute asynchronously. However, if another client calls while the server is working, the new client blocks until its call is accepted, so there is no concurrency for calls overlapping with work. To allow the caller to get further ahead, a larger buffer is needed to store the arguments of the call until the server can process them. Section 7.5.2, p. 350 shows several ways that generic bounded buffers can be built. Hence, the approach is to use a larger internal buffer so the clients become producers adding work to one end of the buffer to allow many clients to get in and out of the server faster, and the server becomes a consumer removing work from the buffer and performing it. However, there are issues:

- Anytime a buffer is used, a programmer should always check if it is useful. That is, unless the average time for production and consumption is approximately equal with only a small variance, the buffer is either always full or empty, and hence unnecessary.
- Assuming the buffer is useful, the mutex property of a task precludes client calls while the server is working, so clients cannot drop off work and the buffer is back to size one. The server could periodically do a non-blocking accept call, using _Else, while processing requests from the buffer. However, this approach is just polling, which is awkward and may be done too often or too infrequently.

Hence, the current server design does not provide much additional concurrency, even after attempting to extend the design with a buffer. These problems can be handled by changing the server design into an administrator.

11.1.2 Administrator

The only way to get a lot more concurrency is to partition the server into multiple tasks, where each task performs the client work. Then as fast as the work appears from the clients, a new task is spawned to perform that work. Like a *bounded* buffer, it may be reasonable to have a bounded number of server tasks rather than an unbounded number, which means eventually a client call could block. The idea is straightforward, but the implementation has to thought out carefully.

'When a server is refactored in this form it is called an **administrator**, which is used to manage a complex interaction or complex work or both. The key idea in the refactoring is that an administrator does little or no work; its job is to manage. Management means delegating work to others, receiving and checking completed work, and passing completed work on. Hence, an administrator is in a cycle accepting external client calls and managing the work, but *not* doing the work (see Fig. 11.1). An absolute way to know if a server is an administrator is whether it never turns itself into a client by calling another task. The reason the administrator makes no direct calls to other tasks is that these calls may block the administrator. Once the administrator is blocked, it cannot accept more client calls or manage work, so the client calls and management backup, resulting in more blocking, causing a cascade effect that can lead to deadlock. Notice, an administrator may still block waiting for client calls or management work to complete. However, in this case, it is self-blocking, i.e., the administrator blocks itself, versus the administrator is blocked by another server. Once the administrator is blocked by another server, it is at the mercy of that server to unblock it in a timely manner.

The detailed structure of an administrator is complex (see Fig. 11.2). An administrator often has several internal buffers where work/results are stored for management purposes. It also manages a pool of *worker* tasks that actually perform the work. Upon creation, each worker task immediately calls its administrator; the administrator never calls a worker task. The administrator accepts calls from the clients as quickly as possible, and from the worker tasks when it needs to based on its management scheme. In other words, an administrator can block its own workers for as along as it wants. Exactly what a worker does is limited only by the imagination of a programmer. Clearly, a worker is providing a thread for extra concurrency, and that thread can execute any code. However, programmers often write specialized workers for particular jobs rather than having a general worker that passed the kind of work to do (i.e., a pointer to a work routine).

The following is a short list of different kinds of workers an administrator might need to perform its management.

- A timer worker calls into the administrator and asks for a notification time. The administrator accepts the timer call and returns a notification time. When the notification time occurs, the timer calls back to the administrator indicating the time has expired and the administrator can return a new notification time or keep the timer worker blocked until it is necessary to return a new notification time.

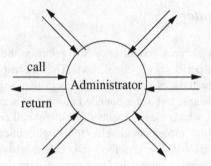

Fig. 11.1 Administrator

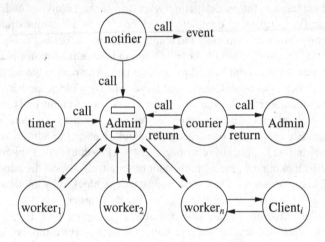

Fig. 11.2 Workers

- A notifier worker perform a blocking wait for an external event, like a key press on a keyboard. Once, the key is pressed, the notifier call the administrator to delivery the value and the administrator accepts the call when appropriate. If the administrator delays processing the call, the notifier work could lose a key press.
- A simple worker calls into the administrator and asks for a unit of work. The administrator accepts the worker call, and the worker takes a work unit from an appropriate buffer and returns with the work. The worker performs the work and calls back to the administrator with the result. The administrator accepts the worker call at an appropriate time. The worker deposits the result in an appropriate buffer, and then checks if work buffer has another work unit, otherwise the worker blocks until the administrator unblocks it because there are no work units from clients. The administrator now processes the result that the work just returned by sending it to another worker for further processing or back to a client. What makes the worker *simple* is that it only communicates with the administrator.

- A complex worker is like a simple worker but it may also communicate directly with the client that dropped off the original work. For example, the worker may need to contact the client and ask for further information, such as colour and size. The client must be aware it maybe contacted by the complex worker and be ready to accept the call.
- A courier worker performs a potentially blocking call on behalf of the administrator. For example, if administrators cannot make direct calls, how can two administrators communicate? To accomplish direct communication, the administrator converts it into a form of indirect communication via the third party courier task. The administrator creates a courier task, which immediately calls into its administrator. The administrator accepts the call, and returns the name of the other administrator and the message for it. The courier then make a direct call to the other administrator to deliver the message. The other administrator accepts the call when appropriate, analyses the message and returns a reply if necessary. The courier now calls its creating administrator and returns the reply from the other administrator. A courier can be used multiple times and there maybe multiple couriers depending the amount of communication with other administrators.

The short list of workers gives the general idea of how flexible the administrator can be with respect to accomplishing its work, and how the administrator fits into the larger design with multiple administrators. It is possible to construct a hierarchy of 10–20 administrators with a CEO administrator at the top and multiple levels of management underneath. Each administrator may manage 10s, 100s or 1000s of workers. Hence, the resulting system may be composed of 10,000s of tasks, but the structure of the system can be easily comprehended, managed and modified.

Some final observations about the implementation of work interaction with the administrator.

- Getting work and returning a result by a worker do *not* require two calls to an administrator. A single call can deliver a return value and pick up new work.

    ```
    work = server.mem( result );
    ```

    The server call passes the result as the argument to the call and receives work through the return value from the call, which may seem backwards. Using a single call for bidirectional communication can significantly reduce complexity and cost.
- After a worker is created it normally calls the creating administrator immediately to get instructions. When the worker next calls the administrator, it returns a result and gets new work. All subsequent calls are of this form. Clearly, the first call is special because there is no result to return, and hence, the first call may have to be handled in a special way.
- A server member called by a worker often has the following pattern:

```
Work Server::mem( T result ) {
    resultBuf1.add_back( result );     // store result for administrator
    if ( workBuf1.empty() ) {          // check if work available
        bench1.wait();                 // wait until work available
    }
    return workBuf1.front();           // return next work unit for processing
}
Server::main() {
    for ( ;; ) {
        _Accept( mem ) {
            workBuf2.push_back( resultBuf1.front() );
            bench2.signalBlock();
        } ... // more accepts
    }
}
```

The client pattern is to save the result, and immediately attempt to return with
new work; otherwise block until new work appears. The server pattern is to
accept its mutex members and move returned results into work for other workers
or as results for clients. In the example, the server transfers the new result from
its result buffer to a different work buffer, and then restart any blocked worker
waiting for that work. It is crucial the server use signalBlock to restart a worker; a
signal would move the worker to the acceptor/signaller stack and the server would
continue to execute. Hence, the worker would wait on the accepter/signaller
stack forever. The signalBlock forces the worker to go ahead of the server, take
the work, and then server continues. Also notice the server does the signalBlock
unconditionally because signalling an empty condition queue is not a problem.
Eventually, a worker will return with a result, and get the new work from the
work buffer.

Using the above patterns, it is possible to build an arbitrarily complex administrator, which now uses buffers in a nonblocking way, to introduce high-levels of
concurrency on the server side of a direct communication.

11.2   Client Side

μC++ (like C++) only provides synchronous call, i.e., the caller is delayed from the
time the arguments are delivered to the time the result is returned (like a procedure
call). In cases where the client does not want the call to block, it is possible to
create an administrator that attempts to make a call as short as possible by buffering
requests and having workers perform the requests. Hence, an asynchronous call is
built out of a synchronous calls.

What if a client wants/needs to have an asynchronous call but the server is not
an administrator? One approach is for the client to create a courier to make the
call, which may or may not block. Another approach is to create a buffer *outside*
of the server into which clients put work that is somehow turned into a call on the
server side (magic). Some programming languages have a special **asynchronous
call** mechanism that performs one of these techniques implicitly. μC++ provides
the former technique via the START and WAIT calls (see Sect. 5.8.4, p. 208), but

not for members. The remaining discussion assumes the server is an administrator supporting asynchronous-call behaviour.

11.2.1   Returning Values

If a client only drops off data to be processed by a server, the asynchronous call is simple. However, most clients invoke a server to do work where the result is subsequently returned to the client. Conspicuous by its absence in the discussion so far is how a client can get this return back from the server. Basically, an asynchronous call returning a result is significantly more complex.

In the case of a result, the asynchrony call is divided into two calls:

```
auto tf = START( f, 8 );        // thread starts in f(8)
S1          // continue execution, do not wait for f
i = WAIT( tf );                 // wait for f to finish
```

The first call specifies the arguments, and creates a micro-server to call the specified routine asynchronously. The time between the two calls allows the calling task to execute asynchronously with the task performing the operation on the caller's behalf. If the result is not ready when the second call is made, the caller blocks or the caller calls again (polling). However, this approach requires a protocol so that when the client makes the second call, the correct result can be found and returned. The following discussion presents three protocols along a spectrum of protocols that attempt to ensure calls and results are correctly matched.

11.2.2   Tickets

A simple protocol to return values is tickets, which have been used before (see Sect. 6.3.8.4, p. 265).

```
int ticket = server.mem(...);
S1          // asynchronous execution
i = server.return( ticket );    // obtain result
```

The first part of the protocol transmits the arguments specifying the desired work and a ticket (like a laundry ticket) is returned immediately. The second call passes the ticket to retrieve the result. The server matches the ticket with a result, and the result is returned if available or the caller is blocked until the result for that ticket is available.

As mentioned, protocols are error prone because the caller may not obey the protocol. For example, a client might never retrieve a result or use the same ticket twice or forge a ticket. However, if a programmer writes both the client and server, there is no chance of these errors (why be malicious to yourself?). Hence, tickets are simple to implement and use, and are an excellent mechanism to handle returning values.

11.2.3   Call-Back Routine

A more advanced protocol to return values is using call-backs (see page 39).

```
uSemaphore avail( 0 );
int result;
void callBack( int &val ) { result = val; avail.V(); }
server.mem( callBack, ... );
S1      // asynchronous execution
avail.P();                          // wait for result to become available
v = result + ...;                   // use result
```

The callback routine is registered with the server, and the server calls the callback
when the result is ready, passing the callback the result value. The programmer is
free to choose any mechanism to inform itself about the completion of the request.
In the example, a semaphore is used to block the client until the server calls the
unblock in the callback. The only restriction is that the callback cannot perform too
much work or block the server. Basically, the callback stores the result and sets an
indicator known to the client. The client must *poll* the indicator, tryP, or block, P,
until the result is available. The advantage is that the server does not have to store
the result, but can drop it off immediately in client storage. Also, the client gets to
choose the synchronization technique.

11.2.4   Future

A future [3] is a mechanism to provide the same asynchrony as above but without
an explicit protocol. The protocol becomes implicit between the future and the task
generating the result. Furthermore, it tries to remove the difficult problem of when
the caller should try to retrieve the results.

In detail, a future is an object that is a subtype of the result type expected by the
client. Instead of two calls as before, a single call is made, passing the appropriate
arguments, and a future is returned.

```
int result = server.mem(...);
S1      // asynchronous execution
v = result + ...;                   // use result, may block
```

In general, the future is returned immediately by the server and it is empty. In other
words, the caller *believes* the call completed and continues execution with an empty
result value. The future is filled in at some time in the *future*, hence the name, when
the result is calculated. If the caller tries to use the future before its value is filled
in, the caller is implicitly blocked. Hence, the trick is to make the programmer
believe the result appeared instantaneously, and the approach relies on the fact that
the empty result is not used immediately so there is time for the server to compute
the result and clandestinely insert it into the future.

The outline for a future implementation is a subtype of the result containing the same kind of information as in the previous callback routine.

```
class Future : public ResultType {
    friend class Server;          // allow server to access internal state
    ResultType result;
    uSemaphore avail;
    Future *link;
  public:
    Future() : avail( 0 ) {}

    operator ResultType() {       // return value
        avail.P();                // wait for result
        return result;
    }
};
```

The result member is where the server places the result, the semaphore avail is used to block the client if the future is empty, and the link field is possibly used by the server to chain the future onto a work list for worker tasks. In C++, the syntax for retrieving the value of the future can be largely seamless with accessing the normal return value, i.e., future usage looks virtually identical to the return type usage. In other languages, like Java, accessing the future is awkward, requiring a getter member, as in result.get(). However, a future is often dynamically allocated so it can escape the block in which it is created. In languages without garbage collection, like C++, the future must be explicitly deleted. So while the goal is for the programmer not to know they are using a future value rather than a normal value, some aspect of the future or programming language implementing the future forces the programmer to differentiate between the two kinds of values.

11.3 μC++ Future

μC++ provides two forms of futures, which differ in their storage-management interface. The explicit-storage-management future (Future_ESM) must be allocated and deallocated explicitly by the client. The implicit-storage-management future (Future_ISM) automatically allocates the required storage and automatically frees the storage when the future is no longer in use. The advantage of Future_ESM is that it allows the programmer to choose the method of allocation, whether on the heap, on the stack, or statically, which can result in more predictable and efficient allocation compared to Future_ISM, which always allocates storage on the heap. The disadvantage of Future_ESM is that the client must ensure that the future is deallocated, but not before the server thread has inserted the result (or the operation has been cancelled).

There is a basic set of common operations available on both types of futures. These consist of client operations, used by a client task to retrieve the return value, and server operations, used by a server task to fill in the value.

11.3.1   Client Operations

The future operations available to a client are:

available –returns **true** if the asynchronous call has completed and **false** otherwise. Note, the call can complete because a result is available, because the
server has generated an exception, or because the call has been cancelled
(through the cancel method, below).

operator() –(function call) returns a copy of the future result. The client blocks
if the future result is currently unavailable. If an exception is returned by the
server, that exception is thrown. A future result can be retrieved multiple times
by any task until the future is reset or destroyed.

operator T –(conversion to type T) returns a copy of the future result. *This kind
of access must be performed only after a blocking access, or after a call to*
available *returns* **true**. This operation is a low-cost way of accessing a future
result *after* the result is known to have been delivered. As with **operator**(), if
the server returns an exception, that exception is thrown.

cancelled –returns **true** if the future is cancelled and **false** otherwise.

cancel –attempts to cancel the asynchronous call associated with the future.
All clients waiting for the result are unblocked, and an exception of type
Future_ESM::Cancellation is thrown at any client attempting to access the
result. Depending on the server, this operation may also have the effect of
preventing the requested computation from starting, or it may interrupt the
computation in progress.

11.3.2   Server Operations

The future operations available to a server are:

delivery(T result) –copy the server-generated result into the future, unblocking
any clients that are waiting for the result. This result is the value returned to
the client. Returns **true** if the result is copied and **false** if the asynchronous
call has already completed.

reset –mark the future as empty so it can be reused, after which the current future
value is undefined.

exception(uBaseEvent *cause) –copy a server-generated exception into the
future. All clients waiting for the result are unblocked, and the exception
cause is thrown at any client attempting to access the result. Returns **true**
if the exception is copied and **false** if the asynchronous call has already
completed.

```
_Event E {};
Future_ISM<int> result;
result.exception( new E );    // exception deleted by future
```

exception deleted by reset or when future deleted

A server may require storage to buffer call arguments and other data needed for cancellation of futures. This storage is allocated as part of the future; hence, the future may also be generic in the type of server-management data. A server exports this type information for use with a future (see Sect. 11.5, p. 583).

Future cancellation affects the server computing the future's value. Depending on the server, cancellation may prevent the requested computation from starting, or it may interrupt the computation in progress. In both cases, the server does not insert a result into the future. If the server computation cannot be interrupted, the server may deliver a result even though the future has been cancelled.

An ESM future's cancel member cannot return until it is known that the server no longer references the cancelled future because the future's storage may be deallocated. Therefore, the server must inform the future if it will or will not deliver a value, by supplying a member in the ServerData type with the following interface:

bool cancel();

It returns **true** if the result of the asynchronous call will not be delivered to the future, and hence the server computation has been interrupted, and **false** otherwise.

An ISM future allows server-specific data to be included in the future through a special constructor parameter, which must implement a similar cancel member. However, no action need be taken by the ISM server, since it is always safe for the client to delete its copy of the future. In this case, the cancel method is purely advisory, allowing the server to avoid unnecessary computation.

11.3.3   Explicit Storage Management

The explicit storage-management (ESM) future (see Fig. 11.3) makes the client responsible for storage management by preallocating the future and passing it as an argument to the asynchronous call.

This kind of future is *not* copyable, i.e., no assignment or pass-by-value is allowed. Both client and server must operate on the same future, since the future is the buffer through which the result is returned. To copy the future would be to create two buffers; a client could wait for a value to be delivered to one buffer, whereas the server could deliver the future to the other buffer. As a result it is necessary to pass the future by pointer or by reference. It is possible for many threads to wait on the same future, so long as each uses a pointer or reference.

It is the client's responsibility to ensure a future continues to exist after a call as long as it is possible for the server to deliver a return value or exception. It is safe to delete the future after **operator**() returns, when available returns **true**, or after cancel returns. Note that because of this guarantee provided by cancel, it may be the case that cancel blocks until the server task acknowledges the cancellation.

```
template<typename T, typename ServerData> _Monitor Future_ESM {
public:
    Future_ESM();

    // used by client
    _Nomutex bool available();            // future result available ?
    T operator()();                       // access result, possibly having to wait
    _Nomutex operator T();                // cheap access of result after waiting

    _Event Cancellation {};               // raised if future cancelled
    _Nomutex bool cancelled();            // future result cancelled ?
    void cancel();                        // cancel future result

    // used by server
    ServerData serverData;                // information needed by server

    bool delivery( T result );            // make result available in the future
    void reset();                         // mark future as empty (for reuse)
    bool exception( uBaseEvent *ex );     // make exception available in the future
};
```

Fig. 11.3   Future: explicit storage management

11.3.4   Example

This example illustrates how a client uses a number of futures to communicate asynchronously with a server:

```
Server server;                          // server thread to process async call
Future_ESM<int, Server::IMsg> f[10];    // created on the stack
for ( int i = 0; i < 10; i += 1 ) {     // start a number of calls
    server.mem( f[i], i, ' c ' );       // async call
}
// work asynchronously while server processes requests
for ( int i = 0; i < 10; i += 1 ) {     // retrieve async results
    osacquire( cout ) << f[i]() << " " <<  // may block on first attempt to retrieve value
                f[i] << endl;           // use value again (cheap access)
}
```

The client creates an array of N futures for **int** values. In general, these futures can appear in any context requiring an **int** value and are used to make N asynchronous calls to the server. For each call to server.mem, a future is passed, in which the server returns a result, along with appropriate arguments, which are used by the server to perform the computation. The client then proceeds asynchronously with the server to perform other work, possibly in parallel with the server (if running multiprocessor). Finally, the client retrieves the results from the server by first performing a blocking access to each future. After that future is retrieved, it can be retrieved again using the cheap nonblocking-form (or the expensive blocking-form, but there is no point in synchronizing more than once for each asynchronous call.)

The key point for explicit futures is that the client preallocates the future storage so the server does not perform any dynamic memory-allocation for the futures,

```
template<typename T> class Future_ISM {
public:
    Future_ISM();
    Future_ISM( ServerData *serverData );

    // used by client
    bool available();                       // future result available ?
    T operator()();                         // access result, possibly having to wait
    operator T();                           // cheap access of result after waiting

    _Event Cancellation {};                 // raised if future cancelled
    bool cancelled();                       // future result cancelled ?
    void cancel();                          // cancel future result

    bool equals( const Future_ISM<T> &other ); // equality of reference

    // used by server
    bool delivery( T result );              // make result available in the future
    void reset();                           // mark future as empty (for reuse)
    bool exception( uBaseEvent *ex );       // make exception available in the future
};
```

Fig. 11.4 Future: implicit storage management

which can provide a substantial performance benefit. In the example, the client is able to use low-cost stack storage for the futures needed to interact with the server.

11.3.5 Implicit Storage Management

The implicit storage-management (ISM) future (see Fig. 11.4) simplifies the future interface relative to Future_ESM by automatically managing the storage required for the asynchronous call.

Unlike the ESM future, an ISM future *is* copyable, i.e., both assignment and pass-by-value are allowed. The ISM future functions as a "handle" or smart pointer [1] that refers to the result value. Any copy of an ISM future refers to the same result value as the original. Although ISM futures may be allocated on the stack, on the heap, or statically, the underlying storage for the result value (and possibly for server-management data as well) is always implicitly allocated on the heap. This storage is freed when all futures referring to that value are destroyed.

Server-specific data (see Sect. 11.3.2, p. 574) can be passed to an ISM future via its constructor. Occasionally it is useful to know whether two futures refer to the result of the same asynchronous call. For this reason, Future_ISM has one member not found in Future_ESM. The member routine equals returns **true** if the argument future refers to the same asynchronous call as this future and **false** otherwise.

11.3.6 Example

This example uses ISM futures similar to the previous example using ESM futures:

```
Server server;                          // server thread to process async call
Future_ISM<int> f[10];                  // created on the stack, but also uses heap
for ( int i = 0; i < 10; i += 1 ) {     // start a number of calls
    f[i] = server.mem( i, ' c ' );      // async call
}
// work asynchronously while server processes requests
for ( int i = 0; i < 10; i += 1 ) {     // retrieve async results
    osacquire( cout ) << f[i]() << " " <<   // may block on first attempt to retrieve value
                 f[i] << endl;          // use value again (cheap access)
}
```

Note that the asynchronous call to the server has the future as its return value, resembling a traditional return call, unlike the ESM future. Also, an ISM future allows the internal server-management data to be (optionally) hidden from the client, because the smart pointer knows when there are no more references to the future.

11.4 Future Access

After a client has created a future, passed it to a server, and then continued asynchronously, it normally accesses the future to retrieve its value. The simplest way to access a future is to call its **operator**() member. If the client's computation is reasonably structured, this approach may provide good asynchrony, with only occasional short-blocking because the future's value is unavailable. However, asynchrony can be curtailed if the client accesses a future too early and blocks when it could do other work. A more complicated way of accessing a future is to check, using the available method, whether the future is accessible before performing a potentially blocking access operation.

When a client creates multiple futures, and correspondingly makes multiple asynchronous calls using these futures, neither of previous approaches may be satisfactory. The client may only be able to proceed when some combination of the future results are available, or it may be able to proceed in different ways depending on the order in which results become available. Although it is possible to use the available method to check for accessibility of a set of futures, it is impossible to use available to wait on a future set without polling the futures (busy waiting). Hence, a more complex future-selection mechanism is necessary. This mechanism can be divided into two basic forms: heterogeneous and homogeneous.

heterogeneous: In this case, there are a number of futures that may have different types. Complicated selection conditions are constructed by naming individual futures in expressions. This style of selection provides great flexibility, but does not scale to large numbers of futures.

homogeneous: In this case, there are a number of futures of related types. The set of futures are stored together in a data structure like a container or array, and hence, must have some notion of common type. Two common selection operations on the futures within the data structure are wait-for-any and wait-for-all, i.e., wait for the first future in the set to become available, or wait for all futures in the set to become available. This style of selection is practical for large numbers of futures, but lacks the flexibility of heterogeneous selection.

11.4.1 Select Statement

μC++ provides a select statement to handle heterogeneous future selection by waiting for one or more available futures based on a logical selection-criteria. The simplest form of the select statement has a single _Select clause, e.g.:

```
_Select( selector-expression );
```

The selector-expression must be satisfied before execution continues. When the selector-expression consists of a reference to a single future, the expression is satisfied if and only if the future is available. For example, in:

```
_Select( f1 );
```

the selector becomes select blocked until f1.available() is true. This select is not equivalent to calling the future access-operator (f1()), which also gets the value, which can throw an exception. More interesting is when multiple futures appear in a compound selector-expression, where the futures are related using logical operators || and && to specify a compound selection criteria, e.g.:

```
_Select( f1 || f2 && f3 );
```

Normal operator precedence applies so the expression is implicitly parenthesized as: (f1 || (f2 && f3)). Execution waits until either future f1 is available or both futures f2 and f3 are available. Hence, for any selector-expression containing an || operator, some futures in the expression may be unavailable after the selector-expression is satisfied. For example, in the above selection expression, if future f1 becomes available, neither, one or both of f2 and f3 may be available.

A _Select clause may be guarded with a logical expression, e.g.:

```
_When ( conditional-expression ) _Select(f1); ≡ if ( conditional-expression ) _Select(f1);
```

The selector task is select blocked while the guard is true and there is no available future. A _When guard is considered true if it is omitted or if its *conditional-expression* evaluates to non-zero. If the guard is false, execution continues without waiting for any future to become available; for this example, the guard is the same as an if statement. Note, a simple select-statement always waits until at least one future is available unless its guard is false.

The complex form of the select statement conditionally executes a specific action *after* each selector-expression evaluates to true:

```
_Select( selector-expression )
    statement                    // action
```

After the selector-expression is satisfied, the action statement is executed; in this case, the action could simply follow the select statement. However, the complex

form of the select statement allows relating multiple _**Select** clauses using keywords
or and **and**, each with a separate action statement. The **or** and **and** keywords relate
the _**Select** clauses in exactly the same way operators || and && relate futures
in a select-expression, including the same operator precedence; parentheses may
be used to specify evaluation order. For example, the previous select statement
with a compound selector-expression can be rewritten into its equivalent complex
form with actions executed for each future that becomes available (superfluous
parentheses show precedence of evaluation):

```
(                                      // superfluous parentheses
  _Select( f1 )
      statement-1                      // action
  or (                                 // superfluous parentheses
      _Select( f2 )                    // optional guard
          statement-2                  // action
      and _Select( f3 )                // optional guard
          statement-3                  // action
      ) // and
) // or
```

The original selector-expression is now three connected _**Select** clauses, where
each _**Select** clause has its own action. During execution of the statement, each
_**Select**-clause action is executed when its sub-selector-expression is satisfied, i.e.,
when each future becomes available; however, control does not continue until the
selector-expression associated with the entire statement is satisfied. For example, if
f2 becomes available, statement-2 is executed but the selector-expression associated
with the entire statement is not satisfied so control blocks again. When either f1
or f3 becomes available, statement-1 or 3 is executed, and the selector-expression
associated with the entire statement is satisfied so control continues. For this
example, within the action statement, it is possible to access the future using the
non-blocking access-operator since the future is known to be available.

An action statement is triggered only once for its selector-expression, even if the
selector-expression is compound. For example, in:

```
_Select( f1 || f2 )
    statement-1
and _Select( f3 )
    statement-2
```

statement-1 is only executed once even though both futures f1 and f2 may become
available while waiting for the selector-expression associated with the entire
statement to become satisfied. Also, in statement-1, it is unknown which of futures
f1 or f2 satisfied the sub-selector-expression and caused the action to be triggered;
hence, it is necessary to check which of the two futures is available.

Note, a complex select-statement with _**When** guards is not the same as a group
of connected **if** statements, e.g.:

```
if ( C1 ) _Select( f1 );              _When ( C1 ) _Select( f1 );
else if ( C2 ) _Select( f2 );         or _When ( C2 ) _Select( f2 );
```

The left example waits for only future f1 if C1 is true or only f2 if C1 is false and
C2 is true. The right example waits for either f1 or f2 if C1 and C2 are true. Like

ESM	ISM
template< **typename** Selectee **>** **class** uWaitQueue_ESM { **public:** uWaitQueue_ESM(); **template<** **typename** Iterator **>** uWaitQueue_ESM(Iterator begin, Iterator end); **bool** empty() const; **void** add(Selectee *n); **template<** **typename** Iterator **>** **void** add(Iterator begin, Iterator end); **void** remove(Selectee n); Selectee *drop(); };	**template<** **typename** Selectee **>** **class** uWaitQueue_ISM { **public:** uWaitQueue_ISM(); **template<** **typename** Iterator **>** uWaitQueue_ISM(Iterator begin, Iterator end); **bool** empty() const; **void** add(Selectee n); **template<** **typename** Iterator **>** **void** add(Iterator begin, Iterator end); **void** remove(Selectee n); Selectee drop(); };

Fig. 11.5 µC++ future types

the _Accept statement, it takes $2^N - 1$ if statements to simulate a compound _Select statement with N _When guards (see page 534).

Finally, a select statement can be made non-blocking using a terminating _Else clause, e.g.:

```
_Select( selector-expression )
    statement                          // action .
_When ( conditional-expression ) _Else  // optional guard & terminating clause
    statement                          // action
```

The _Else clause *must* be the last clause of a select statement. If its guard is true or omitted and the select statement is not immediately true, then the action for the _Else clause is executed and control continues. If the guard is false, the select statement blocks as if the _Else clause is not present.

11.4.2 Wait Queue

µC++ provides two data structures to handle homogeneous future selection. Fig. 11.5 shows the two future types, which have similar behaviour but different approaches to storage management.

To use uWaitQueue_ISM, futures are added to the queue at construction or using the add methods, and are removed using the drop method as each becomes available. uWaitQueue_ESM is similar, except it operates on future pointers. For uWaitQueue_ESM, the client must ensure added futures remain valid, i.e., their storage persists, as long as they are in a uWaitQueue_ESM. For uWaitQueue_ISM, the added futures must be copyable, so ISM futures can be used but not ESM futures; uWaitQueue_ESM is the only queue that can be used with ESM futures.

The operations available on both kinds of queue are:

uWaitQueue_ISM() / uWaitQueue_ESM() –constructs an empty queue.

uWaitQueue_ISM(Iterator begin, Iterator end) / uWaitQueue_ESM(Iterator begin, Iterator end) –constructs a queue, adding all of the futures in the range referenced by the iterators begin and end (inclusive of begin, but exclusive of end). For the ESM queue, it is pointers to the futures that are added to the queue.

empty –returns true if there are no futures in the queue, false otherwise.

add(Selectee n) –adds a single future to the queue (ISM).

add(Selectee *n) –adds a single pointer to a future to the queue (ESM).

add(Iterator begin, Iterator end) –adds all futures in the range given by the iterators begin and end (inclusive of begin, but exclusive of end). For the ESM queue, it is pointers to the futures that are added to the queue.

remove(Selectee n) –removes any futures in the queue that refer to the same asynchronous call as n (ISM).

remove(Selectee *n) –removes any occurrence of the future pointer n from the queue (ESM).

drop –returns an available future from the queue, removing it from the queue. The client blocks if there is no available future. If multiple futures are available, one is chosen arbitrarily to return; other available futures can be obtained by further calls to drop. Calling drop on an empty ISM queue is an error; calling drop on an empty ESM queue returns NULL.

The drop method is an example of "wait-any" semantics in homogeneous selection: execution blocks until at least one future is available. To provide "wait-all" semantics, where execution only continues when all futures are available, a simple loop suffices:

```
uWaitQueue_ISM<Future_ISM<int> > queue; // or ESM
// add futures to queue
while ( ! queue.empty() ) {              // wait for all futures to become available
    queue.drop();
}
```

Other semantics, such as "wait-n" (block until n futures are available), can be obtained using more complex control logic. Indeed, it is possible to use wait queues to simulate some forms of the **_Select** statement:

```
                        uWaitQueue_ISM<Future_ISM<int> > queue;
                        queue.add( f1 ); queue.add( f2 ); queue.add( f3 );
                        for ( ;; ) {
                            queue.drop();
    _Select( f1 )           if ( f1.available() ) {
      statement-1               statement-1; break;
    or _Select( f2 && f3 )  } else if ( f2.available() && f3.available() ) {
      statement-2               statement-2; break;
                            }
                        }
```

However, for more complex selection, the complexity of the simulation grows faster than the complexity of the equivalent **_Select** statement. Furthermore, the **_Select** statement allows for different types of futures (including both ESM and ISM futures) to be mixed in a single selection, whereas the futures in a uWaitQueue must all have the same type.

11.5   Future Server

Fig. 11.6 illustrates an administrator composed of a monitor buffer and worker task. This different pattern simplifies the administrator by using the thread of the client and worker when the amount of work done by the administrator does not justify it having a thread. Both an ESM and ISM version of the server are presented, where the differences are storage management and cancellation of a future. Each server has server-specific data, ServerData, created in each future for use in cancellation. When a client cancels a future associated with this server, member ServerData::cancel is called, and both servers mark the position in the request queue to indicate that future is cancelled. The worker-task type, InputWorker, and an instance of it, is, are local to the server for abstraction and encapsulation reasons. InputWorker reads an $< integer, string >$ tuple and communicates the tuple to the server via a synchronous call to the private mutex-member input, which checks if a future exists with a matching integer key, and if so, places the string into that future as its result value. The ESM server conditionally inserts the string into the future by checking if the future at position value is NULL indicating it has been cancelled. The ISM server does not conditionally insert the string because an empty future is inserted at position value to hold the string if the original future is cancelled. Asynchronous calls from clients are made by calling mutex member request, specifying an integer key and a future to return the associated string read by the input worker. The ESM server resets the future passed to it as it is about to be reused, and the ISM server creates a new future. If the new request is greater than the vector size, the vector size is increased. The future is then buffered in vector reqs until the input worker subsequently fills it in with a value, and server-specific data is filled into the future in case the client cancels the future.

11.6   Executors

An executor is a predefined, generic server with a fixed-size pool of worker threads performing submitted units of work, where work is formed by a routine or functor.

```
class uExecutor {
    enum { DefaultWorkers = 16, DefaultProcessors = 2 };
    public:
    enum Cluster { Same, Sep };              // use same or separate cluster
    uExecutor();
    uExecutor( Cluster clus );
    uExecutor( unsigned int nworkers, Cluster clus = Same );
    uExecutor( unsigned int nworkers, unsigned int nprocessors, Cluster clus = Same );
    template <typename Func> void send( Func action );
    template <typename Func> auto sendrecv( Func action ) ->
            Future_ISM<decltype(action())>;
};
```

The constructor routine has the following form:

ESM	ISM

```
_Monitor Server {
  struct ServerData {

    Server *server;
    int req;

    bool cancel() {
      server->reqs[req] = NULL;
      return true;
    }
    ServerData() {}

  }

  _Task InputWorker {
    Server &is;

    void main() {
      int id;
      string text;

      while ( cin >> id ) {
        getline( cin, text );
        is.input( id, text );
      }
    }
  public:
    InputWorker(Server &is) : is(is) {}
  }
public:
  typedef Future_ESM< string,
          ServerData > FutureType;
private:
  InputWorker iw;
  vector< FutureType * > reqs;

  _Mutex void input(int value, string text) {
    if ( reqs.size() > value ) {
      if ( reqs[value] != NULL ) {
        reqs[value]->delivery( text );
      }
    }
  }
public:
  Server() : iw( *this ) {}

  void request( FutureType *f, int req ) {
    f->reset();
    if ( reqs.size() <= req ) {
      reqs.resize( req + 1 );
    }
    reqs[req] = f;
    f->serverData.server = this;
    f->serverData.req = req;
  }
}
```

```
_Monitor Server {
  struct ServerData :
      public Future_ISM<string>::ServerData {
    Server *server;
    int req;

    bool cancel() {
      server->reqs[req] = Future_ISM<string>();
      return true;
    }
    ServerData(Server *s, int r) :
        server(s), req(r) {}
  }

  _Task InputWorker {
    Server &is;

    void main() {
      int id;
      string text;

      while ( cin >> id ) {
        getline( cin, text );
        is.input( id, text );
      }
    }
  public:
    InputWorker( Server &is ) : is(is) {}
  }
public:
  typedef Future_ISM< string > FutureType;
private:
  InputWorker iw;
  vector< FutureType > reqs;

  _Mutex void input( int value, string text ) {
    if ( reqs.size() > value ) {

      reqs[value].delivery( text );

    }
  }
public:
  Server() : iw( *this ) {}

  FutureType request( int req ) {
    FutureType f( new ServerData(this, req) );
    if ( reqs.size() <= req ) {
      reqs.resize( req + 1 );
    }
    reqs[req] = f;

    return f;
  }
}
```

Fig. 11.6 Server

```
#include <uFuture.h>
#include <iostream>
using namespace std;

int routine() {
    // preform work
    return 3;
}
struct Functor {                              // closure: allows arguments to work
    double x;
    double operator()() {                     // function-call operator
        // preform work
        return x;
    }
    Functor( double x ) : x( x ) {}
} functor( 4.5 );

void uMain::main() {
    uExecutor executor;
    Future_ISM<int> fi[10];
    Future_ISM<double> fd[10];
    for ( int i = 0; i < 10; i += 1 ) {
        executor.submit( fi[i], routine );    // think: fi[i] = executor.submit( routine )
        executor.submit( fd[i], functor );    // think: fd[i] = executor.submit( functor )
    }
    for ( int i = 0; i < 10; i += 1 ) {
        cout << fi[i]() << " " << fd[i]() << " "; // wait for results
    }
    cout << endl;
}
```

Fig. 11.7 Executor example

uExecutor(**unsigned int** nworkers = 4) –creates an executor containing a work
queue and N worker threads, which are created on the current cluster with
the cluster's default stack size.

The member routine send queues a unit of work action, with *no* return value, on a
FIFO buffer in the executor to be eventually executed by one of the worker threads.
The member routine sendrecv queues a unit of work action, with a return value, on a
FIFO buffer in the executor to be eventually executed by one of the worker threads.
Fig. 11.7 shows an example where work is submitted to an executor in the form
of a routine, functor and lambda, and then different types of values (**int**, **double**,
char) are returned.

11.7 Summary

While creating tasks increases concurrency, it does not imply a greater potential
for parallelism. It is crucial to understand communication among active objects to
understand how to enhance concurrency; otherwise, tasks just block and execution

becomes sequential, i.e., one task after another. Using a task to front-end a number of worker tasks is an excellent approach to deal with communication bottlenecks and to allow asynchronous calls. The complexity comes in subsequently returning values from asynchronous execution. A number of approaches are possible, but futures are a commonly used pattern. While futures are suppose to be an invisible form of concurrency, programmers are normally aware they are using futures and restructure code to take advantage of their asynchronous capabilities by making calls earlier before needed to access the result.

11.8   Questions

1. Explain the difference between synchronous and asynchronous communication among tasks, and explain why both are necessary.
2. Name two techniques for implementing asynchronous communication using synchronous communication. (No explanation of the technique is necessary.)
3. a. What makes a *future* safer to use than a *ticket*?
   b. What makes a *future* safer to use than a *callback*?
4. Name three key features of an administrator task.
5. Give an implementation of a future class (including private and public parts) that allows blocking and non-blocking possibilities and has the following interface:

```
class future {
    friend _Task server;

    void set (ResultType result);  // for server
public:
    future();
    ResultType get();       // usual blocking client call - returns result to client
    bool ready();           // non-blocking extension - returns true when result available
};
```

6. What is an administrator server and what does it accomplish?
7. Explain the difference between indirect and direct communication among tasks, and explain why both are necessary.
8. Explain the difference between synchronous and asynchronous communication among tasks, and explain why both are necessary.
9. What is an administrator server and what does it accomplish?
10. What is a *call-back routine*, and how is it used?
11. What is an asynchronous call between tasks, and what is its advantage over synchronous call?
12. Name three different mechanisms used to facilitate returning a value from an asynchronous call. (Do not explain the mechanisms.)
13. Explain why buffering in a server task may not produce additional concurrency.
14. Suggest a change to a server task so that buffering produces additional concurrency.

15. If a language supports asynchronous call, how must the call be implemented?
16. What are the fundamental approaches for increasing server and client side concurrency?
17. Name 3 specific mechanisms to increase client-side concurrency (do not describe them).
18. Why are courier tasks useful in the administrator model?
19. For an asynchronous call between tasks, why is returning a result complex?
20. What is a *future*, and how is it used?
21. Given the outline for an administrator task:

```
_Task Admin {
    uCondition bench;              // workers wait here
  public:
    Job work( ... ) {             // called by worker task
        bench.wait();             // wait for administrator
        return job;               // return new work
    }
  private:
    void main() {
        ... _Accept( work ); ...
        if ( ... ) bench.signal();    // restart worker
        ...
    }
};
```

   a. The given code does not work properly. Explain why.
   b. Correct the line of code so it works properly and explain why this correction fixes the problem.

22. a. Explain why an asynchronous call increases concurrency?
    b. What is the general mechanism for implementing an asynchronous call?
    c. What is the most complex part of an asynchronous call?
23. Once a future has a value, why it is immutable?
24. Explain why very little code should appear in a server's mutex members.
25. What is the general difficulty in returning a value from an asynchronous call?
26. An administrator task is often described as non-blocking, but it must block to work. Explain this contradiction.
27. Explain how a future provides additional concurrency.
28. When is a server task not an administrator task?
29. Why are courier tasks useful in the administrator model?
30. Explain how an exception can be sent from a server to a client task via a future.
31. A future implementation needs the following 3 fields:

```
ResultType result;
uSemaphore avail;
future *link;
```

Explain the purpose of each field.

32. Write the following program, which has user tasks, a keyboard administrator (KBA) task, and a keyboard task, organized in the following way:

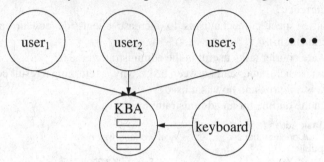

The keyboard task has the following interface:

```
_Task Keyboard {
  public:
    Keyboard( KBA &kba );
};
```

It reads characters from standard input and sends the individual character to the KBA. The whitespace newline character, `'\n'`, is never sent to the KBA from the keyboard task; all other characters are sent, including the other whitespace characters. When the keyboard task encounters end-of-file, it returns the character `'\377'` to the KBA and terminates. Note, characters typed at the keyboard are buffered until RETURN (or ENTER) is typed, and then the whole line is sent to the program. The need to type RETURN before your program sees the data is fine for this assignment.

A user task has the following interface:

```
_Task User {
  public:
    User( KBA &kba, unsigned int taskNo, unsigned int delay );
};
```

It makes requests to the KBA to get characters from the keyboard. If a user task gets the character `'-'`, it terminates and does not print the character `'-'`. Otherwise, it prints its task number (see below) and the character it received. Also, a user task must print its task number when it starts and finishes.

The administrator KBA task has the following interface:

```
_Task KBA {
  public:
    KBA( unsigned int userDelay );
    void nextChar( char ch );   // called by keyboard task
    char getChar();             // called by user task
};
```

It keeps a list of user tasks. Only one of the users in the list is considered to be logically *active*. When the KBA gets a character from the keyboard task, it gives the character to the active user. The KBA deals with the following command characters:

'-'   means terminate the active user and remove it from the user list. The next
task to become active is the next one in the list. If the current active user is
at the end of the list, the remove makes the new active user the one at the
beginning of the list. The character '-' *is* passed to the user task.

'+'   means start a new user task, add it after the currently active task in the list,
and make it the active user task. When a user task is created, a task number is
passed to its constructor. The KBA keeps a counter, which starts at zero (i.e.,
the first task has name 0), and it is incremented by one for each user task
created; the current value of the counter is the task name, and deleting tasks
does not affect the next task name. This uniform naming makes it easier to
check your output. The character '+' is *not* passed to any user task.

'>'   means switch to the next user in the list and make it the active user. If the
current active user is at the end of the list, the switch makes the new active
user the one at the beginning of the list. All subsequent characters are given
to the new active user. The character '>' is *not* passed to any user task.

'@'   means broadcasts the next character to all users. Start with the current
active user and cycle through all users in the same order as for the special
character '>'. The character broadcast to user tasks is not interpreted by the
KBA unless it is the '-' or '\377' character. For '-', terminate each active
user task in turn and remove it from the KBA user list. For '\377' terminate
all users and the KBA. The character '@' is *not* passed to any user task unless
it is preceded by an '@' character.

'&'   sends the last non-command character again to the current user. The
character '&' is *not* passed to the user task. If there is no last character for
any reason, such as an initial input of '+&', the '&' is ignored.

'\377'   means shut down all user tasks, whereupon the KBA terminates. The
character '\377' is *not* passed to any user task and is never printed.

To increase concurrency, the KBA buffers characters from the keyboard
separately for each user task and then processes them in FIFO order for a
particular user task. Hence, a user task only receives data logically sent to
it as the active user. *Note, '-' is the only special character buffered for a
user and is dealt with after any normal characters before it in the buffer.* The
KBA must ensure that even if user tasks are running slowly, the keyboard task
can always send it characters (e.g., between calls to getChar by user tasks,
the keyboard can always continue to make calls). Hence, the active user is
decoupled from the user tasks through the buffers, and the KBA must allow user
tasks to immediately process characters in their buffer or wait for characters to
appear from the keyboard. Finally, if there is no active user (i.e., no user tasks),
characters are ignored instead of buffered, except for '+' and '\377'.

The design rules for an administrator task must be followed in the KBA. The
KBA does not call any blocking operations (except **new** and **delete**), clients
should perform the minimal amount of work in member routines, and the KBA
task-main should do as much administrative work as possible.

The main program should start the KBA and wait for its completion. The KBA should start the keyboard task. Then you can play with the program, creating user tasks, typing characters to each user task, switching between user tasks, and terminating the user tasks. Each user task must print when it starts, when it receives a character (and what the character is), and when it terminates. The keyboard task must print the same as a user task. The KBA task must print any ignored characters (including whitespace characters), any new active tasks, changes to the active task, a deleted task and the subsequent new active task, shut down and any tasks deleted during shut down. Print whitespace characters as two character strings so they are visible, i.e., use character strings like "\t" for tab and "\s" for space. The following is an example of the required behaviour, the exact output format is up to you. (All output spacing can be accomplished using tabs so it is unnecessary to build strings of output messages.) The INPUT column is where the cursor waits for input; thus, user input characters appear in this column as they are typed. Figure 11.8 shows an example KBA output sequence.

The executable program is named kba and has the following shell interface:

    kba [userDelay]

(Square brackets indicate optional command line parameters, and do not appear on the actual command line.) Where the meaning of the parameter is:

userDelay: number of times the user yields to simulate the time required to consume a character. The default value if unspecified is 5.

33. This assignment simulates a simple spy ring using the objects and relationships in Fig. 11.9, p. 592. (Not all possible communication paths are shown in the diagram.) The SpyMaster and Decipher are administrators, all other tasks are different kinds of workers for the two administrators. Each kind of task is discussed in detail below.

a. The SpyMaster task receives encrypted messages from the spies, and passes them for deciphering, via a courier, to the decipher. In addition, once a spy has fulfilled its mission, the spy master sends out a supervisor to terminate it. The spy master has the following interface:

```
_Task SpyMaster {
  public:
    SpyMaster( Gen &data, Decipher &Q );          // data generator and decipher
    void command( char cmd, string spyname );     // user command from keyboard
    void message( string msg );                   // coded message from spy
    void retired();                               // confirmation from supervisor
    void result( int msgtype, string s1, string s2 ); // returns decryption result
                                 // deliberately general to allow individual design
};
```

The keyboard task passes in user commands via the SpyMaster::command member. A spy passes encrypted messages via the SpyMaster::message member, and these messages have to be decrypted. A supervisor confirms completion of a spy termination by calling the SpyMaster::retired member. A courier shuttles encrypted/decrypted messages between the spy master and

```
INPUT KEYBOARD KBA   USERS                  read:c
=====  ========  ===   =====                                        task:0 char:b
                starting                    read:\n
        starting                                                    task:0 char:c
a                                   &d
        read:a                              read:&
        read:\n                             read:d
                    ignore char:a                       cmnd:&, previous character:'c' to user:0
+                                                                   task:0 char:c
        read:+                              read:\n
        read:\n                                                     task:0 char:d
            cmnd:+, new user:0      >e>f>g>
                    task:0 starting         read:>
>>                                          read:e
        read:>                                          cmnd:>, next user:2
        read:>                              read:>
            cmnd:>, next user:0                                     task:2 char:e
        read:\n                             read:f
            cmnd:>, next user:0                 cmnd:>, next user:3
&                                           read:>
        read:&                                                      task:3 char:f
        read:\n                             read:g
            no last character to repeat         cmnd:>, next user:4
abc+&                                       read:>
        read:a                                                      task:4 char:g
        read:b                              read:\n
                    task:0 char:a               cmnd:>, next user:0
        read:c                      @h
                    task:0 char:b           read:@
        read:+                              read:h
        read:&                              read:\n
            cmnd:+, new user:1                  cmnd:@h
                    task:1 starting                         task:0 char:h
                    task:0 char:c                           task:2 char:h
        read:\n                                             task:3 char:h
            cmnd:&, previous character:'c' to user:1        task:4 char:h
                    task:1 char:c       --
-                                           read:-
        read:-                              read:-
        read:\n                                 cmnd:-, delete user:0
            cmnd:-, delete user:1                           task:0 terminating
                    task:1 terminating          cmnd:-, next user:2
            cmnd:-, next user:0             read:\n
++                                              cmnd:-, delete user:2
        read:+                                              task:2 terminating
        read:+                                  cmnd:-, next user:3
            cmnd:+, new user:2          >
                    task:2 starting         read:>
        read:\n                             read:\n
            cmnd:+, new user:3                  cmnd:>, next user:4
                    task:3 starting     space (not actually printed)
&                                           read:\s
        read:&                              read:\n
        read:\n                                             task:4 char:\s
            cmnd:&, previous character:'c' to user:3    >
                    task:3 char:c           read:>
+                                           read:\n
        read:+                                  cmnd:>, next user:3
        read:\n                         j
            cmnd:+, new user:4              read:j
                    task:4 starting         read:\n
>abc                                                        task:3 char:j
        read:>                          ^D (not actually printed)
        read:a                              terminating
            cmnd:>, next user:0                             task:3 terminating
        read:b                                              task:4 terminating
                    task:0 char:a           terminating
```

Fig. 11.8 KBA output

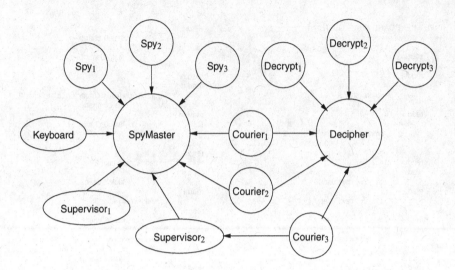

Fig. 11.9 Spy organization

the decipher. The spy master does a random check, 1 in 4, for a compromised spy key. The effect of the compromised key is to turn the spy's important information into nonsense text. The check is performed by a special courier, which is given the spy's key in addition to the encrypted message. Once the special courier has received the decrypted message, it compares the encryption of the first three characters of the decrypted message (using the original key) with the first three characters of the original encrypted message. If they do not match, the spy's key has been compromised. When a spy master learns of a compromised key, a supervisor is sent to terminate the spy.

The SpyMaster receives commands '+' or '-', i.e., plus or minus signs, from the keyboard task. The commands and their arguments are as follows:

+   means create a new spy task, which is done by the spy master. The spy's encryption key and unique name are created by the data-generator object passed to the spy master. You must remember the created spy names to eventually send commands to terminate the spies.

-*name*   means terminate the named spy, which is done by creating a supervisor task, and then remove the spy from the spy master's list. If the named spy does not exist, print a warning message.

'\377'   (octal 377 or decimal 255) means shut down all worker tasks, whereupon the spy master and decipher administrators terminate.

b. The keyboard task reads characters from standard input and has the following interface:

```
_Task Keyboard {
  public:
    Keyboard( SpyMaster &M );
};
```

The character + means pass a + command with an empty string as its argument to the spy master. The character - means pass a - command with the remaining characters (including blanks) on that line as its argument to the spy master. Any other character should be ignored by the keyboard task and a warning message printed. Multiple characters can appear on the same line and each must be handled accordingly, e.g.:

```
++XXX+-Fred
XXX-Mary+
+-
```

where X characters are ignored and "Fred", "Mary+" and "" (empty string) are spy names. When the keyboard task encounters end-of-file, it returns the command '\377' and an empty string as its argument to the spy master, and terminates.

c. A spy task steals secret messages (generated by the data-generator object), encrypts the message and passes the encrypted message to the spy master. It has the following interface:

```
_Task Spy {
  public:
    Spy( SpyMaster &M, Gen &data, string spyname, string encryptionkey );
    void contact( Supervisor &S, int nmsgs );
};
```

A spy generates a message, encrypts it and sends it to the spy master via member SpyMaster::message. Then the spy pauses a random number of seconds, between 3 and 6 inclusive, before sending another message. The following combination of **_Accept** and **_Timeout** (rather than yield)

```
 _Accept ...
or _Timeout( uDuration(number of seconds) );
```

is useful to pause the spy task for periods of time. A spy terminates when a supervisor task invokes its destructor.

Encryption is performed by exclusive-or'ing each character in the message with successive characters in the key, in left-to-right order, cycling around the key characters, e.g.:

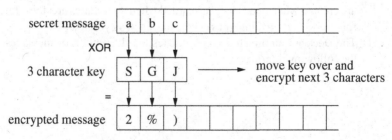

This encryption scheme is reversible, so that encrypting an encrypted message with the same key produces the original message.

d. A supervisor task is created to terminate a spy specified by the spy master. It has the following interface:

```
_Task Supervisor {
public:
    Supervisor( SpyMaster &M, Spy *spyID, string spyname, Decipher &Q );
    void message( string msg );
    void decrypted( string spyname, string spymsg );
};
```

Spies are terminated only by supervisors. The supervisor terminates a spy by deleting it, which implicitly invokes the spy's destructor. Normally, after deleting the spy, the supervisor sends confirmation of termination to the spy master, via member SpyMaster::retired, and to the decipher, via member Decipher::deregisterSpy, and terminates. However, sometimes (half of the time, in fact) a supervisor is a *mole*—an agent secretly working for another spy agency. A mole does not terminate the spy right away. Instead the mole contacts the spy, via the member Spy::contact, and the spy responds by sending encrypted messages to the supervisor, bypassing the spy master. The spy again pauses between messages, as it does when communicating to the spy master. The mole knows this conspiracy cannot be sustained, so only N messages, a random value in the range 1 to 3 inclusive, are passed from the spy to the mole before the mole terminates the spy in the usual way. The value N is passed to the spy via member Spy::contact. A mole hides its actions by using a courier to carry encrypted messages to the decipher, which returns the decrypted message via Supervisor::decrypted.

e. A courier transfers information between the spy master or the supervisor and the decipher. Couriers are specialized to do one of several kinds of transfer. They have the following interface:

```
_Task Courier {                    // abstract class
    virtual void main() = 0;       // main must be defined in derived class
public:
    Courier( Decipher &Q );
};
```

You design courier descendant-types for specific courier jobs, e.g., to register a spy, to carry a message for decryption, etc. Couriers return decryption request results to the requester: the spy master or a mole. Assume couriers are created when needed and discarded when their duties are done. Interfaces for courier descendant types can be designed as you like.

f. The Decipher administrator coordinates the decryption of messages. It has the following interface:

```
_Task Decipher {
public:
    void decrypt( string spyname, string &spymsg );
    void registerSpy( string spyname, string spykey );
    void deregisterSpy( string spyname );
    void done();
};
```

It also simulates the compromise of a spy's key. There is 1 chance in 10 that a spy's key becomes compromised. In the case of a compromise, a registered spy is randomly chosen and each of the first three letters of the key is incremented. To decrypt a message, the decipher creates a Decrypt task, one per message, to perform the work.

A courier from the spy master calls member Decipher::decrypt with a message for decryption. The courier blocks until the message is decrypted directly in the argument to parameter spymsg. Decipher::registerSpy adds a spy name and associated encryption key to an appropriate data structure; Decipher::deregisterSpy removes a named spy from the data structure. The decrypt task uses the Decipher::done member to tell the decipher administrator that it has completed the decryption.

g. The Decrypt task uses the key to decrypt a single message. It has the following interface:

```
_Task Decrypt {
public:
    Decrypt( Decipher &Q, string key, string &msg );
};
```

Decrypting the message occurs directly to the parameter msg—no copy of the message is made. After decrypting a message, the Decrypt task calls Decipher::done to inform the decipher that the work is completed, and terminates.

h. The Gen monitor generates spy names, keys, and messages The interface is:

```
_Monitor Gen {
public:
    Gen();                      // Seeds srand() and sets up lists.
    string generateName();      // Generate a unique spy name.
    string generateKey();       // Generate an encryption key.
    string generateMsg();       // Generate a message.
};
```

i. The main program starts the spy master, and the decipher administrator. The spy master starts the keyboard task. Then you can play with the program, creating spy tasks, watching messages being passed around and terminating the spy tasks. Each spy task must print a starting and terminating output line plus output lines tracing the task's activities, e.g., when a spy sends a message to the spy master.

No interface above can be modified, except for overriding destructors.

Fig. 11.10 shows an example program trace (it can be improved in style and content). Hex numbers (e.g., 0x15de00) are task addresses and used for task ids—see uThisTask() and **this** in the μC++ reference manual. The spy messages have been augmented by tracer numbers, but this is an optional feature of the output.

Note: Since encryption can produce control characters, do not print the encrypted messages if they contain control characters. Line breaks in the messages above are for display purposes only.

By default, characters typed at the keyboard are buffered until RETURN is typed, and then the whole line is sent to your program. The need to type RETURN before your program sees the data is fine for this assignment.

34. Simulate a simple web browser and part of the Internet to retrieve documents from the World Wide Web using the objects and relationships in Fig. 11.11. (Not all possible communication paths are shown in the diagram.) To keep the environment manageable, only a very small set of simplified web pages are used rather than the entire Web. One simplification is that a Uniform Resource Locator (URL) is composed of a topic domain followed by a file name, which contains information germane to that topic, separated by a colon, e.g., art:topics/art/Alexandre_Dumas.

The purpose of each object type required in the assignment is as follows (you may add only a public destructor and private members):

a. A Keyboard task is created by a Browser. It processes simple user commands entered from the keyboard:

f TOPIC   returns the URLs for every document with a topic domain matching TOPIC. The TOPIC is a topic name after the command character and is case-sensitive. If no matches are found, the message "No matches for topic TOPIC." is printed. If matches are found, the TOPIC and a list of URLs are printed.

d URL   displays the contents of the file at the specified URL. The URL is a URL name after the command character and is case-sensitive. If no match is found, the message "URL URL not found." is printed. If a match is found, the URL and file-contents are printed.

p   prints the browser's cache.

c   clears the browser's cache.

k N   sends a courier to the TopicNameServer administrator to kill server N. The N is a server number after the command character. This simulates a server going down after registering with the topic-name server. (Normally, this kind of command is not allowed from a browser.)

q or end-of-file   shuts down the entire system.

You may assume commands have no syntax errors. After a command is entered, the keyboard task calls Browser::keyboard to send the command to the browser.

A Keyboard has the following interface:

Spy Master: starting
    Decipher: starting
Keyboard: starting
+++
Spy Master: creating spy "John Drake"
    Courier 0x15de00: registering (John Drake, xqp)
        Spy John Drake: starting, key = xqp
    Courier 0x15de00: terminating
    Decipher: registered (John Drake, xqp)
        Spy John Drake: delaying 3.
Spy Master: creating spy "Sidney Reilly"
    Courier 0x16ef00: registering (Sidney Reilly, nkx)
        Spy Sidney Reilly: starting, key = nkx
    Courier 0x16ef00: terminating
    Decipher: registered (Sidney Reilly, nkx)
        Spy Sidney Reilly: delaying 5.
        Spy John Drake: sending (1, Mr. Wagner has beautiful moments but
bad quarters of an hour. - Gioacchino Rossini)
        Spy John Drake: delaying 6.
***SpyMaster: checking (1, John Drake)
    Courier 0x180300: checking (1, John Drake)
    Decipher: received message (1, John Drake) to decrypt
        Decrypt 0x188b60: (1, xqp)
        Decrypt 0x188b60: terminating
    Courier 0x180300: terminating
***SpyMaster: checked (1, John Drake) MATCHES original
Spy Master: creating spy "Kelly Robinson"
    Courier 0x180300: registering (Kelly Robinson, yli)
        Spy Kelly Robinson: starting, key = yli
    Courier 0x180300: terminating
    Decipher: registered (Kelly Robinson, yli)
        Spy Kelly Robinson: delaying 6.
-John Drake
Spy Master: retiring "John Drake"
        Supervisor 0x191450: retiring John Drake
        Supervisor 0x191450: is a mole. Contacting John Drake
            for 1 messages
        Spy John Drake: has been contacted by Supervisor 0x191450 who
            wants 1 messages.
        Spy John Drake: sending (2, Behind every great fortune there is
            a crime. - Honore de Balzac)
        Supervisor 0x191450: received (1, (2, John Drake))
    Courier 0x199da0: decrypting (2, Supervisor 0x191450)
    Decipher: received message (2, John Drake) to decrypt
        Decrypt 0x1a2600: (2, xqp)
        Decrypt 0x1a2600: terminating
    Courier 0x199da0: terminating
        Supervisor 0x191450: decrypted (2, Behind every great
            fortune there is a crime. - Honore de Balzac)
        Spy John Drake: terminating
        Supervisor 0x191450: deregistering John Drake
Spy Master: Supervisor 0x191450 reported retirement of spy "John Drake"
        Supervisor 0x191450: terminating
    Decipher: deregistering "John Drake"
        Spy Sidney Reilly: sending (1, A scholar who cherishes the love
of comfort is not fit to be deemed a scholar. - Lao-Tzu (570?-490? BC))
        Spy Sidney Reilly: delaying 4.
SpyMaster: received encrypted (1, Sidney Reilly)
    Courier 0x191450: decrypting (1, Sidney Reilly)
    Decipher: received message (1, Sidney Reilly) to decrypt
        Decrypt 0x166620: (1, nkx)
        Decrypt 0x166620: terminating
    Courier 0x191450: terminating

Fig. 11.10 Spy master: example output

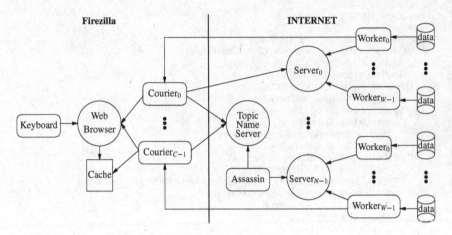

Fig. 11.11 Web browser and simple internet

```
_Task Keyboard {
 public:
     enum Commands { FindTopic, DisplayFile, PrintCache, ClearCache, KillServer, Quit };
     Keyboard( Browser &browser );
};
```

b. A Browser administrator task is created by uMain. It receives and processes
   commands from the Keyboard task and results from Courier tasks. After a
   keyboard command arrives, it is analysed, and results printed immediately by
   the browser if the necessary information is in the browser's cache; otherwise,
   the request is assigned to one of the browser's couriers, if available, selected
   from the fixed-size pool of couriers that the browser creates when it starts.
   If no courier is available, the job must be queued until a courier returns.
   After a courier satisfies a request, it may update the browser's cache so the
   browser can then print the necessary information. Before terminating, the
   browser must complete all queued jobs from the keyboard and wait for any
   active couriers. The keyboard and courier tasks terminate when the browser
   terminates.

   A Browser has the following interface:

```
_Task Browser {
    public:
        struct Job {                                      // Job for a courier
            const Keyboard::Commands kind;                // Kind of job
            std::string argument;                         // URL/Topic from command
            unsigned int server;                          // Server from command
            bool success;                                 // Did the request succeed or fail?
            std::string result;                           // Result of the request

            Job( Keyboard::Commands kind );
            Job( Keyboard::Commands kind, std::string argument );
            Job( Keyboard::Commands kind, unsigned int server );
        };
        Browser( TopicNameServer &tns, const unsigned int poolSize );
        void keyboard( const Keyboard::Commands kind );                    // Keyboard calls with commands
        void keyboard( const Keyboard::Commands kind, const std::string &argument );
        void keyboard( const Keyboard::Commands kind, const unsigned int server );
        Job *requestWork( Job *job );         // Courier calls to return/get job; NULL => terminate
};
```

c. A Courier task is created by a Browser. It calls Browser::requestWork to return the result of its current job and obtain a new job. After obtaining a new job, a courier delays (yield) a random number of times (1..5) before it processes the request of type Job, which contains information to perform one of the following actions:

- To find a topic, the courier requests a list of servers from TopicNameServer:: serversHosting that host the specified topic. It then interacts with each non-zombied server to get file names containing information on the topic. This information is then put directly into the browser's cache. The courier does NOT print the information.

- To display the file contents specified by a URL, the courier requests a list of servers from TopicNameServer::serversHosting hosting the specified topic in the URL. It then interacts with each non-zombied server to check if the specified file-name in the URL is present on that server. The server used a Worker task to interact with the courier for this request. The worker tells the courier if the URL exists on the server by calling Courier::urlExists, and if it exists, also transfers the file contents to the courier by making repeated calls to Courier::putText passing portions of the file content (blocks of approximately 256 bytes) on each call until end-of-file is reached. This information is then put directly into the browser's cache. The courier does NOT print the information.

- To kill a server, the courier calls TopicNameServer::killServer to specify the server to be killed.

After processing a job, a courier returns the job to the browser with field Job::success set to true or false indicating if the request succeeded or failed, and if it succeeded, field Job::result contains an appropriate string of text depending on the kind of request.

A Courier has the following interface:

```
_Task Courier {
  public:
    Courier( TopicNameServer &tns, Cache &cache, Browser &browser,
             const unsigned int id );
    void urlExists( bool exists );    // Worker calls to indicate if url exists on server
    void putText( bool eof, const std::string &text );  // Worker calls to transfer
                                                        // file contents
};
```

d. A TopicNameServer administrator task is created by uMain. It provides services to locate server tasks that host web topics. The servers are created by TopicNameServer from information passed by uMain (constructor parameter servers). Member TopicNameServer::serversHosting returns a pointer to all servers hosting a specified topic domain. As well, member TopicNameServer::killServer provides a mechanism to register a server for termination. A server is terminated via a single specialized Assassin task. The assassin task is created when the TopicNameServer task starts and it calls TopicNameServer::killedServer to obtain the server task to terminate. The assassin terminates when the topic-name server terminates.

A TopicNameServer has the following interface:

```
_Task TopicNameServer {
  public:
    struct ServerInfo {                        // Holds server configuration info
      Server *server;                          // Server address added later
      bool alive;                              // Server zombied ?
      Server::Topic2FileNames t2fns;           // Topics hosted by the server
    };
    typedef std::map<unsigned int, ServerInfo> ServerConfig;

    TopicNameServer( ServerConfig &servers, const unsigned int poolSize );
    ~TopicNameServer();
    std::map<unsigned int, Server *> *serversHosting(
             const std::string &topic );       // Couriers call
                                               // to get list of servers hosting topic
    void killServer( unsigned int id );        // Courier calls to terminate server
    Server *killedServer();                    // Assassin calls to get server; NULL => terminate
};
```

e. An Assassin task is created by a TopicNameServer. It terminates a server by calling Server::kill. After killing a server, it notifies the TopicNameServer by calling TopicNameServer::killedServer to get the next server to terminate.

An Assassin has the following interface:

```
_Task Assassin {
  public:
    Assassin( TopicNameServer &tns );
};
```

f. A Server is an administrator task created by a TopicNameServer. It hosts a number of topics and associated files containing information germane to those topics. For couriers, it provides either a list of hosted files for a topic (Server::getFileNames) or uses a worker task to transmit the entire content of a specific file for a given URL (Server::getFile). A worker is assigned from a fixed-size pool of workers that the server creates when it starts. All workers terminate when the server terminates.

When a server is killed it is not deleted; instead, it goes *zombie* because couriers may have its address and continue to communicate with it. When zombie, a server first completes any outstanding worker requests without accepting any new requests from couriers. (Note, a worker task accesses the t2fns information associated with its server, so the TopicNameServer cannot remove this data (if it is going to) until after the server has stopped all of its workers.) Second, the server goes into a mode where it does no new work and courier calls to Server::getFileNames return NULL and calls to Server::getFile return false.

A Server has the following interface:

```
_Task Server {
  public:
    typedef std::map<std::string, std::vector<std::string> > Topic2FileNames;
    struct Job {                                    // Job for a worker
        const std::string url;                      // URL to look up and transmit
        Courier *courier;                           // Transmit to this courier
        Job( std::string url, Courier *courier = NULL ) : url( url ), courier( courier ) {}
    };
    Server( const unsigned int id, const unsigned int poolSize,
            Topic2FileNames &t2fns );
    _Nomutex unsigned int getId() const;            // Server identifier
    std::vector<std::string> *getFileNames( const std::string &topic ); // Courier calls to
                                                    //   get list of hosted files for topic
    bool getFile( const std::string &url );         // Courier calls to get worker to transmit file
    Job *requestWork( Job *job );                   // Worker calls to get job; NULL => terminate
    void kill();                                    // Kill server so it goes zombie
};
```

g. A Worker task is created by a Server. It calls Server::requestWork to return the result of its current job and obtain a new job. (You may or may not need to use the returned result.) After obtaining a new job, a worker delays (yield) a random number of times (1..5) before it processes the request of type Job, which contains information to look up a URL and transfer its file's content to a courier. A worker communicates directly with the courier requesting a URL transfer.

A Worker has the following interface:

```
_Task Worker {
  public:
    Worker( const unsigned int id, Server &server );
};
```

h. A Cache object is created by a Browser. It contains two independently accessible data structures:

   i. list of topics with associated file names for each topic searched,
   ii. and the contents for each file read.

Since the cache can be accessed simultaneously by both the browser and couriers, use readers/writer mutual-exclusion to control access to both data structures, and use a separate readers/writer lock for each data structure because the data structures are independent critical sections. Note, because the cache is shared, it is possible for the browser, which is an administrator, to block; however, this blocking is short and bounded, and sharing the cache increases concurrency among browser and couriers, in general.

A Cache has the following interface:

```
class Cache {
  public:
    Cache();
    void addFileName( const std::string &topic, const unsigned int server,
                      const std::string &fileName );
    void addUrl( const std::string &url, const std::string &content );
    bool retrieveTopic( std::string &fileNames, const std::string &topic ); // If topic
                                       // present, return concatenated list of file names
    bool retrieveUrl( std::string &content, const std::string &url ); // If url present,
                                       // return the file contents
    void clear();                      // Clear the cache
    void printAll();                   // Print contents of cache
};
```

i. uMain starts by reading in a text configuration file, server.config, from the current directory. The data in the configuration file has the following format:

Server Id	Topic	File Name
0	a	/x/y/data1
0	b	/x/y/data2
1	b	/x/y/data3
1	b	/x/y/data4
2	b	/x/y/data4
4	c	/x/y/data5
4	d	/x/y/data5

Each line consists of a server id, the topic the server hosts, and the name of the file that contains content for that topic. Assume the syntax of the file contents is correct, and the file names are unique and contain no spaces. Read the configuration data into an object of type TopicNameServer::ServerConfig. Then the topic-name server and browser are created. The program terminates when the user types a 'q' or end-of-file is encountered. The output is a simple trace of its execution. Trace output goes to standard output.

The shell interface to the webBrowser program is as follows:

```
webBrowser C W
```

where C specifies the number of couriers in the browser's pool, and W specifies the number of workers in each server's pool. If a pool-size number is less than 1, print an appropriate usage message and exit.

35. WATCola is renown for its famous line of healthy soda pop, which come in the dazzling array of flavours: Blues Black-Cherry, Classical Cream-Soda, Rock Root-Beer and Jazz Lime. The company recently won the bid to provide soda to vending machines on campus. The vending machines are periodically restocked by a WATCola truck making deliveries from the local bottling plant.

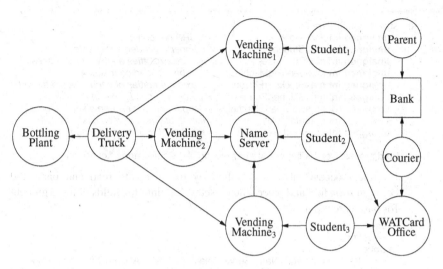

Fig. 11.12 Concession service

This assignment simulates a simple concession service using the objects and relationships in Fig. 11.12. (Not all possible communication paths are shown in the diagram.)

The following constants are used to configure the assignment, and are read from a text file:

```
SodaCost              2    # Manufacturer Suggested Retail Price (MSRP) per bottle
NumStudents           2    # number of students to create
MaxPurchases          8    # maximum number of bottles a student purchases
NumVendingMachines    3    # number of vending machines
MaxStockPerFlavour    5    # maximum number of bottles of each flavour in a
                      #     vending machine
MaxShippedPerFlavour  3    # maximum number of bottles of each flavour generated
                      #     by the bottling plant per production run
TimeBetweenShipments  3    # length of time between shipment pickup
ParentalDelay         2    # length of time between new deposits of funds
NumCouriers           1    # maximum number of couriers in the pool
```

Comments in the file (from # to the end-of-line), as well as blank lines, are ignored. The constants may appear in any order. Any number of spaces/tabs may appear around a constant name, value or comment. You may assume each constant appears in the configuration file, is syntactically correct, its value is within an appropriate range (i.e., no error checking is required), and only one constant is defined per line. You may have to modify the values in the provided sample file to obtain interesting results when testing.

The following types and routines are required in the assignment (you may add only a public destructor and private/protected members):

a. **struct** ConfigParms {
    unsigned int sodaCost;   // *MSRP per bottle*
    unsigned int numStudents;   // *number of students to create*
    unsigned int maxPurchases;   // *maximum bottles a student purchases*
    unsigned int numVendingMachines; // *number of vending machines*
    unsigned int maxStockPerFlavour; // *maximum bottles of each flavour stocked*
    unsigned int maxShippedPerFlavour; // *bottles of each flavour in a shipment*
    unsigned int timeBetweenShipments; // *length of time between shipment pickup*
    unsigned int parentalDelay;   // *length of time between cash deposits*
    unsigned int numCouriers;   // *number of couriers in the pool*
};
void processConfigFile(**const char** ∗configFile, ConfigParms &cparms);

Routine processConfigFile is called by the driver to read and parse the configuration file, and places the parsed values into the fields of the argument for parameter cparms.

b. **_Task** Student {
    void main();
  public:
    Student(Printer &prt, NameServer &nameServer, WATCardOffice &cardOffice,
        unsigned int id, **unsigned int** maxPurchases);
};

A Student's function is to periodically buy some of their favourite soda from a vending machine (a bottle costs whatever the vending machine is charging). Each student is passed an id in the range [0, NumStudents) for identification. A student begins by selecting a random number of bottles to purchase [1, MaxPurchases], a random favourite flavour [0, 3], creates a WATCard via the WATCardOffice with a $5 balance, and obtains the location of a vending machine from the name server. A student terminates after purchasing all the soda initially selected. Before each attempt to buy a soda, a student yields a random number of times in the range [1, 10]. A student then attempts to buy a bottle of soda from the vending machine. Since the vending machine only takes "real" money, the student may have to block until the amount transferred from the WATCardOffice appears on their WATCard. If a courier has lost a student's WATCard during a transfer (see WATCardOffice::Courier), the exception WATCardOffice::Lost is raised when the future value is accessed. In this case, the student must create a new WATCard via the WATCardOffice with a $5 balance, and re-attempt to buy a soda but without yielding as no call to buy has occurred. Note, a courier can lose a student's WATCard during the transfer for the new create so this issue can occur repeatedly. If the vending machine delivers a bottle of soda, the student drinks it and attempts another purchase. If the vending machine indicates insufficient funds, a student transfers the current vending-machine soda-cost plus $5 to their WATCard via the WATCard office. If the vending machine is out of the student's favourite flavour, the student must obtain a new vending machine from the name server. (Hence, a student may busy wait among vending machines until its specific soda appears from the bottling plant.)

c. **class** WATCard {
    WATCard(**const** WATCard &);   *// prevent copying*
    WATCard &**operator**=(**const** WATCard &);
  public:
    WATCard();
    typedef Future_ISM<WATCard *> FWATCard; *// future watcard pointer*
    void deposit(**unsigned int** amount);
    void withdraw(**unsigned int** amount);
    unsigned int getBalance();
  };

The WATCard manages the money associated with a card. When a WATCard is created it has a $0 balance. The courier calls deposit after a funds transfer. A vending machine calls withdraw when a soda is purchased. A student and a vending machine call getBalance to determine the balance. FWATCard is a future pointer to a student's WATCard for synchronizing access to the WATCard between the student and the courier.

d. **_Task** WATCardOffice {
    struct Job {   *// marshalled arguments and return future*
        Args args;   *// call arguments (YOU DEFINE "Args")*
        FWATCard result;   *// return future*
        Job(Args args) : args(args) {}
    };
    _Task Courier { ... };   *// communicates with bank*
    void main();
  public:
    _Event Lost {};   *// lost WATCard*
    WATCardOffice(Printer &prt, Bank &bank, **unsigned int** numCouriers);
    FWATCard create(**unsigned int** sid, **unsigned int** amount);
    FWATCard transfer(**unsigned int** sid, **unsigned int** amount, WATCard *card);
    Job *requestWork();
  };

The WATCardOffice is an administrator task used by a student to transfer funds from their bank account to their WATCard to buy a soda. Initially, the WATCard office creates a fixed-sized courier pool with numCouriers courier tasks to communicate with the bank. (Additional couriers may not be created after the WATCardOffice begins.) A student performs an asynchronous call to create to create a "real" WATCard with an initial balance. A future WATCard is returned and sufficient funds are subsequently obtained from the bank (see Parent task) via a courier to satisfy the create request. A student performs an asynchronous call to transfer when its WATCard indicates there is insufficient funds to buy a soda. A future WATCard is returned and sufficient funds are subsequently obtained from the bank (see Parent task) via a courier to satisfy the transfer request. The WATCard office is empowered to transfer funds from a student's bank-account to its WATCard by sending a request through a courier to the bank. Each courier task calls requestWork, blocks until a Job request is ready and then receives the next Job request as the result of the call. As soon as the request is satisfied (i.e., money is obtained from the bank), the courier updates the student's WATCard. There is a 1 in 6 chance a courier loses a student's WATCard after the update. When the card is lost, the exception WATCardOffice::Lost is inserted into the future, rather than making the future available, and the current WATCard is deleted.

e. **_Monitor** Bank {
    public:
      Bank(**unsigned int** numStudents);
      void deposit(**unsigned int** id, **unsigned int** amount);
      void withdraw(**unsigned int** id, **unsigned int** amount);
    };

The Bank is a monitor, which behaves like a server, that manages student-account information for all students. Each student's account initially starts with a balance of $0. The parent calls deposit to endow gifts to a specific student. A courier calls withdraw to transfer money on behalf of the WATCard office for a specific student. The courier waits until enough money has been deposited, which may require multiple deposits.

f. **_Task** Parent {
    void main();
    public:
      Parent(Printer &prt, Bank &bank, **unsigned int** numStudents,
               unsigned int parentalDelay);
    };

The Parent task periodically gives a random amount of money [$1, $3] to a random student. Before each gift is transferred, the parent yields for parentalDelay times (not random). The parent must check for a call to its destructor to know when to terminate. Since it must not block on this call, it is necessary to use a terminating **_Else** on the accept statement. (Hence, the parent is busy waiting for the call to its destructor.)

g. **_Task** VendingMachine {
    void main();
    public:
      enum Flavours { ... };   // *flavours of soda (YOU DEFINE)*
      _Event Funds {};   // *insufficient funds*
      _Event Stock {};   // *out of stock for particular flavour*
      VendingMachine(Printer &prt, NameServer &nameServer, **unsigned int** id,
               unsigned int sodaCost, **unsigned int** maxStockPerFlavour);
      void buy(Flavours flavour, WATCard &card);
      unsigned int *inventory();
      void restocked();
      _Nomutex unsigned int cost();
      _Nomutex unsigned int getId();
    };

A vending machine's function is to sell soda to students at some cost. Each vending machine is passed an id in the range [0, NumVendingMachines) for identification, MSRP price for a bottle of soda, and the maximum number of bottles of each flavour in a vending machine. A new vending machine is empty (no stock) and begins by registering with the name server. A student calls buy to obtain one of their favourite sodas. If the student has insufficient funds to purchase the soda or the specified soda is unavailable, exceptions Funds or Stock are raised, respectively; otherwise, the student's WATCard is debited by the cost of a soda. (A flag variable is necessary to know when to raise Funds or Stock on the correct task stack.)

Periodically, the truck comes by to restock the vending machines with new soda from the bottling plant. Restocking is performed in two steps. The truck calls inventory to return a pointer to an array containing the amount of each kind of soda currently in the vending machine. The truck uses this information to transfer into each machine as much of its stock of new soda as fits; for each kind of soda, no more than MaxStockPerFlavour per flavour can be added to a machine. If the truck cannot top-up a particular flavour, it transfers as many bottles as it has (which could be 0). After transferring new soda into the machine by directly modifying the array passed from inventory, the truck calls restocked to indicate the operation is complete. The vending machine cannot accept buy calls during restocking. The cost member returns the cost of purchasing a soda for this machine. The getId member returns the identification number of the vending machine. You define the public type Flavours to represent the different flavours of soda.

h. _**Task** NameServer {
```
    void main();
  public:
    NameServer( Printer &prt, unsigned int numVendingMachines,
                unsigned int numStudents );
    void VMregister( VendingMachine *vendingmachine );
    VendingMachine *getMachine( unsigned int id );
    VendingMachine **getMachineList();
};
```

The NameServer is an administrator task used to manage the vending-machine names. The name server is passed the number of vending machines, NumVendingMachines, and the number of students, NumStudents. It begins by logically distributing the students evenly across the vending machines in a round-robin fashion. That is, student id 0 is assigned to the first registered vending-machine, student id 1 is assigned to the second registered vending-machine, etc., until there are no more registered vending-machines, and then start again with the first registered vending-machine. Vending machines call VMregister to register themselves so students can subsequently locate them. A student calls getMachine to find a vending machine, and the name server must cycle through the vending machines *separately* for each student starting from the initial position via modulo incrementing to ensure a student has a chance to visit every machine. The truck calls getMachineList to obtain an array of pointers to vending machines so it can visit each machine to deliver new soda.

i. **_Task** BottlingPlant {
        void main();
    public:
        _Event Shutdown {};   *// shutdown plant*
        BottlingPlant(Printer &prt, NameServer &nameServer,
            unsigned int numVendingMachines, **unsigned int** maxShippedPerFlavour,
            unsigned int maxStockPerFlavour, **unsigned int** timeBetweenShipments);
        void getShipment(**unsigned int** cargo[ ]);
    };

The bottling plant periodically produces random new quantities of
each flavour of soda, [0, MaxShippedPerFlavour] per flavour. The bottling
plant is passed the number of vending machines, NumVendingMachines,
the maximum number of bottles of each flavour generated during
a production run and subsequently shipped, MaxShippedPerFlavour, the
maximum number of bottles of each flavour in a vending machine
MaxStockPerFlavour, and the length of time between shipment pickups by
the truck, TimeBetweenShipments. It begins by creating a truck, performing
a production run, and waiting for the truck to pick up the production run.
The truck then distributes these bottles to initialize the registered vending
machines. To simulate a production run of soda, the bottling plant yields for
TimeBetweenShipments times (not random). The truck calls getShipment to
obtain a shipment from the plant (i.e., the production run), and the shipment
is copied into the cargo array passed by the truck. getShipment throws the
exception Shutdown if the bottling plant is closing down and cargo is not
changed. (Call routine uRendezvousAcceptor before throwing the exception
to prevent raising exception RendezvousFailure at the bottling plant. A flag
variable is necessary to know when to raise Shutdown on the correct task
stack.) The bottling plant does not start another production run until the truck
has picked up the current run.

j. **_Task** Truck {
        void main();
    public:
        Truck(Printer &prt, NameServer &nameServer, BottlingPlant &plant,
            unsigned int numVendingMachines, **unsigned int** maxStockPerFlavour);
    };

The truck moves soda from the bottling plant to the vending machines.
The truck is passed the number of vending machines, numVendingMachines,
and the maximum number of bottles of each flavour in a vending machine
maxStockPerFlavour. The truck begins by obtaining the location of each
vending machine from the name server. Before each shipment from the
bottling plant, the truck yields a random number of times [1, 10] to get a coffee
from Tom Hortons. The truck then calls BottlingPlant::getShipment to obtain a
new shipment of soda; any soda still on the truck is thrown away as it is past
its due date. If the bottling plant is closing down, the truck terminates. To
ensure fairness, the vending machines are restocked in cyclic order starting
at the vending machine *after* the last machine the truck restocked, until there
is no more soda on the truck or the truck has made a complete cycle of
all the vending machines; so there is no guarantee each vending machine

is completely restocked or the entire complement of vending machines is restocked or all the soda on the truck is used. The truck can only restock up to MaxStockPerFlavour for each flavour in each vending machine (see VendingMachine task).

k. **_Monitor** / **_Cormonitor** Printer {
     public:
       enum Kind { Parent, WATCardOffice, NameServer, Truck, BottlingPlant,
                Student, Vending, Courier };
       Printer(**unsigned int** numStudents, **unsigned int** numVendingMachines,
              unsigned int numCouriers);
       void print(Kind kind, **char** state);
       void print(Kind kind, **char** state, **int** value1);
       void print(Kind kind, **char** state, **int** value1, **int** value2);
       void print(Kind kind, **unsigned int** lid, **char** state);
       void print(Kind kind, **unsigned int** lid, **char** state, **int** value1);
       void print(Kind kind, **unsigned int** lid, **char** state, **int** value1, **int** value2);
   };

All output from the program is generated by calls to a printer, excluding error messages. The printer generates output like that in Fig. 11.13. Each column is assigned to a particular kind of object. There are 8 kinds of objects: parent, WATCard office, name server, truck, bottling plant, student, vending machine and courier. Student, vending machine and courier have multiple instances. For the objects with multiple instances, these objects pass in their local identifier [0,N) when printing. Each kind of object prints specific information in its column:

- The parent prints the following information:

State	Meaning	Additional Information
S	starting	
D s,g	deposit gift	student s receiving gift, amount of gift g
F	finished	

- The WATCard office prints the following information:

State	Meaning	Additional Information
S	starting	
W	request work call complete	
C s,a	create call complete	student s, transfer amount a
T s,a	transfer call complete	student s, transfer amount a
F	finished	

```
% soda soda.config 46671
```

Parent	WATOff	Names	Truck	Plant	Stud0	Stud1	Mach0	Mach1	Mach2	Cour0
S	S	S								S
D1,3		R0					S2			
D0,3		R1						S2		
D1,3		R2		S	S1,1				S2	
D1,3	C0,5	N0,0	S	G11	V0	S2,2				t0,5
D1,1	W					V1				
D0,2	C1,5	N1,1								T0,5
										t1,5
			P11							T1,5
			d0,11							
			U0,9							
D0,3	W		D0,0	P			r			
D1,1				G8			R			
D1,3					B3					
...	...	...	...	...	F	...	...	...	...	...
D1,3			P8			L	B1,1			
			d1,8							
			U1,12							
D0,2	C1,5		D1,0	P			r			t1,5
D0,1	W					L	R			T1,5
	C1,5		P4	G4						
			d2,4							
			U2,16							
			D2,0							t1,5
D1,2	W		P					r		T1,5
D1,1				G3	B3		B2,2	R		
D0,1										
D0,3										
D1,1					B1					
...	...	...	...	...	F	...	...	...	...	...
D1,1							B2,1			
...	...	...	F	...	...	...	...	...	...	...
...	...	...	...	F	...	...	...	...	...	...
D0,3										
...	...	...	...	...	...	...	F	...	...	...
D0,3										
...	...	...	...	...	...	...	...	F	...	...
D1,1										
...	...	...	...	...	...	...	...	...	F	...
D0,1										
...	...	F	...	...	...	...	...	...	...	...
D1,2										
D1,2										
...	...	...	...	...	...	...	...	...	...	F
...	F	...	...	...	...	...	...	...	...	...
D1,2										
F	...	...	...	...	...	...	...	...	...	...

```
*************************
```

Fig. 11.13   WATCola: example output

- The name server prints the following information:

State	Meaning	Additional Information
S	starting	
R v	register vending machine	vending machine v registering
N s,v	new vending machine	student s requesting vending machine, new vending machine v
F	finished	

- The truck prints the following information:

State	Meaning	Additional Information
S	starting	
P a	picked up shipment	total amount a of all sodas in the shipment
d v,r	begin delivery to vending machine	vending machine v, total amount remaining r in the shipment
U v,b	unsuccessfully filled vending machine	vending machine v, total number of bottles b not replenished
D v,r	end delivery to vending machine	vending machine v, total amount remaining r in the shipment
F	finished	

States d and D are printed for each vending machine visited during restocking.

- The bottling plant prints the following information:

State	Meaning	Additional Information
S	starting	
G b	generating soda	bottles b generated in production run
P	shipment picked up by truck	
F	finished	

- A student prints the following information:

State	Meaning	Additional Information
S f,b	starting	favourite soda f, number of bottles b to purchase
V v	selecting vending machine	vending machine v selected
B b	bought a soda	WATCard balance b
L	WATCard lost	
F	finished	

- A vending machine prints the following information:

State	Meaning	Additional Information
S c	starting	cost c per bottle
r	start reloading by truck	
R	complete reloading by truck	
B f,r	student bought a soda	flavour f of soda purchased, amount remaining r of this flavour
F	finished	

- A courier prints the following information:

State	Meaning	Additional Information
S	starting	
t s,a	start funds transfer	student s requesting transfer, amount a of transfer
T s,a	complete funds transfer	student s requesting transfer, amount a of transfer
F	finished	

Information is buffered until a column is overwritten for a particular entry, which causes the buffered data to be flushed. If there is no new stored information for a column since the last buffer flush, an empty column is printed. When an object finishes, the buffer is flushed immediately, the state for that object is marked with F, and all other objects are marked with "...". After an object has finished, no further output appears in that column. All output spacing can be accomplished using the standard 8-space tabbing. Buffer any information necessary for printing in internal representation; **do not build and store strings of text for output.**

uMain::main starts by calling processConfigFile to read and parse the simulation configurations. It then creates in order the printer, bank, parent, WATCard office, name server, vending machines, bottling plant and students. The truck is created by the bottling plant; the couriers are created by the WATCard office. The program terminates once all of the students have purchased their specified number of bottles. Note, there is one trick in closing down the system: delete the bottling plant *before* deleting the vending machines to allow the truck to complete its final deliveries to the vending machines; otherwise, a deadlock can occur.

The executable program is named soda and has the following shell interface:

soda [config-file [random-seed]]

config-file is the text (formatted) file containing the configuration constants. If unspecified, use the file name soda.config. seed is the positive seed for the random-number generator. If unspecified, use getpid.

References

1. Alexandrescu, A.: Modern C++ Design: Generic Programming and Design Patterns Applied. Addison-Wesley Professional, Boston (2001)
2. Gentleman, W.M.: Message passing between sequential processes: the reply primitive and the administrator concept. Softw. Pract. Exp. **11**(5), 435–466 (1981)
3. Halstead Jr., R.H.: Multilisp: A language for concurrent symbolic programming. ACM Trans. Progr. Lang. Syst. **7**(4), 501–538 (1985)
4. Lavender, R.G., Schmidt, D.C.: Pattern languages of program design 2. chap. Active Object: An Object Behavioral Pattern for Concurrent Programming, pp. 483–499. Addison-Wesley Longman Publishing, Boston (1996)

Chapter 12
Optimization

One of the most important aspects of a computer is its speed of computation. However, solving problems on a computer is a balancing act between constructing an algorithm to compute a solution, and casting that algorithm into the rigorous and limited structure of a programming language and hardware. A huge amount of time is spent performing optimizations to bridge this gap with the goal of obtaining maximal use of the computer. Often, too much time is focused on optimizing performance for cases where optimal speed is unnecessary. If a computer had infinite memory and speed, no optimizations would be necessary to use less memory or run faster (space/time). However, with finite resources, optimization is useful/ necessary to conserve resources and for good performance. Hence, an algorithm is transformed by a programmer into a programming language, where the programmer tries to utilize a good mix of data structures and control flow to express the algorithm in an optimal way. Then the compiler for the programming language and the hardware for the computer further optimize the program to achieve the best possible execution. Because these latter optimizations are implicit, and hence often beyond the control of the programmer, this chapter gives a general understanding of these optimizations, and discusses their effect on the behaviour and correctness of concurrent programs.

Like having a perfect computer (infinitely large/fast), if programmers were perfect, this discussion would be unnecessary because each program would be written in an optimal way. However, most programs are not written in minimal form or optimal order, so there is potential to optimize for both of these capabilities. For example, the basic concepts in object-oriented, functional, and many software-engineering approaches are seldom optimal on a von Neumann computer.

© Springer International Publishing Switzerland 2016
P.A. Buhr, *Understanding Control Flow*, DOI 10.1007/978-3-319-25703-7_12

12.1   Basic Optimizations

The general forms of compiler and hardware optimizations are:

- **reordering**: By restructuring (refactoring) a program it is possible to introduce micro forms of parallelism available in the hardware to deal with the latency of loading/storing values to/from register and memory. For example, x += 1 requires loading the variable x from memory into a register so it can be incremented and then storing the new value from the register back into variable x in memory. Moving a value to/from register/memory takes time so there is a delay. A program runs faster if this delay can be overlapped in parallel with other work. So the compiler/hardware tries to move the load of x backward in the program as far as possible to start the loading operation *before* the value is actually needed, called **prefetching**, which is like an asynchronous call. Then, in parallel, operations that already have their values can proceed. By the point where the value x is necessary for the increment, the value should be loaded into the register, and hence, no delay is necessary. If the value of x has not appeared by the time it is needed, the computer actually **stalls** (blocks) until the value is loaded. Clearly minimizing stalls increases performance (as it does in a concurrent program). In many ways, x is like a future returned by an asynchronous call to the memory server, and this future is subsequently accessed when needed, which could block if the memory server has not finished the load. So while programmers carefully craft their programs to read well, the compiler and hardware completely tear the program apart moving code all over the place. Prefetching is just one of many reordering optimizations performed by the compiler/hardware to reduce a number of different kinds of latency in a computer.
- **eliding**: Over time, programs grow in size and complexity. However, programmers seldom have the time to ensure all old code is removed as changes are made. Hence, many programs are filled with extraneous code fragments (**dead code**) that no longer perform any function. The hardware always executes dead code. However, the compiler is capable of detecting most dead code and eliding (removing) it before it gets to the hardware. It is surprising how much code can be removed. Again, programmers spend time crafting a program to read well, and the compiler may throw away much of the program, such as getter and setter members used to access data in a class. In the extreme case, a complex program that does not *print* can be elided into the null program, which executes in zero time.
- **replication**: Duplicate code and variables are a maintenance problem because all copies have to be keep consistent. Hence, programmers strive to eliminate duplication using mechanisms like global constants/variables, advanced control-flow, and routines. However, replicating variables and code can shorten access distances by moving a copy closer to where it is used, which correspondingly reduces access latency. For example, a variable is copied into a register from memory to reduce latency, and the variable is kept in the register for the duration of its modification (if possible) to prevent multiple costly loads from memory.

The variable is now duplicated (replicated) in two locations, a register and memory, and these two locations have to be kept logically synchronized, i.e., which location is the true value of the variable. Other forms of replication are multiple hardware pipelines and computational units that allow more micro parallelism in a program.

An optimized program must be isomorphic to its non-optimized counterpart, i.e., both programs produce the same result for fixed input, but the optimized version executes faster. The kinds of optimizations are restricted by the form and structure of the program and the specific execution environment. To understand the effects of optimizations on concurrent programs, it is first necessary to examine sequential optimizations.

12.2 Sequential Optimizations

Most programs are sequential. Even concurrent programs are composed of (large) sections of sequential code executed per thread connected by small sections of concurrent code where threads interact (protected by synchronization and mutual exclusion). Hence, the focus of most programmers, compiler writers and hardware designers is to make sequential execution run as fast as possible. Furthermore, the semantics of sequential execution are significantly simpler to optimization than concurrent execution. Specifically, sequential operations occur in **program order**, while concurrent programs execute in non-deterministic order.

12.2.1 Reordering

Program order introduces dependencies that result in partial orderings among program statements:

- **data dependency** results from the order of reads and writes (R $\Rightarrow$ read, W $\Rightarrow$ write). The following are the 4 orderings of read and write operations on the same variable.

$R_x \rightarrow R_x$	$W_x \rightarrow R_x$	$R_x \rightarrow W_x$	$W_x \rightarrow W_x$
y = x;	x = 0;	y = x;	x = 0;
z = x;	y = x;	x = 3;	x = 3;

reverse lines

z = x;	y = x;	x = 3;	x = 3;
y = x;	x = 0;	y = x;	x = 0;
yes	no	no	no

Which statements can and cannot be reordered without changing program order? The first (left) case can be reordered. That is, it makes no difference if y is assigned before or after z because both variables read the same value from x. In the other three cases, program order is violated if the statements are reordered because x or y has different values for each reordering. Programmers quickly learn that some program orderings matter and some do not.

- **control dependency** results from the conditional nature of control flow. That is, depending on the values of variables, control flow may or may not execute a series of statements.

```
if ( x == 0 ) {          while ( x == 0 ) {
    x = 1;                    x = 1;
    . . .                    . . .
```

reverse lines

```
x = 1;                   x = 1;
if ( x == 0 ) {          while ( x == 0 ) {
    . . .                    . . .
```

no   no

These statements cannot be reordered as the first line determines if the second line is executed.

The key point is that only one of the transformations generates a degree of freedom with respect to reordering optimizations.

Now perform the same reordering analyses with disjoint (independent) variables, i.e., variables with different addresses, e.g., x and y.

- **data dependency**

$$R_x \to R_y \qquad W_x \to R_y \qquad R_x \to W_y \qquad W_x \to W_y$$

```
t = x;          x = 0;          x == 1;          y = 0;
s = y;          y == 1;         y = 3;           x = 3;
```

reverse lines

```
s = y;          y == 1;         y = 3;           x = 3;
t = x;          x = 0;          x == 1;          y = 0;
```

yes   yes   yes   yes

All of these statements can be reordered as there are no dependencies between them.

- **control dependency**

```
if ( x == 0 ) {          while ( x == 0 ) {
    y = 1;                   y = 1;
    . . .                   . . .
```

reverse lines

```
y = 1;                   y = 1;
if ( x == 0 ) {          while ( x == 0 ) {
    . . .                   . . .
```

no   no

These statements cannot be reordered as the first line determines if the second line is executed.

The key point is that for disjoint variables there are more degrees of freedom with respect to reordering optimizations, and both compiler and hardware take advantage of these and other possible reorderings for prefetching.

12.2.2 Eliding

Data-dependency analysis can reveal dead code, which is then removed. For example, if a write/write dependence is detected with no intervening reads:

```
x = 3;  // dead code
 ...    // no read of x
x = 0;  // live code
```

the first write is unnecessary and can be elided. It is surprising how many of these subtle situations occur in large programs. Often the compiler warns about eliding so the programmer can ask "Why am I doing this?".

Control-dependency analysis can reveal unnecessary execution, which is then removed. For example, this loop does not generate any observable computation because no values escape the loop body.

```
for ( int i = 0; i < 10000; i += 1 ) { // unnecessary, no values escape
    int j = i + 2;
}
```

Control-dependency analysis can also refactor from one approach to another, which is more amenable to the particular hardware. For example, recursion is seldom the best approach for iteration, so the compiler detects the tail recursion in the recursive routine and converts it to looping.

tail recursion	looping

`int factorial( int n, int acc ) {`
`    if ( n == 0 ) return acc;`
`    return factorial( n - 1, n * acc );`
`}`
	`int factorial( int n, int acc ) {`
	`    for ( int i = n; i > 0; i -= 1 )`
	`        acc *= i;`
	`}`

12.2.3 Replication

Moore's law [4] states the number of transistors for a processor doubles every 18 months. Notice, this law describes size *not* speed. In fact, the speed of processors is slowly approaching an upper bound of 5-10 GHz, because of power/heat issues. The question remains: what is to be done with all of these transistors? The answer is *replicate* more pathways and computation units. Current processors are composed of complex pathways for data flow, and many general purpose and specialized cores, which introduces increasing parallelism, assuming the software can exploit it. For example, a modern processor chip may have 3-levels of caching, 4-16 cores, 8-32 floating-point units, multiple pipelining units, an array-processing unit and graphics unit (GPU). As well, these computation units interconnect on the memory bus with other specialized I/O processors, such as disks, CD/DVD player, memory cards, USB ports. Each of these I/O devices/controllers has its own processor, some of which are very powerful. These processors run sophisticated algorithms to optimize I/O storage layout, caching, and protocols to minimize the size and cost of data transfers. Overlapping computation with I/O provides a significant form of parallelism. Even before multi-core, multi-processor environments, when computers only had a single CPU, it was possible to obtain program speedup by overlapping computation with I/O channels. While programmers can explicitly access some of these computational units, many are accessed implicit by the compiler and hardware. Essentially, the compiler and hardware are discovering concurrency in a sequential program (see Sect. 5.6, p. 201) and converting small portions of code into a concurrent program that takes advantage of new micro parallelism. Clearly, these new micro-concurrent programs must have corresponding synchronization and mutual exclusion to work correctly. As stated previously, performance gains from discovering concurrency are restricted, but given the amount of parallel hardware, significant benefits are possible.

12.3 Memory Hierarchy

Of all the forms of hardware replication, the complex pathways for data flow, called the memory hierarchy, has a significant affect on concurrency, and so, it is discussed in detail. As pointed out, moving data to/from registers and memory (see Fig. 12.1(a)) takes time, which is mitigated by prefetching. The problem is that there are billions of bytes of memory but only 6–256 registers. Hence, there is a high dynamic circulation of values to/from registers/memory. The compiler makes static guesses as to which variables are highly used and favours these variables with respect to duration of time in registers. Less favoured variables are loaded and stored as needed. Registers are private to each processor, so it is impossible to share or optimize across them. Hence, the register set is completely loaded and unloaded for each context switch among coroutines, tasks and programs, without any consideration of cross execution-state access. Finally, registers have short addresses, 0 to N−1, rather than memory addresses. These short addresses are necessary to keep instruction lengths short, which reduces the time to load instructions from memory.

One way to mitigate register circulation is to add more registers and make them shared, called a cache (see Fig. 12.1(b)). A cache has both register and memory properties, and they are created outside the cores with multiple pathways connecting the cores on the processor chip. The cache is a buffer between the registers and main memory, and multiple buffers are possible, which creates the memory hierarchy. Optimizing data flow along this hierarchy largely defines a computer's speed. Having a basic understanding of the memory hierarchy is essential to understanding performance of both sequential programs and correctness of concurrent programs.

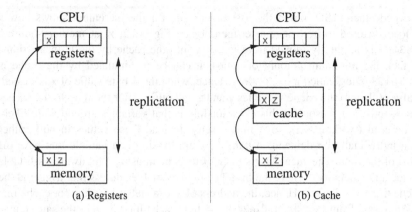

Fig. 12.1 Memory hierarchy

12.3.1   Cache Review

The following is a quick review of cache memory to support subsequent discussion. Cache memory attempts to compensate for the large difference in speed between processor and main-memory speed, which can be as much as 100(0) times (10000(0) times for disk). The approach replicates memory data in increasingly faster but smaller buffers. Hence, a cache is 100(0)s times smaller than main memory but attempts to hold only the highly active values. The reason the approach works is that programs have large amounts of close spatial and temporal accesses. (The same reasoning applies to virtual memory with paging.) That is, small amounts of data are accessed close together and/or at the same time. At any time, a program is manipulating a small **working set** of data, and as the program executes, new working sets are generated and old ones are discarded. Hence, the working set is pulled from memory into the cache, and then these values are rotated through the registers, but the access from register to cache is much faster than memory. As a new working set forms, the values in the old working set are overwritten in the cache, and the new values rotate through the registers. Because the cache is smaller it can be faster, while keeping down cost/power/heat.

The following example illustrates the details of how a cache works to stage data between registers and memory and allow sharing of data among programs. Consider the code fragment:

```
int x, y, z;
x += 1;       ld   r1,0xa3480      // load register 1 from x
              add r1,#1            // increment
              st   r1,0xa3480      // store register 1 to x
```

The code increments x and the assembler code for the increment shows how x is loaded/stored to/from a register/memory. In Fig. 12.2, x, at memory address 0xa3480, is implicitly moved from memory into the cache by the ld instructions. In fact, the minimum amount of data that can be manipulated by the cache is 32/64/128 bytes, called a cache line. Hence, when the 4-byte value of x is loaded, it also pulls into the cache variables y and z and others after them up to the cache-line length. The reason for this extra loading is that variables around x are likely to be used (working set), so it makes sense to load these values in bulk rather than individually on demand. Again, the extra loading is a gamble that pays off most of the time. The cache keeps track of its content using a hardware hash-table (associative memory), where the hash key is the variable address that triggered the cache line to be loaded. Hence, the address of x, 0xa3480, is the key for cache line 1. Addresses from 0xa3480 to 0xa34c0 (64-byte cache line) hash to the same cache line, so this cache is 16-way associative for a word size of 4-byes. That is, each cache address matches with 16 different words of memory. When the cache is full, data is evicted by removing other cache lines. The cache line used the least is usually the best one to remove (LRU); i.e., the cache line for a dissolving working-set. When a program ends, all its addresses are flushed from the memory hierarchy. In theory, caches could eliminate registers, but the small addresses for registers (3-8 bits for 8-256 registers) and the tight binding to the processor still give them a significant performance advantage.

12.3.2   Cache Coherence

Fig. 12.3 shows a 4-core processor with multiple levels of caches, each larger but with diminishing speed (and cost). For example, a processor may have 64K of L1 cache (32K instruction, 32K data) per core, 256K L2 cache per core (combined instruction and data) and 8MB L3 cache shared across cores connected by the system bus. (The system bus connects all the peripherals on a computer: processors, memory and I/O devices.) Data reads logically percolate variables to registers from memory up the memory hierarchy, creating cache copies. It is necessary to eagerly move values up the memory hierarchy to prevent processor stalls (prefetching loads). Data stores logically percolate variables from registers to memory down the memory hierarchy, modifying cache copies. It is advantageous to lazily move values down the memory hierarchy because data may be overwritten multiple times at the highest level so only the last write needs to move all the way to the lowest-level memory. It is lazily writing that produces the performance gain; otherwise, the processor has to wait for values to update memory for each store.

Notice, if the operating system decides to move a program to another processor, all the caching information on the "from" processor becomes invalid and the program's working set has to reform in the cache on the "to" processor, which is expensive. For this reason, the operating system tries to keep a program on the processor where it starts execution. If a program blocks completely, e.g., waiting

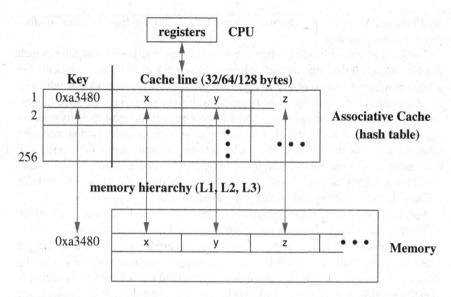

Fig. 12.2 Cache details

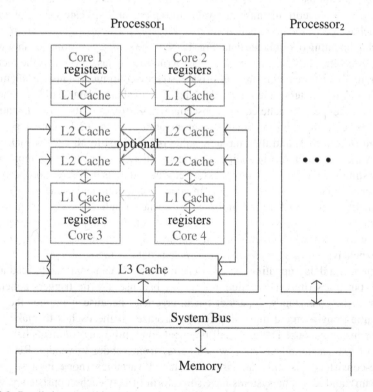

Fig. 12.3 Detailed memory hierarchy

for I/O to occur, there is no alternative but to remove it from the processor so other programs can execute.

Unlike registers, *all* cache values are shared across the entire computer, which can be seen by all the interconnect pathways. Hence, a variable can be replicated in a large number of locations. For a sequential program, it is easy to know which of the duplicate values in the memory hierarchy is the true value, i.e., the value highest up in the memory hierarchy on the executing processor is the most recently updated value. Furthermore, a sequential program has all private variables (not shared with other threads), so its values in the cache are unique, and their modification and movement in the memory hierarchy is independent. For a concurrent program, variables are shared among threads, so there are many duplicate copies of a variable in multiple cache buffers and memory hierarchies on different processors.

Fig. 12.4a shows an example with three threads T_1, T_2 and T_3, each executing on a different core on two different processors, and each accessing the shared variable x. In the execution snapshot, all the values represent variable x duplicated in multiple registers, caches and memory. Which of these values is the true value of x? Clearly, there is no true value and it is impossible to understand the behaviour of execution. What is needed is a mechanism to synchronization the values of x across all the different locations so there is a true value of x. The desired behaviour is for a write to x on one core to cause that value to replace all duplicate values of x in all the caches and in memory, called cache coherence, which is a hardware protocol ensuring updating of duplicate data. Fig. 12.4b is the same execution snapshot where cache coherence has synchronized the last write to x by task T_3 across the memory hierarchy. Notice, registers are still private, so they continue to cause problems. As mentioned, if registers were replaced with cache, all shared data would be coherent.

While the idea of cache coherence seems straightforward, its implementation is complex requiring a bidirectional synchronization. In Fig. 12.4c, core 1 performs a write from 0 to 1, and then the new value is broadcast to all caches sharing the same variable, which update their copy. Clearly, there is a race if two or more writes occur simultaneously. *When* a processor sees an update is a different property than coherence, called cache consistency. In general, each updated cache must send an acknowledgement back to the initial writer cache to indicate synchronization has occurred. Eager cache-consistency means data changes appear instantaneous by waiting for acknowledgements from all caches; however, this approach is complex and expensive. Lazy cache-consistency means data changes take place *eventually*, i.e., there is a delay updating the other caches so cores can continue to read an old value, but not write a new value and read it because a write triggers coherence. Eager cache-consistency is perfect but impractical, because it implies the entire computing environment must stop to synchronize all the caches to make writes appear instantaneous. Therefore, all practical computing environments have some form of lazy cache-consistency, which varies from vendor to vendor. Recapping, cache-consistency is only an issue for shared variables (none in a sequential program), and all cache systems have some form of lazy cache-consistency, which allows reading of stale values. Thus, all concurrent algorithms must be robust enough to handle reading of stale information without failure.

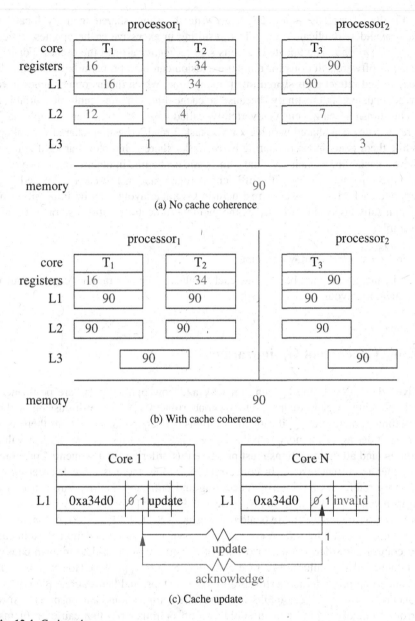

Fig. 12.4 Cache coherence

Finally, if threads continually read/write the same shared memory location, they invalidate duplicate cache lines, resulting in excessive cache updates, called cache thrashing. The updated value is said to *bounce* around the caches. For this reason, software solutions for mutual exclusion can be a problem because threads declare and retract their shared intent many time, which means other caches have to be updated. Interestingly, because a cache line contains multiple variables, cache thrashing can occur inadvertently, called false sharing. For example, task 1 read/writes non-shared variable x while task 2 read/writes non-shared variable y. While there is no apparent sharing by the tasks, there is indirect sharing if x and y share a cache line, which invalidates the same cache line in other caches. The only fix is to separate x and y with sufficient storage (padding) so each is located in a separate cache line. However, restructuring storage layout may be impossible for dynamically allocated variables as the memory allocator positions storage. In this example,

```
      task 1                 task 2
  int *x = new int     int *y = new int;
```

x and y may or may not be on same cache line, and the programmer cannot control the memory layout.

12.4   Concurrent Optimizations

Given the following background on why and how optimizations are performed, it is possible to gage their effects on concurrency [2]. As the discussion so far has hinted, there are significant implications. In sequential execution, there is a strong ordering of memory references, i.e., reading always returns the last value written, and all optimizations must preserve this ordering for a sequential program to generate correct results. In concurrent execution, there is a weak ordering of memory references because of scheduling and buffering, i.e., reading can return strange values (flickering/scrambling Sect. 6.3.7, p. 251), previously written values or values written in the future (staleness/freshness Sect. 9.7.1, p. 463). A concurrent programmer strengthens weak ordering using synchronization and mutual exclusion by controlling order and speed of execution; otherwise, non-determinism causes random results or failure (e.g., race condition, Sect. 8.1, p. 395). However, even if a concurrent programmer performs all the right steps, and hence, creates a correct concurrent program, the compiler and hardware optimizations can conspire to cause errors. In theory, a programmer could turn off optimizations that cause problems, but that presupposes knowledge of what to turn off and how to turn it off. In other words, the set of optimizations vary with compiler and hardware vendor, and new optimizations can be added at any time, making this approach impossible, assuming it is even possible to turn off the offending optimizations. In fact, sequential sections of a concurrent program accessing private variables can be optimized normally. The problems occur crossing concurrent boundaries where shared variables are accessed.

For correctness and performance, identify the concurrent code and only restrict *its* optimization. The following examples (not exhaustive) show different sequential optimizations in memory, cache, processor and compiler that cause failures in concurrent code.

12.4.1 Disjoint Reordering

All of the degrees of freedom in code reordering created by reads and writes on disjoint variable result in significant problems in concurrent code. All four cases are examined.

- $R_x \rightarrow R_y$ allows $R_y \rightarrow R_x$

  Reordering disjoint reads does not cause problems because no ordering information can be determined.

- $W_x \rightarrow R_y$ allows $R_y \rightarrow W_x$

  Reordering disjoint write and read causes problems, e.g., in Dekker's entry protocol:

			temp = you; // *R*
1	me = WantIn; // *W*	1	me = WantIn; // *W*
2	**while** (you == WantIn) { // *R*	2	**while** (temp == WantIn) {
3	...	3	...

  this reordering allows interchanging lines 1 and 2 so both threads read DontWantIn, both set WantIn, both see DontWantIn, and proceed into the critical section.

- $R_x \rightarrow W_y$ allows $W_y \rightarrow R_x$

  Reordering disjoint read and write causes problems, e.g., in using synchronizing flags (see Sect. 5.13, p. 219)

	Prod		Cons		Cons
1	Data = i;	1	**while** (! Insert); // *R*	3	data = Data; // *W*
2	Insert = **true**;	2	Insert = **false**;	1	**while** (! Insert); // *R*
		3	data = Data; // *W*	2	Insert = **false**;

  this reordering allows interchanging lines 1 and 3 for Cons so data is removed before it may have been inserted.

- $W_x \rightarrow W_y$ allows $W_y \rightarrow W_x$

  Reordering disjoint writes causes problems, e.g., in synchronizing flags (see Sect. 5.13, p. 219)

	Prod		Prod
1	Data = i; // *W*	2	Insert = true; // *W*
2	Insert = true; // *W*	1	Data = i; // *W*

  this reordering allows interchanging lines 1 and 2 in Prod so reading of uninserted data can occur.

  Similarly, in Peterson's entry protocol

```
1   me = WantIn; // W        2   ::Last = &me; // W
2   ::Last = &me; // W       1   me = WantIn; // W
```

this reordering interchanging lines 1 and 2 so the race occurs before either task sets its intent and both proceed into the critical section.

- At a higher-level, all of these reorderings can be used by the compiler to violate locking.

```
lock.acquire()        // critical section      lock.acquire()
// critical section   lock.acquire()           lock.release();
lock.release();       lock.release();          // critical section
```

Since routines acquire and release do not references any variables in the critical section, both routine can be moved, or parts of the routines can overlap into the critical section.

The key point is that these sequential optimizations can violate concurrent code in several ways.

12.4.2   Eliding

For high-level languages, the compiler decides when/which variables are loaded into registers. Once a variable is loaded, it can be used multiple times.

```
d = (x + a) * (x - b) / (x + c);
```

The value of variable x can be loaded into a register, where it is used for all of the computations in this expression. In this case, the compiler has elided two of the three loads of variable x. However, once a variable is in a register, no other processor can see it. Eliding loads and stores using registers can cause concurrency problems, e.g., with busy waiting.

```
      T₁                        T₂
...                   register = flag; // one memory read
flag = false // write  while ( register ); // cannot see change by T1
```

Hence, variable flag logically disappears for the duration it is in a register. As a result, task T_2 spins forever in the busy loop, if it reads flag before the write to flag.

12.4.3   Replication

Modern processors increase performance by executing multiple instructions in parallel. Hence, a processor core is actually composed of multiple arithmetic-logical units (ALU) so several independent instructions can occur simultaneously. Essentially, there are a number of internal pools of instructions taken from program order. In the first pool, prefetching of values is started for the instructions that need memory values. Once, the values are available, the instructions move to the next pool to be executed across any free computation unit. Finally, completed instructions are moved to the next pool to store results and/or feed results back into the first pool of available values. The key point is that instructions with independent inputs execute out-of-order. The only requirement is that out-of-order execution preserve program order for a sequential program, because the hardware always assumes every program is sequential. Hence, this parallel execution is allowed to perform all forms of disjoint reordering (see Sect. 12.4.1, p. 627).

Here is another example of a problem resulting from disjoint reordering. A common initialization pattern is double-check locking for the singleton-pattern:

```
    int *ip;              // shared variable
    ...
1   if ( ip == NULL ) {   // no storage ?
2       lock.acquire();   // attempt to get storage (race)
3       if ( ip == NULL ) {  // still no storage ? (double check)
4           ip = new int( 0 );  // obtain storage
5       }
6       lock.release();
    }
```

As part of initializing the execution environment, the shared variable ip must be allocated and initialized for all tasks to use. Assume the tasks start in random order so no task can assume another task has performed the singleton-pattern. Hence, tasks race at start up to perform this operation, but only the first one does the work, and the rest see the completed work and proceed. Each task performs the first check (line 1), and if it succeeds, it means the variable is already allocated and initialized. However, one or more initial tasks may fail the first check and race to acquire the lock (line 2). The thread that acquires the lock performs the second check (line 3) to see if the variable exists, and if not, does the allocation/initialization (line 4) on behalf of the other tasks, and releases the lock (line 6). Other racing tasks now acquire the lock (line 2), perform the second check (line 3) and see the variable exists, so they simply release the lock (line 6). Very quickly, the shared variable is allocated and initialized, so all subsequent arriving tasks only perform the first check.

Now, line 4 is composed of multiple instructions.

```
1   call    malloc      // new storage address returned in r1
2   st      #0,(r1)     // initialize storage
3   st      r1,ip       // initialize pointer
```

After the call to malloc to allocate the storage, register r1 contains the address of the new storage. The first store instruction writes 0 into the integer pointed to by r1 to initialize the variable. The second store instruction writes the address of the new integer into variable ip. Interestingly, these two writes are disjoint, i.e., the address of one is the new storage and the address of the other is ip. Hence, any optimization technique (compiler/hardware) is allowed to interchange these two stores.

```
1   call    malloc      // new storage address returned in r1
3   st      r1,ip       // initialize pointer
2   st      #0,(r1)     // initialize storage
```

Table 12.1 Memory models

Relaxation Model	W → R	R → W	W → W	Lazy cache update
Atomic consistent (AT)				
Sequential consistency (SC)				√
Total store order (TSO)	√			√
Partial store order (PSO)	√	√		√
Weak order (WO)	√	√	√	√
Release consistency (RC)	√	√	√	√

However, this reordering causes a concurrency problem because the shared variable becomes visible to all the tasks *before* it is initialized to 0. As a result, tasks can read an undefined value from ip at the start, causing them to perform erroneous calculations.

Not only can the compiler and hardware cause double-check locking to fail, but so can the cache. Assume task T1 completes the initialization to the two shared memory locations: ip and the storage ip references. Then task T2 sees the updated value for ip in its cache and reads the value referenced by ip. However, T2 can read an old value at this location because of the delay in updating its cache. Again, the cache does not have to update its locations in store order for disjoint variables.

12.5   Memory Models

To help understand the affects of optimization, a taxonomy is created called a memory model [1]. The memory model defines the level (amount) of relaxation (optimizations) from an optimal system with instantaneous updates. As mentioned, instantaneous update is technically impossible because it takes time to perform the update, and stopping the entire computer system to simulate instantaneous update is impractical. (In a distributed system, it is impossible.) Some CPU manufacturers provide multiple levels of relaxation, and one level is set when the computer is initialized (at power on). The fewer relaxations, the safer the concurrent execution but the slower the sequential execution, and vice versa.

Table 12.1 shows most of the popular memory models. Atomic consistent represents an optimal system with read/write events occurring instantaneously, and hence, optimizations are unnecessary. Sequential consistency accepts all events cannot occur instantaneously, and so a task may read old values. Interestingly, sequential consistency is strong enough for all software synchronization and mutual-exclusion algorithms, because busy loops eventually read the new value. Hence, some concurrent programming languages guarantee a sequentially consistency programming model (e.g., Java), which is a convenient environment for sequential and concurrent programmers. Unfortunately, no hardware supports sequential consistency because of the slowdown for sequential programs. As a result, if a programming language provides this model, it has to be simulated by not performing sequential optimizations in the wrong places in concurrent programs, and controlling the hardware at similar locations. Total store order is a good compromise between sequential and concurrent programming, and is provided on the x86 and SPARC architectures. However, software solutions for synchronization and mutual exclusion must be augmented with special pragmas to ensure the compiler and hardware do not corrupt a program. The remaining models partial store order (ARM), weak order (Alpha) and release consistency (PowerPC) increase the default optimization level making sequential programs faster but concurrency more and more difficult, but not impossible because enough mechanisms are supplied to claw back sequential consistency where it is needed.

12.6 Preventing Optimization Problems

All of these optimization problems result from races on shared variables. If shared data is protected by locks (implicit or explicit), the locks define the sequential/concurrent boundaries, and these boundaries can preclude optimizations that affect concurrency. Such environments are called race free because none of the programmer's variables have races because synchronization and mutual exclusion ensure correct behaviour. However, race free does mean there are no races. It means the races are now internal to the locks, and the lock programmer has to cope with all the problems. Hence, a lock provides the necessary protection to preclude concurrent optimization errors at its boundaries and internally. But if this statement is true, why does double-check locking fail as it is protected with a lock? The failure occurs because of the attempt to optimize locking costs by still having a data race at the first check. If double-check locking is converted into single-check locking, the optimization problems disappear.

```
     int *ip;              // shared variable
     . . .
2    lock.acquire();       // attempt to get storage (race)
1    if ( ip == NULL ) {   // no storage ?
4        ip = new int( 0 );  // obtain storage
     }
6    lock.release();
```

As mentioned previously, programmers often over-optimize programs creating self-inflicted problems for very little gain. Hence, optimization issues are best isolated into explicit and implicit locks in the concurrency system, freeing concurrent programmers to develop safe, portable programs.

How does the lock programmer (and lock-free data-structure programmer) make sure the lock is correct? That is, how does a programmer claw back sequential consistency in a more relaxed memory model? There two approaches: ad hoc and formal. The ad hoc approach requires the programmer to manually augment all data races with pragmas that restrict compiler and hardware optimizations, which requires specific knowledge of the compiler and underlying hardware. The ad hoc approach is not portable but often allows a programmer to create an optimal solution.

The formal approach requires the language to choose a memory model and provide a mechanism to abstractly define all locations where data races occur in the program, i.e., a mechanism to indicate all points of sharing. The formal approach is portable across all compilers that implement the language and all hardware on which code is generated, but the results are not always optimal. Because the formal approach depends on the programming language and its memory model and are rather baroque to use, this section examines the ad hoc approach for just the TSO memory model, which is the most common level of default optimization. Many of the ad hoc techniques carry over into the formal approaches. The ad hoc approach uses **volatile** to avoid compile-time reordering and elision, hardware fences to control architectural reordering, pause to mitigate spinning, and data size and alignment to make efficient use of the cache. Each of these items is discussed in detail.

All software solutions and locks have one or more busy waits in the entry/exit protocols.

```
while ( other == WantIn ); // busy wait
```

The compiler is allowed to copy the shared variable into a register making it an infinite loop as this thread never sees the variable other change in memory by another thread. To make this busy loop work, the elided load of the shared variable must be brought back. The mechanism to force loading (and storing) in C/C++/Java is to qualify a variable's type with **volatile**:

```
volatile int other;
```

The compiler copies a **volatile** variable for the minimum duration to perform an operation, e.g., load the value into a register to increment and immediately store the result, even if the variable is immediately used in other computations. Hence, all shared variables used in the entry/exit protocols must be declared with the **volatile** qualifier to prevent problems. However, because **volatile** affects all usages of a variable, it may over-constrain legitimate optimizations in sequential regions.

Because TSO allows reordering loads before stores for disjoint variables, it is necessary to insert a hardware instruction, called a fence, to prevent this optimization. As shown previously, Dekker's algorithm fails for disjoint $W_x \rightarrow R_y$ reordering.

```
1    me = WantIn; // W              1    me = WantIn; // W
                                         Fence();              // prevent reordering
2    while ( you == WantIn ) { // R   2    while ( you == WantIn ) { // R
3    ...                             3    ...
```

Without the fence between the write of me and read of you can be reordered, executing the load of you before the store of me, allowing both threads to simultaneously enter the CS. Platforms with weaker memory models may need additional/stronger fences. Most atomic instructions, e.g., fetch-and-increment, compare-and-assign, have an implicit fence. A few architectures have instructions to force cache invalidation so that values appear sooner with lazy cache-coherency.

While the fence instruction prevents reordering of access to lock data, additional fence instructions may be required to prevent reordering of application data into or outside of the protecting mutual exclusion code. For TSO, the fences within the mutual exclusion code also serve to prevent data accesses within the CS from reordering into or before the entry protocol (lock acquire). Furthermore, reordering of the CS into or after the exit protocol (lock release) is avoided by relying on TSO and the fact that every lock release has at least one store instruction.

Note, the **volatile** qualifier in C/C++ is not as strong with respect to the language memory model as in Java. In fact, the **volatile** qualifier in C was created for use with setjmp/longjmp so variables in the scope of a setjmp are the actual values rather than copied values in registers (see Sect. 3.3, p. 69). This weaker semantics for **volatile** in C is the reason why it is necessary to manually insert memory fences to prevent the hardware from moving loads before stores in the pipeline or in the cache. In Java, this step is handled automatically for all variables declared **volatile**. However, Java may over-constrain accesses, inserting more memory fences than necessary, which can preclude some valid hardware optimizations and hence reduce performance. Alternatively, C11 (IOS/IEC 9899:2011 and stdatomic.h) and features in C++11 now provide Java like **volatile** semantics via new atomic primitives.

The busy-waiting in software solutions for mutual exclusion can cause performance problems, e.g., this busy wait

while (other == WantIn) Pause(); // busy wait

loops around a load (because of the **volatile** qualifier) and compare instruction. As this loop executes, the processor pipeline fills with load/compare instructions, which takes resources (CPU), space (instruction cache) and power (heat). To mitigate these events, many processors have a pause instruction specifically for this situation. The pause instruction is a hint to the processor of a busy loop in progress. The processor has many options: a simple temporal delay, yielding resources to other sibling pipelines, create a speculation barrier to prevent pipeline flooding, reschedule hyper threads on this core, and stop the branch predictor so when the write occurs there are few or no instructions in the pipeline to flush. Hence, a pause instruction should be inserted in tight busy-waiting loops to increase performance.

Often, an algorithm only requires a single bit to store information, such as intent to enter. However, from a performance perspective, it is better to store information in the atomically addressable word size for the underlying computer: intptr_t. Because N is normally ≤ 64, the additional storage cost for using words rather smaller addressable units is minimal. As well, the choice of width can influence the vulnerability to false sharing. There is also a small benefit to align storage on a cache-size boundary, e.g., 64-byte boundary. Specific variables, structures and arrays used in algorithms should be aligned on a cache-size boundary using either memalign for dynamically allocated storage or the following macro for static allocation:

#define CALIGN __attribute__((aligned (64)))

Fig. 12.5 shows the nested version of Dekker's algorithm (see Sect. 6.3.6.1, p. 246) with all the safe techniques required for correct execution in a TSO memory model. The shared variables me, you and Last are declared as **volatile**, and each is aligned on a cache-line boundary. Two fences are added to prevent reading you

```
#define CALIGN __attribute__(( aligned (64) ))  // cache-line alignment
#define Fence() __asm__ __volatile__ ( "mfence" ) // prevent hardware reordering
#define Pause() __asm__ __volatile__ ( "pause" : : : ) // efficient busy wait

enum Intent { DontWantIn, WantIn } Last;

_Task Dekker {
    volatile Intent &me, &you, *&Last;
    void main() {
        for ( int i = 1; i <= 1000; i += 1 ) {
            for ( ;; ) {                          // entry protocol
                me = WantIn;                      // high priority
                Fence();
                if ( you == DontWantIn ) break;
                if ( Last == &me ) {              // high priority ?
                    me = DontWantIn;
                    Fence();
                    while ( Last == &me ) Pause();  // low priority
                }
                Pause();
            }
            CriticalSection();                    // critical section
            Last = &me;                           // exit protocol
            me = DontWantIn;
        }
    }
  public:
    Dekker( volatile Intent &me, volatile Intent &you, volatile Intent *&Last ) :
        me(me), you(you), Last(Last) {}
};
void uMain::main() {
    volatile Intent me CALIGN = DontWantIn, you CALIGN = DontWantIn,
        *Last CALIGN = rand() % 2 ? &me : &you;
    Dekker t0(me, you, Last), t1(you, me, Last);
};
```

Fig. 12.5 TSO-safe Dekker nested

before writing to me and reading Last before writing me, and two pauses are added
in both busy loops. This augmented Dekker's algorithm has been tested on both x86
and SPARC architectures.

12.7   Summary

Modern computers are now too complex to understand by programmers, with
billions of transistors performing non-deterministic actions that are largely invisible.
To achieve the maximum performance obtainable from these computers, the
compiler is enlisted to perform many static optimization steps in preparation for
execution. Then the hardware completes these optimizations dynamically. Virtually
all of these optimizations are for sequential programs/fragments, which constitute
the majority of executed code. As a result, there is a tension between concurrent
programmers and compiler/hardware engineers with respect to the memory model.

Concurrent programmers want ease of use and correctness (strong memory-model), while compiler/hardware engineers want the fastest possible execution for the most common kind of execution (weak memory-model). Unfortunately, the only perfect memory model, instantaneous update, is impossible. As a result, concurrent programmers walk a tight-rope of aggressive optimizations that can invalidate their programs. All of these problems relate to data races that occur outside of traditional locking. Clearly, someone has to write the locks, and hence, deal with these complex issues. This kind of software development is best left to concurrent specialists. The remaining concurrent programmers should leverage this work by ensuring all shared data is properly protected by locks, and hence, never experience these problems. Nevertheless, every concurrent programmer needs to understand these issues, lest they decide to relax their locking and strangely find their programmers no longer work.

12.8 Questions

1. What is *disjoint reordering* with respect to optimization?
2. How can disjoint reordering cause a concurrent program to fail? Give an example illustrating a failure.
3. What execution property are concurrent programmers willing to give up so caching can work efficiently?
4. What is the purpose of a *memory model* with respect to concurrency.
5. Registers are the fastest storage on a computer. Give an example of how register usage causes failure in a concurrent program, and explain a mechanism in C++ to prevent this problem.
6. Name and explain two compiler optimizations that can cause problems for concurrent programs.
7. Explain how CPU caches can invalidate a concurrent program.
8. Why is there a tension between concurrent programmers and hardware engineers with respect to the memory model?

References

1. Adve, S.V., Boehm, H.J.: Memory models: A case for rethinking parallel languages and hardware. Commun. ACM **53**(8), 90–101 (2010)
2. Adve, S.V., Gharachorloo, K.: Shared memory consistency models: A tutorial. Tech. Rep. 7, Western Research Laboratory, 250 University Avenue, Palo Alto, California, 94301, U.S.A. (1995). http://www.hpl.hp.com/techreports/Compaq-DEC/WRL-95-7.pdf, Reprinted in [3].
3. Adve, S.V., Gharachorloo, K.: Shared memory consistency models: A tutorial. Computer **29**(12), 66–76 (1996)
4. Moore, G.E.: Progress in digital integrated electronics. Technical Digest, International Electron Devices Meeting, IEEE pp.11Ǔ13 (1975) 619

Chapter 13
Control Flow Paradigms

This chapter compares and contrasts different approaches to specifying control flow and different implementations of the approaches in programming languages. Thus far, mostly μC++ has been used to specify advanced control flow; it is important to look at other approaches to see if there are strong or weak equivalences among them.

While simplifying the job of programming is a laudable goal, it always comes at some cost. In general, simple problems can be solved with simple solutions and complex problems can *only* be solved with complex solutions. Always beware of simple solutions to complex problems because usually some aspect of the complexity is ignored in the solution, which requires one or more compromises, or the complexity is hidden away beyond a programmer's control. Be especially wary of implicit concurrency (see Sect. 5.6, p. 201), where compilers convert sequential programs into concurrent ones, e.g., by converting sequential looping into parallel looping by creating a thread to execute each loop iteration. Unfortunately, there are significant limitations on the capabilities of such systems. Many concurrent situations, like readers and writer, simply do not exist in a sequential form, and hence, cannot be expressed through such systems. In some cases the compromises in these systems are acceptable, but in many cases, they are not. Finally, some concurrent systems are unsound because the compiler is unaware that the program is concurrent. All concurrent library approaches have this problem because the compiler may perform valid sequential optimizations that invalidate a concurrent program (see Sect. 12, p. 615).

13.1 Coroutines

While coroutines occur less infrequently in programming, that does not imply a lack of usefulness. A few old programming languages support coroutines [11, 27, 29, 36], and a few new programming languages are attempting to support

© Springer International Publishing Switzerland 2016   637
P.A. Buhr, *Understanding Control Flow*, DOI 10.1007/978-3-319-25703-7_13

them (see Sect. 13.1.1, p. 641). A language without coroutines results in awkward solutions for an important class of problems, e.g., automata, resulting in code that is difficult to generate, understand and maintain (see Chap. 4, p. 125).

The first language to provide a comprehensive coroutine facility was Simula [35]. The Simula constructs are more general than those in μC++, but too much generality can be dangerous, e.g., like a **goto** versus a **while** loop. μC++ attempts to restrict the coroutine constructs, forcing a particular coding style and limiting control transfer, in an attempt to make using coroutines easier. Like structured programming, only certain control patterns are allowed to simplify the understanding of a program. The difficulty in introducing restrictions is to ensure the restricted forms easily and conveniently cover the common cases but do not preclude the esoteric ones, albeit with some additional work. In fact, one reason coroutines are not a standard programming mechanism is the complexity and problems resulting from earlier facilities that are too general. μC++ attempts to make coroutines an accessible programming facility.

Simula provides three constructs for coroutining: Call, Detach and Resume. Call and Detach work like μC++ resume and suspend for building semi-coroutines, and Resume works like resume for building full coroutines.

In μC++, the kind of object is indicated by its type, e.g., coroutine or task, and it becomes this kind of object on creation and essentially remains that kind of object for its lifetime. (While a terminated coroutine is a class object and a terminated task is a monitor, these transformations occur only once and are not used in most programming situations.) In Simula, any object can become a coroutine depending on what is executed in its constructor, and convert back, possibly multiple times during its lifetime. The first Detach statement executed in an object's constructor causes the object to become a coroutine by changing it so it has its own execution state; control then suspends back to the declaration invoking the constructor, leaving the constructor suspended. Hence, in Simula, the constructor and the coroutine main are combined in the same block of code. Combining these two blocks of code requires a special facility called **inner** to allow inheritance to work correctly, otherwise the coroutine code for a base class is executed instead of the derived class. (See Sect. 13.2.2.1, p. 658 for details of **inner**.) To allow inheritance in μC++, the constructor and coroutine main are separate routines, and all constructors in a derivation chain are executed but only the coroutine main of the most derived class is started as the coroutine. The μC++ coroutine structure can be mimicked in Simula by placing the coroutine code in a routine called main, calling this routine at the end of the constructor, but detaching just before the call. (This simple simulation does not handle inheritance, which requires using **inner**.) Hence, control returns back to the declaration after the constructor code is executed and the first activation of the coroutine calls main. It is also possible to eliminate the Detach before the call to main, so control continues directly into main until the first Detach is encountered. This style can be mimicked in μC++ by putting a call to resume at the end of the constructor to start main (see Fig. 4.6, p. 134b).

Semi-coroutining is performed using the Call and Detach pairing, where Call corresponds to a resume in a member routine and Detach corresponds to a suspend in the coroutine main. Simula Call explicitly specifies the target coroutine to be activated, as in Call(X). The current active coroutine becomes inactive and the target coroutine, i.e., X, becomes active. In μC++, resume makes the current coroutine inactive and the target coroutine is implicitly the **this** of the coroutine member containing the call to resume. In Simula, coroutine X can make its caller active by executing Detach, which is like suspend. However, Detach is subtlety different from suspend because it de-activates **this** and activates the caller versus de-activating the current coroutine and activating the caller. Therefore, a matching Detach for a Call must be executed from *within* the coroutine's code. In μC++, it is possible for a coroutine to suspend itself in another coroutine's member because the current coroutine does not change on the call.

Notice the Call mechanism allows one coroutine to transfer control to another coroutine without calling one of its member routines. In μC++, each call to resume and suspend is located inside one of the member routines of a coroutine, which results in an encapsulation of all activations and de-activations within the coroutine itself, making the coroutine the only object capable of changing this property. As a result, it is only necessary to look at a coroutine's definition to understand all its activation and de-activation points, excluding external calls to other coroutine members performing suspend and resume. Furthermore, calling a member routine is consistent with normal object-oriented programming and provides a mechanism for passing argument information to the coroutine in a type-safe way. μC++ semi-coroutining can be mimicked in Simula by always calling a coroutine member and that member contains aCall(THIS *type-name*[1]) to activate the coroutine.

Full-coroutining is performed using Resume, where Resume corresponds to resume in a member routine. Simula Resume specifies the target coroutine to be activated, as in Resume(X). The current coroutine becomes inactive and the target coroutine, i.e., X, becomes active. Through this mechanism it is possible to construct arbitrarily complex resume-resume cycles among coroutines, exactly as in μC++. While Call appears to have the same capability as Resume, because both specify a target coroutine, Call cannot be used to construct cycles. The target coroutine of a Call is actually attached to the calling coroutine, i.e., turned back into an object, until it does a Detach, whereupon the target is turned back into a coroutine (like the initial Detach). It is illegal to Resume a coroutine that is in the attached state because it is not a coroutine.

Like Call, the Resume mechanism allows one coroutine to transfer control to another coroutine without calling one of its member routines, with the same problems. μC++ full coroutining can be mimicked in Simula by always calling a coroutine member and that member contains a Resume(THIS *type-name*) to activate the coroutine. Interestingly, the semantics of Detach change when a coroutine is resumed instead of called: Detach transfers back to the block sequence containing the object's lexical type rather than transferring back to the last caller, as in semi-coroutining. From a μC++ perspective, this semantics would normally cause the implicit coroutine associated with uMain to become active.

---

[1]Having to specify the type name for THIS is a peculiarity of Simula.

A Simula coroutine terminates when its constructor completes, at which point, an implicit Detach is executed. The behaviour of this Detach depends on whether the terminating coroutine was called or resumed. In μC++, a coroutine terminates when its coroutine main completes, at which point, the coroutine's starter is resumed (see Sect. 4.7, p. 145). Unlike μC++, the semantics of Simula Detach preclude transferring back to a terminated coroutine, because either the caller or the lexical block containing the definition must exist.

Fig. 13.1 shows the Simula version of the semi-coroutine output formatter discussed in Sect. 4.2, p. 132, written in the μC++ coroutine style. Interestingly, using the μC++ coroutine style deals with another problem with Simula coroutines: the inability to pass and return information with Call/Resume/Detach. By embedding all coroutine transfers within object members and using communication variables, it is possible to pass and return information among Simula coroutines is a type-safe way. The coroutine formatter, FmtLines, is passed characters one at a time by calls to member prt and formats them into blocks of 4 characters and groups the blocks of characters into groups of 5. Notice the coroutine code is placed in a private member called main, and this routine is called at the end of the constructor, after the Detach. Also, the Call in member prt explicitly specifies THIS as the coroutine to be activated. In this specific example, the Call in member prt could be replaced by a Resume for two reasons. First, the instance of the coroutine, fmt is not programmatically terminated. The main block simply terminates and the coroutine is garbage collected at the end of the program. Second, if the coroutine is programmatically terminated, it restarts the main block because it was previously resumed (not called), and the type of the coroutine instance, FmtLines, is located in that block. In this simple program, it is coincidence that the implicit Detach on termination just happens to activate the same block regardless of whether the terminating coroutine is called or resumed; in general, this is not the case.

Fig. 13.2, p. 642 shows the Simula version of the full coroutine producer/consumer discussed in Sect. 4.9.2, p. 159, written in the μC++ coroutine style. The program is almost identical to the μC++ version, but notice the use of Call instead of Resume in member routine stop for the last activation of the consumer by the producer. The Call ensures the final implicit Detach at the end of cons acts like a suspend to re-activate prod and not the main block, which is suspended at the Resume in member routine start. When prod terminates, it was last resumed, not called, by cons, and therefore, its final implicit Detach re-activates the main block in start. The Resume in start cannot be a Call because that would attach prod to the main block making it impossible for cons to resume prod, because prod would no longer be a coroutine.

Finally, Simula coroutines have further complexity associated with the ability to nest blocks in the language. However, this capability does not exist in most other object-oriented programming languages nor does it contribute to the notion of coroutines, and therefore, this capability is not discussed here.

```
BEGIN
    CLASS FmtLines;
        HIDDEN ch, main;                ! private members;
    BEGIN
        CHARACTER ch;                   ! communication;

        PROCEDURE main;                 ! mimic uC++ coroutine main;
        BEGIN
            INTEGER g, b;

            WHILE TRUE DO BEGIN        ! for as many characters;
                FOR g := 1 STEP 1 UNTIL 5 DO BEGIN ! groups of 5;
                    FOR b := 1 STEP 1 UNTIL 4 DO BEGIN ! blocks of 4;
                        OutChar( ch );
                        Detach;             ! suspend();
                    END;
                    OutText( "  " );
                END;
                OutImage;               ! start new line
            END;
        END;

        PROCEDURE prt( chp );
            CHARACTER chp;
        BEGIN
            ch := chp;                  ! communication
            Call( THIS FmtLines );      ! resume();
        END;
        ! FmtLines constructor code;
        Detach;                         ! return to declaration;
        main;                           ! call main as last line of constructor;
    END FmtLines;
    ! uMain::main equivalent;
    REF(FmtLines) fmt;                  ! objects are references;
    INTEGER i;

    fmt :- NEW FmtLines;
    FOR i := Rank( ' ' ) STEP 1 UNTIL Rank( 'z' ) DO BEGIN
        fmt.prt( Char( i ) );
    END
END;
```

Fig. 13.1 Simula semi-coroutine: output formatter

13.1.1 Generators

Some languages, e.g., Alphard [33], CLU [26], Sather [30], Python [32], JavaScript [13], and C# [14] provide a limited form of coroutine solely for the purpose of constructing generators (see Sects. 2.9, p. 41 and 4.5, p. 136) for use in iterating. The key difference between a generator and a coroutine is that a generator is stackless while a coroutine is stackfull. Only a coroutine can call an arbitrary number of routines and suspend, or construct a full coroutine.

The generator in Python is presented as an example. A Python generator is a stackless, semi-coroutine so it cannot call out of the generator and **yield**. As well,

```
BEGIN                                              CLASS Producer;
  CLASS Consumer( prod );                            HIDDEN cons, N, money, receipt, Main;
    REF(Producer) prod; ! constructor parameter;   BEGIN
    HIDDEN p1, p2, status, done, Main;               REF(Consumer) cons;
  BEGIN                                              INTEGER N, money, receipt;
    INTEGER p1, p2, status;                          PROCEDURE main;
    BOOLEAN done;                                    BEGIN
    PROCEDURE main;                                    INTEGER i, p1, p2, status;
    BEGIN
      INTEGER money, receipt;                          FOR i := 1 STEP 1 UNTIL N DO BEGIN
                                                         p1 := RandInt( 1, 100, p1 );
      money := 1;                                        p2 := RandInt( 1, 100, p2 );
      WHILE NOT done DO BEGIN                            OutText( "prod delivers: " );
        OutText( "cons receives: " );                   OutInt( p1, 3 ); OutText( ", " );
        OutInt( p1, 3 );                                OutInt( p2, 3 ); OutImage;
        OutText( ", " );                                status := cons.delivery( p1, p2 );
        OutInt( p2, 3 );                                OutText( "prod status: " );
        status := status + 1;                           OutInt( status, 3 ); OutImage;
        OutText( " and pays $" );                     END;
        OutInt( money, 3 ); OutImage;                  cons.stop;
        receipt := prod.payment( money );              OutText( "prod stops" ); OutImage;
        OutText( "cons receipt #" );                 END;
        OutInt( receipt, 3 ); OutImage;              INTEGER PROCEDURE payment( moneyp );
        money := money + 1;                            INTEGER moneyp;
      END;                                           BEGIN
      OutText( "cons stops" ); OutImage;               money := moneyp;
    END;                                               OutText( "prod payment of $" );
    INTEGER PROCEDURE delivery( p1p, p2p );            OutInt( money, 3 ); OutImage;
      INTEGER p1p, p2p;                                Resume( THIS Producer );
    BEGIN                                              receipt := receipt + 1;
      p1 := p1p;                                       payment := receipt;
      p2 := p2p;                                     END;
      Resume( THIS Consumer );                       PROCEDURE start( Np, consp );
      delivery := status;                              INTEGER Np;
    END;                                               REF(Consumer) consp;
    PROCEDURE stop;                                  BEGIN
    BEGIN                                              N := Np;
      done := TRUE;                                    cons :- consp;
      Call( THIS Consumer );                           Resume( THIS Producer );
    END;                                             END;
    ! Consumer constructor code;                     ! Producer constructor code;
    status := 0;                                     receipt := 0;
    done := FALSE;                                    Detach;
    Detach;                                           main;
    main;                                           END Producer;
  END Consumer;                                     ! uMain::main equivalent;
                                                    REF(Producer) prod;
                                                    REF(Consumer) cons;
                                                    prod :- NEW Producer;
                                                    cons :- NEW Consumer( prod );
                                                    prod.start( 5, cons );
                                                  END;
```

Fig. 13.2 Simula full-coroutine: producer/consumer

```
def Fibonacci( n ):                    # coroutine main
    fn = 0;  fn1 = fn
    yield fn                           # suspend
    fn = 1; fn2 = fn1; fn1 = fn
    yield fn                           # suspend
    # while True:                      # for infinite generator
    for i in range( n - 2 ):
        fn = fn1 + fn2; fn2 = fn1; fn1 = fn
        yield fn                       # suspend

f1 = Fibonacci( 10 )                   # objects
f2 = Fibonacci( 10 )
for i in range( 10 ):
    print next( f1 ), next( f2 )       # resume
for fib in Fibonacci( 15 ):            # use generator as generator
    print fib
```

(a) Fibonacci iterator

```
def Format():
    try:
        while True:
            for g in range( 5 ):            # groups of 5 blocks
                for b in range( 4 ):        # blocks of 4 characters
                    print( (yield), end=' ' ) # receive from send
                print( ' ', end=' ' )       # block separator
            print()                         # group separator
    except GeneratorExit:                   # destructor
        if g != 0 | b != 0:                 # special case
            print()

fmt = Format()
next( fmt )                                 # prime generator
for i in range( 41 ):
    fmt.send( 'a' )                         # send to yield
```

(b) Formatter iterator

Fig. 13.3 Python iterators

a generator is a routine versus class so there is only a single interface, i.e., only one kind of value can be return. Fig. 13.3a shows a generator for producing the Fibonacci numbers. The structure of the generator is identical to the μC++ coroutine version (see Fig. 4.4, p. 131). The calls to **yield** are equivalent to suspend, but return the coroutine result for the single interface. The generator is written to produce a fixed number of values so it can be used in both Python iterative contexts. Two generator objects are created, f1 and f2, and then the first 10 Fibonacci numbers are printed from each generator by calling the next operation to resume the generator. The second loop creates the generator and the **for** implicitly calls the next to resume the generator on each loop iteration.

Fig. 13.3b shows a generator for formatting text. The structure of the generator is identical to the μC++ coroutine version (see Fig. 4.6, p. 134b), except for the use of an exception versus a destructor for object termination. Here, the **yield** works the opposite from the Fibonacci generators, producing a value rather than returning a value. The values produced are the characters sent to the generator. One generator is created and next is used to resume the generator so it is primed to receive the first character at the **yield**. (μC++ primes the coroutine with a resume in the coroutine's constructor.) The loop passes characters to the generator via send, which takes only one argument, and resumes the generator at the **yield**. When the generator restarts at its last suspend, the **yield** produces the passed character to print, loops appropriately and suspends in the print at the **yield**.

13.2   Thread and Lock Library

As the name implies, a thread and lock library is a set of routines providing the ability to create a new thread of control, and a few locks to control synchronization and mutual exclusion among threads. As is shown in Chap. 7, p. 313, working at this level is too detailed and low level for solving even a medium-complex concurrent-application. Furthermore, all concurrent libraries are either unsound or inefficient because the compiler has no knowledge that a program using the library is concurrent. Even given these significant problems, there are still many thread libraries being developed and used. While thread libraries have been written for many languages, only ones associated with C and C++ are discussed here, as that is sufficient to present the fundamental ideas and approaches.

13.2.1   Pthreads

The most popular thread library is POSIX Pthreads [7]. Because Pthreads is designed for C, all of the Pthreads routines are written in a non-object-oriented style, i.e., each routine explicitly receives the object being manipulated as one of its parameters. All non-object oriented library approaches are based on the START/WAIT model discussed in Sect. 5.8.4, p. 208. Hence, routines are used both to create a new thread of control and as the location for the new thread to start execution. In contrast, μC++ uses a declaration of a task type to start a new thread, and the thread implicitly starts execution in the task's main member routine.

13.2.1.1   Thread Creation and Termination

The routine used to start a new thread in Pthreads is:

```
int pthread_create( pthread_t *new_thread_ID, const pthread_attr_t *attr,
    void * (*start_func)(void *), void *arg );
```

The type of a thread identifier is pthread_t, analogous to uBaseTask in μC++. However, a thread identifier is not a pointer to a thread because there is no thread object, or if there is one, it is an internal structure opaque to programmers. In μC++, the opaque thread object is hidden inside a task object, through implicit inheritance from uBaseTask, and the address of the task object is used to indirectly identify a thread.

The thread creation routine returns two results: one through the routine return value and the other through the first argument. The return value is a return code, versus an exception, indicating if the thread is successfully created. If the thread is successfully created, the first argument is assigned the thread identifier of the newly created thread. The second argument is a pointer to a structure containing attribute information for controlling creation properties for the new thread. The attribute information controls properties such as interaction with the operating-system kernel threads, termination properties, stack size and scheduling policy. If the default attributes are sufficient, the argument can be set to NULL. Similar properties can be specified in μC++ through arguments to uBaseTask and via cluster schedulers. The last two arguments are a pointer to the routine where the thread starts execution and a pointer to a single argument for the starting routine. In effect, the new thread begins execution with a routine call of the form:

```
start_func( arg );
```

If more than one argument needs to be passed to start_func, the arguments must be packed into a structure, and the address of that structure used as the arg value (see message passing in Sect. 13.3, p. 665).

The following example:

```
void *rtn( void *arg ) { ... }
int i = 3, rc;
pthread_t t;                          // thread id
rc = pthread_create( &t, NULL, rtn, &i );   // create new thread
if ( rc != 0 ) ...                    // check for error
```

starts a new thread, with default attributes, beginning execution at routine rtn and passes a pointer to i as the argument of rtn. pthread_create assigns the new thread identifier into the reference argument t only if the creation is successful, and returns a return code indicating success or failure of the thread creation.

Notice the type of parameter arg for rtn is **void** * to allow a pointer of any C type to be passed from the caller, through pthread_create, and assigned to arg in a starting routine. As a result, the original type of the argument is lost when the pointer arrives in the start routine. Therefore, it is the start routine's responsibility to cast the argument pointer back to the original type. As well, since all arguments are passed by reference, the start routine may need to copy the argument if it is shared. Therefore, the first line of a typical start routine looks like:

```
void *rtn( void *arg ) {
    int a = *(int *)arg;      // cast and copy argument
    ...
```

For all C library approaches, passing arguments to the start routine is type unsafe, as the compiler cannot ensure correct data is received by the start routine. For example, a programmer can pass an argument pointer of any type to rtn, through pthread_create, and rtn then dereferences it as an integer. Violating the type system in this way defeats the purpose of using a high-level language and relies on programmers following strict coding conventions without making errors.

A thread terminates when its starting routine returns or the thread calls pthread_exit. (There is no counterpart to pthread_exit in μC++.) Termination synchronization (see Sect. 5.8.5, p. 210) is possible using routine:

```
int pthread_join( pthread_t target_thread, void **status );
```

The thread join routine returns two results: one through the routine return value and the other through the second argument. The return value is a return code, versus an exception, indicating if the thread is successfully joined. If the thread is successfully joined, the second argument is assigned a pointer to a return value from the terminating thread. The first argument is the thread identifier of the thread with which termination synchronization is performed. The calling thread blocks until the specified thread, target_thread, has terminated; if the specified thread has already terminated, the calling thread does not block.

It is possible to pass a result back from the terminating thread, either through the starting routine's return-value or through routine pthread_exit. The value is received from the terminating thread through the reference parameter status, which is a pointer to an argument of unknown type. If more than one return value needs to be passed to the caller, the results must be packed into a structure, and the address of that structure passed back to the caller. If the calling thread is uninterested in the return value, the argument can be set to NULL.

The following example:

```
void *rtn( void *arg ) {
    ...
    int *ip = malloc( sizeof(int) );        // allocate return storage
    *ip = 3;                                 // assign return value
    return ip;                               // return pointer to return storage
}
int i, *ip, rc;
rc = pthread_join( t, &ip );                 // wait for result
if ( rc != 0 ) ...                           // check for error
i = *ip;                                     // copy return data
free( ip );                                  // free storage for returned value
```

has the calling thread wait for thread t to terminate and return a pointer to an integer return value. pthread_join returns a return code indicating success or failure of the join, and if successful, assigns the return pointer into the reference argument ip.

Notice the awkward mechanism needed to return a value because the storage for the terminated thread no longer exists after it finishes. Therefore, the terminating thread must allocate storage for the return value and the caller must subsequently delete this storage. Some of this complexity can be eliminated by using global shared variables or passing a return storage area as an argument to the start routine, so new storage does not have to be allocated for the return value. Also, the type of parameter status and the return type from the starting routine are **void** * to allow a pointer of any C type to be passed from the starting routine, through pthread_join, and assigned to status in a call to pthread_join.

For all C library approaches, passing return values from the start routine is type unsafe, as the compiler cannot ensure correct data is received by the caller of pthread_join. For example, a programmer can return a pointer of any type through pthread_join and the caller then dereferences it as an integer. Again, violating the type system in this way defeats the purpose of using a high-level language and relies on programmers following strict coding conventions without making errors.

In μC++, the starting routine, i.e., the task main, has no parameters and returns no result. Information is transferred to and from the task main, in a type safe manner, using the task member routines, albeit via copying information through global task variables. Some of this additional copying also occurs with Pthreads because the argument is a pointer that may need its target copied on entry to the starting routine, and the result is a pointer that may need its target copied on termination. In general, the cost of any additional copying is significantly offset by the additional type safety. The μC++ approach to safe communication cannot be directly mimicked in Pthreads because it requires multiple entry points. A routine has only one entry point, which is the starting point at the top of the routine. A class provides multiple entry points that can be invoked during the lifetime of its objects, and each call to an entry point is statically type checked.

Finally, it is possible for a thread to determine its identity through routine:

```
pthread_t pthread_self( void );
```

which is equivalent to uThisTask. As mentioned, the thread identifier returned is not a pointer but an opaque value. For example, a thread identifier could be a subscript into an array of pointers to pthread_t objects for a particular implementation of the thread library. The only operations allowed on an opaque thread-identifier is to pass it into and out of Pthreads routines and to compare thread identifiers using the routine:

```
int pthread_equal( pthread_t t1, pthread_t t2 );
```

Fig. 13.4 illustrates the Pthreads equivalent for starting and terminating threads in a bounded buffer example (see Fig. 7.14, p. 353(b)). The bounded buffer is presented on page 651.

13.2.1.2 Thread Synchronization and Mutual Exclusion

Pthreads provides two kinds of locks, mutex and condition, through which all synchronization and mutual exclusion is constructed. The mutex lock is like a binary semaphore with the additional notion of ownership but no recursive acquisition,[2] so the thread that locks the mutex must be the one that unlocks it, but only once. As a result, a mutex lock can *only* be used for mutual exclusion, because synchronization requires the locking thread be different from the unlocking one. The Pthreads mutex lock has the following interface:

---

[2]Recursive behaviour is available but only as an implementation-dependent option.

```
void *producer( void *arg ) {
    BoundedBuffer *buf = (BoundedBuffer *)arg;
    const int NoOfElems = rand() % 20;
    int elem, i;

    for ( i = 1; i <= NoOfElems; i += 1 ) {          // produce elements
        elem = rand() % 100 + 1;                     // produce a random number
        printf( "Producer:0x%p, value:%d\n", pthread_self(), elem );
        insert( buf, elem );                         // insert element into queue
    }
}
void *consumer( void *arg ) {
    BoundedBuffer *buf = (BoundedBuffer *)arg;
    int elem;

    for ( ;; ) {                                     // consume until a negative element
        elem = remove( buf );                        // remove from front of queue
        printf( "Consumer:0x%p, value:%d\n", pthread_self(), elem );
        if ( elem == -1 ) break;
    }
}
int main() {
    const int NoOfCons = 3, NoOfProds = 4;
    BoundedBuffer buf;                               // create a buffer monitor
    pthread_t cons[NoOfCons];                        // pointer to an array of consumers
    pthread_t prods[NoOfProds];                      // pointer to an array of producers

    ctor( &buf );                                    // initialize buffer
    for ( int i = 0; i < NoOfCons; i += 1 )          // create consumers
        if ( pthread_create( &cons[i], NULL, consumer, &buf ) != 0 ) exit( -1 );
    for ( int i = 0; i < NoOfProds; i += 1 )         // create producers
        if ( pthread_create( &prods[i], NULL, producer, &buf ) != 0 ) exit( -1 );
    for ( int i = 0; i < NoOfProds; i += 1 )         // wait for producer to terminate
        if ( pthread_join( prods[i], NULL ) != 0 ) exit( -1 );
    for ( int i = 0; i < NoOfCons; i += 1 )          // terminate each consumer
        insert( &buf, -1 );
    for ( int i = 0; i < NoOfCons; i += 1 )          // wait for consumers to terminate
        if ( pthread_join( cons[i], NULL ) != 0 ) exit( -1 );
    dtor( &buf );                                    // destroy buffer
}
```

Fig. 13.4 Pthreads: producer/consumer creation/termination

```
pthread_mutex_t mutex;
int pthread_mutex_init( pthread_mutex_t *mp, const pthread_mutexattr_t *attr );
int pthread_mutex_destroy( pthread_mutex_t *mp );
int pthread_mutex_lock( pthread_mutex_t *mp );
int pthread_mutex_trylock( pthread_mutex_t *mp );
int pthread_mutex_unlock( pthread_mutex_t *mp );
```

The type of a mutex lock is pthread_mutex_t. Each mutex has to be initialized and subsequently destroyed. Since there are no constructors or destructors
in C, this step must be done manually through routines pthread_mutex_init and
pthread_mutex_destroy, respectively. It is a common mistake to miss calling one of
these routines for a mutex lock.

The routine pthread_mutex_init is used to initialize a mutex. A mutex is always initialized to unlocked (open) with no owner. The first argument is a pointer to the mutex to be initialized; a mutex can be reinitialized only after it is destroyed. The second argument is a pointer to a structure containing attribute information for specifying properties of the new mutex. The attribute information controls operating system related properties. If the default attributes are sufficient, the argument pointer can be set to NULL.

The routine pthread_mutex_destroy is used to destroy a mutex. Destruction must occur when the mutex is unlocked and no longer in use, which means no thread is currently waiting on or attempting to acquire/release the mutex; otherwise behaviour is undefined (i.e., Pthreads may or may not generate an error for this case).

The routines pthread_mutex_lock and pthread_mutex_unlock are used to atomically acquire and release the lock, closing and opening it, respectively. pthread_mutex_lock acquires the lock if it is open, otherwise the calling thread spins/blocks until it can acquire the lock; whether a thread spins or blocks is implementation dependent. The member routine pthread_mutex_trylock makes one attempt to try to acquire the lock, i.e., it does not block. pthread_mutex_trylock returns 0 if the lock is acquired and non-zero otherwise. pthread_mutex_unlock releases the lock, and if there are waiting threads, the scheduling policy and/or thread priorities determine which waiting thread next acquires the lock.

The condition lock is like a condition variable, creating a list object on which threads block and unblock; however, there is no monitor construct to simplify and ensure correct usage of condition locks. Instead, a condition lock is dependent on the mutex lock for its functionality, and collectively these two kinds of locks can be used to build a monitor, providing both synchronization and mutual exclusion. As for a condition variable, a condition lock can *only* be used for synchronization, because the wait operation always blocks. A condition lock has the following interface:

```
pthread_cond_t cond;
int pthread_cond_init( pthread_cond_t *cp, const pthread_condattr_t *attr );
int pthread_cond_destroy( pthread_cond_t *cp );
int pthread_cond_wait( pthread_cond_t *cp, pthread_mutex_t *mutex );
int pthread_cond_signal( pthread_cond_t *cp );
int pthread_cond_broadcast( pthread_cond_t *cp );
```

The type of a condition lock is pthread_condition_t. Each condition has to be initialized and subsequently destroyed. Since there are no constructors or destructors in C, this step must be done manually through routines pthread_cond_init and pthread_cond_destroy, respectively. It is a common mistake to miss calling one of these routines for a condition lock.

The routine pthread_cond_init is used to initialize a condition. The first argument is a pointer to the condition to be initialized; a condition can be reinitialized only after it is destroyed. The second argument is a pointer to a structure containing attribute information for specifying properties of the new condition. The attribute information controls operating system related properties. If the default attributes are sufficient, the argument pointer can be set to NULL.

The routine pthread_cond_destroy is used to destroy a condition. Destruction must occur when the condition is no longer in use, which means no thread is currently waiting on or attempting to signal/wait on the condition; otherwise behaviour is undefined (i.e., Pthreads may or may not generate an error for this case).

The routines pthread_cond_wait and pthread_cond_signal are used to block a thread on and unblock a thread from a condition, respectively. However, operations on any list must be done atomically, so both operations must be protected with a lock; hence, the need for the companion mutex lock to provide mutual exclusion. For example, given the following mutex and condition:

```
pthread_mutex_t m;
pthread_cond_t c;
pthread_mutex_init( &m, NULL );
pthread_cond_init( &c, NULL );
```

it is straightforward to protect the signal operation on a condition lock by:

```
pthread_mutex_lock( &m );
pthread_cond_signal( &c );      // protected operation
pthread_mutex_unlock( &m );
```

Hence, only one thread at a time is removing and unblocking waiting threads from the condition. Interestingly, Pthreads allows a condition variable to be signalled by a thread whether or not it currently owns the mutex associated with the wait on the condition; hence, implicit locking must occur within the condition variable itself to ensure an atomic removal and unblocking of a waiting task. Nevertheless, Pthreads advises the mutex lock must be held during signalling if predictable scheduling behaviour is desired.

However, the wait operation must be performed with mutual exclusion, as in:

```
pthread_mutex_lock( &m );
pthread_cond_wait( &c );        // protected operation
pthread_mutex_unlock( &m );     // never execute this statement
```

but accomplishing this is problematic because after the mutex lock is acquired, the thread blocks and cannot unlock the mutex. As a result, no other thread can acquire the mutex to access the condition lock; hence, there is a synchronization deadlock. Interchanging the last two lines clearly does not solve the problem, either. To solve this problem, the wait operation is passed the mutex and it atomically unlocks the mutex and blocks on the condition lock, as in:

```
pthread_mutex_lock( &m );
pthread_cond_wait( &c, &m );    // protected operation, and unlock mutex
```

This two-step operation by pthread_cond_wait is the same as that provided by the special version of P in Sect. 7.6.6, p. 370, which atomically Vs the argument semaphore, and then blocks the calling thread if necessary. Similarly, a monitor wait atomically blocks the monitor owner and releases the monitor lock.

pthread_cond_wait has the additional semantics of re-acquiring the argument mutex lock before returning, as if a call to pthread_mutex_lock had been made after unblocking from the condition lock. This semantics slightly reduces the complexity of constructing monitors but allows calling threads to barge into a monitor between a signaller leaving it and the signalled task restarting within it; hence, unless additional work is done, a monitor has the no-priority property (see Sect. 9.13.1, p. 490). pthread_cond_signal unblocks at least one waiting thread in any order from the condition lock; it may unblock more than one, called spurious wakeup. There is no compelling justification for this latter semantics and it only makes constructing a monitor more difficult [6, § 9]. Since signal does not change the mutex lock, the signaller retains control of it (if acquired), so a monitor has the non-blocking property (see Sect. 9.11.3.4, p. 481). As always, a signal on an empty condition lock is lost, i.e., there is no counter to remember signals before waits. pthread_cond_broadcast unblocks all waiting threads from a condition lock, and is necessary in certain cases because there is no operation to check if a condition lock is empty.

Fig. 13.5 illustrates the Pthreads equivalent for the internal-scheduling bounded-buffer monitor in Fig. 9.6, p. 444. The structure BoundedBuffer contains the shared monitor variables. The first field is the single mutex lock corresponding to the implicit monitor lock in Sect. 9.3, p. 434, which provides mutual exclusion among all mutex members. The routines ctor and dtor perform the construction and destruction of the shared variables, by appropriately initializing and destroying the necessary variables. These routines must be called before/after each use of a buffer instance. Routine ctor *does not* acquire and release the monitor lock as the monitor must not be used until after it has been initialized. Routine dtor *does* acquire and release the monitor lock because the monitor cannot be destroyed if a thread is currently using it. (Actually, acquiring the mutex lock is optional if the programmer can ensure no thread is using the monitor when it is destroyed.)

Routines query, insert and remove are equivalent to those in the bounded buffer monitor. Routine query does not acquire and release the monitor lock because it is a non-mutex member; routines insert and remove do acquire and release the monitor lock because they are mutex members and the signals are non-blocking. The waits in insert and remove are no-priority; as a result, calling threads can barge ahead of threads signalled from internal condition locks, which means the state of the monitor at the time of the signal may have changed when the waiting thread subsequently restarts in the monitor. To deal with this problem, each wait is enclosed in a **while** loop to recheck if the event has occurred, which is a busy waiting because there is no bound on service (see Sect. 9.13.1, p. 490).

An additional problem exists when returning values from mutex routines. The values of global monitor variables cannot be returned directly; only local mutex routine variables can be returned directly. For a return, such as:

```
pthread_mutex_unlock( &m );
return v;        // return global monitor variable
```

there is a race condition after unlocking the monitor lock and returning the monitor variable v. If a time-slice interrupt occurs between these two lines of code, another thread can enter a mutex routine and change the value of v before its previous value is returned to the interrupted thread. This problem is exacerbated by returning expression values involving global monitor variables, as in:

```
pthread_mutex_unlock( &m );
return v1 + v2; // return expression involving global monitor variables
```

```
typedef struct {
    pthread_mutex_t mutex;                                      // monitor lock
    int front, back, count;
    int Elements[20];                                          // bounded buffer
    pthread_cond_t full, empty;                               // waiting consumers & producers
} BoundedBuffer;

void ctor( BoundedBuffer *buf ) {
    buf->front = buf->back = buf->count = 0;
    pthread_mutex_init( &buf->mutex, NULL );
    pthread_cond_init( &buf->full, NULL );
    pthread_cond_init( &buf->empty, NULL );
}
void dtor( BoundedBuffer *buf ) {
    pthread_mutex_lock( &buf->mutex );                        // cannot destroy if in use
    pthread_cond_destroy( &buf->empty );
    pthread_cond_destroy( &buf->full );
    pthread_mutex_unlock( &buf->mutex );                      // release before destroy
    pthread_mutex_destroy( &buf->mutex );
}
int query( BoundedBuffer *buf ) {
    return buf->count;
}
void insert( BoundedBuffer *buf, int elem ) {
    pthread_mutex_lock( &buf->mutex );
    while ( buf->count == 20 )
        pthread_cond_wait( &buf->empty, &buf->mutex ); // block producer
    buf->Elements[buf->back] = elem;                          // insert element into buffer
    buf->back = ( buf->back + 1 ) % 20;
    buf->count += 1;
    pthread_cond_signal( &buf->full );                       // unblock consumer
    pthread_mutex_unlock( &buf->mutex );
}
int remove( BoundedBuffer *buf ) {
    int elem;
    pthread_mutex_lock( &buf->mutex );
    while ( buf->count == 0 )
        pthread_cond_wait( &buf->full, &buf->mutex ); // block consumer
    elem = buf->Elements[buf->front];                         // remove element from buffer
    buf->front = ( buf->front + 1 ) % 20;
    buf->count -= 1;
    pthread_cond_signal( &buf->empty );                      // unblock producer
    pthread_mutex_unlock( &buf->mutex );
    return elem;
}
```

Fig. 13.5 Pthreads: bounded buffer

For example, the remove routine for the bounded buffer could return the element directly from the buffer, as in:

```
int remove( BoundedBuffer *buf ) {
    int prev;
    ...
    prev = buf->front;                          // remember current position of front
    buf->front = ( buf->front + 1 ) % 20;
    buf->count -= 1;

    pthread_cond_signal( &buf->empty );         // unblock producer
    pthread_mutex_unlock( &buf->mutex );
    return buf->Elements[prev];                 // return directly from buffer
}
```

Unfortunately, this fails because the contents of the buffer can change by the time the value is returned. The solution is to copy all return values involving global monitor variables into local mutex routine variables before releasing the monitor lock and returning, as in:

```
int temp = v1 + v2;        // make local copy
pthread_mutex_unlock( &m );
return temp;               // return copy
```

It is the programmer's responsibility to detect these situations and deal with them appropriately.

In all these cases, there is no compiler support to ensure a programmer uses mutex and condition locks correctly or builds a monitor correctly. Common errors are to forget to acquire mutual exclusion before signalling or waiting and/or using the wrong mutex lock when signalling and waiting. In general, a programmer must manually perform the following conventions when building a monitor using Pthreads:

1. each monitor must have a single mutex lock for the monitor lock
2. there must be the equivalent of a constructor and destructor to initialize/destroy the monitor lock and any condition variables
3. each mutex member, excluding any initialization members, must start by acquiring the monitor lock, and the lock must be released by all return paths from a member
4. while Pthreads allows signalling even if the signaller currently does not own the mutex logically associated with the condition variable during waits, such signalling can make scheduling behaviour unpredictable; hence, it is a good practice to only signal while holding the mutex logically associated with the condition variable
5. when waiting for an event, it is necessary to recheck for the event upon restarting because of barging
6. global monitor variables, versus local mutex routine variables, cannot be returned directly

Because a Pthreads mutex lock can only be acquired once, a simulated mutex member cannot call another, unlike μC++; if it does, mutual-exclusion deadlock occurs (see possible workaround in Sect. 9.3.1, p. 437).

Some of these programming conventions can be simplified when using Pthreads in C++, by using constructors and destructors. Fig. 13.6 shows the previous Pthreads bounded buffer written in Pthreads/C++. First, the constructors and destructors for the BoundedBuffer class ensure the monitor lock and condition variables are correctly created and destroyed on object allocation and deallocation. Second, a special class MutexMem, which can be used for building any monitor, takes a reference to the monitor lock, and its constructor and destructor acquire and release the monitor lock. An instance of MutexMem, named lock, is then declared at the start of each monitor mutex member. (The name of the instance is unimportant.) Now the scope rules of C++ ensure the constructor of lock is executed before continuing after the declaration, which acquires the monitor lock. As well, the scope rules ensure the destructor of lock is called regardless of where or how the mutex member returns, including exit via an exception, so the monitor lock is guaranteed to be released. Furthermore, expressions in **return** statements are guaranteed to be evaluated and stored in an implicit temporary *before* local destructors are run because a destructor could change global monitor variables referenced in a return expression; hence, global monitor variables can be returned directly. While these C++ features mitigate some of the problems with building Pthreads monitor, there is still ample opportunity for errors.

Finally, a solution to the readers and writer problem written using Pthreads and C++ is presented in Fig. 13.7, p. 656, which has no starvation and no staleness. The solution is problematic because of the signalling semantics of waking up more than one thread and the barging issue because priority is not given to signalled threads. The signalling problem is handled using a queue of private condition locks, like private semaphores in Sect. 7.6.6, p. 370, where a new condition is allocated for each blocking thread. Since there is only one thread blocked on each private condition, a signal can restart at most one thread. The barging issue is handled by not decrementing rwdelay by the signalling thread; instead, the signalled thread removes its node from the list and decrements rwdelay. As a result, a barging thread always sees a waiting thread and blocks, even if the last thread has been signalled from the condition lock. The only addition is a check at the start of StartWrite for rwdelay > 0, because a barging writer could see rcnt and wcnt at zero, but the last reader or writer may have signalled the only waiting thread from a condition lock. This additional check is unnecessary when there is no barging because control of the monitor goes directly to the signalled thread. This simple scheme for handling barging threads only works for problems where all threads wait on the same condition. If threads wait on different conditions after entering the monitor, a more sophisticated technique must be used to deal with barging, involving creation of a special condition on which barging threads wait on entry; threads are then signalled from this special condition when there are no outstanding signals.

```
class MutexMem {                                        // used by any monitor
    pthread_mutex_t &mutex;
  public:
    MutexMem( pthread_mutex_t &mutex ) : mutex( mutex ) {
        pthread_mutex_lock( &mutex );
    }
    ~MutexMem() {
        pthread_mutex_unlock( &mutex );
    }
};
template<typename ELEMTYPE> class BoundedBuffer {
    pthread_mutex_t mutex;
    int front, back, count;
    ELEMTYPE Elements[20];
    pthread_cond_t full, empty;                         // waiting consumers & producers
  public:
    BoundedBuffer() {
        front = back = count = 0;
        pthread_mutex_init( &mutex, NULL );
        pthread_cond_init( &full, NULL );
        pthread_cond_init( &empty, NULL );
    }
    ~BoundedBuffer() {
        {   // cannot destroy if in use
            MutexMem lock( mutex );                     // acquire and release monitor lock
            pthread_cond_destroy( &empty );
            pthread_cond_destroy( &full );
        }   // release before destroy
        pthread_mutex_destroy( &mutex );
    }
    int query() { return count; }

    void insert( ELEMTYPE elem ) {
        MutexMem lock( mutex );                         // acquire and release monitor lock

        while ( count == 20 )
            pthread_cond_wait( &empty, &mutex ); // block producer
        Elements[back] = elem;
        back = ( back + 1 ) % 20;
        count += 1;
        pthread_cond_signal( &full );                   // unblock consumer
    }
    ELEMTYPE remove() {
        MutexMem lock( mutex );                         // acquire and release monitor lock

        while ( count == 0 )
            pthread_cond_wait( &full, &mutex );         // block consumer
        ELEMTYPE elem = Elements[front];
        front = ( front + 1 ) % 20;
        count -= 1;
        pthread_cond_signal( &empty );                  // unblock producer
        return elem;
    }
};
```

Fig. 13.6 Pthreads/C++: bounded buffer

```
class ReadersWriter {
    enum RW { READER, WRITER };              // kinds of threads
    struct RWnode {
        RW kind;                             // kind of thread
        pthread_cond_t cond;                 // private condition
        RWnode( RW kind ) : kind(kind) { pthread_cond_init( &cond, NULL ); }
        ~RWnode() { pthread_cond_destroy( &cond ); }
    };
    queue<RWnode *> rw;                       // queue of RWnodes
    pthread_mutex_t mutex;
    int rcnt, wcnt, rwdelay;
    void StartRead() {
        MutexMem lock( mutex );
        if ( wcnt > 0 || rwdelay > 0 ) {
            RWnode r( READER );
            rw.push( &r ); rwdelay += 1;      // remember kind of thread
            pthread_cond_wait( &r.cond, &mutex );
            rw.pop(); rwdelay -= 1;           // remove waiting task from condition list
        }
        rcnt += 1;
        if ( rwdelay > 0 && rw.front()->kind == READER )
            pthread_cond_signal( &(rw.front()->cond) );
    }
    void EndRead() {
        MutexMem lock( mutex );
        rcnt -= 1;
        if ( rcnt == 0 && rwdelay > 0 )        // last reader ?
            pthread_cond_signal( &(rw.front()->cond) );
    }
    void StartWrite() {
        MutexMem lock( mutex );
        if ( rcnt > 0 || wcnt > 0 || rwdelay > 0 ) {
            RWnode w( WRITER );
            rw.push( &w ); rwdelay += 1;      // remember kind of thread
            pthread_cond_wait( &w.cond, &mutex );
            rw.pop(); rwdelay -= 1;           // remove waiting task from condition list
        }
        wcnt += 1;
    }
    void EndWrite() {
        MutexMem lock( mutex );
        wcnt -= 1;
        if ( rwdelay > 0 )                     // anyone waiting ?
            pthread_cond_signal( &(rw.front()->cond) );
    }
  public:
    ReadersWriter() : rcnt(0), wcnt(0), rwdelay(0) {
        pthread_mutex_init( &mutex, NULL );
    }
    ~ReadersWriter() {
        MutexMem lock( mutex );                // cannot destroy if in use
        pthread_mutex_destroy( &mutex );
    }
};
```

Fig. 13.7 Pthreads/C++: readers and writer

13.2.2   Object-Oriented Thread Library: C++

In the previous discussion, it is shown that C++ features, like constructors and destructor, can be used to simplify writing certain aspects of concurrent programs using a threads and locks library. However, the basic threads and locks library is not designed to fully utilize all the features of an object-oriented language to simplify implementation and/or usage, usually because the library is written in a non-object-oriented language, such as C. This section examines how a threads and locks library can be designed for an object-oriented language, in particular C++. Several different library approaches are examined because there is no library that is clearly the most popular, and there is no standard thread library as part of the C++ Standard Library. As for non-object-oriented concurrency libraries, object-oriented libraries are either unsound or inefficient because the compiler has no knowledge that a program using the library is concurrent.

13.2.2.1   Thread Creation and Termination

In an object-oriented language, the natural way to provide concurrency through a library is to define an abstract class, Thread, that implements the thread abstraction:

```
class Thread {
    // any necessary locks and data structures
  public:
    Thread() {
        // create a thread and start it running in the most derived task body
    }
    // general routines for all tasks, like getState, yield, etc.
};
```

(Thread is like uBaseTask in Sect. 5.10.2, p. 215.) The constructor for Thread creates a thread to "animate" the object. A user-defined task class inherits from Thread, and a task is an object of this class:

```
class T1 : public Thread { ...   // inherit from Thread
```

This approach has been used to define C++ libraries that provide coroutine facilities [24, 34] and simple parallel facilities [3, 12].

When this approach is used, task classes should have the same properties as other classes, so inheritance from task types should be allowed. Similarly, task objects should have the same properties and behaviour as class objects. This latter requirement suggests that tasks should communicate via calls to member routines, since ordinary objects receive requests that way, and since the semantics of routine call matches the semantics of synchronous communication nicely. The body of the task, e.g., the task main, has the job of choosing which member-routine call should be executed next.

When one task creates another, the creating task's thread executes statements in Thread's constructor that create a new thread. The question arises which thread does what jobs in this process? The approach that produces the greatest concurrency has

the new thread execute the new task's constructors and body, while the creating
thread returns immediately to the point of the declaration of the object. However,
the normal implementation of constructors in most object-oriented languages
makes this difficult or impossible if inheritance from task types is allowed. Each
constructor starts by calling the constructors of its parent classes. By the time
Thread's constructor is called, there can be an arbitrary number of constructor
activations on the stack, one for each level of inheritance. For a library approach, it
is impossible for the initialization code for Thread to examine the stack to locate the
return point for the original constructor (most derived) so the creating thread can
return and the new thread can complete the initialization. Only compiler support,
such as marking the stack at the point of declaration or passing implicitly the return
address for the creating thread up the inheritance chain, can make this approach
work. In the absence of compiler support, the creating thread must execute the new
task's constructors, after which the new thread can begin executing the task body,
which inhibits concurrency somewhat.

Thread Body Placement

The body of a task must have access to the members of a task, and the Thread
constructor must be able to find the body in order to start the task's thread running
in it. Therefore, in the library approach, the task body must be a member of the
task type, and there is hardly any other sensible choice. At first glance, the task's
constructor seems like a reasonable choice. However, the requirement that it be
possible to inherit from a task type forbids this choice for most object-oriented
languages. For example, let T1 be a task type, with a constructor that contains
initialization code for private data and the task body. Now consider a second type
T2 that inherits from T1:

```
class T1 : public Thread {          class T2 : public T1 {
    public:                             public:
        T1() {                              T2() {
            // initialization                   // initialization
            // task body                        // task body
        }                                   }
};                                  };
```

T2's constructor must specify a new task body if it overrides or adds new mutex
members. Therefore, it must somehow override the task body in T1's constructor,
but still execute T1's initialization code. Because both are contained in the same
block of code, it is impossible. One solution is to put the body in a special member
routine, like main, which can be declared by Thread as an abstract virtual member
so that task types must supply one.

Simula provides an interesting mechanism, called **inner**, to address this issue. In
a single inheritance hierarchy, an **inner** statement in a constructor (or destructor) of
a base class acts like a call to the constructor (or destructor) of the derived class:

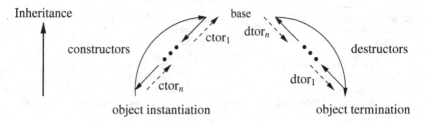

object instantiation   object termination

where the solid-lines are the normal execution path for constructors and destructors
and the dashed-lines are the **inner** execution paths. For example, given:

```
class T1 : public Thread {        class T2: public T1 {
public:                           public:
    T1() { s1; inner; s2; };          T2() : { s3; inner; s4; };
    mem() { ... }                     mem() { ... }
};                                };
T1 t1;
T2 t2;
```

the initialization of t1 executes statements Thread::Thread, s1, and s2, and the
initialization of t2 executes Thread::Thread, s1, s3, s4 and s2, in that order.

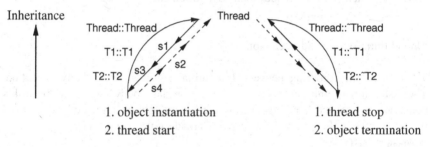

1. object instantiation   1. thread stop
2. thread start   2. object termination

In general, the code before **inner** is executed top-down in the inheritance structure
(as for normal constructor initialization) and code after **inner** is executed bottom-
up, so initialization is composed of two passes: down and then up the constructor
chain. Similarly, for destructors, the code before **inner** is executed bottom-up in the
inheritance structure (as for normal destructor initialization) and code after **inner** is
executed top-down, so termination is composed of two passes: up and then down the
destructor chain. During the initialization of t2, in T1::T1, before the **inner** statement,
t2 is considered to be an instance of class T1. After the **inner** statement, because
initialization is complete, it is an instance of T2, and the meaning of calls to virtual
routines changes accordingly. In this case, a call to mem in s1 invokes T1::mem,
while a call to mem in s2 invokes T2::mem because mem is overridden in T2.

How can **inner** be used to solve the previous problem? By following a convention
of counting down one side of the initialization and then comparing the counter value
on the up side. In this way, it is possible to programmatically locate the most derived
constructor and only the task body of that constructor executes, as in:

```
class T1 : public Thread {          class T2 : public T1 {
   int cnt;                            int cnt;
public:                             public:
   T1() {                              T2() {
      cnt = Thread::cnt += 1;             cnt = Thread::cnt += 1;
      // initialization                  // initialization
      inner;                             inner;
      if ( cnt == Thread.cnt ) // task body   if ( cnt == Thread.cnt ) // task body
   };                                  };
};                                  };
```

Each constructor increments a global class counter in Thread and stores its position in the constructor chain in a local class counter during the execution down the constructor chain. On the way up the constructor chain, only the most derived constructor code is executed because of the conditional check.

However, it is not obvious how **inner** could be added to C++. **inner** must invoke constructors and possibly destructors in the order defined by C++, taking multiple inheritance and virtual inheritance into account. Furthermore, a class can have many constructors, and descendants specify which of their base class's constructors are called. Simula has only one constructor, no destructors, and single inheritance. Finally, this approach relies on programmers following this convention for it to work correctly, which is always a questionable requirement.

Thread Initialization and Execution

There is a strict ordering between task initialization and task body execution. The task's thread must not begin to execute the task body until after the task's constructors have finished. However, in the library approach, the code to start the thread running in the task body appears in Thread's constructor, as in:

```
class Thread {
public:
   Thread() { // create a thread and start it running in the most derived task body ...
   ~Thread() { // wait for thread to terminate ...
   };
```

In C++, the thread creation code is executed first, *before* the constructors of any derived classes. Hence, the new thread must be created in the "blocked" state, and must somehow be unblocked after the most derived constructor finishes. A more subtle problem results from the semantics of initialization. While Thread's constructor is executing, the new task is considered to be an instance of class Thread, not the actual task class being instantiated. This means that, within Thread's constructor, the virtual main routine that contains the task's body is inaccessible.

The most common solution to these problems is requiring an explicit action to unblock the thread *after* all the constructors are executed. In this approach, the Thread class provides a start() member routine that must be called after the declaration of a task, but before any calls to member routines depending on task properties:

```
.  T1 t1;        // declare task object
   t1.start()    // start thread running in most derived task body
```

After the declaration, the constructors have all finished and main refers to the most derived task body. However, this two-step creation protocol opens a window for errors: programmers may fail to start their tasks.

In object-oriented languages with destructors, like C++, a similar interaction exists between task-body execution and task termination. When one task deletes another, it calls the deleted task's destructor. The destructor must not begin execution until after the deleted task's body has finished:

```
{
    T1 t1; ...
} // call destructor for t1 and wait for task body to complete
```

otherwise the object's variables are terminated and storage is released while the thread is still using it. However, the code that waits for the task body to finish cannot be placed in Thread's destructor, because it would be executed last in the destructor sequence, *after* the destructors of any derived classes. Since the thread is still running in the most derived task body and referring to variables at that level, undefined behaviour would result. The task's termination code cannot simply be moved from the destructors to the end of the task body, because that would prevent further inheritance: derived classes would have no way to execute their base class's termination code. Thread could provide a join routine, analogous to start, which must be called before task deletion, but this two-step termination protocol is even more error-prone than the creation protocol, as forgetting the call to join deletes the task's storage with the thread still running.

If an **inner** mechanism is available, it could be used to solve this problem by not starting the thread until after the initialization, as in:

```
class Thread {
public:
    Thread() {
        /* initialization */ inner; /* start thread in most derived task body */
    }
};
```

When the thread is started after **inner**, all the initialization is completed and a reference to main at this point is the most derived one. Thread's destructor would start by waiting for the task body to finish, and then use **inner** to execute the task class's destructors.

More Inheritance Problems

Regardless of whether a concurrency library or language extensions are used to provide concurrency in an object-oriented language, new kinds of types are introduced, like coroutine, monitor and task. These new kinds of types complicate inheritance. The trivial case of single inheritance among homogeneous kinds, i.e., a monitor inheriting from another monitor, is straightforward because any implicit actions are the same throughout the hierarchy. (An additional requirement exists for tasks: there must be at least one task body specified in the hierarchy where the thread starts.) For a task or a monitor type, new member routines defined by a derived class can be accepted by statements in a new task body or in redefined virtual routines.

Inheritance among heterogeneous types can be both useful and confusing. Heterogeneous inheritance is useful for generating concurrent types from existing non-concurrent types, e.g., to define a mutex queue by deriving from a simple queue, or for use with container classes requiring additional link fields. For example, to change a simple queue to a mutex queue requires a monitor to inherit from the class Queue and redefine all of the class's member routines so mutual exclusion occurs when they are invoked, as in:

```
class Queue {                      // sequential queue
  public:
    void insert( ... ) ...
    virtual void remove( ... ) ...
};

class MutexQueue : public Queue { // concurrent queue
    virtual void insert( ... ) {
      // provide mutual exclusion
      Queue::insert(...);          // call base-class member
    }
    virtual void remove( ... ) {
      // provide mutual exclusion
      Queue::remove(...);          // call base-class member
    }
};
```

However, this example demonstrates the dangers caused by non-virtual routines:

```
Queue *qp = new MutexQueue; // subtyping allows assignment
qp->insert( ... );          // call to a non-virtual member routine, statically bound
qp->remove( ... );          // call to a virtual member routine, dynamically bound
```

Queue::insert does not provide mutual exclusion because it is a member of Queue, while MutexQueue::insert does provide mutual exclusion (along with MutexQueue:: remove). Because the pointer variable qp is of type Queue, the call qp->insert calls Queue::insert even though insert is redefined in MutexQueue; hence, no mutual exclusion occurs. The unexpected lack of mutual exclusion results in errors. In contrast, the call to remove is dynamically bound, so the redefined routine in the monitor is invoked and appropriate synchronization occurs. In object-oriented programming languages that have only virtual member routines (i.e., dynamic dispatch is always used), this is not an issue. Nor is there a problem with C++'s private inheritance because no subtype relationship is created, and hence, the assignment to qp is invalid.

Heterogeneous inheritance among entities like monitors, coroutines and tasks can be very confusing. While some combinations are meaningful and useful, others are not, for the following reason. Classes are written as ordinary classes, coroutines, monitors, or tasks, and the coding styles used in each cannot be arbitrarily mixed. For example, an instance of a class that inherits from a task can be passed to a routine expecting an instance of the class. If the routine calls one of the object's member routines, it could inadvertently block the current thread indefinitely. While this could happen in general, there is a significantly greater chance if users casually combine types of different kinds. The safest rule to follow for heterogeneous inheritance is to require the derived kind to be equal or more specific than the base kind with respect to execution properties, e.g., a type with mutual exclusion can inherit from a type without mutual exclusion, but not vice versa.

Multiple inheritance simply exacerbates the problem and it significantly complicates the implementation, which slows the execution. For example, accepting member routines is significantly more complex with multiple inheritance because it is impossible to build a static mask to test on routine entry. As is being discovered, multiple inheritance is not as useful a mechanism as it initially seemed [5, 8].

13.2.2.2   Thread Synchronization and Mutual Exclusion

Synchronization

As suggested in Sect. 13.2.2.1, p. 657, the obvious mechanism for communication among tasks is via calls to member routines, since this matches with normal object communication; however, not all object-oriented concurrency systems adopt this approach. In some library-based schemes (and some languages), communication is done via message queues, called ports or channels [16], as in:

```
MsgQueue<int> Q1, Q2;          // global message queue of integers
class ThreadType : public Thread {
    void main() {              // task body
        Q1.add( 3 );           // add data to message queue
        int i = Q2.remove();   // remove data from message queue
    }
};
```

Particular message queues are shared among tasks that need to communicate, either through global message-queues or passing message-queue arguments. Depending on the kind of message queue, e.g., a prioritized queue, different delivery effects can be achieved. If tasks communicate using message queues, the meaning of publicly available member routines needs to be addressed, because multiple threads may enter and simultaneously access a task's data.

However, a single typed queue per task, such as a queue of integers, is inadequate; the queue's message type inevitably becomes a union of several message types, and static type-checking is compromised. Inheritance from an abstract Message class can be used, instead of a union, but then a task has to perform type tests on messages before accessing them with facilities like C++'s dynamic cast. However, runtime type-checking is still discouraged in C++ design philosophy and has a runtime cost.

When multiple queues are used, a library facility analogous to the μC++ **_Accept** statement is needed to wait for messages to arrive on more than one queue, as in:

```
waitfor i = Q1.remove() || f = Q2.remove ...
```

In some cases, it is essential to also know which message queue delivered the data, i.e., Q1 or Q2, as that knowledge might affect the interpretation of the data or the

next action to be taken. This case is analogous to the code after an accept clause
in a μC++ _**Accept** statement. One approach is for the waitfor statement to return
the message queue identifier from which data was received. A programmer would
then use a **switch** statement to discriminate among the message queue identifiers. A
more general solution requires λ-expressions (anonymous nested routine bodies) to
support a block of code that may or may not be invoked depending on the selection
criteria, e.g.:

```
waitfor i = Q1.remove(), {code-body} || f = Q2.remove, {code-body} ...
```

where the *code-body* is a λ-expression and represents the code executed after a
particular message queue is accepted.

An implementation problem with message queues occurs when multiple tasks
receive messages from the same set of message queues, e.g.:

```
MsgQueue<T1> Q1;
MsgQueue<T2> Q2;
class ThreadType : public Thread {
    void main() {                    // task body
        waitfor i = Q1.remove(), {code-body} || f = Q2.remove, {code-body} ...
    }
};
ThreadType t1, t2;
```

Threads t1 and t2 simultaneously accept messages from the same queues, Q1 and
Q2. It is straightforward to check for the existence of available data in each queue.
However, if there is no data, both t1 and t2 must wait for data on either queue.
To implement this, tasks have to be associated with both queues until data arrives,
given data when it arrives, and then removed from both queues. This implementation
is expensive since the addition or removal of a message from a queue must be
atomic across all queues involved in a waiting task's accept statement to ensure
only one data element from the accepted set of queues is given to the accepting task.
In languages with concurrency support, the compiler can disallow accepting from
overlapping sets of message queues by restricting the waitfor statement to queues
the task declares. Compilers for more permissive languages, like SR [2], perform
global analysis to determine if tasks are receiving from overlapping sets of message
queues; in the cases where there is no overlap, less expensive code can be generated.
In a library approach, access to the message queues must always assume the worst
case scenario.

Alternatively, if the routine-call mechanism is used for communication among
tasks (as in μC++), it is necessary to insert code at the start and exit of each mutex
member to manage selective entry, and provide a facility analogous to the μC++
_**Accept** statement to allow a task to wait for calls to arrive. The code for selective
entry must be provided by the programmer following a coding convention, as is done
at the end of Sect. 13.2.1.2, p. 647 when using Pthreads and C++. Building a library
facility similar to a _**Accept** statement is difficult, e.g., ABC++ [31, p. 8] provides
member routine, Paccept(*task-type*::*member-name*, ...) inherited from Thread, to
control calls to mutex members. However, Paccept has many limitations, like a

restricted number of member names, no mechanism to determine which call is accepted, efficiency problems, and type-safety issues.

Mutual Exclusion

Providing mutual exclusion can be done in the same way as for controlling selective entry by a coding convention of explicitly locking at the start and unlocking at the exit points for each mutex member. Alternatively, the call to each mutex member is modified to perform the necessary mutual exclusion (which could also be done to provide selective entry). For example, in ABC++ [31], calling a mutex member is done indirectly by calling a special routine that then calls the mutex member, as in:

P_call(monitor_object, monitor_type::member, *varible list of up to 7 arguments*);

However, changing the call syntax in this way is usually unacceptable as it often restricts the routine call and makes programs difficult to read. Object-oriented programming languages supporting inheritance of routines, such as LOGLAN'88 [10] and Beta [27], can provide special member code automatically. (The use of **inner** in a constructor is a special case of routine inheritance, where the derived class's constructor inherits from the base class's constructor.) Whatever the mechanism, it must allow the special code to be selectively applied to the member routines. For example, there are cases where not all public member routines require mutual exclusion and where some private members require mutual exclusion. In languages with concurrency support, the compiler can efficiently handle all of these issues.

Finally, mutual exclusion can interact with synchronization, as in internal scheduling, via wait and possibly signal. The wait routine must be passed the monitor mutex-lock, either directly or indirectly through the **this** parameter if the lock is provided via inheritance, along with the condition variable, so it can perform any necessary baton passing to manage the mutex object correctly. However, in first case, users have to be aware of the mutex lock and could pass the wrong lock, and in the second case, having to pass **this** is obscure.

13.3 Threads and Message Passing

The next major style of library approach for concurrency is threads and message passing. Threads are usually created in the same style as in the previous section but synchronization and mutual exclusion are provided by a technique called message passing.

The term message passing has a number of connotation (see Sect. 5.3, p. 195). First, the term is often incorrectly used to imply distributed communication. While it is true that all distributed systems perform message passing, message passing can be performed on shared-memory systems. Second, the term is often used to imply passing data by value rather than by address. While it is true that most distributed

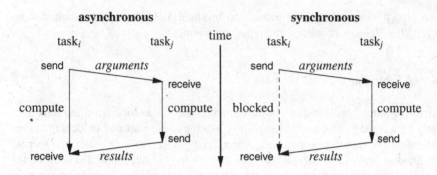

Fig. 13.8 Message passing, send/receive

systems only pass data by value because of the non-shared memories, addresses can be passed in messages for shared-memory systems. However, to ensure portability between distributed and shared-memory systems for programs that might execute on either, it is common practice to preclude passing pointers so that a program does not have to be aware of which environment it is executing on. Here, message passing has only one meaning: an alternative mechanism to parameter passing. That is, in message passing, all communication among threads is transmitted by grouping the data into a single argument and passing it by value. This semantics is a restricted form of parameter passing, where only one parameter is allowed for communication versus any number and type of parameters. If more than one value needs to be passed in a message, the value must be packed into a structure, and the structure passed in the message. While message passing appears to be both syntactically and semantically different from approaches seen thus far, it will be shown that there is a strong equivalence with prior approaches.

The basic mechanism for performing message passing is through two routines, send and receive, which transmit and receive a message, respectively (see MPI Sect. 13.5.4, p. 716). The resulting communication is often asynchronous, and synchronous communication can be simulated (see Fig. 13.8). A third routine, reply, is sometimes available. All three mechanisms are discussed shortly. Messages are usually sent directly from thread to thread, so message passing is a form of direct communication. Each thread involved in message passing has an implicit buffer, analogous to the monitor entry queue, where messages are stored, like call arguments, and senders may wait for messages to be received (accepted).

All message passing approaches are implemented using a library approach, versus augmenting the programming language, and therefore, all concurrent message passing approaches are either unsound or inefficient because the compiler has no knowledge that a program using the library is concurrent. Even given these significant problems, there are still many message passing libraries being developed and used.

13.3.1   Send

Send is the basic mechanism to communicate information to another thread and corresponds to a call of a task's mutex member. The minimum arguments to send are the thread identifier, where the messages are being sent, and the message, which can be empty, e.g., send(Tid,msg). The semantics of send vary depending on the message passing approach. Most message passing approaches support several different kinds of send, and a programmer selects one appropriate to the communication needs. The following is a list of different kinds of message sends.

13.3.1.1   Blocking Send

A blocking send implements synchronous communication, i.e., the sending thread blocks until at least the message has been received. Hence, information is transferred via a rendezvous between the sender and the receiver. For example, a producer thread would send messages to a consumer thread, Cid, by:

```
Producer() {
    for ( ;; ) {
        // produce element and place in msg
        SendBlock( Cid, msg );          // block until the message is received
    }
}
```

Blocking send corresponds to synchronous routine call, where the message corresponds to the argument list.

13.3.1.2   Nonblocking Send

A nonblocking send implements asynchronous communication, i.e., the sending thread blocks only until the message has been copied into a buffer associated with the receiver. The receiver normally gets the messages in the order they are placed into its message buffer. Because a receiver's message buffer can fill, a nonblocking send can temporarily become a blocking send until an empty buffer slot becomes available. Hence, a nonblocking send is only mostly nonblocking; a programmer cannot rely on true nonblocking semantics because that would require infinite buffer space. For example, a producer thread would send messages to a consumer thread, Cid, by:

```
Producer() {
    for ( ;; ) {
        // produce element and place in msg
        SendNonBlock( Cid, msg );       // do not block
    }
}
```

Nonblocking send corresponds to asynchronous routine call, where the message corresponds to the argument list.

13.3.1.3 Multicast/Broadcast Send

Both blocking and nonblocking send can have a multicast and broadcast form, which sends a message to a list of receivers or a special group of receivers or any receiver listening to a particular broadcast. For multicast, the group of receivers is usually defined using some thread grouping mechanism. For example, when tasks are created they may be placed into a named group and that group name can be used for a multicast send; tasks may enter and leave groups at any time during their lifetime. In essence, a multicast send is just a convenience mechanism to send the same message to a number of threads. For broadcast, there may be one or more broadcast channels on which messages are sent and received. When a channel is used for communication, the message passing becomes indirect because there is no specific target thread for the message, i.e., any channel receiver can receive the message. For example, a producer thread can send messages to a list of consumers, CidList, or broadcast to a consumer channel, ConChan, by:

```
Producer() {
    for ( ;; ) {
        // produce element
        MulticastNonBlock( CidList, msg );   // nonblocking form
        MulticastBlock( CidList, msg );      // blocking form
        BroadcastNonBlock( ConChan, msg ); // nonblocking form
        BroadcastBlock( ConChan, msg );    // blocking form
    }
}
```

There is no equivalent to multicast/broadcast send in non-message passing system because routine call is used to initiate the communication. However, both multicast and broadcast can be simulated either by calling a list of tasks or using indirect communication via a monitor.

13.3.2 Receive

Receive is the basic mechanism to receive a communication and corresponds to a task's mutex member. The minimum arguments to receive are the messages being sent, e.g., receive(msg), where msg is an output argument. The semantics of receive vary depending on the message passing approach. Most message passing approaches support several different kinds of receive, and a programmer selects one appropriate to the communication needs. The following is a list of different kinds of message receives.

13.3.2.1 Receive Any

The simplest form of receive is one accepting any message sent to it, called receive any. The receive blocks the calling thread until any message arrives. For example, a consumer thread would receive messages sent from any producer by:

```
Consumer() {
    for ( ;; ) {
        Receive( msg );                    // receive any message
        // consume element from msg
    }
}
```

This kind of receive works like a monitor used only for mutual exclusion purposes, where after processing a call, the next call to any mutex member is processed.

13.3.2.2 Receive Message Specific

A receiver can control messages by indicating the kind of message it is accepting from senders, called receive message specific. The kind of message can be derived automatically from the type of the message or it can be an arbitrary value created by the programmer. The former is safer than the latter. In the latter case, the sender has to explicitly specify the message kind in the send, e.g., SendBlock(Cid,msgId,msg) or embed the message kind at some known location in the message (often the first byte or word of the message). The receive blocks the calling thread until a message of the specified kind arrives, and hence, provides external scheduling. It may be possible to specify a list of acceptable message kinds. For example, a consumer thread would receive only certain kinds of messages sent from producers by:

```
Consumer() {
    for ( ;; ) {
        Receive( msg, msgId );             // receive a message of kind msgId
        Receive( msg, msgIdList );         // receive a message of from any kind in the list
        // consume element from msg
    }
}
```

Receive message specific is like an accept statement, where the kind of accepted message is equivalent to the kind of accepted mutex member. A list of message kinds is like an accept statement with multiple accept clauses, accepting multiple mutex members.

13.3.2.3 Receive Thread Specific

A receiver can control messages by indicating the thread it is accepting messages from, called receive thread specific. The send does not specify any additional information for receive thread specific, but the thread identifier of the sender must be implicitly sent with the message. The receive blocks the calling thread until a message arrives from the specified thread, and hence, provides external scheduling.

It may be possible to specify a list of thread identifiers from which messages are accepted. For example, a consumer thread would receive only messages sent from a particular producer by:

```
Consumer() {
    for ( ;; ) {
        Receive( msg, Pid );           // receive a message from task Pid
        Receive( msg, PidList );       // receive a message from any task Pid in the list
        // consume element from msg
    }
}
```

Receive thread specific is more precise than an accept statement because it indicates a specific thread sending a message not just the kind of message, which might be sent by multiple threads. This capability can only be simulated in μC++ by having a special mutex member (possible private and accessible only through friendship) that is called only by the specific thread. Accepting this mutex member means waiting for the specific thread to call. Interestingly, there is nothing precluding an accept statement from supporting a thread-specific feature, e.g., **_Accept**(Tid, mutex-name).

13.3.2.4 Receive Reply

All the previous receive statements perform two distinct operations. First, an appropriate message is extracted from a thread's message buffer. Second, for blocking sends, the sender is unblocked, ending the rendezvous. There is no reason these two operations have to be bounded together, i.e., it is possible to separate the operations and provide different mechanism for each, called **receive reply** [18]. In this scheme, the receiver blocks until a message arrives but only extracts an appropriate message; unblocking the sender is performed with a separate Reply mechanism. For example, a consumer thread would receive messages sent from any producer by:

```
Consumer() {
    for ( ;; ) {
        Pid = ReceiveReply( msg );    // receive any message
        // consume element from msg
        Reply( Pid );                 // nonblocking
    }
}
```

Since the sender is not implicitly unblocked at the receive, the thread identifier of the sending thread is returned, which must be stored for use in a subsequent reply. Notice if the reply immediately follows the receive, it is identical to a receive any. In this case, the consumer forces the producer to remain blocked until the element is consumed, which may be necessary if there is a side-effect associated with consuming. Interestingly, the receiver is not required to reply immediately to the last sending thread. Instead, the receiver can store the thread identifier of the sender and reply to it at some arbitrary time in the future, which provides internal scheduling. A condition variable can be mimicked by linking together unreplied thread identifiers and replying to them when appropriate events occur.

For blocking send, the reply can also be used as a mechanism to return a result to the original send, as for synchronous call, rather than having the sender perform a second send to obtain a result. In this case, both the send and reply are modified to receive and send a reply message. Notice the role reversal here, where the send becomes a receive and the reply (which is part of a receive) becomes a send. For example, a producer and consumer thread could perform a bidirectional communication by:

```
Producer() {                          Consumer() {
    for ( ;; ) {                          for ( ;; ) {
        // produce element                    Pid = ReceiveReply( recvMsg );
        SendReply( Cid, replyMsg, sendMsg );  // check element
    }                                         Reply( Pid, replyMsg )
}                                             // consume element
                                          }
                                      }
```

In this scenario, the consumer checks the data before replying and sends back a message to the producer indicating if the element is valid; only if the element is valid it is consumed.

13.3.2.5 Receive Combinations

All of the previous receive control mechanisms are orthogonal, and hence, can be applied together in any combination, with the exception that returning a message with reply to a nonblocking send is either an error or the return message is discarded. For example, it is possible to combine all the control mechanisms:

```
Consumer() {
    for (;;) {
        Pid = ReceiveReply( recvMsg, msgIdList, PidList );
        // check element
        Reply( Pid, replyMsg )
        // consume element
    }
}
```

where the consumer only accepts messages of the specified kinds and only from the specified producer identifiers, and then the consumer replies back to the selected sender with a reply message.

13.3.3 Message Format

Message passing systems can specify restrictions on the form and content of the message itself. One restriction mentioned already is disallowing pointers in a message, but there are others.

Another possible restriction is message size. Some message-passing systems allow variable sized messages of arbitrary size (or very large size, e.g., 2^{32} bytes). Other systems chose a fixed sized message, with the size usually falling in the range 32 to 64 bytes. (This range is also the average size of data passed as arguments for a routine call.) The particular size is usually chosen by monitoring communication activity of a variable sized system and finding the average message size, which usually falls in the range 32 to 64 bytes. In some cases, the decision between variable and fixed size messages may depend on the underlying hardware transport mechanism. For example, Ethernet communication channels support variable sized messages while ATM communication channels only support fixed sized messages.

In general, variable sized messages are more complex to implement both in the lower-level software and hardware, and the complexity can slow the implementation, but variable sized messages are easy to use because arbitrarily long messages can be sent and received. On the other hand, fixed sized messages are simple to implement and the implementation is usually very fast, but long messages must be broken up and transmitted in pieces and reconstructed by the receiver, which is error prone.

Combining the two approach leads to the worst of both worlds. Because of the two kinds of messages, many routines have to be written twice: one to deal with variable sized messages and one to deal with fixed sized messages, which doubles every possible problem.

13.3.4   Typed Messages

Most complex applications send and receive a number of different kinds of messages. However, when a message arrives, it is only a string of unknown bytes of some particular length; hence, the receive is normally type-unsafe. It is a common convention in message passing for the first byte or word to contain a value identifying the type of the message. This message code can be used for receive selection, as in receive-message-specific, and/or to assign a meaning to the string of bytes, i.e., is the data three integers or seven pointers. Some message-passing systems implicitly assign the message codes by generating a unique value based on the field types in the message. However, after each receive, there is a **switch** statement performing a dynamic type-check to determine the kind of the message, which is costly and still potentially error prone. This behaviour is in contrast to argument/parameter passing for routine call, which is statically type-safe.

Furthermore, having two forms of communication, i.e., routine/member call and message passing, leads to confusion deciding when to use each. It is much simpler for programmers to have a single consistent mechanism for communication and routine call seems to be the superior approach because of the parameter/argument lists and static type-checking. It is common in message-passing systems to call routines, using arguments for communication, and have the routine pack or unpack the data into or out of a message and performs the send or receive, respectively.

If programmers are going to hide message passing in this way, it begs the question of why use it at all.

Static type-safety and routine call are essential elements of all modern programming-systems. Message passing is type-unsafe and does not follow the standard routine call (arguments/parameters) model. Having to work with two programming models is complex, confusing and largely unnecessary. Therefore, there is no long-term future for the message-passing approach; existing message-passing systems will gradually be supplanted by systems using statically typed routine-call.

13.4 Concurrent Languages

Concurrent languages are programming languages that contain language features that:

1. provide high-level concurrency constructs to simplify the details and complexities of writing concurrent programs
2. inform the compiler that parts of a program are concurrent rather than sequential

The quality, integration and consistency of the features provided in the first point differentiate a good concurrent programming language from an average or bad one. The second point is crucial for correct and efficient code generation, because certain sequential code optimizations invalidate a concurrent program; only when a compiler can differentiate sequential from concurrent code can it highly optimize the former and generate correct code for the latter. Over the years, many languages have provided different styles and mechanisms for concurrency; only a small subset of these languages are discussed. The languages chosen are ones the reader might encounter at some time in their programming career or are historically significant.

13.4.1 Ada 95

The programming language Ada was developed in two major design efforts: one culminating in Ada 83 [22], followed by Ada 95 [23]. Ada 83 provides tasks, which are loosely based on the concept of objects; Ada 95 provides object-based monitors. All the concurrency features are embedded in the language, i.e., there is no library component, so the concurrency features are both sound and efficient.

13.4.1.1 Thread Creation and Termination

Threads are defined in Ada 95 by a special **task type** constructor, as in μC++ with _Task, e.g.:

```
task type Tt is                    -- interface
   entry mem( input : in Integer, output : out Integer ); -- public mutex prototypes
   private
      -- implementation declarations, including more entry member prototypes
end Tt;
task body Tt is                    -- implementation
   -- local declarations for task body, including functions and procedures
   begin                          -- thread starts here
   -- task body (equivalent to constructor and task main in uC++)
      -- all entry member bodies defined within task body
end Tt;
```

The interface and the implementation are separate, with the interface listing the
mutex members, called entries, followed by private variables for the task. Mutex
members can be overloaded, as in C++, and private; private mutex members are used
for scheduling (see **requeue** discussion). This separation is the same as defining all
member bodies outside a class definition in C++, i.e., no inline definitions of routine
members. Unlike μC++, the bodies of the entry (mutex) members are specified
within the task body, which is discussed in the next section. As well, an entry
member can only return a value through an **out** parameter, i.e., members can only be
procedures not functions. The task body is where the new thread begins execution,
and it combines the constructor and the task main of μC++. This concatenation
is possible because there is no inheritance among task types, so separation of
construction from the task main or having an inner facility is not required (see
Sect. 13.2.2.1, p. 658).

Task types and objects can be declared in any Ada declaration context:

```
declare
      type ptype is access Tt;     -- must have named pointer type
      loc : Tt;                     -- local creation
      arr : array(1..10) of Tt;     -- local creation, array
      prt : ptype := new Tt;        -- dynamic creation
begin
      ...
end; -- wait for termination of loc, arr, prt
```

When a task is created, the appropriate declaration initializations are performed by
the creating thread. The stack component of the task's execution-state is created
and the starting point is initialized to the task body. Then a new thread of control
is created for the task, which begins execution at the task body. From this point,
the creating thread executes concurrently with the new task's thread; the task body
executes until its thread blocks or terminates.

A task terminates when its task body terminates. When a task terminates, so
does the task's thread of control and execution-state. As in μC++, storage for a
task cannot be deallocated while a thread is executing, which means a block cannot
terminate until all tasks declared in it terminate. Notice, in the above example, the
access (pointer) variable prt is terminated at the end of the block; this results from
Ada's accessibility rule, which states the duration of a dynamically allocated object
cannot outlive the scope of its access type. Therefore, the dynamically allocated task
referenced by prt cannot exceed the scope of the type ptype and the task object is
implicitly deleted, resulting in the block waiting for the task's termination.

```
with Ada.Numerics.Discrete_Random;
procedure bbmon is
  package Random_Integer is new
    Ada.Numerics.Discrete_Random(Integer);
  use Random_Integer;
  Gen : Generator;

  package IntBuf is -- generic buffer
    new BoundedBufferPkg(Integer, 20);
  use IntBuf;

  type BBptr is access all BoundedBuffer;

  task type producer( buf : BBptr ) is
  end producer;

  task body producer is -- implementation
    NoOfElems : constant Integer := 20;
    elem : Integer;
  begin
    for i in 1..NoOfElems loop
      -- no equivalent to yield
      elem := Random(Gen) mod 100 + 1;
      buf.insert( elem );
    end loop;
  end producer;

  task type consumer( buf : BBptr ) is
  end consumer;
```

```
  task body consumer is -- implementation
    elem : Integer;
  begin
    loop
      buf.remove( elem );
      exit when elem = -1;
      -- no equivalent to yield
    end loop;
  end consumer;

  NoOfCons : constant Integer := 3;
  NoOfProds : constant Integer := 4;
  buf : aliased BoundedBuffer;
begin
  declare
    type conPtr is access all consumer;
    cons : array(1..NoOfCons) of conPtr;
  begin
    declare
      type prodPtr is access all producer;
      prods : array(1..NoOfProds) of prodPtr;
    begin
      for i in 1..NoOfCons loop -- start
        cons(i) := new consumer(buf'access);
      end loop;
      for i in 1..NoOfProds loop -- start
        prods(i) := new producer(buf'access);
      end loop;
    end; -- wait for producers
    for i in 1..NoOfCons loop -- terminate
      buf.insert( -1 );
    end loop;
  end; -- wait for consumers
end bbmon;
```

Fig. 13.9 Ada 95: producer/consumer creation/termination

Unlike μC++, where a task turns into a monitor after its thread terminates, an Ada task does not turn into a protected object (Ada equivalent of a monitor, see Sect. 13.4.1.2). The reason has to do with the placement of a task's entry-members *within* the accept statement rather than having separate member routines, as in C++. Because the entry-members are inlined, it may be necessary to have multiple "overload" versions of the same entry member. In this case, a call to this entry member is ambiguous without an accept statement being executed by the task's thread to differentiate among multiple entry-member definitions.

Fig. 13.9 illustrates the Ada 95 equivalent for starting and terminating threads in a generic bounded-buffer example (see the right-hand side of Fig. 7.14, p. 353). The bounded buffer is presented on page 679. Notice, the interface for both producer and consumer specifies a parameter, called a discriminate, which is equivalent to a template parameter in C++. An argument must be specified when the type is used in the declaration of objects.

13.4.1.2   Thread Synchronization and Mutual Exclusion

Ada 95 provides two mechanisms for mutual exclusion: the protected object (monitor-like) and the task. Both constructs have mutex members, which execute mutually exclusively of one another, and both support synchronization via external scheduling, albeit with some restrictions. However, the mechanisms for external scheduling are different for protected objects and tasks. The default scheduling implementation for both protected objects and tasks has a queue for each entry member (mutex queues) but no single entry-queue to maintain overall temporal order of arrival. (Ada actually uses the term "entry queue" for a mutex queue, but this conflicts with prior terminology.) As a result, when there is a choice for selecting among entry members, an arbitrary selection is made rather than selecting the task waiting the longest. This semantics presents problems in implementing certain solutions to concurrent problems.

Protected Object

An Ada 95 protected type is like a class and has three kinds of member routines: function, procedure and entry:

```
protected type Pt is                    -- interface
    function(...) Op1 return ...;      -- public mutex member prototypes
    procedure(...) Op2;
    entry(...) Op3;
    private
    -- implementation declarations, including more function, procedure, entry members
end Pt;

protected body Pt is                    -- implementation
    function(...) Op1 return ... is begin function-body end Op1;
    procedure(...) Op2 is begin procedure-body end Op2;
    entry(...) when ... Op3 is begin entry-body end Op3;
end Pt;
```

Mutex members can be overloaded, as in C++, and private; private mutex members are used for scheduling (see **requeue** discussion).

Function members are read only with respect to the protected-object's data, while procedure and entry members are read/write. Function members have mutual exclusion with respect to procedures and entries but not with other functions, i.e., multiple function members can run simultaneously but not with a procedure or entry member. Hence, there is a simple built-in readers and writer facility. There is no direct equivalent to function members in μC++ as _Nomutex members have no mutual-exclusion property, and run simultaneously with mutex members; however, it is possible to explicitly code an equivalent facility, as is done with readers in the readers/writer problem. Conversely, there is no equivalent to _Nomutex members in Ada protected objects as all protected-object members acquire some kind of mutual exclusion. Function members have no external scheduling. Procedure members are like simple mutex members in μC++, providing read/write mutual exclusion but no external scheduling. Entry members are equivalent to mutex members in μC++, providing read/write mutual exclusion and a kind of external scheduling.

Operations allowed in a protected object's members are restricted by the requirement that no operation can block. The reason for this severe restriction is to allow non-queued locking mechanisms, e.g., spin lock versus semaphore, to be used to implement the mutual exclusion. Therefore, once a task has entered a protected object it must complete the member and leave without needing to block and be placed on a queue of waiting tasks. A task can make a call to another protected object and delay while attempting to acquire the spin lock for that object; in this case, the task does not have to queue, it can spin. Since a spin lock can only be acquired once, this restriction precludes a call to other members in a protected object, which is too restrictive. To allow some calls within a protected object, Ada differentiates between internal and external calls, e.g.:

```
declare
    protected type Pt is
        - - as above
    end Pt;
    PO : Pt;                        - - declarations
    Other_Object : Some_Other_Protected_Type;

    protected body Pt is            - - implementation
        ...
        procedure Op2 is begin
            Op1;                    - - internal call, like C++ this->Op1
            Op2;                    - - internal call, like C++ this->Op2
            Pt.Op1;                 - - internal call, like C++ this->Pt::Op1
            PO.Op1;                 - - external call, same object
            Other_Object.Some_Op; - - external call, different object
        end Op2;
        ...
    end Pt;
begin
    PO.Op2;                         - - external call
end
```

An internal call is any call to an object's member made through the equivalent of the object's this variable, and such calls do not acquire the protected-object's mutex lock. Otherwise a call is an external call, where there is a further distinction between calls to the same object or a different object.

Given these definitions, the following calls are allowed:

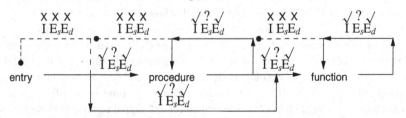

$\sqrt{}$ call allowed, X call disallowed, ? call implementation dependent

I internal call; E_s external call, same object; E_d external call, different object

From left to right, an **entry** member can make internal calls to a **function** or **procedure**, as this does not require the protected-object's mutex lock. An external call is allowed to a **function** or **procedure** in another protected object, but an external call to the same object is defined as an error; however, the implementation can allow the call, but such calls are not portable and should be avoided. An **entry** member cannot call an **entry** member because the call is conditional, which can result in blocking until the condition becomes true; however, blocking is disallowed. A **procedure** member can make internal calls to a **function** or **procedure**, as this does not require the protected-object's mutex lock. An external call is allowed to a **function** or **procedure** in another protected object, but an external call to the same object is defined as an error; however, the implementation can allow the call, but such calls are not portable and should be avoided. A **procedure** member cannot call an **entry** member because the call is conditional, which can result in blocking until the condition becomes true; however, blocking is disallowed. A **function** member can only make internal calls to a **function** because of the read-only property; calls to an **entry** or **procedure** could violate the read-only property because the entry or procedure can change the object. An external call is allowed to a **function** in another protected object, but an external call to the same object is defined as an error; however, the implementation can allow the call, but such calls are not portable and should be avoided. These complex rules, except for the read-only property of functions, could be eliminated by allowing recursive calls for any kind of member at the cost of a more expensive locking mechanism.

Protected-object external scheduling is accomplished using guards at the beginning of entry members, which is a form of restricted automatic-signal monitor (see Sect. 9.11.3.3, p. 480), as in:

    entry insert(elem : **in** ELEMTYPE) **when** count < Elements'length **is** . . .

where the **when** clause on the member definition must be true before a call is allowed to proceed. (The syntax 'length is called an attribute in Ada, where an attribute provides access to both compile time and runtime information, accessing the length of the array.) Notice, this syntax and semantics is almost identical to the conditional critical-region in Sect. 9.2, p. 428. This form of automatic-signalling is external scheduling because a task does not enter the protected object first, possibly reading or changing it, before blocking on the conditional expression. It is restricted because only global protected-object variables can appear in the conditional expression, parameter or local member variables are disallowed. Only entry members can have a **when** clause; functions and procedures cannot. Also, creating an efficient implementation for the conditional expression can be challenging. Since only global protected-object variables are allowed in a conditional expression, the time it takes to find the next task to execute is determined by the cost of re-evaluating the conditional expressions. It is unnecessary to wake up some or all of the tasks to access their local variables, as for general automatic-signal monitors. However, the cost is usually greater than using cooperation with accept statements. Finally, this form of external scheduling suffers the same restrictions as external scheduling in μC++ (see Sect. 9.5.2, p. 449): entry selection cannot depend on local mutex-member values (including parameter values), and once selected, a task cannot block in the mutex-member body using this mechanism. Therefore, some form of internal scheduling is necessary.

While there is no internal scheduling for protected objects, Ada provides a mechanism to simulate it using external scheduling. Rather than using condition variables with signal/wait, a **requeue** statement is provided but it can only be used in an **entry** member. The **requeue** statement terminates the current execution of the entry member and requeues the original call to an equivalent entry member in the current protected object, or another protected object or task so it can be re-accepted at some later time, as in:

```
requeue mem; -- internal requeue to "mem" of current protected object
requeue m.mem; -- external requeue to "mem" of different protected object
```

The requeue is not a call, but a redirection of a call, so it does not specify any arguments, just the new location for the original call to restart. The specified entry member must have the same prototype as the original or have no parameters. The requeued call is then handled as a new entry-member call by the protected object and is subsequently selected by the entry-member guards. The semantics of external requeue to the same object are implementation dependent, and should be avoided.

Unfortunately, Ada requeue suffers the same problems discussed in Sect. 9.5.2.2, p. 453. An entry member working on a request may accumulate complex execution and data state. Unfortunately, the execution location and temporary results cannot be bundled and forwarded to the new entry member handling the next step of the processing because the signature of the new entry member must be the same or empty; hence, there is no way to pass new information. Therefore, the accumulated information must be stored in global protected-object variables for access by the new entry member. Alternatively, the temporary results can be re-computed at the start of the requeued entry member, if possible. In contrast, waiting on a condition variable automatically saves the execution location and any partially computed state.

Fig. 13.10 illustrates the Ada 95 equivalent for the external-scheduling bounded-buffer monitor in Fig. 9.4, p. 439. Unfortunately, the query member has unnecessary mutual exclusion with entry members insert and remove, which inhibits concurrency. Notice the **when** clauses controlling entry into insert and remove. Both conditional expressions only reference global protected-object variables, i.e., count and the array size.

Ada's lack of real internal scheduling via condition locks presents difficulties for certain kinds of problems. For example, the dating service presented in Sect. 9.5.2.1, p. 450 is a problem in Ada because the different compatibility codes require different places to block when waiting for a corresponding partner. Two approaches are presented in Sect. 9.5.2.1, p. 450: arrays of conditions, when the compatibility codes are small and dense, and lists of conditions, when the codes are large and sparse. Ada can handle the former case by using arrays of entry members, called entry families, but the latter case is more difficult as it requires the equivalent of a dynamically allocated condition variable. The array of entry members acts like the array of condition variables, providing a place to requeue and wait for a compatible

```
generic
    type ELEMTYPE is private;              -- template parameters
    Size: in Natural;
package BoundedBufferPkg is
    type BufType is array(0..Size-1) of ELEMTYPE;

    protected type BoundedBuffer is        -- interface
        function query return Integer;
        entry insert( elem : in ELEMTYPE );
        entry remove( elem : out ELEMTYPE );
    private
        front, back, count : Integer := 0;
        Elements : BufType;                -- bounded buffer
    end BoundedBuffer;
end BoundedBufferPkg;

package body BoundedBufferPkg is
    protected body BoundedBuffer is        -- implementation
        function query return Integer is
        begin
            return count;
        end query;

        entry insert( elem : in ELEMTYPE ) when count < Elements'length is
        begin
            Elements(back) := elem;        -- insert into buffer
            back := ( back + 1 ) mod Elements'length;
            count := count + 1;
        end insert;

        entry remove( elem : out ELEMTYPE ) when count > 0 is
        begin
            elem := Elements(front);       -- remove from buffer
            front := ( front + 1 ) mod Elements'length;
            count := count - 1;
        end remove;
    end BoundedBuffer;
end BoundedBufferPkg;
```

Fig. 13.10 Ada 95: protected-object bounded buffer, external scheduling

partner. However, arrays of entry members introduce significant new syntax and semantics into the language, and still cannot handle large, sparse codes.

Fig. 13.11 shows the use of entry families to provide a dating service with small, dense compatibility codes. The two public entry members, Girl and Boy, have three parameters because entry routines cannot return values, so the phone number of a task's partner is returned through the **out** parameter partner. The private entry members are two entry arrays, Girls and Boys, on which tasks wait if there is no available partner with a corresponding compatibility code, plus an additional entry member, Exchange, on which tasks must wait to complete an exchange of phone numbers. The entry Exchange is used in the same way as the condition Exchange in the μC++ monitor solutions.

```
generic
  type ccset is range<>; -- template parameter
package DatingServicePkg is
  type TriggerType is array(ccset) of Boolean;

  protected type DatingService is -- interface
    entry Girl( Partner : out Integer; PhNo : in Integer; ccode : in ccset );
    entry Boy( Partner : out Integer; PhNo : in Integer; ccode : in ccset );
  private
    entry Girls(ccset)( Partner : out Integer; PhNo : in Integer; ccode : in ccset );
    entry Boys(ccset)( Partner : out Integer; PhNo : in Integer; ccode : in ccset );
    entry Exchange( Partner : out Integer; PhNo : in Integer; ccode : in ccset );

    ExPhNo, GPhNo, BPhNo : Integer;
    GTrig, BTrig : TriggerType := (ccset => false); -- initialize array to false
    ExTrig : Boolean := false;
  end DatingService;
end DatingServicePkg;

package body DatingServicePkg is
  protected body DatingService is -- implementation
```

```
entry Girl( Partner : out Integer;        entry Girls(for code in ccset)( Partner:out Integer;
  PhNo : in Integer; ccode : in ccset )     PhNo : in Integer; ccode : in ccset )
  when exchange'count = 0 is                 when GTrig(code) is
begin                                      begin
  if Boys(ccode)'count = 0 then              GTrig(code) := false;
    requeue Girls(ccode); -- no return       ExPhNo := PhNo;
  else                                       Partner := BPhNo;
    GPhNo := PhNo;                           ExTrig := true;
    BTrig(ccode) := true;                  end Girls;
    requeue exchange;  -- no return
  end if;                                  entry Boys(for code in ccset)( Partner:out Integer;
end Girl;                                    PhNo : in Integer; ccode : in ccset )
                                             when BTrig(code) is
entry Boy( Partner : out Integer;          begin
  PhNo : in Integer; ccode : in ccset )      BTrig(code) := false;
  when exchange'count = 0 is                 ExPhNo := PhNo;
begin                                        Partner := GPhNo;
  if Girls(ccode)'count = 0 then             ExTrig := true;
    requeue Boys(ccode); -- no return      end Boys;
  else
    BPhNo := PhNo;                         entry exchange( Partner : out Integer;
    GTrig(ccode) := true;                    PhNo : in Integer; ccode : in ccset )
    requeue exchange;  -- no return          when ExTrig is
  end if;                                  begin
end Boy;                                     ExTrig := false;
                                             Partner := ExPhNo;
                                           end Exchange;
```

```
  end DatingService;
end DatingServicePkg;
```

Fig. 13.11 Ada 95: scheduling using parameter information, solution 1

The two public entry members, Girl and Boy, both have a guard that accepts calls at any time, except when an exchange of phone numbers is occurring within the protected object. The expression exchange'count returns the number of tasks blocked on the mutex queue for member exchange, which is like using empty on a condition queue in μC++ to know if any tasks are blocked on it. The private entry members are all controlled using flag variables, called triggers, to indicate when it is possible to continue execution. The triggers for the entry family members are the arrays GTrig and BTrig, plus the variable ExTrig. Triggers are often used instead of boolean expressions when the boolean expressions become complex and must be reevaluated ever time the protected object becomes inactive.

Both entry members, Girl and Boy, start by checking for a corresponding partner, which is accomplished by checking the number of tasks waiting on the mutex queue for the corresponding entry family, e.g., Boys(ccode)'count. If there is no available partner, a task requeues itself onto the appropriate entry family with the same compatibility code. The current entry member is now terminated and the original call is requeued on the mutex queue for the specified entry family. If there is an available partner, the caller's phone number is copied into the corresponding member variable, GPhNo or BPhNo, respectively, the trigger for the partner entry-family member is set to true, and the task requeues itself on the entry exchange to wait for the partner to wake up and place its phone number in the global variable, ExPhNo. Once a task requeues on exchange, new tasks cannot enter the dating-service object until the exchange is complete.

When the partner is unblocked because its trigger is true, it immediately resets the appropriate trigger, GTrig(ccode) or BTrig(ccode), copies its phone number into the member variable ExPhNo, returns its partner's phone number by assigning from the corresponding global variable, GPhNo or BPhNo, to the output parameter Partner, and finally sets the trigger for the partner blocked on entry-member exchange to true. The entry call returns, completing the original call to the dating service.

When the partner waiting on exchange is unblocked, it immediately resets trigger ExTrig, returns its partner's phone number by assigning from the member variable ExPhNo to the output parameter Partner, and the entry call returns, which completes the original call to the dating service.

Having to use large numbers of trigger flags is the main drawback to this style of controlling tasks with an Ada protected-object. As pointed out in Chap. 2, p. 9, flag variables should be avoided wherever possible, and replaced by explicit control flow. In many cases, Ada protected-objects require the opposite scenario, resulting in a correspondingly poor programming style. Finally, the technique of entry families, i.e., arrays of entry members, does not scale to large, sparse codes.

To handle large, sparse codes requires a different data structure, e.g., linked list, which in turn requires the ability to dynamically create some form of condition variable. Fig. 13.12 shows it is possible to mimic dynamically allocated condition variables in Ada by creating a linked list of Ada protected-objects, and using each one as a condition variable. The protected-object condition has two members, Wait

```
generic
    type ccset is range<>;    -- template parameter
package DatingServicePkg is
    protected type DatingService is    -- interface
        entry Girl( Partner : out Integer; PhNo : in Integer; ccode : in ccset );
        entry Boy( Partner : out Integer; PhNo : in Integer; ccode : in ccset );
    private
    end DatingService;
end DatingServicePkg;


package body DatingServicePkg is

    protected type condition is -- interface          protected body DatingService is -- impl
        entry Wait( Partner : out Integer;                entry Girl( Partner : out Integer;
            PhNo : in Integer; ccode : in ccset );            PhNo : in Integer; ccode : in ccset )
        procedure Signal( PhNop : in Integer );          when true is
    private                                                  N : Elmtp;
        waitTrig : Boolean := false;                     begin
        PhNoEx : Integer;                                    SearchRm( N, boys, ccode );
    end condition;                                           if N = null then -- no partner
                                                                 N := new Node;
    protected body condition is -- impl                          N.ccode := ccode; N.PhNo := PhNo;
        entry Wait( Partner : out Integer;                       girls := Append( girls, N );
            PhNo : in Integer; ccode : in ccset )                requeue N.cond.Wait; -- no return
        when waitTrig is                                     else -- partner
        begin                                                    Partner := N.PhNo;
            Partner := PhNoEx;                                   N.cond.Signal( PhNo );
            waitTrig := false;                               end if;
        end Wait;                                        end Girl;

        procedure Signal( PhNop : in Integer ) is        entry Boy( Partner : out Integer;
        begin                                                PhNo : in Integer; ccode : in ccset )
            WaitTrig := true;                            when true is
            PhNoEx := PhNop;                                 N : Elmtp;
        end Signal;                                      begin
    end condition;                                           SearchRm( N, girls, ccode );
                                                             if N = null then -- no partner
    type Node is record                                          N := new Node;
        ccode : ccset;                                           N.ccode := ccode; N.PhNo := PhNo;
        PhNo : Integer;                                          boys := Append( boys, N );
        cond : condition;                                        requeue N.cond.Wait; -- no return
    end record;                                              else -- partner
                                                                 Partner := N.PhNo;
    package NodeList is new Gen_List( Node );                    N.cond.Signal( PhNo );
    use NodeList;                                            end if;
                                                         end Boy;
    girls, boys : List;                              end DatingService;

end DatingServicePkg;
```

Fig. 13.12 Ada 95: scheduling using parameter information, solution 2

and Signal, used to block and unblock a waiting task, respectively. Because the waitTrig is initialized to false, a call to Wait blocks. The Signal routine resets waitTrig so a call to Wait can now proceed. As well, Signal is used to transfer information from the signalling task into the waiting task for the condition variable, so when a task enters Wait, there is data for it to return to the original call. In this case, the data transferred from signaller to waiting task is the phone number of the signaller. The dating-service protected-object creates two linked lists: one for waiting girl and boy tasks. Each node of the lists contains the compatibility code and phone number of the waiting task, along with the condition variable on which it waits. Tasks call the appropriate entry members of DatingService, which always have true guards. A task then searches the oppose gender list for a compatible partner. If a partner is not found, a node is created, initialized, and linked to the end of the appropriate list. Then the task blocks by requeueing on the Wait member for the condition variable in the node; there is only one task blocked on this condition variable. If a partner is found, the search removes the partner from the list and sets N to point to this partner's node. The partner's phone number is now copied from the node to return to the original call, and the Signal routine is called for the partner's condition variable, passing it the phone number of its partner. When a waiting task unblocks, it copies this phone number back to its original call. Notice, the control logic is simpler in this solution than the previous solution because of the cooperation used.

Task

As described in Sect. 13.4.1.1, p. 673, an Ada 95 task may have both public and private entry-member routines that are equivalent to mutex members in μC++, providing mutual exclusion.

Task external scheduling is accomplished using an accept statement, as in:

```
select
   when expression =>       -- guard
      accept mem(...) do    -- entry member definition
         ...                -- entry member body
      end mem
      ...                   -- executed after accepted call
   or when ...
      ...
   or                       -- optional
      terminate             -- accept destructor
   end select
```

which is very similar to that in μC++. In fact, μC++ adapted the accept statement from Ada for its external scheduling. The main difference is the placement of the entry member body. Instead of having true member routines, entry members are nested within the accept statement, making the accept clause have parameters and a routine body; hence, the static scope of the entry body is different than in μC++. The Ada approach allows different routine bodies for the same entry name in different accept statements. The main problem with placing the entry in the accept statement is that it precludes virtual routine redefinition, which is not an issue in Ada as task types cannot inherit. A further Ada restriction is that the accept statement can only appear in the task body, not any of its local subprograms, which can force an awkward coding style in certain situations. This restriction ensures a nested task cannot call a local subprogram of an enclosing task that subsequently accepts an entry routine of the enclosing task; a task can only accept its own entry routines to ensure correct locking for mutual exclusion. As well, an entry member cannot accept itself because of ambiguity in the resolution of formal parameter names. Finally, the optional terminate clause at the end of the accept statement is chosen when the block containing a local task declaration ends or the block containing the task's access-type ends for dynamic task declaration. The termination clause is like accepting the destructor in μC++.

Like Ada protected-objects, internal scheduling for tasks is accomplished by converting it into external scheduling using the **requeue** statement. The **requeue** statement terminates the current execution of the entry member and requeues the original call to a type-equivalent entry-member in the current task, or another protected object or task so it can be re-accepted at some later time. However, the use of requeue for tasks suffers the same problems as for protected objects with respect to loss of any accumulated execution and data.

Fig. 13.13 illustrates the Ada 95 equivalent for the external-scheduling bounded-buffer task in Fig. 10.6, p. 533. Unfortunately, the query member has unnecessary mutual exclusion with entry members insert and remove, which inhibits concurrency. Like μC++, the **when** clauses control the accepts of insert and remove when the buffer is full or empty, respectively, and the buffer management code has been moved outside of the entry body to maximize concurrency. As well, the loop around the **select** statement is stopped by accepting **terminate**, which immediately terminates the task. Immediate termination prevents a task from cleaning up directly, but garbage collection and controlled types can provide indirect clean up.

The next example is the readers and writer problem. Fig. 13.14, p. 687 shows the first solution to the readers/writer problem in Ada. This solution relies on the built-in semantics provided by Ada protected-objects, i.e., multiple read-only functions can execute simultaneously with mutual exclusion from procedure and entry members, while procedures execute with mutual exclusion with respect to all protected-object members. With this built-in semantics, it is only necessary to make the Read member a function and the Write member a procedure to construct a solution. Notice, the Read routine returns a dummy result because all Ada functions must return a value.

Unfortunately, this trivial solution may suffer starvation and does suffer from staleness. The reason is that the default selection policy chooses arbitrarily *among* mutex queues when multiple queues are eligible. (Other selection policies are available for real-time programming in Ada.) This semantics applies for protected objects with multiple true guards or accept statements with multiple acceptable **accept** clauses. As a result, it is conceivable for starvation to occur if readers and writers are always queued on both entry members and the implementation always chooses one over the other. However, a reasonable implementation for servicing the mutex queues should provide some level of fairness. Nevertheless, the arbitrary selection among queues does result in staleness because temporal order is no longer maintained among the tasks waiting on the different mutex queues. μC++ deals with this problem by having a single FIFO entry queue, instead of multiple FIFO mutex-queues as in Ada.

```
generic
      type ELEMTYPE is private;                        -- template parameters
      Size: in Natural;
package BoundedBufferPkg is
      type BufType is array(0. .Size-1) of ELEMTYPE;

      task type BoundedBuffer is                       -- interface
            entry query( cnt : out Integer );
            entry insert( elem : in ELEMTYPE );
            entry remove( elem : out ELEMTYPE );
      end BoundedBuffer;
end BoundedBufferPkg;

package body BoundedBufferPkg is
      task body BoundedBuffer is                       -- implementation
            front, back, count : Integer := 0;
            Elements : BufType;                        -- bounded buffer
      begin
            loop
                  select
                        accept query( cnt : out Integer ) do
                              cnt := count;
                        end;
                  or when count < Elements'length =>   -- guard
                        accept insert( elem : in ELEMTYPE ) do
                              Elements(back) := elem;     -- insert into buffer
                        end insert;
                        back := ( back + 1 ) mod Elements'length;
                        count := count + 1;
                  or when count > 0 =>                 -- guard
                        accept remove( elem : out ELEMTYPE ) do
                              elem := Elements(front);   -- remove from buffer
                        end;
                        front := ( front + 1 ) mod Elements'length;
                        count := count - 1;
                  or
                        terminate;                      -- task stops here
                  end select;
            end loop;
      end BoundedBuffer;
end BoundedBufferPkg;
```

Fig. 13.13 Ada 95: task bounded buffer, external scheduling

Staleness can only be reduced for the Ada default-selection policy due to the arbitrary selection among mutex queues. One way to reduce staleness is by converting from an external-scheduling style to an internal-scheduling style. Hence, tasks are removed from the public-entry mutex-queues as quickly as possible, and requeued onto a single private-entry mutex-queue, which is FIFO. A consequence of this conversion is that public entries always have open (true) guards to allow immediate entry for subsequent FIFO requeueing, if necessary. However, the arbitrary selection among all acceptable entry members, public and private, means external tasks can barge into the protected object at any time, so the protected object has to be treated as a no-priority monitor. Notice, there is still a small window where multiple tasks can queue on public entry members while the protected-object is

```
protected type ReadersWriter is    -- interface
    function Read(...) return Integer;
    procedure Write(...);
private
    Rcnt : Integer := 0;
end ReadersWriter;


protected body ReadersWriter is    -- implementation
    function Read(...) return Integer is
    begin
        -- read
        return ...;
    end Read;


    procedure Write(...) is
    begin
        -- write
    end Write;
end ReadersWriter;
```

Fig. 13.14 Ada 95: readers/writer, solution 1

active, e.g., if the task in the protected object is time-sliced, and the subsequent arbitrary selection results in staleness due to non-FIFO selection among mutex queues.

Fig. 13.15 shows a solution to the readers/writer problem, which reduces staleness by converting from an external-scheduling to an internal-scheduling style. The solution is based on the Pthreads' solution in Fig. 13.7, p. 656, which is problematic because once a task requeues on rwcond it is impossible to tell if it is a reader or writer task, and there is the barging issue because of arbitrary selection among acceptable entry-members. A task's kind, i.e., reader or writer, is handled by maintaining an explicit queue of these values, which is added to and removed from when a task blocks and unblocks, respectively. The barging issue is handled by checking on entry to StartRead and StartWrite for any blocked tasks waiting to enter rwcond; these blocked tasks have already been waiting, and therefore, have priority over any arriving task. Interestingly, because both reader and writer tasks requeue on the same entry, rwcond, the number and type of parameters of all three members must be identical, which may not always be possible. If the parameter lists are different for the readers and writers, a more complex approach must be used, creating a single list of two kinds of protected-objects using the approach shown in the dating-service solution in Fig. 13.12, p. 683. Again, notice the use of a trigger, rwTrig, to restart waiting tasks from the FIFO mutex queue for rwcond. This trigger is toggled true or false by a restarting task depending on the kind (reader or writer) of the next waiting task on the rwcond mutex queue. Finally, the interface has four members, which must be called in pairs by the user, instead of two members, as in the first solution. In this approach, it is impossible to create the same interface as the first solution with a protected object because all protected-object members acquire some form of mutual exclusion. To achieve the interface of the first solution requires embedding this protected-object within another object that has the correct interface

```
type RWkind is ( READER, WRITER );
package rwlist is new Gen_List( RWkind );
use rwlist;

protected type ReadersWriter is
    entry StartRead(...);
    entry EndRead;
    entry StartWrite(...);
    entry EndWrite;
  private
    entry rwcond(...);

    rw : List := Nil;
    rcnt, wcnt : Integer := 0;
    rwTrig : Boolean := false;
end ReadersWriter;

protected body ReadersWriter is
    entry StartRead(...) when true is
    begin
        if wcnt > 0 or else
            rwcond'count > 0 then
            rw := Append( rw, READER );
            requeue rwcond; -- no return
        end if;
        rcnt := rcnt + 1;
    end StartRead;

    entry EndRead when true is
    begin
        rcnt := rcnt - 1;
        if rcnt = 0 and then
            rwcond'count > 0 then
            rwTrig := true;
        end if;
    end EndRead;
```

```
    entry StartWrite(...) when true is
    begin
        if rcnt > 0 or else wcnt > 0 or
            else rwcond'count > 0 then
            rw := Append( rw, WRITER );
            requeue rwcond; -- no return
        end if;
        wcnt := 1;
    end StartWrite;

    entry EndWrite when true is
    begin
        wcnt := 0;
        if rwcond'count > 0 then
            rwTrig := true;
        end if;
    end EndWrite;

    entry rwcond(...) when rwTrig is
        kind : RWkind;
    begin
        rwTrig := false;
        kind := Element( rw );
        rw := Remove( rw );
        if kind = READER then
            if rwcond'count > 0 and then
                Element( rw ) = READER then
                rwTrig := true;
            end if;
            rcnt := rcnt + 1;
        else
            wcnt := 1;
        end if;
    end rwcond;
end ReadersWriter;
```

Fig. 13.15 Ada 95: readers/writer, solution 2

but no mutual exclusion on the calls; this wrapper object then makes the four calls to the protected object. This structure is accomplished in μC++ by combining no-mutex and mutex members.

Fig. 13.16 shows two approaches for a third solution to the readers/writer problem; the left approach uses a protected-object and the right a task. The solution is based on the right solution in Fig. 9.18, p. 469, which uses external scheduling. For the protected-object solution, the two end members, EndRead and EndWrite, both have true guards as all the control is done in the two start members, i.e., once access to the resource is granted, a task can always end without additional blocking. The guards for StartRead and StartWrite preclude calls if a writer is using the resource or there is a writer delayed because readers are using the resource. After entering StartWrite, a writer delays if readers are using the resource, and requeues its call to wcond. No new readers or writers can start because wcond'count is now 1 so there is no starvation. When the last reader of the current group finishes, it checks for

Protected Object	Task

```
protected type ReadersWriter is
   entry StartRead(...);
   entry EndRead;
   entry StartWrite(...);
   entry EndWrite;
private
   entry wcond(...);
   rcnt, wcnt : Integer := 0;
   wTrig : Boolean := false;
end ReadersWriter;


protected body ReadersWriter is
   entry StartRead(...)
   when wcnt = 0 and then wcond'count = 0 is
   begin
      rcnt := rcnt + 1;
   end StartRead;


   entry EndRead when true is
   begin
      rcnt := rcnt - 1;
      if rcnt = 0 then
         if wcond'count > 0 then
            wTrig := true;
         end if;
      end if;
   end EndRead;


   entry StartWrite(...)
   when wcnt = 0 and then wcond'count = 0 is
   begin
      if rcnt > 0 then
         requeue wcond;
      end if;

      wcnt := 1;
   end StartWrite;


   entry EndWrite when true is
   begin
      wcnt := 0;
   end EndWrite;


   entry wcond(...) when wTrig is
   begin
      wTrig := false;
      wcnt := 1;
   end wcond;
end ReadersWriter;
```

```
task type ReadersWriter is
   entry StartRead(...);
   entry EndRead;
   entry StartWrite(...);
   entry EndWrite;
end ReadersWriter;


task body ReadersWriter is
   rcnt, wcnt : Integer := 0;
begin
   loop
      select
         when wcnt = 0 =>
            accept StartRead(...) do
               rcnt := rcnt + 1;
            end StartRead;
      or
         accept EndRead do

            rcnt := rcnt - 1;
         end EndRead;









      or
         when wcnt = 0 =>
            accept StartWrite(...) do
               while rcnt > 0 loop
                  accept EndRead do
                     rcnt := rcnt - 1;
                  end EndRead;
               end loop;
               wcnt := 1;
            end StartWrite;
      or
         accept EndWrite do

            wcnt := 0;
         end EndWrite;
      or
         terminate;
      end select;
   end loop;


end ReadersWriter;
```

Fig. 13.16   Ada 95: readers/writer, solution 3 (a & b)

a delayed writer and unblocks it by setting wTrig. The unblocked writer resets wTrig
but sets wcnt to 1, so no new readers and writers can enter. When a writer finishes
and sets wcnt to 0, Ada now makes an arbitrary choice between tasks waiting on the
StartRead and StartWrite mutex queues, which maximizes the potential for staleness.

For the task solution, accept statements can be used. However, switching to a
task is inefficient because the task's thread is superfluous; the task's thread mostly
loops in the task body accepting calls to the four entry members. Like the protected-
object solution, the two end members, EndRead and EndWrite, both are accepted
unconditionally as all the control is done in the two start members. The guards
for StartRead and StartWrite preclude calls if a writer is using the resource. After
entering StartWrite, a writer checks for readers, and if present, accepts only calls
to EndRead until that group of readers has finished using the resource. No new
readers or writers can start while the writer is accepting EndRead as it always restarts
after a call is accepted. Notice, the duplicated code in the nested accept because
each accept clause defines a new entry (mutex) body. While the duplicated code
can be factored into a subprogram, the Ada style appears to require more of this
restructuring than the μC++ style. When a writer finishes and sets wcnt to 0, Ada
now makes an arbitrary choice between tasks waiting on the StartRead and StartWrite
mutex queues, which maximizes the potential for staleness.

The readers/writer illustrates the need for basic FIFO service for calls to monitor/
task mutex-members so that a programmer can then chose how calls are serviced.
When the language/system makes arbitrary choices on behalf of a programmer, the
programmer can never regain sufficient control for certain purposes. The only way
to eliminate staleness in Ada is to have the readers and writers call the same entry
member as these calls are serviced in FIFO order. As has been noted, changing the
interface is not always an option; the interface may be given to the programmer via
the specifications.

13.4.2   SR/Concurrent C++

Both SR [2] and Concurrent C++ [17] have tasks with external scheduling using
an accept statement. However, neither language has condition variables or a
requeue statement, so there is no internal scheduling or way to simulate it using
external scheduling. In fact, Ada 83 did not have the **requeue** statement, but it
was subsequently added in Ada'95. Only one feature of these two languages is
discussed: extensions to the accept statement to try to ameliorate the need for
requeue.

The first extension is to the **when** clause to allow referencing the caller's
arguments through the parameters of the called mutex member, as in:

```
select
    accept mem( code : in Integer )
        when code % 2 = 0 do ...              - - accept call with even code
or
    accept mem( code : in Integer )
        when code % 2 = 1 do ...              - - accept call with odd code
end select;
```

Notice the placement of the **when** clause *after* the **accept** clause so the parameter names are defined. When a **when** clause references a parameter, selecting an **accept** clause now involves an implicit search of all waiting tasks on the mutex queue. This search may be large if there are many waiting tasks, and the mutex queue must be locked during the search to prevent a race condition between an appropriate task blocking on the mutex queue and the search missing it. While the mutex queue is locked, calling tasks must busy wait to acquire the lock as there is nowhere else to block. Furthermore, if no waiting task immediately satisfies the **when** clauses, the acceptor blocks, and each arriving call to an open member must either evaluate the **when** expression, or more likely, restart the acceptor task so it can because the expression could contain local variables of the task body. Both SR and Concurrent C select the task waiting the longest if there are multiple waiting tasks satisfying the **when** clause. This semantics is easily implemented if the mutex queue is maintained in FIFO order by arrival, as the first task with a true **when** expression is also the one waiting the longest.

The second extension is the addition of a selection clause to more precisely select when there are multiply true **when** expressions among waiting tasks rather than using order of arrival, as in:

```
select
    accept mem( code : in Integer )
        when code % 2 = 0 by -code do ...     - - accept call with largest even code
or
    accept mem( code : in Integer )
        when code % 2 = 1 by code do ...      - - accept call with smallest odd code
end select;
```

The by clause is calculated for each true **when** clause and the minimum by clause is selected. In essence, the **when** clause selects only those tasks that can legitimately enter at this time (cooperation) and the by clause sub-selects among these legitimate tasks. If there are multiple by expressions with the same minimum value, the task waiting the longest is selected. If the by clause appears without a **when** clause, it is applied to all waiting tasks on the mutex queue, as if **when** true was specified. Notice, the by clause exacerbates the execution cost of executing an accept clause because now *all* waiting tasks on the mutex queue must be examined to locate appropriate ones the minimal by expression.

In all cases, once an accept clause is selected and begins execution it must execute to completion without blocking again with respect to the called resource. Calling other resources may result in blocking, but the called resource has no mechanism (internal scheduling or requeue) to perform further blocking with respect to itself. Therefore, all cooperation must occur when selecting tasks from the mutex queues.

While these two extensions go some distance towards removing internal scheduling and/or requeue, constructing expressions for **when** and by clauses can be complex and there are still valid situations neither can deal with. For example, if the selection criteria involves multiple parameters, as in:

```
accept mem( code1, code2 : in Integer ) ...
```

and the selection algorithm requires multiple passes over the data, such as select the lowest even value of code1 and the highest odd value of code2 if there are multiple lowest even values. Another example is if the selection criteria involves information from other mutex queues such as the dating service where a calling girl task must search the mutex queue of the boy tasks to find a matching compatibility code. While it is conceivable for the language to provide special constructs to access and search all the mutex queues, it is often simpler to unconditionally accept a request, perform an arbitrarily complex examination of what to do next based on the information in the request, and either service or postpone depending on the selection criteria. This avoids complex selection expressions and possibly their repeated evaluation. In addition, it allows all the normal programming language constructs and data structures to be used in making the decision to postpone a request, instead of some fixed selection mechanism provided in the programming language, as in SR and Concurrent C++.

13.4.3 Java

Java is an object-oriented language using a combination of library and language features to provide concurrency. The library features create threads and provide synchronization, and the language features provide mutual exclusion. Unfortunately, library features render any concurrent system unsound. Java deals with this issue by adopting a memory model and giving certain member routines special properties, which is equivalent to making these routines into language constructs.

13.4.3.1 Thread Creation and Termination

Java uses the inheritance approach for associating the thread abstraction with a user defined task type (see Sect. 13.2.2.1, p. 657). The abstraction for the superclass Thread is given in Fig. 13.17. Only those member routines necessary to explain the basic concurrent facilities are presented. This special base class serves the same purpose as the special type uBaseTask in μC++, from which all μC++ tasks implicitly inherit.

As noted, the thread type Thread is like uBaseTask in μC++, and provides any necessary variables and members needed by user subtypes of it, especially the run member, which is the same as the task main in μC++, e.g.:

```
class Thread implements Runnable {
    public Thread();                              // default thread name
    public Thread( String name );                 // set thread name

    public final void setName( String name )      // change thread name
    public final String getName()                 // get thread name
    public static Thread currentThread();          // executing thread
    public static void yield();                   // yield time slice and schedule

    public void run();                            // thread starts here
    public void start();                          // explicitly start thread
    public final void join()                      // termination synchronization
        throws InterruptedException;
}
```

Fig. 13.17 Java thread abstract class

```
class myTask : Thread {          // inheritance
    private int arg;              // communication variables
    private int result;
    public mytask() {...}         // task constructors
    public int result() {...}     // return result after termination synchronization
    // unusual to have more members because no external scheduling
    public void run() {...}       // task body
}
```

Returning a result on thread termination is accomplished by a member that computes a value from the task's communication variables. It is possible to have other members, which means it is possible, in theory, to construct a μC++-like task. However, in practice, there is no external scheduling mechanism so managing direct calls to these member, i.e., direct-communication/rendezvous, is difficult because it necessitates manually constructing some form of accept statement.

The declaration of a thread in Java creates a pointer to a thread object. (All objects in Java are references.) Java defines assignment and equally operations for these pointer values. For example, the following shows Java task creation and termination synchronization:

```
mytask th = new myTask(...);    // create task/thread object and initialized it
th.start();                     // start thread running in "run"
th.join();                      // wait for thread termination
a2 = th.result();               // retrieve answer from task object
```

Like μC++, when the task's thread terminates, it becomes an object, which continues to exist after the termination synchronization, hence allowing the call to member result to retrieve a result in a statically type-safe way.

Java requires explicit starting of a thread after the task's declaration, which is a coding convention that is potential source of error. The problem is that not starting a thread does not necessarily produce an error; a program can continue to use the task as an object, generating correct or incorrect results but having no concurrency. It is possible to mimic starting the thread on declaration by inserting a call to start as the *last* operation of the constructor. It is crucial to strictly follow this convention, because once the thread is started, it is conceivably running in the task at the same time as the thread executing the constructor. Therefore, there is a mutual exclusion issue with respect to completion of object initialization in the constructor and accessing the object in the run member. Unfortunately, as mentioned previously, this technique does not generalize to cover inheritance (see Sect. 13.2.2.1, p. 658) because both the base and derived class constructors start the task's thread. Therefore, explicitly starting a task's thread is not as powerful as implicitly starting the thread after declaration is completed.

However, there are cases where a programmer may not want a task to start immediately after declaration. Can this case be handled by schemes that implicitly start a task's thread after declaration? In μC++, it is trivial to mimic this capability by creating a mutex member start and accepting it at the beginning of the task main:

```
_Task T {
    void main() {
        _Accept( start );          // wait for initial call
        ...
    }
public:
    void start() {}                // no code necessary in member body
    ...
};
```

The same behaviour can be created with internal scheduling by having the task's thread block on a condition variable the start member signals. Thus, there is a weak equivalence between the two approaches as only one can mimic the other trivially.

As mentioned, Java uses a combination of library and language features to provide concurrency. The following situations present problems for the library features with respect to soundness:

```
t.init();                          // modify task object
t.start();                         // start thread
t.join();                          // termination synchronization
i = t.result();                    // obtain result
```

A compiler could interchange either the first two lines or the last two lines, because start or join may not access any variables accessed by init or result. Similar problems can occur with global variables accessed before or after start/join, as these global accesses can be moved a substantial distance with respect to the calls to start/join. Java defines both Thread.start and Thread.join as special routines so the compiler only performs appropriate optimizations.

Fig. 13.18 illustrates Java equivalent for starting and terminating threads in a bounded buffer example (see the right hand side of Fig. 7.14, p. 353). The bounded buffer is presented on page 696.

13.4.3.2   Thread Synchronization and Mutual Exclusion

Java provides an implicit mutex lock and condition variable in each object, through which all synchronization and mutual exclusion are constructed. The hidden Java mutex lock is multiple acquisition, which can be recursively acquired by the thread currently locking it. The following language constructs ensure the thread that locks

```
class Producer extends Thread {
    private BoundedBuffer buf;
    public Producer( BoundedBuffer buf ) {
        this.buf = buf;
    }
    public void run() {
        int NoOfElems = 40;
        for ( int i = 1; i <= NoOfElems; i += 1 ) {
            int elem = (int)(Math.random() * 100);
            System.out.println( "Producer:" +
                this + " value:" + elem );
            buf.insert( elem );
        }
    }
}
```

```
class Consumer extends Thread {
    private BoundedBuffer buf;
    public Consumer( BoundedBuffer buf ) {
        this.buf = buf;
    }
    public void run() {
        for ( ;; ) {
            int elem = buf.remove();
            System.out.println( "Consumer:" +
                this + " value:" + elem );
            if ( elem == -1 ) break;
        }
    }
}
```

```
class BB {
    public static void main( String[] args ) throws InterruptedException {
        int NoOfCons = 3, NoOfProds = 4;
        BoundedBuffer buf = new BoundedBuffer( 10 );
        Consumer cons[] = new Consumer[NoOfCons];
        Producer prods[] = new Producer[NoOfProds];
        for ( int i = 0; i < NoOfCons; i += 1 ) { cons[i] = new Consumer(buf); cons[i].start(); }
        for ( int i = 0; i < NoOfProds; i += 1 ) { prods[i] = new Producer(buf); prods[i].start(); }
        for ( int i = 0; i < NoOfProds; i += 1 ) { prods[i].join(); }
        for ( int i = 0; i < NoOfCons; i += 1 ) { buf.insert( -1 ); } // terminate each consumer
        for ( int i = 0; i < NoOfCons; i += 1 ) { cons[i].join(); }
    }
}
```

Fig. 13.18 Java: producer/consumer creation/termination

the lock also unlocks it: members explicitly declared as synchronized or a member contains a synchronized statement:

```
class mon {           // monitor object
    public synchronized int mem1() {...}
    public int mem2() {
        synchronized( this ) {...}
    }
}
```

The **synchronized** qualifier is identical to the **_Mutex** qualifier in μC++, except it can only appear on a member routine not on the class itself; therefore, it must be repeated for most public members. Synchronized members provide a mechanism to build a simple monitor. Also, the word **synchronized** incorrectly describes the effect it produces, as it generates mutual exclusion not synchronization. The **synchronized** statement specifies a mutex object, as the mutex lock is abstracted within the mutex object. Normally, the object specified in a **synchronized** statement is the current monitor object, i.e., **this**, but it is possible to specify a different monitor object. In general, specifying any object other than **this** seems like poor programming practice, as it implies a monitor object is no longer in control of its mutual exclusion property. The **synchronized** qualifier and statement serve two purposes:

1. indicate to the compiler boundaries for code optimizations involving code movement to ensure soundness for concurrent programs
2. provide a language statement to implicitly acquire the lock on entry to the routine/block and release the lock on exit from the routine/block regardless of whether the block terminates normally or with an exception.

In general, the compiler support for monitor **synchronized** routines should be used rather than explicitly building a monitor using the **synchronized** statement. In other words, let the compiler do the job it is designed to do. However, the **synchronized** statement is very useful to protect a group of logically related objects:

```
A a; B b; C c;           // object a, b, c are logically a single unit
synchronized( a ) {
    ...
    synchronized( b ) {
        ...
        synchronized( c ) {
            ...
        }
    }
}
```

In this case, creating member routines to establish mutual exclusion is unnecessarily complex, versus accessing the data members directly but with mutual exclusion.

The Java condition lock is like a condition variable, creating a list object on which threads block and unblock; however, there is only *one* condition variable implicitly created for each monitor object (like the mutex lock). There is no compelling justification for this latter semantics and it only makes constructing a monitor more difficult (see Sect. 13.4.4, p. 700 for an alternative). Because there is only one condition variable, it can be anonymous, and implicitly known to the operations that use it. The Java condition lock has the following interface:

```
class condition { ... }      // built-in opaque type defined in each mutex object
condition anon;              // built-in declaration in each mutex object
public wait();               // operations manipulate "anon"
public notify();
public notifyall()
```

The routine wait blocks a thread on a condition variable, and routines notify and notifyall unblock threads from a condition variable. As always, operations on a condition must be done atomically, so these operations must be protected within a **synchronized** member or statement. Java atomically releases the monitor lock as part of the call to wait.

wait may unblock spuriously, i.e., not wait at all, and has the additional semantics of re-acquiring the monitor mutex lock before returning, as if a call to acquire the monitor lock had been made after unblocking from the implicit condition variable. This semantics allows calling threads to barge into a monitor between a signaller leaving it and the signalled task restarting within it; hence, unless additional work is done, a monitor has the no-priority property. notify unblocks at least one waiting thread in any order from the implicit condition lock; it may unblock more than one, like Pthreads pthread_cond_signal. There is no compelling justification for this latter semantics and it only makes constructing a monitor more difficult. A signaller retains control of the monitor, so a monitor has the non-blocking property. As always, a signal on an empty condition lock is lost, i.e., there is no counter to remember signals before waits. notifyall unblocks all waiting thread from a condition lock, and is necessary in certain cases because there is no operation to check if the implicit condition lock is empty.

Fig. 13.19 illustrates the Java equivalent for the internal-scheduling bounded-buffer monitor in Fig. 9.6, p. 444. Routines query, insert and remove are equivalent to those in the bounded buffer monitor. Routine query does not acquire and release the monitor lock because it is a non-mutex member; routines insert and remove do acquire and release the monitor lock because they are mutex members through the **synchronized** qualifier. The waits in insert and remove are no-priority (see Sect. 9.11.3.4, p. 481), because after being signalled, a thread implicitly re-acquires the monitor lock as part of returning from call to wait, which means it competes with calling threads to acquire this mutex lock. As a result, calling threads can barge ahead of threads signalled from internal condition locks, which means the state of the monitor at the time of the signal may have changed when the waiting thread subsequently restarts in the monitor (see Sect. 9.13.1, p. 490). To deal with this problem, each wait is enclosed in a **while** loop to recheck if the event has occurred, which is a busy waiting because there is no bound on service (see Sect. 9.13.1, p. 490). The signals in insert and remove are non-blocking (see Sect. 9.11.3.4, p. 481) because the monitor lock is still held by the thread performing the signalling. However, the Java solution is more complex because there is only one condition variable per object and signalled threads are not necessarily restarted in FIFO order. As a result both producers and consumers wait together, and barging and non-FIFO ordering means it is impossible to know what kind of task is unblocked by a signal. Hence, all tasks must be unblocked so one can detect the new state of the monitor and proceed, which is expensive.

Finally, solutions to the readers and writer problem are presented, which have no starvation and no staleness. Java has only one condition variable per object, non-FIFO signalling, barging and spurious wakeup. These issues can be dealt with by using a queue of private condition locks to ensure tasks are signalled in FIFO order. However, managing the queue of private conditions is complex because each object on the queue is more than just a condition queue, it is in fact a monitor with an implicit monitor lock. Therefore, it is easy to cause the nested monitor problem (see Sect. 9.9, p. 471):

```
private synchronized void StartRead() {
    if ( wcnt > 0 || rwdelay > 0 ) {          // writer active or waiting tasks ?
        RWnode r = new RWnode( READER ); // remember kind of task
        rw.push( r ); rwdelay += 1;
        r.wait();                              // nested monitor problem
    ...
```

Because r is itself a monitor, the thread blocks holding two monitor locks, the one for the readers/writer monitor and the one for the node r. The reason is that r.wait()

```
class BoundedBuffer<ELEMTYPE> {
    private int front = 0, back = 0, count = 0;
    private int NoOfElems;
    private ELEMTYPE Elements[ ];

    @SuppressWarnings("unchecked")
    public BoundedBuffer( int size ) {
        NoOfElems = size;
        Elements = (ELEMTYPE[ ])new Object[NoOfElems];
    }
    public int query() { return count; }
    public synchronized void insert( ELEMTYPE elem ) {
        while ( count == NoOfElems )                 // block producer
            try { wait(); } catch( InterruptedException ex ) {}; // release monitor lock
        Elements[back] = elem;
        back = ( back + 1 ) % NoOfElems;
        count += 1;
        notifyAll();                                 // unblock consumers/producers
    }
    public synchronized ELEMTYPE remove() {
        while ( count == 0 )                          // block consumer
            try { wait(); } catch( InterruptedException ex ) {}; // release monitor lock
        ELEMTYPE elem = Elements[front];
        front = ( front + 1 ) % NoOfElems;
        count -= 1;
        notifyAll();                                 // unblock producers/consumers
        return elem;
    }
}
```

Fig. 13.19 Java: bounded buffer, single condition

atomically blocks the thread and releases the mutual-exclusion lock but only for the
RWnode monitor, not the mutual-exclusion lock for the reader/writer monitor. Now
it is impossible for any task to enter the reader/writer monitor to signal the thread
blocked in r, so there is a mutual-exclusion deadlock.

A technique to deal with this problem is to first release the readers/writer monitor
lock and then block on the node. To do this requires using the **synchronized**
statement:

```
private void StartRead() {
    RWnode r = null;
    synchronized( this ) {
        if ( wcnt > 0 || rwdelay > 0 ) {            // writer active or waiting tasks ?
            r = new RWnode( READER );               // remember kind of task
            rw.push( r ); rwdelay += 1;
        } else
            rcnt += 1;                              // do not have to block
    }                                                // release R/W monitor lock
    if ( r != null ) {                              // cannot proceed ? => block
        r.wait();                                   // wait on node monitor
        synchronized( this ) {                      // re-acquire R/W monitor lock
            ...
        }
    }
}
```

Unfortunately, there is now a race condition between signalling and waiting on the
node. The problem occurs if a task is interrupted after it releases the readers/writer

lock but before it waits on node r. Another reader task, for example, might take the node off the list and signal it, and that signal is lost. When the interrupted task is restarted, it blocks having missed its signal, and hence, is synchronization deadlocked. To deal with this problem, the node is made into a simple binary semaphore, which remembers if it is signalled; now if a wait occurs after a signal, the wait is ignored.

Fig. 13.20, p. 701 shows the readers and writer problem written using Java, which has no starvation and no staleness. The basic solution is based on the Pthreads version, with appropriate changes made to eliminate the nested monitor problem. The type RWnode has an additional field beenNotified along with two **synchronized** routines: Notify and Wait. For a thread to signal or wait on nodes of type RWnode, the routines Notify and Wait are called, respectively. The Notify routine acquired mutual exclusion on the node and marks the node as being notified, as well as signalling the condition. If there is no thread blocked on the condition, the signal is lost but the flag is set. The Wait routine acquired mutual exclusion on the node, and only waits if the notification flag is false. Since a node is only used once in this solution, it is unnecessary to reset the notification flag after waiting.

All other code changes from the Pthreads solution are just transformations to deal with the nested monitor problem. The readers/writer monitor lock is acquired to safely examine the monitor variables. When a thread needs to block, it creates a node and chains it onto the list of private conditions. Then, the readers/writer monitor lock is released and a check is made to determine if the thread has to block. If so, the thread calls Wait for the node and either blocks or continues, depending on the value of beenNotified. When a waiting thread restarts, it re-acquires the readers/writer monitor lock, if necessary, and continues as for the Pthreads solution. Notice, all calls to Notify are performed outside the **synchronized** statements for ReadersWriter. This placement is possible because the signalled thread is blocked on a separate monitor in the queue node, and it increases concurrency because the unblocked task immediately executes a **synchronized** statement for ReadersWriter, meaning it does not have to wait for the signaller thread to release monitor ReadersWriter.

Finally, Java has the ability to interrupt a task blocked on a condition variable. In general, this facility is expensive and is used for exceptional situations, such as thread cancellation. However, the interrupt mechanism, in conjunction with exceptions, can be used to explicitly signal an arbitrary task from a condition variable. Hence, it is possible to explicitly build a list of task identifiers blocked on a condition, and subsequently unblock them in any order by selecting a task in the list and interrupting it. This approach is not recommended because it confuses signalling with interrupts, has a high runtime cost, and largely precludes using interrupts for situations like cancellation.

13.4.4   *java.util.concurrent*

The basic Java concurrency mechanisms are extended via a library of additional
capabilities [25]. The library is sound because of the Java memory-model and the
language is concurrent aware. A number of familiar locks are added: Lock (single
acquisition mutex lock), ReentrantLock (multiple acquisition mutex lock), Condition,
Semaphore (counting), CyclicBarrier and ReadWriteLock.

Fig. 13.21, p. 702 shows how the ReentrantLock and Condition locks are used to
build a monitor for a bounded buffer with multiple condition variables. The monitor
lock mlock is explicitly created and managed in the member routines. A condition is
a nested class within ReentrantLock, which implies the condition implicitly knows its
associated (monitor) lock. The two condition variables empty and full are allocated
from the reentrant lock mlock. The **try/finally** pattern is used to ensure the monitor
lock is always released. Scheduling is still no-priority nonblocking, which implies
barging, so the await statements must be in while loops to recheck the waiting
condition. The await atomically blocks and releases its associated ReentrantLock,
mlock.

Warning: there is no connection with the implicit condition variable of an object
and the library locks. Hence do not mix implicit and explicit condition variables, as
they do not work together; use one or the other approaches.

There is no compiler support to ensure a programmer uses mutex and condition
locks correctly or builds a monitor correctly. Like Pthreads, common errors are
to forget to acquire mutual exclusion before signalling or waiting and/or using
the wrong mutex lock when signalling and waiting. As well, a programmer must
manually perform the following conventions when building a monitor:

1. each monitor must have a single mutex lock for the monitor lock
2. there must be the equivalent of a constructor, i.e., an init member, to allocate the
   monitor lock and any condition variables because both are objects
3. each mutex member, excluding any initialization members, must start by
   acquiring the monitor lock, and the lock must be released by all return paths
   from a member
4. when waiting for an event, it is necessary to recheck for the event upon
   restarting because of barging
5. global monitor (object) variables, versus local mutex-member variables, cannot
   be returned directly unless the return is within a try block with a **finally**
   statement that unlocks the monitor lock

Using these conventions, it is possible to construct solutions to other problems, like
readers/writer.

The Java library also provides a few executor administrators with futures (see
Sect. 11.6, p. 583). Fig. 13.22, p. 703 shows a Java and μC++ executor, which are
predefined, generic servers with one or more worker tasks (worker pool). A client
creates work units (Callable objects), which returns a result to be put into the future
by the server. A client calls the executor's submit member to register a work unit, and
the server returns a future to identify the work. Instead of the client just supplying

```
class ReadersWriter {
   enum Kind { READER, WRITER };
   private static class RWnode {
      public Kind kind;
      public boolean beenNotified;

      public RWnode( Kind kindp ) {
         kind = kindp;
         beenNotified = false;
      }
      public synchronized void Notify() {
         beenNotified = true;
         notify();
      }
      public synchronized void Wait() {
         while ( ! beenNotified ) // race ?
            try { wait();
            } catch(InterruptedException ex) {}
      }
   }
   private int rcnt = 0, wcnt = 0, rwdelay = 0;
   private LinkedList<RWnode> rw =
            new LinkedList<RWnode>();

   private void StartRead() {
      RWnode r = null;
      synchronized ( this ) {
         if ( wcnt > 0 || rwdelay > 0 ) {
            r = new RWnode( Kind.READER );
            rw.add( r ); // prepare to block
            rwdelay += 1;
         } else
            rcnt += 1; // no block
      }
      if ( r != null ) { // must block ?
         r.Wait();
         RWnode n = null;
         synchronized ( this ) {
            rcnt += 1;
            rw.removeFirst(); // cleanup
            rwdelay -= 1;
            if ( rwdelay > 0 && // more readers ?
                  rw.getFirst().kind == Kind.READER )
               n = rw.getFirst();
         }
         if (n != null) n.Notify(); // another task ?
      }
   }
```

```
   private void EndRead() {
      RWnode n = null;
      synchronized ( this ) {
         rcnt -= 1;
         if ( rcnt == 0 && rwdelay > 0 )
            n = rw.getFirst();
      }
      if ( n != null ) n.Notify(); // write task ?
   }
   private void StartWrite() {
      RWnode w = null;
      synchronized ( this ) {
         if ( rcnt > 0 || wcnt > 0
               || rwdelay > 0 ) {
            w = new RWnode( Kind.WRITER );
            rw.add( w ); // prepare to block
            rwdelay += 1;
         } else
            wcnt += 1; // no block
      }
      if ( w != null ) { // must block ?
         w.Wait();
         synchronized ( this ) {
            wcnt += 1;
            rw.removeFirst(); // cleanup
            rwdelay -= 1;
         }
      }
   }
   private void EndWrite() {
      RWnode n = null;
      synchronized ( this ) {
         wcnt -= 1;
         if ( rwdelay > 0 )
            n = rw.getFirst();
      }
      if (n != null) n.Notify(); // another task ?
   }
   public void Read() {
      StartRead();
      // read
      EndRead();
   }
   public void Write() {
      StartWrite();
      // write
      EndWrite();
   }
}
```

Fig. 13.20 Java: readers and writer, single condition

```
import java.util.concurrent.locks.*;
class BoundedBuffer<ELEMTYPE> {                        // simulate monitor
    // buffer declarations
    final Lock mlock = new ReentrantLock();           // monitor lock
    final Condition empty = mlock.newCondition(), full = mlock.newCondition();
    public void insert( ELEMTYPE elem ) {
        mlock.lock();
        try {
            while (count == NoOfElems )
                try { empty.await(); } catch( InterruptedException ex ) {}; // release mlock
            // add to buffer
            full.signal();
        } finally { mlock.unlock(); }                 // ensure monitor lock is unlocked
    }
    public ELEMTYPE remove() {
        mlock.lock();
        try {
            while( count == 0 )
                try { full.await(); } catch( InterruptedException ex ) {}; // release mlock
            // remove from buffer
            empty.signal();
            return elem;
        } finally { mlock.unlock(); }                 // ensure monitor lock is unlocked
    }
}
```

Fig. 13.21 Java: bounded buffer, multiple conditions

arguments for the work and the server supplying the code to compute a result from the arguments, the work unit supplies both arguments and code, which the server executes using one of the workers in its worker pool. The client retrieves the result from the future using its get routine, which may block until the result is inserted by the executor.

Finally, the Java concurrency library also provides a number of thread-safe collections, like arrays, queues and hash tables. The collections allow threads to interact indirectly through atomic data-structures, e.g., producer/consumer interact via a thread-safe queue. As well, atomic data-types are provided with associated atomic instructions, which can be used to build lock-free data-structures.

```
int v;
AtomicInteger i = new AtomicInteger();
i.set( 1 );
System.out.println( i.get() );
v = i.addAndGet( 1 );              // i += delta
System.out.println( i.get() + " " + v );
v = i.decrementAndGet();           // --i
System.out.println( i.get() + " " + v );
v = i.getAndAdd( 1 );              // i =+ delta
System.out.println( i.get() + " " + v );
v = i.getAndDecrement();           // i--
System.out.println( i.get() + " " + v );
```

```java
import java.util.ArrayList;
import java.util.List;
import java.util.concurrent.*;
public class Client {
    public static void main( String[] args )
        throws InterruptedException,
            ExecutionException {
        Callable<Integer> work = new
            Callable<Integer>() {
            public Integer call() {
                // do some work
                return d;
            }
        };
        ExecutorService executor =
            Executors.newFixedThreadPool( 5 );
        List<Future<Integer>> futures =
            new ArrayList<Future<Integer>>();
        for ( int f = 0; f < 10; f += 1 )
            // pass work and store future
            futures.add( executor.submit( work ) );
        for ( int f = 0; f < 10; f += 1 )
            System.out.println( futures.get( f ).get() );
        executor.shutdown();
    }
}
```

(a) Java

```cpp
struct Work {  // routine or functor
    int operator()() {
        // do some work
        return d;
    }
} work;

void uMain::main() {
    uExecutor executor( 5 );

    Future_ISM<int> futures[10];
    for ( int f = 0; f < 10; f += 1 )
        // pass work and store future
        executor.submit( futures[f], work );
    for ( int f = 0; f < 10; f += 1 )
        cout << futures[f]() << endl;
}
```

(b) μC++

Fig. 13.22 Executors

13.4.5 Go

The Go programming language provides non-preemptive, user-level threads (like μC++), called **goroutines**) [19]. Go is not object-oriented, so a **go** statement (like START Sect. 5.8.4, p. 208) is used to start a user-level thread running in a routine.

```
go foo( 3, f )    // start thread in routine foo with parameters 3 and f
```

Arguments may be passed to a goroutine but the return value is discarded. All goroutines are anonymous, so direct communication is accomplished using a different mechanism. All threads are terminated (killed) *silently* when the program terminates. Go provides a number of locks (mutex, condition, barrier and readers/writer), and atomic operations. However, the primary mechanism for thread synchronize/communicate is **channels**, based on CSP [21].

A channel is a typed shared buffer with 0 to N elements.

```
ch1 := make( chan int, 100 )    // integer channel with buffer size 100
ch2 := make( chan string )      // string channel with buffer size 0
ch2 := make( chan chan string ) // channel of channel of strings
```

If the buffer size is greater than 0, up to N asynchronous calls can occur; otherwise, a channel call is synchronous. The operator <- performs send/receive; for example, send is done with ch1 <- 1 and receive with s <- ch2. A channel can be constrained to only send or receive; otherwise, it is bidirectional. The ability to pass a channel as a data value through another channel is an important extension over CSP.

The problem with channels is the paradigm shift from routine call. A programmer now has both call/return and channel send/receive. Hence, they must toggle between these paradigms in both declaration and usage within a concurrent program. μC++ uses only the call/return paradigm.

Fig. 13.23 contrasts Go channels and μC++ routine call for synchronous direct-communication. The program transmits three different types of data (integer, float-point and structure) from the main program to the goroutine/task. The Go program has three channels, one of each type of transmitted data; the μC++ program has three different members, one of each type of transmitted data. In the goroutine/task, both languages use a **select/_Accept** statement to block and wait for a communication to occur. The Go program directly assigns the channel argument into the local parameter. The μC++ program indirectly assigns the call argument into a class (communication) variable in the member routine, which is accessed in the task main. Both languages then execute a statement after the data transfer to process (print) the data.

The Go program starts a thread in routine gortn, while μC++ declares a task object, which starts a thread in its task main. The Go program sends data into the appropriate channels, while μC++ calls appropriate member routines. The Go program has to perform a hand-shake with the goroutine to prevent the main program from ending and silently stopping the goroutine. A sentinel value is sent to the goroutine to indicate communication is complete. The routine terminates when the sentinel value is received. The μC++ program performs the hand shake implicitly via deallocation. The main routine waits for the task object gotrn to terminate so it can be deallocated. The gortn task-main terminates when its destructor is called.

Fig. 13.24, p. 706 shows a bounded buffer in Go using mutex/condition locks and a channel to contrast the approaches. Fig. 13.24, p. 706a is very similar to the Java version with ·multiple conditions (see Fig. 13.21, p. 702). The Go **defer** clause is like the Java finally for routine scope, i.e., the **defer** is always executed before returning from the routine, which ensures the mutex lock is always released. The condition locks are associated with a mutex lock at declaration, so waiting on a condition variable atomically blocks and releases the mutex lock. The mutex lock is re-acquired after a goroutine unblocks, so barging is possible, and hence, each wait must recheck its condition in a loop. The corresponding channel version uses a single channel of bounded size to provide asynchronous calls by the producer/consumer until the channel is full or empty. In contrast to the lock version, all necessary locking and synchronization are performed implicitly by the high-level channel.

```
package main
import "fmt"
func main() {

    type Msg struct{ i, j int }
    ch1 := make( chan int )
    ch2 := make( chan float32 )
    ch3 := make( chan Msg )
    hand := make( chan string )
    shake := make( chan string )
    gortn := func() {
        var i int; var f float32; var m Msg
    L: for {
        select { // wait for message
        case <- hand: break L // sentinel
        case i = <- ch1: fmt.Println( i )
        case f = <- ch2: fmt.Println( f )
        case m = <- ch3: fmt.Println( m )

        }
    }
    shake <- "SHAKE" // completion
    }


    go gortn()        // start thread in gortn
    ch1 <- 0          // different messages
    ch2 <- 2.5
    ch3 <- Msg{1, 2}
    hand <- "HAND" // sentinel value
    <-shake           // wait for completion
}
```

```
#include <iostream>
using namespace std;
_Task Gortn {
  public:
    struct Msg { int i, j; };
    void mem1( int i ) { Gortn::i = i; }
    void mem2( float f ) { Gortn::f = f; }
    void mem3( Msg m ) { Gortn::m = m; }
  private:
    int i;  float f;  Msg m;
    void main() {

        for ( ;; ) {

            _Accept( ~Gortn ) break;
            or _Accept( mem1 ) cout << i << endl;
            or _Accept( mem2 ) cout << f << endl;
            or _Accept( mem3 ) cout << "{ "
                << m.i << " " << m.j << "}" << endl;
        }
    }
};
void uMain::main() {
    Gortn gortn;
    gortn.mem1( 0 );
    gortn.mem2( 2.5 );
    gortn.mem3( (Gortn::Msg){ 1, 2 } );
} // wait for completion
```

| (a) Go | (b) μC++ |

Fig. 13.23   Go versus μC++ direct communication

13.4.6   C++11 Concurrency

The C++11 concurrency library adds a Pthread-like interface for concurrency with no high-level language features; hence, threading is kernel threads. The library is sound because C++11 has a memory-model. There are basic mutex and condition locks, and atomic types/operations. There is a thread class, but it is not used for inheritance:

```
class thread {
  public:
    template <class Fn, class... Args> explicit thread( Fn &&fn, Args &&... args );
    void join();                        // termination synchronization
    bool joinable() const;              // true => joined, false otherwise
    void detach();                      // independent lifetime
    id get_id() const;                  // thread id
};
```

Fig. 13.25, p. 707 shows how to start a thread and perform termination synchronization. Even though C++ is object-oriented, threading is based on starting a thread

```go
package main
import "fmt"
import "runtime"
import "sync"

const size = 20
type BoundedBuffer struct {
    lock sync.Mutex
    full, empty *sync.Cond
    front, back, count int
    elements [size] int
}
func initBuffer( buf *BoundedBuffer ) {
    buf.front, buf.back, buf.count = 0, 0, 0
    buf.full = sync.NewCond( &buf.lock )
    buf.empty = sync.NewCond( &buf.lock )
}
func insert( buf *BoundedBuffer, elem int ) {
    defer buf.lock.Unlock()
    buf.lock.Lock()
    for buf.count == size { buf.empty.Wait() }
    buf.elements[buf.back] = elem
    buf.back = (buf.back + 1) % size
    buf.count += 1
    buf.full.Signal()
}
func remove( buf *BoundedBuffer ) int {
    defer buf.lock.Unlock()
    buf.lock.Lock()
    for buf.count == 0 { buf.full.Wait() }
    var elem int = buf.elements[buf.front]
    buf.front = (buf.front + 1) % size
    buf.count += 1
    buf.empty.Signal()
    return elem
}
func main() {
    const times = 20
    var shake chan bool = make( chan bool )
    var buffer BoundedBuffer
    runtime.GOMAXPROCS(2) // kernel threads
    initBuffer( &buffer )
    fmt.Println()
    go func( buffer *BoundedBuffer ) {
        for i := 0; i < times; i += 1 {
            insert( buffer, i )
        }
    } ( &buffer )          // producer
    go func(buffer *BoundedBuffer) {
        for i := 0; i < times; i += 1 {
            fmt.Println( remove( buffer ) )
        }
        shake <- true
    } ( &buffer )          // consumer
    <-shake
} // main
```

(a) Using mutex/condition locks

```go
package main
import "fmt"
import "runtime"

const size = 20
type Buffer interface {
    insert( elem int )
    remove() int
}
type BoundedBuffer struct {
    comm chan int
}
func MakeBoundedBuffer() *BoundedBuffer {
    var buf BoundedBuffer
    buf.comm = make( chan int, size )
    return &buf
}
func ( buf *BoundedBuffer ) insert(elem int) {
    buf.comm <- elem
}

func ( buf *BoundedBuffer ) remove() int {
    return <- buf.comm
}

func main() {
    const times = 20
    shake := make( chan bool )
    buffer := MakeBoundedBuffer()
    runtime.GOMAXPROCS(2) // kernel threads

    fmt.Println()
    go func( buffer Buffer ) { // producer
        for i := 0; i < times; i += 1 {
            buffer.insert( i )
        } // for
    } ( buffer )           // prod
    go func( buffer Buffer ) { // consumer
        for i := 0; i < times; i += 1 {
            fmt.Println( buffer.remove() )
        } // for
        shake <- true
    } ( buffer )           // cons
    <-shake
} // main
```

(b) Using channels

Fig. 13.24 Go: bounded buffer

```
#include <thread>
void hello( const string &s ) {              // callable
    cout << "Hello " << s << endl;
}
class Hello {                                // functor
    int result;
  public:
    void operator()( const string &s ) {     // callable
        cout << "Hello " << s << endl;
    }
};
int main() {
    thread t1( hello, "Peter" );             // start thread in routine "hello"
    Hello h;                                 // thread object
    thread t2( h, "Mary" );                  // start thread in functor "h"
    // work concurrently
    t1.join();                               // termination synchronization
    // work concurrently
    t2.join();                               // termination synchronization
} // must join before closing block
```

Fig. 13.25 C++11: thread creation and join

running in a routine, using a START/WAIT Sect. 5.8.4, p. 208) mechanism. Any entity that is *callable* (functor) may be used as the target for a starting thread. To make the semantics of starting a thread consistent between routine and functor, the functor is copied so multiple threads can be started in the same routine or functor independently. This semantics implies the original functor object cannot be used to return a result, like a Java thread-object, as no thread actually executes in this object. Hence, return values from threads requires a more complex mechanism. The mechanism to start a thread is declarative, and the join is an executable statement. The declaration provides a unique handle to the thread for subsequent joining. Passing multiple arguments uses C++11's variadic template feature to provide a type-safe call from thread constructor to the *callable* routine. The thread starts implicitly at the point of declaration.

The life-time of a thread cannot exceed the life-time of its handle unless the thread is detached. This semantics is also true for block created threads in μC++, but μC++ waits for these threads to terminate at the end of the block rather than generating an error. Like Go, detached threads, t1.detach(), are silently terminated (killed) if the program terminates. Hence, some other form of synchronization is necessary with the main program and detached threads, because once a thread is detached, it is non-joinable. Finally, beware dangling pointers to local variables for detached threads:

```
{
    string s( "Fred" );          // local variable
    thread t( hello, s );
    t.detach();
} // "s" deallocated and "t" running with reference to "s"
```

Fig. 13.26 shows a bounded buffer implemented using the C++11 locks, which is identical in structure to the Pthreads version (see Fig. 13.5, p. 652). The condition

```
#include <mutex>
class BoundedBuffer {                        // simulate monitor
    // buffer declarations
    mutex mlock;                             // monitor lock
    condition_variable empty, full;
    void insert( int elem ) {
        mlock.lock();
        while (count == Size ) empty.wait( mlock );  // release lock
        // add to buffer
        full.notify_one();
        mlock.unlock();
    }
    int remove() {
        mlock.lock();
        while( count == 0 ) notempty.wait( mlock );  // release lock
        // remove from buffer
        empty.notify_one();
        mlock.unlock();
        return elem;
    }
};
```

Fig. 13.26 C++11 bounded buffer

locks are associated with a mutex lock by passing the mutex lock to the wait member, so waiting on a condition variable atomically blocks and releases the mutex lock. The mutex lock is re-acquired after a thread unblocks, so barging is possible, and hence, each wait must recheck its condition in a loop.

Finally, there is an asynchronous call mechanism for increasing client-side concurrency with futures to obtain results.

```
#include <future>
big_num pi( int decimal_places ) {...}
int main() {
    future<big_num> PI = async( pi, 1200 );  // PI to 1200 decimal places
    // work concurrently
    cout << "PI " << PI.get() << endl;        // block for answer
}
```

Here the thread handle is embedded in the future and used to retrieve the result from get. The calling thread blocks if the result is unavailable. As for join, if a call to get is not made, the thread from an asynchronous call is silently terminated when the program ends.

13.5   Concurrent Models

Concurrency models are language-independent approaches for writing concurrent programs based on some encompassing design philosophy. Models are largely language independent and can be introduced into existing sequential languages or incorporated from the start into new languages. In general, models adopt a single

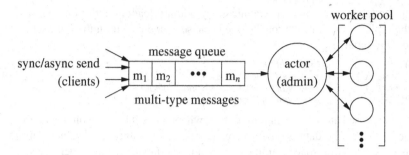

Fig. 13.27 Actor model

approach/methodology that can be used to solve most problems, but at the cost of solving some problems well and others poorly.

13.5.1   Actor Model

The Actor model [20] is essentially a message passing system with a complex abstraction for receiving messages. Fig. 13.27 shows the Actor model defines a task front-ended by a message queue containing all the messages sent to it. Associated with each Actor at the back-end is a list of behaviours, which are (worker) threads that receive consecutive communications from the Actor message queue. A behaviour is restricted to receiving a single message from its actor message queue but has no restriction on the number of sends to other actors. This restriction allows a behaviour to send a message to its underlying actor without deadlocking, possibly even recursively if the next behaviour to receive the message is the same as the one that sent it. An Actor is a task as there is always one behaviour (thread) active in the Actor. Two popular programming languages using actors are Erlang [15] and Scala.

The Actor model can be implemented in a number of ways, e.g. two implementations are given in [1, p. 38-43]. While the model requires that Actors be objects, these objects could be implemented as package- or class-based objects. If the message queue is polymorphic in the message types, type checking is dynamic. Messages are normally sent asynchronously.

13.5.2   Linda Model

The Linda model [9] is based on the concept of a **tuple space**, which is a multiset of tuples, i.e., duplicates are allowed, that is accessed associatively by threads for synchronization and communication. Threads are created in the Linda model through the tuple space, and communicate by adding, reading and removing data from the tuple space. It is a "tuple" space because elements within the multiset are grouped into tuples, e.g.:

```
( 1 )                 // 1 element tuple of int
( 1.0, 2.0, 3.0 )     // 3 element tuple of double
( "Peter", 1, 2 )     // 3 element tuple of char [], and 2 integers
( 'M', 5.5 )          // 2 element tuple of char, double
```

A tuple is accessed atomically and by content, where content is based on the number of tuple elements, the data types of the elements, and possibly their values. Often there is only one tuple space implicitly known to all threads; hence, operations on the tuple space do not have to name it. Work has been done for multiple tuple spaces, which requires explicit tuple names. Because of its simplicity, the Linda model can be incorporated into many programming languages and systems. Usually the language in which the Linda model is embedded is used as a prefix to denote the particular kind of Linda, as in Ada-Linda, C-Linda, etc.

At least 4 operations are available for accessing the tuple space:

1. The read operation reads a tuple from the tuple space. To indicate which kind of tuple to read, a tuple pattern is specified. A pattern indicates both the number of elements in the matching tuple and the keys which must match both in type and value with corresponding fields of a tuple in the tuple space, e.g.:

   ```
   read( 'M', 34, 5.5 );
   ```

   blocks until a matching 3 field tuple with values ('M', 34, 5.5) appears in the tuple space. A variable can be used instead of a constant, e.g.:

   ```
   int i = 34;
   read( 'M', i, 5.5 );
   ```

   Such a read can be used for synchronizing with the thread generating the particular tuple, i.e., the reader cannot proceed until the write has occurred.

   A general form of pattern matching is possible using a type rather than a value, e.g.:

   ```
   int i;
   read( 'M', ?i, 5.5 );
   ```

   blocks until a matching 3 field tuple with values ('M', **int**, 5.5) appears in the tuple space (i is of type **int**), where **int** matches any integer value. After a match is found, the value for any type match is copied from the tuple space into the corresponding variable in the argument list. In this example, the value of the type match is copied into the variable i after a match is found.

2. The in operation is identical to the read operation, except it removes the matching tuple from the tuple space so it cannot participate in further associative searching.

3. The out operation writes a tuple to the tuple space, e.g.:

   ```
   out( 'M', 34, 5.5 );
   ```

   adds the tuple ('M', 34, 5.5) to the tuple space. The out operation is non-blocking. A variable can be used instead of a constant, e.g.:

```
int i = 34;
out( 'M', i, 5.5 );
```

4. The eval operation is identical to the out operation, except any routine argument is implicitly executed with its own thread, e.g.:

```
int f( int, bool );
int i = 34;
eval( 'M', f( i, true ), 5.5 );
```

adds the tuple ('M', f(i, true), 5.5) to the tuple space, with a new thread executing routine f. In contrast, out evaluates all arguments sequentially before the tuple is added to the tuple space. Subsequent reading of this tuple, e.g.:

```
read( 'M', ?i, 5.5 );
```

blocks until both the tuple is available *and* the thread executing argument f has terminated.

The operation names in Linda are from the perspective of the tuple space rather than the program, e.g., in moves data out of the tuple space into the program. Some Linda systems also provide non-blocking versions of and read: inp and readp. If a matching tuple is not found immediately, control returns with a boolean result indicating failure to obtain data.

It is possible to create a binary semaphore to provide mutual exclusion or synchronization by appropriately inserting and removing an element from the tuple space:

Mutual Exclusion	Synchronization	
	Task$_1$	Task$_2$

in("semaphore");
// *critical section*
out("semaphore");
	in("semaphore");
	S2
		S1
		out("semaphore");

For mutual exclusion, the semaphore element must be initially inserted into the tuple space, which corresponds to setting the semaphore to open (1). Tasks then race to remove the semaphore element from the tuple space to enter the critical section. On exit from the critical section, the semaphore element is written back into the tuple space to reset it. The atomicity on operations provided by the tuple space provides an N-task solution for mutual exclusion. Hopefully, there is some bound on access to the element by multiple tasks or starvation can result. For synchronization, the semaphore element must not be inserted into the tuple space, which corresponds to setting the semaphore to closed (0). The task that writes the element into the tuple space marks the completion of an operation, which the other task detects by reading the element. The reading task only blocks if the element is not yet written.

Fig. 13.28 illustrates the Linda equivalent for the semaphore bounded-buffer monitor in Fig. 7.14, p. 353. The tuple space is already a buffer, and handles the unbounded-buffer case since a producer can insert elements into the tuple space and never blocks (but could block if the tuple space fills). A consumer implicitly blocks if there is no element in the tuple space when it attempts to remove one. To simulate a bounded buffer, it is necessary to block the producer

```
int producer( int id ) {
    const int NoOfElems = rand() % 20;
    int elem, i, size;
    for ( i = 1; i <= NoOfElems; i += 1 ) {         // produce elements
        elem = rand() % 100 + 1;                    // produce a random number
        in( "bufferSem" );                          // wait for empty buffer slot
        out( "buffer", elem );                      // insert element into tuple space
    }
    return id;
}
int consumer( int id ) {
    int elem;
    for ( ;; ) {
        in( "buffer", ?elem );                      // remove element from tuple space
        out( "bufferSem" );                         // indicate empty buffer slot
        if ( elem == -1 ) break;                    // consume until a negative element
        // consume element
    }
    return id;
}
int main() {
    const int bufSize = 5, NoOfCons = 3, NoOfProds = 4;
    int i, id;
    for ( i = 0; i < bufSize; i += 1 )              // number of buffer elements
        out( "bufferSem" );
    for ( i = 0; i < NoOfCons; i += 1 )             // create consumers
        eval( "consumer", consumer( i ) );
    for ( i = 0; i < NoOfProds; i += 1 )            // create producers
        eval( "producer", producer( i ) );
    for ( i = 0; i < NoOfProds; i += 1 )            // wait for producer to terminate
        read( "producer", ?id );
    for ( i = 0; i < NoOfCons; i += 1 )             // terminate each consumer
        out( "buffer", -1 );
    for ( i = 0; i < NoOfCons; i += 1 )             // wait for consumers to terminate
        read( "consumer", ?id );
}
```

Fig. 13.28 Linda: producer/consumer bounded buffer

when the buffer is conceptually full, e.g., to prevent producers from filling the tuple
space. Synchronization blocking for the producers is accomplished by simulating
a counting semaphore. The main program inserts N buffer elements into the tuple
space. Each producer removes a buffer element before inserting an element into the
tuple space; when there are no elements, the producer blocks. An element is inserted
back into the tuple space by the consumer only after an element has been removed
from the tuple space, indicating an empty buffer slot. This solution handles multiple
consumers and producers because insertion and removal of elements from the tuple
space is atomic.

Fig. 13.29, p. 714 illustrates the Linda equivalent for the semaphore readers and
writer solution in Fig. 7.23, p. 372 using C++-Linda. This solution uses a private
semaphore to deal with the need to atomically block and release the entry lock.
To ensure FIFO service, a queue indicating the kind of waiting task, i.e., reader or
writer, is maintained. To simulate the entry semaphore, the name "entry" *plus* the

address of the ReadersWriter object is used. The object address allows multiple entry semaphores to occur in the tuple space simultaneously. Similarly, to uniquely name the private semaphores, each private semaphore has the name "privSem" *plus* the address of the list node holding the kind of task. As in the semaphore solution, an interrupt between tuple operations in("entry", **this**) and out("privSem", &r) is not a problem because the blocking task adds its node *before* releasing the entry lock. Any subsequent release of the private lock is remembered in the tuple space until the blocking task can remove it.

As can be seen from the Linda example programs, the facilities provided are at the level of threads and locks (see Sect. 13.2, p. 644). Furthermore, there is essentially no abstraction or encapsulation facilities in the tuple space. As well, sharing the tuple space with multiple applications can easily result in problems with incorrect retrieval unless tuples are tagged with unique values; some work has been done with multiple tuple spaces. Notice also that the Linda primitives have a variable number of parameters, which most languages do not support, and depend on the type system of the language, which varies greatly among languages. There is also a dichotomy between the kinds of data structures in the language and those allowed in the tuple space, e.g., pointers. Therefore, the Linda primitives must be constructs in the programming language in which they are embedded not merely library routines. There are also efficiency considerations for the associative tuple-search since each removal from the tuple space checks both types and values. Linda is dynamically type-safe as a side-effect of the selection from the tuple-space. What is unclear about the Linda model is the canonical form for the type of a tuple, particularly if tuples are allowed to come from different languages with potentially incompatible type systems.

13.5.3 OpenMP

OpenMp [4] is a collection of compiler directives, library routines and environment variables described for shared-memory concurrency in C, C++ and Fortran programs. The concurrency is implicit thread management (programmer hints) using a 1-to-1 threading model (kernel threads) and some explicit locking. Language compilers support the OpenMP API with #pragma directives.

```
#pragma omp ...
```

The concurrency model is similar to COBEGIN/COEND (see Sect. 5.8.3, p. 207), where a team of threads is created and each thread executes a section of code. When team threads complete, synchronize and terminate, the initial thread continues.

```
class ReadersWriter {
    enum RW { READER, WRITER };              // kinds of threads
    struct RWnode {
        RW kind;                             // kind of thread
        RWnode( RW kind ) : kind(kind) {}
    };
    queue<RWnode *> rw;                      // queue of RWnodes
    int rcnt, wcnt, rwdelay;
    void StartRead() {
        out( "entry", this );
        if ( wcnt > 0 || rwdelay > 0 ) {
            RWnode r( READER );
            rw.push( &r ); rwdelay += 1;     // remember kind of thread
            in( "entry", this ); out( "privSem", &r );
            rw.pop(); rwdelay -= 1;          // remove waiting task from condition list
        }
        rcnt += 1;
        if ( rwdelay > 0 && rw.front()->kind == READER )
            in( "privSem", rw.front() );
        else
            in( "entry", this );
    }
    void EndRead() {
        out( "entry", this );
        rcnt -= 1;
        if ( rcnt == 0 && rwdelay > 0 ) in( "privSem", rw.front() ); // last reader ?
        else in( "entry", this );
    }
    void StartWrite() {
        out( "entry", this );
        if ( rcnt > 0 || wcnt > 0 ) {
            RWnode w( WRITER );
            rw.push( &w ); rwdelay += 1;     // remember kind of thread
            in( "entry", this ); out( "privSem", &w );
            rw.pop(); rwdelay -= 1;          // remove waiting task from condition list
        }
        wcnt += 1;
        in( "entry", this );
    }
    void EndWrite() {
        out( "entry", this );
        wcnt -= 1;
        if ( rwdelay > 0 ) in( "privSem", rw.front() );     // anyone waiting ?
        else in( "entry", this );
    }
  public:
    ReadersWriter() : rcnt(0), wcnt(0), rwdelay(0) {
        in( "entry", this );
    }
    ...
};
```

Fig. 13.29 Linda: readers and writer

```
#include <omp.h>
... // declarations of i, p1, p2, p3
int main() {
    int i;
    #pragma omp parallel sections num_threads( 4 ) // start 4-thread team
    { // COBEGIN
        #pragma omp section
        { i = 1; }
        #pragma omp section
        { p1( 5 ); }
        #pragma omp section
        { p2( 7 ); }
        #pragma omp section
        { p3( 9 ); }
    } // COEND (synchronize)
}
```

The pragma states there are 4 sections of code in the following block. When the
block is entered by the initial thread, it creates 4 new threads for each of the
sections. The initial thread then waits at the end of the block until all threads in
the block terminate, before continuing execution. Variables outside a section are
shared; variables inside a section are thread private. Hence, variable i is shared but
only accessed by one thread in the first section.

If all sections are the same, there is a short-hand form. For example, in
concurrently adding up the rows of a matrix (see Sect. 5.12, p. 218), each section
performing a summation is identical except for the particular row.

```
int main() {
    const unsigned int rows = 10, cols = 10;      // sequential
    int matrix[rows][cols], subtotals[rows], total = 0;

    // read matrix
    #pragma omp parallel num_threads( rows )   // start rows-thread team
    {                                          // concurrent
        unsigned int row = omp_get_thread_num(); // row to add is thread ID
        subtotals[row] = 0;
        for ( unsigned int c = 0; c < cols; c += 1 ) {
            subtotals[row] += matrix[row][c];
        }
    }                                          // wait for all threads to finish
    for ( unsigned int r = 0; r < rows; r += 1 ) {   // sequential
        total += subtotals[r];
    }
    printf( "total %d\n", total );
}
```

It just happens the thread identifiers are numbered from 0 to N−1, so the thread id
is used to determine the row to sum. A more formal way to accomplish the same
effect is with the **for** directive, which provides a user defined iteration numbers.

```
#pragma omp parallel for                      // start rows-thread team
for ( unsigned int r = 0; r < rows; r += 1 ) {   // concurrent
    subtotals[r] = 0;
    for ( unsigned int c = 0; c < cols; c += 1 ) {
        subtotals[r] += matrix[r][c];
    }
}                                              // wait for all threads to finish
```

In this case, the loop index r is a unique interaction value in each section, which is used to determine the row to sum.

The programmer is responsible for any overlapping sharing among threads, so there are a number of synchronization, mutual exclusion and atomic directives. For example, there is a barrier pragma for synchronizing threads:

```
int main() {
    #pragma omp parallel num_threads( 4 )      // start 4-thread team
    {
        sleep( omp_get_thread_num() );
        printf( "%d\n", omp_get_thread_num() );
        #pragma omp barrier                    // wait for all threads to arrive
        printf("sync\n");
    }                                          // wait for all threads to finish
}
```

·and a critical section pragma for mutual exclusion among threads:

```
int main() {
    int i;
    #pragma omp parallel num_threads( 4 )      // start 4-thread team
    {
        #pragma omp critical
        {
            i += 1;                            // safely increment shared variable
        }
    }                                          // wait for all threads to finish
}
```

13.5.4 MPI

Message Passing Interface (MPI) [28] is message-passing library-interface specification for C and Fortran programs (C++ support is depreciated). MPI addresses the message-passing programming-model, where data is transferred among the address spaces of processes for computation. A message-passing specification provides portability across shared-memory multiprocessor computers and heterogeneous computer-clusters/networks. MPI is intended to deliver high performance with low latency and high bandwidth without burdening users with details of the shared-memory architecture or network. MPI provides point-to-point send/receive message-passing operations for exchanging data among processes.

MPI supports dynamic type-checking of messages. Each message describes the type of the message: basic type, array or structure (no pointers). The data types must match between sender and receiver. The data types are language specific and an MPI binding is created for each language type. For example, the following is a subset of the C type bindings (minus **unsigned** variants).

MPI datatype	C
MPI_C_BOOL	_Bool
MPI_CHAR	char
MPI_SHORT	signed short
MPI_INT	signed int
MPI_LONG	signed long
MPI_LONG_LONG	signed long long
MPI_FLOAT	float
MPI_DOUBLE	double
MPI_LONG_DOUBLE	long double

Message passing can be synchronous, asynchronous or buffered. MPI Send and Recv are the two most used message-passing constructs.

```
int MPI_Send(
    const void *buf,         // send buffer
    int count,               // # of elements to send
    MPI_Datatype datatype,   // type of elements
    int dest,                // destination rank
    int tag,                 // message tag
    MPI_Comm communicator    // normally MPI_COMM_WORLD
);
int MPI_Recv(
    void *buf,               // receive buffer
    int count,               // # of elements to receive
    MPI_Datatype datatype,   // type of elements
    int source,              // source rank
    int tag,                 // message tag
    MPI_Comm communicator,   // normally MPI_COMM_WORLD
    MPI_Status *status       // status object or NULL
);
```

buf is the location of the data to be sent or received. count is the number of elements of the data type in the message to be sent/received. If count is greater than one, it implies an array of data values. datatype is one of the MPI bindings describing the type of elements in the buffer. It is the programmers responsibility to correctly match the binding. dest/source is the process that the message is to be sent/received to/from. tag controls the kind of send/receive, i.e., receive specific or any. The remaining parameters are unnecessary for this discussion and normally set to MPI_COMM_WORLD and NULL, respectively.

Fig. 13.30 shows an MPI producer/consumer. The producer performs a send specific to the consumer and sends an array of ten integers. After sending the data, a sentential value of -1 is sent to indicate end of communication. The consumer performs a receive specific from the producer, receives the array of integers and checks for the sentinel value. The amount of asynchronous execution depends on the amount of implicit buffering between producer and consumer. Hence, the sender blocks if the buffer fills, and the receive blocks until data is sent (rendezvous).

MPI runs N copies of the same program, using kernel threads to run each copy, with no shared data among the processes. For the producer/consumer, two copies are started: one for the producer and one for the consumer, distinguished by *rank*. The main program of each copy initializes MPI and then asks for its process rank, which is the MPI process identifier, numbered 0 to $N-1$, for N processes. The idea

```
#include <mpi.h>
enum { PROD = 0, CONS = 1 };
void producer() {
    int buf[10];                                    // transmit array to consumer
    for ( int i = 0; i < 20; i += 1 ) {             // generate N arrays
        for ( int j = 0; j < 10; j += 1 ) buf[j] = i;
        MPI_Send( buf, 10, MPI_INT, CONS, 0, MPI_COMM_WORLD );
    }
    buf[0] = -1;                                     // send sentinel value
    MPI_Send( buf, 1, MPI_INT, CONS, 0, MPI_COMM_WORLD ); // only send 1 value
}
void consumer() {
    int buf[10];
    for ( ;; ) {
        MPI_Recv( buf, 10, MPI_INT, PROD, 0, MPI_COMM_WORLD, NULL );
        if ( buf[0] == -1 ) break;                  // receive sentinel value ?
        for ( int j = 0; j < 10; j += 1 ) printf( "%d ", buf[j] );
        printf( "\n" );
    }
}
int main( int argc, char *argv[ ] ) {
    MPI_Init( &argc, &argv );                       // initializing MPI
    int rank;
    MPI_Comm_rank( MPI_COMM_WORLD, &rank );
    if ( rank == PROD ) producer(); else consumer(); // decide on kind
    MPI_Finalize();
}
```

Fig. 13.30   MPI producer consumer

is that each process examines its rank and then decides how it is going to behave. In this case, the process with rank 0 behaves as the producer, and the process with rank 1 behaves as the consumer. When the producer/consumer finishes, MPI is shut down.

An MPI program is compiled and run using MPI commands:

```
$ mpicc bb.cc          # use C compiler
$ mpirun -np 2 a.out   # 2 processes needed (must match number in program)
```

It is crucial the number of processes specified on the run command match with the number expected by the program.

A send is always process specific and message specific, i.e., the receiver must be specified and the message must be fully described. For example, CONS is the receiver, and 0 denotes message specific (no other option is allowed).

```
MPI_Send( &v, 1, MPI_INT, CONS, 0, MPI_COMM_WORLD );
```

In contrast, the receive can be both sender and message specific, i.e., block until a specific sender with a specific kind of message occurs, which allows very precise control on the rendezvous. (μC++ only allows message-specific discrimination.) For example, receive specific (PROD), message specific (0):

```
MPI_Recv( &v, 1, MPI_INT, PROD, 0, MPI_COMM_WORLD, NULL );
```

receive any, message specific (0):

```
MPI_Recv( &v, 1, MPI_INT, MPI_ANY_SOURCE, 0, MPI_COMM_WORLD, NULL );
```
receive specific, message any:
```
MPI_Recv( &v, 1, MPI_INT, PROD, MPI_ANY_TAG, MPI_COMM_WORLD, NULL );
```
and receive any, message any:
```
MPI_Recv(&v,1,MPI_INT,MPI_ANY_SOURCE,MPI_ANY_TAG,MPI_COMM_WORLD,NULL);
```

Unfortunately, MPI does not provide send/receive/reply and it is awkward to simulate it using send/receive. Fig. 13.31 shows the simulation of send/receive/reply with the double cost of communication to respond with an answer. Finally, MPI provides additional concurrency in the form of not blocking until the message is sent. If send buffers are congested, a send may block for an arbitrary period until there is room in the buffer. As well, the receiver always blocks until a message is sent. Fig. 13.32 shows the send and receive can be started but the caller does not block. Both MPI_Isend and MPI_Irecv returned a ticket immediately and the caller executes asynchronously until the completion of the operation is required. That is, until another send must occur or the received data is required, respectively. The synchronization occurs at the MPI_wait, which matches the ticket with the asynchronous operation, and block if the matching operation is incomplete. The wait can occur for *any* request in an array of requests:

```
MPI_Request reqs[20];             // outstanding requests
int index;
MPI_Waitany( 20, reqs, &index, NULL ); // wait for any receive
```

or for *all* request in an array of requests:

```
int buf[20][10];                  // all data
MPI_Request reqs[20];             // outstanding requests
MPI_Waitall( 20, reqs, NULL );    // wait for all receives
```

Fig. 13.33, p. 721 shows the MPI program to concurrently adds up the rows of a matrix (see Sect. 5.12, p. 218), using powerful synchronization/communication mechanisms Bcast, Scatter, Gather and Reduce. Fig. 13.34, p. 721 shows how these operations work. Crucial to understanding this program is a *trick* provided by MPI defining a one to many relationship. One of the N processes is arbitrarily designated as the primary process, called the *root*; in this example, process 0 is designated as the root. Then the set of operations Bcast, Scatter, Gather and Reduce are defined to have one semantics for the root, and for all other processes, the semantics does the opposite. Hence, all of the commands in this set have a duality. This trick allows a single code-image to behave in two different ways. Therefore, when reading the code, one meaning is for the root and another meaning for the other processes.

The program begins with process 0 (root) reading the matrix size and values; the other processes skip this step and have no size or values in their private copy of the program variables. Therefore, the first operation is to broadcast to the other processes the size of a row (number of columns in a row). The broadcast is performed by Bcast sending the row size to all other processes created by the command line flag -np. However, notice that there is no receive after the broadcast

```
enum { PROD = 0, CONS = 1 };
void producer() {
    int v, a;
    for ( v = 0; v < 5; v += 1 ) {         // generate values
        MPI_Send( &v, 1, MPI_INT, CONS, 0, MPI_COMM_WORLD ); // send
        MPI_Recv( &a, 1, MPI_INT, CONS, 0, MPI_COMM_WORLD, NULL ); // block for reply
    }
    v = -1;                                // send sentinel value
    MPI_Send( &v, 1, MPI_INT, CONS, 0, MPI_COMM_WORLD );
    MPI_Recv( &a, 0, MPI_INT, CONS, 0, MPI_COMM_WORLD, NULL ); // block for reply
}
void consumer() {
    int v, a;
    for ( ;; ) {
        MPI_Recv( &v, 1, MPI_INT, PROD, 0, MPI_COMM_WORLD, NULL );
        // examine message
        if ( v == -1 ) break;              // receive sentinel value ?
        MPI_Send( &a, 1, MPI_INT, PROD, 0, MPI_COMM_WORLD ); // send reply
        a = v + 100;
    }
    MPI_Send( &a, 0, MPI_INT, PROD, 0, MPI_COMM_WORLD ); // send reply
}
```

Fig. 13.31 MPI simulate send/receive/reply

```
void producer() {
    int buf[10];
    MPI_Request r;
    for ( int i = 0; i < 20; i += 1 ) { // generate N arrays
        for ( int j = 0; j < 10; j += 1 ) buf[j] = i;
        MPI_Isend( buf, 10, MPI_INT, CONS, 0, MPI_COMM_WORLD, &r );
        // work during send
        MPI_Wait( &r, NULL );              // wait for send to complete
    }
    buf[0] = -1;
    MPI_Isend( buf, 1, MPI_INT, CONS, 0, MPI_COMM_WORLD, &r ); // only send 1 value
    MPI_Wait( &r, NULL );
}
void consumer() {
    int buf[10];
    MPI_Request r;
    for ( ;; ) {
        MPI_Irecv( buf, 10, MPI_INT, PROD, 0, MPI_COMM_WORLD, &r );
        // work during receive
        MPI_Wait( &r, NULL );              // wait for receive to complete
        if ( buf[0] == -1 ) break; // sentinel value ?
        for ( unsigned int j = 0; j < 10; j += 1 ) printf( "%d", buf[j] );
        printf( "\n" );
    }
}
```

Fig. 13.32 MPI future communication

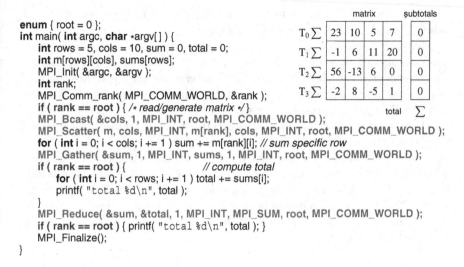

```
enum { root = 0 };
int main( int argc, char *argv[ ] ) {
    int rows = 5, cols = 10, sum = 0, total = 0;
    int m[rows][cols], sums[rows];
    MPI_Init( &argc, &argv );
    int rank;
    MPI_Comm_rank( MPI_COMM_WORLD, &rank );
    if ( rank == root ) { /* read/generate matrix */}
    MPI_Bcast( &cols, 1, MPI_INT, root, MPI_COMM_WORLD );
    MPI_Scatter( m, cols, MPI_INT, m[rank], cols, MPI_INT, root, MPI_COMM_WORLD );
    for ( int i = 0; i < cols; i += 1 ) sum += m[rank][i]; // sum specific row
    MPI_Gather( &sum, 1, MPI_INT, sums, 1, MPI_INT, root, MPI_COMM_WORLD );
    if ( rank == root ) {                    // compute total
        for ( int i = 0; i < rows; i += 1 ) total += sums[i];
        printf( "total %d\n", total );
    }
    MPI_Reduce( &sum, &total, 1, MPI_INT, MPI_SUM, root, MPI_COMM_WORLD );
    if ( rank == root ) { printf( "total %d\n", total ); }
    MPI_Finalize();
}
```

Fig. 13.33 MPI sum matrix rows

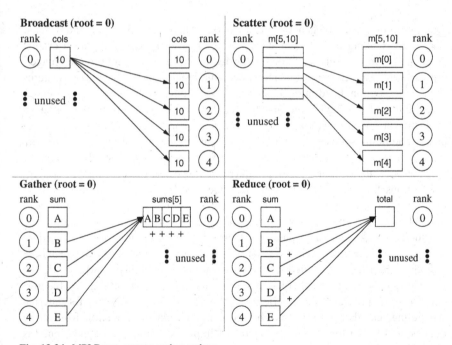

Fig. 13.34 MPI Bcast, scatter, gather, reduce

to read the value. The reason is that Bcast is defined to send for the root, and for all other processes, it does the opposite, i.e., it receives.

The second operation is to broadcast (scatter) the matrix rows to the other processes using Scatter. Remember, only the root has data in its matrix. For the root, Scatter performs a broadcast, and for the other processes, it performs a receive into the row designated by rank; the remainder of matrix is undefined. All processes now sum their particular row of the matrix.

The third operation is to retrieve (gather) the subtotals for each row from the processes to the root using Gather. For the root, Gather does a receive and places a value into the sums array at position rank of the sender; otherwise, the other processes do a send to the root of their row subtotal. The root then adds the subtotals for all the rows. An alternative approach is to use Reduce, which is the same as Gather but also takes an action to be performed on each received message by the root. In this case, the action is MPI_SUM, meaning sum the values that are received in variable sum of the root.

13.6   Summary

Simula coroutines are too general because of direct activation in the Call and Resume statements, making it easy to make mistakes. However, coroutines are a crucial language feature, which are under-supported in modern programming-languages. Furthermore, coroutines must be integrated with other high-level language-features such as exception handling and concurrency. Pthreads concurrency is neither object-oriented nor high-level, and hence, there is little help from the language in writing a concurrent program. The low-level concurrency features and type-unsafe communication conspire to make writing a concurrent program difficult and error prone. While it is possible to mimic high-level concurrency constructions, e.g., monitor, there is only a weak equivalence because of the complex coding-conventions that must be followed. Message passing is a very simple form of thread communication using a small set of primitives (send/receive/reply). However, the lack of static type-safety and the shift from standard routine call (arguments/ parameters) makes message passing an unacceptable technique in most modern programming languages. Ada design suffers from two designs in two different time periods, which are not unified due to backwards compatibility issues. While the Ada design is high-level, there is a strange mixture of non-orthogonal features coupled with programming restrictions imposed by using requeue for internal scheduling, guards for protected-objects, non-deterministic selection from entry queues, and trying to allow many forms of implementation. Java concurrency is object-oriented and high-level but it over-simplifies concurrent programming to the point where it is difficult to solve even medium-difficult problems. The design decision to make all objects monitors with a single condition queue per monitor and no-priority semantics for signalling significantly complicates writing concurrent programs. General concurrency models, such as actors and tuple spaces, attempt to oversimplify the complexity of concurrent programming. Concurrency is inherently complex and will always require a reasonable level of sophisticated language-constructs to deal with the complexity.

13.7 Questions

1. Explain the difference between *stackless* and *stackfull* coroutines.
2. Name two coroutine features that cannot be performed with stackless coroutines.
3. What is the intrinsic problem with all thread libraries built from a sequential programming-language?
4. Why is a library approach for concurrency, like Pthreads, potentially unsafe?
5. Many concurrent systems provide a mutex and condition lock rather than an explicit monitor construct. Why is it difficult to simulate a monitor with these locks?
6. Explain why the wait routine for a condition lock in the pthread concurrency library needs two parameters:

   pthread_cond_wait(pthread_cond_t *cond, pthread_mutex_t *mutex);

7. Why does a nonblocking send operation potentially block?
8. Explain how receive *any* differs from receive *specific* and why this difference is important.
9. Given the communication primitives send(tid, msg) and receive(tid, msg), show how a client sends a request for work to a server and then retrieves the result.
10. Explain each of the 3 operations in send/receive/reply and how the *send-receive-reply* message-passing mechanism works.
11. Explain the advantage of having an explicit reply in send/receive/reply over just send/receive.
12. Message passing with send/receive/reply does not have condition variables, yet internal scheduling is still possible. Explain how to simulate internal scheduling with send/receive/reply.
13. Explain why message passing requires dynamic type-checking.
14. Name the type of monitor that exists in Ada. Be specific.
15. Explain why an Ada monitor cannot solve the *dating-service* problem.
16. Given only one entry routine for boy tasks and one for girl tasks, can the dating-service problem be written using an Ada monitor? If not, why not?
17. Ada does not have condition variables so there is no internal scheduling; instead it has a requeue statement. Explain how the requeue statement in Ada may be used to simulate internal scheduling using external scheduling.
18. What are the disadvantages of an Ada requeue statement?
19. Explain why Ada requeue is not as powerful as internal scheduling.
20. Why do many concurrent languages attempt to use only external scheduling?

21. Explain why a Java task must be explicitly started after a task is declared rather than being implicitly started as in μC++. Why is this a poor design decision?

22. Explain why a Java task must have an explicit join for termination synchronization rather than implicit joining as in μC++.

23. Java and pthreads both use no-priority monitor semantics. Give an advantage and disadvantage of adopting this semantics.

24. A common but erroneous Java implementation of a barrier lock for N tasks is:

```
class Barrier {                        // monitor
    private int N, count = 0;
    Barrier( int N ) { this.N = N; }
    synchronized void block() {
        count += 1;                    // count each arriving task
        if ( count < N )               // barrier not full ? => wait
            try { wait(); } catch( InterruptedException e ) {}
        else                           // barrier full
            notifyAll();               // wake all barrier tasks
        count -= 1;                    // uncount each leaving task
    }
}
```

Explain the pathological (unusual) scenario where this solution fails to work.

25. C++11 threads are implemented by pthreads. As a result, what threading model does C++11 use and is there an disadvantage to this model?

26. μC++/Java start a thread in object member main/run. Go/Pthreads start a thread running in a routine. Briefly suggest why these design decisions were made in these systems.

27. How does an actor in the Scala programming language receive requests?

28. Given the following Linda operations blocking read(), blocking in() and non-blocking out() (see Sect. 13.5.2, p. 709), show how to build *mutual exclusion* and *synchronization* using these operations.

29. Sketch an implementation of a semaphore in the Linda programming environment. Show P() and V() operation.

30. OpenMP uses #pragma to specify concurrency in a C/C++ program. Explain the kind of concurrent system supported by this approach.

31. How does MPI provide dynamic type-checking of messages?

32. Briefly explain two operations (exact signature not needed) that demonstrate how the *message passing interface* (MPI) is geared towards scientific computation.

33. Message Passing Interface (MPI) uses an interesting trick with operations like Bcast, Scatter, Gather to make them work when multiple threads execute exactly the same code. Briefly explain this trick.

34. For each of the entries in the table below, fill in with either a **Yes** or a **No**, if the feature of the first column is part of the language or library. Note, the feature must be an actual part of the language/library, not something simulated, in order for you to fill in a **Yes**.

Language/library feature	Ada	Java	Pthreads
Monitor			
Direct communication			
Internal scheduling			
External scheduling			

35. For each of the entries in the table below, fill in with either a **Yes** or a **No**, if the language provides that feature. If the feature is not implicitly provided, but can be simulated, count it as **Yes**.

Language	Internal Scheduling	External Scheduling	Condition Variable	Direct Communication
Pthreads				
Ada95				
Java				

References

1. Agha, G.A.: Actors: A Model of Concurrent Computation in Distributed Systems. MIT Press, Cambridge (1986)
2. Andrews, G.R., Olsson, R.A., Coffin, M., Elshoff, I., Nilsen, K., Purdin, T., Townsend, G.: An overview of the SR language and implementation. ACM Trans. Progr. Lang. Syst. **10**(1), 51–86 (1988)
3. Bershad, B.N., Lazowska, E.D., Levy, H.M.: PRESTO: A system for object-oriented parallel programming. Softw. Pract. Exp. **18**(8), 713–732 (1988)
4. Board, O.A.R.: Openmp application program interface, version 4.0. Tech. rep. (2013). http://www.openmp.org/mp-documents/OpenMP4.0.0.pdf
5. Bretthauer, H., Christaller, T., Kopp, J.: Multiple vs. single inheritance in object-oriented programming languages. what do we really want? Tech. Rep. Arbeitspapiere der GMD 415, Gesellschaft Für Mathematik und Datenverarbeitung mbH, Schloß Birlinghoven, Postfach 12 40, D-5205 Sankt Augustin 1, Deutschland (1989)
6. Buhr, P.A., Harji, A.S.: Concurrent urban legends. Concurrency Comput. Pract. Exp. **17**(9), 1133–1172 (2005)
7. Butenhof, D.R.: Programming with POSIX Threads. Professional Computing. Addison-Wesley, Boston (1997)
8. Cargill, T.A.: Does C++ really need multiple inheritance? In: USENIX C++ Conference Proceedings, pp. 315–323. USENIX Association, San Francisco, California, U.S.A. (1990)
9. Carriero, N., Gelernter, D.: Linda in context. Commun. ACM **32**(4), 444–458 (1989)
10. Ciesielski, B., Kreczmar, A., Lao, M., Litwiniuk, A., Przytycka, T., Salwicki, A., Warpechowska, J., Warpechowski, M., Szalas, A., Szczepanska-Wasersztrum, D.: Report on the programming language loglan'88. Tech. rep., Institute of Informatics, University of Warsaw, Pkin 8th Floor, 00-901 Warsaw, Poland (1988)
11. Dahl, O.J., Myhrhaug, B., Nygaard, K.: Simula67 Common Base Language. Norwegian Computing Center, Oslo Norway (1970)
12. Doeppner, T.W., Gebele, A.J.: C++ on a parallel machine. In: Proceedings and Additional Papers C++ Workshop, pp. 94–107. USENIX Association, Santa Fe, New Mexico, U.S.A (1987)

13. ECAM International, Rue du Rhone 114, CH-1204 Geneva, Switzerland: ECMAScript 2015 Language Specification JavaScript (2015). 6th Edition

14. ECMA International Standardizing Information and Communication Systems: C# Language Specification, Standard ECMA-334, 4th edn. (2006)

15. Erlang/OTP System Documentation, 1430 Broadway, New York, New York 10018: Erlang Reference Manual User's Guide, Vertion 7.0 (2015).   http://www.erlang.org/doc/pdf/-otp-system-documentation.pdf

16. Galletly, J.: OCCAM 2: Including OCCAM 2.1, 2nd edn. UCL (University College London) Press, London (1996)

17. Gehani, N.H., Roome, W.D.: The Concurrent C Programming Language.   Silicon Press, Summit (1989)

18. Gentleman, W.M.: Message passing between sequential processes: the reply primitive and the administrator concept. Softw. Pract. Exp. **11**(5), 435–466 (1981)

19. Griesemer, R., Pike, R., Thompson, K.: Go Programming Language.   Google (2009). http://golang.org/ref/spec

20. Hewitt, C., Bishop, P., Steiger, R.: A universal modular ACTOR formalism for artificial intelligence. In: Proceedings of the 3rd International Joint Conference on Artificial Intelligence, pp. 235–245. Standford, California, U.S.A. (1973)

21. Hoare, C.A.R.: Communicating sequential processes. Commun. ACM **21**(8), 666–677 (1978)

22. Ichbiah, J.D., Barnes, J.G.P., Firth, R.J., Woodger, M.: Rationale for the Design of the ADA Programming Language. Under Secretary of Defense, Research and Engineering, Ada Joint Program Office, OUSDRE(R&AT), The Pentagon, Washington, D.C., 20301, U.S.A. (1986)

23. Intermetrics, Inc.: Ada Reference Manual, international standard ISO/IEC 8652:1995(E) with COR.1:2000 edn. (1995). Language and Standards Libraries

24. Labrèche, P.: Interactors: A real-time executive with multiparty interactions in C++. SIGPLAN Not. **25**(4), 20–32 (1990)

25. Lea, D.: java.util.concurrency.   Oracle (2014).   http://docs.oracle.com/javase/7/docs/api/java/-util/concurrent/package-summary.html

26. Liskov, B., Atkinson, R., Bloom, T., Moss, E., Schaffert, J.C., Scheifler, R., Snyder, A.: CLU Reference Manual, *Lecture Notes in Computer Science*, vol. 114. Springer, New York (1981)

27. Madsen, O.L., Møller-Pedersen, B., Nygaard, K.: Object-oriented Programming in the BETA Programming Language. Addison-Wesley, Boston (1993)

28. Message Passing Interface Forum, University of Tennessee, Knoxville, Tennessee: MPI: A Message-Passing Interface Standard, Version 3.1 (2015).   http://www.mpi-forum.org/docs/-mpi-3.1/mpi31-report.pdf

29. Mitchell, J.G., Maybury, W., Sweet, R.: Mesa language manual. Tech. Rep. CSL–79–3, Xerox Palo Alto Research Center (1979)

30. Murer, S., Omohundro, S., Stoutamire, D., Szyperski, C.: Iteration abstraction in sather. ACM Trans. Progr. Lang. Syst. **18**(1), 1–15 (1996)

31. O'Farrell, W.G., Eigler, F.C., Pullara, S.D., Wilson, G.V.: ABC++. In: G.V. Wilson, P. Lu (eds.) Parallel Programming in C++, Scientific and Engineering Computation Series, pp. 1–42. MIT Press, New York (1996)

32. van Rossum, G.: Python Reference Manual, Release 2.5. Python Software Foundation (2006). Fred L. Drake, Jr., editor

33. Shaw, M. (ed.): ALPHARD: Form and Content. Springer, New York (1981)

34. Shopiro, J.E.: Extending the C++ task system for real-time control. In: Proceedings and Additional Papers C++ Workshop, pp. 77–94. USENIX Association, Santa Fe, New Mexico, U.S.A (1987)

35. Standardiseringskommissionen i Sverige: Databehandling – Programspråk – SIMULA (1987). Svensk Standard SS 63 61 14

36. Wirth, N.: Programming in Modula-2, 4th edn. Texts and Monographs in Computer Science. Springer, New York (1988)

Chapter 14
μC++ Grammar

The grammar for μC++ is an extension of the grammar for C++ given in [1, Annex A]. The ellipsis in the following rules represents the productions elided from the C++ grammar.

function-specifier :
...
mutex-specifier
mutex-specifier :
_Mutex *queue-types$_{opt}$*
_Nomutex *queue-types$_{opt}$*
queue-types :
< class-name >
< class-name , class-name >
class-key :
mutex-specifier$_{opt}$ **class**
...
mutex-specifier$_{opt}$ **_Coroutine**
mutex-specifier$_{opt}$ **_Task** *queue-types$_{opt}$*
_Event
statement :
...
accept-statement ;
select-statement ;
_Disable *(exception-)identifier-list$_{opt}$ statement ;*
_Enable *(exception-)identifier-list$_{opt}$ statement ;*
jump-statement :
break *identifier$_{opt}$;*
continue *identifier$_{opt}$;*
...
accept-statement :
or-accept

© Springer International Publishing Switzerland 2016
P.A. Buhr, *Understanding Control Flow*, DOI 10.1007/978-3-319-25703-7_14

or-accept timeout-clause
or-accept else-clause
or-accept timeout-clause else-clause
or-accept :
accept-clause
or-accept **or** *accept-clause*
accept-clause :
when-clause$_{opt}$ **_Accept** (*(mutex-)identifier-list*) *statement*
select-statement :
or-select
or-select timeout-clause
or-select else-clause
or-select timeout-clause else-clause
or-select :
and-select
or-select **or** *and-select*
and-select :
select-clause
and-select **and** *select-clause*
select-clause :
when-clause$_{opt}$ (*or-select*)
when-clause$_{opt}$ **_Select** (*(selector-)expression*) *statement*
when-clause :
_When (*expression*)
else-clause :
when-clause$_{opt}$ **_Else** *statement*
timeout-clause :
or *when-clause*$_{opt}$ **_Timeout** (*(time-)expression*) *statement*
try-block :
try *compound-statement handler-seq finally*$_{opt}$
handler :
_CatchResume (*exception-declaration*) *compound-statement*
_CatchResume (*lvalue . exception-declaration*) *compound-statement*
catch (*exception-declaration*) *compound-statement*
catch (*lvalue . exception-declaration*) *compound-statement*
finally :
_Finally *compound-statement*
throw-expression :
. . .
_Throw *assignment-expression*$_{opt}$
_Resume *assignment-expression*$_{opt}$ *at-expression*$_{opt}$
at-expression :
_At *assignment-expression*

Reference

1. International Standard ISO/IEC 14882:1998 (E), www.ansi.org: Programming Languages – C++ (1998)

Index

Printed in the United States
By Bookmasters